# 1985-86
# EVANGELICAL
# Sunday School Lesson
# COMMENTARY

## THIRTY-FOURTH ANNUAL VOLUME

Based on the

## Evangelical Bible Lesson Series

### Editorial Staff

James E. Humbertson—EDITORIAL DIRECTOR

O. W. Polen—EDITOR IN CHIEF

O. C. McCane—GENERAL DIRECTOR OF PUBLICATIONS

James E. Humbertson—EDITOR,
CHURCH SCHOOL LITERATURE

### Lesson Exposition Writers

A. D. Beacham, Jr.                    Charles W. Conn

Donald G. Bennett                    Homer G. Rhea, Jr.

### Published by

**PATHWAY PRESS**                    **Cleveland, Tennessee**

Lesson treatments in the *Evangelical Sunday School Lesson Commentary* for 1985-86 are based upon the outlines of the Evangelical Bible Lesson Series prepared by the Evangelical Curriculum Commission (formerly the Curriculum Commission of the National Sunday School Association).

# TABLE OF CONTENTS

## SPRING QUARTER LESSONS

## SUMMER QUARTER LESSONS

# INTRODUCING THE 1985-86 COMMENTARY

The *Evangelical Sunday School Lesson Commentary* contains in a single volume a full study of the Sunday school lessons for the months beginning with September, 1985, and running through August, 1986. The twelve months of lessons draw from both the Old Testament and New Testament in an effort to provide balance and establish relationship between these distinct but inspired writings. The lessons in this 1985-86 volume are drawn from the first year of a seven-year cycle, which will be completed in August, 1992. (The cycle is printed in full on page 14 of this volume.)

The lessons for the *Evangelical Commentary* are based on the Evangelical Bible Lesson Series Outlines, prepared by the Evangelical Curriculum Commission. (The Evangelical Curriculum Commission is a member of the National Association of Evangelicals.) The lessons in this volume are drawn from the Old and New Testament and taken together with the other annual volumes of lessons in the cycle, they provide a valuable commentary on a wide range of biblical subjects.

The 1985-86 commentary is the work of a team of Christian scholars and writers who have developed the volume under the supervision of Pathway Press. All the major writers, introduced on the following pages, represent a team of ministers committed to a strictly evangelical interpretation of the Scriptures. The guiding theological principles of this commentary are expressed in the following statement of faith:

1. WE BELIEVE the Bible to be the inspired, the only infallible, authoritative Word of God.

2. WE BELIEVE that there is one God, eternally existing in three persons: Father, Son, and Holy Spirit.

3. WE BELIEVE in the deity of our Lord Jesus Christ, in His virgin birth, in His sinless life, in His miracles, in His vicarious and atoning death through His shed blood, in His bodily resurrection, in His ascension to the right hand of the Father, and in His personal return in power and glory.

4. WE BELIEVE that for the salvation of lost and sinful men, personal reception of the Lord Jesus Christ and regeneration by the Holy Spirit are absolutely essential.

5. WE BELIEVE in the present ministry of the Holy Spirit by whose cleansing and indwelling the Christian is enabled to live a godly life.

6. WE BELIEVE in the personal return of the Lord Jesus Christ.

7. WE BELIEVE in the resurrection of both the saved and the lost—they that are saved, unto the resurrection of life; and they that are lost, unto the resurrection of damnation.

8. WE BELIEVE in the spiritual unity of believers in our Lord Jesus Christ.

# USING THE 1985-86 COMMENTARY

The *Evangelical Sunday School Lesson Commentary* for 1985-86 is presented to the reader with the hope that it will become his weekly companion through the months ahead.

The fall quarter 1985 begins a new seven-year cycle of lessons which will be completed with the summer quarter 1992. The twenty-eight quarters of studies will draw from both the Old and New Testaments. Also a number of studies will be topical in nature as attention is focused on contemporary issues. A complete listing of the topics that will be included in the seven-year cycle, is printed on page 14 of this volume.

Quarterly topics for the 1985-86 volume are as follows:

Fall quarter—"Truths From Genesis." In this series of lessons, chapters 1-24 of Genesis are considered.

Winter quarter—"Hebrews." This is a book study on the important New Testament Book of Hebrews.

Spring quarter—"The Patriarchs." Studies in this quarter focus on chapters 25-50 of Genesis.

Summer quarter—"The Bible and Critical Issues." Ranging from studies on personal integrity to that of family and service to humanity through the church, this quarter focuses on day-to-day living issues.

The lesson sequence used in this volume is prepared by the Evangelical Curriculum Commission. (The Evangelical Curriculum Commission is a member of the National Association of Evangelicals.)

The specific material used in developing each lesson is written and edited under the guidance of the editorial staff of Pathway Press.

STUDY TEXT: At the opening of each week's lesson, you will see printed the Study Text. These references point out passages of Scripture that are directly related to the lesson, and it is advisable for you to read each one carefully before beginning the lesson study.

TIME and PLACE: A time and place is given for each lesson. Where there is a wide range of opinions regarding the exact time or place, the printed New Testament works of Merrill C. Tenney and Old Testament works of Samuel J. Schultz are used to provide the information.

PRINTED TEXT and CENTRAL TRUTH: The printed text is the body of Scripture designated each week for verse-by-verse study in the classroom. Drawing on the Study Text the teacher delves into this printed text, expounding its content to the students. Although the printed text contains different insights for each teacher, the central truth states the single unifying principle that the expositors attempted to clarify in each lesson.

DICTIONARY: A dictionary, which attempts to bring pronunciation and clarification to difficult words or phrases, is included with most lessons. Pronunciations are based on the phonetic system used by Field Enterprises Educational Corporation of Chicago and New York in *The World Book Encyclopedia.* Definitions are generally based on *The Pictorial Bible Dictionary,* published by Zondervan Publishing Company, Grand Rapids, Michigan.

EXPOSITION and LESSON OUTLINE: The heart of this commentary —and probably the heart of the teacher's instruction each week—is the exposition of the printed text. This exposition material is preceded by a lesson outline, which indicates how the material is to be divided for study. These lesson outlines are not exhaustive, but provide a skeleton for the teacher to amplify upon and to build around.

REVIEW and DISCUSSION QUESTIONS: Immediately following the expository material in each lesson are five review questions. These questions are designed as discussion starters, along with the discussion questions appearing throughout the expository material. The review questions also serve to restate the major bits of information in the text and may be supplemented by questions of your own drawn from the expository material.

GOLDEN TEXT HOMILY: The golden text homily for each week is a brief reflection on that single verse. As the word *homily* implies, it is a discourse or sermon on a particular point. The homily may often be used effectively to give the lesson a life-related slant.

SENTENCE SERMONS: Two or more sentence sermons—popular and pithy single-line thoughts on the central truth of the lesson—are included each week.

EVANGELISTIC APPLICATION: The evangelistic application relates the general theme of the week's lesson to the ongoing task of evangelism. The theme of the lesson (but not necessarily of the lesson text) is used to make this application. At times the emphasis of the section bears on direct evangelism of class members who may not be Christians; at other times the emphasis bears upon exhorting the class members to become more involved in evangelizing others.

ILLUMINATING THE LESSON: In this section, illustrative material is provided for the teacher to use to support the lesson at whatever point seems most appropriate.

DAILY DEVOTIONAL GUIDE: The daily devotional guides are included for the teacher to use in his own devotions throughout the week, as well as to share with members of his class.

## EXPOSITION WRITERS

Writers for the expository materials for the 1985-86 volume are as follows:

The lesson expositions for the fall quarter (September, October, November) were prepared by the Reverend A. D. Beacham, Jr. (M.Div., Th.M., D.Min.) a former faculty member of Emmanuel College, who is currently pastor of the prestigious Pentecostal Holiness Church of Franklin Springs, Georgia.

The Reverend Dr. Beacham is a graduate of Emmanuel College, University of Georgia, and Union Theological Seminary in Virginia. He holds three graduate degrees including the Master of Divinity, Master of Theol-ogy, and Doctor of Ministry, all from Union Theological Seminary.

Dr. Beacham is an ordained minister of the Pentecostal Holiness Church, and is a Chaplain with the rank of Captain in the U.S. Army Reserve.

In addition to his duties as pastor, Dr. Beacham regularly writes the *Teen Teacher* quarterly for his denomination, and contributes articles to the Advocate. In 1983 Dr. Beacham completed a full-length volume entitled *A Brief History of the Pentecostal Holiness Church*. He is a member of the Evangelical Curriculum Commission and other professional associations.

Lesson expositions for the winter quarter (December, January, February) were written by the Reverend Homer G. Rhea, Jr.

The Reverend Mr. Rhea is pastor of the Woodlawn Church of God, Columbia, Mississippi. Before accepting his present position, he served as editorial administrative assistant at the Church of God Publishing House, Cleveland, Tennessee; and in conjunction with the Editor in Chief, prepared the *Church of God Evangel*, the official journal of the denomination. Reverend Rhea was reared and educated in Mississippi, where he served in the pastoral ministry for over fifteen years. He is an ordained minister in the Church of God and has held positions as district overseer and member of the Mississippi State Council and the State Youth and Christian Education Board.

The Reverend Mr. Rhea is author of the Instructor's Manual to the Church Training Course *Highlights of Hebrew History* by Charles Conn; *A New Creation: A Study of Salvation* for the Christian Faith Series of the International Correspondence Program. He is also a frequent contributor of articles to the *Church of God Evangel* and Youth and Christian Education *Leadership* magazine.

Lesson expositions for the spring quarter (March, April, May) were written by the Reverend Charles W. Conn (Litt.D.), former president of Lee College and current Church Historian for

the Church of God, and lecturer of Christian Life Seminars.

Before going to Lee College in 1970, Dr. Conn spent eight years on the Executive Committee of the Church of God, including a four-year term as general overseer of the denomination. He is a well-known writer in the Evangelical church world and is the author of thirteen books published by Pathway Press. He served for ten years as editor in chief of Church of God publications, during which time he served on various boards and committees of the National Sunday School Association (NSSA), the National Association of Evangelicals (NAE), and the Evangelical Press Association (EPA).

Recognized for his depth in Bible studies, church history, and the role of the church in the contemporary world, Dr. Conn is in constant demand as a speaker at national and international conferences and conventions.

Lesson expositions for the summer quarter (June, July, August) were written by the Reverend Donald G. Bennett, (B.A., M.Div.), pastor of the Church of God in Willard, Ohio. Before accepting his pastoral position, the Reverend Mr. Bennett was an instructor in the Department of Religion at Lee College, Cleveland, Tennessee.

Reverend Bennett is a graduate of Lee College, and holds the M.Div., from Southwestern Baptist Theological Seminary.

# GOLDEN TEXT HOMILY WRITERS

French L. Arrington, Ph.D.
Professor of New Testament Greek and Exegesis
Church of God School of Theology
Cleveland, Tennessee

Terry A. Beaver
Pastor, Church of God
Bradley, Illinois

Richard Y. Bershon
Chief, Chaplain Service
VA Medical Center
Tomah, Wisconsin

Ralph Brewer
Editorial Administrative Assistant
Church of God Publishing House
Cleveland, Tennessee

Noel Brooks, D.D. (Retired)
Writer, *Adult Sunday School Teacher* Quarterly
International Pentecostal Holiness Church
Oklahoma City, Oklahoma

Karl L. Bunkley, (Retired)
Former General Sunday School President
International Pentecostal Holiness Church
Oklahoma City, Oklahoma

James R. Burroughs
Chaplain (Major) U.S. Army
Fort Jackson, South Carolina

Edward Call
Head Librarian
West Coast Christian College
Fresno, California

Eugene C. Christenbury, Ed.D.
Associate Professor
Lee College
Cleveland, Tennessee

Larry D. Cripps
Chaplain (LT), CHC, USN
Millington, Tennessee

Ralph S. Douglas
Chaplain (LT) 1st Marine Division
Camp Pendleton, California

James L. Durel
Chaplain, Director of Prison Ministry
Chicago, Illinois

Calvin Eastham
Chaplain (LT) U.S. Army
Fort Hood, Texas

Kenneth K. Foreman
Director of Christian Education
Messenger Publishing House
Joplin, Mississippi

Chancel E. French
Associate Pastor
North Cleveland Church of God
Cleveland, Tennessee

Ted Gray
Pastor, Church of God
Henrietta, Texas

Thomas Griffith, Jr., D.Min.
Administrative Dean
West Coast Christian College
Fresno, California

Marcus V. Hand
Editor, *Lighted Pathway*
Church of God Publishing House
Cleveland, Tennessee

William M. Henry, Jr.
Instructor, Missions and New Testament Greek
West Coast Bible College
Fresno, California

James E. Humbertson, D.Min.
Editorial Director, *Evangelical Commentary*
Pathway Press
Cleveland, Tennessee

Robert Humbertson, Ph.D.
(Deceased) Former, Chairman Language Arts
Department
Lee College
Cleveland, Tennessee

Leroy Imperio, Th.D.
(Retired) Former Pastor
Elkins, West Virginia

Robert Jenkins
Chaplain, DIVARITY Chaplains Office
Fort Campbell, Kentucky

W. E. Johnson (Retired)
Former Executive Secretary
Church of God World Missions
Cleveland, Tennessee

Raymond Lankford
Chaplain, Mississippi Department of Corrections
Parchman, Mississippi

James N. Layne, D.Min.
Pastor, Cornerstone Church
Cleveland, Tennessee

David Lemons, D.D.
Faculty Member
Church of God School of Theology
Cleveland, Tennessee

**10**

F. J. May
Associate Professor
Church of God School of Theology
Cleveland, Tennessee

Levy Moore
Chaplain, Emmanuel College
Franklin Springs, Georgia

Christopher C. Moree
Editor of Missions Publications
Church of God
Cleveland, Tennessee

Richard L. Pace
Chaplain (LT)
Fort Benning, Georgia

Ronald M. Padgett
Director Chaplaincy Services
Mississippi Department of Corrections
Parchman, Mississippi

Luther E. Painter, D.Min.
Assistant Professor of Religion
Lee College
Cleveland, Tennessee

Benjamin Perez
Chaplain (Major)
Air Force Chaplain School USAF
Maxwell, AFB, Alabama

Wayne S. Proctor
Pastor, Church of God
Lexington, Kentucky

O. W. Polen, D.D.
Editor in Chief
Church of God Publishing House
Cleveland, Tennessee

Jerry Puckett
Plant Superintendent
Church of God Publishing House
Cleveland, Tennessee

John E. Renfro (LT)
Office of the Command Chaplain
Millington, Tennessee

John J. Secret
Chaplain (CPT) Captain, USAF
A.P.O., New York

Philip Siggelkow
President, International Bible College
Moose Jaw, Saskatchewan, Canada

David Smartt
Chaplain (CPT) Captain, U.S. Army
Fort Stewart, Georgia

Henry J. Smith, D.Min.
President, East Coast Bible College
Charlotte, North Carolina

Paul Stewart
Chaplain (CPT) Captain, USAF
Fairchild, AFB, Washington

Fred Swank
Pastor, Church of God
Monroe, Michigan

Robert B. Thomas, D.Litt.
Chaplain/Lee College
Cleveland, Tennessee

Fred Whisman
Cost Analyst
Church of God Publishing House
Cleveland, Tennessee

Mrs. Florie Brown Wigelsworth
Chaplaincy Staff
Mississippi Department of Corrections
Parchman, Mississippi

Charles G. Wiley
Pastor, Church of God
Pine Bluff, Arkansas

Jimmy D. Wood
Former Editor of Family Training
Hour Curriculum
Church of God Publishing House
Cleveland, Tennessee

## SCRIPTURE TEXTS USED IN LESSON EXPOSITION

| 1 Thessa- | | | | 7:22 | Winter/L. 7 |
|---|---|---|---|---|---|
| lonians | 5:22 | Summer/L. 10 | | 8:6 | Winter/L. 7 |
| 2 Thessa- | | | | 9:11-24 | Winter/L. 8 |
| lonians | 3:10-12 | Summer/L. 14 | | 10:19-31 | Winter/L. 9 |
| 1 Timothy | 2:9, 10 | Summer/L. 10 | | 11:1-10 | Winter/L. 10 |
| | 5:1-4 | Summer/L. 8 | | 12:1-8, | |
| | 6:9-11 | Summer/L. 5 | | 11-15 | Winter/L. 11 |
| 2 Timothy | 3:12 | Summer/L. 7 | | 12:18-27 | Winter/L. 12 |
| Hebrews | 1:1-11 | Winter/L. 1 | | 13:1-17 | Winter/L. 13 |
| | 2:1-10 | Winter/L. 2 | James | 5:13-16 | Summer/L. 8 |
| | 3:12 | Winter/L. 3 | 1 Peter | 1:17 | Summer/L. 6 |
| | 4:3 | Winter/L. 3 | | 2:13-17 | Summer/L. 2 |
| | 4:14 | Winter/L. 5 | | 3:1-7 | Summer/L. 4 |
| | 5:10 | Winter/L. 5 | | 5:5-7 | Fall/L. 7 |
| | 5:11 | Winter/L. 6 | 1 John | 3:17, 18 | Summer/L. 8 |
| | 6:8 | Winter/L. 6 | Revelation | 14:13 | Summer/L. 9 |

## SCRIPTURE TEXTS USED IN GOLDEN TEXT HOMILIES

| Genesis | 1:27 | Summer/L. 6 | | 8:18 | Summer/L. 7 |
|---|---|---|---|---|---|
| | 2:7 | Fall/L. 2 | Romans | 8:28 | Spring/L. 10 |
| | 2:24 | Summer/L. 3 | | 12:10 | Spring/L. 4 |
| | 6:3 | Fall/L. 5 | 1 Corin- | | |
| | 8:1 | Fall/L. 6 | thians | 6:20 | Summer/L. 10 |
| | 12:2 | Fall/L. 8 | | 13:4 | Spring/L. 8 |
| | 15:1 | Fall/L. 11 | | 15:54 | Summer/L. 9 |
| | 24:40 | Spring/L. 1 | | 15:57 | Spring/L. 5 |
| | 28:15 | Spring/L. 6 | Ephesians | 5:33 | Summer/L. 4 |
| | 32:26 | Spring/L. 7 | Colos- | | |
| Deuteron- | | | sians | 1:16 | Fall/L. 1 |
| omy | 30:19 | Spring/L. 2 | 1 Timothy | 2:1 | Fall/L. 12 |
| 1 Kings | 8:56 | Spring/L. 13 | Hebrews | 2:3 | Winter/L. 2 |
| Psalm | 2:7 | Winter/L. 1 | | 4:3 | Winter/L. 3 |
| | 133:1 | Fall/L. 9 | | 4:16 | Winter/L. 5 |
| Isaiah | 9:6 | Winter/L. 4 | | 6:12 | Winter/L. 6 |
| Micah | 6:8 | Summer/L. 1 | | 7:25 | Winter/L. 7 |
| Matthew | 5:16 | Summer/L. 2 | | 9:28 | Winter/L. 8 |
| | 6:14 | Spring/L. 11 | | 10:23 | Winter/L. 9 |
| | 6:33 | Summer/L. 14 | | 11:1 | Winter/L. 10 |
| | 7:12 | Fall/L. 10 | | 11:4 | Fall/L. 4 |
| | 28:19 | Summer/L. 12 | | 11:6 | Fall/L. 13 |
| Luke | 12:15 | Summer/L. 5 | | 12:14 | Spring/L. 3 |
| John | 8:31, 32 | Summer/L. 11 | | 12:14 | Winter/L. 11 |
| | 14:26 | Spring/L. 12 | | 12:28 | Winter/L. 12 |
| Romans | 1:22 | Fall/L. 7 | | 13:15 | Winter/L. 13 |
| | 5:18 | Fall/L. 3 | James | 1:12 | Spring/L. 9 |
| | 6:11 | Summer/L. 13 | 1 John | 3:18 | Summer/L. 8 |

# ACKNOWLEDGMENTS

Many books, magazines, and newspapers have been used in the research that has gone into this 1985-86 *Evangelical Commentary*. A few of the major books that have been used are listed below.

## Bibles

*King James Version,* Oxford University Press, Oxford, England
*New American Standard Bible,* A. J. Holman Co., Publishers, New York, New York
*New English Bible* (NEB), Oxford University Press, Oxford, England
*New International Version* (NIV), Zondervan Publishing House, Grand Rapids, Michigan
*The Berkeley Version,* Zondervan Publishing House, Grand Rapids, Michigan

## Commentaries

*Clarke's Commentary,* Abingdon-Cokesbury, Nashville, Tennessee
*Commentaries on the Old Testament* (Keil & Delitzsch), Eerdmans Publishing Co., Grand Rapids, Michigan
*Ellicott's Bible Commentary,* Zondervan Publishing House, Grand Rapids, Michigan
*Expositions of Holy Scriptures* (Alexander MacLaren), Eerdmans Publishing Co., Grand Rapids, Michigan
*The Broadman Bible Commentary,* Volumes 10 and 11, Broadman Press, Nashville, Tennessee
*The Interpreter's Bible,* Abingdon Press, New York, New York
*The Letters to the Corinthians,* William Barclay, Westminster Press, Philadelphia, Pennsylvania
*The Pulpit Commentary,* Eerdmans Publishing Co., Grand Rapids, Michigan
*The Wesleyan Commentary,* Eerdmans Publishing Co., Grand Rapids, Michigan
*The Expositor's Greek Testament,* Eerdmans Publishing Co., Grand Rapids, Michigan

## Illustrations

*Dictionary of Illustrations for Pulpit and Platform,* Moody Press, Chicago, Illinois
*I Quote,* George W. Stewart Publishers, Inc., New York, New York
*3,000 Illustrations for Christian Service,* Eerdmans Publishing Co., Grand Rapids, Michigan
*Knight's Master Book of New Illustrations,* Eerdmans Publishing Co, Grand Rapids, Michigan
*Notes and Quotes,* The Warner Press, Anderson, Indiana
*The Pointed Pen,* Pathway Press, Cleveland, Tennessee
*The Speaker's Sourcebook,* Zondervan Publishing House, Grand Rapids, Michigan
*1,000 New Illustrations,* Al Bryant, Zondervan Publishing Co., Grand Rapids, Michigan
*The Encyclopedia of Religious Quotations,* Fleming H. Revell Co., Old Tappan, New Jersey

## General Reference Books

*Harper's Bible Dictionary,* Harper and Brothers Publishers, New York, New York
*The International Standard Bible Encyclopedia,* Eerdmans Publishing Co., Grand Rapids, Michigan
*The Interpreter's Dictionary of the Bible,* Abingdon Press, Nashville, Tennessee
*The World Book Encyclopedia,* Field Enterprises Education Corp., Chicago, Illinois
*Pictorial Dictionary of the Bible,* Zondervan Publishing House, Grand Rapids, Michigan
*Word Pictures in the New Testament* (Robertson), Broadman Press, Nashville, Tennessee

# EVANGELICAL BIBLE LESSON SERIES (1985-92)

| FALL QUARTER (September, October, November) | WINTER QUARTER (December, January, February) | SPRING QUARTER (March, April, May) | SUMMER QUARTER (June, July, August) |
|---|---|---|---|
| 1985 TRUTHS FROM GENESIS (Genesis 1-24) | 1985-86 HEBREWS | 1986 THE PATRIARCHS (Genesis 25-50) | 1986 THE BIBLE AND CRITICAL ISSUES |
| 1986 ISAIAH | 1986-87 PEOPLE WHO MET THE MASTER | 1987 THE LIFE AND TEACHINGS OF MOSES | 1987 THE HOLY SPIRIT IN ACTION |
| 1987 THE JOURNEYS OF ISRAEL | 1987-88 THE TEACHINGS OF CHRIST (Matthew-Mark) | 1988 PAULINE EPISTLES (Eph., Phil., Col., 1 & 2 Thes., 1 & 2 Tim., Titus, Phil.) | 1988 THE CHRISTIAN IN TODAY'S WORLD |
| 1988 LUKE | 1988-89 ACTS | 1989 EARLY DAYS IN CANAAN (Joshua, Judges, Ruth) | 1989 THE FAMILY IN BIBLICAL PERSPECTIVE |
| 1989 GENERAL EPISTLES (1 & 2 Peter, James, Jude, 1, 2, 3 John) | 1989-90 EVANGELISM | 1990 ROMANS AND GALATIANS | 1990 LEARNING FROM PSALMS AND PROVERBS |
| 1990 GOSPEL OF JOHN | 1990-91 GREAT PEOPLE OF THE BIBLE | 1991 LEARNING FROM THE OLD TESTAMENT KINGS | 1991 BEYOND THE NATURAL WORLD (God, Angels, Satan, and Evil Spirits) |
| 1991 THE MAJOR DOCTRINES OF THE BIBLE | 1991-92 THE PROPHETS AND THEIR MESSAGE (Major & Minor) | 1992 1 AND 2 CORINTHIANS | 1992 PROPHECY AND THE END TIMES (Daniel and Revelation) |

# INTRODUCTION
# TO FALL
# QUARTER

The name of the Book of Genesis in Hebrew is the same word as that used for the first phrase of the first verse, "In the beginning." Genesis is rightly called a book of beginnings. This book, as well as all the other books of the Bible, is more than a human document; it is a divinely inspired revelation of God to man. While for hundreds of years critics have attacked its credibility, continued research in the field of archaeology has caused many secular scientists to admit the Bible's historical reliability.

For the next three months we shall study incidents from the Book of Genesis, chapters 1 through 22. We shall at times be disappointed to learn of the first sin, the necessity of God's judgment by the Flood, His discipline at the Tower of Babel and Lot's wrong choice; but we shall balance these disappointments by exploring the wonder of God's creation, thrilling at His Covenant with Noah, and being amazed at His love for the human family.

Give to these lessons the time they invite, and at the end of the quarter of studies you will be wiser, stronger in faith, more determined to avoid sin and the serious consequences thereof, and more settled in your mind to allow God's leadership in every avenue of your life.

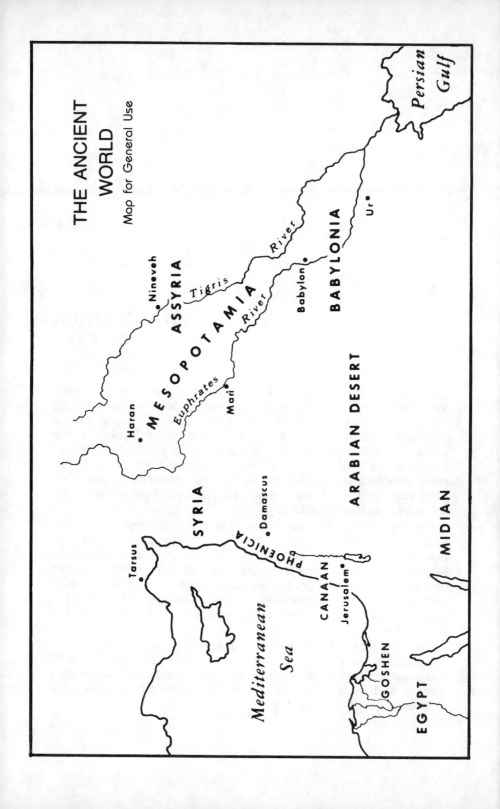

THE ANCIENT
WORLD
Map for General Use

Persian
Gulf

MESOPOTAMIA

ASSYRIA

Nineveh

Tigris

River

Haran

Euphrates

Mari

River

Babylon

BABYLONIA

Ur

SYRIA

Damascus

PHOENICIA

ARABIAN DESERT

Tarsus

Mediterranean
Sea

CANAAN

Jerusalem

GOSHEN

EGYPT

MIDIAN

# Creation

**Study Text:** Genesis 1:1 through 2:3

**Supplemental References:** Job 38:1-21; Isaiah 40:12-31; Colossians 1:15-17; Hebrews 11:1-3

**Time:** Dawn of Creation

**Place:** Universe, Earth, Eden

**Golden Text:** "By him were all things created, that are in heaven, and that are in earth" (Colossians 1:16).

**Central Truth:** God created all things for His glory and proclaimed them good.

**Evangelistic Emphasis:** One must respond affirmatively to the Creator in order to reflect the moral image of God.

## Printed Text

**Genesis 1:1.** In the beginning God created the heaven and the earth.

**2. And the earth was without form, and void; and darkness was upon the face of the deep. And the Spirit of God moved upon the face of the waters.**

3. And God said, Let there be light: and there was light.

**4. And God saw the light, that it was good: and God divided the light from the darkness.**

5. And God called the light Day, and the darkness he called Night. And the evening and the morning were the first day.

**26. And God said, Let us make man in our image, after our likeness: and let them have dominion over the fish of the sea, and over the fowl of the air, and over the cattle, and over all the earth, and over every creeping thing that creepeth upon the earth.**

27. So God created man in his own image, in the image of God created he him; male and female created he them.

**28. And God blessed them, and God said unto them, Be fruitful, and multiply, and replenish the earth, and subdue it: and have dominion over the fish of the sea, and over the fowl of the air, and over every living thing that moveth upon the earth.**

29. And God said, Behold, I have given you every herb bearing seed, which is upon the face of all the earth, and every tree, in the which is the fruit of a tree yielding seed; to you it shall be for meat.

**30. And to every beast of the earth, and to every fowl of the air, and to every thing that creepeth upon the earth, wherein there is life, I have given every green herb for meat: and it was so.**

31. And God saw every thing that he had made, and, behold, it was very good. And the evening and the morning were the sixth day.

17

## LESSON OUTLINE

I. THE UNIVERSE CREATED
   A. When God Works
   B. When God Speaks
II. THE EARTH FORMED AND FILLED
III. MAN AND WOMAN CREATED
   A. Why God Made Humankind
   B. Blessings for Humankind
IV. THE PERFECT CREATION

## LESSON EXPOSITION

INTRODUCTION

Our lessons this quarter will carry us through Genesis 22, which is the account of the great test of faith brought to Abraham through the apparent sacrifice of Isaac, which was the supreme test of obedience. It is the theme of obedience that is part of our journey this quarter. We will move through these opening chapters of the Bible and discover the failure of Adam and God's search for a person (Abraham) and a people (Israel) who will obey through whom the promises of blessing can be imparted in anticipation of the Messiah, Jesus Christ.

In our study of this book, especially in the opening chapters, we will not be primarily concerned with issues of paleontology. My conviction is that these opening chapters of Genesis speak primarily as declarations of Israel's faith concerning this God who has called her into existence through His creative Word. As Gerhard von Rad has commented, "These sentences cannot be easily over-interpreted theologically!"

As you prepare to teach these lessons, and especially Lesson One, keep close attention on the Central Truth. You will find it tempting to be side-tracked down numerous interesting, yet unproductive, roads. Stay with the biblical text and the Central Truth and listen carefully to the voice of the Lord speaking through ancient words.

We should also remember that these words recorded by Moses spoke to the people of Israel throughout their existence. In the glory days of David and Solomon these words from Genesis were heard. In the days following the Babylonian Captivity these words from Genesis were heard. In our day with the Word made flesh in Jesus Christ we still hear these words from Genesis and find the majestic presence of our Lord and Creator.

I. THE UNIVERSE CREATED (Genesis 1: 1-5)

A. When God Works (vv. 1, 2)

**Genesis 1:1. In the beginning God created the heaven and the earth.**

Martin Luther was once asked what God was doing before He created the heaven and earth. Luther, recognizing the absurdity of such a querry, responded, "He was making cane sticks to use on people who ask such questions!" While somewhat comical, the response does point out that our knowledge of God is limited to what He has chosen to reveal to us.

In Genesis 1:1 it speaks of "the beginning." We should not think of it as God's beginning. Rather, it is the beginning of God's special dealing with His creation. Some commentators have suggested that the opening clause is a dependent temporal clause translated as "When God began to create . . . ." However, it should be noted that not all commentators agree with this interpretation. It is of note that "God" is the first proper name in the Bible. We can easily say that without God there is no beginning. God is the Creator who creates creation, according to Walter Brueggemann's word-play. The key word is "created." It is used three times in chapter 1 (vv. 1, 21, 27) "without analogy. It refers to the special action by God and to the special relation which binds" Creator and creation together (quote from Brueggemann, *Interpretation: A Bible Commentary for Teaching and Preaching*, John Knox Press). In fact, it should be noted that the Hebrew word for "created" is used only in the Old Testament to refer to the creative activity of God.

Brueggemann offers the following additional insights into this verse regarding the creation and Creator. The first is that "the creator has a purpose and a will for creation. The creation exists only because of that will. The creator continues to address the creation, calling it to faithful response and glad obedience to his will." The second is that "the creation, which exists only because of and for the sake of the creator's purpose, has freedom to respond to the creator in various ways."

As we shall see, God is involved in creating an order that can be in relationship with Him. It is to our advantage to think of God "covenanting" Himself to the created order in the form of commitment and care.

**2. And the earth was without form, and void; and darkness was upon the face of the deep. And the Spirit of God moved upon the face of the waters.**

---

Discuss some of the more liberal interpretations of the first two verses of Genesis 1. What does secular thought say about creation?

---

While verse 1 implied a powerful presence of God as the Author of creation, verse 2 calls us to remember how close we live to chaos. Note the words of potential terror: "without form, void, darkness, deep." At the same time note the presence of God's Spirit moving over this chaotic situation. Imagine if you can this earth covered with water and in turmoil of the elements. There are no life forms as we know them now. There is no light. It is absolute terror to human existence and must be dealt with by God himself before even the elementary elements of life can find refuge on the earth. God's Spirit "moved" over this chaotic situation providing the opportunity for God's speech in verse 3. The Hebrew "moved" has the sense of "vibrate, tremble, stir" (von Rad, **Genesis**). Von Rad also suggests that "Spirit" (Hebrew **ruah**) is better understood in this passage as "storm of God."

B. When God Speaks (vv. 3-5)

**3. And God said, Let there be light: and there was light.**

**4. And God saw the light, that it was good: and God divided the light from the darkness.**

**5. And God called the light Day, and the darkness he called Night. And the evening and the morning were the first day.**

It is significant that God begins His speech with the creation of light. In many respects this contrasting of light and darkness provides the ongoing lessons of redemptive work. Christ is the "light of the world;" Satan is a deceiver and seeks to keep people from the light (2 Thessalonians 2:9-11; Ephesians 5:8, 12, 13; 1 Thessalonians 5:4-8).

We should also note that "speech" is the medium of divine creation. In this first chapter God's speaking is mentioned fourteen times. Speech is a characteristic of the covenental relationship God has with His creation. The creation has not naturally emanated from God; rather, He has chosen to be in the position of relating to His creation in a unique fashion. If God speaks, then the creation is called to listen and obey. Speech implies an "other." Thus, from verse 3's statement of "God said" we are led in the direction of a special part of creation who will be able to "talk back" or respond to God.

The story is terse and to the point. God speaks and something happens. Speaking and obedience go hand in hand. That is still true today. The Word speaks to us and we are expected to obey.

Verse 4 shows the relationship between God's Word, obedience, and God's value judgment: it is good. "Good" is not meant primarily aesthetically as much as "the designation of purpose" (von Rad). In the New Testament this is picked up by the words to the obedient disciples, "Well done, thou good and faithful stewards."

II. THE EARTH FORMED AND FILLED (Genesis 1:6-25)

(These verses are not in the printed text.)

The progression of establishing the

created order follows in logical style. Before God could create life forms upon the earth, He had to prepare the earth for such life.

In six key places we have God speaking the words of creation in the form of "Let there be . . . " or "Let the . . . " (vv. 6, 9, 11, 14, 20, 24). This pattern corresponds to comments made earlier regarding God's speech and things actually happening. What should be noticed is that sin is missing from these verses. It is a world where God is obeyed. It is a world where His speech is accepted with complete authority. Doubt does not exist. Doubt can only exist where the Word of God is suspect. When the Word of God is met with obedience, sin looses its power and the words of Jesus take full effect regarding "all power [authority]" (Matthew 28:18).

The action of God is said to be completed in "days." We know from 2 Peter 3:8 "that one day is with the Lord as a thousand years." However, for us to engage in the question of 24-hour days as a hallmark for our faith is to miss the central issues that are revealed in the text. The "days" of Genesis 1 should speak to us of the Lordship of God over all days.

The "first day" concluded at 1:5. The "second day" concluded at verse 8. On this second day the "heavens" are established as separate from the watery earth. The Hebrew word for "firmament" described something that was firmly hammered or stamped. Von Rad comments, "The meaning of (firmament) concerns the hammering of the vault of heaven into firmness (Isaiah 42:5; Psalm 136:6)."

The "third day" is found in verses 9-13. Verses 9 and 10 concern the establishing of boundaries for dry ground and the water. We can really say that it completed what was begun on the second day.

Verses 11 and 12 refer specifically to the formation of plant life. What is striking is that God did not separate plant life from the earth as separate creations. The earth is commissioned by God to produce the plant life. There is a real sense of "Mother Earth" in these verses.

Verses 14-19 tell of God's activity on the "fourth day." Verses 14 and 15 tell of the formation of the lights in the heavens. Verses 16-18 specify what those lights were and their purpose. What should be noticed is that God takes complete control over the creation of these lights. Those who worship the sun, the moon, the stars are worshiping the creature rather than the Creator (Romans 1:25). Astrology continues to be a source of spiritual blindness in the world. For those who seek to find their futures written in the stars, Genesis 1:14-19 affirms that these stars were created by God. They are not separate spiritual entities of their own and are not meant by God to be the source of divine guidance. Man lives by the Word of God not by the stars!

You should note in verse 18 that the sun and moon are given positions of "ruling" over the day and night. In God's creative order darkness is not meant to be a sinister force against Him. Already at the beginning God had ordained that light be the rule of His creation.

---

Discuss the concept of darkness as the environment or covering for evil deeds. Why did God provide for a period of darkness as well as light?

---

The "fifth day" is described in verses 20-23. It is the creation of fish in the waters and fowls in the air. Note that only now is the world prepared to support life other than plant life. It is also significant that the key word "create" is used in verse 21 in relation to these forms of animal life. What is also of importance is the word of blessing upon these creatures. In a world accustomed to slaughtering creatures, it is important to note that the first "blessing" of the Bible is directed to these creatures of the sea and the air (verse 22).

The "sixth day" (vv. 24-32) includes the other aspects of the animal kingdom and man. By relating humankind with the animal kingdom God shows the close relationship the two have with one another.

After the creation of the animal order (vv. 24, 25) God speaks a new "Let us make . . ."

## III. MAN AND WOMAN CREATED. (Genesis 1:26-30)

### A. Why God Made Humankind (vv. 26, 27)

**26. And God said, Let us make man in our image, after our likeness: and let them have dominion over the fish of the sea, and over the fowl of the air, and over the cattle and over all the earth, and over every creeping thing that creepeth upon the earth.**

---

How do you feel about man's dominion extending to the moon and perhaps further into space?

---

We have come to the crowning point of God's creation: humankind. In all the previous "let . . . " the focus was away from God. Now, the focus has shifted and God himself has taken on the activity of making mankind. Although Genesis 2 will tell us more of the particulars regarding this creation, it is clear that humankind is made by the Word of God . The "let us" and "our" of this verse have caused many commentators difficulties. However, what we have is the tremendous spiritual insight (although not understood at the time of its writing) that the Holy Trinity was involved in this special act of creation.

The word for "man" is the Hebrew **adam;** thus our English "Adam." It is a generic term and referred to both men and women.

Humankind is made in God's image and likeness. The only other major Old Testament text relating to man's creation is Psalm 8:4-9. In both Psalm 8 and Genesis 1 it is the entire person who is made in God's image. While we cannot press this point too strongly regarding man's physical existence, we must remember that the ancient Hebrew considered the whole person as a unit. The ancient Hebrew did not divide man into categories of spirit, mind, and body. That is primarily Greek thought. Rather, the

ancient Hebrew would have understood that in some marvelous and mysterious way, the whole person is made in God's image. It should be noted that in speaking of the people of Christ, the term "body" is used.

It becomes clear from the remainder of the verse that humankind stands in special relationship with the rest of God's created order. Man is to exercise "dominion" over these things. Thus, as a consequence of being made in God's image, man is able to exercise God-given sovereignty over the other creatures of the earth. Von Rad argues that "image of God" and this exercise of dominion are related in terms of purpose: "Just as powerful earthly kings, to indicate their claim to dominion, erect an image of themselves in the provinces of their empire where they do not personally appear, so man is placed upon earth in God's image as God's sovereign emblem."

**27. So God created man in his own image, in the image of God created he him; male and female created he them.**

It should be noted that three times the key word "created" occurs. This powerfully portrays the special work of God in making humankind. We are told from the front of the book that this is God's special effort. The pages of the Bible will continue to tell this story of God involved in this high point of created order. It should also be noted that twice more it is affirmed that man is made in God's image.

Earlier I wrote of God's covenant with the created order. Here it is clearly seen that God's special relationship to humankind by stamping His image upon him as bonded Him to a particular love for this creature. We have the beginnings of love that will enable God to overlook the tragedy of sin and embark on the quest of returning humankind to its place of covenant.

The verse concluded with the affirmation that both men and women are equal creations of God. Genesis 2 will tell more of how the woman was made; but here in Genesis 1 it is clear that God sees

Himself as the Creator of both and sustainer of both.

B. Blessings for Humankind (vv. 28-30)

**28. And God blessed them, and God said unto them, Be fruitful, and multiply, and replenish the earth, and subdue it: and have dominion over the fish of the sea, and over the fowl of the air, and over every living thing that moveth upon the earth.**

We have the second blessing of the Bible in this verse. The first blessing related to the creatures of the sea and air (v. 22). This blessing includes man's dominion over the recipients of the first blessing. The blessing has five dimensions: (1) Be fruitful—we saw this earlier in reference to the fish and fowls of verse 22.

---

Discuss the use of the term "replenish" as used in verse 28. Does that imply there were persons on the earth at an earlier period? Explain.

---

(2) Multiply—this was also used in verse 22 referring to the fish and fowl. The expression "be fruitful and multiply" is also used of Israel in Genesis 47:27 and Exodus 1:7; it is used in Psalm 107:37, 38 and in Jeremiah 23:3. (3) Replenish—this means to fill, to be full, to be in abundance. (4) Subdue—this word is used in relation to the replenishing of the earth. It has the sense of bringing the earth into bondage. The implication is that the earth is prepared as a place waiting to be brought under control by the efforts of man. This subduing is to be accomplished by man as he fills the earth by population growth. We cannot help but be reminded of Romans 8:19-22 in which the creation, bound by man's sinfulness, longs for the glorious liberty of the sons of God. In this sense, the meek, who shall inherit the earth (Matthew 5:5) shall treat the earth with redeemed subjection and the earth herself shall be blessed rather than cursed by man's sinful exploitation and abuse. Evangelical Christians need to remember that there is a legitimate theology of ecology formulated in Scripture. (5) Have dominion—this word was used in verse 26 and indicates the rule that man has from God over the lower created order.

**29. And God said, Behold, I have given you every herb bearing seed, which is upon the face of all the earth, and every tree, in the which is the fruit of a tree yielding seed; to you it shall be for meat.**

**30. And to every beast of the earth, and to very fowl of the air, and to every thing that creepeth upon the earth, wherein there is life, I have given every green herb for meat: and it was so.**

This passage should take the sting out of vegetarian jokes! It is a striking picture of humankind and the animal kingdom living in perfect harmony. Animals were not originally meant to be killed and eaten and skinned by people. And people were not meant to be killed and eaten by raging animals. Each had his place in the created order. Add to this the insights in verse 28 on dominion and you get a clear picture of the nature of this dominion. Man was not made to exercise the power of life and death over the animal kingdom; that power was always reserved for God. Dominion did not mean the power to kill; dominion meant the power to protect and name.

The plant kingdom was made available to both people and animals. The reason being that the plant world came from the earth and was meant to return to the earth. People and animals have life. We should not think that animals have a "soul." That is not the intention of the text; however, it is clear that blood is found in both and it is through the blood that life flows.

That is why when sin entered human experience, animals were slain for clothing as well as sacrifice. Sin disrupted the natural harmony and the world has not been the same since.

IV. THE PERFECT CREATION (Genesis 1:31 through 2:3)

**31. And God saw every thing that he had made, and, behold, it was very**

**good. And the evening and the morning were the sixth day.**

Von Rad observed, "This 'Behold, it was very good' of great importance . . . . (and) could also be correctly translated, 'completely perfect' and rightly (referred) more to the wonderful properness and harmony than to the beauty of the entire cosmos."

Prior to verse 31, God had always called the creation, "good." At verse 31 God is seen as proclaiming the entire creation as "very good." This needs to be heard in our generation. The created order did not have sin as part of its existence. Sin comes into the world where people can doubt the Word of God. Plants and animals were not made to doubt God's Word. They naturally obeyed the order of creation. Only man was made in the image of God; it would prove the basis for faith and the basis for disobedience.

In the meantime, the created order of God was good, and is good. We must carefully hear this Word from Genesis 1 and reject any theology that tells us the world of physical objects is inherently evil. Such a view leads to a dualism of soul and flesh that tears asunder the will of God in redeeming the whole person.

In Genesis 2:1 we find a summary statement regarding the heavens and earth. This statement implies a continuing effect in that God was in process in making the world.

Verse 2 sets the stage for the special day of God known as the Sabbath. It is our day of rest because it was first of all God's day of rest. The "rest" of God implies that the creation was complete, the process had ended. It had tremendous implications for God and humankind. That God could "rest" meant that humankind was especially protected and free from evil. It also served to sanctify the created order for His purposes.

It is striking to note that after the "seventh day" there is no reference to the regular formula of "and the evening and the morning were . . . ." This implies that the Sabbath is still open to the future. It implies there is a "rest" for the people of God (Hebrews 4:1, 3, 9-11, *New King James Version): "Therefore, since a promise remains of entering His rest, let us fear lest any of you seem to have come short of it." "For we who have believed do enter that rest, as He has said: 'So I swore in My wrath, They shall not enter My rest,' although the works were finished from the foundation of the world."*

*"There remains therefore a rest for the people of God. For he who has entered His rest has himself also ceased from his works as God did from His. Let us therefore be diligent to enter that rest, lest anyone fall after the same example of disobedience."*

**REVIEW QUESTIONS**

1. What is the significance of the word "created" in Genesis 1?
2. What are the implications of God's "speech" (Word) for our lives?
3. What defense can the believer offer to those who believe they can find their fate in the stars?
4. What are the specific blessings God gave humankind in creation?
5. What is the special relationship in creation between the animal world and the human world?

**GOLDEN TEXT HOMILY**

"BY HIM WERE ALL THINGS CREATED, THAT ARE IN HEAVEN, AND THAT ARE IN EARTH" (Colossians 1:16).

In Revelation the Eternal Christ said, "I am Alpha and Omega, the beginning and the ending" (Revelation 1:8).

**In Him** all things were created. Jesus is the ground, the basis, the foundation of all creation. Only in Him do things which exist have any meaning at all. He is the melody in earth's song; He is the words in earth's speech.

**By Him** all things were created. Jesus is the agent of creation. His life-giving being is powerful and explosive, giving form and substance to everything. The wonders of nature and the stars, flesh-and-blood beings, and spirit beings—everything that exists came tripping from His fingers.

**For Him** all things were created. Things which exist were created for His glory. All things came into being to fulfill His purpose. The fact that sin frustrates His purposes at times does not alter the original meaning of creation. Creation exists **for** Him.

**In Him** all things hold together. Jesus is concerned with creation **and** with its maintenance. He is the invisible glue that holds cells together, the invisible force that gives meaning to "energy," and unseen power that guides planets, stars, and galaxies in their prescribed orbits.

The Christian's confidence rests in the fact that in Christ all things have unity and meaning. Ultimately, His aims will be fulfilled. His purposes will be served. His glory will be realized.

This is our hope!—**Marcus V. Hand, Editor** Lighted Pathway, **Church of God Publishing House, Cleveland, Tennessee.**

## EVANGELISTIC APPLICATION

PEOPLE ARE SAVED BY FAITH IN THE SON OF GOD.

One must respond affirmatively to the Creator in order to reflect the moral image of God. We are lost. We are lost because of sin. We are people disobedient to the Word of God and therefore have betrayed the image of God in which we were made. God is at work seeking to restore that lost image through the person and work of Jesus Christ.

Jesus is the epitome of our lost image. Note characteristics of Jesus that have been lost in our lives:

(1) Complete confidence in the Word of God as the only source of life in the world;

(2) Complete faith in the will of His Father;

(3) Absolute obedience to the Word of His Father;

(4) Filled with the Spirit for a life of holiness;

(5) Able to do mighty deeds through the power of the Holy Spirit.

God has willed that no one be lost from the glory of His image; He has provided Jesus Christ as the Way, the Truth, and the Life for being restored.

## ILLUMINATING THE LESSON

I remember an episode on the old "Andy Griffith Show" about Opie being enchanted with a slingshot. The Mayberry sheriff had warned his son to be careful with the slingshot and not aim at windows or living things.

In the episode Opie kills a bird with his sling. Attempts at hiding are made, but the truth finally comes out.

To the viewer there was a sense of gross injustice. One had the feeling that somehow nature had been violated by the reckless actions of the young boy. It was easy to sympathize with his youthful vigor and at the same time feel the sorrow as the child learned the value of life.

While we can understand killing animals for food, it is difficult to understand the wholesale slaughter of whales and seals and other creatures great and small. Paradise meant a lot to the animals as well as the people.

Perhaps the coming kingdom will once again restore that harmony and peace when the lion, the lamb, and the child can lie down together.

## DAILY DEVOTIONAL GUIDE

M. Creator of All Things. Psalm 148:1-13

T. Creator of the Heavens. Isaiah 42:5-7

W. Creator of New Earth. Isaiah 65:17-25

T. Created Through the Word. John 1:1-3

F. Created by Christ. Colossians 1:15-17

S. Created for God's Pleasure. Revelation 4:9-11

September 8, 1985

# Man, A Unique Creation

**Study Text:** Genesis 2:4-25

**Supplemental References:** Psalm 8:1-9; Isaiah 43:1-7; Hebrews 2:5-9

**Time:** The dawn of Creation

**Place:** Garden of Eden

**Golden Text:** "The Lord God formed man of the dust of the ground, and breathed into his nostrils the breath of life; and man became a living soul" (Genesis 2:7).

**Central Truth:** We are created to glorify God and enjoy His creation.

**Evangelistic Emphasis:** Redemption fulfills God's original purpose for man and all creation.

## Printed Text

**Genesis 2:7.** And the Lord God formed man of the dust of the ground, and breathed into his nostrils the breath of life; and man became a living soul.

**8. And the Lord God planted a garden eastward in Eden; and there he put the man whom he had formed.**

9. And out of the ground made the Lord God to grow every tree that is pleasant to the sight, and good for food; the tree of life also in the midst of the garden, and the tree of knowledge of good and evil.

**15. And the Lord God took the man, and put him into the garden of Eden to dress it and to keep it.**

16. And the Lord God commanded the man, saying, Of every tree of the garden thou mayest freely eat:

**17. But of the tree of the knowledge of good and evil, thou shalt not eat of it: for in the day that thou eatest thereof thou shalt surely die.**

18. And the Lord God said, is not good that the man should be alone; I will make him an help meet for him.

**19. And out of the ground the Lord God formed every beast of the field,** and every fowl of the air; and brought them unto Adam to see what he would call them: and whatsoever Adam called every living creature, that was the name thereof.

20. And Adam gave names to all cattle, and to the fowl of the air, and to every beast of the field; but for Adam there was not found an help meet for him.

**21. And the Lord God caused a deep sleep to fall upon Adam, and he slept: and he took one of his ribs, and closed up the flesh instead thereof;**

22. And the rib, which the Lord God had taken from man, made he a woman, and brought her unto the man.

**23. And Adam said, This is now bone of my bones, and flesh of my flesh: she shall be called Woman, because she was taken out of Man.**

24. Therefore shall a man leave his father and his mother, and shall cleave unto his wife: and they shall be one flesh.

**25. And they were both naked, the man and his wife, and were not ashamed.**

25

## LESSON OUTLINE

I. A LIVING SOUL
II. HUMAN RESPONSIBILITY
A. Human Opportunity
B. Human Environment
C. Human Limitations
III. A GOD-ORDAINED RELATIONSHIP
A. Dominion Exercised
B. The Perfect Match

## LESSON EXPOSITION

### INTRODUCTION

In Genesis 1 we saw the general outline of all creation. In Genesis 2 we shall see in more detail the creation of man and woman and their purpose in the overall scheme of God in the earth.

We shall discover that the Garden of Eden is not a romanticized place of carefree inactivity; rather, it is the place of sinless responsibility and labor. We shall see the glorious opportunities facing humankind and the first glimpse of limitations that will haunt us to this day.

As Walter Brueggemann phrases it, we shall discover that human destiny is "to live in God's world, not a world of his own making . . . to live with God's other creatures . . . all of which are to be ruled and cared for . . . to live in God's world . . . on God's terms" (*Genesis*).

### I. A LIVING SOUL (Genesis 2:4-7)

(Verses 4-6 are not in the Printed Text.)

The first part of 2:4 refers to "the generations." It has been suggested that this verse anticipates the genealogical list of Genesis 5 that traces humankind from Adam to Noah (the teacher may wish to read this list as it will not be dealt with in a future lesson).

Verse 5 refers to the fact that rain did not exist and refers to a period prior to the creation of man when the plants and herbs were still in the womb of mother earth. The last part of verse 5 offers an explanation for the apparent slow growth of the plant world: the lack of rain and the fact that there was no man to cultivate it. Verse 6 shows that the earth at this time was watered by dew.

The reader cannot help but notice the very abbreviated story of creation 2:4-6. It simply serves as a prelude to the story of the crowning point of creation: Adam. It seems as if the entire world was waiting for Adam to be made before it could blossom into life. God did not make the earth to be uninhabited. The earth is made for the glory of God through the faithful stewardship of humankind. God planned the earth to need Adam. This plan of God has not been negated and redemption is partly the story of God's efforts to have a New Man (one made by faith in Christ Jesus) for the earth for eternity. Mankind and the earth are bound together in God's eternal plans. This should serve to teach us that our plans are not meant to be so heavenly minded they are of no earthly good. We must never forget that while Satan may control the mind of this world, he does not control the fate of the earth. That belongs to God who holds the title deed to this earth and will redeem it in the glorious appearing of Jesus our Lord.

**7. And the Lord God formed man of the dust of the ground, and breathed into his nostrils the breath of life; and man became a living soul.**

Adam comes from the earth. The wordplay in Hebrew is obvious: Adam (man) —adama (earth). What makes this earthly being a human being is that a special life has been breathed into him by God. The other creatures of the earth have a life of their own that is important, but their life does not contain the breath of God. When God breathes into Adam He breathes the life of His Spirit into the clay vessel. Thus, man becomes a living being. Bonhoeffer in the essay **Creation and Fall** comments, "Man as man does not live without God's Spirit. To live as man means to live as body in Spirit. The human body is distinguished from all non-human bodies by being the existence-form of God's Spirit on earth."

Again, the close relationship between the body being formed by God and the breath of God is important. To be concerned only about the human spirit without regard to the human body is to lose contact with the power of holiness in the world. Man does not have a body; man **is** body and soul. That is why Jesus was raised with a new body. If you believe that the body is simply a resting place for the spirit and that the body has no future with God then you had best excuse 1 Corinthians 15 from your Bible! God has made this human body as the place where His Spirit will dwell (see Paul's argument concerning this in 1 Corinthians 6:19 as it relates to sexual purity). On the basis of this we will one day receive a new glorified body that is free from the impact of sin.

---

Do you think the modern day emphasis on the care of the body is somehow motivated by God? Explain.

---

II. HUMAN RESPONSIBILITY (Genesis 2:8-17)

A. Human Opportunity (vv. 8, 9)

**8. And the Lord God planted a garden eastward in Eden; and there he put the man whom he had formed.**

**9. And out of the ground made the Lord God to grow every tree that is pleasant to the sight, and good for food; the tree of life also in the midst of the garden, and the tree of knowledge of good and evil.**

The expression "Lord God" is rare in the Old Testament. It is used only in Genesis 2 and 3 and only once outside of the Pentateuch.

What strikes us is that God "planted" the garden in which man was to live and work. This marks the garden as a "holy" place as well as a place of "grace." God, not man, had made this place available. It is in this same garden of opportunity that man will disobey. It will take another garden for man to find the hope of eternal life through the resurrection of Jesus. The story of redemption begins with a garden of hope turned into a garden of death. The same story reaches its climax in a garden of death that is turned into a garden of life at the resurrection of Jesus.

Brueggemann observes that this garden is not one of "cheap grace." It is a garden of grace that has a cost: obedience to the Word concerning the tree.

One almost gets the impression that man was made somewhere else on the earth and moved to the garden by God (v. 8). However, the text may simply be affirming that it was there that God made man and intended for him to remain. The garden is known as "Eden." The Hebrew word **eden** means "bliss." The garden is a place for humankind. God did not create man to live in terror of the creation nor to be in turmoil. God created man to be in bliss with Himself and nature. That God did not dwell there is seen from Genesis 3 as God would come and visit in the cool of the day. The garden is the place where man can live in God's world on God's terms.

Verse 9 gives insight into the nature of this garden. It is a place of groves of trees. All the trees that produce the necessities for life are found in the garden. Man does not have to go outside the garden for his fulfillment. All is present for the joy of life! God is not opposed to things pleasant. God created pleasant things for Adam: things pleasant to see and to eat.

Two trees are especially mentioned. The first is the tree of life. There are three references in Proverbs that give insight into the nature of this Tree of Life. It should be noted that in verse 17 that eating from this tree is not prohibited. The first Proverbs reference is 11:30, "The fruit of the righteous is a tree of life"; the second is 13:12, "Hope deferred makes the heart sick, but when the desire cometh, it is a tree of life"; the third is 15:4, "A wholesome tongue is a tree of life: but perverseness therein is a breach of the spirit." Clearer expression is found in the words of the risen Lord in Revelation 2:7, "To him that overcometh will I give to eat of the tree of life, which is in the midst of the paradise of God." It becomes clearer from the witness of the Scriptures that the tree of life is related to righteous living and the power of genuine love.

It should be noted that the tree of life is referenced to being "in the midst of the garden." In Genesis 3, we are informed that the tree of knowledge is also "in the midst of the garden."

This is the only reference in the Bible to the tree of knowledge of good and evil. We will reserve most of our comments concerning this tree until later. However, it should be noted that the tree of life's specified location places it in the midst of the garden. We could almost translate that as "in the middle of the garden." In this sense the text tells us something about the claim of God upon our lives. He seeks to be the center of our lives. Far too many people try to discover God at the edges of life when He is always seeking to be the center of our lives. As long as Adam keeps his thoughts on the tree of life at the center of life he is safe.

B. Human Environment (vv. 10-14)

(These verses are not in the Printed Text.)

A brief attempt is made to give historical location to this garden. It is obviously somewhere in the valley of the Tigris and Euphrates. Rather than trying to geographically locate each river, it serves our purpose of exposition to see the function of these verses in the garden scene.

Verse 10 shows that the life of the four rivers begins in the garden. Out of the garden which has the tree of life flows a river of life that encompasses the entire world. The number four is used in the Bible to symbolize the entire world. Thus, the four rivers show the grace of God coming from the place where He has placed Adam.

In Ezekiel 47:1-12 and Revelation 22:1, 2, the rivers of life are mentioned as providing health and nourishment.

C. Human Limitations (vv. 15-17)

**15. And the Lord God took the man, and put him into the garden of Eden to dress it and to keep it.**

For all who are tired of work, or are lazy, and desire to be in Adam's paradise, take note. The garden was a place of work for Adam. This is no carefree "goin' to lay down my burdens by the riverside." Adam has a vocation from God. He has been given dominion over the earth and must begin to exercise it. If you remember from verse 5, we saw that vegetation had not grown since there was not rain nor man to till the soil. Tilling the soil is not an effect of sin. In our lesson next week we will see how sin adversely affected work. But we must not overlook the fact that work is part of the created order. Adam still labored and sweat; the difference was that the labor was done in harmony with nature.

"Dressing" the garden means to till it. To "keep" the garden means that he is the caretaker of the Lord's vineyard. Adam thus becomes the model for every Christian worker. The garden is still God's garden; but it is a garden made for the purposes of man. The same applies in our service in the fields of harvest for the Lord. The fields and the harvest belong to the Lord; yet they are there so that our lives may reach their fullest in His will and glory.

What attitude should Christians have toward work, either in a secular setting or in a Christian environment?

Again, in verse 15 we have the implication, noted in comments on verse 8, that God created Adam outside the garden and then brought him into it for divine-human vocation.

Before we leave this verse let's make sure we understand fully this vocation that has been given Adam. Vocation is the same as "call." Each person has their call from the Lord. Until that person is matched with their call, they are functioning on a level beneath the will of God. There should not be the situation of a Christian without a call from God. The call will be different for each of us; yet, we must hear our true vocation from God. It still may be a vocation in the secular world; but it becomes our true vocation by the gifts of the Holy Spirit operating in our lives in obedience to the will of God. As Paul wrote in Romans 11:29, "the gifts and calling of God are without repentance."

**16. And the Lord God commanded the man, saying, Of every tree of the garden thou mayest freely eat:**

**17. But of the tree of the knowledge of good and evil, thou shalt not eat of it: for in the day that thou eatest thereof thou shalt surely die.**

We saw in Genesis 1 the first blessings of God to humankind. In Genesis 2:16 we have the first command from God to humankind. The commandment was not meant to restrict man from the goodness of God. All that God has for man is freely available. This includes the tree of life in the middle of the garden. God is not playing games with Adam. God has shown His marvelous grace in which there is fullness of blessing and life. Man is not God's slave; he is free to take charge of this world and exercise the ordained dominion and subdue it. The opportunity from God has come as challenge and promise. It is fullest expression of what it truly means to be human.

Brueggemann comments that this is the permission of God towards man. It is a wonderful freedom that the Apostle Paul rediscovered belong to the person who believed in Christ (1 Corinthians 6:12; 10:23, 26). Creation is to be received with thanksgiving and glory. Those things done in thanks to God cannot be sinful. This freedom takes place within the context of the permit God has given man.

However, verse 17 contains the only prohibition. No attempt is made to explain why Adam should not eat of the tree of the knowledge of good and evil. It is simply and clearly stated that he is to maintain a "hands off" policy. God did not call Adam to live by the fruit of knowledge of moral decisions; He called Adam to live by the fruit of life that comes through His Word. If Adam decides to gain the knowledge of good and evil he decides to replace the Word of God.

A few words of caution should be given. This is not an excuse to be ignorant! Nor is it an excuse to fail to discern between good and evil! Rather, it is a word from God that His wisdom and understanding of good and evil are more accurate than ours will ever be.

If Adam keeps his attention on the tree that claims the center of his life, he will be obedient and know life. If Adam turns to the edges of life to discover his own way, he will discover the horror of evil and the fact that disobedience and death are bedfellows.

In the midst of an otherwise wonderful story, a note of dread has been introduced.

III. A GOD-ORDAINED RELATIONSHIP (Genesis 2:18-25)

A. Dominion Exercised (vv. 18-20)

**18. And the Lord God said, It is not good that the man should be alone; I will make him an help meet for him.**

**19. And out of the ground the Lord God formed every beast of the field, and every fowl of the air; and brought them unto Adam to see what he would call them: and whatsoever Adam called every living creature, that was the name thereof.**

**20. And Adam gave names to all cattle, and to the fowl of the air, and to every beast of the field; but for Adam there was not found an help meet for him.**

The account of Genesis 1 indicated that man and woman were created together. In this chapter we are given more detail concerning how God actually brought about the two human sexes.

An interesting side in this lesson is that God is seen bringing Adam the animals as potential "helpmeets." It would be absurd to think that God had not thought of woman as the suitable companion for man. What the text is meaning to say to us is that man needs someone who is like himself to relate to. The human species is not meant to live alone. Men need women and women need men. This is the divine order. It should also be noted that the making of the helpmeet is something that God decides to do, "I will make him a help meet for him." Thus, the woman is not to be made as an unequal to the man; she also is made from the hand of God.

"Helpmeet" is meant to characterize one who will be a source of encouragement to the man. This encouragement is based on mutuality and equality. It is based on intimate communion. The animals are not able to provide this for the man. The animals are named by Adam. This naming recognizes what they are by nature as well as functions to show man's dominion over the earth. God did not choose to name the animals; that is left entirely to Adam.

Brueggemann observes that God decrees that He will help man find a proper "helper." But God does not commit Himself to be man's helper. The "helper" must be someone like the man; that is, the helper must be creature and not Creator. This does not indicate that God is not in the final sense our "Helper" (such is the meaning of "Comforter" in the Gospel of John); rather, it means that God expects man to use his resources and abilities to help himself in taming the world.

Verse 20 concluded with a note of joy and a note of sadness. The joy comes from the accomplishing of the act of dominion over the animal kingdom. Yet, Adam must be clearly aware that he is alone. For him there has been found no helpmeet. "She" is not present in the garden. **She** cannot come to him to be named. **She** is not a separate creation apart from him. **She** must come from God's special action. **She** must be as new to the earth as was Adam when he was made. **She** will be as special as Adam is.

B. The Perfect Match (vv. 21-25)

**21. And the Lord God caused a deep sleep to fall upon Adam, and he slept; and he took one of his ribs, and closed up the flesh instead thereof;**

**22. And the rib, which the Lord God had taken from man, made he a woman, and brought her unto the man.**

**23. And Adam said, This is now bone of my bones, flesh of my flesh: she shall be called Woman, because she was taken out of Man.**

**24. Therefore shall a man leave his father and his mother, and shall cleave unto his wife: and they shall be one flesh.**

**25. And they were both naked, the man and his wife, and were not ashamed.**

In his essay, **Creation and Fall,** Bonhoeffer calls this section of Genesis, "the strength of the other person." In this section he made the compelling comment, "What man cannot find or do while he is awake God does with him when he is asleep." It expresses clearly the limits of man—he cannot make another person in his own image; God is the Creator and Maker. That principle is behind every successful marriage (and any other successful human relationship): it is not our task to turn the other person into what we expect him to be; it is our task to be used of God freely for the benefit of the other person being made by God for the task He has designed for them.

It has often been commented that the woman was made from the "rib" or "side" of the man. She is not made from the crown of his head to be above him; nor made from his foot to be below him; she is made from his side to be beside him. Only in this fashion can she serve as a true helpmeet. This is not the picture of oppressed womanhood. This is not a place to support chauvinistic male supremacy. This is the place to see that men and women are both special creations of God and have their God-ordained roles to live.

It is important to note in verse 22 that Eve was brought to the man by God. The same action was applied in verse 19 when God brought the animals to Adam to be named. We would be remiss to think that the woman is considered on the same level as the animals (I seriously doubt that I would try arguing that point in a Sunday school class or anywhere else!). Rather, the man is given the opportunity to recognize the woman. He gives her her name. Rather than being a point of dominion (nowhere in the pre-Fall text do we have such a notion of man's dominion over the woman as with the animals), it becomes a point of recognizing her for what she truly is! It is a recognition that liberates. She is "bone of my bones and flesh of my flesh." She is me! It is a recognition of someone special from God who is the true helpmeet.

The play on names in verse 23 is seen in Hebrew. The Hebrew for man in verse 23 is **ish.** The brew for woman is **ishshah.**

Verses 24 and 25 immediately move us to the beauty of the marriage relationship. God wants us to know that Adam and Eve are married in His sight. Note that in verses 24 and 25 the terminology has changed concerning Eve. No longer is she "woman," she is now "wife." Their relationship in the garden is one of inexpressable beauty of husband and wife working together for the purposes of God. Adam is overwrought with joy that God has provided the "wife." The wife is the perfect helpmeet for him and shares in the responsibility of the garden with him before God.

They have become "one flesh." They are not to consider themselves as two separate people who are working out their own lives over the course of time. In God's eyes, they are one flesh. They are the two who have complimented themselves for the one purpose God has for them. They have learned to love together, think together, work together, and love their God together.

The use of "naked" in verse 25 certainly applied to their physical circumstances. Yet, it also applied to the fact that their relationship was "open" and had no hidden agendas. To be "ashamed" is to feel that one is lacking in something. Adam and his wife felt no shame because they were not lacking. They had recognized their completeness in one another.

## REVIEW QUESTIONS

1. What are the two wordplays in the text (see vv. 7 and 23)?

2. What is the relationship between man's body and spirit?

3. What is your understanding of "work" from Genesis?

4. Why is the tree of knowledge restricted from man?

5. What is significant about the man naming the woman?

## GOLDEN TEXT HOMILY

"THE LORD GOD FORMED MAN OF THE DUST OF THE GROUND, AND BREATHED INTO HIS NOSTRILS THE BREATH OF LIFE; AND MAN BECAME A LIVING SOUL" (Genesis 2:7).

If the physical structures of the lower organisms display such admirable proportions and striking adaptations to their environment as to evidence the action of Divine intelligence, much more may the Creator's hand be recognized in the form and symmetry, proportion and adjustment of the human body. An examination of the hand, eye, or brain, of the muscular or nervous systems, instinctively awakens the devout feelings of the Psalmist: "I will praise Thee, O Lord; for I am fearfully and wonderfully made" (Psalm 139:14).

Shown by the personal care and attention which God devoted to its construction, since He designed it to be the noblest of His works, the shrine of an immortal spirit, a prophecy and type of the body of His Son, it becomes a sobering reality that God loves us with a never dying love. This high estimate has been confirmed: by His abundantly and generously sustaining it; taking it into union with Himself, in the person of His Son; and constituting it a partaker of resurrection glory. **Excerpts from Pulpit Commentary**

## SENTENCE SERMONS

MAN IS CREATED to glorify God and to enjoy His creation.

**—Selected**

MAN IS GOD's highest present development, he is the latest thing in God.

**—Samuel Butler**

GOD MADE MAN to be somebody—not just to have things.

**—"Brotherhood Journal"**

MAN IS GOD's CREATION. Everything else is the nursery and nurse of man.

**—Henry Ward Beecher**

## EVANGELISITC APPLICATION

REDEMPTION FULFILLS GOD'S ORIGINAL PURPOSE FOR MAN AND ALL CREATION.

The marvelous state we have seen described in Genesis 1, 2 is lost for us because of sin. Yet, God seeks to restore us in His marvelous image of grace and seeks to renew our lives as examples of people who live by the power of the "tree of life."

This means that as husbands and wives live faithfully before Him as a witness to the world they give His Name an opportunity to be glorified. This does not mean that a charade is played before the world; rather, it means that a couple can live with each other without being "ashamed" and can live before the world without being "ashamed."

It is worth noting that the primary human relationship of the Bible is that of husband and wife. That place is the primary place for witnessing. That place is the primary place for grace to take effect. That place is the primary place for genuine respect and love to be known and shown for the glory of God.

## ILLUMINATING THE LESSON

On our need for someone like us for life and love, Bonhoeffer wrote:

"The first man is alone. Christ was also alone. And we are alone as well. Everyone is alone in his own way: Adam is alone in the expectation of the other person, the community. Christ is alone because only he loves the other person, because he is the way by which mankind has returned to its Creator. We are alone because we have pushed the other person from us, because we hated him. Adam was alone in hope, Christ was alone in the fullness of deity, and we are alone in evil, in hopelessness" **(Creation and Fall).**

Such as it is we are left with only one recourse: turn to the Christ who has made a new body of people, the Church. It is only there, in the context of the community of people who are found in Christ, that we shall discover the cure for our loneliness and hopelessness.

## DAILY DEVOTIONAL GUIDE

M. Created in God's Image. Genesis 5: 1, 2
T. Endowed With Choice. Joshua 24:14-18
W. Honored by God. Psalm 8:1-9
T. Redeemed by Christ. Romans 5:1-11
F. Chastened by Love. Hebrews 12:6-11
S. Rewarded for Faithfulness. Revelation 2:8-10

# The Origin of Sin

**Study Text:** Genesis 3:1-24

**Supplemental References:** John 8:34-44; Romans 5:12-21; 1 Corinthians 15:20-26

**Time:** The Dawn of Creation

**Place:** Garden of Eden

**Golden Text:** "As by the offence of one judgment came upon all men to condemnation; even so by the righteousness of one the free gift came upon all men unto justification of life" (Romans 5:18).

**Central Truth:** Sin came into the world through man's willful transgression of God's law.

**Evangelistic Emphasis:** A person can be saved from his sinful condition only through God's love revealed in Christ.

## Printed Text

**Genesis 3:1.** Now the serpent was more subtil than any beast of the field which the Lord God had made. And he said unto the woman, Yea, hath God said, Ye shall not eat of every tree of the garden?

**2. And the woman said unto the serpent, We may eat of the fruit of the trees of the garden:**

3. But of the fruit of the tree which is in the midst of the garden, God hath said, Ye shall not eat of it, neither shall ye touch it, lest ye die.

**4. And the serpent said unto the woman, Ye shall not surely die:**

5. For God doth know that in the day ye eat thereof, then your eyes shall be opened, and ye shall be as gods, knowing good and evil.

**6. And when the woman saw that the tree was good for food, and that it was pleasant to the eyes, and a tree to be desired to make one wise, she took of the fruit thereof, and did eat, and gave also unto her husband with her; and he did eat.**

7. And the eyes of them both were opened, and they knew that they were naked; and they sewed fig leaves together, and made themselves aprons.

**8. And they heard the voice of the Lord God walking in the garden in the cool of the day: and Adam and his wife hid themselves from the presence of the Lord God amongst the trees of the garden.**

9. And the Lord God called unto Adam, and said unto him, Where art thou?

**10. And he said, I heard thy voice in the garden, and I was afraid, because I was naked; and I hid myself.**

---

**LESSON OUTLINE**

I. THE TEMPTER'S SUBTLETY

A. The Authority of God's Word

B. Satan's Lie Against God

II. THE NATURE OF SIN
  A. Sin's Price of Shame
  B. Sin's Price of Fear
  C. Sin's Price of Irresponsibility
III. THE PENALTY OF SIN
  A. The Hidden Promise
  B. The Woman's Lost Estate
  C. The Man's Lost Estate
  D. East of Eden

## LESSON EXPOSITION

INTRODUCTION

In the previous two lessons we have seen the special grandeur of creation by God. It had been a world of unique harmony among all life-forms. It was a world where men and women were not in competition but in mutual love and support. It was a world where the Word of God reigned supreme and the word of man was in responsive obedience.

Beginning in Genesis 3 we have the story of our world. We are not told how long this blessed harmony lasted from the seventh day to that fateful day that drove humankind *East of Eden* (to borrow John Steinbeck's novel on the human condition). All that is for certain is that a time for decision concerning the Word of God had come for Adam and Eve and that they had faltered in their confidence of that Word. With the turn from God's Word to human words came the expulsion into the world of pain, sorrow, hopelessness, and threat of annihilation that we know at this last quarter of the twentieth century.

As you read this lesson from Genesis 3 be mindful that it is a continuing story that portrays our lives. But also remember that this story of failure in the Garden of Genesis has its story of reconciliation and hope in the Garden of Easter! It will be of value to read Romans 5:12-21 in relation to this text in Genesis. The Romans passage will bring to light for your teaching the powerful Word of grace found in Jesus Christ that offers promise to the dismal scene of Genesis 3.

I. THE TEMPTER'S SUBTLETY (Genesis 3:1-5)
A. The Authority of God's Word (vv. 1-3)
  **1. Now the serpent was more subtil than any beast of the field which the Lord God had made. And he said unto the woman, Yea, hath God said, Ye shall not eat of every tree of the garden?**

We would be remiss to focus our attention too sharply on the serpent. The creature is not the primary character in the episode. That dubious honor belongs to the man and woman. What does concern us about the serpent is what it says concerning God's Word. It should be noticed that the serpent, although made by God, is considered more subtle than the other creatures of the field. We should avoid tacky questions of how an animal was able to speak. What seems more important is that the issue of the Word of God and obedience is directly related to earthly realities. The account in no way seeks to introduce Satan or to apply human sinfulness only to the "spiritual" level. Earthly life and spiritual life are too interconnected to be separated in such a fashion. Thus, it is a creature of the earth who addresses the woman. As stated several times previously, the primary issue is the authority of the Word of God. We have seen in the first two chapters of Genesis that the Word of God is the decisive, creative reality in the world of humankind. Nothing exists separate from the Word of God.

The serpent tells a half-truth about God's Word. Von Rad has penetratingly observed, "The serpent neither lied nor told the truth. One has always seen in the half-truth the cunning of its statement. One should also observe that it speaks no summons; it simply gives men the great stimulus from which decision can be made quite freely." What the serpent had done was to make the woman think that she could operate her life separate from the Word of God, even in defense of the Word of God.

It should be noted that his half-truth is in the form of a question. The serpent seduces the woman by the art of the question. "Hath not God said?" can be the most difficult place of temptation. As we reflect on the nature of temptation, we should note that it concerns the Word. Misquoting the Word or misapplying the Word is always the origin of temptation. This is clearly seen in the accounts of the temptation of Jesus by Satan in Matthew 4:1-11 and Luke 4:1-13. The same is true in our lives. No doubt the specific area of temptation may be power, pride, money, sensuality; but the root area of the temptation is always in relation to the Word of God. In John 15:7, 10 Jesus made clear the relationship of abiding in His words and being fruitful for the kingdom. In 1 Corinthians 10:13 Paul spoke of our victory over temptations through the faithfulness of God. The way of escape and the enduring of the temptation is in relation to the God who is faithful and whose faithfulness is known through the power of His Word.

**2. And the woman said unto the serpent, We may eat of the fruit of the trees of the garden:**

**3. But of the fruit of the tree which is in the midst of the garden, God hath said, Ye shall not eat of it, neither shall ye touch it, lest ye die.**

The woman made the tragic mistake of trying to argue with the tempter regarding the rightness/wrongness of its position. The tempter had been wrong in the argument of verse 1. But it was a calculated wrong meant to engage the women in defending God. The tragedy is that she chose to defend God on the basis of her own wisdom and strength and not on the basis of fleeing the tempter and depending upon the Word to rescue her. She chose to attempt to "rescue" the Word. Such attempts are doomed from the start for they begin with the assertion that the Word is somehow weak and needs our defense. Just the contrary is true: **we** are weak and **we** need the defense of the Word!

The woman made the additional error of claiming something for God that was not part of His Word. She claimed that the tree could not even be touched. Such cannot be found from the Word of God. God only insisted that this tree not be eaten of (Genesis 2:17). By enlarging upon God's Word, she established a righteousness that was man-made and not of God. She committed herself to the rigors of this "law" and was doomed to be judged by it. By

expanding God's Word, she generated a position of weakness for herself that would bring about her downfall. It is as if she was so zealous for God that she stumbled over her own self-righteousness and pride.

B. Satan's Lie Against God (vv. 4, 5)

**4. And the serpent said unto the woman, Ye shall not surely die:**

**5. For God doth know that in the day ye eat thereof, then your eyes shall be opened, and ye shall be as gods, knowing good and evil.**

In verse 1 we saw that the tempter used a misquote of God's Word to engage the woman in conversation. In verse 4 the tempter is able to engage in clear debate with the woman concerning God's Word of judgment. The facade of deceit has been removed and the woman is caught struggling over the very terrain the tempter has established. The tempter has succeeded in moving her to the rather neutral position of judging God's Word on the basis of the tempter's word. She has stepped beyond obedience and is now playing by the tempter's rules.

Verse 4 raised the issue of the ultimate goal of human existence: life or death. By seeking to deny the power of death and the limitations of human existence, the tempter has managed to bring humankind to the very point of this reality and tragic limitation.

---

Discuss some of the present day tactics evil forces use to persuade believers to doubt the Bible or portions of it.

---

Verse 5 promised a future. "Knowing good and evil" should be understood in a broader sense than moral judgment; it should be seen in the sense of knowing everything. The tempter has promised the woman an alternative future to God's future. He has done this by offering his word as an alternative to the Word of God. In telling her that her "eyes would be opened" the tempter was painfully honest. He did not lie there; he simply did not tell her the tragic consequences of being able to see so clearly. Such vision is the vision of those who see themselves distinct from the perspective of the Word of God. To see oneself in disobedience does result in the shame and fear found later in the chapter, but to see oneself in the light of God's future is to be seen in glory and hope.

II. THE NATURE OF SIN (Genesis 3:6-13)

A. Sin's Price of Shame (vv. 6, 7)

**6. And when the woman saw that the tree was good for food, and that it was pleasant to the eyes, and a tree to be desired to make one wise, she took of the fruit thereof, and did eat, and gave also unto her husband with her; and he did eat.**

Sin is costly. The passage in Romans 6:23 tells us clearly that "the wages of sin is death." Sin has a terrible payoff and price that must be paid by all who transgress. The horror is that we cannot bear the price for our own redemption. The price must be paid by Someone else. The price we pay is isolation and death. The price offered by that Person is life and community.

Verse 6 compacts so many things that happened in the life of the woman regarding the temptation to be "limitless." How long "the woman saw" we do not know. There is a silence between verses 5 and 6 in which eternity hangs in the balance. It is the testing time of the spirit in regards to the Word of God and the word of sin. The progression of the temptation in her life should be noted. First she contemplates that the tree is good for food. She has recessed the issue of knowledge until she is ready to receive it without hesitation. That the tree could provide food becomes the basis for questioning how something meant for food could be the source of evil. She has made the decision at this point that the material world is of more eternal value than the spiritual world.

Second, the tree is "pleasant to the eyes." She is engaged in discovering the power of the sensual in human life. Her eyes were meant for her husband and the wonderful order of life found in obedience to the Word. Now she has

discovered that sin is not ugly (at least at first). She has discovered that sin is quite appealing and beautiful and therein lies its deception.

Third, the tree is worthy of "desire" because of its supposed ability to make one capable of transcending human limitations. She has come to the edge of the divine-human frontier and is prepared to step over the boundary of obedience into the world of self-dependency and isolation from God. In such a world man is cursed with the knowledge of good and evil. But such a knowledge does not set free; it only binds and leads to fear and shame. As Von Rad comments, humankind is at the point of deciding "that he is better off as an autocrat than in obedience to God."

The narration runs its course with little hint of horror or despair. There is no indictment from the writer but rather a profound awareness that Eve's story is now everyone's story. It is almost as if sin is not even surprising.

Verse 6 concludes with Eve becoming a temptress. The fact that she included Adam in the sin is a statement of their solidarity as well as the social nature of sin. There is a deception in the world that sin only affects the sinner. Such is not the case. Sin is always social in nature and affects others around us, including our environment.

We should not think of Adam as a victim. He was as much a participant in the sin as was the woman. Conjecture concerning whether Adam was intentionally deceived or why ·he did not ask the origin of the food is not the concern of the text. Both are equally guilty as far as God is concerned. The assessment of blame (vv. 12, 13) upon the woman and then the serpent is perceived as ludicrous in relation to the issue of obedience.

Do you feel that Adam was as much to blame for the sin of Eve as she was? Explain your answers.

**7. And the eyes of them both were opened, and they knew that they were naked; and they sewed fig leaves together, and made themselves aprons.**

The serpent was correct in the assessment that their eyes would be opened. Instead of discovering the power of divine limitlessness they discovered the power of sinful knowledge. When their eyes were opened they discovered they were naked. Shame constitutes the emotional factor of their existence. Their shame exists because they have violated the Life-Word and have seen that their feeble attempt for unlimited life has exposed them as frail and vulnerable people. It should also be noted that the initial response of the sin is directed against one another, not God. Both the man and woman have become acutely aware that they have violated the intimacy that was so precious and wholesome prior to entering these forbidden realms of knowledge.

B. Sin's Price of Fear (vv. 8-10)

**8. And they heard the voice of the Lord God walking in the garden in the cool of the day: and Adam and his wife hid themselves from the presence of the Lord God amongst the trees of the garden.**

The imagery is powerful. Here is mankind, who has just opened the doors of damnation upon human life thinking that he could be all wise, huddling together in shame and fear in the trees, listening to the dominant steps of the Lord God walking in the garden. The "cool of the day" implies the evening when man's work is done and God would join him for times of fellowship. It is a wonderful picture of the fellowship Adam and Eve had with God prior to the sin. What adds to the pain of this situation is that the writer only tells of this relationship when we know the relationship is practically severed.

Adam has not rejected Eve. She is still his wife. They still need each other and cannot exist separately; but now they need each other in shame and fear. The holy fellowship they had in openness and total acceptance has now been divided; yet, they are still together.

**9. And the Lord God called unto Adam, and said unto him, Where art thou?**

**10. And he said, I heard thy voice in the garden, and I was afraid, because I was naked; and I hid myself.**

Verse 9 is the first question by God in the Bible. It is a question that generates a plan of redemption that culminates in the words of Jesus, "the Son of man came to seek and to save the lost" (Luke 19:10). It is of note that God usually did not have to ask where Adam was. The fellowship was so clean and unbroken prior to disobedience. But now, the question is still on God's lips as He seeks His hiding children.

In verse 10 Adam replied to the question of where he was with a statement of his fear. We earlier saw that shame is the emotional quality between people when violation has occurred. When the violator encounters God it is fear that emerges. I may be shamed by you as another person; but I may be slain by God.

Note that the hiding and fear are related to the shame of his nakedness and his awareness that he is exposed.

C. Sin's Price of Irresponsibility (vv. 11-13)

(These verses are not found in the Printed Text.)

The irresponsibility is found in the fact that the man and woman seek to shift the blame regarding their sin. Shame is the feeling that a person is lacking. This embarrassment of the self has caused them to turn from the truth and to continue the sinful effects of disobedience by shifting the blame. We do not have confession in any sense from the man or woman; we have continued hiding in the presence of God. They are talking with God but in circles.

The second question from God came in verse 11 and is directed clearly to them in relation to their sin. When God finds us in our sin He also confronts us with the realities of that sin. Only through such confrontation are we truly freed of the power of sin. The questions posed by God in verse 11 are rhetorical. He already knows the answer and the second part of the verse indicates His clear understanding of their disobedience.

Verse 12, 13 show the response of

man to this direct confrontation that demands truth and repentance. Instead, given the opportunity to repent, the man betrays the woman. She had led him into temptation; now he seeks to leave her betrayed. Also, by the first clause of verse 12, Adam seeks to blame God for his problem as she is described as "the woman whom thou gavest to be with me." The woman in verse 13 shifts her blame to the serpent and accuses him of beguiling her. She has accurately seen the character of Satan as a deceiver. What she has failed to see is that God is giving them an opportunity for grace to be manifested if only they would repent and acknowledge the truth. While the first sin of eating the fruit is inexcusable, the second sin of failing to genuinely repent has cut short a clear revelation of grace.

III. THE PENALTY OF SIN (Genesis 3:14-24)

A. The Hidden Promise (vv. 14, 15)

These verses describe the lot of humankind and its relation to the animal kingdom following the primary act of disobedience. In verses 11-13 we saw that the order of accountability started with the man and then the woman and finally· the serpent. In these verses which describe punishment the order is reversed.

The serpent is given a special curse that makes him separate from the beast of the field. Dust is his lot in life even as dust will become the resting place of mankind. The curse upon the serpent really affects all the animal kingdom. In the first two lessons of this quarter we saw that the zoological world lived in peaceful harmony with the world of man. Animals did not slay man nor did man slay the animals. There was equal protection and purpose in life. Now that situation has been adversely affected. Man and the beast are now at war with each other.

Although it speaks of spiritual realities, we should not take lightly the physical qualities of sin in relation to the serpent. Von Rad observed the situation with these words, "(In the serpent) evil has assumed form, that is inexplicably present within our created world, and that has singled out man, lies in wait for him, and everywhere fights a battle with him for life and death."

Yet in the midst of this terrible reality of nature against man we find a promise from God concerning the ultimate redemption of this order. Verse 15 is a messianic promise of the coming Savior who will become the enemy between the serpent and the woman (who in this sense represents all life). In Christ there is a clear new beginning from God by which every serpent-plagued person can find deliverance and freedom. The power of sin will seek to destroy the Messiah. But in terms of ultimate realities, it will only bruise His heel. The Messiah will deliver a deadly blow to the head of the evil one and thus bring to conclusion the evil begun in this garden.

B. The Woman's Lost Estate (v. 16)

It is worth noting that neither the woman nor the man are specifically cursed. The serpent is clearly cursed in verse 14. What happens to the man and woman is that severe afflictions of what had been their natural order come upon them. It is common language in Christian thought to speak of the curse of sin. Yet, we must remember that God has not damned humankind. There is mercy provided even in the midst of the judgment. They will pay for their sin, but they will not be cursed by God. Sin is cursed, but not the person!

The woman's punishment is directed at the source of her life: child-bearing and her husband. What was meant to be always a source of great joy, childbearing is turned into a place of pain and sorrow.

The punishment also indicates a change in the relationship between the woman and man. We have already seen the seeds of antagonism in the way in which she tempted him and he betrayed her. Now the fundamental quality of their lives is affected. Her desire is for her husband and he shall exercise rule over her. Many modern feminists are offended by this passage; yet there is a measure of grace implicit: her desire is for her own husband, and no other; and only her husband, not another, shall rule over her. She is not turned into chattel; what has changed is the fundamental equality that once existed. The inequality is a sign of sin. The Gospel of Jesus offers a liberation for men and women that enables them to fulfill their ordained destinies in love and honor in the Lord.

There are two extremes we should avoid in the discussion of the situation of the woman after the Fall. The first is to radically reject the Genesis story as being chauvinistic and somehow "anti-woman." That is not the intention of the text: there is grace implicit in the text. The second is to consider the man in such a position of authority that the woman is treated merely as an appendage to his life. The teachings of the remainder of the Bible simply do not support superior claims, especially in light of the liberating gospel of Jesus for husbands and wives. That is one of the beautiful aspects of a man and woman married physically, emotionally, and spiritually in the bond of the love of Christ. Where Christ rules the relationship between husband and wife there is genuineness and openness that can parallel the quality of life prior to the Fall.

C. The Man's Lost Estate (vv. 17-19)

As stated earlier, neither the man nor woman were directly cursed; rather, punishment was afflicted on dominant areas of their lives. For the man the punishment involves the place of livelihood: the ground. What is striking is that the ground is cursed! There is not a greater argument in Holy Scripture for a meaningful Christian ecology than the awareness that human sin has damaged the earth! It is no wonder that the whole creation groans waiting for the revealing of the sons of God (Romans 8:19-22). Christians are called to be redemptive in terms of how we handle natural resources. The earth is hurting because of our sinfulness. Only those who meekly obey the Lord will inherit the earth. The meek are those who remember their proper place in the created order; they are the ones who have the

spiritual vision to see behind the Fall and see the perfect order of God. The meek care for the earth and care seriously.

---

Are the problems of drought the result of the curse or are they the result of poor environmental planning? Are they both? Explain.

---

Because the earth is cursed mankind is forced to exact his livelihood from a more difficult environment. Previously the earth cooperated in bearing the fruit of her womb. Now, even as the womb of Eve is touched with grief, so the womb of earth is touched. The earth has lost its capacity to speak for life; it is now the place of death. The same soil that produces the food to live is the soil that will inherit our earthly bodies (v. 19).

D. East of Eden (vv. 20-24)

Verse 20 seems out of place. Why should Adam wait until this moment to give her a proper name? It is almost as if he has to give her another identity after sin. She is now Eve, mother of all living. It is a penetrating insight into Adam's understanding of what is happening around him. His ground, originally a bountiful source of life, is in rebellion. The woman remains as the source of earthly life. He still needs her, perhaps now more than ever. Even though she was first tempted and brought about this sad circumstance, he still longs for her and acknowledges her power of life.

Verse 21 tells of the death of the animals. God will not let them hide behind the leaves of cursed nature. They must hide behind what He provides. The skins are made by God himself and He clothes both the man and woman. Already the blood must be slain for the covering of sin. There is little doubt we have an oblique reference to early sacrifice. Adam is not asked to slay the animals for the skins; God, who is holy and faithful, will provide for His soon to be wandering couple. Mercy again comes to the surface and we have a glimpse of the future in which the Lamb will be slain for the salvation of the world.

Verse 22 does not contain anxiety from God that the man will actually become as He is. Rather, it is the affirmation that the man has overstepped the boundaries of human life and is on the edge with his commitment to thinking that life is unlimited. To discover the power of the tree of life in such a state of distorted realities would only add to the sorrow that man must face in the world.

In verses 23, 24 the man and woman are driven from the Garden and are left on their own. They are now wanderers on the face of the earth. They have chosen autonomy when He desired obedience. They have chosen isolation when He had desired community.

## REVIEW QUESTIONS

1. In what way is the Word of God the central issue in matters of temptation?

2. How did the woman's enthusiasm for defending God make her prey to sin?

3. How does the progression of the temptation in 3:6 relate to the words of 1 John 2:16?

4. How important is confession and acknowledgement of one's sin to the process of forgiveness?

5. Name some of the ways that grace began to show in the midst of sin?

## GOLDEN TEXT HOMILY

"AS BY THE OFFENCE OF ONE JUDGMENT CAME UPON ALL MEN TO CONDEMNATION; EVEN SO BY THE RIGHTEOUSNESS OF ONE THE FREE GIFT CAME UPON ALL MEN UNTO JUSTIFICATION OF LIFE" (Romans 5:18).

With an added explanation in verse 17 ("For if by one man's offense death reigned by one; much more they which receive abundance of grace and of the gift of righteousness shall reign in life by one, Jesus Christ.") Paul trusts that his readers will understand and accept this twofold conclusion—the universality and absolute effectiveness of salvation by grace through faith. As all men die physically, spiritually, and eternally by sin, so in all these respects they live by grace.

Of course a salvation that is through faith can be rejected. But it was still no less provided "unto all men." Justification is by GRACE as to its means, by FAITH as to its application, and of LIFE as to its effect.

The God kind of righteousness, revealed and experienced, cannot stop with a forensic decree. It must issue in life eternal. Thus only in thought can justification and regeneration be separated. God always accomplishes both in relation to the penitent at the same instant. **Excerpts from** The Wesleyan Bible Commentary

## SENTENCE SERMONS

SIN IS MAN'S declaration of independence of God.
—**"The Encyclopedia of Religious Quotations"**

OUR SENSE OF SIN is in proportion to our nearness to God.
—**Thomas D. Bernard**

THE GREATEST SECURITY against sin is to be shocked at its presence.
—**Thomas Carlyle**

EVERY SIN IS a mistake, as well as a wrong; and the epitaph for the sinner is, "Thou fool."
—**Alexander MacLaren**

TEMPTATIONS NEED NOT be hindrances. As we put them beneath our feet, they lift us to higher ground.
—**Lois F. Blanchard**

## EVANGELISTIC APPLICATION

A PERSON CAN BE SAVED FROM HIS SINFUL CONDITION ONLY THROUGH GOD'S LOVE REVEALED IN CHRIST.

As we have seen in the lesson, God initiated the work of mercy for all humankind in the Garden. The place of sin and transgression has become the very place where God is going to redeem. Although He spoke with judgment, it was tempered with mercy and not death. Although the man and woman were exposed and covered vainly by their efforts with the leaves, He was willing to begin the sacrifice of life that would clothe and protect them.

This sacrificial plan on the part of God has reached to all people east of Eden through Jesus Christ. It is as if God has provided another tree of life on Mount Calvary to be more important than the tree of good and evil of the Garden. A price for redemption had to be paid and God initiated the payment.

There is only one way to find salvation. That way is through faith in Christ who represents God's bountiful mercy.

## ILLUMINATING THE LESSON

D. R. Davis in a 1946 book **Down Peacock's Feathers,** "Now in history we have to face the fact . . . that the human race through the individuals composing it, has willed itself out of the subordinate relation to God, with the fatal result that every individual becomes his own centre . . . Since we are all alike in wanting to be our own centre, we are irrevocably divided from one another. United in sin, we become disunited in everything else. This is the brilliant mess in which humanity finds itself, especially the progressive civilized humanity of to-day." **(The Interpreter's Bible,** Vol. 1)

## DAILY DEVOTIONAL GUIDE

M. Sin's Penalty. 2 Samuel 12:7-12
T. Two Ways of Life. Psalm 1:1-6
W. Sin's Universality. Romans 5:12-14
T. Sin's Remedy. Romans 5:15-21
F. Believer's Protection. Ephesians 6:10-20
S. Believer's Hope. 1 John 1:1-10

# The Spread of Sin

**Study Text:** Genesis 4:1-26

**Supplemental References:** Psalm 10:1-11; Mark 7:14-23; James 1:12-15

**Time:** Soon after Creation of man

**Place:** Probably near the Garden of Eden.

**Golden Text:** "By faith Abel offered unto God a more excellent sacrifice than Cain, by which he obtained witness that he was righteous, God testifying of his gifts: and by it he being dead yet speaketh" (Hebrews 11:4).

**Central Truth:** Sin follows a pattern which, if allowed to go unchecked, results in great tragedy and death.

**Evangelistic Emphasis:** Sin brings tragedy and death, but redemption through Christ brings forgiveness and life.

## Printed Text

**Genesis 4:3.** And in process of time it came to pass, that Cain brought of the fruit of the ground an offering unto the Lord.

**4. And Abel, he also brought of the firstlings of his flock and of the fat thereof. And the Lord had respect unto Abel and to his offering:**

5. But unto Cain and to his offering he had not respect. And Cain was very wroth, and his countenance fell.

**6. And the Lord said unto Cain, Why art thou wroth? and why is thy countenance fallen?**

7. If thou doest well, shalt thou not be accepted? and if thou doest not well, sin lieth at the door. And unto thee shall be his desire, and thou shalt rule over him.

**8. And Cain talked with Abel his brother: and it came to pass, when they were in the field, that Cain rose up against Abel his brother, and slew him.**

9. And the Lord said unto Cain, Where is Abel thy brother? And he said, I know not: Am I my brother's keeper?

**10. And he said, What hast thou done? the voice of thy brother's blood crieth unto me from the ground.**

11. And now art thou cursed from the earth, which hath opened her mouth to receive thy brother's blood from thy hand;

**12. When thou tillest the ground, it shall not henceforth yield unto thee her strength; a fugitive and a vagabond shalt thou be in the earth.**

13. And Cain said unto the Lord, My punishment is greater than I can bear.

**14. Behold, thou hast driven me out this day from the face of the earth; and from thy face shall I be hid; and I shall be a fugitive and a vagabond in the earth; and it shall come to pass, that every one that findeth me shall slay me.**

15. And the Lord said unto him, Therefore whosoever slayeth Cain, vengeance shall be taken on him sevenfold. And the Lord set a mark upon Cain, lest any finding him should kill him.

**16. And Cain went out from the presence of the Lord, and dwelt in the land of Nod, on the east of Eden.**

---

## LESSON OUTLINE

I. UNACCEPTABLE WORSHIP
   A. Mystery of Election
   B. Temptation at the Altar
II. PREMEDITATED MURDER
   A. Death of a Brother
   B. Sin Exposed
III. JUDGMENT AND MERCY
   A. The Earth Recoils
   B. The Marks of Cain
   C. Hope of New Life

## LESSON EXPOSITION

### INTRODUCTION

The effects of sin's deception upon the husband and wife in the Garden reached into their very home and brought jealousy and death among their children.

We want to watch carefully a number of things as we study Genesis 4. It is very easy to read too much into the material based on prior assumptions. There are three areas that come to attention:

First, we should note the central theme of God's sovereignty to accept whom He desires.

Second, we should note that the doctrine of original sin (based on Genesis 3) did not negate Cain's responsibility nor did it make sin his sole option.

Third, we should note that grace and not damnation stands as the last words of this text.

I. UNACCEPTABLE WORSHIP (Genesis 4:1-7)

A. Mystery of Election (vv. 1-5)

**1. And Adam knew Eve his wife; and she conceived, and bare Cain, and said, I have gotten a man from the Lord.**

**2. And she again bare his brother, Abel. And Abel was a keeper of sheep, but Cain was a tiller of the ground.**

Throughout the Old Testament the Hebrew "yadah" (know) is used to describe intimate sexual relations. It is an important verb because it connotes that sexual relations are more than merely physical but also involve spiritual realities of truly knowing the other person. It is intimate knowledge and sharing of oneself that makes it so powerful and deemed for the sanctity of marriage. Such knowledge between the man and the woman produces life.

The personal name "Cain" has a double meaning. As related to the Hebrew verb "gotten" in verse 1, it means "to get, acquire, to create." It also has the meaning of "spear." Cain as the firstborn, is mentioned in several places in the Bible. In the three places of the New Testament, he is not mentioned with any degree of kindness. In Hebrews 11:4, the two brothers are mentioned together with Abel's offering being "by faith" and "more acceptable" to God than Cain's. Why this was the case is not told other than the possible use of the expression "by faith" as the interpretive key. In 1 John 3:12 Cain is mentioned as a murderer and evil. The question is clearly answered regarding why Cain murdered his brother: "because his own deeds were evil and his brother's righteous." However, that still does not answer the question of the sacrifice being rejected. The final passage regarding Cain is in Jude 11 in which Cain's life is characterized as a "way" in which deceivers can walk. Again, interpretive issues are at stake regarding what constitutes the "way of Cain."

Abel's name means "breath, futility, vapor, nothingness." From the beginning of the story, the Hebrew reader could have foreseen the fate of Abel simply by his name. Why Eve named her child in this fashion is left to conjecture. Perhaps he was more weakly appearing than the elder brother.

Three times in the New Testament Abel is mentioned. The first is Matthew 23:35 in which Jesus indicted the Pharisees as hypocrites because of the way they treated the prophets before Him and would treat Him. Abel's blood is mentioned as being innocently shed because of religious reasons. (The parallel to this is found in Luke 11:51.) The next reference is Hebrews 11:4 in which both Cain and Abel are mentioned. (See the comments previously on this text regarding Cain.) Abel's sacrifice is accepted by God, apparently on the basis of faith. Although Abel died, he still speaks through his faith to continual generations. The message of his faith is not easily discerned from Genesis 4, but it is obvious that later Jewish and Christian writers saw tremendous implications from the life of the innocent Abel. The final passage is Hebrews 12:24 in which the shed blood of Christ is compared to the shed blood of Abel. Abel's blood cried out for vengeance and justice; the blood of Christ cries out for redemption and mercy.

Verse 2 tells us of the occupations of the two men. Some commentators have suggested that Abel's offering was more pleasing because it involved the shedding of blood. I do not find that interpretation convincing. Israel had numerous sacrifices by which the fruit of the land would be offered. There seems to be little or no indication that God prefers shepherds over farmers! What does stand out is that both Cain and Abel have purposeful occupations and are contributors to the purposes of God in the world.

**3. And in process of time it came to pass, that Cain brought of the fruit of the ground an offering unto the Lord.**

**4. And Abel, he also brought of the firstlings of his flock and of the fat thereof. And the Lord had respect unto Abel and to his offering:**

**5. But unto Cain and to his offering he had no respect. And Cain was very wroth, and his countenance fell.**

The great mystery of God's power to show mercy to whom He desires (Exodus 33:19) is given its first revelation in this event at the place of worship. The pattern of the older brother coming in second place to the younger brother in God's blessing continues throughout the Bible: Jacob and Esau (Genesis 25:23), Leah and Rachel (Genesis 29:21-30; 30:22-24), Joseph and his brothers (Genesis 37), David and his brothers (1 Samuel 16), and the parable of the prodigal son (Luke 15:11-32).

It is this important aspect of the majesty of God that dominates the first part of the text. From the insights of verses 3-5, it is clear that God is the primary problem in the text, not Cain nor Abel. God is free to accept or not accept the offering. There is a divine mystery in His will that causes upheaval and yet accomplishes His purpose of redemption.

Verse 3 tell us that Cain offered his sacrifice to the Lord. "In the process of time" is another way of saying "and it came to pass." The time of this event is not nearly as important as where this scene took place: the altar of sacrifice. We are not told the origin of the offering practice nor what purpose it was given. Cain has done what you would expect a farmer to do: he has given from his crops, apparently in an act of gratitude. No comment is made in verse 3 regrading the Lord's attitude towards Cain's offering. That is reserved until verse 5.

---

How do you account for the presence of evil tendencies in Cain's life at this time?

---

Abel's offering is described in verse 4 in some detail. It is emphasized that he brought the firstlings of his flock and offered the entire animal, including the fat portions. Yet, there is no internal reason why God would choose Abel's offering over Cain's. In fact, Abel is doing exactly what a shepherd would do: offer from his flock. Perhaps the closest we can come to a reason for the Lord's acceptance of Abel's is that the sacrifice of blood was more pleasing. Even if that is the case, it still does not imply that God could not be pleased with sacrifices derived from the fruit of the ground; even the Levitical system knew of offerings that came from the ground.

Verse 5 tersely gives the decision by the Lord: rejection of Cain and his sacrifice. What becomes more important than the actual offering and rejection is the response of Cain to the situation. We must keep in mind that the altar is the site of this rejection. Cain had come expecting some degree of blessing and acceptance from God. What he found was rejection. Von Rad comments, "Hot resentment had risen in Cain, which had distorted even his body! He envies God's pleasure in his brother."

We must not overlook the significance of the expression "His countenance fell." It is a classic expression of the way man feels when he realizes God has not accepted him. It is the ultimate rejection and Cain must either deal with God in terms of the anger (wroth) or deal with the jealousy that is looming towards the brother. Such a situation still addresses the people of God as we gather to offer our praise and worship and discover that sometimes God does seem to favor others over ourselves. In such a situation we must carefully examine verses 6 and 7 as they offer words of warning and hope.

B. Temptation at the Altar (vv. 6, 7)

**6. And the Lord said unto Cain, Why art thou wroth? and why is thy countenance fallen?**

**7. If thou doest well, shalt thou not be accepted? and if thou doest not well, sin lieth at the door. And unto thee shall be his desire, and thou shalt rule over him.**

As we reflect on Cain's experience at the door of the place of sacrifice, we must remind ourselves that Cain's dilemma has originated from God's prerogative to accept or reject according to His will. We must also remember that his rejection of Cain has created another situation by which he still might be accepted by God. Will he turn to God in repentance or will he turn on his brother in anger?

In verse 6 the Lord speaks to Cain as if nothing of great significance has happened. That a person's sacrifice might not be accepted is apparently not a major problem to the Lord. It is not the rejected sacrifice that is the problem. The problem is what Cain will do with this God who maintains His freedom to act. It is as if God assumed that Cain would appreciate this fact of God's nature.

That point should not be left simply to the past. The same thing happens today. There are Christians who have had the experience of praying for something and expecting God's blessing only to discover that God blessed someone else and not us. It generates feelings of jealousy and insecurity. It strikes at the pride of our own self-righteousness and forces us beyond the limits of a God who works at our request to the God who is free in His will. When God blesses someone else and not us then we are faced with the same dilemma that faced Cain. We too are left questioning this God; we too must discover what God's response is for us in the midst of our rejection.

Thus verse 7 presents the options available to Cain and us as we face the problem of God's freedom. Note that verse 7 knows nothing of humankind being bound to sin. Cain has not inherited from Adam a tendency to sin so that he has no other options. God generously moved Cain from the spector of rejection at the altar to the place of acceptance if he would only "do well." To "do well" is God's invitation to Cain to trust in the Lord in spite of what has happened. It is an invitation to faith. It is an invitation to not be so wrapped up in himself that he cannot be free for the future God has for him.

In the midst of this invitation God tells Cain that "sin lieth at the door." According to some modern translations the wording is "sin is couching at the door; its desire is for you, but you must master it." Sin is seen as an active, personal force seeking to disrupt the harmony between God and Cain. Sin has not been present in the rejection of the sacrifice; that rejection is purely from the perspective of God's freedom to choose. Sin is present in the response of Cain. That Cain is "wroth" and it shows on his face (vv. 5, 6) is still not a matter of sin. What is the occasion for sin is that Cain will leave the place of the altar not reconciled to his God or brother. At the door is where Cain must decide for or against God. Sin has a "desire" for Cain. It seeks to consume and control him. Brueggemann observes, "Sin lusts after Cain with an animal hunger. The term 'desire' is telling here. It is the same word used in Genesis 3:16 to describe the perverted inclination of the woman for the man in the disordered affair of the garden."

Yet, the verse concludes with a word of hope from the Lord concerning the power of sin. Sin is not all-powerful. Cain has in his ability the power to say "no" to sin. Cain can "rule" over sin if he will. While this is a word of hope, it is also a word of pain concerning the human condition after the Fall. Man must take responsibility for his own actions. He can choose to obey or choose to disobey. While the choice was man's before the Fall, it was a choice still grounded primarily in obedience and close communion with God. Expelled from the Garden, Cain is left with an invitation from God but also with the crucible of self-responsibility. It is that crucible that sin seeks to devour as it waits lurking at the door.

II. PREMEDITATED MURDER (Genesis 4:8-10)

A. Death of a Brother (v. 8)

**8. And Cain talked with Abel his brother: and it came to pass, when they were in the field, that Cain rose up against Abel his brother and slew him.**

Von Rad exclaims in his commentary on this verse, "And now occurs the first murder, . . . Cain who had the opportunity to rule over sin (v. 7) has now become the one who is ruled over."

What did they talk about? Was it a deceptive lure to lead Abel into the field of death? Was it an attempt to understand what happened at the altar, an attempt

that somehow went sour? Was it an argument over whom God loved best? Was it mere chitchat that covered a lurking pain that would erupt in fury and death? All we know is that time passed on and led to the rendezvous that marks the murderous course of life. Note the progression of death: first, an animal is slain to cover Adam and Eve following their sin; second, more animals are slain in sacrifice by Abel; third, the sacrificer of animals is himself slain to appease the fury of his brother.

B. Sin Exposed (vv. 9, 10)

**9. And the Lord said unto Cain, Where is Abel thy brother? And he said, I know not: Am I my brother's keeper?**

---

Discuss the extent of our accountability as being "our brother's keeper."

---

It should be noted the sequence of the questions posed by God towards sinful man. The first question was "Where are you?" (Genesis 3:9). The second question is "Where is your brother?" (4:9). Those two questions stand together as we measure the impact of sin. First of all, sin separates us from God so that we are lost. Secondly, sin separates us from our brothers so that we are lost from them. When community with God is shattered, all human community is threatened. The same is true today when we consider this nation's stance on abortion. We are people lost from God and thus are lost from our unborn brothers of the future.

Cain lied to the Lord. He knew where his brother was; he had killed him. But in order to avoid the confrontation with the lie, he turned the question back to God. It is interesting to note the power of the question, "Am I my brother's keeper?" It was a pun effect, "Am I the shepherd's shepherd?" The answer surprisingly, is "no." Cain is not his brother's keeper. He is his brother's brother; and there is a big difference. Cain assumed he was his brother's keeper and thus slew him. If Cain had remained his brother's brother then the weak Abel would have lived. While Cain was correct in his reply to the

Lord, he was in error in that he failed to obey his own advice.

**10. And he said, What hast thou done? the voice of thy brother's blood crieth unto me from the ground.**

Cain had violated a most sacred trust: the relationship between life and God in another person. Abel's life belonged to God, not Cain. By attacking Abel, Cain had assaulted what was God's possession: Abel's life.

The cry of the Lord, "What hast thou done?" is one of utter disbelief and horror. This is not a simple question offered by the Lord. It is a horried stricken cry that continues to echo down through human history from Cain to Auschwitz to contemporary forms of injustice. It even has a parallel in the cry of another Son of God from the Cross. "My God, my God, why hast thou forsaken me?"

The Lord is able to hear the spilt blood of Abel cry from the ground. The sounds of injustice do not end with death; they continue to ring in God's ears and our ears as long as men have memories. One of the most pathetic sights in our generation has been the pictures of hundreds of mothers and wives stalking the streets of Argentina wondering where their lost sons and daughters were killed and buried. Abel's blood continues to cry out (Hebrews 12:24), but it is a cry birthed in injustice. The blood of Jesus cries out, but it is birthed in the love of God.

III. JUDGMENT AND MERCY (Genesis 4:11-16, 25, 26)

A. The Earth Recoils (vv. 11, 12)

**11. And now art thou cursed from the earth which hath opened her mouth to receive thy brother's blood from thy hand.**

**12. When thou tillest the ground, it shall not henceforth yield unto thee her strength; a fugitive and a vagabond thou shalt be in the earth.**

As noticed last week regarding the effect of the "curse of sin" upon Adam and Eve, it did not directly affect them in the sense that the curse was placed upon them. Rather, the curse was upon those things which made up the source of their life. The same principle holds true in God's relationship to Cain. The curse is not placed directly upon Cain; only a mark that points to the curse is placed upon him. (Yet, even that mark is two-edged: curse and blessing.)

The curse is actually upon the ground in relationship to Cain. The earth could not receive a greater burden than what was received in Adam's disobedience. However, the earth is specifically called to be cursed in relation to Cain. The man who made his livelihood from the ground and used the fruit of the ground to sacrifice to God is now cut off from the ground. Cain had fertilized the earth with the blood of his brother. The earth under his feet and plow was thus polluted and could never be a source of life to him again.

The language of verse 11 is so powerful. Cain's hand had been instrumental in bringing sustaining life from the ground. In his fury he turned his hand back upon the ground and fed it the brother's blood. By his own hand he brought death to himself, his brother, and his land. The effects of disobedience reach dimensions that we seldom see in advance. Sin's pervasive power seeks to bring death in every way possible. That is why disobedience is so painful for all who are involved. Sin is never just personal; it is socially destructive.

Cut off from the strength of the land, Cain is destined to a life of wandering in the earth. It is suggested that his descendants were Kenites who inhabited the fringes of Israelite society. The Kenites were worshipers of Israel's God yet were not part of the covenant community. Along with a sister tribe, the Rechabites, they are mentioned in 1 Kings 20:41; 2 Kings 10:15; 1 Chronicles 2:55; Jeremiah 35; Ezekiel 9:4; and Zechariah 13:6.

B. The Mark of Cain (vv. 13-16)

**13. And Cain said unto the Lord, My punishment is greater than I can bear.**

**14. Behold, thou hast driven me out this day from the face of the earth; and from thy face shall I be hid; and I shall be a fugitive and a vagabond in the earth; and it shall come to pass,**

**that every one that findeth me shall slay me.**

**15. And the Lord said unto him, Therefore whosoever slayeth Cain, vengeance shall be taken upon him sevenfold. And the Lord set a mark upon Cain, lest any finding him should kill him.**

**16. And Cain went out from the presence of the Lord, and dwelt in the land of Nod, on the east of Eden.**

Cain had experienced double rejection. First his sacrifice had been rejected; second, his source of livelihood, the earth, had rejected him. It is little wonder that he exclaims that his punishment is too great. It is a cry of desperation before the Lord. That the Lord heard his cry should speak to us of the Lord's mercy. Just as the Lord heard the cry of Abel's blood, He has now heard the lament of the threat of life from Cain. Cain is helpless as was Abel. Therein marks the difference between God and man. Cain slew Abel in his helplessness; God marks Cain for life in the midst of his helplessness.

Is man's difficulty in earning a living always an example of God's judgment for sin? Defend your answer.

In verse 14, Cain exclaimed that he would be cut off from everything familiar. The face of the earth would no longer confront with a smile. The face of God is hidden in the mystery of guilt and forgiveness. The fear reached its climax in the cry, "everyone that findeth me shall slay me" (v. 14). The slayer has become the fugitive.

God responded mercifully to Cain by reaffirming that the power of life and death belongs solely to Him. While Cain had found mercy in the midst of his sin, the slayer of Cain would find vengeance sevenfold. The mark was apparently some type of visible sign; perhaps a tatoo.

Verse 16 gives the predicament of all since Cain. Each of us lives east of Eden in the land of Nod. The actual place is long since lost; but the Hebrew word means "restlessness, wanderer." It is the place of fear that others will slay us once they discover who we are. It is the price

paid for the hiding of our emotions and real selves lest we not be accepted and someone else slay us with rejection.

Ever since Adam began hiding from God in the garden, like Cain, we have joined in hiding in fear. The good news of Jesus is that God has initiated the way to move us from the places of fear to the places of trust. In Christ, God has committed Himself not to slay us. God has committed Himself to be for us and not against us. God has committed Himself to love us and reconcile us to Himself (Romans 5:1-11; 8:31-39; 2 Corinthians 5:17-19).

C. Hope of New Life (vv. 25, 26)

It is important that Christians remember that death is not the last word. Life is the last word! Even though Abel no longer walked the face of the earth, God brought life again in the birth of Seth. It is through the lineage of Seth that the Messiah, Jesus Christ, was born (Luke 3:38). The life-theme is so vivid in this sense as we consider that God has chosen newness and life for us. Cain, though plagued with the curse of rejection, is also the outsider who will ultimately find himself back home in the saving work of Christ.

The note at the conclusion of verse 26 is significant. In order to fully understand it we must remember that the Hebrew used several names for God. One name was "Elohim" which often referred to God as a Creator-God (Genesis 1:1). Here we have the use of "Yahweh" as a proper name for God. This name in Hebrew is usually translated with the English Lord. The emphasis of this divine name was upon the covenant-making quality of the Lord. Thus, He was seen to be a Lord in direct relationship with His creation. It is not until the time of Moses that the full revelation took place under the auspices of this name. What is of note is that from very early times people worshiped the same Lord who revealed Himself to His covenant partner Abraham, His covenant people Israel at Sinai, and all people in Jesus Christ the Lord.

**REVIEW QUESTIONS**

1. How does the New Testament treat Cain and Abel? What texts support your view?

2. In your opinion, why did God reject Cain's sacrifice?

3. What is the significance of the expression concerning Cain, "his countenance fell"?

4. What avenue of opportunity did God give Cain to escape from the temptation to sin?

5. What is the meaning of the "mark upon Cain"?

## GOLDEN TEXT HOMILY

"BY FAITH ABEL OFFERED UNTO GOD A MORE EXCELLENT SACRIFICE THAN CAIN, BY WHICH HE OBTAINED WITNESS THAT HE WAS RIGHTEOUS, GOD TESTIFYING OF HIS GIFTS: AND BY IT HE BEING DEAD YET SPEAKETH" (Hebrews 11:4).

There are several key points of importance in the account of Cain and Abel in relation to their offerings to God. First of all a look at their names reveals much. In Genesis 4:3-12 we are given a clear picture. Cain's name meant "acquisition," thus he was a type of the mere man of the earth. His religion was void of any adequate sense of sin, or need of atonement. Among some of his characteristics and deeds are (1) self-will in worship; (2) anger toward God; (3) refusal to bring a sin-offering; (4) murder of his brother; (5) lying to God; and (6) becoming a fugitive and a vagabond in the earth.

On the other hand Abel's name meant "exhaltation" or "that which ascends," thus he was a type of the spiritual man. His sacrifice was one in which atoning blood was shed; therefore, this was his confession of sin and the expression of his faith in a vicarious sacrifice. Our vicarious sacrifice is none other than the Lord Jesus Christ proclaimed by John as "the Lamb of God, which taketh away the sin of the world" (John 1:29). Abel's offering is contrasted with Cain's offering of fruit of his own works. This is proclaiming in the very beginning of the human race the primal truth that the shedding of blood is essential in the remission of sin.

Second is the striking fact that "by faith" Abel offered unto God. This implies that a previous instruction for faith is taking God at His word. This is also in line with Romans 10:17 where the Apostle Paul writes: "So then faith cometh by hearing, and hearing by the word of God." How vitally important for Christians to hear the Word of God and walk in faith, doing everything "by faith."

Thirdly, Cain's bloodless offering was a refusal of the divine way. The Lord God Jehovah even made a last appeal to Cain (Genesis 4:7) to still bring the required offering and to be accepted by Him. But Cain was self-willed in his worship and refused to come God's way. Likewise the appeal is still going out to all those who are unsaved. All that is required is to bring themselves to the Lord Jesus Christ, confess their sins, and be saved through faith in His shed blood at Calvary.

**—William M. Henry, Jr., Professor of New Testament Greek and Missions, West Coast Christian College, Fresno, California**

## SENTENCE SERMONS

JEALOUSY IS a horse the devil likes to ride.

**—Selected**

SIN FOLLOWS a pattern which, if allowed to go unchecked, results in great tragedy and death.

**—Selected**

WHATEVER IS BEGUN in anger ends in shame.

**—"Speaker's Sourcebook"**

SIN MAY BE clasped so close we cannot see its face.

**—Trench**

## EVANGELISTIC APPLICATION

SIN BRINGS TRAGEDY AND DEATH, BUT REDEMPTION THROUGH CHRIST BRINGS FORGIVENESS AND LIFE.

Redemption in Christ must speak more loudly in our lives than the blood of Abel. Abel's blood cries for revenge. Yet we are not redeemed by that blood; we are redeemed by the blood of Christ that cries for reconciliation and mercy.

This point must be made in terms of

our living with other brothers and sisters in faith. The world is watching to see if we really practice what we preach! Our best evangelism is made as we truly love one another. As Jesus commented, "By this they shall know that you are my disciples, that you love one another." That is the foundation of effective evangelism in the church.

All our pietistic plans and efforts to win the lost and be holy will be of little value if they are not grounded in our love one for the other. This means that we are to rejoice when God blesses the other person and not us. It means we speak words of life and not of death concerning one another. It means we seriously remember whose blood it is that has redeemed us.

## ILLUMINATING THE LESSON

In a poetic sermon titled "Come Sweet Death," the author David Napier relates the cry of Abel's blood:

What have you done? The voice of Abel's blood is crying to me from the ground. The voice of Abel's blood, a thousand, thousand voices crying to me from the bloody ground!

O Absalom, my son, my son, who took the life of Amnon, son of mine; the voice of Amnon, Absalom, is crying to me from the ground. O bleeding son of mine, the son your brother (son of mine) despised; my son rejected, smitten, and afflicted; my son my wounded son, my dying son, subjected to the public ways of dying and all the countless, private, hidden ways in battle, execution, inquisition; in lethal oven or in lethal humor; in lynching by the hand of brutal brother; or brutal psychological exclusion (a quiet but effective form of lynching); and always wholesale murder by neglect.

My son, my son! The voice of Abel's blood is crying to me from the ground. O Christ, O Jesus Christ, my son, my dying son.—**Come Sweet Death,** United Church Press

## DAILY DEVOTIONAL GUIDE

M. Sin Punished. Joshua 7:10-12
T. Mercy Granted. Psalm 94:17-22
W. Gratitude Expressed. Romans 7:21-25
T. Grace Extended. Ephesians 2:1-10
F. Safety Confirmed. 2 Thessalonians 1:3-7
S. Judgment Foretold. 2 Thessalonians 1:8-10

# A Wicked Society

**Study Text:** Genesis 6:1 through 7:24

**Supplemental Reference:** Isaiah 54:1-10; Matthew 24:38, 39; Luke 17:20-27; 2 Peter 2:4-9

**Time:** Traditional Chronology dates the flood around 2400 B.C.

**Place:** Somewhere in Asia Minor

**Golden Text:** "The Lord said, My Spirit shall not always strive with man" (Genesis 6:3).

**Central Truth:** Though God is merciful, all who continue in sin will be judged.

**Evangelistic Emphasis:** A merciful God calls men to repentance.

## Printed Text

**Genesis 6:1.** And it came to pass, when men began to multiply on the face of the earth, and daughters were born unto them,

**2. That the sons of God saw the daughters of men that they were fair; and they took them wives of all which they chose.**

3. And the Lord said, My spirit will not always strive with man, for that he also is flesh: yet his days shall be an hundred and twenty years.

**4. There were giants in the earth in those days; and also after that, when the sons of God came in unto the daughters of men, and they bare children to them, the same became mighty men which were of old, men of renown.**

5. And God saw that the wickedness of man was great in the earth, and that every imagination of the thoughts of his heart was only evil continually.

**6. And it repented the Lord that he had made man on the earth, and it grieved him at his heart.**

7. And the Lord said, I will destroy man whom I have created from the face of the earth; both man, and beast, and the creeping thing, and the fowls of the air; for it repenteth me that I have made them.

**7:11. In the six hundredth year of Noah's life, in the second month, the seventeenth day of the month, the same day were all the fountains of the great deep broken up, and the windows of heaven were opened.**

12. And the rain was upon the earth forty days and forty nights.

**13. In the selfsame day entered Noah, and Shem, and Ham, and Japheth, the sons of Noah, and Noah's wife, and the three wives of his sons with them, unto the ark;**

14. They, and every beast after his kind, and all the cattle after their kind, and every creeping thing that creepeth upon the earth after his kind, and every fowl after his kind, every bird of every sort.

51

**15. And they went in unto Noah into the ark, two and two of all flesh, wherein is the breath of life.**

16. And they that went in, went in male and female of all flesh, as God had commanded him: and the Lord shut him in.

---

## LESSON OUTLINE

I. MAN'S WICKEDNESS
  A. The Spread of Wickedness
  B. Source of Evil Thoughts
II. GOD'S DISPLEASURE
III. NOAH'S SALVATION
  A. A Righteous Person Called
  B. Sanctuary Described
  C. Provision for the Future
  D. Days of Judgment

## LESSON EXPOSITION

INTRODUCTION

It is important to keep in mind the sequence of events that happens in the opening chapters of Genesis. The first two chapters write of a world ordered by God. It is a world given over to His purposes where sin, though present, does not exercise influence. The third chapter, without any explanation or hint of trouble, opens with the active presence of sin. It seems as if sin needed the cooperation of humankind in order to truly work its destructive will. The earthly paradise comes to a swift end and the principles of self-will and disobedience spread like a raging fire across the landscape of Adam's children. If sin killed man in Genesis 3, then brother-man killed brother-man in Genesis 4. We come to Genesis 6 in this lesson and discover that the iniquity along the lines of men and women and the entire order is in upheaval.

As you prepare to teach this lesson, keep in mind that Lesson 6 will also deal with the Noah story. Lesson 5 will focus primarily on the wickedness of Noah's generations (note the topic). Lesson 6 will focus on God's redemptive response through the man Noah. I have drawn this to your attention so that you will not feel any need to rush through these chapters (6-9). The principles found in these two lessons warrant your careful attention.

Let me suggest you study both lessons together in your preparation. You will likely want to keep your spoken comments directed at the specific lesson; however, your knowledge of the entire focus will add greatly to your ability to speak with insight to your class.

I. MAN'S WICKEDNESS (Genesis 6:1-5)

A. The Spread of Wickedness (vv.1-4)

**1. And it came to pass, when men began to multiply on the face of the earth, and daughters were born unto them,**

**2. That the sons of God saw the daughters of men that they were fair; and they took them wives of all which they chose.**

**3. And the Lord said, My Spirit shall not always strive with man, for that he also is flesh: yet his days shall be a hundred and twenty years.**

**4. There were giants in the earth in those days; and also after that, when the sons of God came in unto the daughters of men, and they bare children to them, the same became mighty men which were of old, men of renown.**

These verses introduce us to a time in human history that is shrouded in mystery and myth. The Bible has little to offer that helps to clarify the events related in Genesis 6:1-4. Much of what we can offer is conjecture. Yet we can only get the dim outlines of realities that are long past in human history.

We are introduced to three areas of concern about the early days of human life: the union of the sons of God and the women of earth, the days of the giants **(the Nephilim),** and God's decision to limit the sphere of His Spirit among the human creatures of earth.

The debate continues regarding who are these "sons of God" who united with earthly women and produced the mighty men of old. Some commentators have considered them to be men of a superior human race. Other commentators see them as beings from the heavenly realms.

The second group mentioned are the "giants" of verse 4. The Hebrew word for "giants" in this passage is **Nephilim,** a title by which they are called in numerous English sources. In Numbers 13:33, the **Nephilim** are mentioned as descendants of Anak. Giants are referred to in Deuteronomy 2:21; 3:11 (implied); Ezekiel 32:21, 27 (especially if **Nephilim** is translated with the sense of "strong ones" or "heroes" (Von Rad); Amos 2:9.

The third area is found in verse 3 and is God's decision to place firm limits on the course of mankind. It is a verse of judgment on a world gone mad. It seems that in a world where evil has mixed so intimately with the life of flesh, God is constrained to limit the activity of His life-giving Spirit among men. It has been suggested that the "hundred and twenty years" refers to a period of time between which God levied this judgment and the coming of the Flood **(The Interpreter's Bible).**

What should be noted is that the absence of the Spirit of God is equivalent to a sentence of death upon mankind. Life is found in the Spirit of God. When God no longer strives with a person or society, then death is the inevitable result.

B. The Source of Evil Thoughts (v.5)

**5. And God saw that the wickedness of man was great in the earth, and that every imagination of the thoughts of his heart was only evil constantly.**

---

In what ways is the world situation of today reminiscent of Noah's day?

---

W. R. Bowie records this tidbit of serious humor, "What is the shape of the earth?" asked a schoolteacher, and one small pupil replied, "My daddy says the shape of the earth is a mess."

While that story has a humorous side to it, there is no humor in the intent of the text that God say the wickedness of man. We should not pass too quickly over the first words of this verse, "God saw. . . ." We live in a world where man thinks that the Creator either does not exist or the Creator is not concerned with what the creature does. It is a world where God's vision is denied. It is a world blinded by the darkness of the evil one. But it is still a world that God sees. What a fearful word that is! God is not ignorant of the evil designs of our lives. We deceive ourselves into thinking that we can live irresponsibly without due penalty; yet, He sees our disobedience and allows sin to work its destructive course in our lives.

God saw the wickedness of man. The same Hebrew word is used for "wickedness" and "evil" in this verse. If anything, it intensified the meaning of great wickedness and great evil. It should also be noted that God ascribes this evil to man. Man is the recipient of blame regarding this invasion of evil that has corrupted God's plan. Note that the devil is not mentioned in the text. Man stands completely responsible before God for this great wickedness in the earth. The popular expression, "The devil made me do it," is not acceptable to God. God holds humankind responsible for willful disobedience.

The source of this evil in man is seen in man's thoughts and his imagination. The Hebrew word for imaginations is used five times in the Old Testament. In Genesis 8:21 (part of the Noah story), it is used to describe evil imaginations; in Deuteronomy 31:21, it is used in a negative sense of evil plans; in 1 Chronicles 28:9; 29:18, it is used positively in relation to David's prayer at his death.

The word thoughts has the sense of devices. With the two concepts together (imagination and thoughts) we can see that imagination is related to what a person can begin to envision for the future. Thoughts become more specific plans and devices of the mind to actually accomplish the imaginations.

II. GOD'S DISPLEASURE (Genesis 6:6, 7)

**6. And it repented the Lord that he**

**had made man on the earth, and it grieved him at his heart.**

**7. And the Lord said, I will destroy man whom I have created from the face of the earth; both man, and beast, and the creeping thing, and the fowls of the air; for it repenteth me that I have made them.**

It has been said that the saddest words in Holy Scripture are found in verse 6. The translation of the **New International Version** speaks forcefully, "The Lord was grieved that he had made man. Another modern translation reads," The Lord was sorry that he had made man." The **New English Bible** reads the closing statement in verse 7 as the Lord saying, "I am sorry that I ever made them." Whatever translation the intent is painfully clear: God regretted making man.

The heart of God and the heart of man were meant to be in communion and harmony. But out of man's heart has come imaginations and thoughts of rebellion. The heart of God is cut to the core as the heart of man fails. Brueggemann has observed that this picture of God is not one of anger but of grief. God is mourning because man has placed himself in the position of death spiritually and thereby death physically on a large scale. Man has chosen the way of rebellion and death while this God longed for man to choose the way of life and blessing. It should be noted that the word "grieved" in verse 6 is the same word used in 3:16 to describe the pain the woman experiences in childbirth because of sin. It is the language of children gone bad; it is the language of mourning parents.

God had such high hopes for his created order. This is vividly expressed in his hopes for Israel found in Jeremiah 3:19; the pain and grief of these hopes is found in Jeremiah 3:20. God acknowledges the utter failure of His people.

The language of verse 7 is hard. The Hebrew expression "destroy" has the sense of "wash away" (Von Rad). It is a scene of God choosing to destroy practically all life because of His great sorrow.

It may be that God's decision to destroy the animal kingdom is related to man's tendency to worship these creatures and use them as models for worship rather than truly worship God. (See Romans 1 for more on this matter of idolatry.) What is part of this lesson is the question of the wrath of God. God's wrath is not petty anger but grows out of deep remorse for man's decision for sin. God's holiness and His love demand that grief be His response to this disobedience. It has been said that grief is a love word (Fay Angus); that is correct.

This grief of God finally manifests itself in His wrath. We should note that the wrath of God is God's willingness to let the world go its way to destruction (Romans 1:24, 26, 28). God's wrath is seen in His apparent permission to allow sin to run its evil course of destruction in the world. His mercy is seen in His specific acts of discipline (such as the flood) where the wages of sin are finally collected but also where the free gift of His mercy can begin to take effect (Noah).

III. NOAH'S SALVATION

(Genesis 6:8 through 7:24; Only 7:11-16 are in the printed text.)

A. A Righteous Person Called (6:8-10).

From the Fall in Genesis 3 to the world of evil in 6:7, we have seen the earth and humankind caught in an ever deepening pit of death and rebellion. God's announcement in 6:6, 7, seemed so total and absolute. Yet, in verse 8 God offers a new alternative. God affirms that faithlessness is not the final word in the world but that faithfulness will have a place in His sight.

Righteous Noah has been kept from the story of the evil world so that he can emerge as God's source of salvation. Yet the text makes clear that Noah has not deserved this position on the basis of his own righteousness; like all men, he too must find "grace in the eyes of the Lord." It is God's mercy extended to a new world that is revealed to Noah. Noah is an agent of salvation because he is a recipient of grace! God's unmerited favor stands behind all of His love and compassion towards us.

Verse 9 begins with a statement of Noah's generations. You would think that immediately there would follow the naming of his physical posterity, the sons. But they are reserved for verse 10, almost as an afterthought. Noah's true legacy (generation) is found in the description of himself before God: "a just man and perfect in his generations, and Noah walked with God" (v. 9). What a fitting commentary the Bible gives us regarding the legacy we leave at death. We do not leave the future only sons and daughters to carry on human life; we also leave our own effects of righteousness or unrighteousness. They are the real marks of our lives upon the world.

As Brueggemann comments, "Noah is the bearer of an alternative possibility." God's working in the world is not locked in; God always has a way to accomplish His ways of salvation! The alternative way from that of the destruction of the world is found in the three affirmations regarding Noah.

First, he is called a righteous man. It is important that we connect this righteousness with God's covenant. Noah's righteousness consists in the fact that He believes God's Word and trusts God as his Creator. He really believes God has committed Himself to him and he responds by obedience.

Second, he is "perfect." A better way of thinking of this is that he is blameless before God as he has lived. He is not stained with the guilt of his world. He is a man given to God and thus can hear God speak the words of deliverance.

Third, he walked with God. The expression is seldom used in the Bible. It seems that after the Flood man walks before the Lord but not with Him.

B. Sanctuary Described (6:14-16)

With the previous introduction of Noah, we find that God not only is concerned to preserve a remnant but that He actually provides a way for that remnant to be saved.

It should be noticed that Noah is instructed to "make thee an ark." God is not going to make the sanctuary for him; Noah is a clear example of what it is to

work out one's salvation in fear and trembling (Philippians 2:12). While salvation is completely from God and grace is indeed unmerited favor, it is also true that we have the responsibility of responding faithfully in our own life. God's covenant of grace which Noah begins to receive by this call issues forth in man's joyful obedience to the good news of salvation.

The gopher wood was perhaps cypress. The dimensions indicated by cubits measure approximately 489 feet in length, 81 feet wide, and 49 feet high. The interior was composed of rooms and had three stories for storage. The roof is perhaps to be understood as a window for visibility. In order to further secure the vessel, it was coated on the inside with pitch.

In principle this sea-going sanctuary is an early example of the earthly and heavenly sanctuaries described in both Testaments. This is seen in that both have specific dimensions given by God and both serve the same purpose of protection and preservation from sin and judgment.

C. Provision for the Future (6:17 through 7:16; 7:11-16 are in the printed text).

Chapter 6 has three areas of concern and a final statement concerning Noah. The first area of concern is in verse 17 where God's word of judgment is specified. Here it is clear that God's intention is to "wash away" sin and through Noah provide a new humanity that will obey. As we know, this did not reach its fullness until the time of Jesus Christ who came and washed away sin and became the true source of newness for all mankind. Noah serves as an example of Christ in that he is the one chosen to preserve the future. One major difference is the fact that Christ seeks to save even those who are lost in Noah's flood!

The second concern in verse 18 in which the word of judgment of verse 17 is followed by the word of covenant. Covenant is God's decision to be "for" humankind even in the midst of judgment. This covenant has not originated out of nothing. Rather, its source is found in

God's love for His creation. We have earlier seen that God's heart is broken by man's disobedience. Now we find that God's broken heart is still a heart of commitment and love.

The third section of concern is in verses 19-21 where this covenant is extended to the animal kingdom and properties of the plant world for food as well as seed for the future. The expression "keep them alive" is found in verses 19 and 20. As we saw in Genesis chapters 1 and 2 man lived in harmony with the animal kingdom, but that harmony was broken by sin. Now we see Noah preserving God's other creatures who cannot provide for themselves. This is truly a statement of man's rightful role of exercising dominion over the creation.

The final verse (22) concludes this section with the affirmation of Noah's obedience. He did what God commanded. It must have been a source of great ridicule for him to make such a vessel expecting something he and those around him had never seen (a storm of this magnitude). Yet, in the face of tremendous peer pressure and public abuse Noah did what God commanded. Perhaps that one verse is the telling statement of how the Christian lives in the midst of a wicked society.

Most of 7:1-10 restates the final portion of chapter 6. Additions regarding the time of the flood and continued statements of Noah's obedience are made.

**11. In the six hundredth year of Noah's life, in the second month, the seventeenth day of the month, the same day were all the fountains of the great deep broken up, and the windows of heaven were opened.**

The picture presented is one of great detail. God is specific about when the judgment is to begin. Let there be no doubt, there is a day of judgment that comes upon sin. It also tells of the origins of the Flood. The Hebrew is graphic in describing the fact that the entire cosmos is involved in this catastrophe. The fountains of the deep erupt in spewing forth a torrent of water from the earth and the heavens open in sending torrents

of water upon the earth. In Genesis 4, the blood of Abel cried for justice. In Genesis 7, the waters of the earth arise to cover the foulness of man's inhumanity and disobedience.

**12. And the rain was upon the earth forty days and forty nights.**

This repeats the affirmation of 7:4 that it would rain non-stop for 40 days and nights. It is basically a statement of the totality of the catastrophe that came upon the earth. It is as if the primeval darkness of Genesis 1:2 had again engulfed the earth and man's condition is hopeless, except for that bobbing piece of gopher wood.

**13. In the selfsame day entered Noah, and Shem, and Ham, and Hapheth, the sons of Noah, and Noah's wife, and the three wives of his sons with them, into the ark.**

In what ways is the Church typical of the ark?

In the midst of the darkness comes the revelation that God has a future with Noah's family safely huddled in the ark. Noah will not be left alone in the earth (as was Adam at the beginning). Woman, the bearer of human fruit, is present and part of the new order that will come from the ark of safety.

**14. They, and every beast after his kind, and all the cattle after their kind, and every creeping thing that creepeth upon the earth after his kind, and every fowl after his kind, every bird of every sort.**

**15. And they went in unto Noah into the ark, two and two of all flesh, wherein is the breath of life.**

**16. And they that went in, went in male and female of all flesh, as God had commanded him: and the Lord shut him in.**

The same point of the provision for the future regarding husband and wife (verse 13) is made for the animal kingdom in male and female of each kind. The account emphasizes that life is still the intention of God.

The account closes with the fact that God was the preserver of Noah in the midst of this great destruction. God shut Noah in the ark.

D. Days of Judgment (7:17-24)

The terrible days of destruction caused by the deluge are described in these verses. It should be noted that the safety of the ark of promise and covenant is kept above the raging waters. It is elevated "above the earth." The earth has become the place of destruction; to be above the earth is to be safe.

The prevalence of the waters is intensified in progressive in order from verses 17-20. Note in verse 19 that all the high mountains are covered; verse 20 indicates they were covered completely.

The effects of the Flood are described in verses 21-23. The death scene begins with the animals and concludes with man. Perhaps man managed to survive longer than any other creature due to his innate abilities; yet, he too fell prey to the destruction that was wasting at noonday. Verse 23 shows that God's judgment was behind this destruction as the total scene is revisited.

The last part of verse 23 lamely mentions that only Noah and those in the ark were left alive. While still present, the word of grace is left to a few. It is a profound statement that the chapter ends with the haunting words of verse 24, "And the waters prevailed upon the earth an hundred and fifty days."

## REVIEW QUESTIONS

1. What things would cause the Spirit of God to no longer strive with humankind?

2. How would you describe the wickedness of humankind today? What clear manifestations exist to prove your point?

3. What is the relationship between "imaginations" and "thoughts"?

4. What is significant about the heart of God being broken as He saw sin?

## GOLDEN TEXT HOMILY

"THE LORD SAID, MY SPIRIT SHALL NOT ALWAYS STRIVE WITH MAN" (Genesis 6:3).

"The time of God patience and forbearance towards provoking sinners is sometimes long, but always limited: reprieves are not pardons" (Matthew Henry).

David said, "As for man, his days are as grass: as a flower of the field, so he flourisheth. For the wind passeth over it, and it is gone; and the place thereof shall know it no more" (Psalm 103:15, 16).

James said, "For what is your life?" He answered, "It is even a vapour, that appeareth for a little time, and then vanisheth away" (James 4:14).

Since man's existence on earth is limited, the Spirit's striving with man is limited. There comes the time when we pass from this life to the next. "It is appointed unto men once to die, but after this the judgment" (Hebrews 9:27). Men ought to heed the call of the Spirit to repentance today because they have no assurance that they will be alive tomorrow to hear His call. "Prepare to meet thy God," the Prophet Amos declared (4:12). It is today that men should prepare for the inevitable encounter with God. Today they have life and opportunity. Tomorrow they may be in the presence of God. If they have responded in their lifetime to the wooings and strivings of the Holy Spirit and have believed on the Son of God, they shall have everlasting life. If they have not believed on the Son, they shall not see life. "The wrath of God abideth on [them]" (John 3:36).

As believers on the Lord Jesus Christ, we must constantly remind the unsaved that they should heed the voice of the Holy Spirit today as He strives with them. They may not be alive tomorrow to hear His voice.—**Robert Humbertson, (Deceased) Former Chairman, Language Arts Department, Lee College, Cleveland, Tennessee** (Editor's note: Soon after Dr. Humbertson wrote this homily, he was called from this life to his eternal reward.)

## SENTENCE SERMONS

BECAUSE GOD is just, He must punish

sin; because He is merciful, He will forgive those who repents.

—**Selected**

LET IT PROFIT thee to have heard by terrible example, the reward of disobedience.

—**Milton**

COURAGE IS that virtue which champions the cause of right.

—**Cicero**

THE BEST SAFEGUARD for the young generation is a good example by the older generation.

—**Epictetus**

## EVANGELISTIC APPLICATION

THOUGH GOD IS MERCIFUL, ALL WHO CONTINUE IN SIN WILL BE JUDGED.

A merciful God calls men to repentance. The reason He does this is because He knows of His providential care and love. God knows the power of this sin by the suffering of His own Son, Jesus. On Good Friday God could no longer look upon His Son who had willingly taken the stigma of sin upon Himself. It was this self-sacrifice on the part of God that make it possible for repentance to be man's hope.

Yet God himself knows the power of repentance, for it is part of His nature as well. Not that God needs to repent of sin; rather, God is capable of changing His will in accordance with principles of grace and mercy.

This should be a point of great hope for all who feel condemned by sin. God is not the author of condemnation; Satan is the great accuser. God is the author of hope and repentance. God is not predisposed to bring destruction upon our lives; rather, He is predisposed to offer mercy and everlasting life.

## ILLUMINATING THE LESSON

The power of the Christian life is joy and hope in the face of discontinuity. The churches have never accepted this easily. Endless theologies have been constructed to ease the discontinuity, to reduce the conflict, to find some accommodation between Christ and the world, to affirm the world on its own terms, to secure a comfortable place in the world, and to find our hope there after all. The placing of false hope in the world and its power to save itself has always been and continues to be a great treat to the church.

What the church must always seek is the gracefulness of life lived in discontinuity and conflict. It is the gracefulness of living an ordinary and normal life in Christ which is so extraordinary and abnormal in the world. Partaking of the riches of that life, one which the world regards as a scandal, is the source of our joy.

From **The Call to Conversion** by Jim Wallis (Harper & Row, 1981).

## DAILY DEVOTIONAL GUIDE

M. Judgment Needed. Exodus 32:1-6

T. Judgment Demanded. Exodus 32:7-10

W. Judgment Stayed. Exodus 32:11-14

T. Judgment Which Is Just. Romans 2:1-12

F. Judgment in God's Hands. Romans 12:9-21

S. Judgment Finalized. Revelation 20:7-15

# God Remembers

**Study Text:** Genesis 8:1 through 9:17; Hebrews 11:7

**Supplemental References:** Psalm 36:5-7; 119:89-93; Lamentations 3:22-26; 2 Peter 1:1-4

**Time:** Traditional chronology dates the flood at about 2400 B.C. However, it could be as early as 8000 B.C.

**Place:** The region of Asia Minor

**Golden Text:** "God remembered Noah, and every living thing, and all the cattle that was with him in the ark" (Genesis 8:1).

**Central Truth:** God is faithful to remember His promises.

**Evangelistic Emphasis:** God is merciful and will forgive those who repent.

## Printed Text

**Genesis 8:13.** And it came to pass in the six hundredth and first year, in the first month, the first day of the month, the waters were dried up from off the earth: and Noah removed the covering of the ark, and looked, and, behold, the face of the ground was dry.

**14. And in the second month, on the seven and twentieth day of the month, was the earth dried.**

15. And God spake unto Noah, saying,

**16. Go forth of the ark, thou, and thy wife, and thy sons, and thy sons' wives with thee.**

17. Bring forth with thee every living thing that is with thee, of all flesh, both of fowl, and of cattle, and of every creeping thing that creepeth upon the earth; that they may breed abundantly in the earth, and be fruitful, and multiply upon the earth.

**18. And Noah went forth, and his sons, and his wife, and his sons' wives with him:**

**19:1.** And there came two angels to Sodom at even; and Lot sat in the gate of Sodom: and Lot seeing them rose up to meet them; and he bowed himself with his face toward the ground;

**9. And they said, Stand back. And they said again, This one fellow came in to sojourn, and he will needs be a judge: now will we deal worse with thee, than with them. And they pressed sore upon the man, even Lot, and came near to break the door.**

10. But the men put forth their hand, and pulled Lot into the house to them, and shut to the door.

**11. And they smote the men that were at the door of the house with blindness, both small and great: so that they wearied themselves to find the door.**

12. And the men said unto Lot, Hast thou here any besides? son in law, and thy sons, and thy daughters, and whatsoever thou hast in the city, bring them out of this place:

**13. For we will destroy this place, because the cry of them is waxen great before the face of the LORD; and the LORD hath sent us to destroy it.**

## LESSON OUTLINE

## LESSON EXPOSITION

### INTRODUCTION

The lesson last week focused on the terrible plight of humanity caught in the death-web of sin. It was a powerful statement of God's wrath and pain at the ever-increasing effects of sin from Adam's disobedience.

The lesson this Sunday takes an entirely different track. God has moved beyond the intention to destroy and is committed to "remember" in order to save and preserve for the future.

### I. FAITH REWARDED (Genesis 8:1-22; Hebrews 11:7)

A. The Crisis Ends (8:1-12)

(These verses are not in the Printed Text.)

The crisis of the flood comes to an end as God "remembers" Noah. The topic for the lesson, "God Remembers," vividly captures the thrust of these verses. That God remembers means that He has turned away from wrath and turned towards salvation. That God remembered also means that humankind and animals are not forgotten. It is a terrible thing to be forgotten. Each of us knows the personal anguish of being ignored, of being treated as if we did not exist. Yet, the gospel is that God has chosen to remember His water-filled creation.

There are numerous references in the Old Testament to the fear of being forgotten by God, such as Psalm 10:11, "He says to himself God has forgotten" **(New International Version).** Other references include Psalms 13:1; 42:9; Isaiah 49:14; Lamentations 5:20. Brueggemann has observed that in contrast to God, "The flood not only has no memory. It means to destroy and set us in a world of utter amnesia."

This new world of creation is strikingly similar to the first order of creation. The wind of God blew over the earth (8:1) bringing order out of the chaos of the deep. This wind is the divine "ruah" (spirit) of God that is God's way of bringing order to the disordered world. The wind of God is the wind that makes it possible for all life to take place on earth. Without the blowing of this wind Noah and his family would be trapped in the wooden vessel awaiting the onslaught of death.

God's mercy is shown Noah as the ark finally came to rest on the mountains of Ararat. Von Rad observed that this "resting" of the ark is the result of God's remembering. "The importance of this event is emphasized in the text by a pun on the verb "nuah" (rest) which is the root of Noah's name.

The specific mountain is not named; however, the mountain range is identified as Ararat. This would place the location in the area of present-day Armenia (Turkey).

These verses indicate that the process of the earth coming back to order was slow. Noah cannot rush God's way. He can only participate as God has ordained. The raven is sent in verse 7 but does not return to the ark. From verse 5 it is clear that mountaintops are visible to Noah and perhaps the raven has found a way to survive. Yet, Noah knew he needed more than the absence of the raven.

Three times a dove is sent from the ark. On the second effort the dove returned with an olive leaf giving indication that plant life was beginning to resume in the lower elevations. The final dove is sent and does not return indicating that life can be lived to the fullest on the drying earth.

B. New Beginning Offered (vv. 13-22)

**13. And it came to pass in the six**

hundredth and first year, in the first month, the first day of the month, the waters were dried up from off the earth: and Noah removed the covering of the ark, and looked, and behold, the face of the ground was dry.

**14. And in the second month, on the seven and twentieth day of the month, was the earth dried.**

Earlier it was commented on how slow the process was of getting out of the ark. It took a lengthy period for the earth to finally be dry enough for humans to begin cultivation and civilization. It was nearly two months from the time that Noah removed the covering of the ark to the time that God finally spoke for him to leave the ark.

An important lesson is apparent: Noah did not move until he heard God speak. How tempting it would have been to leap from the ark and turn the animals loose prior to the earth being fully dry. Think of how crowded it had become (as well as other unsavory aspects of the domicile)! Yet, Noah was a man who trusted God completely.

Patience is a key word to successful Christian living. We must learn to not act until we hear from God. This means learning to delay gratification for a greater purpose. In a recent book, **The Road Less Traveled,** writer Scott Peck observed that delaying gratification is an important lesson of mature living. He observes that for us to develop the capacity to delay gratification, "it is necessary . . . to have self-disciplined role models, a sense of self-worth, and a degree of trust in the safety of their existence." Each of these became part of Noah's life as he learned to "wait upon the Lord."

**15. And God spake unto Noah saying,**

**16. Go forth of the ark, thou, and thy wife, and thy sons, and thy sons' wives with thee.**

**17. Bring forth with thee every living thing that is with thee, of all flesh, both of fowl, and of cattle, and of every creeping thing that creepeth upon the earth; that they may breed abundantly in the earth, and be fruitful, and multiply upon the earth.**

**18. And Noah went forth, and his sons, and his wife, and his sons' wives with him:**

Finally God spoke. Earlier it was noted that the "wind of God" was similar to the opening verses of Genesis 1 when He brought order from the chaos. In these verses we find a repetition of the original order of creation regarding humankind and the animal kingdom. Von Rad has pointed out that Noah and the animals were not allowed to leave the ark until God had spoken the word. It was not God's intention for "human vitality and arbitrariness" to "seize the fresh earth; God Himself liberated the earth for the survivors."

Although not a part of the Printed Text, verses 19-22 give a broader view of God's willingness to start fresh on the earth. A number of points of startling hope come from this fresh beginning. The first is that Noah affirmed the majesty of the Lord and offered sacrifices to Him. Noah was a deeply humbled man by the experience in the ark. He was the lone survivor and the future of the world rested in his wisdom and loins. He submitted himself to the Lord of mercy by this act of burnt offerings on the altar.

The second thing is that God found the sacrifice to be pleasing. It should be remembered this is only the second sacrifice mentioned in the Bible to this point. The first sacrifice ended in the death of Abel (Genesis 4). That was a story of rejection and God's displeasure. This story in Genesis 8 is one of God's acceptance. The odor of the sacrifice came as a "sweet savor" to Him. The Old Testament contains a number of references to sweet savors before the Lord: Exodus 29:18, 25, 41; Leviticus 1:9, 13, 17; 3:5, 16. Three places in the writings of Paul relate to these sweet savors: 2 Corinthians 2:15; Ephesians 5:2; Philippians 4:18. The 2 Corinthians passage relates what it is to move from death to life, "For we are a fragrance of Christ among those who are being saved and among those who are perishing" **(New American Standard Bible).** We find in Ephesians 5:2 a call to walk in love even as Christ did and gave Himself as an offering and sacrifice to God as a fragrant aroma. Finally Philippians 4:18 is Paul's thanksgiving for the gift sent him by the Philippian Christians as an acceptable sacrifice, well pleasing to God.

A third point of the newness is that God decreed never to curse the earth because of man's evil again. As observed in Lesson Three, the earth received part of the curse that came upon Adam in his disobedience. In Genesis chapters 6-8 the earth again paid the price for man's rebellion. At the end of Genesis 8 God affirmed that He would not unleash His complete wrath upon the earth in the future. Man still must pay for his sins and rebellion (except for those who believe in Christ) and will face the judgment. But God is committed to redeem His earth.

In 1 Peter 3:20, 21, a New Testament interpretation is given of the flood. It is compared to water baptism.

C. A Hero of Faith (Hebrews 11:7)

While verse 7 is the primary verse, the focus of verse 6 should not be overlooked. Verse 6 tells us what constitutes true faith. First, faith is that quality that pleases God. In fact, God will not be pleased with anything less than faith. Our moralistic codes, as much as they offer a good life, do not please God as does faith. Second, those who please God in faith are those who believe that He is. This is far more than a philosophical agreement that a god of some sort is in heaven. This is a commitment of the self at its deepest levels that God truly is. It is the affirmation of God's self-revelation as Yahweh, "I am that I am." Third, faith knows that the God who is, is the God who is intimately related to His creation. Thus, He is the God who rewards those who seek Him. These rewards are found in salvation, mercy, righteousness, and a life lived pleasing before Him.

Noah was truly a man who pleased God by his faithfulness in the time of trial. Note what faith did for Noah: First, it warned him of the flood that

was coming. This was a faith that could be touched with the gift of prophecy. Second, he acted upon the vision of the future by constructing the ark God commanded. The ark became a symbol of salvation to those who believed and a symbol of condemnation to those who did not believe. Third, by his faith in God's work and God's future Noah joined ranks with those who were certified as righteous before God by faith. Thus he is an appropriate forerunner of the great hero of faith, Abram.

II. COMMISSION RENEWED (Genesis 9:1-7)

A. Limits Defined (vv. 1-4)

**1. And God blessed Noah and his sons, and said unto them, be fruitful, and multiply, and replenish the earth.**

How do you interpret the term "replenish?" Does it suggest there was a prior race on the earth? Explain.

Noah is the man blessed by God. Such a person is always the recipient of God's Word, the recipient of God's saving acts of mercy, and the leader into the future. The passage in Genesis 9:1 provides the answer to the question of whether or not God's original command for humanity still holds. The answer is a resounding "Yes" from God. That original command was expressed in 1:28 in which man was called to "be fruitful." Humanity still has the opportunity to fill the earth and be harbingers of righteousness.

In verses 2 and 3 the order is changed from the original command. It was clear in Genesis 1 that humankind and the animals were meant to live in peaceful cohabitation. Man was primarily a vegetarian prior to the Flood. Now, after the Flood a man is given permission to eat of the animal kingdom. God has given the permission for man to take as nourishment from this kingdom. Why this order was changed is uncertain. Perhaps it indicated that the plant kingdom would not respond as quickly for normal life and man needed the nourishment from the animals. Regardless, it is clear that a change has taken place.

However, that change is given clear limits in verse 4. While the animal may be eaten for food, the blood may not be used for food. This is God's reminder to humanity that all life, whether animal or human, still belongs to Him. As an act of mercy the human may eat the animal; but as an act of remembrance and submission he is not to eat of the blood.

B. God and Man (vv. 5-7)

This section concludes with the call to be fruitful that began in verse 1. Yet, in the midst of this positive call comes the clear word from God that He has set limits.

Verses 5 and 6 indicate that God is not going to tolerate the shedding of human blood without some form of vengeance. The act of vengeance is given to man. Yet it is clearly defined so as not to support wanton destruction. If a man kills another man, that man must be prepared to be killed himself. It is the **lex talionis** "an eye for an eye" principle.

God allows for human justice to be practiced. Yet it must be remembered such allowance is made within the structure of 9:1, 7 that calls for life to be multiplied. It must also be remembered that these allowances for human justice are also made within the framework that life belongs to God.

III. COVENANT-SIGN GIVEN (Genesis 9:8-17)

A. Protection Guaranteed (vv. 8-11)

(These verses are not in the Printed Text.)

All biblical theology is ultimately "covenant theology." For those persons who grew up in the Reformed tradition (Calvinist churches) the language of covenant is not new. But many from the Wesleyan traditions are not familiar with this significant biblical concept. It is the basis of all of God's dealings with His creatures.

Most of the covenants in the Bible imply an agreement between a greater

person (or power) and a lesser one. The greater promises to provide specified blessings (or protection) in exchange for specified acts of obedience from the lesser. In this sense they are called conditional covenants and have the language of "if . . . then." Examples are found in Joshua 24 at the covenant-making ceremony at Shechem; the book of covenant Exodus 24:7 which comprises Exodus 20:23 through 23:33. Each of these are covenants in which Israel was bound to obey the Lord.

The other type of covenant in the Bible is one in which Yahweh binds Himself to keep the covenant. The two most important are those to Abraham (Genesis 15, 17) and David (2 Samuel 7). The Noah covenant in Genesis 9 is an example of this commitment made by Yahweh.

**9. And I, behold, I establish my covenant with you, and with your seed after you;**

**10. And with every living creature that is with you, of the fowl, of the cattle, and of every beast of the earth with you; from all that go out of the ark, to every beast of the earth.**

This covenant to Noah is spelled out regarding those who are to share its benefits. The mercy reaches to Noah's family and his descendants (which would include all future humankind since all other human life had been destroyed.) It also reaches to all the animals who had been on the ark and all future animals. The emphasis is clear in verse 9 that it is Yahweh Himself who is making this covenant. This is based on the faithfulness of His Word which cannot be broken by any human effort. This principle of the power of God's Work is found in Romans 3:3, 4, "If some did not believe, their unbelief will not nullify the faithfulness of God, will it? May it never be! Rather, let God be found true, though every man be found a liar" **(New American Standard).** The grass may wither and the flowers fade, but the Word of God will stand forever is the testimony of Isaiah 40:8. Thus, the emphasis of Genesis 9:9 is that God's Word is faithful.

**11. And I will establish my covenant**

**with you; neither shall all flesh be cut off any more by the waters of the flood; neither shall there any more be a flood to destroy the earth.**

The truthfulness of God's promise to His creatures is found in verse 11. Never again will the sin of man which so painfully broke God's heart allow God to move beyond His commitment to seek and save rather than destroy by flood. This promise is made to all life forms. The earth was devastated by human disobedience. God has reaffirmed His commitment that the earth will be His place for His prized creature, man, to give Him glory by faithful exercise of dominion and worship.

---

How do you feel about the so-called potential for the human race being "wiped off the earth" by nuclear war?

---

Even if man after Noah falls from the way of obedience, God is still committed to save. What begins with this covenant to Noah concludes with the New Covenant established at the death and resurrection of Jesus.

B. God's Sure Promise (vv. 12-17)

**12. And God said, This is the token of the covenant which I make between me and you and every living creature that is with you, for perpetual generations:**

**13. I do set my bow in the cloud, and it shall be for a token of a covenant between me and the earth.**

In the previous point it was observed that God is faithful to His covenant promise. That faithfulness is given a form that humans can see and be reminded of in the midst of the storms that rage the earth: the rainbow.

It has been observed that the Hebrew word translated "bow" in verse 13 is usually used to describe a weapon of war. Von Rad observes the significance of this as God putting "aside His bow." It is a marvelous statement that God's position of emnity with man is ended (at least on the level of total destruction).

While that bow still gathers in the skies following a storm as a covenant sign, God has given another covenant sign that reaches further than the bow: the Cross of Christ.

The bow is a promise; the Cross is the realization of the promise. The bow is seen after the storm as a sign; the Cross stands present in the storm as God's mighty refuge. The bow could not save from sin; the Cross offers forgiveness. The bow could not keep Noah's generation from further rebellion; the Cross sanctifies from inbred sin.

It is the covenant of the Cross that is the true statement that God remembers! The Cross is also that supreme statement that the warfare between God and man is ended. Even as the "bow of war" has been placed by God as the "bow of covenant," so also the Cross is the place of reconciliation where God has signaled the end of our hostility with Him (Romans 5:1-10).

## REVIEW QUESTIONS

1. What are some of the parallels between the first creation in Genesis 1, 2 and this second opportunity for mankind in Genesis 8, 9?

2. What significance is there for us in the fact that Noah did not leave the ark until God had clearly spoken?

3. What is the significance of Noah's offering to the Lord?

4. How do Christians today please God?

5. Discuss "covenant" and God's commitment to us in Jesus Christ.

## GOLDEN TEXT HOMILY

"AND GOD REMEMBERED NOAH, AND EVERY LIVING THING, AND ALL THE CATTLE THAT WAS WITH HIM IN THE ARK" (Genesis 8:1).

God remembered the promise He had made Noah in the sixth chapter of Genesis for he was righteous in the sight of God—a just and perfect man in his generation.

Having found grace in the eyes of the Lord (Genesis 6:8) God made a covenant with Noah for he had done all that God had commanded him to do.

Remembrance came before God as Noah carried out his work of building an ark in obedience to God's command which was for the preservation of mankind.

God remembers Noah as the righteous seed that was preserved to again populate the world. It would be from Noah that all the kingdoms of the world would again commence. For Noah as well as all living things with him in the ark would receive the blessing.

You can be certain that God always remembers where we are, and for what purpose we are here. He remembers His promise and is faithful to forgive those who repent of their sins.
**—Leroy Imperio, TH.D., (Retired), Former Pastor, Elkins, West Virginia**

## SENTENCE SERMONS

GOD IS FAITHFUL to remember His promises.
**—Selected**

WHAT MUST BE borne becomes lighter with patience.
**—Shakespeare**

WE BELIEVE that the task ahead of us is never as great as the Power behind us.
**—Selected**

PATIENCE IS the virtue of a donkey that trots beneath his burden and is quiet.
**—George Granville**

## EVANGELISTIC APPLICATION

GOD IS MERCIFUL AND WILL FORGIVE THOSE WHO REPENT.

The Bible tells us that God is capable, in His divine love, of casting our sins into the sea of forgetfulness and never remembering them again. That God remembers is meant to be a sign of hope for all who are lost.

We may go through life thinking that God is determined to "get us." We see God as an angry figure who remembers our sins and holds them over our heads. Yet, He is a God who is seeking to forget our sins. But He cannot forget unless we repent. For Him to forget without

our repentance would be for Him to license sin. But when we confess our sins, we discover that He is indeed faithful and just to forgive us our sins!

We discover then that God truly is committed to remembering us in His covenant with Christ Jesus. That is part of what it means for us to be "in Christ." We are placed in the covenant-remembering position before God and our sins are removed and our lives are sanctified in His presence.

## ILLUMINATING THE LESSON

In Jonah 3:1, we are told that "the Word of the Lord came unto Jonah a second time." That principle is behind God's Word coming to the family of man in the life of Noah. The post-flood generation(s) became the focus of the Word of the Lord coming again to man.

The wonder is that God's Word continued to come down to man, time and time again. That Word reached its apex with the coming of the Word made Flesh, Jesus Christ. It is that Word that will come again, the second time, to complete the job of redemption begun and finished on Calvary.

The floods have overwhelmed the lives of many people. They have been floods of pain and regret from sins committed that came home to nest. Many of these people are people who have heard the Word once or more in their lives; yet, who continued in their willful disobedience. The gospel is that Good News that God continually speaks again to those whose lives are washed up. To be washed ashore on the sands of God's kingdom is to finally be saved.

## DAILY DEVOTIONAL GUIDE

M. Repulsive Wickedness. Isaiah 5:8-12

T. Extensive Judgment. Psalm 9:16-18

W. Redemptive Grace. Titus 2:11-14

T. Active Faith. Hebrews 11:8-12

F. Precious Promises. 2 Peter 1:1-4

S. Responsive Worship. Psalm 66:1-4

# Dangers of Pride

**Study Text:** Genesis 11:1-25; 1 Peter 5:5-7

**Supplemental References:** Psalm 19:7-12; Romans 1:18-32; 2 Thessalonians 2:8-12

**Time:** Traditional chronology dates this lesson around 2091 B.C. It could, however, be as early as 8000 B.C.

**Place:** Babel

**Golden Text:** "Professing themselves to be wise, they became fools" (Romans 1:22).

**Central Truth:** Success comes only when we labor within God's will.

**Evangelistic Emphasis:** Salvation comes not by human works but by the work of Christ on Calvary.

## Printed Text

**Genesis 11:1.** AND the whole earth was of one language, and of one speech.

**2. And it came to pass, as they journeyed from the east, that they found a plain in the land of Shinar; and they dwelt there.**

3. And they said one to another, Go to, let us make brick, and burn them throughly. And they had brick for stone, and slime had they for morter.

**4. And they said, Go to, let us build us a city and a tower, whose top may reach unto heaven; and let us make us a name, lest we be scattered abroad upon the face of the whole earth.**

5. And the LORD came down to see the city and the tower, which the children of men builded.

**6. And the LORD said, Behold, the people is one, and they have all one language; and this they begin to do: and now nothing will be restrained from them, which they have imagined to do.**

7. Go to, let us go down, and there confound their language, that they may not understand one another's speech.

**8. So the LORD scattered them abroad from thence upon the face of all the earth: and they left off to build the city.**

9. Therefore is the name of it called Babel; because the LORD did there confound the language of all the earth: and from thence did the LORD scatter them abroad upon the face of all the earth.

**1 Peter 5:5. Likewise, ye younger, submit yourselves unto the elder. Yea, all of you be subject one to another, and be clothed with humility: for God resisteth the proud, and giveth grace to the humble.**

6. Humble yourselves therefore under the mighty hand of God, that he may exalt you in due time:

**7. Casting all your care upon him; for he careth for you.**

## DICTIONARY

**Shinar (SHINE-ahr)—Genesis 11:2**—The word means "two rivers," and it indicates the plain between the rivers Euphrates and Tigris, today found in the country of Iraq.

**Babel (BAY-buhl—Genesis 11:9**—The word means "to confound" and refers to the confounding of the language by God because of sin. The city was built on the plain of Shinar, and was on the site of the city of Babylon.

---

## LESSON OUTLINE

I. SELF-WILL EXPRESSED
    A. Human Desire to Expand
    B. Human Glory Desired
II. GOD'S DISAPPROVAL
    A. God's Revulsion
    B. The Foundation of Confusion
    C. Human Fragmentation
III. NEED FOR HUMILITY
    A. Humility Brings Grace
    B. Humility Brings God's Care

## LESSON EXPOSITION

INTRODUCTION

This lesson brings us to the close of the first part of Genesis. Chapters 1 through 11 of Genesis contain the story of God's creation gone astray in disobedience. Adam's sin was not removed by the Flood. The principle remained active and reached a new apex with the Tower of Babel. The movement from the original man, Adam, to the larger class of men at Babel left in its debris the death of Abel, the wandering of Cain, the unbelief of Noah's generation, and the confusion of human understanding.

Out of the confusion of Genesis 11 God will begin with a new man Abraham, and make a new community that will be bound in faith, hope, and love in Jesus Christ.

It will be of value for the teacher to read Acts 2 in relationship to Genesis 11. In Acts 2 we find the sending of the Holy Spirit. This chapter also provides insight into the healing that God seeks for the world cursed by its continual efforts to raise Babel in each generation.

I. SELF-WILL EXPRESSED (Genesis 11:1-4)

One of the fundamental aspects of sin

has been human self-centeredness and willfulness. Psychiatrist Gerald May comments that there is a fundamental difference between "willingness" and "willfulness." He writes that "willingness" implies a surrendering of one's self-separateness, an entering-into, an immersion in the deepest processes of life itself . . . . Willingness is saying yes to the mystery of being alive in each moment." He further defines willfulness as "the setting of oneself apart from the fundamental essence of life in an attempt to master, direct, control, or otherwise manipulate existence. . . . . Willfulness is saying no, or perhaps more commonly, 'Yes, but.' " May further elaborates by writing that "willingness" notices this wonder (of the mystery of life) and bows in some kind of reverence to it. Willfulness forgets it, ignores it, or at its worst, actively tries to destroy it" **Will and Spirit,** Harper and Row 1982).

It is a sad commentary on life that willfulness, the desire to do things our way, is so often the characteristic that marks our existence. Until we learn the meaning of surrender to the will of God we will not know what it is to be fully free for the purposes of God in the world.

A. Human Desire to Expand (vv. 1, 2)

**1. And the whole earth was of one language, and of one speech.**

**2. And it came to pass, as they journeyed from the east, that they found a plain in the land of Shinar; and they dwelt there.**

The redundancy of verse 1 emphasized the fact that people could understand one another. The background for this verse is found in 10:9, 10 with a reference to Nimrod who was a mighty hunter before the Lord (thus the migratory background). We are further told that Nimrod's kingdom included Babel (Babylon) in the land of Shinar (11:2). Another reference is 10:15 and the note that the earth was divided (an obvious reference to Genesis 11) during the days of Pelag. Chapter 10 of Genesis concludes with a grand picture of the families, nations, and languages after the time of Noah. It may be that this section of Genesis 10 is meant to reflect realities following the disruption of the Tower of Babel rather than how things stood prior to the Tower.

The note in verse 1 sets the stage for man unified against God. There are several different translations for the last part of verse 1: "one language and a common speech" **New International Version;** "a single language and used the same words" **New English Bible.** The later contains a footnote that offers "used few words." Whatever the case may be it is clear that men were able to understand one another.

It is of particular note in verse 2 that people began to migrate. This places the origins of human life east of Palestine. The Garden of Eden was thought to have been between the Euphrates and Tigris Rivers. It seems that emerging civilizations are related to migrations. These migrations cause the moving peoples to find a common bond of unity in language, religion, and other aspects of culture.

The migration is from east to west as these peoples come to the land of Shinar. Shinar is clearly a reference to Babylon. The plain probably refers to the northern sections of the Tigris and Euphrates River valleys.

It is the same situation today. Man is constantly seeking new horizons of adventure and growth. The old saying is true: the grass does seem greener on the other side! Yet, in hidden ways, God is accomplishing His purpose described in Genesis 1 and 2 to have man exercise dominion over the earth. Sooner or later man was going to have to leave the Garden in order to fulfill the divine mandate. The sad aspect is that man chose to be

in sin while fulfilling the mandate. Yet, God's will is still being accomplished.

---

Why is self-centeredness so damaging to a person or nation?

---

B. Human Glory Desired (vv. 3, 4)

**3. And they said one to another, Go to, let us make brick, and burn them throughly. And they had brick for stone, and slime they had for morter.**

**4. And they said, Go to, let us build us a city, and a tower, whose top may reach unto heaven; and let us make a name, lest we be scattered abroad upon the face of the whole earth.**

The vanity of human pride is exposed in these verses. Von Rad observed that verse 3 told the weakness of their effort. "Their joy in their inventiveness—they use asphalt as mortar—is shown in the Hebrew text by appropriate puns . . . . the material that men used for their gigantic undertaking was perishable and unsatisfactory!"

Verse 4 gives a number of key insights into the dynamics of this culture. First, they desire to build a city. Note the use of the personal pronoun "us" in the text. There is no regard for God and His standards. This city is to be a city for "us" and "our" values. All of man's arrogance and terrible discrimination are hidden in this verse. Note also the emphasis upon "Go to" (also used in verse 3). Here is man in his assertive self. The motto of the "can do" generation is clearly expressed here. This poses a continual problem: Is the Word of God against growth and achievement? The answer is yes and no. Yes, God is opposed to such growth when it occurs at the expense of justice and righteousness and the purposes of His kingdom. On the other hand, no, God is not opposed to human effort when it occurs in a framework of trust in Him and seeks to accomplish the goals of the kingdom. Does this mean that all human effort that does not happen by faith is sinful? No, but it does mean that sin is able to take advantage of those efforts in easier fashion.

The second area of concern is the

reference to the tower whose top reaches into the heavens. It is a mistake to assume this tower meant to enter heaven itself. Rather, the tower is man's effort to achieve fame. It was meant to last as a monument to human effort. It should be noted there are such monuments that exist today: the Pyramids in Egypt and even our own historical sites in the United States (Washington Monument, Statue of Liberty). While they move the soul with deep emotion they are still like the tower at Shinar—efforts of human fame.

The third area is the desire to make a name. Neither individuals nor societies want to be forgotten. Thus, even our grave-markers are made of lasting stone and engraved with our vital information. Nations and cultures do the same engraving! This desire for a name is rooted in deep anxiety and lack of trust in God. That is why the church does not carry its own name in the Bible. The church goes by the name of the One who has conquered death and hell: Jesus Christ. Whenever a denomination or local congregation becomes so engrossed in its own name that it forgets who it really belongs to and whose name it really serves that body ceases to be the body of faith and becomes the body of the plain of Shinar.

All of this is related to fear and anxiety. Verse 4 closed with the fear of man being scattered. The fear of being scattered is indicative of a number of contemporary problems. One, there is the fear of being vulnerable to the forces of nature. Surely the memories of the Flood were part of human experience. Such memories are no different from today's memories of Hiroshima and Nagasaki. The "nuclear winter" does provide for our deep spiritual discontent and vulnerability. Second, to be scattered is to be alone in the world. It is to be cut off from human contact and communion. Man cut off from communion with God must find substitutes wherever possible. That is still part of the human condition under sin: man trembling in his fear, faking it with great cities and avenues of fame.

---

How should a Christian react toward the generosity of persons who give large sums of money, but have no concern for spiritual matters? How can they be helped?

---

## II. GOD'S DISAPPROVAL (Genesis 11:5-9)

### A. God's Revulsion (vv. 5, 6)

**5. And the Lord came down to see the city and the tower, which the children of men builded.**

**6. And the Lord said, Behold, the people is one, and they have all one language; and this they begin to do: and now nothing will be restrained from them, which they have imagined to do.**

That God came down to see the works of men of the plain indicates the smallness of their efforts in light of His eternal grandeur. One commentator wrote that the Lord came near "because he dwells at such tremendous height and their work is so tiny. God's movement must therefore be understood as a remarkable satire on man's doing." It should also be noted that the city and tower are clearly seen to be the work of the children of men. God is not involved in approving this effort. Calvin commented that Genesis 11 "embodies a truth of permanent validity —the futility and emptiness of human effort divorced from the acknowledgement and service of God" (quoted in **Interpreter's Bible,** Vol. 1).

There is no doubt that God desires unity. Yet, the oneness of the people of the plain is a unity on the verge of the demonic. They have just begun to isolate themselves further from the purposes of God.

God's intervention is for the sake of humanity. God has seen into the future regarding the effects of man's demonic efforts and knows the destruction and dehumanizing that will result from it. He also knows that this realm into which man is entering will know little of earthly limits.

The modern world is quickly approaching the time when there will again be one primary language of influence. Perhaps it will not be so much a spoken tongue as it will be the language of technology, science, computers, international business, or a dominant political philosophy. Whatever the case may be, Christian responsibility is to use the language clearly and boldly as a witness to the gospel of Christ.

## B. The Foundation of Confusion (v. 7)

**7. Go to, let us go down, and there confound their language, that they may not understand one another's speech.**

Language is powerful. Words create and become the avenue for the thoughts of man becoming realized and communicated into existence. Without language, thought is jumbled confusion. Practically nothing is possible without language. Even the Bible records that the "word of the Lord" created this world. When God chose to send the Redeemer it was in the "Word made flesh."

Thus, in order to prevent man from becoming the agent of his own destruction God came down and confounded human speech. The "let us" of verse 7 parallels the "let us" of verses 3 and 4. In verses 3 and 4 we saw the collected efforts of men to preserve their own lives. As Reinhold Niebuhr has so clearly pointed out, the collective will of the group is less moral than that of an individual **(Moral Man and Immoral Society).** God's "let us" indicates the total involvement of the Godhead in seeking to preserve humankind.

While Paul is correct in 1 Corinthians 14:33 that God is not a God of confusion, it is true that God does seek to confound the foolishness of human pride. The word for "confound" is the Hebrew word **balal.** It has the meaning of "mix, mingle." It is only used in Genesis 11:7, 9. It is obvious the play on words in verse 9 regarding "Babel" and "balal." Another Hebrew word is used more often in the Old Testament to describe God's confounding of humanity. The word is **bosh** and has the sense of "making ashamed, blushing." Thus, God's confounding of human pride leaves man aware of his lack of ability to save himself and ultimately control his destiny.

Twice in 1 Corinthians 1:27 the Apostle Paul used the Greek for "confound" to make the point of God's power: "But God hath chosen the foolish things of the world to confound the wise: and God hath chosen the weak things of the world to confound the things which are mighty." The Apostle Peter in his first letter wrote:

"Wherefore also it is contained in the scripture, Behold, I lay in Sion a chief corner stone, elect, precious: and he that believeth on him shall not be **confounded"** (2:6).

However, the most significant use of this word in relation to Genesis 11 is found in Acts 2:6: "Now when this was noised abroad, the multitude came together, and were **confounded,** because that every man heard them speak in his own language." In the introduction is mentioned the relationship between Genesis 11 and Acts 2. That relationship is seen in the fact that Pentecost is God's solution to the arrogance of man in his quest for language. The new language of the people of God is the language of the Holy Spirit. It is the thoughts, tongue, and words of Spirit-filled humanity submitted to the lordship of Christ in the world. The redeemed do not build cities and towers for themselves: rather they seek a city whose builder is God. Their tower is the tower of strength in the Word of God. In Genesis 11 men were confounded by the fact that they could not understand. In Acts 2 men are confounded with the fact that they can understand the good news of God.

## C. Human Fragmentation (vv. 8, 9)

**8. So the Lord scattered them abroad from thence upon the face of all the earth: and they left off to build the city.**

When men cannot understand one another they cannot accomplish their deeds. This simple fact is reality to all of us. Until our children learn words and their meanings we cannot expect them to obey us. Those who have studied foreign languages know how frustrating such study is until words and sentences begin to take meaning.

Even those who speak the same language may discover they cannot work together unless words have the same intention and meaning for all parties. Next time you are asked for directions, try giving them this, "Go down the road a fer piece and you'll see a clump of trees, don't turn there," and look at the confounded expression staring back at you!

The failure of language meant the failure of the effort to build the city. It should also be noted that this scattering was the work of the Lord. Not all human fragmentation is of the devil. God has purposes which are moving humanity beyond its tendency to find refuge in the crowd. This is true from a reading of the early chapters of the Book of Acts. There it is clear that it took persecution in the Jerusalem church to scatter the church into the other regions of Palestine and into the farthest regions of the earth.

How do you suppose the people reacted to the language problem? Who did they blame?

Earlier in 11:4 the people of Shinar had feared this scattering. Yet, it was necessary for God's purposes to be fulfilled.

**9. Therefore is the name of it called Babel; because the Lord did there confound the language of all the earth: and from thence did the Lord scatter them abroad upon the face of all the earth.**

The relationship between "balal" (confounding) and the name of the place as Babel has already been mentioned. Popularly it is called the "Tower of Babel." Yet realistically Babel relates to the entire effort and God's action upon it.

God's action had two aspects. The first was punitive. The loss of common language was judgment upon the migrants for seeking to build their own reputation at the expense of acknowledging God. The second was preventive. This was God's merciful way of keeping man from realizing the terror of his own power outside of God's law and will.

Do we have any modern-day examples of God's stepping in to delay or destroy a project of self-exalting interest?

III. NEED FOR HUMILITY (1 Peter 5:5-7)

This is an appropriate conclusion to a lesson on the pride of life shown in the plain of Shinar. God's way to unity and achievement is through humility and submission. Love, faith, and hope are the characteristics of the hard workers of God.

The Book of 1 Peter is written to people who are scattered abroad (1:1). But these folk are elected of God, sanctified of the Spirit, and obedient to their calling through the blood of Jesus (1:2). The hope these scattered persons have is the Resurrection. It is a "lively hope." The building which concerns these people is that "spiritual house" whose foundation and chief stone is Jesus Christ (2:5-7).

A. Humility Brings Grace (vv. 5, 6)

**5. Likewise, ye younger, submit yourselves unto the elder. Yea, all of you be subject one to another, and be clothed with humility: for God resisteth the proud, and giveth grace to the humble.**

**6. Humble yourselves, therefore under the mighty hand of God, that he may exalt you in due time:**

Much of 1 Peter deals with suffering and the sober attitude of the believer. It also focuses on the meaning and means of submission within the Christian fellowship and home.

Chapter 5 begins with an admonition to the elders of the churches. "Elders" is the translation of the Greek, **presbyteros.** It has the meaning of "leader, pastor." It connotated one who was in a position of spiritual authority in the church. Peter considered himself to be an elder (5:1). Such elders were to serve the Lord willingly as they cared for the flock of God. Peter's concern for the flock of God certainly reflects the Lord's instructions to him in John 21. Elders were to be examples to the flock. This life was to be lived knowing that the Chief Shepherd in His appearing would provide a crown of glory.

These are important words to all church leaders who are tempted to build their own towers of reputation and name. God's flock is not there to be fleeced for any reason. The Chief Shepherd, our Great Elder, is watching over His flock and calls His elders to account.

The "younger" of verse 5 refers to those persons in the fellowship who are not in positions of spiritual authority as well as their chronological age. These younger ones are to be faithfully and lovingly submitted to the elder (the Greek is plural for elder). The focus for our lesson is that arrogant self-positioning is the same as the arrogant building of the tower. To fail to be in submission to those in authority is to loose God's judgment upon us in order to discipline us into the fold of His eternal purposes.

The focus quickly shifts in verse 5 to indicate that the submission is a mutual reality in which all the members are to submit to one another in humility. It is important to note that "subjection" is not the primary focus of this material. The primary focus is "humility." Those who genuinely humble themselves before God will not be caught in false humility and will not be trapped into thinking that humility is weakness. To be clothed with humility is to be covered and protected by the grace of God. Thus, Peter quoted from Proverbs 3:34. God will resist the arrogant of His people but He seeks to express His love via grace.

The humility of the Christian is under the "mighty hand of God." This is another expression for God's power. Those who submit to the power of God in their lives will discover that God has a perfect time for the glory He has for us. Tragically too many Christians are not willing to patiently endure in their loving service. They want their glory and reward now. In exchange for their impatience they get positions for which they are not spiritually prepared and often cause great harm in the church. Perhaps the greatest witness a Christian can make is his or her willingness to wait for God's time!

B. Humility Brings God's Care (v.7)

**7. Casting all your care upon him; for he careth for you.**

Such humility and knowledge of God's perfect timing enables us to truly know that God cares. Thus, we can deliver to Him all the burdens of life and be freed in our spirits for the special work He has in our lives.

(The teacher may wish to refer to **Evangelical Commentary** for April 29, 1984, pp. 298, 299 for more detailed discussion of this passage in 1 Peter 5.)

## REVIEW QUESTIONS

1. What is the significance of the migrating spoken of in Genesis 11:2?

2. What are some of the fears involved in man's anxiety about being "scattered"?

3. How is God's punitive and preventive love expressed in this story?

4. How does Acts 2 relate to Genesis 11?

5. How does God's grace and care relate to our attitude of humility?

## GOLDEN TEXT HOMILY

"PROFESSING THEMSELVES TO BE WISE, THEY BECAME FOOLS" (Romans 1:22).

In the world we can see God. This is Paul's argument in the context from which the Golden Text is taken. If we look at the world we see that suffering follows sin. Break the laws of agriculture—your harvest fails. Break the laws of architecture—your building collapses. Break the laws of health—your body suffers. Paul was saying "look at the world, and see how it is constructed! From a world like that you know what God is like." The sinner is left without excuse.

Paul goes on another step. What did the sinner do? Instead of looking out to God, he looked into himself. He involved himself in vain speculations and thought he was wise, while all the time he was a fool. Why? He was a fool because he made his ideas, his opinions, his speculations the standard and law of life, instead of the will of God. The sinner's folly consisted in making "man the master of things." He found his standards in his own opinions and not in the law of God. He lived in a self-centered instead of a God-centered universe. Instead of walking looking out to God he walked looking into himself, and like any man who does not look where he is going, he fell.

The world has changed little since Paul's day. Humankind still seeks answers to life's problems by looking inward instead of in the direction of God. And like those to whom Paul wrote there is the tendency for the undisciplined mind, to feel that he is wise and thus become a fool. **Excerpts from** *The Letter to the Romans,* **by William Barclay**

## SENTENCE SERMONS

SUCCESS COMES only when we labor within God's will.

**—Selected**

A MAN's PRIDE shall bring him low: but honour shall uphold the humble in spirit.

**—Proverbs 29:23**

PRIDE IS the only disease known to man that makes everyone sick except the one who has it.

**—Buddy Robinson**

NOTHING IS as hard to do gracefully as getting down off your high horse.

**—Franklin Jones**

## EVANGELISTIC APPLICATION

SALVATION COMES NOT BY HUMAN WORKS BUT BY THE WORK OF CHRIST ON CALVARY.

Paul wrote to the Ephesian Christians that God's great grace had been shown to us in the riches of Jesus Christ. Even when we were dead in sin, God made us alive in Christ. He then emphasized that it is by grace we are saved (Ephesians 2:4, 5).

This salvation by faith leads to God doing His work in us. We are God's "workmanship, created in Christ Jesus to do good works, which God prepared in advance for us to do" (Ephesians 2:10 **New International Version**).

To become a Christian is to embark on a new journey of life. Our former occupation may not change; but what we accomplish for the kingdom will change radically!

Grace does not set us free from sin for our own works; it sets us free for the discipline of God. Thus, disciples are the people of grace! Grace is the avenue by which God invites us to participate in meaningful life.

## ILLUMINATING THE LESSON

W. R. Bowie in the **Interpreter's Bible** commented on the arrogance of nations: "Immense material resources, scientific inventiveness, the mobilization of unprecedented military might, economic mastery, the control of atomic energy—are not these at last the bricks out of which the tower may be built that will enable a nation to supplant the sovereignty of God? 'The Third Reich will last for a thousand years'; 'America, God's Country' —is there not in all of these an element of that same blind pride of power which became obsessed with building the tower that ultimately must be confounded? The picture of the Tower of Babel still confronts us with its prophecy."

## DAILY DEVOTIONAL GUIDE

M. Peril of Pride. Deuteronomy 8:11-20
T. Result of Pride. Isaiah 14:12-17
W. Judgment on Pride. Isaiah 14:18-27
T. Destructiveness of Pride. Proverbs 16:16-19
F. Pride Denounced. James 2:1-9
S. Antidote to Pride. 1 Corinthians 13: 1-10

# Responding to God's Call

**Study Text:** Genesis 11:26 through 12:9

**Supplemental References:** Exodus 3:1-10; Isaiah 6:1-8; Mark 1:16-20

**Time:** About 2000 B.C.

**Place:** Ur of Chaldees, Haran

**Golden Text:** "I will make of thee a great nation, and I will bless thee, and make thy name great; and thou shalt be a blessing" (Genesis 12:2).

**Central Truth:** Obedience to God makes possible the fulfilling of His divine purpose.

**Evangelistic Emphasis:** God uses obedient servants in His plan for redeeming mankind.

## Printed Text

**Genesis 11:31.** And Terah took Abram his son and Lot the son of Haran his son's son, and Sarai his daughter in law, his son Abram's wife; and they went forth with them from Ur of the Chaldees, to go into the land of Canaan; and they came unto Haran, and dwelt there.

**32. And the days of Terah were two hundred and five years: and Terah died in Haran.**

**12:1.** Now the Lord had said unto Abram, Get thee out of thy country, and from thy kindred, and from thy father's house, unto a land that I will shew thee:

**2. And I will make of thee a great nation, and I will bless thee, and make thy name great; and thou shalt be a blessing:**

3. And I will bless them that bless thee, and curse him that curseth thee: and in thee shall all families of the earth be blessed.

**4. So Abram departed, as the Lord had spoken unto him; and Lot went** **with him: and Abram was seventy and five years old when he departed out of Haran.**

5. And Abram took Sarai his wife, and Lot his brother's son, and all their substance that they had gathered, and the souls that they had gotten in Haran; and they went forth to go into the land of Canaan; and into the land of Canaan they came.

**6. And Abram passed through the land unto the place of Sichem, unto the plain of Moreh. And the Canaanite was then in the land.**

7. And the Lord appeared unto Abram, and said, Unto thy seed will I give this land: and there builded he an altar unto the Lord, who appeared unto him.

**8. And he removed from thence unto a mountain on the east of Beth-el, and pitched his tent, having Beth-el on the west, and Hai on the east: and there he builded an altar unto the Lord, and called upon the name of the Lord.**

9. And Abram journeyed, going on still toward the south.

74

## DICTIONARY

**Terah (TEA-rah)—Genesis 11:31**—The father of Abraham, Haran, and Nahor. He may have been a wealthy merchant.

**Abram (AA-brum)—Genesis 11:31**—The first of the great patriarchs, father of Isaac, and founder of the Hebrew nation under God. Abram's name was changed to Abraham at the time of his circumcision. Abram means "great father."

**Lot (LAHT)—Genesis 11:31**—Abraham's nephew, who accompanied him on many journeys. His name means "covering."

**Sarai (SAY-ri)—Genesis 11:31**—Abraham's wife. Her name was changed to Sarah in Genesis 17:15 and means "princess."

**Ur—Genesis 11:31**—Probably the city located in Southern Mesopotamia about 150 miles from the Persian Gulf, which may have flowed near it in biblical times.

**Chaldees (KAL-dees)—Genesis 11:31**—The people of the southern part of Babylonia, between the Tigris and Euphrates Rivers.

**Canaan (KAY-nun)—Genesis 11:31**—The land between the Jordan River and the Mediterranean Sea, roughly. It was Abraham's land of promise and the land in which God's chosen nation, Israel, was to dwell. It carries the name of Israel today. The name comes from Canaan, a son of Ham, who was one of Noah's sons.

**Haran (HAY-run)—Genesis 12:4**—A city that still exists on a branch of the Euphrates River.

**Sichem (SIGH-kem)—Genesis 12:6**—An ancient city, called Shechem (SHE-kem) in other parts of the Old Testament and Sychar (SIGH-kar) in John 4:5. It was situated near Mount Gerizim (GER-i-zim) in Canaan.

**Moreh (MO-rey)—Genesis 12:6**—The word refers to oak trees. It was Abram's first stopping place in Canaan. It also figures in the story of Jacob, Joshua, and Gideon.

**Canaanite (KAY-nun-night)—Genesis 12:6**—A member of one of the tribes that inhabited the Promised Land; these people were descendants of Canaan and were non-Israelites.

**Bethel (BETH-el)—Genesis 12:8**—The word means "house of God" and refers to a Canaanite city once called Luz (Joshua 18:13). As Abram's worship place, it was God's house.

**Hai (HAY-eye)—Genesis 12:8**—A Canaanite city near Bethel. The word means "a heap of ruins." Known elsewhere in the Bible as Ai, it truly became a heap of ruins when Joshua conquered it (Joshua 8:28).

---

## LESSON OUTLINE

I. DIVINE CALL

    A. Change-Factors in Life

    B. The Call to Blessing

II. HUMAN RESPONSE

    A. A Total Response

    B. A Realistic Response

III. GOD'S PROMISE

    A. The Worship Response

    B. The Progressing Journey

## LESSON EXPOSITION

INTRODUCTION

We begin our study of the great patriarchs of Israel's faith. Abram, as he is called until Genesis 17, is the great hero of faith for the New Testament. Without him, the promises of God remain hidden. He is the man whose obedience in faith results in the righteousness of God being proclaimed as a reality in his life.

Through the remainder of this quarter we will study the life and times of this great faith-walker. We will discover that he is a man like ourselves with faults, sins, and hopes. We will also discover that he is a man that God has blessed and through him will bless the entire world. Out of his seed will come the promised Messiah to redeem Israel and save the decadent gentile world.

Since Abraham is such an important figure in the biblical story, we should note how he is considered in the New Testament.

He first appears in the accounts of the ministry of John the Baptist in Matthew 3:9 and Luke 3:8. John took issue with the Jews who claimed a special righteousness because they had Abraham as their father. The Baptizer preached that God could raise up children of Abraham for His glory from the stones on the ground.

The next major area in which he appears in the Gospels is John 8:31-59, a discourse account of a controversy Jesus had with the Jews. Verse 31 indicates that these Jews at first believed in Him. They sought to justify their position by appealing to their relationship to Abraham (v. 33). Jesus replied that their relationship to Abraham did not keep evil intentions from entering their hearts (v. 37). The conflict intensified to the point that the Jews accused Jesus of having a demon (v. 48). Jesus replied that those who keep His word will not die. The Jews ridiculed Him by questioning whether He was "greater than our father Abraham, which is dead?" (v. 53). Jesus replied that Abraham rejoiced to see His day. This the Jews could not comprehend and Jesus in verse 58 affirmed His preexistence to Abraham. The text concluded with the Jews picking up stones to throw at Him for what they perceived to be blasphemy.

Not until the writings of Paul do we find a more detailed discussion of Abraham in the plan of salvation. Both Romans 4:1-25 and Galatians 3:6-29 show that Abraham's faith preceded the coming of the law of Moses and that Abraham was counted righteous by God prior to the act of circumcision. On this basis, Abraham is the man of faith who stands as our example. He shows that only by faith can a person be saved. He also shows that it is through faith that the promises of God are given and kept by God. In Romans 4 he is further developed as the example of God's power to create—out of nothing—the son Isaac (both Abraham and especially Sarah were too old to bear children). By this feat of bringing life to one as though dead, God proves His ability to raise Jesus from the dead for our salvation.

I. DIVINE CALL (Genesis 11:26 through 12:3)

A. Change-Factors in Life (11:26-31)

(Verses 26-30 are not in the printed text.)

The story of Abraham begins with little fanfare. It concludes an extensive genealogy begun in 11:10 with the generations of men being scattered over the earth. In 11:26 the father of Abraham, Terah, is listed as a member of the genealogy family tree. In verse 26, we are told that Terah had three sons: Abram, Nahor, and Haran. In verse 27, we are told that Haran had a son named Lot (who later appears in the story). Lot is thus Abram's nephew. In verse 28, we are further told that Haran died leaving the son behind. Perhaps this helps explain the special concern Abram had throughout his life for Lot.

The end of verse 28 gives the first information on the geographical locale of this family: Ur of the Chaldees. Ur was located on the Euphrates River approximately 100 miles from the Persian Gulf in modern Iraq. Major excavations in the 1920s by Woolley showed a city that had occupants as far back as 2,600 B.C. Abraham's family can be dated in Ur from 2000-1,800 B.C. Thus, the city was already old by the time his family left. There were private homes (many homes in present-day Iraq are built in similar fashion) and the city had a natural harbor. The city contained a sacred area to the moongod, Nanna. In the center of the sacred area stood a ziggurat that dates around 2,200-2,100. Thus, it was a sight that Abraham's family had seen and perhaps even worshiped.

While in Ur, the men took wives. Abram's wife was Sarai. Her name apparently means "princess" as it is derived from the word for "prince." In Genesis 20:12, we are told that Abram and Sarai were half-siblings. Terah was her father, but she and Abram had different mothers. Thus, the comment in Genesis 20 that she was Abram's sister was true. She was apparently a woman of remarkable grace and beauty. She was near 65 years old when Abram came into the land of Canaan. Yet, her age did not adversely affect her natural beauty. In the Dead Sea Scrolls there is a document entitled "Memories of the Patriarchs." This document tells of her beauty when she was taken by Pharaoh in Genesis 12:10-20.

The account tells of the visit of three Egyptian dignitaries who saw her: "They kept bestowing (compliments upon her for her) godly (grace) and wisdom." After returning to Pharaoh these dignitaries related to him her beauty: "How comely is the shape of her face . . . and finespun are her tresses! How beautiful her eyes! How delicate is her nose and the whole lustre of her countenance! How fair are her breasts, and how comely withal is her complexion! How comely too are her arms, and how perfect her hands! How (delightful) are her hands to behold, how lovely her palms, how long and slender are her fingers!" And the account goes on to further describe her. (This particular translation of the Scrolls is by T. H. Gaster published by Doubleday.)

After all that has been said about her beauty, the Genesis text brings us to what will be the issue of Abram's faith: his beautiful wife is barren and can have no children (v. 30).

**31. And Terah took Abram his son, and Lot the son of Haran his son's son, and Sarai his daughter in law, his son Abram's wife; and they went forth with them from Ur of the Chaldees, to go into the land of Canaan; and they came unto Haran, and dwelt there.**

Sometime between 2000-1,800 B.C., this family migrated from east to west. They left Ur and went in a northwesterly direction following the Euphrates until they settled in Haran. We should not think that this was an isolated event of one family moving. Rather, they were part of a greater migration of peoples that was taking place across the Fertile Crescent. We know from ancient history that Ur was a weakened political power at this time; this may explain why the family chose to leave.

It is clear that the family had original intentions to go to Canaan. For reasons unknown they settled in Haran. It has been suggested that Terah became sick and the family remained in Haran until his death (v. 32). Whatever the case, this was a family that had not completed the purposes God had for it.

One of the striking aspects of this story is the passive role of Abram during this migration. He is a man caught up in something bigger than himself. This is manifested in three ways: First, from a sociological standpoint, he was under direction of his father during this move. It seems to have been at the initiation of the father that Abram is part of this move. His family responsibilities were something bigger than his own desires, and he was bound to them. Many people think that responsibilities are not of God; that is far from the truth. God usually works out His will in our keeping those commitments that are genuine and meant to be kept. In fact, there may often be little we can do about these things, as they are larger than we are!

Second, the apparent political situation in Ur was larger than Abram. It was out of his control and his family chose to leave a country that had little future.

Third, Abram was caught up in the web of the providence of God. God's purposes are often hidden in the midst of normal human events. There is no indication that Abram was in communion with Yahweh during this journey or that the family had any serious understanding that God was behind this move.

It should be a source of great hope for believers to realize that our lives are hidden with Christ and the circumstances and events of life will be revealed and understood at His coming (Colossians 3:3). What are some of the change factors you are facing in life? Are members of your class facing retirement? loss of jobs? dissolution of the family? Each of these are crucial times and require much courage and support as we face them. Yet, these change points can be tremendous avenues of turning our life around and serving God in new and refreshing ways regardless of our age. For the person who is confined to a nursing home the change point can offer an opportunity to be in intercessory prayer for a local church or group of people.

B. The Call to Blessing (Genesis 11:32 through 12:3)

**32. And the days of Terah were two hundred and five years: and Terah died in Haran.**

**12:1. Now the Lord had said unto Abram, Get thee out of thy country, and from thy kindred, and from thy father's house, unto a land that I will show thee.**

Why do you suppose God did not tell Abram at this time where He was leading Him?

What was Haran for Abram? Perhaps it was a place of delay of the purposes of God. It is also possible that it was an intentional place of waiting that God ordained. The relationship between 11:32 and 12:1 should not be passed over. Only after the death of Terah does the Word of the Lord come to Abram. Earlier it was observed that Abram was under the influence of something larger than himself. The situation in Ur was well past and no longer exercised control over him. The second factor concerned his father, Terah. Now that his father is dead Abram is directly responsible before God for hearing and obeying God's voice. Perhaps Abram had spent his life listening to the voice of God through his

father's intentions. But the time comes in every person's life when he must hear for himself the voice of God and must obey or not obey.

For Abram the place of waiting—Haran—became the place of death. In some respects death must occur before we can proceed with hearing and obeying God. There may actually be situations where parents or their youngsters are standing in the way of obeying God and it takes a literal death before that person is free. More often than not the death is spiritual and involves attachments that are not in harmony with the kingdom of God.

Only after the father died was Abram addressed by the Lord. Note the focus of 12:1. Abram is to leave the country of Haran and his kinfolk and his father's house. There is a call for genuine separation so he can see what God has for him. God's promise and plan is specific for Abram and can be witnessed. Faith enables us to grasp God's blessings and call for our lives and act obediently.

Does God lead Christians today in a similar manner as He did Abram? Explain.

**2. And I will make of thee a great nation, and I will bless thee, and make thy name great; and thou shalt be a blessing:**

**3. And I will bless them that bless thee, and curse him that curseth thee: and in thee shall all families of the earth be blessed.**

In 1 Thessalonians 5:9, Paul tells us that God has not destined us for wrath but for salvation. This salvation is spelled out in Ephesians 1 as the purposes of God in Christ are related to the blessings God has for us in Him.

Abram is the Old Testament example who tells us that we are destined for glory in God's call. Note that the word **bless** occurs five times in verses 2 and 3. The focus of this unconditional covenant by God towards man is found in the fact that it is God who is the personal pronoun "I." In each instance of blessing, God is the author. All that Abram is to be for himself and for the world is found in the gracious power of the almighty "I." God alone is capable of making this happen. Abram will participate by faith and obedience, but the reality of the blessing depends completely on the faithfulness of God to His Word. Abram believes that God's Word is true and acts accordingly.

These promises to Abram are still valid today. Those who bless Abram's seed will themselves be blessed; those who curse his seed will bring that curse upon themselves. An example of this is given in Numbers 22-24 which tells of the effort of Balaam to curse Abram's seed, but his curses come out as blessings. Abram's seed today is composed of his natural heirs, the Jews, and his spiritual heirs —believers in Christ (whether Jew or Gentile). In Romans 11:28-31, Paul points out that regarding the gospel unbelieving Jews are enemies of God for the sake of Gentiles being included in the blessings of faith. But regarding election, the Jews are beloved by God because of their faithful forefathers. God's gifts and call are irrevocable in relation to these unconditional covenants He has made with the patriarch Abram. This should cause all Christians to be in great prayer for the salvation of the Jews as heirs of Abram. When the policies of a nation turn against the Jews, that nation alines itself with curses from God.

II. HUMAN RESPONSE (Genesis 12:4-6)

A. A Total Response (vv. 4, 5)

**4. So Abram departed, as the Lord had spoken unto him; and Lot went with him: and Abram was seventy and five years old when he departed out of Haran.**

Abram heard and obeyed the voice of God in his life. The way to blessing for ourselves, as well as being a blessing to others, is through obedience. If there is rebellion in your heart and life against God's will then you cannot expect His blessings.

Four things come to mind as we reflect on Abram's ability to hear God speak. These things are related to help-ing us grow in our knowledge of His will and Word. First, we mature in our understanding of the fact that we do have a place in God's plans. This maturing moves us past our childish expressions of faith and moves us to really trust in Him. Second, there is a maturing that enables us to know how to interpret the circumstances of our lives. Third, there is a maturing that sees the Bible not as a law book but as God's Word for life. Fourth, a maturing that enables us to see that we are part of God's plans that are larger than us. We belong to the community of faith and our lives are defined in relation to God's people.

**5. And Abram took Sarai his wife, and Lot his brother's son, and all their substance that they had gathered, and the souls that they had gotten in Haran; and they went forth to go into the land of Canaan; and into the land of Canaan they came.**

It should be noted that in obedience to the voice of God Abram took his family and moved. This was a total commitment by Abram to the way of God. We will see in Lesson 10 just how important it is to make a total commitment to the Lord.

The fact that Abram took his family indicates that the entire family submitted to the ways of God. The New Testament tells of the conversion of the Philippian jailer and the subsequent conversion of the entire household (Acts 16). This principle should not go unnoticed in our world today. Husbands who accept Christ have a responsibility to seek to order their home and family after the ways of God. Obviously, this is often difficult; yet, the Lord provides strength and wisdom as this is done with love and Christian discipline.

B. A Realistic Response (v. 6)

**6. And Abram passed through the land unto the place of Sichem, unto the plain of Moreh. And the Canaanite was then in the land.**

"Sichem" is the site of "Shechem." It is about 350 miles to the south of Haran. There was a famous place of worship at Moreh. The word "plain" can mean "oak."

The note at the end of verse 6 indicates that Abram was not going to find a fairytale kindgom awaiting him. It was a land that had to be conquered. It was a land wherein others dwelt; yet, God had given it to Abram.

One point that should be made is that faithful service to the Lord takes place in the midst of an unbelieving world. We do not witness to those who already are followers of Christ; our witness is to those who have not heard or who have rejected. Thus, the call of God will often lead us into the midst of a sinful and perverse generation. Christian service is the way of the Cross. God does not promise wealth or material prosperity. He does not promise good health or absolute safety. The Christian can obey because he knows that all things work for good to those who love the Lord and are called according to His purposes, (Romans 8:28). Regardless of the suffering, for a person to be in the will of God is the most important place in the world.

III. GOD'S PROMISE. (Genesis 12:7-9)

A. The Worship Response (vv. 7, 8)

**7. And the Lord appeared unto Abram, and said, Unto thy seed will I give this land: and there builded he an altar unto the Lord, who appeared unto him.**

The earlier covenant from God in 12:1-3 did not contain explicit reference to the seed of Abram. He knew from God that he was to be the father of a great nation. This could have easily meant in the sense of a great empire gained by wealth and power. That was not the way God desired to bring about the promise of His will. As we know from Zechariah 4:6, God's purposes are accomplished by His Spirit, not by might nor by power.

Verse 7 points that Abram's understanding of God's will is in another direction. He was to begin a journey of faith that would lead to the miracle work of God in

the birth of Isaac. It is this question of the son born from Abram's seed which will be the center of Abram's faith-struggle throughout Genesis. This journey would one day lead to another miraculous birth is the coming of the Savior, Jesus Christ.

It is evident that Abram was able to trust God's Word of promise concerning his seed evident from the reference that he built an altar and worshiped the Lord. This particular altar is not given a specific name other than being near the oak of Moreh. Lack of specifics does not mean the location is insignificant; rather, attention is put on the fact that this altar represents a place which every person of faith must come to. Its particular name is as various as one's own name. It is the place where one glimpses the power, wonder, and majesty of God submits himself to His way.

The verse begins and ends with the fact that the Lord "appeared" unto Abram. How does God appear to people? Do we actually see Him? This seems unlikely since the Scriptures indicate that no one can look upon God and live. A clue is given in the Gospel of John where Jesus describes His relationship with the Heavenly Father. The John 5:19 and 20 reference is made by Jesus that "The Son can do nothing of himself, but what he seeth the Father do: for what things soever he doeth, these also doeth the Son likewise. For the Father loveth the Son, and sheweth him all things that himself doeth."

From these verses in John, it is clear that Jesus could "see" what His Father was doing and desired of Him. This "seeing" was possible because of the love the Father has for the Son and because the Son has complete faith and confidence in the Father who has sent Him.

This same love of the Lord is given to Abram. God loves Abram and desires that Abram be a man of faith who can "see" what God is desiring! Thus, within the context of hearing God's promise, of worshiping Him in Spirit and in truth, we are able to "see" with eyes of faith the marvelous things that God has for those whom He calls and loves! Thus we can have confidence that God will reveal Himself to us in such a way that, by faith, we can affirm He has appeared!

One of the important aspects of faith that needs to be rediscovered is that faith "sees" in mind and spirit what it is that God will accomplish. This is part of the "visionary" work of the Spirit enabling us to truly believe and act in faith.

**8. And he removed from thence unto a mountain on the east of Beth-el, and pitched his tent, having Beth-el on the west, and Hai on the east: and there he builded an altar unto the Lord, and called upon the name of the Lord.**

"Hai" is the site "Ai" in the Bible. Note that Abram moved to the site of a mountain in order to "see" what God had for him. He moved the place of worship and "pitched his tent." This is a statement of contentment in Abram's spirit. It is as if a major hurdle has been leaped and the man of faith is able to rest in what God has promised. Such a place of rest is a place of worship. It is a place of moving beyond the pressure of the call and being at peace with the God of the call.

B. The Progressing Journey (v. 9)

**9. And Abram journeyed, going on still toward the south.**

Abram is a man of movement. After finding the place of worship and peace on the mountain, he continues to move throughout the land that is his in God's will. The "south" is the **Negeb.** It is more of a desert area but indicates Abram journeyed the length of Canaan.

The life of faith is a life that is open to the "moving" of the Spirit. It is not an irresponsible life; rather, it is the ultimate act of responsibility towards the Creator and His invitation to obedience. Abram is free from those things that stood in his way at the end of Genesis 11. He is a stranger in the land of Canaan; yet, he is confident that he is a stranger in God's will. Thus, he experiences a tremendous liberty that comes to those sons and daughters who have made faith and God's Word their standard!

## REVIEW QUESTIONS

1. How is Abram's faith discussed in Paul's writings in Romans 4 and Galatians 3?

2. What are the three areas of life that controlled Abram's life prior to God's direct call in 12:1?

3. What are some areas of life that must "die" before we can hear and obey God's voice?

4. How do we share in the blessings God promised Abram in 12:1-3?

5. In what ways are the "Canaanites" still in the areas of our life?

## GOLDEN TEXT HOMILY

"AND I WILL MAKE OF THEE A GREAT NATION, AND I WILL BLESS THEE, AND MAKE THY NAME GREAT, AND THOU SHALT BE A BLESSING" (Genesis 12:2).

In this passage is the call by which Abraham was removed out of the land of his nativity into the land of promise. This was designed to try his faith and obedience and also to separate him and set him apart for God's use.

Abraham's response was much like Christians today. We are willing to go part of the way—Abraham went only half way from Ur of the Chaldeans to Canaan and spent some five years in Haran.

God said "Get thee out of thy country." By this precept Abraham was put to the test—could he willingly leave his native soil and dearest friends to go along with God?

All of God's precepts attended with promises to the obedient. In Genesis 12: 2, 3, God made Abraham six promises: (1) I will make thee a great nation. (2) I will bless thee. (3) I will make thy name great. (4) Thou shalt be a blessing. (5) I will bless those that bless thee and curse those that curseth thee. (6) In thee shall all the families of the earth be blessed.

The sixth was the promise of a Messiah. Jesus Christ is the great blessing of the world. It is a great honor to be related to Christ. This made Abraham's name great that the Messiah was to descend from his loins. It was Abraham's honor to be His descendant by nature; it will be ours to be His brethren by grace. (See Matthew 12:50.) Obedience to God makes possible the fulfilling of His promises.

Moses failed to reach the promised land because he disobeyed God.

Jonah got in great trouble because he failed to carry out God's instructions.

The simple truth is that we cannot have Jesus Christ and all His blessings apart from His teachings. Our devotion to Him can only be expressed in loving obedience to His commandments.— **W. E. Johnson, (Retired), Former Executive Director World Missions, Church of God, Cleveland, Tennessee.**

## SENTENCE SERMONS

OBEDIENCE TO GOD makes possible the fulfilling of His divine purpose.
**—Selected**

IF YE BE WILLING and obedient, ye shall eat the good of the land.
**—Isaiah 1:19**

FAITH IS NOT a sense nor sight, nor reason, but taking God at his word.
**—A. B. Evans**

IF THE WILL of God is our will, and if He always has His way, then we always have our way also.
**—Hannah Whitall Smith**

## EVANGELISTIC APPLICATION

GOD USES OBEDIENT SERVANTS IN HIS PLAN FOR REDEEMING MANKIND.

God uses obedient servants in His plan for redeeming mankind. This is seen first of all in the fact that the Redeemer himself became truly man in flesh and died for us. Jesus, as the Word made flesh, is the Savior and Servant of God for the sake of salvation. He is not only the object of salvation but also an example to us of a faithful servant.

An obedient servant has certain characteristics: First, the servant is willing to listen to the call of God. Second, the servant is willing to obey the call of God. Third, the servant counts the cost of obedience and enters into the realm of faithful service with full knowledge and intention. Fourth, the servant worships the Lord for His call and power to fulfill His Word. Fifth, the servant finds rest and peace in the love of the Lord.

Such characteristics enhance our capacity to be used for redemptive love.

## ILLUMINATING THE LESSON

Walter Brueggemann has observed that Abram's journey in Genesis 12 is developed two ways in the New Testament:

"Christian discipleship is understood as a following of 'the way' " (Matthew 8:22; 9:9; 10:38). "The 'way' " . . . is the way of Jesus, the way of the Cross, the way of suffering, the way to Jerusalem. The term marks Christians as those who live in a way contrasted to every fixed and settled form of life. They pursue a God who finally will be at peace with no human arrangement that falls short of the kingdom in its practice of justice and freedom.

"In . . . Hebrews 11, Abraham and Sarah are presented as people who claimed no home. They only pursued a risky promise. . . . Such a pursuit of promise can never be one-generational. Each generation trusts that if the promise is not now fulfilled, it will be given to a next generation. Thus, the text stands in opposition to the one-generational ideology of our culture which demands everything now."

## DAILY DEVOTIONAL GUIDE

M. Action Requested. Joshua 1:1-6
T. Faithfulness Required. Joshua 1:7-9
W. Commitment Expressed. Isaiah 6:1-8
T. Invitation Accepted. Matthew 4:18-22
F. Vigilance Expected. Matthew 25:1-13
S. Obedience Remembered. Hebrews 11:8-19

# Settling Differences

**Study Text:** Genesis 13:1-3

**Supplemental References:** Genesis 26:17-33; Matthew 6:19-34; Acts 9:26-29

**Time:** Around 2000 B.C.

**Place:** Egypt and Canaan

**Golden Text:** "How good and how pleasant it is for brethren to dwell together in unity!" (Psalm 133:1)

**Central Truth:** We should always seek God's help in making decisions.

**Evangelistic Emphasis:** Believers witness to the world by manifesting a Christlike attitude in the midst of controversy.

### Printed Text

**Genesis 13:1.** And Abram went up out of Egypt, he, and his wife, and all that he had, and Lot with him, into the south.

**2. And Abram was very rich in cattle, in silver, and in gold.**

3. And he went on his journeys from the south even to Beth-el, unto the place where his tent had been at the beginning, between Beth-el and Hai;

**4. Unto the place of the altar, which he had made there at the first: and there Abram called on the name of the Lord.**

5. And Lot also, which went with Abram, had flocks, and herds, and tents.

**6. And the land was not able to bear them, that they might dwell together: for their substance was great, so that they could not dwell together.**

7. And there was a strife between the herdmen of Abram's cattle and the herdmen of Lot's cattle: and the Canaanite and the Perizzite dwelled then in the land.

**8. And Abram said unto Lot, Let there be no strife, I pray thee, between me and thee, and between my herdmen and thy herdmen; for we be brethren.**

9. Is not the whole land before thee? separate thyself, I pray thee, from me: if thou wilt take the left hand, then I will go to the right; or if thou depart to the right hand, then I will go to the left.

**10. And Lot lifted up his eyes, and beheld all the plain of Jordan, that it was well watered every where, before the Lord destroyed Sodom and Gomorrah, even as the garden of the Lord, like the land of Egypt, as thou comest unto Zoar.**

11. Then Lot chose him all the plain of Jordan; and Lot journeyed east: and they separated themselves the one from the other.

**12. Abram dwelled in the land of Canaan, and Lot dwelled in the cities of the plain, and pitched his tent toward Sodom.**

13. But the men of Sodom were wicked and sinners before the Lord exceedingly.

## DICTIONARY

**Canaanite (KAY-nan-ite)—Genesis 13:7**—A member of one of the tribes that inhabited the promised land; they were descendants of Canaan and were non-Israelites.

**Perizzite (PAIR-iz-zite)—Genesis 13:7**—One of the ten doomed tribes of Canaan. They inhabited the mountainous region which they eventually yielded to the tribes of Ephraim and Judah. A small group of them remained in the time of Solomon, and were by him used for bond service (1 Kings 9:20).

**we are brethren—Genesis 13:8**—Blood relatives. In the society of the time, strife was especially avoided among kinsmen.

**the whole land before thee—Genesis 13:9**—Abram, being the elder, has first choice, but he waives his right in the interest of peace.

**Jordan (JOR-dun)—Genesis 13:10**—The river that flows from between Mt. Hermon and Mt. Lebanon to the Sea of Galilee and on to empty into the Dead Sea. The Hebrew meaning of the word is "descender." This is because it falls nearly 2,500 feet in its short course.

**Sodom (SAH-dum)—Genesis 13:10**—A wicked city on the shore of the Dead Sea, the lowest point on earth.

**Gomorrah (ge-MOR-ruh)—Genesis 13:10**—A city near Sodom and equally wicked.

**Zoar (ZO-ahr)—Genesis 13:11**—A small town near Sodom and Gomorrah, but at a higher elevation and probably southeast of the Dead Sea.

---

## LESSON OUTLINE

I. STRIFE AMONG BRETHREN
  A. Turning From a Wrong Decision
  B. The Curse of "More"
II. A GENEROUS PROPOSAL
III. CONTRASTING CHOICES
  A. The Lust of the Eyes
  B. The Blessings of Trust

## LESSON EXPOSITION

### INTRODUCTION

The teacher will do well to read carefully the remainder of Genesis 12:10-20. That story will have significance in the total understanding of Abraham's attitude to allow Lot to choose first. It will show that Abraham had moved from an initial weak faith, which led to the troubles in Egypt, to a man of abiding faith which led to the blessings of the Promised Land.

Although Lot had been introduced in 11:27, 31, in Genesis 13 there begins a series of stories in which Lot becomes dependent upon Abraham's faith and power to deliver him from the effects of evil.

I. STRIFE AMONG BRETHREN (Genesis 13:1-7)

A. Turning From a Wrong Decision (vv. 1-4)

**1. And Abram went up out of Egypt, he, and his wife, and all that he had, and Lot with him, into the south.**

**2. And Abram was very rich in cattle, in silver, and in gold.**

As mentioned in the Introduction the events of 12:10-20 are important in understanding this part of the story of Abraham. In Genesis 12:10-20, the story is told of how a person can miss the will of God in the midst of a crisis. Abram had been told to go to Canaan. He was not told by God to go to Egypt. The south of Canaan, where Abram settled (12:9), was hit by famine. We know today from reports concerning East Africa and Ethiopia how devastating such famines can be. Yet, Abram chose not to trust in the Lord to supply his every need. God is able to bring springs from the desert for those who will trust and obey His Word. The only famine that the person of God should fear is the famine of hearing of the Word of God. In Amos 8:11, 12, such a famine is described: "The days are coming," declares the Sovereign Lord, "when I will send a famine through the land—not a famine of food or a thirst for water, but a famine of hearing the words of the Lord. Men will stagger from sea to sea and wander from north to east, searching for the word of the Lord, but they will not find it" **(New International Version).** Abram experienced such a famine. The Word was not heard by him because he apparently did not seek it. How tempting it is in the midst of a crisis to act out of our own knowledge and understanding and fail to rely upon the Word of the Lord. Abram's call was to live by faith, not by sight or anxiety.

Unless we have a clear word from the Lord regarding our actions, we are often wise to simply remain still and wait for His guidance. Patience is a difficult Christian virtue; yet it is so close to the knowledge of God that it is a fruit of the Spirit. Thus, God will give direction and provide for us as we submit to wait before Him. To act from anxiety and fear is never a good Christian motive. To act from the fear of God and the witness of His Word and Spirit provides clear direction.

Abram's decision to turn to Egypt endangered his wife. It was a partial truth that she was his sister (half-sister through the same father). What he failed to tell was the entire truth, thus jeopardizing her role in the future plans of God. It is clear from 12:12, 13 that Abram was a man filled with fear. Fear is the end result of running from God's purposes. It is not that Abram meant to run from God. His intentions were to preserve himself. He had yet to learn that God's will was to preserve him. Security could only be found in what God ordained. That is why salvation is never a matter of one's own effort; it is always by grace so that we know with certainty that God has saved us.

One of the ironies of the entire situation in Egypt is that Abram did not lose in terms of material blessings. Verse 2 tells us that he returned "very rich" in material things. While this seems to be a contradiction, the remainder of Genesis 13 shows that this wealth became a source of conflict within the family. It also shows that the wealth became the source of

another opportunity for Abram to exercise his faith in God.

The "south" of verse 1 is the area of the desert, the Negeb. On a map this area would be near Beersheba.

**3. And he went on his journeys from the south even to Beth-el, unto the place where his tent had been at the beginning, between Beth-el and Hai.**

**4. Unto the place of the altar, which he had made there at the first: and there Abram called on the name of the Lord.**

The journey from Egypt brought Abram back to his beginnings. Bethel was located near the border of the tribal territories of Ephraim to the north and Benjamin to the south, approximately 20 miles north of modern Jerusalem.

Acts of sin require that we return to the place of the altar to hear again from God and begin our journey in His will. Abram's sin in going to Egypt was that he acted on an authority other than the Word from God. By returning to the altar, he placed himself back in the territory God had given him and also placed himself back under the framework of the covenant promise of Genesis 12:1-3.

Verse 4 concludes with Abram calling upon the name of the Lord. In Genesis 12:10-20 the Lord's name is used only to indicate that it was He who brought afflictions on the house of Pharaoh. There is no indication that Abram called on the Lord's name in Egypt. To call on the name of the Lord is to affirm one's submission to His authority and lordship. The Scriptures contain numerous references to calling upon the Lord's name (Psalms 55:16; 80:18; 105:1; 145:18; Isaiah 41:25; Romans 10:13). To call upon His name means to know Him and be known by Him. It means that the Lord is ready to hear and answer. It means that He longs for fellowship with us in prayer and obedience.

For Abram it also meant that he had returned to the place where he could do the will of God.

B. The Curse of "More" (vv. 5-7)

**5. And Lot also, which went with**

**Abram, had flocks, and herds, and tents.**

**6. And the land was not able to bear them, that they might dwell together: for their substance was great, so that they could not dwell together.**

**7. And there was a strife between the herdmen of Abram's cattle and the herdmen of Lot's cattle: and the Canaanite and the Perizzite dwelt then in the land.**

Material things in themselves are not evil. But, as Paul wrote to Timothy, "the love of money is the root of all evil" (1 Timothy 6:10). Money is the outward commercial symbol of possessions. To love things of substance as possessions more than to love the Creator of possessions is the root of evil in all situations of life.

With Abram and Lot we have clear contrast on how people of faith are to deal with their material blessings. This is an important lesson in our generation. As citizens of Western civilization, most of us are relatively well-off compared to the remainder of the world. To have material blessings is not immoral—assuming they are gained in a moral way. It is our attitude and what we do with our blessings that answers the question of morality regarding our wealth.

---

Discuss the danger of a materialistic "mind set" in a world where so many have not needed food and shelter. To what extent are we obligated to share?

---

These verses tell us that Abram's entire family benefitted from the stay in Egypt. Lot returned with his uncle and members of the two families soon discovered they could not dwell together in peace. The Hebrew word for "dwell" is the usual word for "sitting, remaining." The **Brown, Driver, Briggs Hebrew Lexicon** comments that it meant "to have their abode together." Thus, we are presented with a tragic picture of family disruption. The wealth of the two families has created barriers. It should be noted that the text makes no moral judgment on this situation. That is a fact of life: more wealth means the

need for more room, especially among sheepherders. So, the fact is treated as a reality of life. Yet, it generated a situation in which Lot moved away from the center of the original call to Abram. Lot, by his wealth, is led to believe that he can make it on his own. His self-sufficiency becomes an avenue of sin in his life.

**Substance** is the Hebrew **recosh** which meant "property, goods." It was used to describe movable goods of all kinds, but clearly referred to flocks (see Genesis 31:18; 36:7).

Their possession became the source of "a strife." This reading by the **King James Version** seems to indicate there was one conflict. Actually the focus is upon the fact that there were numerous conflicts between the two herds. It is also pointed out that the conflict does not seem to have directly involved either Lot or Abram. They are called upon to settle the matter before it becomes more devisive and perhaps violent.

The word for "strife" in the Hebrew is **rib** (pronounced as "riv" with a soft "b"). While used in various ways in the Old Testament, its use in Proverbs is of special note: "A wrathful man stirreth up strife: but he that is slow to anger appeaseth strife" (15:18); "Better is a dry morsel, and quietness therewith, than an house full of sacrifices with strife" (17:1); "It is an honour for a man to cease from strife: but every fool will be meddling" (20:3); "As coals are to burning coals, and wood to fire; so is a contentious man to kindle strife" (26:21).

In the New Testament there are several instances in which Christians are warned against strife. Paul mentions in Galatians 5:20 that strife is one of the works of the flesh and those who do such things will not inherit the kingdom of God. In Philippians 2:3, Paul warns that Christian service should not be done in strife. In 2 Corinthians 12:20 he expressed concern that he would visit the Corinthian church and discover the presence of strife in the congregation. In James 3:14, strife is an agent of boasting and therefore distorts the truth. James further indicated in verse 16 that strife created confusion and the possibility of every kind of evil work.

Verse 7 of Genesis 13 concludes with a reference to the presence of the Canaanites and Perizzites in the land. In 12:6 it was noted that the Canaanite was in the land when Abram first arrived (see Lesson 8). They were sources of trouble and indicated that the Promised Land was not to be taken lightly but would have to be subdued by the righteous faith of people such as Abraham. It is of interest that after Abram's stay in Egypt his return finds alongside the Canaanites another semi-nomadic group called "Perizzites." The meaning of their name is obscure; however, the **Interpreter's Dictionary of the Bible** indicates that the name perhaps meant "dweller of the open country." They are mentioned 23 times in the Old Testament—four times in connection with the Canaanites. That they continued to be present in Israel is clear from 1 Kings 9:20 where they are mentioned as slave labor used by Solomon. The 1 Kings passage indicates that they were one of the groups that Israel failed to utterly destroy during the time of the occupation under Joshua and the judges.

It is obvious that they are enemies of the purposes of God. Their presence along with the strife of Abram and Lot is of special note. Dissension always brings in its wake "every kind of evil" (James 3:16).

Earlier comments were made regarding the neutral character of material items. They could either be a source of blessing or a source of cursing. Christians are to remember that our blessings are primarily spiritual and relate to the coming of the kingdom of God. When we focus our attention too much on material blessings we open a door for Satan to cause conflict and lead us to make choices that are not in the will of God. Only by being free from the control of our material blessings can we exercise "lordship" over them rather than them controlling us.

II. A GENEROUS PROPOSAL (Genesis 13:8, 9)

**8. And Abram said unto Lot, Let there be no strife, I pray thee, between me and thee, and between my herdmen and thy herdmen; for we be brethren.**

---

Discuss the "how to" and merits of settling strife as early as possible when issues that divide congregations develop.

---

Abram offers the peace treaty to Lot. His offer is based on one primary theme: we are brothers! This theme has two major implications.

The first implication is personal. Abram does not desire to see this dispute come between him and his nephew. It is important that personal relationships be kept pure before the Lord. When we have discord among ourselves we place barriers that limit communication and the effective work of love in our life. Christian unity means that the brethren love one another. This is a crucial sign for our witness to the world of the effectiveness of the death and resurrection of Jesus. Our love one for the other reflects the love that the Son has for us and the love the Father has for the Son.

The second aspect of this theme is that our disputes affect others. Sin always has corporate dimensions. The excuse used in this generation—"it doesn't matter what I do as long as no one gets hurt"—is a lie from the pit of hell. Sin seeks to deceive us into believing that only our lives are affected by disobedience. But that is far from the truth. All strife has ramifications for the future. The sins of the fathers do get passed to their children. How sad it is to watch persons continue to harber bitterness over issues long ago that concerned persons now dead. A tremendous amount of spiritual energy goes into such wasted life.

The call to unity at the close of verse 8 is based on the brotherhood between Abram and Lot. That brotherhood has been expanded in Jesus Christ to include all people. Regardless of the color of the skin or the national origin we are brothers and sisters together in Christ Jesus. As Paul wrote so powerfully to the Galatian Christians: "Ye are all the children of God by faith in Christ Jesus. For as many of you as have been baptized into Christ have put on Christ. There is neither

Jew nor Greek, there is neither bond nor free, there is neither male nor female: for ye are all one in Christ Jesus. And if ye be Christ's, then are ye Abraham's seed, and heirs according to the promise" (3:26-29).

**9. Is not the whole land before thee? separate thyself, I pray thee, from me: if thou wilt take the left hand, then I will go to the right; or if thou depart to the right hand, then I will go to the left.**

After affirming the unity of their relationship as brothers, Abram did a most unusual thing: He gave up his rights for the sake of Lot and the will of God. It was within his legitimate power as the head of the family to choose first.

Is it always proper to "prefer your brother when the option of choice exists"? Explain your answer.

His denial of choice indicated that he had moved past the point of acting out of panic as he did in the flight to Egypt 12:10. He matured in his faith to the point that he was willing to trust God for the present and the future. Abram's response goes counter to the mood of our society that says to "assert yourself." We are people accustomed to knowing and claiming our rights. While this is certainly good in our democratic society, it is not the way of the kingdom of God. The kingdom way is the way of denial and submission to the Lord of lords and to one another as brothers and sisters in Christ.

Abram has also moved past his problem of trusting in God to provide in the midst of famine situations. Abram could have acted out of anxiety that Lot would get all the best land. Yet, he chose to place his future completely with God. He chose the way of God's security rather than man's insecurity. He gave up his human prerogatives for the sake of giving God room to operate in his life.

Brueggemann has observed the relationship between this story and Luke 12:13-21. In the passage from Luke, Jesus is confronted with a brother who feels

that he has been wronged in the matter of a family inheritance. Jesus invited the man to step back from that strife and place his trust in God rather than in riches (v. 15). The man who trusts in material things for his life will discover such a life concludes with death (vv. 20, 21). Following the story Jesus continued to relate how God will supply our every need as we trust in Him. The three things that can distort our relationship with God and our brothers regarding material things are (1) coveteousness (12:15), (2) anxiety (12:22, 25), and (3) little faith (12:28).

The relationship of these accounts in Luke to Genesis 12:10 through 13:18 is that Abram learned how not to covet nor be anxious nor be of little faith regarding the power of God to provide.

III. CONTRASTING CHOICES (Genesis 13:10-13)

A. The Lust of the Eyes (vv. 10-13)

**10. And Lot lifted up his eyes, and beheld all the plain of Jordan, that it was well watered every where, before the Lord destroyed Sodom and Gomorrah, even as the garden of the Lord, like the land of Egypt, as thou comest unto Zoar.**

As the subtitle suggests, 1 John 2:16 is a striking New Testament commentary on Lot's choice. Those verses are worth reading to see the full implications of a choice like Lot's: "love not the world, neither the things that are in the world. If any man love the world, the love of the Father is not in him. For all that is in the world, the lust of the flesh, and the lust of the eyes, and the pride of life, is not of the Father, but is of the world. And the world passeth away, and the lust thereof: but he that doeth the will of God abideth forever" (1 John 2:15-17).

Instead of lifting his spirit to the Lord, Lot lifted his eyes to the world. Lot's situation could have been different. The Lord would have provided room for both herds, if he had trusted the Lord with his future.

The land of the Jordan plain was obviously a beautiful place prior to the destruction of Sodom and Gomorrah. Yet it was also a place of terrible sin. Von Rad commented on this land as "unheard of beauty" and "unheard of depravity."

The Jordan plain refers to the lower part of the Jordan River Valley that began about 25 miles north of the Dead Sea and included the Dead Sea area in its dimensions **(Interpreter's Bible).** Zoar was a city near Sodom and Gomorrah. The reading of the Authorized Version gives the impression that Zoar was near Egypt; the actual case is that even as Egypt was a beautiful land, so was the Jordan plain as one approached it from Zoar.

**11. Then Lot chose him all the plain of Jordan; and Lot journeyed east: and they separated themselves the one from the other.**

**12. Abram dwelled in the land of Canaan, and Lot dwelled in the cities of the plain, and pitched his tent toward Sodom.**

**13. But the men of Sodom were wicked and sinners before the Lord exceedingly.**

Lot continued to be the major character in this part of the story. The mention of Abram is brief but it contains the positive statement that he remained in Canaan, the land promised in 11:31.

The comment in verse 11 that "Lot journeyed east" is of interest. The original family migration was from the east to west. It is as if Lot is going backwards. To live "east" is to live away from God in the opening part of Genesis. Adam and Eve are forced from the garden "east of Eden" (3:24). Cain is forced to wander in the land of Nod, "east of Eden" (4:16). Lot turned his tent towards the wicked city of Sodom. It is an intentional choice that placed opportunity ahead of the righteous call of God.

It is clear there were more cities in this plain than Sodom and Gomorrah. Because of his flocks, Lot lived near them for the commerce they provided. Yet, the influence of Sodom was manifested in the entire area. Verse 13 emphasized just how evil and wicked these men were. Their wickedness was something that was stench before the Lord.

B. The Blessings of Trust (vv. 17, 18)

(These verses are not in the Printed Text.)

The contrast between Abram and Lot is on several levels. The first is that Abram learned to trust God with his future while Lot was concerned with self-survival. Another contrast is in the way both men relate to God. There is no communication between God and Lot over the choice of the Jordan plain. But in 13:14 the Lord tells Abram to "Lift up now thine eyes. . . ." In 13:10 Lot lifted his eyes and saw with the lust of the flesh. Abram did not lift his eyes until instructed by the Lord. How important it is to wait on the Lord! While Lot saw in one direction, the east, Abram was invited by God to look in every direction! Lot pitched his tents in the vicinity of Sodom; Abram went to Hebron and built an altar to the Lord. Lot will run for his life from Sodom; Abram is given the freedom to "walk" through the land and enjoy its promise from the Lord regarding the future.

For the person who learns to "trust in the Lord with all thine heart; and lean not unto thine own understanding" (Proverbs 3:5) the Lord will provide marvelous blessings that have eternal purposes. It means that all material blessings from God are recognized as gifts from Him to be used for His glory. To joyfully submit to His lordship is to learn to love and trust Him as a caring eternal Father.

**REVIEW QUESTIONS**

1. How does Abram's choice in 12:10-20 contrast with his choice in 13:1-3?

2. Does material gain cause discord in families today? What about in the church? What can Christians who are growing in wealth do to keep such discord from happening?

3. What does the New Testament say about "strife" in the church?

4. What are the implications of being brothers for the way we solve problems in the church?

# 90

5. What happens to our "rights" as we trust in the Lord?

## GOLDEN TEXT HOMILY

"HOW GOOD AND HOW PLEASANT IT IS FOR BRETHREN TO DWELL TOGETHER IN UNITY!" (Psalm 133:1).

A little boy saw two nestling birds peaking at each other and asked his older brother what they were doing. "They are quarreling," the elder brother replied. "But they cannot be," insisted the little boy, "they are brothers."

One of the most beautiful descriptions of the church in the Bible is that of a family—"the Household of Faith." Because of our relationship to God through Christ and our adoption into His family, we are not only sons and daugthers of God but brothers and sisters in the truest sense. Paul reminds us that "we are members one of another" (Ephesians 4:25) and "by one Spirit are we all baptized into one body" (1 Corinthians 12:13).

The term "unity" in scriptural context refers to the harmonious function of the body of Christ in fulfilling the will of God on the earth and in directing energy and resources toward the expansion of His kingdom. The unity of brotherhood is premised upon three things: (1) mutuality of faith, (2) the power of the Holy Spirit and (3) the reality of God's love flowing from heart to heart.

The spiritual unity of which the Bible speaks is not a sporadic or temporary experience. It is a state of being in which every believer should daily live. Like the precious ointment with which Aaron the high priest was anointed and the refreshing dew that gave life to the mountains of Zion, unity should pervade the entire atmosphere of all our activity.

Unity does not mean that there will be no differences of opinion among the brethren. It does mean, however, that because of our unique relationship to God and to one another, our goals are greater than our differences. The common ground of faith we share provides a secure foundation on which to build for the future. The cords that bind us together must always be strong—so strong that

self-interests are laid aside for the best interests of the entire body. "Be devoted to one another in brotherly love," said Paul. "Honor one another above yourselves" (Romans 12:10, **New International Version).** Brethren dwelling together in unity—this is good—this is pleasant declared the psalmist.—**J. Ralph Brewer, Editorial Administrative Assistant, Church of God Evangel, Cleveland, Tennessee.**

## SENTENCE SERMONS

DISSATISFACTION WITH our condition is often due to the false idea we have of the happiness of others.
—**Churchman**

KEEP CLEAR OF a man who does not value his own character.

HE WHO FALLS in love with himself will have no rivals.
—**Franklin**

WE SHOULD BE as generous with a man as we are with a picture which we are always willing to give the benefit of the best light.
—**Emerson**

## EVANGELISTIC APPLICATION

BELIEVERS WITNESS TO THE WORLD BY MANIFESTING A CHRISTLIKE ATTITUDE IN THE MIDST OF CONTROVERSY.

Believers witness to the world by manifesting a Christlike attitude in the midst of controversy. As Henri Nouwen comments in **Clowning in Rome,** one of the things the world can say about us is "See how they love one another." It is always a sad situation when Christians part without being reconciled one to the other. Our unity is found in our love and respect for each other.

The world will accept our witness even when we disagree among ourselves as long as the world sees the love of Christ in us. Christian unity does not mean killing debate or avoiding controversy. Rather, it means acting in the Spirit of Christ in the midst of that debate.

Paul's letters to Christians contain references to the fact that the heathen world is judging us to see the merits of our proclamation. We are called to be different and the world really desires that we actually be different. The world, although bound by deceit and sin, still longs for the truth to set it free.

## ILLUMINATING THE LESSON

In **Celebration of Disciple** (Harper & Row, 1978), author Richard Foster speaks of "The Discipline of Simplicity." Here is a collection of quotes from that chapter.

"Simplicity is freedom. Duplicity is bondage. Simplicity brings joy and balance. Duplicity brings anxiety and fear."

"The Christian Discipline of simplicity is an inward reality that results in an outward lifestyle. . . . We deceive ourselves if we believe we can possess the inward reality without its having a profound effect on how we live. To attempt to arrange an outward lifestyle of simplicity without the inward reality leads to deadly legalism."

"We must clearly understand that the lust for affluence in contemporary society is psychotic. It is psychotic because it has completely lost touch with reality. We crave things we neither need nor enjoy." According to Arthur Gish in **Beyond the Rat Race,** "We buy things we do not want to impress people we do not like."

## DAILY DEVOTIONAL GUIDE

M. Choosing to Serve. Joshua 24:11-21
T. Choosing to Follow. Ruth 1:11-18
W. A Wrong Choice. Mark 10:17-22
T. A Selfish Choice. Luke 12:16-21
F. A Deferred Choice. Acts 24:10-26
S. A Righteous Choice. Hebrews 11:23-28

# November 3, 1985

# Concern for Others

**Study Text:** Genesis 14:1-24
**Supplemental References:** Exodus 32:25-34; Luke 10:25-37; Romans 9:1-5
**Time:** Around 1950-1900 B.C.
**Place:** Dan, Hobah, and Valley of Shaveh
**Golden Text:** "All things whatsoever ye would that men should do to you, do ye even so to them" (Matthew 7:12).
**Central Truth:** God is pleased with those who are concerned about the needs of others.
**Evangelistic Emphasis:** Concern for the lost is an essential characteristic of all Christians.

## Printed Text

**Genesis 14:14.** And when Abram heard that his brother was taken captive, he armed his trained servants, born in his own house, three hundred and eighteen, and pursued them unto Dan.

**15.** And he divided himself against them, he and his servants, by night, and smote them, and pursued them unto Hobah, which is on the left hand of Damascus.

16. And he brought back all the goods, and also brought again his brother Lot, and his goods, and the women also, and the people.

**17. And the king of Sodom went out to meet him after his return from the slaughter of Chedorlaomer, and of the kings that were with him, at the valley of Shaveh, which is the king's dale.**

18. And Melchizedek king of Salem brought forth bread and wine: and he was the priest of the most high God.

**19. And he blessed him, and said,**

**Blessed be Abram of the most high God, possessor of heaven and earth:**

20. And blessed be the most high God, which hath delivered thine enemies into thy hand. And he gave him tithes of all.

**21. And the king of Sodom said unto Abram, Give me the persons, and take the goods to thyself.**

22. And Abram said to the king of Sodom, I have lift up mine hand unto the Lord, the most high God, the possessor of heaven and earth,

**23. That I will not take from a thread even to a shoelatchet, and that I will not take any thing that is thine, lest thou shouldest say, I have made Abram rich:**

24. Save only that which the young men have eaten, and the portion of the men which went with me, Aner, Eshcol, and Mamre; let them take their portion.

---

**DICTIONARY**

**Hobah (HO-bah)—Genesis 14:15—**A place north of Damascus.

**Chedorlaomer (KED-or-lay-OH-mur)—Genesis 14:17—** King of Elam, East of Babylonia, inhabited by Indo-Europeans; later part of Persia-modern Iran.

**Valley of Shaveh (SHA-veh)—Genesis 14:17—**Called the "king's dale"; identified by some as the same place Absalom erected a memorial to himself.

**Melchizedek (mel-KI-zuh-dek)—Genesis 14:18—**King of Salem as well as priest. Salem is a place identified with Jerusalem.

**Aner (AH-nerh)—Genesis 14:24—**An Amorite and ally to Abraham.

**Eshcol (ES-coil)—Genesis 14:24—**An Amorite and ally to Abraham.

**Mamre (MAM-ree)—Genesis 14:24—**An Amorite who was confederate of Abraham. Also the name of a place north of Hebron.

---

## LESSON OUTLINE

I. TROUBLED TIMES
   A. Rebellion in the Empire
   B. Victims in War
II. ACTIVE CONCERN
   A. Prepared to Act
   B. Rescue Accomplished
III. THANKS TO GOD
   A. Response to a Blessing
   B. True Independence

## LESSON EXPOSITION

### INTRODUCTION

Jesus prayed to the Father concerning His disciples, "I pray not that thou shouldest take them out of the world, but that thou shouldest keep them from the evil. As thou hast sent me into the world, even so have I also sent them into the world" (John 17:15, 18).

The principles of that prayer are clearly seen in the life of Abram. From the beginning of his call in Genesis 12:1-3 Abram is meant to be a man involved in the world for the sake of blessing. In our lessons this quarter we primarily focus on Abram's relationship to God. Yet, other passages in Genesis show us that Abram was involved in the world: Genesis 12:10-20, with Pharaoh; Genesis 18:22-33, interceded for Sodom and Gomorrah; and Genesis 20, the conflict with Abimelech.

Our lesson from Genesis 14 fits this pattern and shows us the life of the man of faith in the midst of international conflicts. Personal faith is never separated from the realities of the world. If our faith

cannot address nuclear war, world hunger, sanctuary for refugees, and a host of other concerns, then our faith is indeed poor and our understanding of the lordship of Jesus inadequate for effective living in the world.

### I. TROUBLED TIMES (Genesis 14:1-13)

A. Rebellion in the Empire (vv. 1-11)

(These verses are not in the Printed Text.)

Although not part of the Printed Text, an understanding of 14:1-13 is essential in comprehending all of Genesis 14. These verses show us that Abram was part of something larger than himself in the world. (See Lesson Eight for more discussion of this theme of Abram being part of something larger than himself.) While in Genesis 11 we see him being carried along by these events, in Genesis 14 we see a man whose faith has matured and is capable of acting responsible in the world in accordance with the will of God.

These verses show us an international conflict which affects Abram indirectly. It is a conflict rooted in the rebellion of the city-states of the Jordan plain against their ruling states. Four kings (and kingdoms) are seeking to bring back under submission five kings (kingdoms).

The four kingdoms of authority are named in 14:1. From verse 4 it is clear that Chedorlaomer was the head of this confederacy. Efforts to concretely identify these kings with known historical characters is difficult. It has been suggested that Amraphel of Shinar was the Babylonian king Hammurabi. Shinar is clearly Babylon but such identification cannot be made with certainty regarding the kings. It has also been suggested that Arioch was the Mari king Arriwuku. Chedorlaomer is an Elamite name meaning "slave of Lagamer." (Lagamer was an Elamite divinity.) While the conjectures are interesting, Von Rad is correct in asserting that we cannot be certain about any of these.

This should not be taken to mean that the events described did not happen. It simply means that the kings named are not clearly recorded in other ancient accounts.

The reference in verse 1 to "Tidal king of nations" needs to be understood in the sense of "nations" referring to the "goi'im"—for example, the Gentiles. The events described apparently took place sometime near the end of the 1700's B.C. or early 1600's B.C.

Verse 2 named the five kings of the Jordan plain who were rebelling against Chedorlaomer. Three particular names and sites are of interest to us. Bera is the king of Sodom and Birsha is the king of Gomorrah. Also, the king of Zoar (see Genesis 13:10) is not specifically named and Zoar's alternate, Bela, is given.

After being under Chedorlaomer's rule for 13 years these city-states rebelled. It appears the rebellion was widespread as Chedorlaomer's forces engaged on an extensive campaign described in verses 5-7. The connection of Sodom and Gomorrah draws our attention back to Genesis 13 and the choice of Lot to live near these cities. Immediately we understand that his choice of living near such immorality without clear direction from God was a poor one. We are given insight into the situation of Sodom and Gomorrah. Not only were they cities that practiced terrible immorality, they were places where the spirit of rebellion was active.

After concluding the campaign against surrounding territories (v. 7), Chedorlaomer was met by the rebellious forces in the Valley of Siddim (called the salt sea in verse 3). While the actual battle is not described, it is clear that the rebellion was practically crushed with the defeat of the kings of Sodom and Gomorrah. The terrain of the valley contained slime pits into which the defeated armies fell during their confused retreat. These pits were actually bitumen pits.

Verse 11 tells that the forces of Chedorlaomer were victorious and ravished the cities of Sodom and Gomorrah after which they withdrew.

B. Victims in War (vv. 12, 13)

(These verses are not in the Printed Text.)

William T. Sherman was absolutely correct in his American Civil War observation that "War is hell." With the advent of instant media we are able to see firsthand the ravages of war around the world. Revelation shows the natural progression of the horror of war with the three horsemen of war, famine, and death (Revelation 6:3-8). All wars produce refugees and innocent civilian casualties.

Discuss the basic causes of war and oppression of people. Is the Christian church able to do anything to reduce wars?

The war described in Genesis 14 is no different. In all likelihood Lot and his family were part of a number of people who were taken as slaves of the victorious armies of Chedorlaomer. It is of note too that Lot's possessions were also taken and apparently not destroyed. These goods refer to his flocks. Since Lot did not live in the cities but in the surrounding fields, it is likely that his flocks were taken as food support for the avenging army.

However, Lot was not left without a divinely appointed avenue of assistance. Verse 13 tells of an escapee who found Abram at his encampment near Mamre and related what had happened.

There are a number of interesting historical references in verse 13. First, Abram is called a "Hebrew." We know there were Semites in Ur during the time that Abram and family lived there. The second historical note is that Mamre was the name of an Amorite who had also migrated to Canaan from eastern Mesopotamia. Because of their common background, these peoples were allies and were able to dwell together. It should also be noted that Abram is living in an area that belonged to the Amorites. Thus, the promise of the giving of the land (Genesis 13) was not something to be realized immediately.

## II. ACTIVE CONCERN (Genesis 14:14-16)

### A. Prepared to Act (v. 14)

**14. And when Abram heard that his brother was taken captive, he armed his trained servants, born in his own house, three hundred and eighteen, and pursued them unto Dan.**

The fact that Lot is called "brother" in this verse should simply indicate the love that Abram had for Lot. It shows a closer feeling of relationship between the two men. It also shows that the division in Genesis 13 did not result in permanent disruption of the family.

The verse also contains three observations concerning Abram's household. It is obvious that the household was large and that Abram had taken great care to develop an effective and loyal household. First we are told that Abram **armed** his servants. The Hebrew word has the sense of "empty out, as in draw forth the sword." The image is of men who have their sword at the ready, unsheathed. It was used in Exodus 15:9, Leviticus 26:33, and five times in Ezekiel (5:2, 12; 12:14; 28:7; 30:11). The second factor of the household is that the men were trained. The same Hebrew word is used in Proverbs 22:6 "Train up a child in the way he should go: and when he is old, he will not depart from it." The word had the sense of "dedicate, make experienced, be submissive." The *Brown, Drive, Briggs Hebrew Lexicon* observed, "his tried and trusty men." Finally, we are told that these men were born in Abram's own house. This means that from their youth they had been brought up in the values of Abram and the knowledge of his call from God.

These three elements continue to be essential in our ability to act effectively for the Lord. We must be people who are prepared to bear effective witness to the power of God. Our sword today is the Word of God. Our weapons are the weapons of righteousness and justice. Although based on a different Hebrew verb, the Greek of 1 Peter 4:1 tells us, "Forasmuch then as Christ hath suffered for us in the flesh, arm yourselves likewise with the same mind: for he that hath suffered in the flesh hath ceased from sin." Our weapons of spiritual warfare are exactly those used by Jesus in His defeat of sin on the cross: submission to the will of God, humility, obedience, and faith in the power of God to redeem and make alive.

Such effective use of arms comes only by being trained in the way of the faith. The disciplined life is the only effective life for Christians. This discipline is not a rigidity; rather, it is the freedom from the dominion of sin in every aspect of life so that we are liberated to serve God with wholeness of mind, spirit, and flesh.

Finally, such effective persons are those who have been trained from youth to be for God. Abram gives a godly example of what an effective household should be for the sake of redemption. This verse should raise serious questions to three groups of people. The first are Christian parents. How effectively do we arm our children for the warfare of life? Do we teach them the Word of God each day? Is memorization of the Word important in our homes? Do we expect our children (preteens as well as teens) to read Christian literature? Do they have examples from us regarding memorization of the Word and reading the Word? The second group is composed of pastors and others who lead the flock of God. Do pastors train the flock of God entrusted to them in being effective soldiers of the Cross? Do we teach our people or do we just preach tired phrases? Do we model the Christian life so our flock can have an example to follow? Can we, like Paul, encourage our congregations to imitate us (1 Thessalonians 1:6; 4:1, 2)? The third group is you, the Sunday school teacher! Is your preparation a last-minute event on Saturday evening? Do you take the time to allow the principles of each lesson to become part of your life? These are important issues for all Christians. A serious study of Genesis 14:14 provides great insight into the ways of God.

---

As a body of believers is it imperative that we ban together to fight the forces of evil? How are we doing it?

---

B. Rescue Accomplished (vv. 15, 16)

**15. And he divided himself against them, he and his servants, by night, and smote them, and pursued them unto Hobah, which is on the left hand of Damascus.**

**16. And he brought back all the goods, and also brought again his brother Lot, and his goods, and the women also, and the people.**

Verse 14 indicated that Abram finally caught the elements of Chedorlaomer's army that was holding Lot in northern Canaan (Dan). Dan was the northernmost tribe of Israel near the modern area of southern Lebanon.

Once there, Abram undertook a night maneuver that divided his forces (usually a dangerous move from a military standpoint) and effectively routed those holding his kinsman, Lot. While God is not specifically mentioned in this account, it is clear that His hand was working through the abilities of Abram to plan what turned out to be an excellent and daring maneuver.

Verse 15 shows that the route continued into modern Syria near Damascus. It is approximately 150 miles from Hebron (the plain of Mamre) to Damascus. It was about 120 miles from Hebron to the territory of Dan. This meant that Abram on his rescue mission went north the length of the Jordan River to the Sea of Galilee and continued north past Mount Hermon. It is likely the mission took him north of the Latani River, a site of importance in recent Israeli/Palestinian conflicts in southern Lebanon. This was not new territory to Abram as he had passed through it from Haran into Canaan. It simply shows the extent of the rescue mission.

Verse 16 shows the extent of the victory of the mission as all of Lot's possessions

and family are brought into safety. The old evangelistic hymn "Rescue the Perishing" is a fitting commentary on this lifesaving effort to Abram. Oh, that every captive soul to sin had an Abram to take the time and pay the cost to go the extra miles for salvation!

III. THANKS TO GOD (Genesis 14:17-24)

A. Response to a Blessing (vv. 17-20)

**17. And the king of Sodom went out to meet him after his return from the slaughter of Chedorlaomer and of the kings that were with him, at the valley of Shaveh, which is the king's dale.**

It's just like Satan to come against us following a great victory! The king of Sodom was not killed in the earlier victory of Chedorlaomer but escaped to cause difficulty for Abram. After Abram's victory near Dan, he returned with the spoils of victory including the family of Lot. The king of Sodom, while introduced here, later seeks to assert himself and his claim upon Abram (the focus of vv. 21-24). The king's dale is a reference to a site called the King's Valley.

**18. And Melchizedek king of Salem brought forth bread and wine: and he was the priest of the most high God.**

We are introduced to this shadowy figure found in several other places in the Bible. His name means "King of Righteousness." **Salem** means "peace" and seems to be related to the city later called Jerusalem. Thus, Melchizedek served as priest of the area that would later be the home of the Lord through His Temple and the site of the death and resurrection of Jesus (see Psalm 76:2 for reference to Salem).

The only other place Melchizedek is mentioned in the Old Testament is Psalm 110:4. This Messianic psalm shows the power of the Son of God in subduing the enemies of the Lord. God affirmed that His Son would be a "priest for ever after the order of Melchizedek" (v. 4). In the New Testament Melchizedek is given detailed treatment in the Book of Hebrews.

In Hebrews 5:6 the title is quoted from Psalm 110:4 and is used to show the Sonship of Jesus and His role as high priest for the sins of the people. In 5:10 the figure of Melchizedek is used to refer to Jesus as the One who through His suffering became the source of eternal salvation to all who obey. In 6:20 the figure is used to describe the mission of Jesus as eternal priest on our behalf in the Holy of Holies.

The largest exposition of Melchizedek is Hebrews 7:1-17. In this passage reference is made to the account in Genesis 14 in which Abram is a victor and is blessed by Melchizedek. His name is translated in this passage and comparison is made between him and Christ as the Son of God. Verse 3 is of special note as it indicates that he had no genealogy nor record of birth or death. Thus, his life is applied to the life of the Son of God who is the Alpha and Omega of all things.

Verses 4-10 illustrate the submission of Abram by giving a tithe to Melchizedek. The point here is that Abram's faith begins this submission, but is also continued into the law where the tribe of Levi paid tithes to Melchizedek (thus Christ) since Levi existed in Abram's sperm.

This argument is carried further in 7:11-17 to show that Christ, as the fulfillment of Melchizedek, is the ultimate high priest and through Him comes a change in the priesthood by which men are to be saved. God has changed the priestly line from that of Levi to that of Judah. Christ is thus a high priest not by the dictates of the law but by the power of the Resurrection that has made His life indestructible. Thus, the power of God and grace are the characteristics of His priestly line—not obedience to the law, or family descent.

It is of note that Genesis 14:18 shows Melchizedek bringing bread and wine to Abram. These are obvious symbols of the Lord's Supper. It is as if Melchizedek, as a type of Christ, is serving to this man of faith the power of the death and resurrection of Jesus! Thus, Abram is not disconnected from the eternal purposes of God in Christ Jesus! He too shares in the benefits of His glorious death and victory by faith and submission to Christ in Melchizedek.

**19. And he blessed him, and said, Blessed be Abram of the most high God, possessor of heaven and earth:**

**20. And blessed be the most high God, which hath delivered thine enemies into thy hand. And he gave him tithes of all.**

As if out of the blue, Melchizedek blessed Abram. Abram did nothing to earn that blessing; rather, it came as a gift from the Lord. As in Genesis 12:1-3, the word **bless** dominates the passage. Three times the Hebrew is used.

Abram is blessed because he belongs to the same God that Melchizedek belongs unto: the "most high God." This God is the God who possesses heaven and earth. It reminds us of Genesis 1:1 where Elohim (God) is called Creator of heaven and earth. The Hebrew for **possess** was used in the Old Testament to refer to God's activity in creating (Deuteronomy 32:6; Psalm 139:13; Proverbs 8:22, referring to the creation of wisdom). It also was used of God's victorious redemption of His people (Exodus 15:16; Isaiah 11:11; Psalm 74:2). Both senses are used when we think of Abram. First, Abram's family is the new family God has redeemed for the purposes of creating a new people holy to His name. Second, Abram engages in the mission of redeeming even as God is Redeemer.

Verse 20 continued the blessing of Melchizedek by focusing on the fact that it was God who had delivered Abram's enemies into his hands.

The last part of verse 20 is not part of Melchizedek's blessing. Rather, it is the record of what Abram did in response to the blessing: he freely paid tithe to Melchizedek.

By paying tithe, Abram asserting his submission to this King of Righteousness. The significance of tithing is revealed in Malachi 3:8-12. It is sad that so many Christians think of tithing in terms of law; it is an obligation imposed upon them. Yet, from Genesis 14 it was not demanded. Abram gave the tithe as a sign of his willing obedience and submission to the One who had brought the bread and the wine. Tithing thus became Abram's way of stating whom he would submit unto.

Tithing requires discipline. It is so easy in this consumer oriented society to become saddled to the hilt with debts. Most of our debts are the result of choosing to live a lifestyle based on the priorities of worldly success. We are tied to "keeping up" with everything from the Joneses to today's advertising.

Yet, tithing teaches us to submit to another way. Even for those who find it hard to make ends meet each month, it is important to **first** give to God that 10 percent. What if I cannot pay other creditors? Offer your submissive heart to God by faithfully paying the tithe and ask God to give you the discipline and wisdom to deal with your current debts. There is simply no excuse for a Christian failing to be faithful in this matter. It does not guarantee that God will help you win a lottery; God is not bought by an action. What tithing does do is make a genuine statement to ourselves and society that we are going to live by the principles of God's Word.

B. True Independence (vv. 21-24)

**21. And the king of Sodom said unto Abram, Give me the persons, and take the good to thyself.**

**22. And Abram said to the king of Sodom, I have lift up mine hand unto the Lord, the most high God, the possessor of heaven and earth,**

**23. That I will not take from a thread even to a shoe-latchet, and that I will not take any thing that is thine, lest thou shouldest say, I have made Abram rich:**

**24. Save only that which the young men have eaten, and the portion of the men which went with me, Aner, Eschol, and Mamre; let them take their portion.**

In verse 20 Abram asserted his submission to God by paying tithes. In verses 22 and 23, Abram asserts his independence from the way of the world by refusing to take anything from the king of Sodom.

Verse 21 is a powerful statement of how Satan works. Note that he offers Abram all the possessions (the goods) if Abram will just give him the persons.

Satan is more than willing to offer us that compromise: he will give us wordly possessions in exchange for the souls of our families. How many Christians have unwittedly taken that bargain and found material blessing but also found spiritual bankruptcy in their personal lives? Abram has chosen to live in complete dependence upon God. He is not going to stand before the Lord and say that the world has made him what he is. Anything that he accomplished in life would be solely from the hand of God.

## REVIEW QUESTIONS

1. What are the three characteristics of Abram's household that made it effective in delivering Lot?

2. How can you make these three elements effective in your own home? Church?

3. How did Abram submit to the Lord?

4. How did Abram affirm his independence from the king of Sodom?

5. Is tithing important for Christians?

## GOLDEN TEXT HOMILY

"ALL THINGS WHATSOEVER YE WOULD THAT MEN SHOULD DO TO YOU, DO YE EVEN SO TO THEM" (Matthew 7:12).

This scripture is commonly referred to as the Golden Rule: "Do unto others as you would have them do unto you." As you know, this scripture is located in the last chapter of Christ's Sermon on the Mount (Matthew 5-7). Upon examining the entire sermon, we must conclude that Jesus is primarily dealing with not only the action, but to a greater extent, the intent of the action. We find in this verse the foundation stone of Christian ethics; furthermore, Christ related to this act as being the pivot point of the Law and the prophets.

This command of Christ encompasses every relationship we have with each other. Note His words "all things"—which leaves nothing out. So this action of doing unto others as you would have them do unto you, becomes a way of living, and not just isolated acts. The person who is loving God with all his mind, soul and strength will strive to act and react within the principle of the Golden Rule.

The action of doing makes us take an inward look at our own lives and needs. We must ask ourselves: "How do I wish to be treated?" "Am I in control of my feelings?" "Are my ethics in line with that which God has commanded?" For our response to others is not a reaction to their acts, but an action based on Christ in us.

The ability to live within the Golden Rule can only be achieved by a close relationship with Christ through the Word. It is my humble opinion that the Golden Rule can only be fully expressed within the life of a Christian. The unregenerated cannot understand this higher level of life.—**Raymond O. Lankford, CADC D.D. Chaplain, Chicago, Illinois.**

## SENTENCE SERMONS

GOD IS PLEASED with those who are concerned about the needs of others.
**—Selected**

CHARITY IS A VIRTUE of the heart, and not just of the hands.
**—Joseph Addison**

THE LIONS never get out of the road of the man who waits to see the way clear before he starts.
**—Anonymous**

FONDLY DO WE HOPE, fervently do we pray, that the mighty scourge of war will speedily pass away.
**—Abraham Lincoln**

IT IS THE BUSINESS of the church to make my business (war) impossible.
**—Sir Douglas Haig**

## EVANGELISTIC APPLICATION

CONCERN FOR THE LOST IS AN ESSENTIAL CHARACTERISTIC OF ALL CHRISTIANS.

Concern for the lost is an essential characteristic of all Christians. This concern is more than mere sentiment. The passage in Genesis 14 shows Abram going on a long and dangerous journey to rescue Lot.

In this age of "instant" everything, it is easy to become impatient with the task of evangelism. We tend to give up on the lost if they do not come to the church or respond to the altar call. We fail to realize that the lost are truly "lost" and need someone to take the long and difficult journey to where they are in order to bring them back into the fold.

How easy it would have been for Abram to have chased after Lot for a week or 50 miles and just given up. But that is not the characteristic of effective witnesses in the world. Effective witnesses are people who have been liberated from the prevailing social values of our day and are ruled by the power of the Holy Spirit. May God make our concern a long-term venture for the sake of the kingdom.

## ILLUMINATING THE LESSON

In **Celebration of Discipline: Paths to Spiritual Growth,** Foster lists ten principles regarding a life of economic simplicity:
1) "Buy things for their usefulness rather than their status."
2) "Reject anything that is producing an addiction in you. . . . Refuse to be a slave to anything but God."
3) "Develop a habit of giving things away."
4) "Refuse to be propagandized by the custodians of modern gadgetry."
5) "Learn to enjoy things without owning them."
6) "Develop a deeper appreciation for the creation."
7) "Look with a healthy skepticism at all 'buy now, pay later,' schemes."
8) "Obey Jesus' instructions about plain, honest speech."
9) "Reject anything that will breed the oppression of others."
10) "Shun whatever would distract you from your main goal."
(Harper & Row, 1978, pp. 78-82)

## DAILY DEVOTIONAL GUIDE

M. A Leader's Concern. Exodus 32:25-34
T. Love for Strangers. Deuteronomy 10:17-19
W. Love in Action. Luke 10:25-37
T. A Father's Love. Luke 15:11-24
F. The Ultimate in Love. John 15:12-17
S. Self-Giving Love. Romans 9:1-5

# God's Everlasting Covenant

**Study Text:** Genesis 15:1-21; 17:1-27

**Supplemental References:** Genesis 21:1-21; Exodus 24:6-8; Matthew 26:26-29; Hebrews 6:13-20

**Time:** Around 1900 B.C.

**Place:** Canaan

**Golden Text:** "I am. thy shield, and thy exceeding great reward" (Genesis 15:1).

**Central Truth:** God's Word is certain and His promises everlasting.

**Evangelistic Emphasis:** God's greatest promise is eternal life through Jesus Christ His Son.

### Printed Text

**Genesis 15:1.** After these things the word of the Lord came unto Abram in a vision, saying, Fear not, Abram: I am thy shield, and thy exceeding great reward.

**2. And Abram said, Lord God, what wilt thou give me, seeing I go childless, and the steward of my house is this Eliezer of Damascus?**

3. And Abram said, Behold, to me thou hast given no seed: and, lo, one born in my house is mine heir.

**4. And, behold, the word of the Lord came unto him, saying, This shall not be thine heir; but he that shall come forth out of thine own bowels shall be thine heir.**

5. And he brought him forth abroad, and said, Look now toward heaven, and tell the stars, if thou be able to number them: and he said unto him, So shall thy seed be.

**17:6. And I will make thee exceeding fruitful, and I will make nations of thee, and kings shall come out of thee.**

7. And I will establish my covenant between me and thee and thy seed after thee in their generations for an everlasting covenant, to be a God unto thee, and to thy seed after thee.

**8. And I will give unto thee, and to thy seed after thee, the land wherein thou art a stranger, all the land of Canaan, for an everlasting possession; and I will be their God.**

20. And as for Ishmael, I have heard thee: Behold, I have blessed him, and will make him fruitful, and will multiply him exceedingly; twelve princes shall he beget, and I will make him a great nation.

**21. But my covenant will I establish with Isaac, which Sarah shall bear unto thee at this set time in the next year.**

---

**LESSON OUTLINE**

I. PROMISE OF THE COVENANT

  A. Promise Given

B. Covenant Made

C. Dream of the Future

II. RENEWAL OF THE COVENANT

A. God's Almighty Power
B. The Covenant Established
III. HEIRS OF THE COVENANT
A. New Identity
B. The Future Considered

## LESSON EXPOSITION

INTRODUCTION

Great themes emerge from the two chapters studied in this lesson. One of the most significant of those themes is that of "justification by faith." Developed from Genesis 15:6, this verse was used by Paul to explain the priority of faith over law in establishing the right(eous) relationship with God. As we come to this verse in our study, we will further develop the New Testament understanding of this righteousness by faith.

Another great theme is that of "covenant." Although briefly discussed in previous lessons, this lesson will show the relational quality of this commitment by God to His creatures.

I. PROMISE OF THE COVENANT (Genesis 15:1-21)

A. Promise Given (vv. 1-6)

**1. After these things the word of the Lord came unto Abram in a vision, saying, Fear not, Abram: I am thy shield, and thy exceeding great reward.**

The expression "word of the Lord came" is not a frequent expression outside the prophets; however, it is used extensively in the Old Testament prophets. Thus, one gets the impression that Abram is being addressed as God's prophet. In a sense he is. He is God's prophet because out of his life will come the future God has ordained for salvation.

The "word of the Lord" also tells us that God is the reality behind the covenant making that occurs in Genesis 15. This is not a psychological trick that childless Abram has played on himself. This is not the invention of Satan; this is a creating Word that will usher in the new. Because it is God's Word, Abram is called to absolute trust and is given solid ground upon which to trust.

One of the questions many people face in life is "how do I hear God's voice?" In this passage we are told that the Word of the Lord (that is God's voice) came to Abram in a vision. The word translated "vision" in verse 1 is formed from the Hebrew noun **chazon.** It was a word used extensively by the Old Testament prophets to describe the manner in which the Word of the Lord came unto them. It was used at least 8 times by Ezekiel and 11 times by Daniel. A clear use in relation to the classical prophets is Isaiah 1:1: "The vision of Isaiah . . . which he saw concerning Judah."

A closely related form of our word has the sense of "light, place of seeing, window." Thus, a vision is the avenue used by God to reveal His thoughts and purposes. It is the window through which we see the will of God. David Napier comments, "The mystery of the vision is the mystery of the Word—the mystery of God's disclosure of Himself and of the meaning of history in the light of His effective infringement upon it, His reign over it, and of His purpose ultimately to redeem all history" **(Interpreter's Dictionary of the Bible).**

If a "vision" is one of the windows of God uses for communication, how does it affect me such that I can hear His voice? A clue is given by the opening words of 15:1, "After these things." The "things" are the events of Genesis 14. In that chapter (Lesson 10), Abram delivered Lot from captivity and asserted his dependence upon God and independence from the world. Thus, Abram has become a man dedicated completely to the purposes of God. In such a condition of submission to the lordship of God in Christ, the believer is moved to the place where God can visit in a marvelous fashion. The mind that is renewed after the Spirit and is seeking the mind of Christ is free to ask the Lord to "show" His will. This asking then requires a patient waiting in silence and meditation upon His Word. This opens the imagination to the purposes of God and obediently seeks to visualize what God is desiring. The Christian who submits to spiritual life in this direction need not fear the onslaught of Satan to deceive as long as the desire to "see" is kept in balance with the revealed Word of God in Scripture and genuine confession and praise to Christ in prayer.

What Abram saw he also heard. It is clear he saw a "shield" and "great reward." He heard the Lord tell him not to be afraid and what He was for him. "Fear not" is an important phrase. It is only natural that humanity be fearful in the presence of God's revealed will. Yet, God speaks to us that His holiness is meant to release us from the power of fear for the sake of joyful service. Here is a brief listing of other passages in the Bible where the command to "fear not" is given: Genesis 21:17; 26:24; 35:17; 43:23; 46:3; 50:19, 21; Exodus 20:20; Deuteronomy 1:21; 3:2; Joshua 8:1; 10:25; Judges 6:10, 23; Ruth 3:11; 1 Samuel 4:20; 22:23; 23:17; 2 Samuel 9:7; 13:28; Matthew 1:20; 10:26, 28, 31; Luke 1:13, 30; 2:10; 5:10; 8:50; 12:7, 32; John 12:15; Revelation 1:17.

There is a clear reason why Abram does not have to be afraid: The Lord is his "shield." Also used in Psalms 3:3; 28:7; 33:20, "shield" indicates the protective power of God over Abram's life. In Ephesians 6:16 reference is made to the "shield of faith." The shield of faith enables the believer to quench the flaming darts of Satan. It functioned as a barrier against which efforts of Satan would be dashed. In this sense the connection between faith, the shield, and the righteousness that comes by faith is important. Faith knows that God truly loves us; love knows that God can be trusted to be faithful. Thus, love casts out fear and makes the way possible for faith to march in triumph over the darts of Satan.

The "exceeding great reward" is referenced specifically to God himself. Yet, it is also a reward that is understandable in Abram's experience. The great reward probably encompasses the promise of the land and the promise of the heir.

**2. And Abram said, Lord God, what wilt thou give me, seeing I go childless, and the steward of my house is this Eliezer of Damascus?**

**3. And Abram said, Behold, to me thou hast given no seed: and, lo, one born in my house is mine heir.**

Abram's response to the Lord reveals his fear of the future: He is childless. How can God's Word come true if there is nothing in the present to guarantee the future? In these verses we see the first of two attempts by Abram to accomplish God's will. In this case, he suggests, that God's will can be accomplished by using what is already available—namely, the household slave, Eliezer.

The use of a slave as a legal heir was common in the ancient world. The Nuzi text (records of a city by that name that relates to social practices in the 1500-1600 B.C.; they are written in Akkadian and give insight into a number of activities that occurred during the period of the patriarchs) shows that in such cases the slave was responsible to provide a proper funeral for his former master and then would inherit the property.

In 11:30 we were told that Sarai was barren. The import of that statement begins to loom on the horizon of God's dealings with Abram. What is at stake is the faithfulness of God's Word. What is also at stake is the faithfulness of Abram in every aspect of obedience.

Earlier I commented that this was the first of two ways that Abram attempted to accomplish God's will. The second way is discussed in Genesis 16 in which Abram and Sarai agree for Abram to impregnate the household maid, Hagar. Out of this relationship is born Ishmael. Rather than a source of blessing, this child became a source of curse and frustration. The important thing for us to remember is that when we commit to do God's will, we must remember that we are also committing to do God's will way!

**4. And, behold, the word of the Lord came unto him, saying, This shall not be thine heir; but he that shall come forth out of thine own bowels shall be thine heir.**

In response to Abram's concern about accomplishing God's will, God indicated that He would take responsibility for accomplishing His will. This would be through Abram's own body. The barrenness would become fruitful. God would perform the miracle in the life of the man of faith.

**5. And he brought him forth abroad, and said, Look now toward the heaven, and tell the stars, if thou be able to number them: and he said unto him, So shall thy seed be.**

Abram's vision carried him outside to see the expanse of the heavenlies. In order to show the power of His Word, God asked Abram to number the stars. Obviously he could not. Yet, the point was clear to him: God was more than capable of fulfilling His Word.

It is in response to this promise that Abram believed in the Lord. It was a specific belief in which Abram understood that God was all-powerful. It made him see the limitations of human effort in the light of God's unlimited power. This was faith at its apex—a faith that saw the future wrapped in the loving care of God. It was a faith that understood that God was completely faithful to His Word. It was a faith that did not consider human understanding to be the final word. Just as Abram resisted the king of Sodom's efforts to make him rich, so he also resisted the thinking of the world to limit the power of God.

This faith became the basis for Paul's understanding of Christian faith. In Romans 4:22, 23 portions of Genesis 15:6 are quoted. But Romans 4 in its entirety is an argument to support Paul's claim in Romans 3:21-31 that righteousness is now manifested apart from the law through faith in Jesus Christ for all who believe. Paul argued that only by faith could a person be saved. No works of the law on any level could pay the price of sin. Sin was so evil that it took advantage of the law through the weakness of the flesh. Only faith can appropriate the grace and mercy available through Christ Jesus.

The fourth chapter of Romans became a commentary on the reality of this faith by appealing to the Father of faith, Abram. Paul showed that Abram was justified

before God prior to the coming of the law of Moses. If works had been the basis of Abram's salvation then he could have boasted before God. Yet, it was not on account of any works by Abram that he was counted righteous; it was purely on account of his faith. In Romans 4:13 Paul shows that the promise God made to Abram and his seed that they should inherit the world came through the righteousness based upon faith. Faith makes us descendents of Abram and thus heirs of the blessings God has promised to Abram and his seed. Abram's faith believed that God could give life to the dead and call into existence things that do not exist (4:17). Hope pointed him to the future that God held in His hands and would make real through the faithfulness of His Word. Even his age and the natural age of Sarah did not make him waver considering what God had promised!

In Galatians 3:6-18 another Pauline argument regarding the covenant of Genesis 15 is given. The issue in Galatians is more sharply related to the law than in Romans 4. In Galatia Christians are turning from the way of faith back to salvation by works. Paul was so deeply concerned with this that he started the chapter so expressing profound surprise that the Galatian Christians had been "bewitched." The working of the Holy Spirit and the faith of Abram are closely related. The Spirit of Christ does His work in relation to faith—not works of the law. As Paul commented in 3:7, "It is men of faith who are the sons of Abraham" **(King James Version).** It is through this faith that the Gentiles can share in the promised blessings. Thus, Abram's seed in Genesis 15 would not only be Jews by natural descent, but would become a vast multitude from around the world who believed in the lordship of Jesus.

Because of his faith, righteousness was counted to him. **Counted** means "what God thinks about a person." God could count a person as His enemy (Job 19:11). According to Psalm 32:2, a man knew that he was blessed when God did not count his iniquity against him. With Abram, God counts, reckons, and considers him to be righteous. This "righteousness" can be meant in a number of ways. Some consider it simply a change in the way God looks at a person. Others consider it to be of a moral character that is implanted in the life of the person. Perhaps the best way to understand this righteousness is in light of covenant. In a new commentary on Romans, New Testament scholar Paul Achtemeier comments on this covenantal righteousness: "To be 'just' or 'righteous' is to uphold the covenant; to be 'unrighteous' is to act in such a way that the covenant is broken. What upholds the relationship is 'righteous'; what destroys the relationship is 'unrighteous.' . . . 'Righteousness' is not a 'quality' or a conformity to some legal norm. Rather, it is a positive relationship to God growing out of His power to restore through Jesus Christ His gracious lordship over us, a lordship which our idolatrous rebellion had turned into a wrathful lordship . . . Righteousness does not describe something God is . . . so much as it describes something God does. God's righteousness is His power by which He breaks the power of sin and sets aside its corruption, restoring sinners to a positive relationship with Himself" (**Romans** John Knox Press, 1985, pp. 61-66).

B. Covenant Made (vv. 7-11)

(Verses 7-11 are not in the Printed Text.)

Abram's response to the Lord regarding this promise of the future was a question. He desired to know how he would possess this future. God's response is enigmatic. The call of faith was not meant to answer every question concerning the future. Faith was meant to trust completely in God in every area of life.

To show His faithfulness, God initiated a covenant making ceremony in which various animals were literally divided and placed in rows so that Abram and God could walk between them as signs of covenant righteousness.

At best it is a mysterious ceremony. Death was necessary for the covenant to be completed. Abram was responsible for bringing forth the animals God required and for keeping the birds of prey away from the carcasses.

C. Dream of the Future (vv. 12-21)

(Verses 12-21 are not in the Printed Text.)

The covenant was good news and bad news. The bad news is prefigured in the horror of great darkness that came upon Abram in his sleep. This passage should aid us in dispelling naive notions that God's will is always to accomplish. That is far from the truth. The future is not always bright even for the people of God. Obedience may bring difficult and painful experiences; yet, God is faithful to perform His Word. He is more interested in accomplishing the purposes of redemption than establishing our personal happiness according to wordly standards. Christians submit to His absolute lordship and offer themselves to the altar of sacrifice for the sake of the kingdom of God.

Abram is given a vision of the captivity of his seed in Egypt. They shall suffer under Pharaoh but in the end God will deliver them. Abram himself will die in peace. But the future of his people will be bound together with cords of suffering and redemption.

II. RENEWAL OF THE COVENANT (Genesis 17:1-8)

A. God's Almighty Power (vv. 1-4)

(Verses 1-4 are not in the Printed Text.)

After the abysmal failure of Genesis 16, the Lord appeared to Abram again and renewed the covenant initiated in Genesis 15.

Among the things we should note, is that a number of years had elapsed since Abram last clearly heard God's call. It seems from Genesis 16:3 that Abram dwelt in the land of Canaan ten years prior to the birth of Ishmael. Abram was eighty-six years old when Ishmael was born (Genesis 16:16). Thus, Abram was about seventy-five or seventy-six when he arrived in Canaan from Haran (Genesis 12:4). In Genesis 15:1-16 is given the last clear Word of God for Abram. We are not told his age; although it is clear he was younger than eighty-six. That means nearly 13 years elapsed before Abram heard a clear call from God regarding how He was going to keep His Word.

The implications of that time lapse for us are staggering. We are people who live in the age of "instant anything." We know little of what it means to wait long periods of time. If we do not get our satisfaction soon, we drop what we are doing and go to something else. If God does not answer us soon, we drop Him and go to another god.

Patience is not a quality of American life. It is not a quality of much of American spiritual life. Just as Pepsi tells us we are part of the "now generation," many preachers preach a "now-gospel." While there is truth in the assertion of God's "now-presence," it is also important for Christians to understand that God's plans reach far ahead of our timetables. Abram had to come to a point where he understood that all his times were in God's hands. God is not bound to satisfy our frustrated personal clocks; we are bound to come to terms with the fact that He holds time and eternity in His hands.

For Abram it was 13 years since he last heard God. He must have known that Ishmael was not in the will of God. How easy it would have been to have given up on the promises of God and turned into rebellion and served the gods of Canaan. Yet, he remainded faithful even though he knew he had failed. He knew that God would not fail!

At ninety-nine years of age, the Lord spoke to him. In Genesis 17:1 there is a powerful invitation and authorization from God to live in obedience and trust. It began with the acknowledgement of who God was—El Shaddai. Although usually translated as "God Almighty," this title for God has the meaning of "self-sufficient, omnipotent." From Exodus 6:3 it is clear this was the title normally used by God as He appeared to the patriarchs Abraham, Isaac, and Jacob. In four other places in Genesis it is found: In Genesis 28:3 it is

found on the lips of Isaac as he addressed Jacob. In 35:11 God identifies Himself by this name as He tells Jacob that He is going to change his name to Israel (very similar situation as found in Genesis 17 and the changing of Abram's name to Abraham). In 43:14 the elderly Jacob used this title as he spoke to his sons who were preparing to return to Egypt and face Joseph. In 48:3 Jacob used the title as he spoke to Joseph.

It is clear that "El Shaddai" is a covenant-making God who is deeply committed to Abram's offspring culminating in the formation of Israel. It should also be noted that this name appears twice in connection with name changes that relate to expanded posterity.

In light of this, Abram is authorized to walk before the Lord blamelessly. We should not think of the last part of 17:1 as a command meant to burden Abram; rather, it is God's divine authorization for Abram to live holy. It is as if God is returning to the man who had turned from Him and is reaching out His hand and offering permission for holiness to be the core of Abram's life. "Perfect" is not meant in the sense of moral faultlessness as much as it means covenantal relationship.

On the basis of this relationship, the Lord will make "my covenant" and "multiply thee exceedingly." Grace dominates the passage. Abram has done nothing to deserve what God is saying to him. For 13 years he has had the reminder of the Ishmael he birthed when he failed to obey the Lord. Now, at the edge of one hundred years old, God reaffirmed His faithful Word.

Abram's response is humble submission (v. 3). The Lord continued to talk with him (vv. 4-22) and emphasized the power of the covenant and the promised heir.

B. The Covenant Established (vv. 5-8)

**5. Neither shall thy name any more be called Abram, but thy name shall be Abraham; for a father of many nations have I made thee.**

**6. And I will make thee exceeding fruitful, and I will make nations of**

**thee, and kings shall come out of thee.**

The covenant decree of God was more than an announcement of grace, it was a grace that worked a change in Abram's life and inner being.

The presence of the Almighty God creates the power for change in our lives. In the ancient world, a person's name was indicative of their personality. While that dimension is usually missing in the modern world, the fact that the inner self can be changed by grace is still true. The human self is not the clear reflection of how Adam was created. Sin has marred the human personality. We are in need of the presence of Christ in our life so that He can do His sanctifying work of making us into the image of God that we are destined unto. Christ in us truly is the hope of glory. His personality heals the damaged places of our life and sets us free from the chains of the past for the freedom of the future. That future is a productive future in the purposes of the kingdom of God. For Abram, it meant a productivity related to birthing new generations of peoples called by the name of the Lord. That may be the case for us in terms of our own families. It may also be the case in terms of new ventures of faith we are beckoned unto.

Note that Abram was promised nations and kings (v. 6). The "nations" is clearly a reference to Israel and perhaps other Gentile nations that would serve the Lord through faith. The kings obviously refer to the kings of Israel and most especially to the King of Kings, Jesus Christ.

**7. And I will establish my covenant between me and thee and thy seed after thee in their generations for an everlasting covenant, to be a God unto thee, and to thy seed after thee.**

Again the language of grace dominates the passage as it is clear that the Lord is the one who establishes this covenant. It is marvelously comforting to know that it is primarily His Word on the line rather than our word or Abram's word. We, like Abram, can fail the Lord. But God is completely faithful and cannot lie.

This covenant is an everlasting covenant between God and Abraham. The significance of this is found in Romans 9-11. These chapters by Paul show that the rejection of the Jews was not by God's fault but by their unbelief. Because of this disobedience the Gentiles became the heirs of grace. Yet His love continues strong for the descendants of Abraham according to the flesh, "But of Israel he says, 'All day long have I stretched forth my hands to a disobedient and gainsaying people' " (Romans 10:21). Paul began Romans 11 by asking if God had rejected "his people." The answer is a resounding "No!' " God is still faithful to keep the word of His promise. His everlasting covenant with Abraham is the basis for the future hope of Israel. The patriarchs are the roots of the olive tree described in 11:17-24. The Jews were the natural branches that had to be pruned off due to their failure to produce fruit worthy of repentance. The Gentiles who repented were thus engrafted into the tree of the promises to Abraham. Yet Gentiles must be careful not to boast of their new position in Abraham's blessings. The purpose of the salvation of the Gentiles is to bring Israel back on her knees to God Almighty and thereby bring in the full blessings of the kingdom of God in Christ.

**8. And I will give unto thee, and to thy seed after thee, the land wherein thou art a stranger, all the land of Canaan, for an everlasting possession; and I will be their God.**

The covenant faithfulness of God is shown in two ways. First, Abram will have posterity from his own seed that will become a great nation. Second, this great nation will inherit the land which God gave Abram following Lot's decision in Genesis 13. Acts of righteousness and trust lead into the future. Abram's faithfulness in trusting the Lord at the end of Genesis 13 payed off in the land of milk and honey for the promised people.

This eternal covenant made to Abram in Genesis 17 is made valid to us in Jesus Christ's death and resurrection. Through faith in Christ we share in these covenantal blessings. We are part of a great nation—men and women from around the world who confess their citizenship with the kingdom of God. We have a great King: Jesus the risen Lord. Our great land of inheritance is heaven and the redeemed earth and heaven at His coming.

The last part of this verse, "I will be their God," is echoed in Revelation 7:9-17 where He is present with those who have suffered for His name and are present in heaven worshiping Him night and day.

III. HEIRS OF THE COVENANT (Genesis 17:15-22)

(Only verses 20, 21 are in the Printed Text.)

A. New Identity (vv. 15, 16)

(Verses 15 and 16 are not in the Printed Text.)

The covenant of circumcision is described in verses 9-14. Every male child born in the house of Abram's faith was to be brought to the Lord on the eighth day of life to be circumcised. This act symbolized the act of sanctification. Circumcision affects the male organ of reproduction. From the male, life comes through this organ. It holds the seed of the future. Circumcision is a sign of the future being given completely to God.

Even as Abraham's name was changed in verse 5 from "exalted father" to "father of many nations," Sarai's name is changed. It is interesting that no explanatory note is given to indicate the precise meaning of her name. "Sarah" means "princess" and the change may reflect the note in verse 16 that kings shall come from her womb.

B. The Future Considered (vv. 17-22)

(Verses 19, 22 are not in the Printed Text.)

In verses 17, 18 Abraham's initial response is one of humorous unbelief. The scene is admittedly silly: can a one hundred-year-old man and a ninety-year-old woman have a child together? As far as the man is concerned it is physically possible. But is is unlikely that a woman of that age would continue to issue a monthly egg. That is what adds to the

miracle of this story: God performs a miracle in the life of the woman to produce what is missing. Because of this, the child Isaac is born.

It is interesting that Abraham's understanding had not caught up with his faith! Verse 18 sees Abraham wishing that Ishmael could be the child of the promise! This should not be taken as rebellious unbelief; rather, it is the natural tendency to only see the limits of human possibility and not understand the unlimited power of God! That is why in Romans 4 Paul related the birth of Isaac to the resurrection of Jesus. As far as the situation between Abraham and Sarah was concerned, she was as good as dead because her body did not produce the ovum of life. Yet God miraculously produced life in her. The same happened with Jesus. He who was dead through crucifixion and the sting of suffering wounds was brought back to life without having His flesh suffer in the grave!

The name "Isaac" means "laughter." Verse 19 shows God's understanding as He takes Abraham's laughter of misunderstanding and turns it into the joy of the new birth.

**20. And as for Ishmael, I have heard thee: Behold, I have blessed him, and will make him fruitful, and will multiply him exceedingly; twelve princes shall he beget, and I will make him a great nation.**

**21. But my covenant will I establish with Isaac, which Sarah shall bear unto thee at this set time in the next year.**

These verses tell us a great deal about the grace of God. It is a grace that reaches into the sins of the past and offers redemptive love. Although Ishmael was born out of man's effort to accomplish God's will, God mercifully offered the promise of a future.

As verse 21 indicates, however, the covenant of blessing still remained with Isaac. The sins of our past are forgiven and can be turned to redemptive purposes in Christ. Yet, those forgiven sins never reach the place of blessing that God brings upon complete obedience. To obey from a pure heart is better than to be forgiven for wrongs committed. Some people live by the popular saying, "It's easier to get forgiveness than permission." That may be the way the world lives and thinks, but it is not the way of righteousness of God. It is a far better thing for the believer to be sanctified in thought and deed and living in obedient response to God's faithful Word.

## REVIEW QUESTIONS

1. How does the Holy Spirit illuminate the will of God today?

2. Why is the command to "fear not" so important in obeying God's will?

3. What are the two ways Abram tried to do in order to accomplish God's will prior to the birth of Isaac?

4. What is the significance of the title, "God Almighty?"

5. Why is it important that faith preceded the rite of circumcision?

## GOLDEN TEXT HOMILY

"I AM THY SHIELD, AND THY EX-CEEDING GREAT REWARD" (Genesis 15:1).

The story of redemption was first hinted of in the Garden of Eden (Genesis 3:15). Now some 2000 years after the creation and fall of man, 400 years after the Flood, in a world lapsed into idolatry and wickedness, God called Abraham to become the founder of a nation having for its object the redemption of mankind.

God made a **covenant** with Abraham, a righteous man, believing in monotheism (one God), that his descendants (1) should inherit the land of Canaan, (2) become a great nation, and (3) all nations should be blessed through them.

God made many promises to Abraham, and in the end He actually made a promise which He (God) confirmed with an oath. When God made this special promise to Abraham, since He was not able to swear by anyone greater, He swore by Himself. This made it doubly binding.

This promise was that all of Abraham's descendants would be blessed; therefore, that promise was to the Christian church,

for the church is the true Israel and the true seed of Abraham. That blessing came true in Jesus Christ. Now, let us look at the key word in this lesson, a word in which the whole of Jesus' work and intention is enshrined. It is the word **covenant.** Jesus spoke of His blood being the blood of the covenant. What Jesus meant by that was that a covenant is a relationship between two people; when two people enter into a covenant, they enter into a relationship with each other.

But the covenant of which Jesus spoke was not a covenant between man and man; it was a covenant between God and man. In Matthew 26:26-30 what Jesus was saying at the Last Supper was this: "Because of My life, and above all because of My death, a new relationship is now possible between you and God." Christ was saying to them, "You have seen Me; and in Me you have seen God; I have told you. I have shown you. How much God loves you. He loves you even enough to suffer this that I am going through." That is what God is like. Because of what Jesus did for mankind, the way for them is open to all the blessings of God in this new relationship. When Jesus spoke these words, He was on His way to Calvary, but He was also on His way to the throne of the kingdom of God, to seal forever the covenant God made to Abraham that through Him all nations of the world would be blessed.—**James N. Layne, D.Min., Pastor, Cleveland, Tennessee.**

## SENTENCE SERMONS

FAITH IS DEAD to doubt, dumb to discouragement, and blind to impossibilities.

**—"The Defender"**

THE PROMISES of God, like Himself, are unchangeable and eternal.

**—Selected**

YOU CAN REST the weight of all your anxieties upon God, for you are always in His care.

**—Paraphrase of 1 Peter 5:7**

GOD'S WORD is certain and His promises everlasting.

**—Selected**

## EVANGELISTIC APPLICATION

GOD'S GREATEST PROMISE IS ETERNAL LIFE THROUGH JESUS CHRIST HIS SON.

This promise is seen vividly in the words of Jesus to His disciples at the Last Supper. He took the cup and told them that this was His blood shed for the sins of the world. He spoke of this as the cup of the new covenant.

The work of Jesus at the Cross is the point that all of God's dealings with Abraham were looking forward to. Abraham longed to see Jesus' day and rejoice in it.

This means that our evangelism must include all people. No one is omitted from the atoning blood of Christ. As it is true that all have sinned, it is also true that all can be saved in Him. It is this multitude of redeemed people from around the world who make up the new nations that Abram was promised. These peoples are joint heirs with Christ and are rulers together with Him as He manifests His glory and power. We are citizens of the coming kingdom. We joyfully announce a new government that is established upon His shoulders and that is one of peace and righteousness in the Holy Spirit.

Christian evangelism has worldwide implications because of what has happened on the Cross.

## ILLUMINATING THE LESSON

Carlo Carretto comments "that contemplation is not so much a matter of watching God as of being watched by God." Abram spent 13 years without hearing the voice of God. Yet he was constantly being watched by God. He was never out of God's providential care. He was on that journey described by Carretto: "When you have passed beyond the stages where sentiments, hymns, preoccupation with your own salvation, immediate results and easy achievements matter, and have reached the realm of mystery, then you understand what this world is. . . . Yes, God is there before you, watching you. His look is creative, capable of achieving the impossible. And just as He looked on the chaos at the beginning, hovered over the waters with the smile of His favor, and drew forth the cosmos, so, looking at you with the same favoring smile, He realizes the final purpose of creation: love. . . .

"Take courage, then: God loves you . . . .

"Let yourself go; let Him take hold of you."

(From **In Search of the Beyond**)

## DAILY DEVOTIONAL GUIDE

M. Human Ingenuity. Genesis 16:1-6
T. Divine Revelation. Genesis 16:7-16
W. Son of Promise. Genesis 21:5-12
T. New Name. Genesis 35:9-15
F. Promised Son. John 1:1-13
S. Final Word. Hebrews 1:1-12

# Intercessory Prayer

**Study Text:** Genesis 18:16 through 19:29
**Supplemental References:** Deuteronomy 9:13-21; 2 Kings 19:1-19; John 17:1-26
**Time:** Around 1900 B.C.
**Place:** Sodom and Gomorrah, plains of Mamre
**Golden Text:** "I exhort therefore, that, first of all, supplications, prayers, intercessions, and giving of thanks, be made for all men" (1 Timothy 2:1).
**Central Truth:** God hears and responds to the prayers of those who intercede for others.
**Evangelistic Emphasis:** God's mercy and grace are sufficient for the salvation of any individual.

## Printed Text

**Genesis 18:23.** And Abraham drew near, and said, Wilt thou also destroy the righteous with the wicked?

**24. Peradventure there be fifty righteous within the city: wilt thou also destroy and not spare the place for the fifty righteous that are therein?**

25. That be far from thee to do after this manner, to slay the righteous with the wicked: and that the righteous should be as the wicked, that be far from thee: Shall not the Judge of all the earth do right?

**32. And he said, Oh let not the Lord be angry, and I will speak yet but this once: Peradventure ten shall be found there. And he said, I will not destroy it for ten's sake.**

33. And the Lord went his way, as soon as he had left communing with Abraham: and Abraham returned unto his place.

**19:12. And the men said unto Lot, Hast thou here any besides? son in law, and thy sons, and thy daughters, and whatsoever thou hast in the city, bring them out of this place:**

13. For we will destroy this place, because the cry of them is waxen great before the face of the Lord; and the Lord hath sent us to destroy it.

**24. Then the Lord rained upon Sodom and upon Gomorrah brimstone and fire from the Lord out of heaven;**

25. And he overthrew those cities, and all the plain, and all the inhabitants of the cities, and that which grew upon the ground.

**26. But his wife looked back from behind him, and she became a pillar of salt.**

27. And Abraham gat up early in the morning to the place where he stood before the Lord:

**28. And he looked toward Sodom and Gomorrah, and toward all the land of the plain, and beheld, and, lo, the smoke of the country went up as the smoke of a furnace.**

29. And it came to pass, when God destroyed the cities of the plain, that God remembered Abraham, and sent Lot out of the midst of the overthrow, when he overthrew the cities in the which Lot dwelt.

## LESSON OUTLINE

I. A PERSISTENT PLEA
  A. God's Concern for Abraham
  B. God's Concern for Righteousness
  C. The Power of Intercession
II. SIN AND MERCY
  A. The Horror of Sin
  B. Escape Provided
III. RETRIBUTION
IV. PRAYER ANSWERED

## LESSON EXPOSITION

INTRODUCTION

The topic of this lesson, "Intercessory Prayer," is an appropriate approach to a world of sin prefigured in the stories of Sodom and Gomorrah. These two cities were part of Abram's and Lot's life in Genesis 14 (Lesson Ten). We saw the rebellious attitude of these cities of the plain. In Genesis 19 we will discover more about the terrible moral blight that characterized this area. A further study of other passages where these two cities are mentioned in the Bible will show us more of the terror of sin that dominated them. The folly of Lot's choice and the wisdom of Abraham's in Genesis 13 is never clearer than in this story.

I. A PERSISTENT PLEA (Genesis 18:16-33)

A. God's Concern For Abraham (vv. 16-19)

(Verses 16-19 are not in the Printed Text.)

It is important that the teacher read all of Genesis 18. The story of the promised birth of Isaac is continued with the arrival of three visitors to Abraham's home. It is evident immediately that they are divine visitors with a message to confirm the promise of God regarding the birth from Sarah and himself. The story has a comical edge as Sarah is caught laughing in the tent about the news she overheard the men give Abraham. Upon being confronted about her laughing, she denied it; however, the Lord rebuked her and indicated she did laugh.

That part of the story is left hanging until Genesis 21. The story of the three visitors takes an interesting turn. Originally messengers of grace to Abraham, they become messengers of destruction to Sodom.

In Genesis 18:16-19 we learn of the struggle God had regarding how much Abraham should be involved in the destructive plans. Abraham journeyed with the three visitors until they came to the hills overlooking the plain. From there the men went their way into the city to face humiliation. But Abraham is left with God. It is this time of being before God that became the basis for intercession.

Why would God be concerned about hiding the destruction from Abraham (v. 17)? Rather than thinking that God actually doubted Himself, it is better to think that this question is posed to provide an understanding of the role of faith in the world. It is clear from John 17:15, 17 that Jesus was concerned that His disciples be kept free of the evil influence of the world—but not free from being an influence upon the world. That lies behind the question of verse 17. The man of faith, Abraham, is not meant to live isolated from the terrors of sin and its horrible effects on society. People of faith are given a specific task in the world: intercession. Many Christians think their task is primarily one of judgment and condemnation; but this story illustrates that God seriously seeks to save Sodoms and Gomorrahs. God also seriously raises up people who are willing to intercede for the lost places and people of the world.

Henri Nouwen illustrates this principle of intercession with a story from the desert Christian fathers of Egypt: "A brother . . . committed a fault. A council was called to which Abba Moses was invited, but he refused to go to it. Then the priest sent someone to say to him, 'Come, for everyone is waiting for you.' So he got up and went. He took a leaking jug, filled it with water, and carried it with him. The others came out to meet him and said to him, 'What is this, Father?' The old man said to them, 'My sins run out behind me, and I do not see them, and today I am coming to judge the error of another.' When they heard that they said no more to the brother but forgave him" **(The Way of the Heart).**

The story illustrates that Abraham's faith was based on grace. He knew himself that he was an undeserving recipient of forgiveness and grace. Only one who comprehends this is capable of interceding with sincerity for the terrible sinful places of our world. How different Abraham is from Jonah. Jonah sees Nineveh (the same as Sodom in **his** book!) and longs to see fire and brimstone rained upon them. His very preaching was designed to bring them under indictment and then the sentence of death was to follow. Yet, they understood Jonah's God better than he did! They knew that He might forgive them and change His mind of the judgment that was due.

Verses 18 and 19 point to the fact that one way the blessing of Abraham is come upon himself and then upon the world is through this genuine encounter with sin.

B. God's Concern For Righteousness (vv. 20, 21)

(Verses 20 and 21 are not in the Printed Text.)

These verses introduce us to the horror of life in Sodom and Gomorrah. The evil being done in these cities is described as being cried against in the heavenlies. The word of the awful sin has come to God and He desires to examine it. We should not think that God was not aware of what was actually happening in Sodom; rather, the writer makes the story alive by having the Lord visit the cities for a firsthand look at the sin! It provides an explanation for those who face terrible sins and wonder where God is. He is present and closer than you realize! He will not allow sin to continue to go unpunished. As terrible as the Nazi treatment of the Jews was, God had a time in which that modern nightmare came to an end.

The word **cry** has the sense of "utterance of horror, distress, alarm, sorrow." It is used with great frequency in the Old Testament when those who are being treated unjustly raise their voices in lament to the lord. The intent of this is expressed clearly in Proverbs 21:13: "Whoso stoppeth his ears at the cry of the poor, he also shall cry himself, but shall not be heard."

The sin (not yet explained) of Sodom is called "very grievous." The word "grievous" is based on the Hebrew **cabod. Cabod** is often translated as "glory," but also has the sense of "heaviness." As used in Genesis 18:20 it refers to sin as a heavy burden. It is oppressive and a vexation. It weighs down human society and crushes people under its weight.

In Genesis 19 we are given more insight into one of the sins that dominated the cities: homosexuality. However, as further reference to other uses of these in the Bible illustrates, homosexuality was just one expression of the sin that crushed the spirits of people. Sodom and Gomorrah are referred to 18 times outside of Genesis. These include 4 times in Isaiah (1:9, 10; 3:9; 13:19), 3 times in Jeremiah (23:14; 49:18; 50:40), once in Lamentations (4:6), and 6 times in Ezekiel 16 (vv. 46, 48, 49, 53, 55, 56). Other aspects of sin that relate to the spirit of Sodom and Gomorrah are as follows:

a. A multitude of sacrifices without obedience (Isaiah 1:10).

b. Severe injustice caused by class partiality (Isaiah 3:9).

c. Forsaking the covenant of God (Deuteronomy 29:23).

d. A nation that is empty of God's counsel (Deuteronomy 32:32).

e. God's prophets guilty of lies and adultery (Jeremiah 23:14).

f. A life of pride, plenty of food, and prosperous ease, with no aid for the poor and needy (Ezekiel 16:49).

It is clear that the sin has corrupted the entire society of Sodom. It is a byword even today to describe the breakdown of society's obligation to care for the poor and live righteously before the Lord.

The cities are referred to ten times in the New Testament. Jesus contrasted those cities that refused to believe in the gospel with Sodom and Gomorrah. On the Day of Judgment it will be more tolerable for Sodom than for those cities that have rejected the gospel (Matthew 10:15). The reason this is the case is that the only true foundation that can change society is the gospel of the kingdom of God.

Other places where the cities are mentioned in the New Testament include Luke 10:12, 17:29; Romans 9:29; 2 Peter 2:6; Jude 7; and Revelation 11:8.

God's concern for righteousness reaches every society of the world. The gospel of the kingdom is the Good News that all oppressed peoples are longing to hear. Sometimes the secular world describes its compassion more clearly than the church. Several months ago relief efforts for Ethiopia were heightened by the recording of "We Are the World, We Are the Children." Concern and action for those who are on the edges of life is part of the Good News that Christians are to bear gladly and with wise effectiveness.

C. The Power of Intercession (vv. 22-33)

Intercession begins as one "stands" before the Lord as Abraham did in 18:22. To stand before the Lord is to place oneself in a position of humble power.

Walter Brueggemann makes the interesting observation that God allows Abraham the honor of teaching Him about His own graciousness. As a former teacher I can testify that teaching is the best way to learn. God allows Abraham to "teach Him" so that Abraham may fully learn who He is!

**23. And Abraham drew near, and said, Wilt thou also destroy the righteous with the wicked?**

**24. Peradventure there be fifty righteous within the city: wilt thou also destroy and not spare the place for the fifty righteous that are therein?**

**25. That be far from thee to do after this manner, to slay the righteous with the wicked: and that the righteous should be as the wicked, that be far from thee: Shall not the Judge of all the earth do right?**

In his intercession, Abraham appeals to the very nature of God. He has already experienced the grace of this God and knows that blessings belong to those who bless His name. Thus, on the basis of what Abraham already knows he appeals to God to be God. A righteously

indignant man may choose to destroy Sodom with wicked and righteous alike; but God is not like a man. God is God and is bound to His nature.

Intercession presupposes that God is willing to "change His mind." This is not a careless action on the part of human intercessors; rather, it is the knowledge that God is not locked into the future. God responds to repentance! That is the entire message of the gospel: God is willing to be changed by the power of righteousness.

It is in the light that Abraham's standing before God in verse 22 is so important. There are four key elements that intercessors must have operating in their lives. The first is a righteousness based on faith in the life of the intercessor. We do not stand before God on the basis of our own works or abilities; like Abraham, we stand before God on the basis of faith.

Second, we must be committed to doing God's will God's way. We must submit every aspect of our intercession to God. We must not work God into a corner (as if we could!) so that He is expected to work in only one acceptable way.

Third, like, Abraham, we must be sanctified in heart and flesh. Holiness must be a living reality in our life. This holiness is a holiness born of heart-love, not born of works.

Fourth, the intercessor must be aware of who he is in Christ. We are heirs of grace in Christ Jesus. He is our Elder Brother interceding before the Father!

Abraham, on the basis of the four things mentioned above, negotiated with God for two things. First, he argued for the salvation of Sodom. It did not matter if there were only ten righteous people left in the evil city, God was willing to let it stand. The implications of this are crucial. It means that a few righteous people are powerful influences in the world. Often we are deceived by Satan into thinking that we must be large in numbers before we can influence the world. Such thinking goes hand in hand with democratic notions of rule by popular vote. But that is not the way of the kingdom of God. God's rule is exercised by a few people interceding with effectual righteousness.

The second thing is that Abraham negotiated for the family of Lot. I am reminded of a phrase in one of the late Keith Green's songs, "I pledge my head, my wife, my son, to heaven for the gospel." Our intercession must begin within our own home. How sad it is to be so concerned for the sins of the world that we ignore the love-needs of our own spouse and children. Also, the intercession for Lot is Abraham's tacit admission that in the final analysis the decision belongs to God regarding the fate of Sodom. If ten righteous cannot be found to save the city; then at least allow Lot's family to be saved on the basis of Abraham's righteousness! This is consistent with Abraham's position before the king of Sodom in Genesis 14. Abraham was not going to give Sodom the people and at this time of destruction he was not going to give Lot over to death.

Richard Foster, in **Celebration of Discipline** (Harper & Row, 1978), has a number of penetrating insights into intercessory prayer. He writes, "Prayer catapults us onto the frontier of the spiritual life. It is original research in unexplored territory . . . Real prayer is life creating and life changing . . . To pray is to change. Prayer is the central avenue God uses to transform us. If we are unwilling to change, we will abandon prayer as a noticeable characteristic of our lives."

Foster lists several things that are of value in intercessory prayer. First, prayer is a learning process. Even the disciples asked Jesus to teach them how to pray (Luke 11:1). This liberates us from the idea that we have to pray "perfect" prayers in the fashion of a more experienced prayer warrior.

Second, prayer is not tentative in intercession. It has a clear goal in mind and prays with "vision." While "if it be Thy will" prayers should not be ignored,

it is important to intercede with fervent intention for the desires of the heart.

Third, such fervent praying should illicit within us a real expectation that change is going to occur. This is not the naive expectation of a child; rather, it is the maturing expectation of a person in Christ.

Fourth, effective intercessory prayer is prayer that originates out of communion with God. It may be quiet and filled with silence. But it begins with profound awareness that we are addressing the Lord of Lords. Thus, intercessory prayer becomes an exercise in listening to the voice of God as well as speaking our own concerns. Related to this aspect of prayer is praying in the Spirit. The eighth chapter of Romans (vv. 18-27) provides an excellent context for understanding prayer in a Spirit-given language. By this prayer the Holy Spirit intercedes through our spirit according to the will of God.

Fifth, compassion becomes a hallmark of the intercessor. This compassion is an ability to "feel" the pain (certainly emotional and spiritual and perhaps physical) that another person is experiencing. Compassion becomes the expression of love for that person and our intercession ceases from being mere words.

**32. And he said, Oh let not the Lord be angry, and I will speak yet but this once: Peradventure ten shall be found there. And he said, I will not destroy it for ten's sake.**

**33. And the Lord went his way, as soon as he had left communing with Abraham: and Abraham returned unto his place.**

These verses bring us to the conclusion of the intercession. Abraham's appeal to God on the basis of His divine mercy concluded with grace being shown in wonderful measure.

Verse 33 tells us that intercession is a special place of encounter between people and God. Out of His grace He enters into this place of intercession with us. We enter it by practicing those things seen in the life of Abraham and comments made on intercession in the previous section.

II. SIN AND MERCY (Genesis 19:1-23)

A. The Horror of Sin (vv. 1-11)

(These verses are not in the Printed Text.)

The visiting angels came into Sodom and met Lot at the gate. It was common practice in the ancient world for men to sit at the gates to exchange information and practice economic exchange.

Apparently Lot recognized something about them that moved his spirit. He entreated them to stay in his home overnight. At first they refused his offer and planned to find abode in the streets. It is clear from 19:3 that Lot knew the reputation of the city and "greatly pressed" the men to stay with him. Lot knew the men would be sexually assaulted in the city streets.

Near time for retiring for the night, Lot realized that the house was surrounded by men of all ages seeking the visitors. But their desire for the men was not confined to greetings. They desired to "know" them. The Hebrew word for "know" is often used in the Old Testament to describe sexual relations. Thus, a large crowd of homosexual men gathered at the door demanding the visitors.

Lot offered his daughters, who were virgins, to the men but they refused (compare Judges 19:22-25). The anger of the men was evident as they turned on Lot and accused him of acting as a judge over them. Little did they know that the two visitors were actually their judges. The two visitors displayed their power for Lot and struck the raging crowd blind so that the men had to depart from the door of the house.

Although other sins of Sodom were mentioned in the exposition of "God's Concern for Righteousness," it is clear that homosexuality was a serious problem facing the city. We live in a day when sexual perversions of all varieties are practiced openly. We should not think that this later part of the twentieth century is the only time these things have happened (Genesis 19 testifies against that!). What is significant today is that popular opinion seems to support any lifestyle as acceptable. In a democratic society this is almost inevitable. But for the Christian this poses a serious area of conflict. Christians are called to bear witness to the world of another way to live: the way of righteousness ordained by God. We are in a period of historical uncertainty as our society struggles with political change brought by factions representing all segments of our culture. This is not the place to discuss various approaches to a Christian's involvement in the political sphere. But it is clear that Christians are having to wrestle with bearing witness to the sins of our society and offering changes. The greatest change needed is a change of the heart that comes from genuine repentance. Legislative changes may be good or bad and have no degree of permanence. But the change that comes from the Spirit of God in the life of individuals, families, and society is genuinely transforming and crosses all political ideologies.

While individual Christians will have to decide their own political preferences, all Christians can submit themselves to the Word of God and the righteousness found in Christ. We are primarily citizens of the kingdom of God. Paul makes it clear in 1 Corinthians 6:9, 10 that persons who indulge in a lifestyle of practices contrary to the will of God will not inherit the kingdom of God. In Romans 1:26, 27 sexual perverseness is seen as a consequence of idolatry. Those who love the world more than God will ultimately find themselves engaged in a variety of sinful possessions that lead to death and destruction.

As seen from Genesis 19, this happened in Sodom. Sodom reached such a low level of depravity that God's only recourse was destruction. It was a destruction brought upon itself by its failure to acknowledge the God of truth. It appears that much of our society (perhaps all of Western society) is headed in the same direction. God is still looking for intercessors for this depraved world. He is looking for a few righteous men and women who will commit their families and lifestyles to be controlled by His Spirit as a testimony to the world of the redeeming grace of God.

B. Escape Provided (vv. 12-13)

**12. And the men said unto Lot, Hast thou here any besides? son-in-law, and thy sons, and thy daughters, and whatsoever thou hast in the city, bring them out of this place:**

**13. For we will destroy this place, because the cry of them is waxen great before the face of the Lord; and the Lord hath sent us to destroy it.**

Lot, by his poor choice in Genesis 13, found himself in the midst of a terrible temptation. Yet, we know that God always provides a way of escape from the snare of temptation (1 Corinthians 10:13). For Lot, that way was the way of obedience to the voice of the Lord revealed in the two visitors.

In response to Abraham's intercession (19:29) the invitation to salvation was extended to Lot's family. Originally the invitation was meant for all members of the family. But it was not taken seriously by Lot's son-in-law nor apparently by his sons.

In verse 13 the visitors spoke of "destroying" the cities of the plain. The word **destroy** is used frequently in Genesis. In Genesis 6:13, 17 it is used to describe God's reaction to the world of sin prior to the Flood. In Genesis 9:11, 15 it is used to describe God's covenant not to destroy the world by flood in the future. In 13:10 it referred to the land of Sodom which was to be destroyed. In 18:28, 31, 32 it is used in Abraham's negotiations with God over the fate of Sodom. It is used in 19:13, 14, 29 to describe the actual destruction. It is also of note that the same Hebrew word is used in Numbers, Joshua, and Judges to describe how the Israelites were to deal with the inhabitants of the land who were to be removed. It seems to be a key word to describe God's response to unrepentant, depraved sin.

A sad element is added to this passage in verse 16. Lot is reluctant to leave. What a powerful statement to the power of the world to attract a person into the place of destruction. The Hebrew for "linger" has the sense to "delay." In Arabic it means "slow walk." It aptly describes a person not sanctified in heart to obey the word of the Lord. In Psalm 119:60 it is used in a positive sense in relation to the Word of God, "I made haste, and delayed not to keep thy commandments." The power of sin is so deceiving. Even though we know that the Word of God is true, we often allow ourselves to be blinded to the horror of the sin around us in order to enjoy the comforts of the world. Verse 16 adds that it was only because of the Lord's mercy that he was forceably brought forth from the city.

Lot's attachment to the world of Sodom continued to be a possible snare as he argued with the visitors regarding the site of refuge (vv. 18-21). Lot compromised for the city of Zoar.

III. RETRIBUTION (Genesis 19:24-26)

**24. Then the Lord rained upon Sodom and upon Gomorrah brimstone and fire from the Lord out of heaven.**

"Rain" is used several times in the Bible to describe God's action of judgment. It connotates a saturing of divine judgment upon a place; the place was covered with destruction. It is used in Exodus 9:18 and Psalms 11:6 in this fashion. Brimstone is referred to in Psalm 11:6 and Ezekiel 38:22. In the New Testament brimstone functions as "divine fire" (Luke 17:29; Revelation 9:17, 18; 14:10; 19:20; 20:10; 21:8).

**25. And he overthrew those cities, and all the plain, and all the inhabitants of the cities, and that which grew upon the ground.**

The destruction was total. It was a firestorm of tremendous magnitude. Perhaps the closest we can come in this age to understanding the extent of the destruction is to think of the effects of a nuclear blast. Vegetation is severly damaged from this fire-storm from heaven. The actual physical dynamics of how God performed this are beyond us. How He did it is not nearly as important as why He did it! In reflecting on the Day of the Lord, Peter forsees the last days of the earth to be a time of judgment from severe fire (2 Peter 3:7, 10, 12).

**26. But his wife looked back from behind him, and she became a pillar of salt.**

Earlier we noted Lot's hesitancy about leaving Sodom and then his hesitancy to go where the visitors commanded him. Now we see that his wife's attachments were as strong. The family was warned not to look back at the destruction. She turned and was slain as she saw. Again, the actual physical dynamics are not given. What is significant is that the way of salvation is so important that one can never afford to turn back to the old ways that lead to death.

IV. PRAYER ANSWERED (Genesis 19:27-29)

**27. And Abraham gat up early in the morning to the place where he stood before the Lord:**

**28. And he looked toward Sodom and Gomorrah, and toward all the land of the plain, and beheld, and, lo, the smoke of the country went up as the smoke of a furnace.**

**29. And it came to pass, when God destroyed the cities of the plain, that God remembered Abraham, and sent Lot out of the midst of the overthrow, when he overthrew the cities in the which Lot dwelt.**

There is a time to intercede and then a time to depart from interceding. Abraham interceded till his heart was free of the burden and left the issue with God. How tempting it would have been for Abraham to have run into Sodom and tried to rescue Lot. Yet, that was not the way God desired. Abraham's role was intercessory prayer; God's role was to work out the way of salvation.

Abraham returned to the place of presence before the Lord to see the results of the destruction. Verse 28 vividly captures the total destruction that covered the horizon. What he saw was in terrible contrast to what had been seen in the early controversy of Genesis 13:10. The

allurement of sin through the lust of the eyes had turned to charred remains of a desolate land.

The lesson concludes with a reminder that God did answer Abraham's prayer. The intercession for Sodom did not press God to allow total unrighteousness to remain. Abraham wisely stopped the negotiations at ten people. But God did remember to save Lot. The phrasing of the language is important. Lot is saved because "God remembered Abraham." Intercessory prayer touches the heart of God. Such prayers are not forgotten in the heavenlies. It is appropriate that the Book of Revelation calls to our attention the power of prayer (5:8). God's righteous people do make a difference in the world.

**REVIEW QUESTIONS**

1. In what way did God show His desire to save Sodom?

2. Name other aspects of sin that are related to Sodom in the Old Testament.

3. Why is homosexuality such a serious sin?

4. How does an intercessory "stand" before the Lord?

5. In what ways do Christians today exhibit the same behavior as Lot in lingering in Sodom?

**GOLDEN TEXT HOMILY**

"I EXHORT THEREFORE, THAT, FIRST OF ALL, SUPPLICATIONS, PRAYERS, INTERCESSIONS, AND GIVING OF THANKS, BE MADE FOR ALL MEN" (1 Timothy 2:1).

Paul's expression **I exhort therefore first of all that supplications, prayers, intercessions, thanksgivings be made for all men** is a logical transition from his general charge to wage a good warfare on behalf of the truth (cf. 1:18) to his outline of specific duties. There will be real warfare between the forces of evil and the forces of righteousness. True believers compose a worshiping fellowship, and among true worshipers prayer is primary. It is essential to victory over their spiritual foes. A prayerless church is a powerless and defeated church, but a praying church is a conquering church (cf. Acts 4:23-31; 12:1-19, 24).

The **words Paul uses** to describe prayer seem to have different shades of meaning, and there is overlapping between the first three. Nevertheless, they appear to be cumulative and serve to emphasize the duty enjoined. He was primarily concerned that true believers' prayer and praise should include all classes and conditions of men.

**Supplication** expresses the sense of need, the greatest of which is for God's pardoning grace, or forgiveness of sins. The word **prayer** conveys the idea of reverence, or homage because of the character of God. It involves **heartfelt reverence** and "an habitual listening for His voice, and a natural talking to Him about everything."

**Intercessions** are importunate, intensified petitions offered to God in behalf of another. The word also conveys the idea of confidence that the intercessions are in accordance "with the Spirit of the Great Mediator." Thanksgiving is an element that is too often missing in both private and public prayer. The privilege of petitioning God to meet needs carries with it the obligation to praise Him for all He has done in response to our prayers. This kind of praying is universally binding on the churches. It is their standing duty. The failure of the Church to pray in accordance with this exhortation is one of its great sins today.

The scope of prayer, **for all men, for kings and all that are in high places,** is a rebuke to the narrowness that characterizes so much of the Church's praying. The tendency is to classify the needy in categories such as "those likely to be won to the gospel," "those not likely to be interested in the gospel message," and "those whom it is impossible to win to Christ through the gospel." Paul's personal experience (cf. 1:12-15) and God's abundant provision for the salvation of all men (cf. John 3:16; 2 Peter 3:9) rebuke such an attitude. The gospel is for all men: high, low, rich, poor, learned, ignorant, of any race or rank. All whom God has created, He is willing to save.

—**Excerpts from Wesleyan Bible Commentary,** Vol. V.

## SENTENCE SERMONS

GOD HEARS AND RESPONDS to the prayers of those who intercede for others.
—**Selected**

PRAYER REQUIRES more of the heart than of the tongue.
—**Adam Clarke**

TO GET NATIONS back on their feet, we must get down on our knees first.
—**Letter to Editor: "Des Moines Register"**

PRAYER OPENS OUR EYES that we may see ourselves and others as God sees us.
—**Clara Palmer**

## EVANGELISTIC APPLICATION

GOD'S MERCY AND GRACE ARE SUFFICIENT FOR THE SALVATION OF ANY INDIVIDUAL.

That is why intercessory prayer for the lost is so important. Such prayer unleashes powerful spiritual forces that have an unseen impact on the lost person. We often think that saving the lost is a matter of physical presence at the "right" religious service. We think that a setback in life will turn the person to the Lord. While these are important, they are not as important as the unseen spiritual battle waging for that person's soul.

In 2 Corinthians 10:3, 4 the Apostle Paul, perhaps the most effective evangelist in 2,000 years, wrote that our warfare was not against the physical things of the world and thus our weapons were not physical weapons. Our weapons are the weapons of the Spirit because the great enemy is spiritual.

Growing churches are often evangelistic churches—they are also praying churches. They are people who have begun to understand the power of spiritual warfare and intercessory prayer for the lost. Such prayer is not some chance arrangement prior to revival efforts; it is the intentional effort of the people of God who are genuinely concerned for the lost world.

## ILLUMINATING THE LESSON

Henri Nouwen, in **The Way of the**

**Heart** (Ballantine Books, 1981), comments on the relationship of ministry, spirituality, and compassion:

"We reach the point where ministry and spirituality touch each other. It is compassion. Compassion is the fruit of solitude and the basis of all ministry.

"Let us not underestimate how hard it is to be compassionate. Compassion is hard because it requires the inner disposition to go with others to the place where they are weak, vulnerable, lonely, and broken. But this is not our spontaneous response to suffering. What we desire most is to do away with suffering by fleeing from it or finding a quick cure for it.

"It is in solitude that his compassionate solidarity grows. In solitude we realize that nothing human is alien to us, that the roots of all conflict, war, injustice, cruelty, hatred, jealously, and envy are deeply anchored in our own heart. In solitude our heart of stone can be turned into a heart of flesh, a rebellious heart into a contrite heart, and a closed heart into a heart that can open itself to all suffering people in a gesture of solidarity."

## DAILY DEVOTIONAL GUIDE

M. Pray With Definiteness. Psalm 27:1-4

T. Pray With Fear. Psalm 145:18-21

W. Pray With Persistence. Luke 18:1-18

T. Pray With Thanksgiving. 1 Thessalonians 5:17-24

F. Pray With Boldness. Hebrews 4:14-16

S. Pray With Fervency. James 5:16-18

# Faith and Obedience

**Study Text:** Genesis 22:1-9

**Supplemental References:** Numbers 13:26-30; Romans 4:13-25; Hebrews 11:8-12, 17-19

**Time:** Around 1900 to 1850 B.C.

**Place:** Mount Moriah, Canaan

**Golden Text:** "Without faith it is impossible to please him: for he that cometh to God must believe that he is, and that he is a rewarder of them that diligently seek him" (Hebrews 11:6).

**Central Truth:** God's covenant blessings come through faith and obedience.

**Evangelistic Emphasis:** Only Jesus Christ can atone for the sins of the world.

## Printed Text

**Genesis 22:1.** And it came to pass after these things, that God did tempt Abraham, and said unto him, Abraham: and he said, Behold, here I am.

**2. And he said, Take now thy son, thine only son Isaac, whom thou lovest, and get thee into the land of Moriah; and offer him there for a burnt-offering upon one of the mountains which I will tell thee of.**

3. And Abraham rose up early in the morning, and saddled his ass, and took two of his young men with him, and Isaac his son, and clave the wood for the burnt-offering, and rose up, and went unto the place of which God had told him.

**4. Then on the third day Abraham lifted up his eyes, and saw the place afar off.**

5. And Abraham said unto his young men, Abide ye here with the ass; and I and the lad will go yonder and worship, and come again to you.

**6. And Abraham took the wood of the burnt-offering, and laid it upon Isaac his son; and he took the fire in his hand, and a knife; and they went both of them together.**

7. And Isaac spake unto Abraham his father, and said, My father: and he said, Here am I, my son. And he said, Behold the fire and the wood: but where is the lamb for a burnt-offering?

**8. And Abraham said, My son, God will provide himself a lamb for a burnt-offering: so they went both of them together.**

9. And they came to the place which God had told him of; and Abraham built an altar there, and laid the wood in order, and bound Isaac his son, and laid him on the altar upon the wood.

**10. And Abraham stretched forth his hand, and took the knife to slay his son.**

11. And the angel of the Lord called unto him out of heaven, and said, Abraham: and he said, Here am I.

**12. And he said, Lay not thine hand upon the lad, neither do thou any thing unto him: for now I know that thou fearest God, seeing thou hast**

**not withheld thy son, thine only son from me.**

13. And Abraham lifted up his eyes, and looked, and behold behind him a ram caught in a thicket by his horns: and Abraham went and took the ram,

and offered him up for a burnt-offering in the stead of his son.

**14. And Abraham called the name of that place Jehovah-jireh: as it is said to this day, In the mount of the Lord it shall be seen.**

---

**LESSON OUTLINE**

I. AN UNUSUAL COMMAND
 A. Standing Before God
 B. The Word Heard
II. AMAZING FAITH
 A. The Word Obeyed
 B. The Hope of God's Provision
III. DIVINE PROVISION
 A. The Fear of the Lord
 B. The Provision Made
 C. The Covenant Reaffirmed

**LESSON EXPOSITION**

INTRODUCTION

Since Genesis 12 we have followed Abraham's journey with this God who has laid claim to him. It has been a journey characterized by an insistent demand upon faith. In Genesis 22 we come to the climax of the story of Abraham and discover that this "faith" is an "anguished faith" (Brueggemann). We discover that Abraham must choose between the actual promise of God as revealed in the birth of Isaac and the God of the promise as revealed in his call. The fundamental issue is idolatry. Will Abraham trust God even if God takes back the sign of the promise? That is the struggle for all God's people who hear and obey the call to live by faith.

I. AN UNUSUAL COMMAND (Genesis 22:1, 2)

A. Standing Before God (v. 1)

**1. And it came to pass after these things, that God did tempt Abraham, and said unto him, Abraham: and he said, Behold, here I am.**

That God would tempt His own people is a theological point that drives us to despair. The closest parallel comment in the Bible to God "tempting" Abraham

outside of Genesis is Hebrews 11:17. Here the Greek word **peirazo** is used and shows that Abraham's trial was a trial of his faith, "By faith Abraham, when he was tried, offered up Isaac." The word "tried" has the sense of discovering what kind of a person Abraham was. It was used in a positive sense to refer to God or Christ putting people to the test to prove themselves true. It would be a way that God used to build the confidence of faith. Such a view is also found in 1 Corinthians 10:13, "There hath no temptation taken you but such as is common to man: but God is faithful, who will not suffer you to be tempted [**peirazo**] above that ye are able; but will with the temptation [**peirazo**] also make a way to escape, that ye may be able to bear it."

The other New Testament passage that bears on this is James 1:13. In this passage two different Greek words are used to describe "temptation, tempting." The word used three times is **peirazo** (the same root word used in Hebrews 11 and 1 Corinthians 10). The other word is **aspeirastos** which has a linguistic relationship to **peirazo**. This is the only time this word is used in the New Testament. A translation of this verse from Greek gives this reading,"Let not him who is being tempted **(periazo)** say 'I am being tempted **(periazo)** by God'; for God is not tempted **(aspeirastos)** with evil, and He does not tempt **(peirazo)** any man."

As we noted from Hebrews 11:17, **peirazo** has the sense of proving what is good in a man and is used in a positive sense. **Aspeirastos** is used in James with the sense of coming from evil. Thus, the James passage makes it clear that God's testing of a person is not founded in evil designs. When man is tested and the origin of that testing is from evil then it works in cooperation with man's passion (James 1:14). Thus, the Christian is called to recognize that God may be at work in the midst of a test (or temptation) to prove His righteousness and to prove the victory of faith verses sin. But the temptation is not designed from or for evil for the person. As 1 Corinthians 10:13 shows, God provides a way of escape in the temptation.

The Hebrew word used in Genesis 22:1 is **nasah.** Brueggemann observes that this word and another Hebrew word for testing both point to God's desire to have a loyal people unto Himself. "Testing is no marginal notion in the faith of Israel. It occurs only in a faith in which a single God insists upon undivided loyalty. . . . Testing is unnecessary in religious of tolerance. The testing times for Israel and for all of us who are heirs of Abraham are those times when it is seductively attractive to find an easier, less demanding alternative to God."

The point of this brief word study on tempting has been to show that Abraham faced a real temptation. He was not just walking through this experience with the idea that God really would not demand the life of Isaac. Such an attitude would have been a denial of the trustworthiness of the Word of God he had received and would be a denial of his own commitment to this God. The possibility of the death of Isaac was extremely real and that is what made the temptation so powerful and fearful. It forced Abraham to answer a fundamental question, "Would he serve a God who made such demands?" His answer was "Yes!"

The second point of this verse is found in the response of Abraham to the voice of God, "Behold, here I am." Three times in the narrative Abraham gives this response to questions (vv. 1, 7, 11). As Brueggemann comments, Abraham is a man who "stands before a word. He is addressed. He answers immediately and faithfully. He does not flinch from answering. There are not reasons within his own person to dispute, delay, or resist the address."

It is imperative that the person of faith know where they are in life. This is far more than geographical information; it is a statement of a person's relationship before God. Such a person can hear the voice of God and recognize it. When we are out of touch with our inner self, we are "lost." We are unable to "center down" and hear the voice of God. We hear many other voices and respond to them. But the voice of God is lost in the business of life. A silence before the Lord in which the competing voices of the world loose their power enables us to recognize God's voice and obey.

Brueggemann mentioned that Abraham did not "dispute, delay, or resist the address." Each of those is important. In previous studies in this quarter we have seen how Abraham did all three. In each instance a crisis of faith and obedience was caused in his life. Yet, at this most important time, Abraham is able to hear, recognize, and obey the voice of God. He is able to do this because he trusts the God who has called him. His life is not his own; his life has come from God. The same is true for Isaac. As Jesus spoke nearly two thousand years later, unless a man lose his life, he will not find it.

B. The Word Heard (v. 2)

**2. And he said, Take now thy son, thine only son Isaac, whom thou lovest, and get thee into the land of Moriah; and offer him there for a burnt-offering upon one of the mountains which I will tell thee of.**

In 2 Chronicles 3:1 Moriah is identified with the site of the Temple in Jerusalem. It is the place of sacrifice. There is a heaviness in the word from the Lord. Isaac is Abraham's "only son." How can this be in the light of Ishmael? Has God forgotten that Abraham birthed another child? No! But God knows that Abraham has birthed only **one** son of promise! There can be no substituting for this one son. The son of promise is the son God demands to satisfy His desire for obedience.

This son is further understood to be the one "whom thou lovest." Isaac is loved because of his relationship to the promise. He is the child born out of grace and obedience. He is the child whose name means "laughter."

Both of these remind us of the relationship of the heavenly Father to the Son. The Son is God's "only Son." The Son is the one God loves. It is because of this love between the Father and Son that the Son's life of obedience and joy before the Father can bring about our salvation.

The word for "burnt-offering" is the same as used in the remainder of the Old Testament to describe a sacrificial offering for sin. "It was a voluntary offering that could be offered every morning and evening, every sabbath day, the first day of every month, the seven days of unleaven bread, and the day of Atonement" (**Young's Analytical Concordance to the Bible**). It was a type of Christ who was offered as a sacrifice for sin (Hebrews 10:10). The type of animal offered varied so that all could participate in this offering of self-dedication and thanksgiving. As it relates to the death of Jesus, it is of note that the Lord's Supper (where His death is remembered) is often called by the Greek for thanksgiving, **eucharist.**

II. AMAZING FAITH (Genesis 22:3-10)

A. The Word Obeyed (vv. 3-5)

**3. And Abraham rose up early in the morning, and saddled his ass, and took two of his younger men with him, and Isaac his son, and clave the wood for the burnt-offering, and rose up, and went unto the place of which God had told him.**

**4. Then on the third day Abraham lifted up his eyes, and saw the place afar off.**

**5. And Abraham said unto his young men, Abide ye here with the ass; and I and the lad will go yonder and worship, and come again to you.**

As noted above, Abraham did not delay in obeying the voice of God. The necessary things for the journey were accomplished with little fanfare. There was no indication that anyone else knew the nature of this trip to the mountains.

The expression "clave the wood" simply means Abraham cut the wood before the journey began.

The journey lasted three days. We are told nothing of the conversation during the journey. Yet, verse 4 is full of implications regarding Abraham's vision of another death that would occur on that mountain centuries later. The man of faith lifted his eyes of faith and saw "afar off" the only Son of God on the cross. The writer of Hebrews comments on this passage:

"Abraham reasoned that God could raise the dead, and figuratively speaking, he did receive Isaac back from death" (11:19, **New International Version**).

Discuss briefly some of the thoughts that were likely in Abraham's mind on this journey.

We are told in verse 5 that Abraham and the lad Isaac went to "worship" on the mountain. The Hebrew for worship in this verse is **shachah** which means to "bow oneself down." It described a physical positioning of oneself before the Lord. It was a sign of submission in the presence of one who is greater. No doubt Abraham was deeply burdened with the possibilities facing him; yet, his first thought was to worship the Lord.

It should be noted that this same word is used in Genesis 24:26, 48, 52 to describe the attitude of Abraham's servant who has gone to find a wife for Isaac. It is used extensively in the Old Testament with a pronounced usage in passages that warn of worshiping other gods (Deuteronomy 4:19; 8:19; 11:16; 17:3).

Its usage in Genesis 22 indicates a profound submission to the will of God on Abraham's part. He is a man who has learned that time belongs to God. In Hebrews 10:35, 36 we are told not to cast away our confidence in God's faithfulness because such faithfulness and confidence results in a great reward. In order to have this confidence we are instructed (10:36) to have patience "that, after ye have done the will of God, ye might receive the promise." Thus, Abraham is no longer afraid to trust God with everything, including the sign of the promise (Isaac). As a man over 100 years of age he is not panicky about God's ability to provide. If God desires the life of Isaac, then God will provide another heir. He is going to worship this God regardless of the cost.

This is an important lesson to be learned in our life today. We often approach sacrifices for God with a sense of dread. Yet, none of us are called to make the kind of sacrifice imposed upon Abraham. We fret and argue with God regarding His claims upon our life. Abraham teaches us the liberating power of worship. Such worship acknowledges that God is God. It acknowledges that with God all things are possible. It knows the freedom of a personal walk with this Lord of life. It knows that God is on the side of life regardless of the outward signs. Such worship is truly worship in spirit and truth.

It is the same today. When we go to the mount of God we worship at the feet of the sacrificed Son of God. Yet, we worship not one who is dead but one who is alive. We are thereby called to present our bodies as living sacrifices. This presentation is indeed a reasonable service in the sight of God.

B. The Hope of God's Provision (vv. 6-10)

**6. And Abraham took the wood of the burnt-offering, and laid it upon Isaac his son; and he took the fire in his hand, and a knife; and they went both of them together.**

The story is powerfully and simply told. One can easily imagine the scene as the old man walks side-by-side with his doomed son. The old man's hands are filled with the weapons of death: the fire to consume the corpse of his son, and the knife to slay the son. The young man Isaac is burdened with the wood of his own funeral pyre. This would have been a rather large amount of wood in order for it to have accomplished the burning required by ancient

burnt offerings. It is truly a cross to be borne on the road of Isaac's calvary. The closing statement moves the viewer to tears: "they went both of them together." The father who knows and the son who is wondering are taking the journey together. Abraham will not allow the son to be alone. As painful as these steps are, they are steps to be taken together in faith.

**7. And Isaac spake unto Abraham his father, and said, My father: and he said, Here am I, my son. And he said, Behold the fire and the wood: but where is the lamb for a burnt-offering?**

This is the second instance where Abraham was addressed and indicated he knew where he was. How crucial it was to know exactly where he stood with God at this time. The son's question is not without significance. The lad has recognized all the elements for a burnt offering and knows they have come to worship. But the sacrifice is not apparent to him.

**8. And Abraham said, My son, God will provide himself a lamb for a burnt-offering: so they went both of them together.**

Abraham's response echo's down the corridors of eternity. This is the supreme statement of 'faith: God will provide. An amazing thing is told us about Abraham's God: He tests and He provides. That God provides means that only He is the source of life. Brueggemann comments on this provision, "In a world beset by humanism, scientism, and naturalism, the claim that God alone provides is as scandalous as the claim that He tests."

Brueggemann also draws upon the insights of theologian Karl Barth in this passage. Barth observed that the translation of the Hebrew word for "provide" is usually translated "see." For Abraham to have said that God will "see" the situation would have lessened the power of God's hand in this episode. Barth connects "provide" with its Latin roots **pro-video,** meaning "to see before, to see to, to see about." Thus, God's provision is in reality His "seeing about" us and our needs. God's "providence" is thus an extension of His divine provision for the needs of His creatures. Abraham's faith expressed a profound understanding that God was "seeing about" the business of their lives. He could trust God to somehow, someway, provide. This trust even included the death of Isaac if need be. God's Word was so certain that Abraham was willing to place everything before His all-seeing eyes in obedience.

That God will provide should set us free to live in absolute trust and confidence in His Word. Nothing is more important than faithful obedience. No job or degree or financial security is more important than the freedom to obey knowing He will provide. This is the basis of Christian confidence: God is faithful.

**9. And they came to the place which God had told him of; and Abraham built an altar there, and laid the wood in order, and bound Isaac his son, and laid him on the altar upon the wood.**

**10. And Abraham stretched forth his hand, and took the knife to slay his son.**

Obedience is far more than lip service. We can offer God complacent obedience. Such complacent obedience does not concentrate on delays or arguments with Him. Rather, it pretends to go through the motions. It fails to take seriously His Word and His command. It presumes to know more about what He desires than He has actually given. It is ultimately a lie and knows nothing of life-giving faith.

Why do you think God allowed the test to go as far as He did before stopping Abraham?

But that is not the faith of Abraham. All has been done in full accordance with the directions God had given. Abraham is not ahead of schedule nor behind. Even as the wood is laid in order, so

also Abraham's obedience has been in order. Nothing at all is told of Isaac's response. He is incidental to the story as if his death really would not affect God's covenantal promises at all. And that is exactly the case. God could bring forth another Isaac from the womb of Sarah. What counts in this story is the faith of Abraham.

III. DIVINE PROVISION (Genesis 22:11-19)

A. The Fear of the Lord (vv. 11, 12)

**11. And the angel of the Lord called unto him out of heaven, and said, Abraham, Abraham: and he said, Here am I.**

This is the third time Abraham has identified his place before the Lord. In verse 10 the man of faith had raised the knife to slay the son. In verse 11 the angel beckons him twice. It is as if Abraham is so intensely absorbed in the scene that the angel must strive to gain his attention. More than ever it was important that Abraham know "Here I am." He never lost touch of his place before the Lord. He always knew how to listen and discern God's voice from the other voices crying in his heart. We must not think Abraham is in some mad stupor so that he can go through the action of killing the son. Rather, he is keenly alert to all around him and especially alert to the voice of God speaking.

The voice of the angel comes from heaven. Here is clear testimony that God has been "seeing" (**pro-video**) all along.

**12. And he said, Lay not thine hand upon the lad, neither do thou any thing to him: for now I know that thou fearest God, seeing thou hast not withheld thy son, thine only son from me.**

The "fear of the Lord" is revealed to be behind the testing of Abraham and the provision of God. Ironically Abraham's obedience shifted the focus of the situation. Abraham provided obedience and God was put to the test! In both instances, God and Abraham were faithful. God was faithful to His covenant word and Abraham was faithful to his God.

In this lesson there are several elements that give us insight into living a life under the liberating control of the fear of God. The first is that a life lived in the fear of the Lord is a life lived in contact with itself and God. Abraham always knew where he was with God. Abraham never acted out of compulsion or fear of man in this chapter. He was able to "hear" God and recognize His voice. Second, Abraham had a heart of ready obedience. He did not rush into the sacrificial act outside of God's timing. But he listened for the timing of the obedience. Third, Abraham kept silent about the inner discussion and word from God. This does not mean that we should not get wise counsel in times of decision; but it does mean that obedience is most fruitful when born out of a heart given completely to God's voice. In the booklet **The Way of the Heart,** Henri Nouwen writes of silence that it makes us pilgrims, that it guards the fire of the Holy Spirit within us, and that silence teaches us to speak.

The fear of the Lord is not a paralyzing fear. The fear of what men think of us paralyzes us from genuine actions of love and faithfulness to God. But the fear of the Lord sets our priorities straight.

In Psalm 34:11, 13, 14 were given profound insight into living a life of fear before the Lord. Verse 11 tells us that the fear of the Lord can be taught. Thus, it means that it is not some secret mystery that God keeps for only a few of His children. It means that the knowledge of this lifestyle affects the way we think and decide about life. Verses 13, 14 give six components of the fear of the Lord being learned in our lives. The first three are (1) keep thy tongue from evil, (2) thy lips from speaking guile (lies), (3) depart from evil. Note how these relate to the tongue and speaking what we have deep inside us. The mouth speaks the intentions of the heart. Ultimately there is no way to deceive the mouth. If the heart is bitter and full of lies, then the mouth will utter the spirit of that bitterness. The last three are (1) do good, (2) seek peace and (3) pursue peace. Note how these are related to the principles of the kingdom of God and relate to the Beatitudes in Matthew 5.

B. The Provision Made (vv. 13, 14)

**13. And Abraham lifted up his eyes, and looked, and behold behind him a ram caught in a thicket by his horns: and Abraham went and took the ram, and offered him up for a burnt-offering in the stead of his son.**

**14. And Abraham called the name of that place Jehovah-jireh: as it is said to this day, In the mount of the Lord it shall be seen.**

As noted earlier, the words "see," "look" and "provide" are the same in Hebrew. In verse 13 Abraham "looked" and found the provision of the Lord. This theme of God's provision is echoed in 1 Corinthians 10:13 where we are told God makes a way (provides) for escape in the midst of the temptation. God knew exactly when to halt Abraham's hand and provide the ram. If Abraham had tried to obey based on human calculations of when God would intervene he would have tempted God and failed the test. His faith would not allow him to tempt God in such a fashion. He knew that such manipulations were nothing more than signs of unbelief. He obeyed as if God was actually going to take the life of Isaac. His hope of God's provision was not predicated on prior understanding of what God could do. He was firmly convinced that God was able to give him whatever He desired. Thus, obedience became the watchword of his life.

The Christological implications of these verses are strong. God has provided His Lamb on the mount of provision. Jesus Christ has been sent by God to take the place of all the Isaacs of this world. We are marvelously set free from the bondage of the burnt offering for our own sins; Jesus has paid them all. Now we offer ourselves as living sacrifices (Romans 12:1).

C. The Covenant Reaffirmed (vv. 15-19)

(These verses are not in the printed text.)

The word of blessing was again given to Abraham after this act of obedience. This was the climatic and closing episode of faith in Abraham's life. His life is not tested again. While he did live much longer after this (outliving Sarah) we are left with the impression that his faith cannot be shaken by anything. His concern shifted to the future of Isaac and the choice of a bride (Genesis 24).

Verse 18 gives the key to the blessings of the covenant for Abraham: "thou hast obeyed my voice." Such a theme runs throughout the Bible and is still true today. Obedience brings together faith, hope, and love in a dynamic trio of commitment to the Lord of the covenant.

## REVIEW QUESTIONS

1. How do we stand before the Lord in this generation as Abraham did in Genesis 22:1, 7, 11?

2. What comparisons do you see between the sacrifice of Jesus and this story?

3. What is the significance of the "burnt offering"?

4. What are your thoughts on God's ability to provide?

5. Discuss the "fear of the Lord" as it relates to obedience.

## GOLDEN TEXT HOMILY

"WITHOUT FAITH IT IS IMPOSSIBLE TO PLEASE HIM: FOR HE THAT COMETH TO GOD MUST BELIEVE THAT HE IS, AND THAT HE IS A REWARDER OF THEM THAT DILIGENTLY SEEK HIM" (Hebrews 11:6).

Man was created to please God. "For thy pleasure they are and were created" (Revelation 4:11). Man is a faith creature made with a capacity to believe. We believe the natural phenomena such as sunrise, tide, springtime, and harvest with or without a salvation experience. There is, however, another dimension of faith which relates to the spiritual and which comes as the hearing of holy truth, "So then faith cometh by hearing and hearing by the Word of God" (Galatians 10:17).

God is offended when mankind, from whom He proposed to be pleased, disbelieved Him. Consider His wrath when Israel refused to believe God for the conquest of Canaan. God said, "How long will this people provoke me? and how long will it be ere they believe me?" (Numbers 14:11). "I have sworn in my wrath, if they shall enter into my rest" (Hebrews 4:3).

Without faith it is impossible to please God, but with faith we can please Him. Thus according to this text we are to believe that God is and that He rewards.

We believe that God is the ever existent One. He is. He always was. He will ever be. He said of Himself to Moses, "I am that I am" (Exodus 3:14). While in the Bible no effort is made to prove the existence of God it is replete with evidence. Moreover we are so surrounded with timing evidence that the psalmist declares, "The fool hath said in his heart, There is no God" (Psalms 14:1).

If there were no God, how did the concept of His being get into the hearts of all the people of all colors, tribes and nations around the world both now and from the earliest record of mankind?

If there is no God of holiness, from whence came the ideas of truth, love, service, righteous measurements and confidence in future retributions?

If there is no God, from whence came a functioning universe in which billions of people live and are sustained? Can there be a watch without a watchmaker?

God rewards them that diligently seek Him. God is not a passive, nonseeing, nonfeeling, noncaring monarch. To store up our faith in this wise, loving and caring God the context of this text lists three categories of champions of faith. They are as follows:

(1) Champions of faith with **citations.** This means there is given for each one respectively a candid history. They are Able, Enoch, Noah, Abraham, Sarah, Isaac, Jacob, Joseph, Moses, and Rahab.

(2) Champions of faith with **honorable mention.** The commentary concerning them is a terse composite one. They are

Gideon, Barak, Sampson, Jeptha, David, and Samuel.

(3) Champions of faith unnamed. While we do not know their names, we know of them that they were mocked, scourged, imprisoned, stoned, trampled, slain, exiled, destitute, afflicted, and tormented. The Lord said of them that, the world was not worthy and that they obtained a good report.

You will never experience any circumstance of life concerning which you would not relate to someone or some situation in this record. In it all, God is desirous of pleasure of witnessing your faith regardless of the norms or the extremes. Faith thus applied brings:

(1) Salvation
John 3:16
(2) Victory
1 John 5:4
(3) Freedom in
prayer
James 1:6
(4) Peace with God
Romans 5:1
(5) Justification
Galatians 2:16

It is worth it all that "your names are written in heaven" (Luke 10:20).
**—David Lemons D.D., Faculty Member, Church of God School of Theology, Cleveland, Tennessee.**

## SENTENCE SERMONS

THROUGHOUT THE BIBLE, . . . when God asked a man to do something, methods, means, materials and specific directions were always provided. The man had only one thing to do: obey.
**—Elisabeth Elliot**

GOD HAS NEVER been able to use any man in a large way who could not be trusted in an emergency.
**—"Speaker's Sourcebook"**

TRUST IN GOD is an antidote for fear of men.
**—Selected**

THERE ARE NO miracles to men who do not believe in them.
**—Anonymous**

## EVANGELISTIC APPLICATION

ONLY JESUS CHRIST CAN ATONE FOR THE SINS OF THE WORLD.
The death of Isaac would only have

proved one thing: God can provide another son to Abraham's obedience. Isaac's death had no atoning value. Isaac, although a son of promise, was not sinless; he was not the Son of God incarnate. God had never demanded human sacrifice for sins but only animal sacrifice.

But the time was coming, in the fulness of time, when the divine-human sacrifice would be made. That time came when Jesus the Messiah was lifted upon the cross and slain as the Son of God. Because of His sinless obedience God raised Him from the dead and gave Him the name of Lord of lords.

Our witnessing to Him must draw attention to Him. If He is lifted up He will draw all men unto Himself. If we lift up anything or anyone else before the lost we are lifting up a false savior. How sad it is that Christians often talk about their church to the unsaved. The unsaved will not be saved by believing in a church that has all the right programs and special ministries. Those ministries and programs may help bring the lost to see Christ, but they themselves offer no salvation. The lost are saved as we bear witness to the Son of God who has died for the world.

## ILLUMINATING THE LESSON

"The types of the completeness of the Redemption, as that the sun gives light to all, indicate only completeness . . . .

"Jesus Christ the Redeemer of all. Yes, for He has offered, like a man who has ransomed all those who were willing to come to Him. If any die on the way, it is their misfortune; but, so far as He was concerned, He offered them redemption. That holds good in this example, where he who ransoms and he who prevents death are two persons, but not of Jesus Christ, who does both these things. No, for Jesus Christ, in the quality of Redeemer, is not perhaps Master of all; and thus, in so far as it is in Him, He is the Redeemer of all.

"When it is said that Jesus Christ did not die for all, you take advantage of a fault in men who at once apply this exception to themselves; and this is to favour despair, instead of turning them from it to favor hope. For men thus accustom themselves in inward virtues by outward customs" (from **Pascal's Penses**).

**DAILY DEVOTIONAL GUIDE**
M. Declaration of Faith. Numbers 13:26-30

T. Reward of Faith. Joshua 14:6-13

W. Object of Faith. John 12:37-50

T. Walk of Faith. 2 Corinthians 4:8-18

F. Work of Faith. Hebrews 11:1-6

S. Trial of Faith. 1 Peter 1:1-9

# INTRODUCTION
# TO WINTER
# QUARTER

The lessons for the winter quarter (December, January, February) mark a departure from the Old Testament studies that have occupied us for the last three months. The studies this quarter are taken from the Book of Hebrews and will show the relationship between the Old Testament and New Testament teachings better than a study of any other book of the Bible.

From the series of studies you will see how Christ fulfills the Old Testament rites and worship systems, and how much better the way of Christ is than the way of Moses. The lessons lift up some profound teachings, and at the same time set forth a logical and understandable explanation of the plan of God through Old Testament and New Testament times.

Those who lack orientation to the total meaning and plan of the Bible will find this study of the Book of Hebrews most beneficial. The lessons also contain much practical teaching for developing one's devotional and intellectual Christian life.

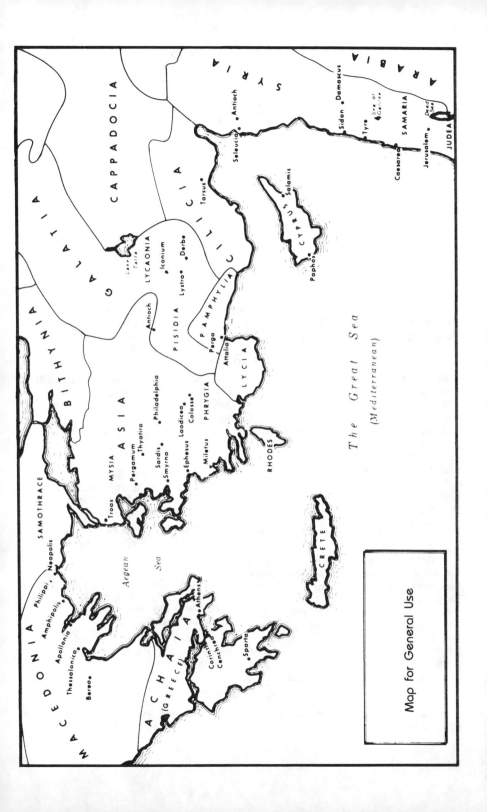

Map for General Use

# God's Exalted Son

**Study Text:** Hebrews 1:1-14

**Supplemental References:** 2 Samuel 7:4-17; Psalm 2:1-12; Luke 1:26-33; Acts 2:30-36; Colossians 1:15-18

**Time:** Opinions vary ranging from 40-90 A.D. But conservative scholars suggest a date of late 60's.

**Place:** Opinions differ, but generally thought to have been written from the city of Rome.

**Golden Text:** "Thou art my Son; this day have I begotten thee" (Psalm 2:7).

**Central Truth:** God reveals Himself fully in the person and work of Jesus Christ.

**Evangelistic Emphasis:** People are saved by faith in the Son of God.

## Printed Text

**Hebrews 1:1.** GOD, who at sundry times and in divers manners spake in time past unto the fathers by the prophets,

**2. Hath in these last days spoken unto us by his Son, whom he hath appointed heir of all things, by whom also he made the worlds;**

3. Who being the brightness of his glory, and the express image of his person, and upholding all things by the word of his power, when he had by himself purged our sins, sat down on the right hand of the Majesty on high;

**4. Being made so much better than the angels, as he hath by inheritance obtained a more excellent name than they.**

5. For unto which of the angels said he at any time, Thou art my Son, this day have I begotten thee? And again, I will be to him a Father, and he shall be to me a Son?

**6. And again, when he bringeth in the firstbegotten into the world, he saith, And let all the angels of God worship him.**

7. And of the angels he saith, Who maketh his angels spirits, and his ministers a flame of fire.

**8. But unto the Son he saith, Thy throne, O God, is for ever and ever: a sceptre of righteousness is the sceptre of thy kingdom.**

9. Thou hast loved righteousness, and hated iniquity; therefore God, even thy God, hath anointed thee with the oil of gladness above thy fellows.

**10. And, Thou, Lord, in the beginning hast laid the foundation of the earth; and the heavens are the works of thine hands:**

11. They shall perish; but thou remainest; and they all shall wax old as doth a garment;

---

## DICTIONARY

**at sundry times and in divers manners—Hebrews 1:1**—Many times and in many ways

**express image of his person—Hebrews 1:3**—Exactly like God the Father

**sceptre—Hebrews 1:8**—Generally an ornately carved and bejeweled rod or cane, carried by a ruler as a symbol of his authority. The sign of Christ's authority was His holy life.

**oil of gladness—Hebrews 1:9**—Oil was symbolic for healing and was also used in inaugurating rulers. The joy that Christ gives heals pains and hardships.

**wax old—Hebrews 1:11**—Wear out

---

## LESSON OUTLINE

I. GOD SPEAKS TO MAN
  A. The Prophets
  B. The Son
  C. The Glory

II. CHRIST SUPERIOR TO ANGELS
  A. The Angels
  B. The Angels Worship
  C. The Angels Minister

III. CHRIST'S EVERLASTING REIGN
  A. The Throne
  B. The Never-Ending Life
  C. The Intercessor

## LESSON EXPOSITION

### INTRODUCTION

The Bible is a book of God's self-revelation. Any concept of God that does not conform to that revelation is false. Man is without excuse in his search for an understanding of the nature and attributes of God. They are clearly revealed in His Word.

God employed various methods to make Himself known to men. The clearest expression is seen in His Son, Jesus Christ. The first chapter of the Book of Hebrews establishes this fact. It sets forth the superiority of Christ to all things animate and inanimate. The radiance of God's glory is seen in Him. He is the exact representation of the Father.

The passage before us contains some of the most beautifully expressed truths in God's Word. Its language is sublimely stated. Its magnificent teachings will open our understanding to many of the wonders of the God whom we serve.

I. GOD SPEAKS TO MAN (Hebrews 1:1-3)

A. The Prophets (v. 1)

**Hebrews 1:1. GOD, who at sundry times and in divers manners spake in time past unto the fathers by the prophets,**

The writer of Hebrews begins by drawing a contrast between Jesus and the prophets. The prophets were recognized as instruments through whom God revealed His will to men. In fact, Amos asserted: "Surely the Lord God will do nothing, but he revealeth his secret unto his servants the prophets," (Amos 3:7).

The message of the prophet was tailored to the age in which he lived. He always voiced those truths that spoke to the needs of his hearers. But at the same time, the revelation which they gave was only a fragment of God's truth. In fact, Barclay points out that many times the prophets were characterized by one idea. "For instance," he wrote, "**Amos** is **'a cry for social justice.'** **Isaiah** had grasped the **holiness of God. Hosea,** because of his own bitter home experience, had realized the wonder of **the forgiving love of God. . . .** No prophet had grasped the whole round orb of truth; but with Jesus it was different. Jesus was not a part of the truth; He was the whole truth. . . . The prophets were the **friends** of God; but Jesus was the **Son.** The prophets grasped **part** of the mind of God; but Jesus **was** the mind of God. . . . The writer of the Hebrews . . . is not saying that there is a **break** between the Old Testament revelation and that of the New Testament; he is stressing the fact that there is **continuity,** but continuity that ends in **consummation**."

The prophets used a variety of methods to convey the revelations which God had given them. On some occasions, they merely spoke the word from the Lord. At other times they used dramatic action to get the message across. For instance, Ahijah the prophet used a new cloak to present a message to Jeroboam. He tore the cloak into twelve pieces and gave ten pieces to Jeroboam. He then explained that God was going to tear the kingdom out of Solomon's hand and give Jeroboam ten tribes (read 1 Kings 11:29-32).

The days of the prophets, as known in the Old Testament, were past. A new day and a new revelation had begun. The prophets had been singally successful in fulfilling their calling, but the world had yet to see God revealed in His greatest and most magnificent works.

B. The Son (v. 2)

**2. Hath in these last days spoken unto us by his** Son, whom he hath appointed heir of all things, by whom also he made the worlds;

In this verse, the writer takes us out of the past and brings us into the present. Not only did God speak in yesteryear, He speaks today. When God speaks His message calls for completed, decisive action. His word is the final authority, and that word has come to us in the person of His Son.

God spoke many times, in many ways, to man in bygone days; but in the new revelation God spoke in one moment, in one word—Jesus—far more than He had ever said before. In this word, in fact, He said all that ever needs to be said.

The actual word **Jesus** does not appear in the Book of Hebrews until chapter 2; but we know, of course, that the reference to God's Son meant Jesus.

So, man not only received a new message, but this message came by no less than the Son of God, the truth of which was almost overwhelming to the early Christians. God had previously revealed Himself primarily through things and, at most, through persons of lesser importance. But the new revelation came by a Person—a Person of highest rank—the Son of God himself.

The appointment of the Son of God as heir of all things was made by the triune God at some time in the remote past. One of the Trinity would be the bearer of Redemption's message to the world. Redemption would be brought to man by no less means than God himself in the person of the Son being born among men.

The preexistent Son was an active agent in creation. Of Him John wrote: "In the beginning was the Word, and the Word was with God, and the Word was God. The same was in the beginning with God. All things were made by him; and without him was not any thing made that was made . . . the world was made by him" (John 1:1-3, 10). When the work of creation was finished, as recorded in Genesis, creation was then full, complete, and final. There was no place for further creative acts. And the Son was active in this work of creation.

C. The Glory (v. 3)

**3. Who being the brightness of his glory, and the express image of his person, and upholding all things by the word of his power, when he had by himself purged our sins, sat down on the right hand of the Majesty on high;**

If one wants to see the glory of the Father, he has only to look at the glory of the Son. Jesus is described as the brightness or radiance of God's glory. God is revealed in the Son so that the whole world may know what God is like. Jesus is the reflection of the Father.

Jesus is also described as the express image or exact representation of the Father. He is the imprint of all the character traits of the Father. As a perfect coin is the exact duplicate of the die that cuts, molds, and imprints it, so the Son, being made perfect, is the exact duplicate of His Father. Through Christ, God has revealed Himself in a form man can comprehend.

Believers also share the nature and characteristics of divinity. God created man in His own image. That image was deeply marred when sin entered through Adam and Eve. But, in Christ man's nature is changed. He becomes a new creation. In all the things the believer says and does, and in the demeanor of his life, others should hear, see, and perceive that he is a partaker of the divine nature.

The writer of Hebrews also said that Jesus sustains all things by His powerful words. John shared that same thought when He wrote: "Thou art worthy, O Lord, to receive glory and honour and power: for thou hast created all things, and for thy pleasure they are and were created" (Revelation 4:11). Paul also wrote: "All things were created by him, and for him: And he is before all things, and by him all things consist" (Colossians 1:15, 16).

The same power required in creating is required in sustaining creation. Christ upholds all things by the power of His word.

A message that appears many times in the Book of Hebrews is that Jesus provided purification for our sins. This is why the Son was conceived, why He was born, why He ministered, why He died, why He rose again, why He ascended to the Father, and why He will come again.

Having finished His earthly mission, Christ returned to the Father, and there sits on the Father's right hand. As the believer's Advocate, He serves as attorney, pleading the cases of the redeemed before the Father and presenting their prayers to Him.

Discuss the significance of Christ's position at the right hand of the Father, in relationship to the believer.

II. CHRIST SUPERIOR TO ANGELS (Hebrews 1:4-7)

A. The Angels (v. 4)

**4. Being made so much better than the angels, as he hath by inheritance obtained a more excellent name than they.**

Angels were important to the Jews. They were aware of how active angels had been in the Old Testament economy. They could picture the vision of Isaiah when he saw "the Lord sitting upon a throne, high and lifted up, and his train filled the temple. Above it stood the seraphims: each one had six wings; with twain he covered his face, and with twain he covered his feet, and with twain he did fly. And one cried unto another, and said, "Holy, holy, holy, is the Lord of hosts: the whole earth is full of his glory" (6:1-3).

They remembered the experience of Elisha when he awoke in Dothan surrounded by a great host. His servant wondered what they would do. But Elisha prayed, "Lord, I pray thee, open his eyes, that he may see. And the Lord opened the eyes of the young man; and he saw: and, behold, the mountain was full of horses and chariots of fire round about Elisha" (2 Kings 6:17).

They also recalled the experience of Daniel when a heavenly messenger touched him and assured him that God heard his prayer the day he uttered it. He added that the prince of the Persian kingdom had hindered the delivery of the message. Also, Michael, one of the chief princes, came to the aid of the messenger. Thus, Daniel was given a vision of the future (see Daniel 10:10-14).

Obviously, many of the Jews had a healthy respect for angels. Now, the writer of the Book of Hebrews is saying to them that there is one who is far superior to the angels, even Jesus Christ, the Son of God.

His superiority is indicated in the previous verse where we are told that when the Son completed His earthly task, He assumed His rightful place at the right hand of God. No angel had ever occupied such a position. It was reserved for the Son alone.

B. The Angels Worship (vv. 5, 6)

**5. For unto which of the angels said he at any time, Thou art my Son, this day have I begotten thee? And again, I will be to him a Father, and he shall be to me a Son?**

**6. And again, when he bringeth in the firstbegotten into the world, he saith, And let all the angels of God worship him.**

The writer continues his argument that the Son is superior to angels. He poses the question of the Father-Son relationship which no angel could claim. His statements remind us of the uniqueness of the Son. Christ was, after all, the greatest One who ever lived upon earth. His ministry was more magnanimous than we could ever describe. His death and resurrection mean salvation for all mankind. His eternal presence with God the Father as intercessor is our one greatest source of help in everyday life. We have everything it takes to make us complete in Him. Paul stated it this way: "For in him dwelleth all the fulness of the Godhead bodily. And ye are completed in him" (Colossians 2:9, 10).

The Father-Son relationship is a beautiful picture. Each is a vital and integral part of the other. Each is an essential part of the completeness of the relationship. When one sees the Father, he sees the Son; when one sees the Son, he sees the Father. Jesus said, "I and my Father are one" (John 10:30).

The writer speaks of God bringing His firstborn into the world. This act seems to refer to the formal presentation of Jesus to the world as Savior, yet man—but, as a man in higher position than any other man.

Then, the angels of God are called upon to worship the Son. However important the angels are in the service of the Lord, they are on a lesser level than that of the Son. They are to recognize His superiority and His majesty, and bow down and worship Him. They must align themselves with every other creature in paying homage to the Son of God. He is worthy of that adoration.

C. The Angels Minister (v. 7)

**7. And of the angels he saith, Who maketh his angels spirits, and his ministers a flame of fire.**

Commentary of this verse, A. B. Davidson wrote: "When His angels are sent forth as messengers they are made winds (Psalm 104:4), when they minister before the throne of His glory they are flames of fire."

Angels are still God's servants actively ministering in our world. In His book, *Angels: God's Secret Agents*, Billy Graham shares the following story.

In the early days of the World War II, Britian's air force saved it from invasion and defeat. In her book, *Tell No Man*, Adela Rogers St. John describes a strange aspect of that weeks-long air war. Her information comes from a celebration held some months after the war, honoring Air Chief Marshall Lord Hugh Dowding. The King, the Prime Minister and scores of dignitaries were there. In his remarks, the Air Chief Marshall recounted the story of this legendary conflict where his pitifully small complement of men rarely slept, and their planes never stopped flying. He told about airmen on a mission who, having been hit, were either incapacitated or dead. Yet their planes kept flying and fighting; in fact, on occasion pilots in other planes would see a figure still operating the controls. What was the explanation? The Air Chief Marshall said he believed angels had actually flown some of the planes whose pilots sat dead in their cockpits.

That angels piloted planes for dead men in the battle for Britian we cannot finally prove. But we are absolutely sure from the Word that angels are actively involved in our world. They are fulfilling the mission God has given to them. They are our allies in God's service.

III. CHRIST'S EVERLASTING REIGN (Hebrews 1:8-14)

A. The Throne (vv. 8-10)

**8. But unto the Son he saith, Thy throne, O God, is for ever and ever: a sceptre of righteousness is the sceptre of thy kingdom.**

**9. Thou hast loved righteousness, and hated iniquity; therefore God, even thy God, hath anointed thee with the oil of gladness above thy fellows.**

**10. And, Thou, Lord, in the beginning hast laid the foundation of the earth; and the heavens are the works of thine hands:**

This passage has God the Father referring to the Son as God. Although such a statement is rarely made by the Father, it underscores the fact that Christ is God. And being God, His throne is an everlasting throne. For those who are tired of the fading, failing things of this world, and who are looking for something that will last, their search can end with Christ. John records these words from Jesus: "I am Alpha and Omega, the first and the last: . . . I am he that liveth, and was dead; and, behold, I am alive for evermore" (Revelation 2:11, 18).

The Father also said that righteousness would be the scepter of Christ's Kingdom. You can always depend upon Him to follow a straight path. He will not bend toward anything contrary to the unmatchable holiness and righteousness of divinity. Only those with perverted vision imagine that they see fault in Him for He is free of all imperfections. He is God and He is qualified to purify and redeem man from sin. He has both a maximum love for righteousness and a maximum hatred for wickedness. Because He holds to that frame of mind, the Father has set Him above all others and anointed Him with the oil of joy.

Again, the Father ascribes the works of creation to Christ. He laid the foundations of the earth. The heavens are the works of His hands.

The believer has in Christ One whose throne will last forever; One whose righteousness is heralded by the Father; and One to whom creative acts are ascribed. Thus, faith in Him promises an unending life and sustaining grace through His great power. He is our source of hope.

B. The Never-Ending Life (vv. 11, 12)

**11. They shall perish; but thou remainest; and they shall wax as old as doth a garment;**

**12. And as a vesture shalt thou fold them up, and they shall be changed: but thou art the same, and thy years shall not fail.**

The Father continued by saying that the things which Christ created will perish, but that He would remain. He likened the fading of created things to the wearing out of a garment.

When you buy a new dress or suit, you give little thought to the fact that it will eventually be worn out or be discarded. After wearing it and cleaning it a few times, you begin to lose your attachment to it. It appears to be fading, wearing out, and soon you reckon that it is useless. The time comes when you toss it aside or give it to someone less fortunate. But God said that it is not that way with the Son. He is forever.

Everyone raves at the appearance of a newborn baby. Its skin is tender; its eyes are searching; and its actions are uncertain. Little thought is given to any change that will eventually come in that baby. But changes will come. Gradually the skin will become calloused, the eyes will become dull, the limbs will become gnarled, the steps will become slow, and the body's movements will become labored. From that vantage point, we will understand that the decaying process began at birth. This is a natural human phenomenon which we cannot avoid.

What a different perspective the spiritual side of life offers. When we know Christ, our spirit remains tender, our eyes are fixed on God, and our actions are motivated by a desire to please God. We maintain a loving, lovable disposition throughout life. Not only that, but we also partake of His eternal life. When other things fail and falter, we will be sustained through the marvel of His grace.

C. The Intercessor (vv. 13, 14)

**13. But to which of the angels said he at any time, Sit on my right hand, until I make thine enemies thy footstool?**

**14. Are they not all ministering spirits, sent forth to minister for them who shall be heirs of salvation?**

The Father again asserts the superiority of the Son over angels. He asks a question which requires no answer. At the same time, He gives assurance that the Son sits at the right hand of the Father. In that position, Christ fills an intercessory role for believers. Our case is presented by One who bears flesh and understands its weakness. He empathizes with us and seeks to guide us in the right direction.

What comfort this truth offers to the believer.

The Father also puts the enemies of Christ on notice that one day they will be mere footstools for the Son. Those who dare to make war with Him will eventually be vanquished. Victory belongs to the Lord. It behooves all men to give their allegiance to Him. Paul wrote of a day when "at the name of Jesus every knee should bow, of things in heaven, and things in earth, and things under the earth; And that every tongue should confess that Jesus Christ is Lord, to the glory of God the Father" (Philippians 2:10, 11).

Verse fourteen describes the function of angels in our world today. They are sent to serve believers. If we have received salvation, we have every right to expect the ministry of angels. We may not always be aware of how they are working or even when they are at work, but they are ministering spirits sent from God to assist us in our service for Him.

Though Christ is superior to angels, this doesn't diminish their importance nor distract from the ministry God has given them.

## REVIEW QUESTIONS

1. What were some of the weaknesses of the prophets as compared to Christ?

2. What is meant by the expression "whom he hath appointed heir of all things?"

3. Discuss the superiority of Christ when compared to angels.

4. What is the function of God's created angels in the world?

5. What Christological truths have you gained from the study of this lesson?

## GOLDEN TEXT HOMILY

"THOU ART MY SON; THIS DAY HAVE I BEGOTTEN THEE" (Psalm 2:7).

The second psalm is a powerful, royal psalm used in ancient Israel at the coronation of the king. It demonstrates clearly that God was sovereign in setting up of the Davidic kings of Israel. Despite the conspiracy of other nations,

or the plots of the people, God said, "Yet have I set my king upon my holy hill of Zion" (v. 6).

In verse seven, the divine decree of the Lord is given: "Thou art my son; this day have I begotten thee." As the Old Testament reveals (2 Samuel 7:14; Psalm 89:26, 27) this decree meant that the king was "begotten" or "brought forth" and was considered to be God's son and God's anointed.

The writers of the New Testament saw this passage as being far more than a psalm to be read at the coronation of a king in Israel. They interpreted it in the light of its prophetic, messianic message. In Paul's message (Acts 13:33), he quotes from the second psalm and declares these words to be fulfilled in Jesus Christ and His resurrection from the dead. Again, in Hebrews 1:5, this psalm is quoted to demonstrate that Jesus Christ is the exalted Son of God and is superior to all prophets, all angels, and all of creation.

Thus, in the person of Jesus Christ we see the fulfillment of all the hopes and prophecies of the Hebrew people in regard to their king. Jesus Christ, God's Son and God's anointed King of Kings and Lord of Lords.—**F. J. May, Associate Professor, Church of God School of Theology, Cleveland, Tennessee**

## SENTENCE SERMONS

GOD REVEALS HIMSELF fully in the person and work of Jesus Christ.
**—Selected**

JESUS CHRIST, the condescension of divinity, and the exaltation of humanity.
**—Phillips Brooks**

GOD BE THANKED for that good and perfect gift, the gift unspeakable: His life, His love, His very self in Christ Jesus.
**—Maltbie D. Babcock**

THE DYING JESUS is the evidence of God's anger toward sin; but the living Christ is the proof of God's love and forgiveness.
**—Lorenz Eifert**

## EVANGELISTIC APPLICATION

PEOPLE ARE SAVED BY FAITH IN THE SON OF GOD.

Salvation is an act of God whereby He

imparts to the believer spiritual life. This impartation of spiritual life follows saving faith in Christ. John wrote of Jesus: "But as many as received him, to them gave he power to become the sons of God, even to them that believe on his name: Which were born, not of blood, nor of the will of the flesh, nor of the will of man, but of God" (John 1:12, 13).

In his natural state, every man is spiritually dead. His plight is altered only by life-giving grace applied by the Holy Spirit. Jesus said: "Except a man be born of water and of the Spirit, he cannot enter into the kingdom of God" (John 3:5). Spiritual birth is just as necessary as physical birth. Thus Paul could say to the Ephesians, "you hath he quickened, who were dead in trespasses and sins" (2:1).

## ILLUMINATING THE LESSON

F.B. Meyer once said, "Christ was born of a woman; yet He made woman. He ate in hunger, drank and thirsted; yet He caused the corn to grow on the mountains, and poured the rivers from His crystal chalice. He needed sleep; yet He slumbers not and needs not to repair His wasted energy. He wept; yet He created the lachrymal duct. He died; yet He is the ever-living Jehovah, and made the tree of His cross. He inherited all things by death; yet they were His before by inherent right. What else can we do but bow in reverence before such a stupendous miracle."

## DAILY DEVOTIONAL GUIDE

M. Christ's Coming Foretold. Isaiah 42: 1-4

T. Christ's Ministry Foretold. Isaiah 61: 1-3

W. Christ's Suffering Foretold. Isaiah 53: 1-12

T. Christ's Resurrection Foretold. Psalm 16:5-11

F. Christ, the Faithful Witness. Revelation 1:4-6

S. Christ's Ultimate Triumph. Revelation 19:11-16

# Our Perfect Salvation

**Study Text:** Hebrews 2:1-18
**Supplemental References:** Psalm 8:1-9; Isaiah 53:1-12; Luke 24:25-27, 44-48; John 1:29-37
**Time:** Around 65-70 A.D.
**Place:** Probably Rome
**Golden Text:** "How shall we escape, if we neglect so great salvation" (Hebrews 2:3).
**Central Truth:** Failure to heed the Word of God will result in tragic consequences.
**Evangelistic Emphasis:** The heart of God reaches out to the lost.

## Printed Text

**Hebrews 2:1.** Therefore we ought to give the more earnest heed to the things which we have heard, lest at any time we should let them slip.

**2. For if the word spoken by angels was stedfast, and every transgression and disobedience received a just recompence of reward;**

3. How shall we escape, if we neglect so great salvation; which at the first began to be spoken by the Lord, and was confirmed unto us by them that heard him;

**4. God also bearing them witness, both with signs and wonders, and with divers miracles, and gifts of the Holy Ghost, according to his own will?**

5. For unto the angels hath he not put in subjection the world to come, whereof we speak.

**6. But one in a certain place testified, saying, What is man, that thou** art mindful of him? or the son of man, that thou visitest him?

7. Thou madest him a little lower than the angels; thou crownedst him with glory and honour, and didst set him over the works of thy hands:

**8. Thou hast put all things in subjection under his feet. For in that he put all in subjection under him, he left nothing that is not put under him. But now we see not yet all things put under him.**

9. But we see Jesus, who was made a little lower than the angels for the suffering of death, crowned with glory and honour; that he by the grace of God should taste death for every man.

**10. For it became him, for whom are all things, and by whom are all things, in bringing many sons unto glory, to make the captain of their salvation perfect through sufferings.**

## LESSON OUTLINE

I. GOD'S WORD IS STEADFAST

   A. Heeding What We Hear

   B. Ignoring a Great Salvation

   C. Testifying to That Salvation

II. GOD'S PURPOSE FOR MAN

   A. Considering Man's Position

B. Crowning Man
C. Subjecting Everything to Man
III. THE CAPTAIN OF SALVATION
  A. Seeing Jesus
  B. Belonging to the Same Family
  C. Destroying the Devil
  D. Helping Those in Need

## LESSON EXPOSITION

### INTRODUCTION

In the first chapter of Hebrews, we were told that God spoke to the Hebrew fathers through the prophets; also, that He has spoken to us through His Son. His revelation has been recorded, and we have it in the form of His Word.

We are admonished in this second chapter to give careful attention to God's Word. Our salvation depends upon our reaction to what He has said. If we heed His message, our hope of redemption is realized. If we neglect that message, our doom is inevitable.

Obviously, we cannot underestimate the importance of heeding the Word of the Lord. Not only is our eternal destiny determined by our attitude toward the Word, but our daily lives are also affected. The quality of our life rises or falls in exact proportion to our commitment to obey the instructions and guidelines set forth in the Scriptures. May this lesson serve to remind us to be more alert to what the Lord is saying to us.

I. GOD'S WORD IS STEADFAST (Hebrews 2:1-4)

A. Heeding What We Hear (v. 1)

**Hebrews 2:1. Therefore we ought to give the more earnest heed to the things which we have heard, lest at any time we should let them slip.**

The word **therefore** directs our attention back to the previous chapter. In that passage we were told that God's Son is superior to angels and that God has spoken to us through Him. Since we know the Son has spoken, we must now pay much closer attention to what we have heard.

We might dismiss the statements of another as unworthy of our attention. We might even ignore the advice of an angelic being. But we dare not turn a deaf ear to the voice of the Lord Himself. He deals only in truth. We ought, therefore, to pay the greatest attention to what He says.

The danger of not listening to Him is that we begin to drift away. The picture is that of a ship drifting aimlessly in the harbor. Left to itself it will land on the rocks. Likewise, no one can keep his life on a steady course who does not obey the words of Jesus.

Seldom does a soul deliberately turn away from Christ. The departure starts with a gradual and slow drifting from Him, and ends with the soul shipwreck and hopelessly lost.

B. Ignoring a Great Salvation (vv. 2, 3)

**2. For if the word spoken by angels was stedfast, and every transgression and disobedience received a just recompence of reward;**

**3. How shall we escape, if we neglect so great salvation; which at the first began to be spoken by the Lord, and was confirmed unto us by them that heard him;**

The message spoken by angels was binding. Most commentators conclude that this is a reference to the giving of the law. This understanding is based on Stephen's statement about the fathers of Israel. He said that they "received the law by the disposition of angels" (Acts 7:53). While God Himself gave the law to Moses, it is true that angels were involved in the events that accompanied the giving of the law.

Any violation of the law is met with just punishment. Any disobedience is acknowledged with an appropriate penalty. One does not have the liberty to transgress the law of God or to disregard the commandments of the Lord. The precepts of God are irrevocable. If He has set certain conditions or assigned certain consequences to His law, they cannot be altered. The conditions must be met; the consequences must be faced. It behooves us to walk within the bounds of His Word. The rewards for doing so are as satisfying as the results for not doing so are devastating.

The writer of Hebrews suggests that if the message of angels carries such great weight; the message which came directly from Christ is even weightier. The great plan of salvation was first announced by the Lord Himself. It was also confirmed by those who heard Him.

Does man need the salvation the writer speaks of? Consider Hamlet's oft-quoted tribute to man, "What a piece of work is a man!" Or think of Sophocles' celebration of the greatness of man, "He is master of all in this life except death, which alone can conquer him." Or, think of Pascal's quiet word, "By space the universe encompasses and swallows me up like an atom; by thought I comprehend the world."

Surely man's gifts are worthy of praise. He has tamed many of the forces of nature, belittled space, and turned the storm into his instrument. He has built great cities and controls vast interests. He has prolonged human life, eased the curse of drudgery, and opened the door to nature's plenty. There is in man a dimension which escapes the formulas of sciences, since man in this dimension creates the sciences. His art, his music, his literature, all refuse to let us discount him. The record of human nobility is inspiring. In the encounter with God man reaches his greatest height. Here is his grandeur, his high destiny.

But there is also the tragic story of man's failure. Endowed with knowledge, he has invented destruction. Given freedom, he has chosen slavery. Made in God's image, he has disfigured himself by commerce with the demonic. Made to be master, he is a slave to his fears. Made to walk amidst the beauties of heaven, he wades through the mire. Made for steady peace and abiding joy, his heart is in torment. Made to stand erect with the dignity of God upon his face, his face is brutalized by lust. Made for love, he hates. Made for strength, he is too weak to throw off the shackles of his sin (Adapted from *The Interpreter's Bible*).

These facts make the question, "Does man need salvation?" a rhetorical question. The obvious answer is yes.

C. Testifying to That Salvation (v. 4)

**4. God also bearing them witness, both with signs and wonders, and with divers miracles, and gifts of the Holy Ghost, according to his own will?**

---

Discuss the timelessness of the admonitions through nature and the written Word.

---

The plan of salvation was devised in the eternal counsels of God. It was provided in time through the death, burial, and resurrection of Christ. It is administered in the present age through the operation of the Holy Spirit. It was announced first by Christ, and then confirmed by those who heard Him. Paul summed up this plan in these words: "I declare unto you the gospel . . . By which also ye are saved, . . . how that Christ died for our sins according to the scripture; And that he was buried, and that he rose again the third day according to the scriptures" (1 Corinthians 15:1-4).

In addition to the announcement by Christ and the confirmation by His followers, God has used other means to testify of the salvation He has provided. Signs, wonders, and various miracles from His hand have all borne witness to the efficiency of redemption in Christ. Through the manifestation of the gifts of the Holy Spirit which He has distributed according to His will, God has confirmed the gospel.

II. GOD'S PURPOSE FOR MAN (Hebrews 2:5-8)

A. Considering Man's Position (vv. 5, 6)

**5. For unto the angels hath he not put in subjection the world to come, whereof we speak.**

**6. But one in a certain place testified, saying, What is man, that thou are mindful of him? or the son of man, that thou visitest him?**

The greatness of God's salvation is seen in the scope of its provision. It not only brings present salvation; it also assures escape from eternal damnation. In addition, it offers a glorious future to all who embrace its provisions. As mighty and glorious and marvelous as the angels are, they are not going to govern the coming world. Man is. That is, the men who have been redeemed by God's grace. Both angels and the world will be under their jurisdiction. Paul wrote: "Do you know that the saints shall judge the world? and if the world shall be judged by you, are ye unworthy to judge the smallest matters? Know ye not that we shall judge angels? how much more things that pertain to this life?" (1 Corinthians 6:2, 3).

In *The Dawn of World Redemption,* Eric Sauer suggests this whole universe over which believers will rule will be populated. "Has God any pleasure in dead matter? Is He not the God of the living? Can inanimate matter praise Him, the Lord of all life (Psalm 30:9)? If only our small earth . . . carries organic life . . . then the fiery splendour of the millions of suns, which yet illuminate nothing, were only 'a vast meaningless and purposeless firework in the dead universe,' and all the stars and heavenly bodies were only burning or burned out craters!"

The writer of Hebrews now turns to the Book of Psalms to raise some questions about man. The verse in the Psalms which precedes this verse (6) speaks of the majesty of the universe. David's thoughts turned to the heavens, the moon and the stars. He knew they were the work of God's fingers; that God had set them in place. When he pondered this magnificent, immeasurable universe, he wondered about the smallness and insignificance of man. How could God possibly be mindful of man, or care about Him? But He does.

In *Exploring Hebrews,* John Phillips wrote: "Throughout the Old Testament era God visited men. He visited Adam in the Garden of Eden. He visited Abraham, Hagar, Jacob, Moses, Joshua, Gideon, Samson's parents, Elijah, Daniel, and the three young Hebrews in the fiery furnace. He visited with Israel in the wilderness and tramped the hot sands of Sinai in their company. He dwelt among them in the glory cloud in the promised land. Best of all, He visited men in the person of the Lord Jesus. It is a fact of eternal astonishment that God's delights should be with the sons of men."

B. Crowning Man (v. 7)

**7. Thou madest him a little lower than the angels; thou crownedst him with glory and honour, and didst set him over the works of thy hands:**

In the order of created beings, man ranks a little lower than the angels. Below man in the order of the universe are animals, plants, and inanimate objects.

There are a number of ways in which angels excel over man. They are faster and more powerful. Also, they operate in all three spheres of the heavens as well as upon the earth.

Several translations render this verse "For a little while" man is made lower than the angels. These versions remind us of the day when we will be made like Jesus and will reign as coheirs with Him.

Not only did God make man just a little lower than the angels, but He also crowned him with glory and honor. Paul wrote that man "is the image and glory of God" (1 Corinthians 11:7). Surely this says something for the vast potential God has placed in every man.

Then, God put man in charge of the works of His hands, and even says that there is nothing that is not subject to him. The Fall has marred and misdirected much of man's dominion. But it seems possible that if sin had not corrupted man's power, he could have, under God, extended the paradise of Eden over all the earth.

C. Subjecting Everything to Man (v. 8)

**8. Thou hast put all things in subjection under his feet. For in that he put all in subjection under him, he left nothing that is not put under him. But**

**now we see not yet all things put under him.**

When God created man and placed him in the perfect environment of the Garden of Eden, He intended that man should have dominion over every thing. He even mentioned the fish of the sea, and the birds of the air, and every living creature that moves on the earth (see Genesis 1:26-31). Clearly, God excluded nothing in His act of subjecting everything to man.

Yet God's intention for man has not been fully realized. At the present time, everything is not subject to man. But that is man's fault. As a result of his sin, the ground is cursed and many of the animals are no longer domesticated (see Genesis 3:17-19). Man must engage in painful toil as he obtains food to eat by the sweat of his brow.

Man will not enjoy the total dominion that God intended for him until all things are restored to God. The ultimate effect of salvation will bring that about. Then a new earth will offer a new opportunity to fullfil the role God wanted man to complete originally. Are you ready to be a part of that new age?

III. THE CAPTAIN OF SALVATION (Hebrews 2:9-18)

A. Seeing Jesus (vv. 9, 10)

**9. But we see Jesus, who was made a little lower than the angels for the suffering of death, crowned with glory and honour; that he by the grace of God should taste death for every man.**

**10. For it became him, for whom are all things, and by whom are all things, in bringing many sons unto glory, to make the captain of their salvation perfect through sufferings.**

The failure of man is here contrasted with the triumph of Jesus. Our attention is turned from man whose sin keeps him from having all things subjected to him and is focused on Jesus who brought to completion the work which the Father had given Him to do.

In order to do the work of redemption, Jesus was made a little lower than the

angels. He came to that lowly position from His exalted place in Heaven. There angels vailed their faces and cried, "Holy, holy, holy" in His presence.

Having become a man, Jesus suffered death for men. The Old Testament prophets could never fully understand this, nor could the Lord's disciples (see 1 Peter 1:11 and Matthew 16:22). They could not picture the Messiah dying. They could only envision Him in glory and triumph.

At the cross, Christ was crowned with glory and honor. Although a crown of thorns was all that was visible, God slipped a royal diadem over His brow and He regained the dignity and distinctiveness man lost in the Fall.

In His death, the Lord showed forth the majesty of the grace of God. He did not go to the cross because man deserved Him to go, but only because the love and mercy of God constrained Him. It was not nails that held Him to the cross; it was love, divine love. How matchless and marvelous is that love!

The statement that Jesus "should taste death for every man" is a strong one. It does not mean that He sampled death, or barely nibbled at it, but that He experienced it in all of its ramifications. He felt its physical agony; He experienced its psychological distress; He even knew its spiritual dimension of the separation of a person from God, the torture of the second death. His suffering for us cannot be overstated.

Christ's death was in behalf of all men. Through His death, He has made life possible for everyone. The invitation reads, "And the Spirit and the bride say, Come. And let him that heareth say, Come. And let him that is athirst come. And whosoever will, let him take the water of life freely" (Revelation 22:17). Everyone who accepts that invitation experiences the life which Christ alone can give.

The writer tells us that Christ was made "perfect through suffering." What he means by "perfect" is the bringing to completion of the work Christ was sent to do. The Lord became man in order to pay the penalty for man's sin. This He did by His crucifixion, resurrection, and ascension. Thus, He is described as the Captain of our salvation.

B. Belonging to the Same Family (vv. 11-13)

**11. For both he that sanctifieth and they who are sanctified are all of one: for which cause he is not ashamed to call them brethren,**

**12. Saying, I will declare thy name unto my brethren, in the midst of the church will I sing praise unto thee.**

**13. And again, I will put my trust in him. And again, Behold I and the children which God hath given me.**

Every believer should read this passage with pride. We are told that we belong to the same family as Christ does. He is the One who makes men holy and we are the ones who have been made holy. His Father has become our Father. We have entered a brother to brother relationship with Christ. We have been accepted into the family of God.

Because of this new relationship, Christ is not ashamed of us. When God came down into the Garden of Eden in the cool of the day, Adam and Eve were ashamed to be seen of Him because of their sin. God had every right to be ashamed of them as well. But, in Christ, all of that has changed. Made holy by His grace, the Lord proudly calls us His brothers. Not only that, He openly and joyfully confesses that we are His brothers in the presence of the great congregation in Heaven. It is as though He would parade us before the heavenly host and say, "Here am I, and here are the children God has given me."

What responsibilities rest on the children of God as brothers and sisters to Christ? Any comparisons to the human family?

C. Destroying the Devil (vv. 14, 15)

**14. Forasmuch then as the children are partakers of flesh and blood, he also himself likewise took part of the same; that through death he might**

**destroy him that had the power of death, that is, the devil;**

**15. And deliver them who through fear of death were all their lifetime subject to bondage.**

Christ identified with man by taking to Himself a human nature. He was a divine person with a divine nature, but He also had a human nature and experienced a human life in its total expression, yet without sin (Hebrews 4:15).

Jesus shared in our humanity not only to redeem us but also to destroy the devil. By His death, He accomplished both objectives. At the time of the Fall, God said to the serpent, "And I will put enmity between thee and the woman, and between thy seed and her seed; it shall bruise thy head, and thou shalt bruise his heel" (Genesis 3:15). At the cross Jesus fulfilled that prophecy.

Satan held the threat of death over all men. But Christ wrestled the keys of death from his hands at Calvary. Later, the Lord could say to John, "Fear not; I am the first and the last: I am he that liveth, and was dead; and, behold, I am alive forevermore, Amen; and have the keys of hell and of death" (Revelation 1:17, 18). Now no believer has any reason to live in the fear of death. Death is for him just a passageway to a better, more abundant life.

D. Helping Those in Need (vv. 16-18)

**16. For verily he took not on him the nature of angels; but he took on him the seed of Abraham.**

**17. Wherefore in all things it behoved him to be made like unto his brethren, that he might be a merciful and faithful high priest in things pertaining to God, to make reconciliation for the sins of the people.**

**18. For in that he himself hath suffered being tempted, he is able to succour them that are tempted.**

Some of the angels fell by way of transgression. There is no evidence that any means of redemption has been provided for them. Men also sinned against God. But in their case, Christ came to their rescue. What a contrast. Christ did not take upon Himself the nature of angels, instead He took upon Himself the nature of man.

In taking upon Himself a human nature, Christ was made like His brothers in every way. He had all the characteristics of an ordinary man. He did not wear a halo, or have a glow emanating from Him. Also, He was merciful in contrast to the self-serving officers of His day. Again and again, His heart was moved with compassion as He observed the needs of the people. In addition, He was faithful to God who sent Him. More than one time did the Father acknowledge that faithfulness and express His pleasure in the Son. Then, Christ made the sacrifice that completely satisfied the righteous demands of God for sin. Thus, He is able to help those who come to Him for assistance, and who look to Him for help.

## REVIEW QUESTIONS

1. What is the general focus of this lesson?

2. Why was it so necessary for the writer of the Book of Hebrews to admonish people to be attentive to God's written Word?

3. Discuss the honored position man was given in God's creative order (verse 7).

4. When will mankind enjoy total dominion that God intended for him at creation?

5. Since Christ was both human and divine, do you think He felt the total impact of temptation as we do? Explain.

## GOLDEN TEXT HOMILY

HOW SHALL WE ESCAPE, IF WE NEGLECT SO GREAT SALVATION'' (Hebrews 2:3).

In the history of the Hebrew people God had shown the validity and seriousness of His message. Those to whom the message had come had been disposed to slight it, either because of the improbability of the matter, or the mean appearance of the messenger. And behind both of these considerations it

might also be that the message was very unpalatable. But however the message might appear to men, it was God's message, therefore necessary to be sent.

We might be negligent of the great salvation. Our own personality, with its great powers and with the claims which God has upon it, we may allow to go to wreck and ruin, instead of submitting to the process whereby God would save us, and make us capable of glorifying Him in a perfect way.

"How shall we escape," is a question parallel to that of Paul in Romans 2:3 "How shalt thou escape the judgment of God?" The question is not of escaping from the danger by some other means than what God has provided. It is as to how we shall get away from God's doom upon us for deliberately and persistently neglecting His loving provisions.

Over against such neglect there is an admonition for close attention to God's provision.—**Excerpts from** *Pulpit Commentary*

## SENTENCE SERMONS

FAILURE TO HEED the Word of God will result in tragic consequences.

**—Selected**

THE BOOKS OF MEN have their day and grow obsolete. God's Word is like Himself, "the same yesterday, today, and forever."

**—Robert Payne Smith**

NOBODY EVER OUTGROWS Scripture: the Book widens and deepens with our years.

**—Charles Spurgeon**

WHEN GOD MEASURES a man He puts the tape around the heart instead of the head.

**—Selected**

## EVANGELISTIC APPLICATION

THE HEART OF GOD REACHES OUT TO THE LOST.

Jesus Christ reveals the heart of God. His plea with Jerusalem is touching: "O Jerusalem, Jerusalem, thou that killest the prophets, and stonest them which are sent unto thee, how often would I have gathered thy children together, even as a hen gathereth her chickens under her wings, and ye would not" (Matthew 23:37).

Obviously Christ would have provided their need if they would have turned to Him. Likewise today, when men turn to God in their guilt, He pardons them. When they bring their troubles to Him, He offers comfort. When they cast their cares upon Him, He shows how much He cares for them. When they bring their sickness to Him, He gives to them a healing touch. When they reveal to Him the sadness of their heart, He exchanges that sadness for joy.

## ILLUMINATING THE LESSON

Of all the fears of man, the fear of death is the greatest. The author of Hebrews is very correct when he describes the fear of death as subjecting people to bondage.

But, again, Christ is the answer. Through Him the bonds of fear are broken, and we become free indeed. We must still recognize the fact of death, but we do not have to fear death. We must still respect death, but we are not forced to kneel in homage before it. We may not want to die, and it is quite normal for us to feel this way; but when we know death must be faced, we will then find a fortitude of spirit to carry us through.

## DAILY DEVOTIONAL GUIDE

M. Forgiveness for Sin. Psalm 79:8-10
T. Joy in God's Salvation. Isaiah 12:1-6
W. Strength for the Weak. Isaiah 40:29-31
T. The Lamb Slain. John 1:29-37
F. God's Love. John 3:14-17
S. The Church Redeemed. Revelation 5:9-13

# Rest Through Faith

**Study Text:** Hebrews 3:1 through 4:13

**Supplemental References:** Numbers 13:17-33; Psalms 95:1-11; 106:1-48; Mark 6:1-6; Luke 7:1-10; Romans 4:13-25

**Time:** Around A.D. 65-70

**Place:** Probably Rome

**Golden Text:** "We which have believed do enter into rest" (Hebrews 4:3).

**Central Truth:** Trust and obedience lead believers into spiritual rest.

**Evangelistic Emphasis:** Faith opens the door to salvation and spiritual rest.

## Printed Text

**Hebrews 3:12.** Take heed, brethren, lest there be in any of you an evil heart of unbelief, in departing from the living God.

**13. But exhort one another daily, while it is called To day; lest any of you be hardened through the deceitfulness of sin.**

14. For we are made partakers of Christ, if we hold the beginning of our confidence stedfast unto the end;

**15. While it is said, To day if ye will hear his voice, harden not your hearts as in the provocation.**

16. For some, when they had heard, did provoke: howbeit not all that came out of Egypt by Moses.

**17. But with whom was he grieved forty years? was it not with them that had sinned, whose carcases fell in the wilderness?**

18. And to whom sware he that they should not enter into his rest, but to them that believed not?

**19. So we see that they could not enter in because of unbelief.**

4:1. Let us therefore fear, lest, a promise being left us of entering into his rest, any of you should seem to come short of it.

**2. For unto us was the gospel preached, as well as unto them: but the word preached did not profit them, not being mixed with faith in them that heard it.**

3. For we which have believed do enter into rest, as he said, As I have sworn in my wrath, if they shall enter into my rest: although the works were finished from the foundation of the world.

## DICTIONARY

**provocation—Hebrews 3:16—**Rebellion

**Egypt—Hebrews 3:16—**The land where the Jews had lived in bondage for four hundred years.

## LESSON OUTLINE

I. HEARING GOD'S VOICE
  A. The Faithful One
  B. The Rebellion
  C. The Encouragers
  D. The Confident Ones
II. EXAMPLES OF UNBELIEF
  A. The Rebellious
  B. The Sinful
  C. The Disobedient
III. GOD'S SPIRITUAL REST
  A. The Unbelieving
  B. The Believers
  C. The Rest
  D. The Word

## LESSON EXPOSITION

### INTRODUCTION

The Book of Hebrews contrasts Christ with others. He has been shown in the previous lessons to be superior to prophets and angels. In today's study, He is shown to be greater than Moses. To convince the Hebrews that there is one greater than Moses was no easy task. But the writer does just that.

Today's lesson also speaks to the folly of unbelief. No matter how great the provisions God has made, they must be appropriated. If one does not receive them, they cannot benefit him. And that appropriation is made by faith. The people of Israel missed so much because of their lack of faith. Are we guilty of the same folly?

This lesson also deals with the fruits of faith. It focuses on the spiritual rest available to the people of God. It challenges us to reach out by faith and grasp the blessings that are all around us. What others have lost through their unbelief, we are called upon to receive by faith.

### I. HEARING GOD'S VOICE (Hebrews 3: 1-15)

#### A. The Faithful One (vv. 1-6)

(Hebrews 3:1-6 is not included in the printed text.)

Three great thoughts are set forth in this passage. First, Christ is greater than

Moses. He is worthy of greater honor than Moses. Moses was a servant who faithfully discharged his duty; Christ is a Son who is faithful over His Father's house. Therefore, says the author, we should fix our thoughts on Jesus.

Second, God is the builder of everything. All that is good and constructive in this life can be traced to Him. And for those who love Him, He makes all things work together for their good. He can take the reverses of life and turn them around to produce positive good. He ever works to build men up and to bring the best to them.

Third, believers are an integral part of His economy in this age. We are His house. And we are to steadfastly persist in the hope we have in Christ. In *A Commentary on the Epistle to the Hebrews*, P. E. Hughes wrote: "Security in Christ does not absolve one from personal responsibility; quite the contrary, for the regenerate man is under total obligation to God." Seriousness in believing should manifest itself in seriousness concerning doctrine and conduct.

#### B. The Rebellion (vv. 7-11)

(Hebrews 3:7-11 is not included in the printed text.)

In a simple expression the author of Hebrews affirms the divine inspiration of the Scripture. When he wrote "as the Holy Ghost saith," he was speaking of an Old Testament passage. Thus the statements of Psalm 95:7-11 and the words of the Holy Spirit are synonymous. The writer obviously penned his words under the sovereign superintendence of the Spirit.

The passage before us contains words of warning with a note of urgency about them. The reader is called upon to give immediate attention to what is being said. He is also urged to be sensitive to the voice of the Spirit. Especially is he not to harden his heart.

The author reminds us of the attitude of the Israelites from the time they left Egypt until their entrance into Canaan. For 40 years they showed a rebellious attitude, and thereby tested the patience of God. In Rephidim they complained because they had no water. At Morah they were unhappy that the water was bitter. In the "wilderness of sin" their complaint was that there was no bread. When God sent them bread from heaven, they got tired of this manna and began to murmur because they had no meat to eat.

Finally, God responded to their provocation in holy anger. Gromack says that this "is always the divine response to the deliberate disobedience of God's revealed, righteous will." Thus, those who were guilty of rebellion were excluded from the land of Canaan: they died in the wilderness. They missed the blessing of the promised land.

C. The Encouragers (vv. 12, 13)

**Hebrews 3:12. Take heed, brethren, lest there be in any of you an evil heart of unbelief, in departing from the living God.**

**13. But exhort one another daily, while it is called To day; lest any of you be hardened through the deceitfulness of sin.**

The author calls for personal soul-searching that we turn not away from God. Salvation is an individual affair. No one can believe for another. Each person is responsible for his standing with God. On a regular basis we should pray the prayer of the psalmist: "Search me, O God, and know my heart: try me, and know my thoughts: And see if there be any wicked way in me, and lead me in the way everlasting" (Psalm 139:23, 24).

The great danger the reader faced was developing an unbelieving heart. Faith is at the center of all Christian endeavor. In fact, the writer of Hebrews later said, "But without faith it is impossible to please him: for he that cometh to God must believe that he is, and that he is rewarder of them that diligently seek him" (11:6).

The result of a sinful and unbelieving heart is apostasy. It leads to an attitude that refuses to cleave to, trust in, or rely upon the Lord. The ultimate outcome is a denial of the faith and a forfeiture of the blessings and benefits of knowing God.

While we are each personally responsible for our own salvation, we also have an obligation to encourage others in Christ. We are admonished to give daily attention to the needs of other believers. There is no time to become lax in our concern for those about us. By pulling together and building one another up in the Lord, we can all be victorious.

The author indicates that we will not always be able to give encouragement. We are, therefore, to do our best while there is still time, "while it is called To day." Jesus warned that the time will come when no man can work. He therefore urged us to seize the moment, to make the most of the opportunities that are before us.

The result of our comfort to other believers is that they do not fall into the trap of spiritual hardening of the heart. The delusive glamor of sin can sometimes produce such hardening. Along with the sin of unbelief, Gromack points out that "sin can also deceive through riches (Matthew 13:22), lusts (Ephesians 4:22), philosophy (Colossians 2:8), and unrighteousness (2 Thessalonians 2:10)."

D. The Confident Ones (vv. 14, 15)

**14. For we are made partakers of Christ, if we hold the beginning of our confidence stedfast unto the end;**

**15. While it is said, To day if ye will hear his voice, harden not your hearts, as in the provocation.**

When we were converted we became a partaker of the divine nature. Peter wrote, "Whereby are given unto us exceeding great and precious promises: that by these ye might be partakers of the divine nature, having escaped the corruption that is in the world through lust" (2 Peter 1:4).

The author of Hebrews says that we share in the nature of Christ. By this he means that we share in all that Christ has for us. According to John Phillips this word **confidence** is translated "title deed" elsewhere. It was used by the Greeks for documents kept in official archives, relating to a person's ownership of a piece of property. Phillips adds that the believer's title deeds to salvation are all in Christ, and he is thus as secure as Christ himself can make him.

The believer is admonished to hold firm that title deed which he acquired when he first found Christ. It is not enough that we start well, we must maintain to the very end the original assurance we gained. Lenski wrote, "The saddest thing in the world is to see a noble beginning made in the Christian faith and then to have this lost before the end arrives."

When we think of someone going back in his spiritual experience, it is always someone else, never ourselves, who would do such a dastardly thing. But we should not avoid the warning flags that tell us that we too may become apostate unless we submit ourselves to God's demands upon our life and unless we are careful in our devotion and service to Him.

In *Why Men Go Back*, Charles W. Conn clearly warns: "It is high time that all of us as Christians arise from the dust and loose ourselves from the fetters that carelessness has put around us: . . . We are God's people, and He is prodding us through His Holy Spirit. In sleeping numbness we can drowsily turn our backs and forget it. We must awake and put on the strength of His Spirit and the beautiful garments of His holiness. We must shake ourselves from the dust, arise, and sit in His presence. We must loose ourselves from the bands of careless living, or even we shall sleep the sleep of death."

II. EXAMPLES OF UNBELIEF (Hebrews 3:16-19)

A. The Rebellious (v. 16)

**16. For some, when they had heard, did provoke: howbeit not all that came out of Egypt by Moses.**

God brought the Israelites out of Egypt with a mighty display of His power. Their deliverance was in keeping with the promise God had made them. His faithfulness along with His ability and willingness to keep His Word should have inspired confidence in the people. It is surprising that they so readily turned away from Him.

The Israelites were the repository of divine truth in their day. Through their prophets, God made His will known. When they rebelled against Him, they were doing so in spite of the truth they had been taught. Moses heard the truth from his mother and chose to identify with the people of God. He renowned the pleasures of sin and the privileges of Egyptian royalty to serve the living God. The people, on the other hand, heard the truth from Moses and others, refused to walk in it, and ultimately rebelled against God.

These rebels provoked God to anger. Their rejection of the truth and resolve to walk in their own willful way called forth His wrath. He still reacts to rebellion in that way.

B. The Sinful (v. 17)

**17. But with whom was he grieved forty years? was it not with them that had sinned, whose carcases fell in the wilderness?**

A variety of words are used by various translaters to describe the attitude of God toward the rebellious of Israel: **displeased, exasperated, disgusted, incensed, and indignant.** Those are attitudes that we need to avoid. Our aim should be to have God's approval, to know that He is pleased with us, and to have Him smile upon us.

The Israelites sinned against God. Sin is falling short of His standard, missing the mark He has set, breaking the law He has given. Sin always breaks the heart of God and alienates one from Him. It behooves us to keep a daily watch over our life that we do not fall into the snare of the evil one and displease God.

Because of the sin of these rebels, a whole nation fell dead in the wilderness. Their corpses lay scattered throughout the desert. It is not likely that every person who died in the wilderness was a rebel. Nevertheless, the entire nation suffered because of the judgment of God upon the rebels. Likewise, our conduct affects many others and wrong conduct causes much pain.

## C. The Disobedient (vv. 18, 19)

**18. And to whom sware he that they should not enter into his rest, but to them that believed not?**

**19. So we see that they could not enter in because of unbelief.**

Two groups of people are discussed in this passage: the disobedient and the unbelieving. In the strongest terms, God vowed that these would never enter the rest of Canaan. This same disposition of heart will keep one out of the eternal rest He offers to all believers.

The world is always looking for a bargain. Many a storekeeper has made money by taking an 89-cent article that no one would buy, marking it up to 98 cents, and saying it is something very special. A pile of advertising folders was laying on the counter of a railroad ticket office. There in large letters was the interesting offer, "$5,000 for 25 cents." This looked worth investigating. But like many of the world's offers, and like all of Satan's offers, there was a hitch to it. If the whole truth had been printed, it would have read, "$5,000 for 25 cents and your life." Or else, "$5,000 for 25 cents and two eyes." Or again, "$5,000 for 25 cents and both hands." The money part of the offer was less attractive by the time the details were known.

The devil comes with the word, "The whole world for just a bit of worship of me." It sounds attractive, but the omitted words should be added: "and the loss of your soul." This is what Christ indicated when He said, "What shall it profit a man, if he shall gain the whole world, and lose his own soul?" (Mark 8: 36). Yet there are many at Satan's bargain counters, willing to pay the present price but unmindful of the second payment. (Adapted from *Let Me Illustrate* by Donald Grey Barnhouse, published by Fleming H. Revell.)

Do you not suppose that the rebels

in the wilderness would have acted differently if they had thought of the final outcome? Will it not pay us to look beyond the present and to consider the final consequences of what we are doing?

Jesus Christ offers an abundant life to those who will believe in Him and obey Him. There are no hidden surprises or second payments. What He offers is real, and is eternal in duration.

## III. GOD'S SPIRITUAL REST (Hebrews 4: 1-13)

## A. The Unbelieving (vv. 1, 2)

**4:1. Let us therefore fear, lest, a promise being left us of entering into his rest, any of you should seem to come short of it.**

**2. For unto us was the gospel preached, as well as unto them: but the word preached did not profit them, not being mixed with faith in them that heard it.**

One of the worst things we can do is to assume an attitude that says, "I've got it made." Living in this age, belonging to a certain denomination, being reared in a Christian home, none of these things guarantee that we are going to make it. Since our spiritual relationship is a personal matter, we must carefully work out our own salvation.

It is easy for us to look at the Israelites and say, "That could never happen to me." But if we live as carelessly as they lived, it can happen to us. With this in mind, we ought to approach every decision prayerfully. Weighing the consequences of our action can help us avoid doing something that will be a detriment to the soul.

This verse contains the good news that the promise of entering His rest still stands. Abraham was promised entrance into the land of Canaan for his offspring based on faith in the promises of God. Likewise, we are assured of eternal life when by faith we come out of our spiritual bondage. What a positive hope is set before us.

Again, the author of Hebrews gives us

a warning. We have had the gospel preached to us, just as they did. What we do with it makes all the difference in the world. How we listen to the gospel and what we really hear is important. If we listen objectively with an open mind and a receptive heart, the gospel will do us good.

On the other hand, if we do not grasp by faith the truth being shared with us, our listening is in vain. The message heard by the Israelites was of no value to them because they did not combine their hearing with faith. When the Word of God is responded to as a divinely authoritative message, it will bring results.

B. The Believers (v. 3)

**3. For we which have believed do enter into rest, as he said, As I have sworn in my wrath, if they shall enter into my rest: although the works were finished from the foundation of the world.**

The writer confidently announced that believers have entered into the rest which God has provided. We entered at the time of our conversion. We continue in that rest as we render service to the Master. But the greater fulfillment of that rest will come in the future. In Psalm 95:11 God referred to this future rest though on a negative note. The unfaithful—those who erred in their heart, who did not know the ways of God—will not enter into His rest.

Then, the writer made a distinction between the creation rest and the salvation rest. In Genesis 2:1, 2, Moses declared, "Thus the heavens and the earth were finished, and all the host of them. And on the seventh day God ended his work which he had made; and he rested on the seventh day from all his work which he had made."

C. The Rest (vv. 4-11)

(Hebrews 4:4-11 is not included in the printed text.)

The word **rest** is used in three different ways in the Bible. Sometimes, it speaks of sleep though this application is not found in the Book of Hebrews. At other times, it refers to ceasing from work and is used of God in that sense

in this passage. The third use addresses the position of spiritual rest to which a believer may attain.

This rest was secured for the believer at Calvary. There Christ finished the work of redemption. Through Christ, we have already entered into rest. We have ceased from religious works to gain divine favor, and have appropriated an abundant life by faith, by resting in the divine provision.

The author encourages the reader to make sure he has entered into the rest of God. Entering His rest is so important that we are exhorted to make every effort to enter. There is a note of urgency, of giving immediate attention, of being decisive. That sense of momentous consequence is followed by a clear warning. To follow Israel's example of disobedience will result in failure for the reader too.

D. The Word (vv. 12, 13)

(Hebrews 4:12, 13 is not included in the printed text.)

The Word of God is alive. Because it is alive it accomplishes the purpose God has for it. Speaking through Isaiah, God said: "For as the rain cometh down, and the snow from heaven, and returneth not thither, but watereth the earth, and maketh it bring forth and bud, that it may give seed to the sower, and bread to the eater: So shall my word be that goeth forth out of my mouth: it shall not return unto me void, but it shall accomplish that which I please, and it shall prosper in the thing whereto I sent it" (Isaiah 55:10, 11).

Charles Erdman wrote that the Word of God searches a man's "inmost desires and motives. It makes evident whether or not he is really seeking for purity and holiness and fellowship with God, or whether lower desires are dominating his soul." He added: "We are responsible to a living God whose all-seeing eye none can escape. He knows perfectly all our disobedience and unbelief, yet He is ready to grant all needed grace as we draw near to Him in the name of Christ."

**REVIEW QUESTIONS**

1. What admonitions did the writer of

Hebrews give in verses 12 and 13?

2. How are we made partakers of Christ according to verse 14?

3. Why is it important not to "harden your heart?"

4. What is meant by term "the provocation" as used in verse 15?

5. What price did Hebrews, who came out of Egypt, pay for their unbelief? What price do we pay because of unbelief?

## GOLDEN TEXT HOMILY

"WE WHICH HAVE BELIEVED DO ENTER INTO REST" (Hebrews 4:3).

God used Moses to bring Israel out of Egypt's bondage. Life in Egypt was very hard, not only because of the physical work and labor, but also because purpose was lacking and satisfaction was gone. There was no longer joy in life. The Israelites were not strangers to hard work before Egypt, but during their stay they lost everything that was meaningful to life.

However, God had promised Israel to bring them out of Egypt and take them to a land of blessing and rest. God's timing came, and He raised up Moses to lead Israel out of Egypt—but the people did not follow God in obedience and faith. As a result, God said they would never enter His rest. The only men of that generation who were allowed to enter the rest God had prepared for Israel were Caleb and Joshua, two faithful and obedient Israelites.

God has rest for Christians today, but many never find that rest because of the same reasons Israel did not. God has given us great promises and opportunities to live in faith, yet many Christians choose to live in bondage and disobedience. Can Christians live in faith and walk in disobedience at the same time? No! The rest God offers us is based on our obedience to His Word, as well as our quality of Christian life. When we live in obedience to His Word we are also walking in faith.

Faith and obedience place us into God's rest. Jesus said, "I am come that they might have life, and that they might have it more abundantly" (John 10:10). In God's kingdom here on earth, God expects His people to work, but because faith and obedience are working in their life, they also abide in His rest. **—Levy Moore, Chaplain, Emmanuel College, Franklin Springs, Georgia.**

## SENTENCE SERMONS

TRUST AND OBEDIENCE lead believers into spiritual rest.

**—Selected**

FAITH MUST have adequate evidence, else it is mere superstition.

**—Archibald Hodge**

## EVANGELISTIC APPLICATION

FAITH OPENS THE DOOR TO SALVATION AND SPIRITUAL REST.

The Scripture repeatedly exhort men to turn to God, to repent, and to believe. . . . Therefore God, in His kindness and mercy . . . produces repentance (Acts 5:31; 11:18; 2 Timothy 2:25) and faith (Romans 12:3; 2 Peter 1:1) in his heart.

According to His promise, God now actually saves all those who repent and believe (Mark 1:15; John 1:12; 5:24; Acts 3:19; 15:11; Romans 10:9-11). On the basis of these conditions He regenerates them (John 3:3, 5, 14), justifies them (Romans 5:1), grants them His Spirit (Galatians 3:5, 15), sanctifies them (Acts 26:18), keeps them (Romans 11:20; 1 Peter 1:5), establishes them (Isaiah 7:9), and even heals their bodies (James 5:15). Thus, God is the Author and Finisher of salvation. From beginning to end we owe our salvation to the grace of God which He has decided to bestow upon sinful men (Henry Clarence Thiessen in *Introductory Lectures in Systematic Theology*).

## DAILY DEVOTIONAL GUIDE

M. Unbelief Blinds Spiritually. Numbers 13:31-33

T. Unbelief Limits God's Power. Psalm 78:40-42, 56, 57

W. Faithfulness to God Rewarded. Malachi 3:13-18

T. Man's Unbelief. Mark 6:1-6

F. Extraordinary Faith. Luke 7:1-9

S. Faith's Victory. 1 John 5:1-5

# December 22, 1985

# God's Gift to the World

## (Christmas Lesson)

**Study Text:** Isaiah 7:10-16; 9:1-7; 11:1-10
**Supplemental References:** Genesis 3:14, 15; Micah 5:1, 2; Luke 2:1-11; Galatians 4:4-7; Philippians 2:5-11
**Time:** Isaiah ministered from 740 B.C. until about 680 B.C. Christ was born between 6 B.C. and 4 B.C.
**Place:** Isaiah ministered in the Southern Kingdom (Judah). Jesus was born in Bethlehem of Judah (Judah).
**Golden Text:** "Unto us a child is born, unto us a son is given: and the government shall be upon his shoulder" (Isaiah 9:6).
**Central Truth:** The course of history is moving toward the establishment of Christ's kingdom on earth.
**Evangelistic Emphasis:** God's mercy and forgiveness of sins are extended to all through Jesus Christ.

### Printed Text

**Isaiah 7:10.** Moreover the Lord spake again unto Ahaz, saying,

**11. Ask thee a sign of the Lord thy God; ask it either in the depth, or in the height above.**

12. But Ahaz said, I will not ask, neither will I tempt the Lord.

**13. And he said, Hear ye now, O house of David; Is it a small thing for you to weary men, but will ye weary my God also?**

14. Therefore the Lord himself shall give you a sign; Behold, a virgin shall conceive, and bear a son, and shall call his name Immanuel.

**15. Butter and honey shall he eat, that he may know to refuse the evil, and choose the good.**

16. For before the child shall know to refuse the evil, and choose the good, the land that thou abhorrest shall be forsaken of both her kings.

**9:6. For unto us a child is born, unto us a son is given: and the government shall be upon his shoulder: and his name shall be called Wonderful, Counsellor, The mighty God, The everlasting Father, The Prince of Peace.**

7. Of the increase of his government and peace there shall be no end, upon the throne of David, and upon his kingdom, to order it, and to establish it with judgment and with justice from henceforth even for ever. The zeal of the Lord of hosts will perform this.

**11:1. And there shall come forth a rod out of the stem of Jesse, and a Branch shall grow out of his roots:**

2. And the spirit of the Lord shall rest upon him, the spirit of wisdom and understanding, the spirit of counsel and might, the spirit of knowledge and of the fear of the Lord.

155

## DICTIONARY

**Ahaz (A-has)—Isaiah 7:10**—The name means "he has grasped" and may be descriptive of the character of this man who was king of Judah for twenty years (735-715 B.C.).

**house of David—Isaiah 7:13**—Nation of Judah.

**virgin—Isaiah 7:14**—Literally "a young maiden" (who most naturally would be a virgin)

**Immanuel (e-MAN-you-el)—Isaiah 7:14**—The name means "God with us." It is one of the titles of Jesus, the Messiah.

**Jesse—Isaiah 11:1**—The son of Obed and the father of King David; an ancestor of the Lord.

**Branch—Isaiah 11:1**—One of the Messiah's titles, prophetic of His being born in the lineage of David.

## LESSON OUTLINE

I. A SAVIOR PROMISED
   A. King Ahaz
   B. The Sign
   C. The Wasted Land
II. A SON GIVEN
   A. A Great Light
   B. A Mighty Governor
   C. A Great King
III. A KINGDOM DESCRIBED
   A. The Branch
   B. The Spirit
   C. The Restoration
   D. The Glorious Light

## LESSON EXPOSITION

### INTRODUCTION

With the birth of Jesus Christ, God broke into the history of man in a very dramatic fashion. Of course, this was not the first time He had moved to the center of the stage of human activity.

When God's children were held in bondage in Egypt, He came to their rescue. This episode also began with a baby—baby Moses in the bulrushes. Someone has said that "God floated His navies of deliverance into this land in the tears on a baby's cheek." He raised this baby to manhood and maturity and through him set His people free.

This entry of God into the affairs of men in Moses' day was but a prediction of the greater deliverance He would bring through Christ. The Lord's coming was not only to bring physical deliverance but spiritual deliverance as well.

The appearance of Christ on the stage of human history was disturbing to the worldly powers. The king was so enraged by the news of one born to be king of the Jews that he ordered the slaughter of the innocent infants of Bethlehem. Later, the religious leaders were so intimidated by the Lord that they orchestrated His crucifixion.

But, as Charles J. Rolls wrote, "The potentialities of Christ are unpredictable, the prerogatives of Christ are unpronounceable and the purposes of Christ are unpreventable." Therefore, His mission will not fail. The course of history is rapidly moving toward that ultimate fulfillment when Christ will establish His kingdom upon the earth. And may God hasten the day.

### I. A SAVIOR PROMISED (Isaiah 7:10-16)

A. King Ahaz (vv. 10-12)

**Isaiah 7:10. Moreover, the Lord spake again unto Ahaz, saying,**

**11. Ask thee a sign of the Lord thy God; ask it either in the depth, or in the height above.**

**12. But Ahaz said, I will not ask, neither will I tempt the Lord.**

The prophets provide a valid background for much of the Christian message. The day in which Isaiah wrote was dark and dismal. The nation was under the rulership of a weak and wicked king, Ahaz. The prophet's aim, among other things, was to show that a better day was coming. Light would replace the darkness and strength would replace weakness, while wickedness would give way to righteousness. He foretold the day of the Messiah through whom the God of all hope will provide an answer to the problems of mankind.

Ahaz came to the throne of Judah in about 741 B.C. at a very young age. He was 20 years old when he succeeded his father, Jotham. He is described as an idolater who caused his son to pass through the fire, and who sacrificed and burnt incense on high places and under green trees (see 2 Kings 16:3, 4).

At one point in his reign, Ahaz was unsuccessfully besieged in Jerusalem by the army of Rezin, king of Syria, and Pekah, king of Israel. During this period and before the invading force arrived, Isaiah was sent to urge Ahaz to trust in the Lord rather than rely on outside forces. But Ahaz was not ready to accept Isaiah's guidance.

Isaiah even invited Ahaz to seek a sign from the Lord when he realized that the king questioned the divine origin of the prophet's message. The Lord would confirm his word and satisfy the mind of the king. Ahaz was given the privilege of choosing the sign and the place where it would be displayed—either above or below.

But Ahaz refused. He did so, he claimed, on the basis of not tempting God. His real reason, however, was that he had already decided to seek help from Assyria. He, therefore, did not feel the need to trust in God and to wait quietly upon Him for victory.

B. The Sign (vv. 13, 14)

**13. And he said, Hear ye now, O house of David; Is it a small thing for you to weary men, but will ye weary my God also?**

**14. Therefore the Lord himself shall give you a sign; Behold, a virgin shall conceive, and bear a son, and shall call his name Immanuel.**

Isaiah's attention turns now to the house of David—the princes and rulers. They, too, are responsible for this decision to find the answer to Judah's problems in a source other than God. They had departed from the example set for them by him whose name their chamber bore. David was a man after God's own heart who kept his confidence in God. They were looking to others for help.

Isaiah warns his hearers that their rejection of his message was also a rejection of God. Even trying the patience of a prophet was no light matter, but they were testing the patience of God. Their public rejection of a sign God offered was a direct insult to the Lord. Such an insult demanded the severest reproof.

Although Ahaz had rejected God's help and refused a sign from Him, God would still give a sign to His people, Isaiah declared. In spite of the rebellion of Ahaz, God always has been and always will be the great Deliverer of His people.

The sign which the Lord would give is expressed in the words, "Behold, a virgin shall conceive." Matthew tells us that this virgin will not conceive by the ordinary course of nature, but by the gracious influence of the Holy Spirit (Matthew 1:18-25).

Isaiah said that the mother would give the child His name. Normally this privilege was reserved for the Father. This act itself speaks of the child being conceived in such a manner as not to have a father on earth.

Also, the prophet said that His name would be Immanuel. It is a name befitting the only begotten Son of God. The name means, "God with us." There would not be one before Him or after Him that could be compared to Him. He is unique in His extraordinary excellence and authority.

C. The Wasted Land (vv. 15, 16)

**15. Butter and honey shall he eat, that he may know to refuse the evil, and choose the good.**

**16. For before the child shall know to refuse the evil, and choose the**

**good, the land that thou abhorrest shall be forsaken of both her kings.**

There was a custom among the Jews —a custom they still observe—to cause a child to taste butter and honey, as soon as he is born, before receiving suck. Since this custom was to be observed with Jesus, it indicated that His upbringing would be the same as that of other children. Thus Luke could write of Him, "And Jesus increased in wisdom and stature, and in favour with God and man" (Luke 2:52).

The prophet also told us that Jesus would reach an age in which He could distinguish between good and evil. This indicates that His development as a human being would parallel that of other human beings. It also shows how low Christ stooped in order to be our Savior. He identified with man in every respect, therefore, He understands our weaknesses and is eager to help us.

In verse 16, Isaiah moved from the sublime theme of Immanuel to more mundane matters that concerned King Ahaz. The child referred to is not the Messiah and the countries mentioned were lands that Ahaz personally abhorred.

The child spoken of here may well be the son of the prophet (see Isaiah 8:4). If this is the case, Isaiah is saying that before this child was grown, both Israel and Syria would be without their kings. At least it happened that way. Before Isaiah's son was grown, both Rezin of Syria and Pekah of Israel were removed from the land of the living. About 730 B.C. Tiglathpileser of Assyria overran both kingdoms.

## II. A SON GIVEN (Isaiah 9:1-7)

### A. A Great Light (vv. 1-5)

(Isaiah 9:1-5 is not included in the printed text.)

During World War II when bombers were invading England, the people were instructed to turn off all the lights in their houses. They were told not even to burn a flashlight or light a candle unless the curtains were closed. The reason for this was that the pilots could see the tiniest light and the peoples' lives would be endangered.

Light dispels darkness. No matter how dark the night, light will penetrate through the darkness. Darkness had turned into despair for God's people in Isaiah's day. But he had for them a message of hope. They would see a great light that would drive away the blackness of the midnight. That light, of course, is the Lord Jesus Christ.

Not only has God sent the light of Christ to His people, He has greatly increased their joy by doing so. The prophet used two figures to describe their joy—a harvest and a victory. Most of the people of Judah, at the end of the eighth century B.C., lived on farms. The season of greatest rejoicing for them came at harvesttime. They also understood the excitement of men dividing the spoil after a great victory had been won. Yet nothing could equal the joy of the good news of the birth of Christ as Prince of Peace.

The Prince of Peace will bring an end to all warfare. The weapons of warfare can be burned for fuel of fire, and can serve the useful purposes of heating and cooking.

### B. A Mighty Governor (v. 6)

**Isaiah 9:6. For unto us a child is born, unto us a son is given: and the government shall be upon his shoulder: and his name shall be called Wonderful, Counsellor, The mighty God, The everlasting Father, The Prince of Peace.**

The prophecy of this passage reaches its climax in this verse. The Messiah for whom His people had longed would be born as a child. He comes as the gift of the God of love (see John 3:16). And the government would be vested in Him.

Then Isaiah gives a list of titles which reflect both the character and the mission of the Messiah. He shall be called Wonderful. He would be wonderful in the whole bearing of His life. He would even be majestic in death and resurrection.

Christ would also be called Counsellor. In that title resides the thought of His great wisdom and His ability to guide and direct the affairs of men. On numerous occasions, the Master displayed that wisdom astonished the men who heard Him.

The Messiah would also be called The Mighty God. This is a reference to His divine nature. He would be both God and man. No one else could ever make that claim.

Then, the Lord would be called The everlasting Father. This name may be more properly rendered, the Father of eternity. As such it denotes His everlasting duration.

Finally, the Messiah would be called "The Prince of Peace." By this title the people of God would understand that He would be a peaceful prince. The tendency of His administration would be to restore and to perpetuate peace.

### C. A Great King (v. 7)

**7. Of the increase of his government and peace there shall be no end, upon the throne of David, and upon his kingdom, to order it, and to establish it with judgment and with justice from henceforth even for ever. The zeal of the Lord of hosts will perform this.**

The reign of the Messiah would be without end. His government would increase continuously, ever growing and expanding. The centerpiece of His kingdom would be peace. The earth has not yet seen the kind of prosperity and the quality of peace that He will bring. The strongest hopes the hearts of men have held will be fulfilled in Him.

The Messiah would sit upon the throne of David. He was to be a descendent of David. God chose David out of a humble background for the purpose of reigning over His people. For the most part, David was faithful to that calling and was in the administration of his government a man after God's own heart. Because of this, he enjoyed a long and prosperous reign. The Messiah, too, would rule over the people of God and would establish the throne of David forever.

Justice and righteousness would be the guiding principles of Christ's kingdom. He will not be influenced by partiality or prejudice. The constitution under which He will govern may be stated in one word—uprightness. He will love righteousness and hate wickedness. His everlasting duration and His righteousness go hand in hand (see Psalm 47:2). In His righteous reign, the Messiah will fulfill the intense and ardent desire of God for the establishment of this kingdom. The zeal of the Lord Almighty will accomplish this.

### III. A KINGDOM DESCRIBED (Isaiah 11: 1-10)

#### A. The Branch (vv. 1, 2)

**Isaiah 11:1. And there shall come forth a rod out of the stem of Jesse, and a Branch shall grow out of his roots:**

**2. And the spirit of the Lord shall rest upon him, the spirit of wisdom and understanding, the spirit of counsel and might, the spirit of knowledge and of the fear of the Lord.**

The ten verses we study in this section are entirely Messianic. In the previous chapter, God pronounced judgment upon Assyria. He had used that nation to punish His people for their waywardness. Assyria was itself an evil nation and although God used them He did not overlook their wickedness. They, too, were punished.

In this chapter, Isaiah has a message of hope for the remnant of Israel. Judah might be compared to a stump that appeared to be dead. But from that stump a twig would grow and the branch which came forth would be the Messiah. Thus, the fairest of earthly flowering shrubs sprang out of what seemed to be barren soil and brought forth fruit worthy of heaven.

The prophet foretold that the Spirit of the Lord would be upon the Messiah. This prophecy was fulfilled at Jesus' baptism. He, then, exercised His ministry in the fulness of the spirit.

The Spirit provided Christ with the equipment He needed to accomplish the work He came to do. These qualities may be divided into three groups: (1) His intellectual powers—wisdom and knowledge: He ever was, and ever will be the personification of wisdom and understanding. (2) His practical gifts—counsel and might: Christ has the ability to advise, with unerring intelligence, in every situation, no matter how perplexing it may be; (3) His spiritual resources—knowledge and fear of the Lord: As perfect man, Christ abounded in the fear of the Lord, never taking one step that was not ordered by God's Word. Even on the throne of all the earth, the highest qualification is "the fear of the Lord."

B. The Spirit (vv. 3-5)

(Isaiah 11:3-5 is not included in the printed text.)

The prophet presents a definitive statement of the rulership of the Messiah. He will take pleasure in the fear of the Lord. He will be guided by and devoted to the Lord in all that He does. Also, He will not judge things by their outward appearance. He will look beyond what the eye can see and the ear can hear. He will not be persuaded by flowery speeches or ingenious defenses. Rather, He will weigh all the evidence carefully and by an impartial examination of the true merits of the case, He will make a decision.

A careful examination of the life of Jesus shows that He was never influenced by an undue regard to rank, honor, or office. His opinions were always impartial; His judgments, without bias or favoritism. He knew what was in man, saw the true state of the heart, and, therefore, was not deceived or imposed upon as human judges are.

From such a ruler the downtrodden of the earth could be sure of justice, administered with mercy. Christ was a friend to the poor and to the meek.

There is another side to the Messiah. Isaiah prophesied that He would strike the earth with the rod of His mouth. The reference is to the ungodly inhabitants. This statement implies that the earth will be extraordinary wicked when He comes to judge and reign. He will not hesitate to pronounce judgment on the apostates. He will render judicial decisions that will affect the wicked.

What comfort to know that we have a king who can bare His almighty arm and smite the kingdom of evil! With His breath He can blow away every refuge of lies. What comfort also to be reminded that His government will be established in righteousness, and faithfulness will be its supporting pillar.

C. The Restoration (vv. 6-9)

(Isaiah 11:6-9 is not included in the printed text.)

The Apostle Paul wrote of a time when the creature would be delivered from the bondage of corruption into which man's sin brought it: "For the earnest expectation of the creature waiteth for the manifestation of the sons of God. For the creature was made subject to vanity, not willingly, but by reason of him who hath subjected the same in hope. Because the creature itself also shall be delivered from the bondage of corruption into the glorious liberty of the children of God" (Romans 8:19-21).

The prophet has drawn a lovely picture of the peaceful happiness of the regenerated earth. There will be no bloodshed among the creatures for they will no longer be carnivorous. They will return to their original food, the green herb (see Genesis 1:30). This perfect unbroken joy will be based on the knowledge of the Lord. The earth will be full of His knowledge as the waters cover the sea.

D. The Glorious Light (v. 10)

(Isaiah 11:10 is not included in the printed text.)

The Messiah is both Jesse's Root and Jesse's Branch. He shall be manifested in such resplendent majesty as to be a banner around which the people of the earth will rally. The whole earth will share in the joy of Him who is both the root and offspring of David.

John gave us a description of the future city of God, the holy Jerusalem, which descends out of heaven from God: "Having the glory of God: and her light was like unto a stone most precious, even like a jasper stone, clear as crystal; And had a wall great and high, and had twelve gates, and at the gates twelve angels, and names written thereon, which are the names of the twelve tribes of the children of Israel: On the east three gates; on the north three gates; on the south three gates; and on the west three gates. And the wall of the city had twelve foundations, and in them the names of the twelve apostles of the Lamb" (Revelation 21:11-14).

John also wrote that the nations of the earth would walk in the light of this glorious city; and that the kings of the earth would bring their glory and honor into it (see Revelation 21:23-26).

## REVIEW QUESTIONS

1. Who was king while Isaiah was prophet in the chapters we consider today?

2. What sign was promised Ahaz and the people of Judah?

3. What are some of the names ascribed to Christ in today's lesson?

4. What unusual qualities, according to Isaiah 11:2, did the prophet say the Messiah would possess?

5. What is the significance of the "girdle of Christ" as presented in this lesson?

## GOLDEN TEXT HOMILY

"FOR UNTO US A CHILD IS BORN, UNTO US A SON IS GIVEN: AND THE GOVERNMENT SHALL BE UPON HIS SHOULDER" (Isaiah 9:6).

Like Jeremiah, John the Baptist, and some others, Christ's work and ministry was decided before He was born. Coming as a babe and growing to adulthood as other human beings was a part of His destiny. But he was not merely a human being; He was also the Son of God, and that was much more important than being the Son of Mary. The scope of His destiny included the role of Savior for all believers; the perfect and eternal sacrifice to God for sin; and the head of the Church. Upon the Church was placed the responsibility to discipline and govern, according to the Scriptures. God's heritage upon the

earth until Christ returned to take it out of the world.

The phrase "for unto us a child is born" is in itself inadequate to designate this particular Child, because even though He was a human child, He was truly God in the flesh. He came to fill an unequaled and irreversible role previously planned for the Messiah. He was truly human in every sense of the word, but also the God-man who accepted the role of humanity and became one of us that He might lift all who believe on Him out of the encumbrance of the flesh to be like Him and with Him in eternal glory. He came to us a babe destined to become King of all kings and Lord of all lords!—**Robert Pruitt, Communications Minister, "Voice of Salvation," Cleveland, Tennessee.**

## SENTENCE SERMONS

THE NAME OF Jesus is not so much written as plowed into the history of the world.
—**Ralph Waldo Emerson**

THE NATURE OF CHRIST'S existence is mysterious, I admit; but this mystery meets the wants of man. Reject it and the world is an inexplicable riddle, believe it, and the history of our race is satisfactory explained.
—**Napoleon Bonaparte**

JESUS CHRIST IS the condescension of divinity and the exaltation of humanity.
—**Phillips Brooks**

## EVANGELISTIC APPLICATION

GOD'S MERCY AND FORGIVENESS OF SINS ARE EXTENDED TO ALL THROUGH JESUS CHRIST.

Who can fathom the distance a sin-stained soul is from God? Yet the love of God is so great that it reaches across that wide gulf and redeems and delivers man.

Through Christ redemption is available to every man. The luster of His glory reaches an unlimited distance, and each man may reflect some of its rays. His immortality and incorruptibility are complete and continual, and everyone may derive life and immortality from Him. Every individual may become a facsimile of Christ, bearing the very virtues of His character, and wearing the impress of His image. Through repentance and faith, any man may have the hope of a painless life in a deathless home where we shall see His face and be like Him in His endless kingdom.

## ILLUMINATING THE LESSON

A distinguished pastor from Britain was crossing the Atlantic on an east-bound steamer, where he met one of our foremost statesmen. The minister asked the American, "What's the matter with your country? What does America need?" The visitor was thinking about the mismanagement and corruption of vast American cities.

"Sir," replied the statesman, "America needs an emperor." "You astound me! As a statesman revered at home and abroad, do you confess that your government is a failure?"

"Sir," said the statesman, "America needs an emperor, and His name is Jesus Christ."

All men need the Savior and He is available to all men.

## DAILY DEVOTIONAL GUIDE

M. Promise of Deliverance. Genesis 3: 14, 15

T. Promise of Comfort. Isaiah 40:1-5

W. Promise of Joy. Isaiah 61:1-3

T. God's Great Gift. John 3:16-18

F. Peace With God. Romans 5:1-5

S. God's Grace. Titus 2:11-15

# Our Great High Priest

**Study Text:** Hebrews 4:14 through 5:10

**Supplemental References:** Genesis 14:18-20; Psalm 110:1-7; Malachi 2:4-7; Matthew 27:50-54; 1 John 2:1, 2

**Time:** Around A.D. 65-70

**Place:** Probably Rome

**Golden Text:** "Let us therefore come boldly unto the throne of grace, that we may obtain mercy, and find grace to help in time of need" (Hebrews 4:16).

**Central Truth:** The believer's steadfastness in the faith is made possible by the priestly ministry of Christ.

**Evangelistic Emphasis:** God has provided a way by which all men can approach Him and receive mercy and grace.

## Printed Text

**Hebrews 4:14.** Seeing then that we have a great high priest, that is passed into the heavens, Jesus the Son of God, let us hold fast our profession.

**15. For we have not an high priest which cannot be touched with the feeling of our infirmities; but was in all points tempted like as we are, yet without sin.**

16. Let us therefore come boldly unto the throne of grace, that we may obtain mercy, and find grace to help in time of need.

**5:1. For every high priest taken from among men is ordained for men in things pertaining to God, that he may offer both gifts and sacrifices for sins:**

2. Who can have compassion on the ignorant, and on them that are out of the way; for that he himself also is compassed with infirmity.

**3. And by reason hereof he ought, as for the people, so also for himself, to offer for sins.**

4. And no man taketh this honour unto himself, but he that is called of God, as was Aaron.

**5. So also Christ glorified not himself to be made an high priest; but he that said unto him, Thou art my Son, to day have I begotten thee.**

6. As he saith also in another place, Thou art a priest for ever after the order of Melchisedec.

**7. Who in the days of his flesh, when he had offered up prayers and supplications with strong crying and tears unto him that was able to save him from death, and was heard in that he feared;**

8. Though he were a Son, yet learned he obedience by the things which he suffered;

**9. And being made perfect, he became the author of eternal salvation unto all them that obey him;**

10. Called of God an high priest after the order of Melchisedec.

## DICTIONARY

**high priest—Hebrews 4:14**—The chief priest. He represented all the Jewish nation before God and to him alone were reserved the privileges of entering the most holy place in the Temple and of performing certain rites.

**throne of grace—Hebrews 4:16**—God's throne from whence He dispenses His unmerited favors.

**Aaron (AIR-run)—Hebrews 5:4**—The first high priest of Israel and the brother of Moses.

**Melchisedec (mel-KIZ-uh-deck)—Hebrews 5:6**—The priest and the king of Salem (the ancient Jerusalem), to whom Abraham paid tithes (Genesis 14:18).

---

## LESSON OUTLINE

I. TEMPTED, YET SINLESS
   A. A Great High Priest
   B. A Sympathetic High Priest
   C. A Merciful High Priest

II. APPOINTED BY GOD
   A. A Compassionate High Priest
   B. An Honorable High Priest
   C. A Divinely Appointed High Priest

III. THE AUTHOR OF SALVATION
   A. A Unique High Priest
   B. A Perfect High Priest
   C. A Called High Priest

## LESSON EXPOSITION

INTRODUCTION

The passage in Hebrews 4:14 directs our attention to the priesthood of Jesus Christ. This is not the first reference in the book to Him as High Priest. Already the writer has said, "Wherefore in all things it behooved him to be made like unto his brethren, that he might be a merciful and faithful high priest in things pertaining to God, to make reconciliation for the sins of the people" (2:17). Also, "Wherefore, holy brethren, partakers of the heavenly calling, consider the Apostle and High Priest of our profession, Christ Jesus" (3:1).

In chapter 4 the writer compares the priesthood of the Son with the priesthood of Aaron and the Levitical order. The Son is shown to be superior. For all that the Levitical order accomplished, it was but a type of that higher order represented in Jesus Christ. Christ fulfilled the demands of the Law while Aaron and his group were only shadows of things to come.

The author also shows that the complete fulfillment of the priestly purpose is realized in Christ, and in Christ alone. While the priests of Israel served a useful purpose, they never reached the heights to which our Lord climbed as High Priest. Only He can stand in the presence of a holy God, representing others who, in themselves, are defiled. Standing for us, He can never fail.

And standing in Him, we can never fail. Our steadfastness in the faith is made possible by the priestly ministry of the Lord. He has not only converted us, He keeps us and sustains us with His grace. At the right hand of the Father, He pleads our case. While He is praying for us, Satan will be frustrated in His attempts to stop us, even as he was when he tried to destroy Simon Peter. We have a great High Priest.

I. TEMPTED, YET SINLESS (Hebrews 4:14-16)

A. A Great High Priest (v. 14)

**Hebrews 4:14. Seeing then that we have a great high priest, that is passed into the heavens, Jesus the Son of God, let us hold fast our profession.**

Under the Law, the priest held a unique position. He was appointed of God, separated to his office and task, consecrated with the washing of water and anointing oil, and wore distinguishing garments and ornaments: the robe, the mitre, and the breastplate. His work consisted of teaching the people, offering sacrifices, and burning incense before the Lord.

Then, the high priest was set apart from the other priests. He represented the Jewish nation in annual intercessory prayer, and came forth to bless the people in the name of the Lord. Also, to him alone was reserved the privilege of entering the most holy place in the Temple—the Holy of Holies.

In this verse, the author proves that our High Priest is incomparably exalted above Aaron and his successors. He supports this fact by a twofold proof: our High Priest has ascended into heaven, and His name is Jesus Christ, the Son of God.

*Pulpit Commentary* states: "The high priest of the Law passed through the veil to the earthly symbol of the eternal glory; the 'great High Priest' has passed through the heavens to the eternal glory itself." He was gloriously received into the highest heaven and sat down at the "right hand of the Majesty on high" (Hebrews 1:3).

The Son of God was given the earthly name "Jesus." He took upon Himself human nature that He might offer Himself unto God. He could make reconciliation for the sins of the people only by becoming man. He bore our nature, the nature that had sinned, yet He was not touched by sin; therefore, He was able to make atonement with God for us through His own blood.

By receiving Him "into the heavens," God testified that He was satisfied with the sacrifice Christ had made. At the right hand of the Father, Christ continues to carry on His high priestly office. He intercedes for the church; He is the Mediator.

Understanding that we have such "a great high priest," we are exhorted to "hold fast our profession"—our faith and trust in Jesus. That trust must continually manifest itself in obedience and love. It must not be an inward trust only. There must be an open confession of our faith in Christ before men.

B. A Sympathetic High Priest (v. 15)

**15. For we have not an high priest which cannot be touched with the feeling of our infirmities; but was in all points tempted like as we are, yet without sin.**

In all things Christ was tempted like as we are. This is shown to a great degree in the story of His temptation in the wilderness. Man is vulnerable in the area of his spiritual life (his relationship to God), in the realm of his physical life (his hunger for food), and in the matter of his aspiration and ambition (his desire to possess kingdoms). The temptation of our Lord as recorded shows Him in each of these areas, yet completely victorious over every attack. It is because He entered into these experiences so completely on the human level that He is able to be gentle with the erring.

Although He is great, He is not beyond caring for us. He understands our weaknesses, our infirmities, our vulnerable points. He sympathizes with us in every temptation. *Jameson, Fausset, Brown Commentary* states: "Though exalted to the highest heavens, He has changed His place, not His nature and office in relation to us; His condition, but not His affection."

Through the Apostle Paul, the Lord has promised: "There hath no temptation taken you but such as is common to man: but God is faithful, who will not suffer you to be tempted above that ye are able; but will with the temptation also make a way to escape, that ye may be able to bear it" (1 Corinthians 10:13).

Christ is our great example in the matter of temptation. Though tempted, He was absolutely in all things without sin. He identifies with us in our trials. Let us emulate Him in all things. He is our model for safe conduct from this sin-infested world to the secure shores of eternal bliss.

C. A Merciful High Priest (v. 16)

**16. Let us therefore come boldly unto the throne of grace, that we may obtain mercy, and find grace to help in time of need.**

Believers are encouraged to come boldly to the throne of grace. In *God's Last Word to Man,* G. Campbell Morgan makes this comment about the phrase "the throne of grace": "In that phrase we have a revelation of God; the Throne necessarily speaking of authority, sovereignity; while grace unveils the deepest fact in the nature of God. John, in the course of his writings in one sentence, declared, 'God is love.' " We fall short of the mark when we speak of love as an attribute of God. Love is His very essence. Grace is love in action. Thus the Throne speaks of law, and grace speaks of love . . . in order to appropriate the activities of grace, there must be submission to the authority of the Throne."

There is but one way whereby we may approach this throne with boldness—through Jesus Christ. To "come boldly" implies a freedom and liberty in speaking. It also implies a spiritual confidence of acceptance with God through the work of Jesus Christ. We, in Christ, knowing His nature as our great High Priest, can with assurance approach the throne of grace.

We are encouraged to approach the throne of grace that we may "obtain mercy" and "find grace" to help in the time of need. "The time of need" is a proper and seasonable time. "Help" is also something that is fit and seasonable—as to the purposes of God who gives it, as to the needs of the persons who receive it, as to the moment when it is given, and as to the end for which it is given.

There will be times in the course of our Christian experience when we will need special aid. At such times, suitable help will be available from God. He is the God of all grace (2 Corinthians 9:8). A fountain of living waters is with Him for refreshment of every weary and thirsty soul. If we "obtain mercy" and "find grace," we shall have "help."

II. APPOINTED BY GOD (Hebrews 5:1-6)

A. A Compassionate High Priest (vv. 1, 2)

**Hebrews 5:1. For every high priest taken from among men is ordained for men in things pertaining to God, that**

**he may offer both gifts and sacrifices for sins:**

The function of the high priest is expressed in these words: "that he may offer both gifts and sacrifices for sin." "Sin which excludes the God-made man from fellowship with the God who made him, and loves him, must be dealt with in some way in order that he may find his way back to God. It is this function which is perfectly fulfilled in Jesus, the Son of God" (G. Campbell Morgan). He offered the ultimate sacrifice of Himself in order to make restoration to God possible.

The qualification for being a high priest includes an ability to bear with the weaknesses and sinful provocations of the ignorant and erring. The ignorant are those who do not know, and the erring are those who, knowing, either willfully or unwillfully wander from the way. Either group can test the patience of those committed to serve them. And yet the priest or minister who has the best interest of His people at heart will find a way to address their needs.

The compassion of the high priest of old for the ignorant and erring was prompted by a consideration of His own condition. He found himself compassed about with infirmity. He could, therefore, sympathize with other men in their weakness. In a fuller sense than the high priest of old, Jesus Christ knows the feeling of our infirmity. He was a "man of sorrows, and acquainted with grief" (Isaiah 53:3). His sacrifice was the once-and-for-all perfect gift in our behalf. His provision is all we need.

B. An Honorable High Priest (vv. 3, 4)

**3. And by reason hereof he ought, as for the people, so also for himself, to offer for sins.**

**4. And no man taketh this honour unto himself, but he that is called of God, as was Aaron.**

The high priest of old stood in no less need of atonement than did the people. There was no one who could offer sacrifices for his sins; therefore, he had to do it for himself. He was to offer sacrifices for himself in the same way and for the same reasons as he offered sacrifices for the people.

Also the mere fact that a man had the qualifications of a high priest did not necessarily mean that he would fill that office. So sacred was that vocation that no man could, on his own, decide to be a priest. He had to be called of God and anointed. It was so sacred a matter that the responsibility for appointing a priest rested with God, and not with man.

When Aaron was called, he was actually separated and consecrated unto the office of the high priest. This was accomplished by special sacrifices made by another for him. The extraordinary manner of his calling demonstrated that the responsibility for his appointment rested with God.

In his book *Let Me Illustrate,* Donald Grey Barnhouse tells the interesting story of God's call to an uneducated minister in Scotland who began to preach among his fellow workmen with great power. Soon his witness took him far beyond the confines of the mining towns. Someone asked him how he had received his call to preach. He replied, "Oh, I had such a burden on my soul for those who did not know the gospel, I argued with the Lord that I had no education and no gift. But He said to me, 'Jamie, you know what the sickness is, don't you?' " I answered, 'Yes, Lord. The remedy is the Lord Jesus Christ.' " And He said to me, 'Jamie, just take the remedy to those who are sick.' That is my call to preach."

C. A Divinely Appointed High Priest (vv. 5, 6)

**5. So also Christ glorified not himself to be made an high priest; but he that said unto him, Thou art my Son, to day have I begotten thee.**

**6. As he saith also in another place, Thou art a priest for ever after the order of Melchisedec.**

The author of this epistle quotes from Psalm 2:7 to show that the office of the high priest was conferred upon Christ by

the Father: "Thou art my Son; this day have I begotten thee." Aaron did not take this honor upon himself, and neither did Christ. Both were called of God to the office of the high priest.

Christ's appointment was made because of His Sonship. Only this qualified Him to be a high priest. None but the divine Son could have fulfilled the office. Christ did not constitute Himself the Son of God, but was from everlasting the only begotten of the Father. On His Sonship depended His being called of God to priesthood.

It is also clear that all the mediatory power of Christ is received from God the Father. His relation to the church as Prophet, Priest, and King is by divine appointment. This is both a mystery and a truth of great magnificence. The Godhead is seen working in unison for the redemption of mankind.

A second quote from the Book of Psalms is given by the writer. This time he refers to Psalm 110:4, "Thou art a priest for ever after the order of Melchizedek."

This call of Christ had no need of outward ceremony to express it, as did the call of Aaron. Yet it had a glory that no ceremony could express. It consisted of the words of God spoken immediately to the Son, and not to any others concerning Him. It indicated God's infinite love and acquiescence in the person of Christ as High Priest.

III. THE AUTHOR OF SALVATION (Hebrews 5:7-10)

A. A Unique High Priest (v. 7)

**7. Who in the days of his flesh, when he had offered up prayers and supplications with strong crying and tears unto him that was able to save him from death, and was heard in that he feared.**

This prophecy concerning Melchisedek is a clear prophecy of the eternal priesthood of Christ, yet the Jews vainly seek to apply it to David. John Calvin wrote: "We know that it was unlawful for kings to exercise the priesthood. It was for this crime of meddling in an office that was not his that Uzziah provoked the wrath of God and was smitten with leprosy (2 Chronicles 26:19). It is therefore quite certain that neither David nor any other of the kings is referred to here."

What information we have about Melchizedek is found in Genesis 14:18-20. He is described as a priest of the most high God to whom Abraham paid tithes. The writer of Hebrews says of him that he had "neither beginning of days, nor end of life" (Hebrews 7:3). He is also referred to as the "King of Salem" (Hebrews 7:2).

Further, it was a rare and almost unique occurence for the same person to be both a king and a priest. Melchizedek, therefore, provides a pattern of the Messiah. It is as if the writer of Hebrews was saying that Christ's royal dignity will not hinder Him from performing the task of priesthood as well.

He who is unique in His high-priestly ministry was subjected to much suffering in the days of His flesh. By the word **flesh** is meant human nature not yet glorified, with all its infirmities. Among those infirmities were hunger, thirst, weariness, sorrow, grief, fear, pain, wounding, and death itself. By the "days of his flesh" is meant His last days on earth, when His suffering, His sorrow, His trials, and His temptations came to a head.

At that time He endured the bitterest agonies of spirit. He prayed with tears, thus bearing witness to the supreme anguish of His spirit. By "tears" and "strong crying" the writer's intention is to express the force of Jesus" grief.

B. A Perfect High Priest (vv. 8, 9)

**8. Though he were a Son, yet learned he obedience by the things which he suffered;**

**9. And being made perfect, he became the author of eternal salvation unto all them that obey him.**

Jesus was God's own Son, the only begotten of the Father, yet He "became obedient unto death, even the death of the cross" (Philippians 2:8).

This was the commandment of His Father, that He should lay down His life, and He obeyed. He experienced in Himself the difficulties involved in obedience, and understood how greatly grace is needed. He therefore looks with pity and compassion upon us in our efforts towards obedience; He stands ready to give us the help we need.

Through His suffering, He is "made perfect." Since Christ is our **perfect** High Priest, the salvation He offers is complete. He is its author because by His sacrifice and by His intercession, salvation is effected in our life. Christ—by His Spirit, His grace, and His glorious power—actually communicates salvation unto us. And this salvation is "eternal": It is endless, unchangeable, and permanent.

This salvation is assured to all who obey Him. No one who obeys Him will be denied, and no one else will be given this glorious gift.

It is Christ alone who is the cause of our salvation; yet He will save none but those who obey Him. He came to save sinners, but not such as choose to continue in their sins. The gospel is full of grace, of mercy, and of pardon to all those who will obey.

Using this passage as a basis for our belief, we can boldly affirm "that Jesus Christ is the only begotten Son of the Father . . . that Jesus was crucified, buried, and raised from the dead; that He ascended to heaven and is today at the right hand of the Father as the intercessor."

C. A Called High Priest (v. 10)

**10. Called of God an high priest after the order of Melchisedec.**

In this verse the author reaffirms what he has already said about the role of Jesus as High Priest. He was not in this position of His own choosing. Rather, He was designated to that role by God the Father. Knowing that His calling was from the Father, He willingly carried out in a perfect manner the task assigned to Him.

There is always complete harmony of function between the Father and the Son. In fact, on more than one occasion the Father interrupted the affairs of men to break in and announce of Jesus, "This is my beloved Son; I am well pleased with Him."

The writer tells us again that Jesus is a high priest after the order of Melchisedek. Melchisedek's priesthood was superior to the Aaronic priesthood. Likewise, Christ's priesthood was of the highest nature and continues in His **person** forever.

## REVIEW QUESTIONS

Discuss the role of the Jewish high priest as compared to a lower-order priest.

2. Why is the high priestly function of Christ so much superior to the high priests which preceded Him?

3. List some of the human temptations Jesus encountered on earth. Do you feel He felt temptation the same as we do? Explain.

4. In Melchisedek's role as both king and priest he provided the pattern of Christ's high-priestly function. Explain this role.

5. Discuss the concept of "the priesthood of all believers."

## GOLDEN TEXT HOMILY

"LET US THEREFORE COME BOLDLY UNTO THE THRONE OF GRACE, THAT WE MAY OBTAIN MERCY, AND FIND GRACE TO HELP IN THE TIME OF NEED" (Hebrews 4:16).

The idea of standing before the throne of an all-powerful God who is capable of destroying both body and soul can be a horrifying thought. In the wilderness, the Israelites trembled in the presence of God and begged Moses to stand before God for them. Most of us are keenly aware of our sins and, like Adam, we would rather look for a place to hide from the holy throne of God than stand before Him in our own righteousness.

God, however, demands that we present ourselves before His throne in order to receive forgiveness. In the Old Testament this was accomplished by the high priest going into the veiled Most Holy Place to make atonement for the sins of the people in order that the judgments of God would not come upon them. All others were prohibited from entering the Most Holy Place.

The work of Jesus Christ changed the way of approaching God. As a result of His sinless life and sacrificial death, the throne of judgement has become a throne of grace; the closed veil has become an open door; and the prohibition has become an invitation.

Our attitude of approaching God no longer has to be one of fear but one of boldness. Through our faith in Christ we can be confident that God will forgive our sins, not because we deserve forgiveness but because Christ has provided it for us. We can be confident as well that we will be able to find the sustaining grace of God when we need it most. Because of Christ we can receive both forgiveness of past sins and the power to live an overcoming life at God's throne of mercy and grace.— **Richard L. Pace, Chaplain (Captain), Fort Benning, Georgia**

## SENTENCE SERMONS

THE BELIEVER'S STEADFASTNESS in the faith is made possible by the priestly ministry of Christ.

**—Selected**

GOD CLOTHED HIMSELF in vile man's flesh so He might be weak enough to suffer woe.

**—John Donne**

SALVATION IS FREE because someone else paid.

**—"The Encyclopedia of Religious Quotations"**

THE LOVE OF GOD is no mere sentimental feeling; it is redemptive power.

**—Charles Clayton Morrison**

## EVANGELISTIC APPLICATION

GOD HAS PROVIDED A WAY BY WHICH ALL MEN CAN APPROACH HIM AND RECEIVE MERCY AND GRACE.

J. Wilbur Chapman once related this story of one of his friends who was a boyhood companion of Robert Lincoln,

the son of Abraham Lincoln. He entered the Civil War and went to the front.
When Robert Lincoln found that his friend
was a private soldier, he said to an ac-
quaintance, "Write, and tell him to write
to me, and I will intercede with Father,
and get him something better."

The young soldier said, "I never took
advantage of the offer, but you do not
know what a comfort it was to me.
Often after a weary march I would throw
myself on the ground and say, 'If it becomes beyond human endurance, I can
write to Bob Lincoln and get relief; and
I would rather have his intercession than
that of the Cabinet, because he is the
son.'"

Every true Christian knows that he
has the best Friend possible at the court
of heaven in the Son of God, who "ever
liveth to make intercession" for us (Walter
B. Knight in *Knight's Master Book of
New Illustrations*).

## ILLUMINATING THE LESSON

There is an important distinction
between a model and an example which
needs to be kept in view. F. W. Robertson skillfully explains that distinction:
"You copy the outline of a model; you
imitate the spirit of an example. Christ
is our example, not our model. You might
copy the life of Christ, make Him a model
in every act, and yet you might not be
one whit more of a Christian than before.

"On the other hand, you might imitate
Christ, get His Spirit, breathe the atmosphere of thought that He breathed, do
not one single act which He did, but
every act in His Spirit; . . . The spirit
of His self-devotion might have saturated
your whole being, and penetrated into
the life of every act, and the essence
of every thought. Then Christ would have
become your example; for we can only
imitate that of which we have caught
the spirit" (Robert Tuck in *The Preacher's Homiletic Commentary*).

## DAILY DEVOTIONAL GUIDE

M. The Way of Blessing. Joshua 1:6-9

T. A Wise Choice. Joshua 24:14-18

W. God's Word Is Precious. Psalm 19:7-14

T. Eternal Life Through Christ. John 6:47-51

F. Power Through Christ's Name. Acts 3:12-16

S. More Than Conquerors. Romans 8:31-39

# Spiritual Maturity

**Study Text:** Hebrews 5:11 through 6:12

**Supplemental References:** Isaiah 6:1-9; Matthew 13:10-17; 1 Corinthians 3:1-9; Ephesians 4:11-16; 2 Peter 1:1-11; 1 John 3:1-10

**Time:** Probably A.D. 65-70

**Place:** Probably Rome

**Golden Text:** "Be not slothful, but followers of them who through faith and patience inherit the promises" (Hebrews 6:12).

**Central Truth:** God's Word directs and equips the believer to mature in Christ.

**Evangelistic Emphasis:** God's love compels the Christian to warn others against the danger of apostasy.

## Printed Text

**Hebrews 5:11.** Of whom we have many things to say, and hard to be uttered, seeing ye are dull of hearing.

**12.** For when for the time ye ought to be teachers, ye have need that one teach you again which be the first principles of the oracles of God; and are become such as have need of milk, and not of strong meat.

13. For every one that useth milk is unskilful in the word of righteousness: for he is a babe.

**14.** But strong meat belongeth to them that are of full age, even those who by reason of use have their senses exercised to discern both good and evil.

6:1. Therefore leaving the principles of the doctrine of Christ, let us go unto perfection; not laying again the foundation of repentance from dead works, and of faith toward God,

**2. Of the doctrine of baptisms, and of laying on of hands, and of resurrec-**tion of the dead, and of eternal judg**ment.**

3. And this will we do, if God permit.

**4. For it is impossible for those who were once enlightened, and have tasted of the heavenly gift, and were made partakers of the Holy Ghost,**

5. And have tasted the good word of God, and the powers of the world to come,

**6. If they shall fall away, to renew them again unto repentance; seeing they crucify to themselves the Son of God afresh, and put him to an open shame.**

7. For the earth which drinketh in the rain that cometh oft upon it, and bringeth forth herbs meet for them by whom it is dressed, receiveth blessing from God:

**8. But that which beareth thorns and briers is rejected, and is nigh unto cursing; whose end is to be burned.**

171

## LESSON OUTLINE

I. IGNORANCE REPROVED
   A. Being Slow to Learn
   B. Living on Milk
   C. Using Solid Food
II. GROWTH ENCOURAGED
   A. Going on to Maturity
   B. Falling Away
   C. Receiving the Blessing
III. VICTORY ASSURED
   A. Being Confident
   B. Helping Others
   C. Possessing the Inheritance

## LESSON EXPOSITION

INTRODUCTION

The goal toward which every believer should be moving is maturity in Christ. The Apostle Paul presents us with this challenge: "And he gave some, apostles; and some, prophets; and some, evangelists; and some, pastors and teachers; For the perfecting of the saints, for the work of the ministry, for the edifying of the body of Christ: Till we all come in the unity of the faith, and of the knowledge of the Son of God, unto a perfect man, unto the measure of the stature of the fulness of Christ: That we henceforth be no more children, tossed to and fro, and carried about with every wind of doctrine, by the sleight of men, and cunning craftiness, whereby they lie in wait to deceive; But speaking the truth in love, may grow up into him in all things, which is the head, even Christ: From whom the whole body fitly joined together and compacted by that which every joint supplieth, according to the effectual working in the measure of every part, maketh increase of the body unto the edifying of itself in love" (Ephesians 4:11-16).

In an attempt to clarify what the apostle is saying, the *New International Version* makes two important distinctions in its translation. Verse 12 is translated "to prepare God's people for works of service, so that the body of Christ may be built up." Verse 16 is rendered that the whole body "grows and builds itself up in love, as each part does its work."

In the church whose members are moving toward maturity, each individual has found his place of service and is doing his part to enhance the cause of Christ. By this gauge a church may measure the degree of maturity it has attained. Having determined where it stands, a church can take steps to overcome its weaknesses.

I. IGNORANCE REPROVED (Hebrews 5: 11-14)

A. Being Slow to Learn (vv. 11, 12)

**Hebrews 5:11. Of whom we have many things to say, and hard to be uttered, seeing ye are dull of hearing.**

**12. For when for the time ye ought to be teachers, ye have need that one teach you again which be the first principles of the oracles of God; and are become such as have need of milk, and not strong meat.**

The subject with which the writer has been dealing is the priestly ministry of Christ. There is much more to be said about this facet of Christ's work. The author apparently feels that his time is limited for addressing such a large theme and later confesses that he has written a short letter. Knowing precisely what to write in a short span of time became a problem for him.

Another problem he faced was that this subject was hard to explain. He wanted to interpret what he was writing in a manner that those who read it would perceive the biblical truth it offered. All truth has to be presented in a way that it can be understood. Only when we understand a matter can we apply its principles to our life.

The writer's problem was complicated by the fact that his readers were slow to learn. The indication is that they had no desire to explore new truths. The situation was made more difficult because they were disinterested by personal choice. Apparently they had been interested at an earlier time, but their doubts had destroyed that concern.

The writer says that his readers had not followed the natural processes of spiritual growth. Peter described that process thusly: "As newborn babes, desire the sincere milk of the word, that ye may grow thereby" (1 Peter 2:2). The tragedy with these folk was that they had never left that state of infancy. They had been saved a long time, but they had not matured in Christ. They should be teaching others by now, but they still needed to be taught even the elementary matters of Christian life and conduct.

These readers had regressed to the point that they needed someone to refresh their memory about the most basic truths of God's Word. They needed to be reminded of man's lost condition and of his inability to save himself. Also, they had forgotten the meaning of the Jewish sacrificial system and its fulfillment in the death and resurrection of Christ.

Learning is a two-way street. Both the teacher and the student are involved. If either fails to do his part, learning will not take place.

B. Living on Milk (v. 13)

**13. For every one that useth milk is unskilful in the word of righteousness: for he is a babe.**

The readers of this letter were on a spiritual milk diet. Milk is great for babes, but it is hardly an adequate diet for adults. A milk diet, in a spiritual sense, refers to the earliest stages of the Christian faith. These believers had not advanced beyond their starting point in Christ. They could not handle strong meat; therefore they lacked solid nourishment.

In their infantile state of mind they did not have enough experience to determine what was right and what was wrong. They needed someone to tell them what to do and how to do it. They could not turn to the Scriptures to find solutions to their problems. Every believer should reach a level of spiritual maturity

in which he can find guidance in God's Word.

In *Stand Bold in Grace*, Robert G. Gromack offers these thoughts: "There is a difference between maturity and spirituality and between immaturity and carnality. Maturity involves time, growth, and experience, whereas spirituality stresses a believer's momentary relationship to the Holy Spirit. A believer who is walking in the Spirit is spiritual because he wants to be controlled by Him, but that same Christian may be immature if he has just been saved for a short time (Galatians 5:16). . . . The goal of each saint should be maturity and spirituality. . . . The readers were basically immature with periodic lapses into carnality."

Perhaps a moment of personal examination would be in order. How much have you advanced in Christ since your conversion? Have you gone beyond the elementary stages of the Christian life? Are you still on a milk diet, or have you begun to take solid food? Are you now a mature Christian who has found spiritual nourishment that is producing growth?

C. Using Solid Food (v. 14)

**14. But strong meat belongeth to them that are of full age, even those who by reason of use have their senses exercised to discern both good and evil.**

Not everyone arrives at maturity in the same way. Circumstances of life may force some into maturity sooner than others. For example, a lad's father dies and much of the responsibility for the support of the family falls to him. He begins to act in ways that he would not have acted, had his father not died, until a few years later. Thus, he is, in a sense, rushed into maturity. But whether one comes to maturity early or later, the results are the same. As a mature person he is ready to give support, rather than crave it or depend upon it. He dares to stand alone if need be; to be an oak, not a vine.

Mature Christians are said to be full-grown men and women. They are grown-up people who act like grown-up people. Paul expressed it this way: "When I was a child, I spake as a child, I understood as a child, I thought as a child: but when I became a man, I put away childish things" (1 Corinthians 13: 11). Having reached this level of maturity, they are ready for solid food. No more milk only, but strong meat now.

Mature believers have learned how to make sound decisions. They have made mistakes over the years, but they have learned from them. Now they know more about what they ought to do and what will only result in trouble. They have also discovered that the Word of God speaks to their particular situation. It is not a book written for the first century only. It has spoken to people in every age, and the full-grown Christian finds in its pages the guidance that leads to victorious living.

The person who has become mature in Christ is sensitive to the way he lives. He sees dangers that a less mature person would never see. He is careful to order his life to conform to the principles of God's Word. He is able to distinguish right from wrong. His keen perception tells him what is good for him and what is bad for him. He therefore avoids the pitfalls to which many others fall prey.

II. GROWTH ENCOURAGED (Hebrews 6:1-8)

A. Going on to Maturity (vv. 1-3)

**Hebrews 6:1. Therefore leaving the principles of the doctrine of Christ, let us go on unto perfection; not laying again the foundation of repentance from dead works, and of faith toward God,**

**2. Of the doctrine of baptisms, and of laying on of hands, and of resurrection of the dead, and of eternal judgment.**

**3. And this will we do, if God permit.**

This passage begins with the word **therefore:** It calls to our attention what has been said previously. The author has shown that his readers have not developed in their spiritual experience. He

is now saying to them that it is time to begin to mature. They had gotten no further than the elementary teachings about Christ, and so they needed to move into other areas of His unsearchable riches.

The author then identifies those things which he regards as elementary, and warns against laying a second foundation. Once the foundation is lain, one begins to erect the building. The foundational matters he refers to are repentance and faith. They are the two sides of the coin of conversion. A man must repent of his sins and place his faith in Jesus Christ in order to be saved. Once he has done that his past sins are under the blood and his name is written in the Lamb's Book of Life. He never has to repeat that procedure again with reference to his past.

Neither is there any necessity for repeated baptisms. The believer's baptism is based on the once-for-all-time sacrifice which Christ made. It symbolizes a public identification with Christ in His death and resurrection.

Also the laying on of hands was practiced under the Law (Leviticus 1:4; 16: 21) as well as by Jesus (Matthew 19:13; Mark 7:32, 33) and His apostles (Acts 6:6; 8:17; 1 Timothy 4:14; 5:22). It symbolized recognition, identification, and approval.

The two other themes mentioned are the resurrection of the dead and eternal judgment. Believers must not stop with these six truths but are challenged to explore all facets of divine truth. The author then asserts that he and the readers will go on from immaturity to maturity, as God permits and enables.

B. Falling Away (vv. 4-6)

**4. For it is impossible for those who were once enlightened, and have tasted of the heavenly gift, and were made partakers of the Holy Ghost,**

**5. And have tasted the good word of God, and the powers of the world to come,**

**6. If they shall fall away, to renew them again unto repentance; seeing they crucify to themselves the Son**

of God afresh, and put him to an open shame.

There are four **impossibles** in the Book of Hebrews. The first one affirms that it is impossible for God to lie (6:18); the second, it is impossible for the blood of sheep and goats to take away sin (10:4); the third, "without faith it is impossible to please [God]" (11:6); the fourth impossible is in this passage. It declares that it is impossible for those who have experienced the grace of God and have become apostates to be brought again to repentance (vv. 4-6).

The writer ties this warning to the preceding admonition to move from infancy to maturity. The implication is that our failure to grow may result in regression. And that regression can lead to apostasy.

The writer offers a list of characteristics common to all believers. He speaks of being enlightened. Believers have discovered the truth; they have received Him who is the Light of the world. He writes of tasting the sweetness of the heavenly gift. Perhaps he had the words of the psalmist in mind, "O taste and see that the Lord is good: blessed is the man that trusteth in him" (Psalm 34:8). The author also talks of receiving the Holy Spirit. The Spirit is the seal and guarantee of our inheritance in Christ Jesus. He guides us into the things the Lord would have us do and then enables us to do them. Then the author writes of realizing how good the Word of God is. Only in God's Word can we find the true meaning of life. What a different perspective we have of life when we see it from the viewpoint of the Bible. Finally the writer speaks of feeling the mighty powers of the world to come, of being touched by the spiritual resources of the eternal world. In this present age the believer experiences the wonder and blessedness of the age to come.

Then the author projects a tragic picture. It is possible to fall away after having experienced all that is mentioned. And the consequences are far-reaching. As William Barclay observes: "Every person who, to save his life or comfort, denies Christ, aims a body-blow at the Church, for it means that his life and comfort are dearer to him than his religion; it means that Jesus Christ is not really his Lord; it means that there is something more precious to him than Jesus Christ. . . . When we sin we crucify Christ again. Sin does not only break God's law; again and again it breaks God's heart . . . . When we sin the world will say: 'So that is all that Christianity is worth. So that is all this Christ can do. So that is all the Cross achieved.' It is bad enough when a church member falls into sin in that he brings shame to himself and discredit on his church; but what is worse is that he draws men's taunts and jibes and jeers on Christ. He shames his Lord and makes men laugh at the Cross."

C. Receiving the Blessing (vv. 7, 8)

**7. For the earth which drinketh in the rain that cometh oft upon it, and bringeth forth herbs meet for them by whom it is dressed, receiveth blessing from God:**

**8. But that which beareth thorns and briers is rejected, and is nigh unto cursing; whose end is to be burned.**

The author turns to nature and agriculture to illustrate the truth he is conveying. He draws a sharp distinction between obedience and disobedience in the life of a follower of the Lord Jesus Christ.

The richness of the land is determined by the quality of the goods it produces. When the ground drinks in the rain and yields a useful crop to those for whose benefit it is cultivated, it can be said that it is land which has the blessing of God upon it. Likewise, the believer who is bearing fruit and moving toward maturity is pleasing God and receiving of His blessings. The amount of fruit one bears will vary from individual to individual. One's background and opportunity for development in Christ will be factors in his growth and productive skills. When one walks in obedience to God, he can depend upon the blessings of God in his life.

The life of disobedience is likened

to land that only produces thorns and thistles. Such living meets with divine disapproval. It is regarded as worthless; it has lost its value. It indicates that one has become reprobate.

In a state of disobedience one is on the verge of being cursed. He stands in danger of the judgment of God upon his life because of his conduct.

The final fate of the disobedient is burning even as a crop that is worthless is used for fuel. All that stems from carnality will be consumed because it has no eternal value. It behooves the believer to walk in obedience.

III. VICTORY ASSURED (Hebrews 6:9-12)

A. Being Confident (v. 9)

(Hebrews 6:9 is not included in the printed text.)

The author now expresses a strong vote of confidence in his readers. Although he has given them this stern warning, he is fully persuaded that they are going to walk in obedience. The writer used great wisdom in his approach. He pointed out the problem that they could face, but expressed his conviction that they would go on to maturity.

These words must have been encouraging to the readers. How helpful it can be to have someone express their belief that you are going to make it, that you have what it takes to be victorious. This kind of language is found in many different places in the Bible. Dr. Paul Tournier, in his book, *A Doctor's Casebook,* has a paragraph on what he calls the personalism of the Bible. "God says to Moses, 'I know thy name' " (Exodus 33:17). He says to Cyrus, "I am the Lord which call thee by thy name" (Isaiah 45:3). These texts express the essence of the personalism of the Bible. One is struck, on reading the Bible, by the importance in it of personal names. Whole chapters are devoted to long genealogies. When I was young I used to think that they could well have been dropped from the biblical Canon. But I have since realized that these series of proper names bear witness to the fact that, in the biblical

perspective, man is neither a thing nor an abstraction, neither a species nor an idea, that he is not a fraction of the mass, as the Marxists see him, but that he is a person.

B. Helping Others (vv. 10, 11)

(Hebrews 6:10, 11 is not included in the printed text.)

Continuing to reassure his readers, the author reminds them that God is not unfair; therefore, He will not lose sight of anything that they have done. The Lord takes note of all that we do even to the giving of a cup of cold water to one of His disciples. Jesus said, "And whosoever shall give to drink unto one of these little ones a cup of cold water only in the name of a disciple, verily I say unto you, he shall in no wise lose his reward" (Matthew 10:42).

These readers have manifested love by helping God's people, and they were still showing that love. This is one of the best ways to demonstrate that salvation is genuine. John wrote: "We know that we have passed from death unto life, because we love the brethren. He that loveth not his brother abideth in death" (1 John 3:14).

The author then expresses an earnest desire that the readers will continue on the path of love and obedience to the very end. They must not waver and hesitate and doubt in their journey. Their resolution must be marked by a firm conviction that this is the course God has set before them and that He will fulfill His promise to them.

The goal which God has set for every believer is maturity. We should never be satisfied until we have obtained that objective. It is a lifetime pursuit. There is no point at which we can stop and say we have arrived. We must always be striving toward the goal.

C. Possessing the Inheritance (v. 12)

(Hebrews 6:12 is not included in the printed text.)

The author now warns the readers about the danger of becoming lazy in their search for the goal. Many things could happen that would cause them to become careless and approach their work in a halfhearted fashion. Such disinterest was to be avoided. The goal was attainable if they continued to diligently seek after it.

The writer encouraged them to follow the example of those who had inherited the promises. There was no point in patterning their lives after those who had failed. Wisdom dictated that they observe and emulate those who are now enjoying the blessings of God's promises.

Two key elements must be cultivated if the goal is to be reached—faith and patience. John Phillips wrote: "God's promises have a **trust** element in them which is to be grasped by faith and a **time** element in them which is to be grasped by patience."

## REVIEW QUESTIONS

1. What were some of the problems the writer of Hebrews addressed in today's lesson?

2. What thoughts are conjured up when the phrase "living on a spiritual milk diet" is used?

3. What is meant by the phrase "spiritual maturity?"

4. Is it possible for a Christian to attain perfection in this life? Explain.

5. List some of the benefits you have obtained from the study of this lesson.

## GOLDEN TEXT HOMILY

"BE NOT SLOTHFUL, BUT FOLLOWERS OF THEM WHO THROUGH FAITH AND PATIENCE INHERIT THE PROMISES" (Hebrews 6:12).

The scope of the appeal in the Golden Text reminds us of the words of Paul, who said that he had not attained; but, leaving the things that were behind, he was pressing forward to those that were before. The ideal Christian, in the parable of our Lord, represents unbroken progress from blade to ear, and from the ear to full corn in the ear. Believers are to seek the full assurance of hope, which has a mighty and purifying power;

for "we are saved by hope"; and if it is like a ship with outspread sails under a vigorous breeze, the vessel moves with speed to the desired haven. To enjoy this hope there must be a resistance to that torpor and drowsiness which lead us to say, "A little more sleep, a little more slumber, and a little more folding of the hands to sleep." The voice of inspiration is, "Be vigilant"; "Let us not sleep, as do others"; "Awake thou that sleepest, and arise, and Christ shall give thee light." Encouragement is supplied to perseverance from the success which others have attained. "The spirits of just men made perfect" are already reaping the blessed results of their earnest pursuit and unwearied diligence. Faith prompted them to begin and continue the career, and gave them patience to endure the contrast between present trial and future glory. To stimulate in this course, believers are urged to imitate their example, that they may share in the blessedness which they now enjoy.

Excerpts from **Pulpit Commentary.**

## SENTENCE SERMONS

GOD'S WORD DIRECTS and equips the believer to mature in Christ.
**—Selected**

THE GOAL TOWARD which every believer should be moving is maturity in Christ.
**—Homer G. Rhea, Jr.**

IN THE CHURCH where members are moving toward maturity, each person has found his place of service and is doing his part to enhance the cause of Christ.
**—Homer G. Rhea, Jr.**

CHRISTIANS WHO MOVE the world are those who do not let the world move them.
**—"Moody Monthly"**

WHEN A CHRISTIAN ceases to grow he begins to decay.
**—Clate Risley**

## EVANGELISTIC APPLICATION

GOD'S LOVE COMPELS THE CHRISTIAN TO WARN OTHERS AGAINST THE DANGER OF APOSTASY.

There is nothing comparable to God's

love. It is a vital part of His being and has existed for as long as He has existed—forever. Dr. Robert G. Lee observed that God's love has no fluctuation or cessation. It is a love which seeks no benefits for Himself and bestows everything. It is inexhaustible in its benevolences and pours forth in springs that know no drought, and have no hindered outflow. The sun that shines shall set, the summer streams shall freeze, the deepest wells go dry, but not so with God's love.

God's love constrains us to warn others against going astray. We do so from the standpoint of what they will lose and what they will suffer. But we also do so from the viewpoint of what they will miss. To lose out on this love is the tragedy of tragedies. No sadder fate could befall an individual than to lose the warmth of God's compassionate love.

## ILLUMINATING THE LESSON

True faith does not look at the obstacles, but rather at God. A dear old woman had a very beautiful faith; she was obedient, and obedience is the only beauty of faith. Someone said to her, "I believe that if you thought the Lord told you to jump through a stone wall, you would jump."

The old lady replied, "If the Lord told me to jump through a wall, it would be my business to jump, and it would be His business to make the hole."

It would be impossible to define more simply the exact relationship between obedience and faith. Here is the essence of true faith. Although we do not understand every step of the way by which we must walk, we are fully persuaded that whatsoever God has promised, He is able to perform (Romans 4:21), and we leave all of the matters that are not comprehended to the mind and heart of the God whom we know to be the loving heavenly Father, through Jesus Christ, our Lord (from *Let Me Illustrate*, by Donald Grey Barnhouse).

## DAILY DEVOTIONAL GUIDE

M. Spiritual Success. Joshua 1:5-9
T. Spiritual Fruitfulness. Psalm 1:1-3
W. Spiritual Benefits. Psalm 103:1-5
T. Ministering to Others. 2 Corinthians 8:1-8
F. Spiritual Growth. 2 Peter 1:5-11
S. Living in God's Love. Jude 20-25

# Christ Our Mediator

**Study Text:** Hebrews 7:15 through 8:13

**Supplemental References:** Job 23:1-17; John 17:1-26; Romans 8:28-34; 1 Timothy 2:1-7; 1 John 2:1, 2

**Time:** Generally thought to have been written around A.D. 65-70

**Place:** Probably Rome

**Golden Text:** "He is able to save them to the uttermost that come unto God by him, seeing he ever liveth to make intercession for them" (Hebrews 7:25).

**Central Truth:** Christ's presence at the right hand of God guarantees the perpetual fulfillment of the covenant which He mediates.

**Evangelistic Emphasis:** God's mercy toward sinners is expressed through Christ's death on the cross.

## Printed Text

**Hebrews 7:22.** By so much was Jesus made a surety of a better testament.

**23. And they truly were many priests, because they were not suffered to continue by reason of death:**

24. But this man, because he continueth ever, hath an unchangeable priesthood.

**25. Wherefore he is able also to save them to the uttermost that come unto God by him, seeing he ever liveth to make intercession for them.**

26. For such an high priest became us, who is holy, harmless, undefiled, separate from sinners, and made higher than the heavens;

**27. Who needeth not daily, as those high priests, to offer up sacrifice, first for his own sins, and then for the people's: for this he did once, when he offered up himself.**

28. For the law maketh men high priests which have infirmity; but the word of the oath, which was since the law, maketh the Son, who is consecrated for evermore.

**8:1. Now of the things which we have spoken this is the sum: We have such an high priest, who is set on the right hand of the throne of the Majesty in the heavens;**

2. A minister of the sanctuary, and of the true tabernacle, which the Lord pitched, and not man.

**3. For every high priest is ordained to offer gifts and sacrifices: wherefore it is of necessity that this man have somewhat also to offer.**

4. For if he were on earth, he should not be a priest, seeing that there are priests that offer gifts according to the law:

**5. Who serve unto the example and shadow of heavenly things, as Moses was admonished of God when he was about to make the tabernacle: for, See, saith he, that thou make all things according to the pattern shewed to thee in the mount.**

6. But now hath he obtained a more excellent ministry, by how much also he is the mediator of a better covenant, which was established upon better promises.

## DICTIONARY

**surety of a better testament—Hebrews 7:22—** Guarantee of a better agreement or covenant.

**suffered—Hebrews 7:23—**Allowed

**intercession for them—Hebrews 7:25—**Pray for, take the part of, and intervene for them.

**infirmity—Hebrews 7:28—**Weakness

**example and shadow—Hebrews 8:5—**Pattern and copy.

**the mount—Hebrews 8:5—**Mount Sinai

**mediator—Hebrews 8:6—**A person who negotiates to bring about peace, agreement, and reconciliation between two other parties.

---

## LESSON OUTLINE

I. HIS PRIESTLY MINISTRY
   A. An Endless Life
   B. An Ever-Living Savior
   C. The Holy One
   D. A Perfect Sacrifice

II. HIS EXALTED POSITION
   A. The Majestic High Priest
   B. The Sufficient Sacrifice
   C. The New Covenant

III. HIS BETTER COVENANT
   A. A More Excellent Ministry
   B. The Mediator
   C. A New Knowledge

## LESSON EXPOSITION

INTRODUCTION

The unique character of Christ's high-priestly ministry is the subject of this passage. The whole priesthood of the Hebrew people had been Levitical, of the order of Aaron. Jesus was not of the tribe of Levi, but of Judah. He was not, therefore, a priest of the Aaronic order; but, as the writer says, He was a priest after the order of Melchizedek.

Melchizedek did not come to his office by the right of succession. In fact, there was no established priesthood in his day. He was raised up and immediately called of God to be a priest. Likewise Christ had no successors on earth, and was a priest only after an extraordinary call.

As a type of Christ, Melchizedek was a "king of righteousness," a "king of peace," and one who had "neither beginning of days, nor end of life." Furthermore, Abraham paid tithes to him.

Jesus Christ is "King of righteousness, and after that also . . . King of peace." He is really and truly the "priest of the most high God." He is the Son of God. He alone abides as priest forever.

The function of the priesthood consisted of aiding the people in being accepted by God, in experiencing present righteousness, and in looking forward to future blessedness. If the Levitical priesthood could not aid the people in this way—despite whatever use it may have had for a season—it could not serve permanently. Since the Levitical order could not accomplish this end, it was necessary for "another priest" of another order to arise and execute the office of the priest in compliance with the call and appointment of God.

Where could another priest be found? Who could possibly fulfill such high expectations? Only one person qualified—the Lord Jesus Christ! If we examine His record we discover that He fulfilled the Law; He provided the perfect sacrifice.

I. HIS PRIESTLY MINISTRY (Hebrews 7:15-28)

A. An Endless Life (vv. 15-21)

(Hebrews 7:15-21 is not included in the printed text.)

The effort to prove that Melchizedek's priesthood was superior to the Aaronic priesthood continues. Abraham, though founder of the Jewish people, gave tithes to Melchizedek. The office of Levi was subject to change and death; the office of Melchizedek was permanent and perpetual. Melchizedek had "neither beginning of days, nor end of life" (Hebrews 7:3). His priesthood continued in principle even after his death. Likewise, Christ, not being of the priestly order, and not being numbered with them, still was high priest. His priest-hood was of the highest nature and continues in His person forever. The very fact that Melchizedek and the Messiah belonged to another order of the priesthood indicated the imperfection of the Levitical order.

Those to whom the Book of Hebrews was written had confessed that Jesus of Nazareth was the Christ. The writer, therefore, shows not only that the ancient priesthood was abolished, but also that Jesus, the new priest, had taken the place of the old. There could be no return to the old order, for Jesus was not of the old order.

Many good things were contained in the Law. Much guidance for good living was given therein. Instruction in the faith and in the fear of God was found there. Yet, the part of the Law relating to the sacrificial system was gone forever.

The ceremonial Law was abolished because it was weak and futile. The ceremonies, which had no substance in themselves, had no power. All the types and shadows likewise had no substance in themselves, having reference to Christ: they all derived their power and effect from Him. They could do nothing or effect nothing of themselves. All their power depended on Christ alone. The moment types and shadows were separated from Christ, they had nothing left but weakness. In short, no benefit was found in the ancient ceremonies except as they related to Christ.

B. An Ever-Living Savior (vv. 22-25)

**Hebrews 7:22. By so much was Jesus made a surety of a better testament.**

**23. And they truly were many priests,** **because they were not suffered to continue by reason of death:**

**24. But this man, because he continueth ever, hath an unchangeable priesthood.**

**25. Wherefore he is able also to save them to the uttermost that come unto God by him, seeing he ever liveth to make intercession for them.**

God put Himself on oath. He asserted in an oath that His counsel was immutable, that it could not be changed, that whatever the appearances of the hour might be, that whatever the passing of the years might bring, the one thing that remained certain was the immutability of His divine counsel.

Herein God accommodated Himself and His method to meet man in his need, but man needed more than a declaration. God, therefore, made an oath through His Son, who became a fellowman with man.

In this way Christ was made the guarantee of a better covenant. He was made a guarantee according to the singular and absolute promise of God. His appointment to the office of high priest was confirmed, ratified, and made irrevocable by His death.

With reference to the Aaronic order of the priesthood, it was made weak by its break in continuity by the death of the priests. On the other hand, the priesthood of Christ was permanent. From the first moment of His being a priest, Christ abode so always, without interruption or intermission. It followed then that He had an "unchangeable priesthood," a priesthood that would not pass from one person to another.

Because the Son is One whose personality transcends all human measurements and limitations, He is able to bring complete salvation to them that approach God through Him.

That word **uttermost** is a great word, which has a double meaning. It carries with it the thought of "all" and "extent." In Christ there is fullness of provision in quantity and fullness of provision in duration. He saves all, no matter how deep in sin they may be.

Only God alone knows how great is the work of saving to the uttermost. He saw that the continual intercession of Christ was needful and expedient unto the salvation of souls and His own glory.

Thus the word **salvation** is represented in all its fullness and glory. We are able to say, looking back, we were saved; looking to the present, we may say, we are saved; and lifting our eyes to the future, we can say, we shall be saved. "For now is our salvation nearer than when we believed" (Romans 13:11).

C. The Holy One (v. 26)

**26. For such an high priest became us, who is holy, harmless, undefiled, separate from sinners, and made higher than the heavens.**

Our High Priest is the kind that we would expect an all-wise God to give and the kind that we need. Where else could we find a high priest who could make atonement for our sin and supply us with the grace to walk before God in an acceptable manner? We stood in need of a high priest like this, and it became the wisdom and grace of God to give such a one to us.

What a description we are given of our High Priest! He is holy. He is pure in His nature. Elsewhere He is called the Holy One. We are called upon to exhibit holiness in our life.

Christ is harmless. His life is free of evil, guile, fraud, and sin. He "did no sin, neither was guile found in his mouth" (1 Peter 2:22). The Lord is eternally free from malice or craftiness. His motivations are absolutely blameless.

Our High Priest is undefiled. There is no blemish in Him. He has never been morally polluted or stained by outside sinful pressures.

Christ is separate from sinners. He is separate from us not because He rejects us from His society, but because He has the exceptional attribute of holiness in its purest form. He is free from all uncleanness. Christ ate with publicans and sinners, but He never condoned their sin.

Also, our High Priest is made higher

than the heavens. He is no longer on the earth, but is exalted to a throne of majesty above the heavens. He is in a state of glory at the right hand of the Majesty on high. He is, therefore, higher even than other sacred inhabitants of those heavenly places.

D. A Perfect Sacrifice (vv. 27, 28)

**27. Who needeth not daily, as those high priests, to offer up sacrifice, first for his own sins, and then for the people's: for this he did once, when he offered up himself.**

**28. For the law maketh men high priests which have infirmity; but the word of the oath, which was since the law, maketh the Son, who is consecrated for evermore.**

The author points out two further defects in the Levitical priests. First, in the old priesthood the high priest offered sacrifices for his own sin. How could he approah God for others when he himself needed forgiveness? Second, the Aaronic priest offered various sacrifices every day; therefore, it followed that there was no true atonement: if the cleansing had to be repeated, obviously sin remained.

What a contrast in Christ! He needed no sacrifice inasmuch as He was not tainted by any stain of sin. His sacrifice was such that its once-for-all oblation sufficed to the end of the world. He offered Himself—in the Holy of Holies He presented His own blood—not for Himself, but for you and me. The Apostle Peter wrote of Christ: "Who his own self bare our sins in his own body on the tree, that we, being dead to sins, should live unto righteousness: by whose stripes ye were healed" (1 Peter 2:24).

Since the Law did not set up true priests, this fault needed to be corrected. It has been corrected by the word of God's oath, for Christ is the Son of God, subject to no fault, but adorned and endowed with supreme perfection. He reigns as king and priest. He is our contemporary and He never changes. The winds of the ages have long since erased the footprints of the

Galilean from the sands of Palestine's roadways and byways, but He still lives. He who walks through the centuries walks into men's hearts and lives!

## II. HIS EXALTED POSITION (Hebrews 8:1-5)

### A. The Majestic High Priest (vv. 1, 2)

**Hebrews 8:1. Now of the things which we have spoken this is the sum: We have such an high priest, who is set on the right hand of the throne of the Majesty in the heavens;**

**2. A minister of the sanctuary, and of the true tabernacle, which the Lord pitched, and not man.**

The expression "this is the sum" means "this is the chief point" or "this is the most important thing." The author then refers to the spiritual nature of Christ's work and points out that our High Priest works on a spiritual plane.

This concept is most important because it shows our relationship to this High Priest. The Jews derided the Christians for having no visible high priest; but on behalf of the Christian community the writer declares a relationship with an invisible, spiritual High Priest who was exalted in glory and dignity far above all earthly priests.

Observe the contrast in posture between the older priests and Christ. They stood before God in His earthly sanctuary. But Christ sat down, indicating the unchangeable stability of His state and condition.

Christ ministered from the true tabernacle. He was seated at the right hand of the throne of God in the heavens, while the earthly priests only ministered in a temple built by human hands. Christ was seated in the sanctuary, which was the spiritual, heavenly counterpart of the earthly Holy of Holies, in which the ancient high priest ministered alone.

In a sense, Christ himself is the true tabernacle. He was the body and substance of all the types—of priests, sacrifice, tabernacle, altar, and what belonged thereto. The pitching of the true tabernacle then was the work of God alone, without any service or ministry of men.

### B. The Sufficient Sacrifice (vv. 3, 4)

**3. For every high priest is ordained to offer gifts and sacrifices: wherefore it is of necessity that this man have somewhat also to offer.**

**4. For if he were on earth, he should not be a priest, seeing that there are priests that offer gifts according to the law.**

The principal function of the high priest was to offer gifts and sacrifices. The people might bring their offerings unto God, but only the priest could offer them on the altar. If Jesus Christ, the Son of God, the high priest of the New Testament, was to fulfill this function, He had to have something to give to God. What did He have to offer? Himself. Through this offering He was able to discharge the office of priesthood.

The office of the priesthood demonstrates that men cannot find favor with God except by sacrifice. To rush into the presence of God, bypassing Christ and His atoning death, is fatal presumption. The wrath that rages in the heart of God, because of our sins, must be appeased. Neither man nor angel is good enough to produce this appeasement. There must be an acceptable sacrifice. Unless we come with the perfect sacrifice of Christ, the unspotted Lamb, God will not be favorably inclined toward us. If, however, we base our approach to God upon Christ's work, we shall find acceptance.

In referring to the death of Christ, the writer stresses the spiritual fruit derived from that sacrifice. Physically, Christ died as all men die; but as priest He made divine atonement for the sins of the world. Outwardly He shed His blood, but inwardly and spiritually He brought cleansing. In short, He died on earth, but the power and efficacy of His death came from heaven. What a High Priest we have!

### C. The New Covenant (v. 5)

**5. Who serve unto the example and shadow of heavenly things, as Moses**

**was admonished of God when he was about to make the tabernacle: for, See, saith he, that thou make all things according to the pattern shewed to thee in the mount.**

The writer speaks of the priests in this verse. Their service included everything assigned to them in the worship of God. However, this service was an example, a representation, a shadow of heavenly realities. Although it was an inferior form of worship, it was, nevertheless, necessary; for it looked to what was higher.

The importance of the service of the priests and the building of the tabernacle is seen in the instructions given to Moses at Mount Sinai. God warned Moses to exercise great caution in carrying out His directions so that there would be no mistake. Rabbinic writers concluded that Moses had a vision of the heavenly tabernacle, or that a visible representation of it was exhibited to him on the Mount. Moreover, he was divinely admonished to make the tabernacle after the fashion that was shown to him. Whatever the cost in time and material, it had to be a true representation of the one in heaven. (See Exodus 25:40; Acts 7:44.)

Three important things may be learned from this verse: We learn first from it that the ancient rites were not brought about by chance for God to keep His people busy with them as if in a child's game, and that the building of the tabernacle was not an empty pursuit. There was a real spiritual meaning in everything, in that Moses was commanded to do everything according to the original pattern which was heavenly.

Second, we are here informed that all those forms of worship which men allow themselves to invent by their own ingenuity and contrary to the command of God are false and spurious.

In the third place, we must learn from this that there are no true religious symbols except those which conform to Christ. It is not permissible for us to invent anything we like, but it belongs to God alone to show us according to the pattern that was showed them (John Calvin).

III. HIS BETTER COVENANT (Hebrews 8:6-13)

A. A More Excellent Ministry (v. 6)

**6. But now hath he obtained a more excellent ministry, by how much also he is the mediator of a better covenant, which was established upon better promises.**

In contrast with the ministries of the priests of old, the Lord Jesus Christ has received a ministry far superior to theirs. The excellence of His ministry was in proportion to the excellence of the covenant of which He served as the mediator. This covenant is said to be a superior covenant, implying that there was another covenant of which He, though the author, was not the mediator.

The other covenant was none other but that which God made with the children of Israel on Mount Sinai. The sublimer covenant, of which Christ was the mediator, was the covenant of grace. In this covenant—established upon better promises—all things were founded in promises of continuous mercy and grace, as well as in future blessedness. This covenant brought to the church the highest privileges and advantages. It also placed every believer under obligation to live a holy and fruitful life, unto the glory of God.

Because the first covenant had its limitations, the better covenant was needed. There was no fault in the first covenant itself; but it was insufficient to the perfection and salvation of the Church. Therefore, God in His wisdom and grace provided for the Church a new and better covenant.

B. The Mediator (vv. 7-9)

(Hebrews 8:7-9 is not included in the printed text.)

The prophet charges the people with faithlessness because they received the Law, but did not stand fast in the faith. Therefore, the Law was the covenant that, God complained, was broken by the people. To remedy this evil, He promises a new and different covenant to replace the old one.

In a strict sense, this new covenant was made with the house of Israel and with the house of Judah. Both were mentioned because the tribes of Israel were divided into two kingdoms. The promise was given that all the elect would be gathered into one body again. But, in a broader sense, the covenant was made to the whole church of God— Jews and Gentiles together—unto whom grace was actually communicated.

God's new covenant communicated more grace and mercy to the church than the Israelites ever partook of. And greater blessing carried greater warning: the church was to live before God in an acceptable manner, lest she perish like her fathers of old.

The covenant God made with the house of Israel was made on the day that He took them by the hand and led them out of slavery. The writer of Hebrews increases the magnitude of their desertion by reminding them of their great blessing. Because of their sin, there was no advantage in their having been once adopted as His people if God had not come to their aid with a new kind of remedy. What an illustration of the grace of God, that He would make a new covenant in spite of the sin of those who broke the former!

C. A New Knowledge (vv. 10-13)

(Hebrews 8:10-13 is not included in the printed text.)

God could not enter into a new covenant with men to be "to them a God," and for them to be to Him "a people," while man was still fallen and sinful. So God provided a Mediator of this new covenant, Jesus Christ, who would cleanse repentant man of his sin. Through Jesus God would secure all the good things of the covenant, both as to grace and glory. In the covenant God became the Mediator's Master, and the Mediator became the Servant of God in a peculiar manner. It is peculiar because God, the Mediator's Master, became the Father; Christ, the Mediator, became the Son; and we, the covenant people, became "heirs . . . and joint-heirs with Christ" (Romans 8: 17).

The day is coming, says the Lord, when everyone, great and small, will know Him. It is the work of the Holy Spirit to illuminate our minds so that we might know the will of God and turn our hearts to obey it. Common, ordinary men were not to be shut off from heavenly wisdom; great and noble men could not attain that wisdom through human efforts and learning. Thus God joined together the low and humble with the high and proud. The Spirit works equally in all and is Master of all, "for all shall know me" (v. 11).

## REVIEW QUESTIONS

1. Relate the priestly role of Old Testament Melchizedek to Christ in today's lesson.

2. Name some of the weaknesses of the Old Testament ceremonial law.

3. What do we mean when we call the worship room in our churches today sanctuaries?

4. In what ways is Christ to be compared to a sacrificial lamb?

5. What is your definition of the word "mediator?"

## GOLDEN TEXT HOMILY

"HE IS ABLE ALSO TO SAVE THEM TO THE UTTERMOST THAT COME UNTO GOD BY HIM, SEEING HE EVER LIVETH TO MAKE INTERCESSION FOR THEM" (Hebrews 7:25).

The theme of the Book of Hebrews is to show the superiority of Christ to that which has gone before and to that which is to come.

When the writer says, "he is able to save," he is indicating that the priest-hood of Christ combines intercession with the power to save. It should be noted this is the third time His ability has been stressed in this Epistle. In chapter 2:18, we are told that because of His temptations in the flesh, "He is able to succour [help] them that are tempted." In 4:15 it is indicated that because of the days of his humanity we have a high priest who is able to sympathize with us when we are tempted. The Golden Text (7:25) gives to us the great assurance that "he is able to save" (deliver) even in the utmost circum-stances. This truth about the ability of Christ is of great importance to the Christian faith. It is basic to everything in the believer's life and experience.

He is able to save "to the uttermost." The phrase means "completely," and is found in only one other place in the Scripture—Luke 13:11. The Satan-afflicted woman "was bowed together, and could in no wise lift up herself." A more accurate description of her condition is given in the **New English Bible** indicating she was "unable to stand up straight." What a picture of too many believers today—they face ever downward looking at earthly things. With no power to lift themselves unto God, definitely hampered, they are Satan-bound. Christ instantly made straight the bent back; so now as our High Priest, He can save completely those who draw near unto God by Him, because "he is always living to plead on their behalf." **(New English Bible).—L. E. Painter, D. Min., Assistant Professor of Religion, Lee College, Cleveland, Tennessee.**

## SENTENCE SERMONS

CHRIST'S PRESENCE at the right hand of God guarantees the perpetual fulfillment of the covenant which He mediates.
**—Selected**

JESUS, MY SHEPHERD, Brother, Friend
My prophet, Priest, and King,
My Lord, my life, my Way, my end,
Accept the praise I bring.
**—Anonymous**

CHRIST CAME NOT to preach the gospel, but that there might be a gospel to preach.
**—Griffith Thomas**

THE MEDIATORAL PROCESS which began historically with Christ's incarnation, and was continued through His humiliation and exaltation, reached its full perfection in the session at the right hand of God.
**—H. Orton Wiley**

## EVANGELISTIC APPLICATION

GOD'S MERCY TOWARD SINNERS IS EXPRESSED THROUGH CHRIST'S DEATH ON THE CROSS.

In Germany many years ago a man was working high up on the steeple of a church. Suddenly he lost his footing and fell headlong to the ground beneath. Grazing on the grass in the churchyard

was a lamb. The body of the man fell on the lamb, and thus his fall was broken. The lamb perished, but the man was saved. As a token of his gratitude he carved in one of the stones over the doorway of the church the figure of a lamb.

Every true church of Christ has that lamb, as it were, carved in the stones of its wall. "Behold the Lamb of God, which taketh away the sins of the world" (Clarence Edward Macartney in *Macartney's Illustrations*).

The beautiful thing is that the grace and mercy of God are provided for all sorts of sins. When sinners turn to the Cross, God remembers their sins no more. When our guilt is lifted, we have peace with God.

## ILLUMINATING THE LESSON

Dr. Robert L. Sumner tells of a doctor who died in Chicago and left a will which completely wiped out all the unpaid medical fees owed by his patients. The attorney who filed the doctor's will estimated that the unpaid bills totaled around $25,000. The good doctor's actions completely and finally cancelled every one of the debts. No heir can ever in the future collect a single dime of the $25,000 total. The once-indebted ones are forever free from the obligations.

Sumner says, "In a much grander and nobler sense, of course, that is part of what happened on the cross of Calvary. There our staggering debt of sin was cancelled once and for all in behalf of each individual willing to accept it."

What a thrill to know that the payment accepted for sins need never be made again. Sin once forgiven is sin forever forgiven. And God never has, never can, never will demand two payments for one debt (Robert G. Lee in *Sourcebook of 500 Illustrations*).

## DAILY DEVOTIONAL GUIDE

M. Divine Protection. Job 1:8-12
T. Gratitude for Forgiveness. Psalm 103:12-22
W. Christ Prays for Us. John 17:20-26
T. Sons of God. Romans 8:14-18
F. Heirs of God. Galatians 4:1-7
S. Fellowship with God. 1 John 1:1-4

# Our Great Redemption

**Study Text:** Hebrews 9:1-28

**Supplemental References:** Exodus 24:3-8; Leviticus 16:1-34; Luke 4:16-21; 1 Peter 1:18-22

**Time:** Probably A.D. 65-70

**Place:** Probably written from Rome.

**Golden Text:** "Christ was once offered to bear the sins of many; and unto them that look for him shall he appear the second time without sin unto salvation" (Hebrews 9:28).

**Central Truth:** Christ's death provides eternal redemption for all who believe.

**Evangelistic Emphasis:** Christ's death provides eternal redemption for all who believe.

## Printed Text

**Hebrews 9:11.** But Christ being come an high priest of good things to come, by a greater and more perfect tabernacle, not made with hands, that is to say, not of this building;

**12. Neither by the blood of goats and calves, but by his own blood he entered in once into the holy place, having obtained eternal redemption for us.**

13. For if the blood of bulls and of goats, and the ashes of an heifer sprinkling the unclean, sanctifieth to the purifying of the flesh:

**14. How much more shall the blood of Christ, who through the eternal Spirit offered himself without spot to God, purge your conscience from dead works to serve the living God?**

15. And for this cause he is the mediator of the new testament, that by means of death, for the redemption of the transgressions that were under the first testament, they which are called might receive the promise of eternal inheritance.

**16. For where a testament is there must also of necessity be the death of the testator.**

17. For a testament is of force after men are dead: otherwise it is of no strength at all while the testator liveth.

**18. Whereupon neither the first testament was dedicated without blood.**

19. For when Moses had spoken every precept to all the people according to the law, he took the blood of calves and of goats, with water, and scarlet wool, and hyssop, and sprinkled both the book, and all the people,

**20. Saying, This is the blood of the testament which God hath enjoined unto you.**

21. Moreover he sprinkled with blood both the tabernacle, and all the vessels of the ministry.

**22. And almost all things are by the law purged with blood; and without shedding of blood is no remission.**

23. It was therefore necessary that the patterns of things in the heavens should be purified with these; but the heavenly things themselves with better sacrifices than these.

**24. For Christ is not entered into the holy places made with hands, which are the figures of the true; but into heaven itself, now to appear in the presence of God for us:**

**LESSON OUTLINE**

I. FIGURES OF HEAVENLY THINGS
  A. The Most Holy Place
  B. The High Priest
  C. The New Order
II. CHRIST'S PERFECT SACRIFICE
  A. The Heavenly Tabernacle
  B. The Sacrifice
  C. The Cleansing
III. REDEEMED BY HIS BLOOD
  A. Mediator of the New Testament
  B. Remission of Sin
  C. Intercession of Christ
  D. Appearance of Christ

**LESSON EXPOSITION**

INTRODUCTION

In today's lesson we look at the eternal redemption which is provided through Christ's death. Emphasis is placed on the superior work of our eternal High Priest. The nature of His sacrifice is such that it is able to cleanse the "conscience from dead works to serve the living God." It is a once-for-all sacrifice in that He offered Himself "through the eternal Spirit."

Emphasis is also placed on the accessibility of our great High Priest. Wherever is found the soul who will come to God through Him, there He is found as priest, ready to provide redemption and acceptance. No longer does the individual have to go to a certain place, for Christ is everywhere present.

Christ hides all who come to Him. They need no longer look with dread to a day of future judgment. Instead they rejoice in the glorious hope of His own second coming. Only through Christ's sacrificial death may such hope be entertained. Christ's blood, however, satisfies the justice of God. What a privilege to live under this better plan!

I. FIGURES OF HEAVENLY THINGS (Hebrews 9:1-10)

A. The Most Holy Place (vv. 1-5)

(Hebrews 9:1-5 is not included in the printed text.)

The first covenant was tied to the Levitical sacrificial system. The system operated in an earthly tabernacle. The men who labored there were godly men and the Israelites who worshiped there were spiritual people. The sanctuary was a "set apart place" or a "holy place."

The tabernacle was divided into two rooms. The first room called the sanctuary was the place were the priests performed their daily ministries. Inside this room was a lampstand which provided light for that area. Across the room was a table on which twelve loaves of bread representing the twelve tribes of Israel were arranged in two rows of six each.

A curtain separated this area from the Most Holy Place. This room was known as the "Holy of Holies." Here God visited His people in a special way.

The writer speaks of a golden censer. This censer was used by the high priest on the Day of Atonement. He filled it with burning coals of fire from off the altar, sprinkled incense upon the coals, and caused smoke to cover the mercy seat.

Inside the Holy of Holies was the Ark of the Covenant, which was a chest containing the tables of Law that God had given Moses on Mount Sinai. The top of the chest was called the mercy seat, on which two cherubims of gold knelt with their wings outspread. It was under the canopy of their wings that the Shekinah, the visible representation of God, rested. It was here that the high priest annually sprinkled the blood of sacrifice for the sins of the nation.

B. The High Priest (vv. 6, 7)

(Hebrews 9:6, 7 is not included in the printed text.)

After the tabernacle was erected, the priestly duties began. The priests served in the first room, the Holy Place, every day (9:6). They lit the seven lamps on the lampstand every evening and trimmed the wicks each morning (Exodus 27:20, 21; 30:7). They burned incense on the altar of incense during the offering of the morning and the evening sacrifices

(Exodus 30:7, 8). They replaced the twelve loaves of bread on the table of showbread every Sabbath (Leviticus 24: 5-9).

Only the high priest could go into the second chamber, the Holy of Holies, and he could only enter on one day of the calendar year, the Day of Atonement (9:7). He could not enter "without blood." He actually entered the sacred room twice on that day: the first time to sprinkle the blood of the bullock upon the mercy seat for the atonement of his personal sins and the second time to sprinkle the blood of a goat upon the mercy seat for the atonement of the nation (Leviticus 16:11-16). The atonement was made on account of the sins which the people have ignorantly committed. A difference was made between sins committed presumptuously and those done out of ignorance, although both were still defined as sins (Numbers 15:22-31). No sacrifice could be offered for presumptuous sins (Robert G. Gromacki).

This complex system of ritual and worship continued until the coming of Christ. Each year the high priest followed this same procedure. This mode of worship was not intended to continue forever, for it only foreshadowed the work of the true High Priest, the Lord Jesus Christ.

C. The New Order (vv. 8-10)

(Hebrews 9:8-10 is not included in the printed text.)

The Holy Spirit sought to teach the people through the ceremonials and rituals of the tabernacle. One lesson they might learn is that they did not through this system have direct access to God. The people were not allowed to enter the Holy of Holies where God made Himself known. As long as the tabernacle was standing, they knew there must be a better way whereby they could approach God.

Another thing they needed to learn was that the gifts and sacrifices being offered were not able to clear the conscience of the worshiper. Outwardly they knew that they were ceremonially ac-

ceptable, but inwardly they recognized that the animal sacrifices did not remove the personal guilt of their sins. Since these sacrifices were incapable of cleansing and renewing the inner man, their conscience reminded them of their sins and condemned them.

The author mentions four areas of the legalistic code: the dietary regulations (meats); the controls on beverages (drinks); the various ceremonial immersions (divers washings); and the judgments which guided social behavior (carnal ordinances). These external regulations, they needed to learn, will be in force only until the time for the new order. The prophet Isaiah spoke of that day: "The voice of him that crieth in the wilderness, Prepare ye the way of the Lord, make straight in the desert a highway for our God. Every valley shall be exalted, and every mountain and hill shall be made low: and the crooked shall be made straight, and the rough places plain: And the glory of the Lord shall be revealed, and all flesh shall see it together: for the mouth of the Lord hath spoken it" (Isaiah 40:3-5). This prophecy spoke of the coming of the Lord Jesus Christ and the establishing of the new order.

II. CHRIST'S PERFECT SACRIFICE (Hebrews 9:11-14)

A. The Heavenly Tabernacle (v. 11)

**11. But Christ being come an high priest of good things to come, by a greater and more perfect tabernacle, not made with hands, that is to say, not of this building.**

The heavenly tabernacle out of which Christ ministers is described as a greater and more perfect tabernacle—a tabernacle not fashioned by human hands. It is openly affirmed that the habitation of God could not be in the Temple Solomon built, because it was made with hands. The whole majesty of God could only dwell in a temple not made by human hands.

On a hot August day in Florence, after visiting the great Duomo, where Savonarola thundered against the iniquities of the city, and the beautiful St. John's

Church, with its marvelous gateway, I sought out a Protestant place to worship. It was an evangelical church of no great dimensions, in an obscure part of the city. The service was one familiar to all Protestants; and, although I did not understand much that he was saying, I could tell that the preacher spoke in simple earnestness to his people. On the wall over his head were the words: "There is one God and one mediator between God and men, the man Christ Jesus" (1 Timothy 2:5). However neglected this idea may be in popular teaching and preaching, however lost sight of in popular Christianity today, no one can read the New Testament without having presented to him the fact that the kingdom of God is a kingdom of redemption and of meditation, and that the Mediator, the one who stands between man and God and reconciles man to God and God to man, is the eternal God man, Christ Jesus (Clarence Edward Macartney in *Macartney's Illustrations*).

B. The Sacrifice (vv. 12, 13)

**12. Neither by the blood of goats and calves, but by his own blood he entered in once into the holy place, having obtained eternal redemption for us.**

**13. For if the blood of bulls and of goats, and the ashes of an heifer sprinkling the unclean, sanctifieth to the purifying of the flesh.**

Upon His ascension, Christ entered once for all into the real sanctuary; that is, into heaven, the residence of God. Satan, the world, death, and hell had been conquered. Peace and reconciliation had been made by the blood of the Cross. The covenant had been confirmed. Eternal redemption had been obtained. All power had been committed unto Him. Therefore, He entered heaven triumphantly, as our high priest, into the holy place, the temple of God, to apply the benefits of His sacrifice to the church. This He did once—only once—for all.

Christ did not enter by the blood of animals; He entered in by His own blood, when He offered Himself unto God. By this offering, He was given the

right to administer His priestly office in heaven. The apostle Peter properly evaluated the meaning of the shed blood of Christ: "Forasmuch as ye know that ye were not redeemed with corruptible things, as silver and gold, from your vain conversation received by tradition from your fathers; But with the precious blood of Christ, as of a lamb without blemish and without spot" (1 Peter 1:18, 19).

This is the heart of the gospel, the object of the admiration of angels and men unto all eternity. What heart can conceive or what tongue can tell the wisdom, grace, and love that are contained in this blessed Truth! This alone is the stable foundation of faith in our access to God.

The redemption which Christ secured on Calvary lasts forever. It makes possible a forgiveness that is eternal in both quality and scope because it is based on the riches of His grace. Paul wrote: "In whom we have redemption through his blood, the forgiveness of sins, according to the riches of his grace" (Ephesians 1:7). Every believer has found release from the penalty of sin through this marvelous work of Christ in his behalf.

C. The Cleansing (v. 14)

**14. How much more shall the blood of Christ, who through the eternal Spirit offered himself without spot to God, purge your conscience from dead works to serve the living God?**

The emphasis is again on the blood of Christ and its effectual work in the salvation of the soul. He shed His blood voluntarily—He "offered himself." In doing so, He set an example which we would do well to follow in Christian service. The ultimate goal of every Christian should be to offer himself unto God. Paul wrote: "I beseech you therefore, brethren, by the mercies of God, that ye present your bodies a living sacrifice, holy, acceptable unto God, which is your reasonable service" (Romans 12:1). God is looking for people who will serve Him voluntarily. In fact, all true service to God is voluntary.

Also, Christ offered Himself without spot. His life was sinless; therefore, His offering was without blemish. Thus, it was acceptable unto God. He functioned as both priest and sacrifice "through the eternal Spirit." Only the spotless Son of God could remove the corruption, penalty, and guilt brought to man by sin and replace it with tranquillity and love. Paul declared: "Therefore being justified by faith, we have peace with God through our Lord Jesus Christ" (Romans 5:1). And, "There is therefore now no condemnation to them which are in Christ Jesus, who walk not after the flesh, but after the Spirit" (Romans 8:1).

Then, Christ's sacrifice was a spiritual sacrifice. He "offered himself . . . through the eternal Spirit." His sacrifice was not only human but divine. Its character was not temporary and changeable, but permanent and eternal. The effect of such a sacrifice was cleansing and life: "How much more shall the blood of Christ . . . purge your conscience from dead works to serve the living God."

Consider Paul's thoughts on service to God: "I beseech you therefore, brethren, by the mercies of God, that ye present your bodies a living sacrifice, holy, acceptable unto God, which is your reasonable service. And be not conformed to this world: but be ye transformed by the renewing of your mind, that ye may prove what is that good, and acceptable, and perfect, will of God" (Romans 12:1, 2).

III. REDEEMED BY HIS BLOOD (Hebrews 9:15-28)

A. Mediator of the New Testament (vv. 15-21)

**15. And for this cause he is the mediator of the new testament, that by means of death, for the redemption of the transgressions that were under the first testament, they which are called might receive the promise of eternal inheritance.**

**16. For where a testament is, there must also of necessity be the death of the testator.**

**17. For a testament is of force after men are dead: otherwise it is of no strength at all while the testator liveth.**

**18. Whereupon neither the first testament was dedicated without blood.**

**19. For when Moses had spoken every precept to all the people according to the law, he took the blood of calves and of goats, with water, and scarlet wool, and hyssop, and sprinkled both the book, and all the people,**

**20. Saying, This is the blood of the testament which God hath enjoined unto you.**

**21. Moreover he sprinkled with blood both the tabernacle, and all the vessels of the ministry.**

A testament or will is made by a living man; but while he lives, it is of no value. In order for it to be effectual, the testator must die.

Thus, the writer stresses the purpose of Christ's death. The better covenant that God was making with man could only be ratified and valid as it was sealed by the death of Christ. Without the shedding of His blood, the new testament was meaningless. But when His blood was shed, the hope expressed in this covenant could be realized by any who would accept its promise by faith.

A testament or will gives instruction as to the distribution of a person's goods after his death. Upon His death, Christ, the testator, bequeathed His goods to His heirs. All the goods of grace and glory belonged to the Lord Jesus Christ, for He was "appointed heir of all things" (Hebrews 1:2). In His death, He bequeathed "all things" unto His people, appointing them to be heirs of God and coheirs with Himself.

Moses was the mediator between God and man in the administration of the Law (Galatians 3:19). He spoke "every precept" audibly. He read the Law—the old covenant—in the audience of the people. The Law itself justified Moses in this reading; he spoke "according to the Law."

Moses, then, mixed the blood of the sacrificial beasts with water to make it distributable. He took a bunch of hyssop bound up with scarlet wool and, dipping it into the basins, sprinkled the blood until it was all spent in that service. One half of it he sprinkled on the altar, and the other half he sprinkled on the people—the twofold distribution signifying atonement and purification.

Everything about the people that was not sprinkled with the blood was impure and unclean. Because of their uncleanness and their transgressions, the Tabernacle itself and all its vessels—the Ark of the Covenant, the mercy seat, the altar of incense, etc.—were purified every year with blood on the Day of Atonement. The end result was to purge the people from their uncleanness.

B. Remission of Sin (vv. 22, 23)

**22. And almost all things are by the law purged with blood; and without shedding of blood is no remission.**

**23. It was therefore necessary that the patterns of things in the heavens should be purified with these; but the heavenly things themselves with better sacrifices than these.**

The word **almost** indicates that some things were cleansed differently. But any other element of cleansing derived its power from the sacrifices. There was no remission without blood.

Just so, there is neither purity nor salvation apart from Christ. His blood is both necessary and sufficient to cleanse all sin. Men are shut off from the favor of God because of their sin. The only way to appease God's wrath is by the atonement of the blood.

When we understand the nature of sin, we also understand why the cost for its remedy was so high. Sin manifests itself as lawlessness in that it is a transgression of the law (John 3:4). It is a grievous malady that contaminates the whole of man's being (Isaiah 1:4, 5; Romans 3:10-18). Sin is an obscuring cloud, which hides the face of God's blessing (Isaiah 59:2). Sin is a binding cord, which holds man in its power (Proverbs 5:22). It is a tyrannical owner, who embitters the lives of his slaves (Nehemiah 9:37). It is a disturber of rest, which causes disorder and anxiety (Psalm 38:3). Sin is a robber of blessing, which strips and starves the soul (Jeremiah 5:25). It is a terrible devastation, which brings untold desolation. It is a terrible devastation, which brings untold desolation (Micah 6:13). It is a tripper-upper, which continually overthrows the sinner

to his hurt (Proverbs 13:6). It is a record writer, which leaves its indelible mark upon the committer (Jeremiah 17:1). Sin is a betraying presence, which "will not" no matter what pains are taken to hide it (Ezekiel 21:24). It is a sure detective, which turns upon the sinner and finds him out (Numbers 32:23). It is an accusing witness, which points its condemning finger at the prisoner in the bondage of sin (Isaiah 59:12). Sin is a sum of addition which accumulates its weight to the condemnation of the sinner (Isaiah 30:1).—(Adapted from *Sourcebook of 500 Illustrations* by Robert G. Lee.)

In verse 22, we are given a contrast between the earthly and the heavenly. Under the law there were symbols and types of spiritual things. But under the new covenant there were no symbols and types—only realities. Thus, the heavenly sanctuary was the reality, of which the earthly tent was a copy. Therefore, it was cleansed with a better sacrifice— even the sacrifice of Christ, the Son of God.

C. Intercession of Christ (v. 24)

**24. For Christ is not entered into the holy places made with hands, which are the figures of the true; but into heaven itself, now to appear in the presence of God for us.**

Christ did not enter into the man-made sanctuary, but into the heavenly sanctuary. The purpose of His entrance into the sanctuary was "to appear in the presence of God for us."

Such appearance expresses the duration of time from the entrance of Christ into heaven unto the consummation of all things. Christ not only entered into heaven after His death, but He is in heaven now as our high priest. He is in heaven now as our advocate. His presence there is testimony of His continuing love, care, and compassion for us.

To what extent are we following Christ in the role of intercessor? Are there not countless millions who are lost and who will die without hope unless they find Jesus Christ? Are we praying for them? There are friends and neighbors and relatives who have not discovered new life in Christ. Are we praying for them? Others may use their abilities in a different way than us. But what greater service could we render than to enter our secret closet where we can get close to God and intercede for others in prayer? The work of interceding has no glamour in it, but its rewards are great. Too see one soul come to Christ for whom we have prayed more than compensates for all the time and effort involved. No other work comes so close to the heart of Christian service.

D. Appearance of Christ (vv. 25-28)

(Hebrews 9:25-28 is not included in the printed text.)

Our understanding of Christ's priesthood revolves around the word **once.** The **one** sacrifice of Christ is valid **once** and for all; it need never be repeated. Its effectiveness is so comprehensive, so vast in scope, that it has taken away "the sins of many." It is sufficient for all mankind.

**Once** is contrasted with oftentimes. Again and again, year after year, a sacrificial animal had to be slaughtered under the old covenant. The word **often** betrays the inadequacy of the Old Testament order. The work of Christ is not marked by the word **often** but by the word **once.** But **once** means "once and for all."

Christ's offering of Himself turns our gaze toward the consummation of the ages. Death happens once, to each individual; it cannot be repeated; but after death comes judgment. Likewise, Christ's death happened once; it cannot be repeated. But just as man must appear once again, after death, at judgment, so will Christ appear a second time—not in lowliness, but in glory. His coming again will differ from His first coming, in that it will not be related with the sin of men. When He comes the second time, He will bring the consummation of redemption.

This passage calls attention to the finished work of redemption, the present reality of redemption, and the promised future realization of Redemption. Before our spiritual eyes stands the crucified Christ, the eternal high priest, and the coming Savior. We await the ultimate revelation of Christ, our high priest.

## REVIEW QUESTIONS

1. What good was the sacrifice of animals in the Old Testament days?

2. What, according to verses 16 and 17, makes a legal will effective?

3. How did Moses dedicate the first covenant?

4. What, according to verse 22, is the one thing that is absolutely necessary for sins to be remitted?

5. What truths of this lesson are applicable to our day-to-day living?

## GOLDEN TEXT HOMILY

"CHRIST WAS ONCE OFFERED TO BEAR THE SINS OF MANY; AND UNTO THEM THAT LOOK FOR HIM SHALL HE APPEAR THE SECOND TIME WITHOUT SIN UNTO SALVATION" (Hebrews 9:28).

A successful advertising campaign refers to its product as the "real thing." It implies that all others are nothing more than imitations and, therefore, inferior to their product. Original works of art are sometimes considered priceless because of their extraordinary beauty or because of the reputation of the artist. Copies or reproductions of valuable originals may look like the real thing but cannot stand up under close examination.

In order for the estrangement between God and mankind to be removed, something had to be done about its underlying cause—namely sin. This sin was so pervasive and its consequences so far reaching that no ordinary means could be used to eliminate it. Something special had to happen. God had promised in the garden (Genesis 3:15) that the power of sin would be broken.

The sacrificial system was introduced by God as a temporary means of dealing with the sins of the people. It was imperfect that the sacrifices had to be offered over and over again. It was also imperfect in that the blood offered was of animals, different in essence from the people whose sins it was intended to cover.

What was needed was a better sacrifice. God had already made provision for it, and the temple sacrifices were but a shadow of what was to come. They were clues that represented the "real" sacrifice that was to be made by Christ himself. When Jesus took upon Himself the sins of the world, He did not offer up the blood of another. He shed

His own blood, the very "blood of God" which had infinite worth. This incredible act of love was sufficient to deal with the issue of sin once and for all.

Christ will come again, and at this second coming He will not be concerned with sin. That account was settled at his first coming. Rather He comes "unto them that look for him." A telling characteristic of true believers is that they are looking for His return and eagerly await the completion of their salvation, for He comes "unto salvation." Our great redemption has been accomplished by Christ on the Cross and will be consummated in heaven where we will eternally be with the Lord. Paul said when the trumpet sounds "the dead in Christ will rise first. After that, we who are still alive and are left will be caught up with them in the clouds to meet the Lord in the air. And so we will be with the Lord forever" (1 Thessalonians 4:16, 17; *New International Version*).

We rejoice and take comfort in the work of Christ and in our hope for the future. Jesus came and broke the power of sin. He will come again to receive those who look for Him into eternal fellowship in heaven. Praise God for this great redemption!—**Benjamin Perez, Chaplain (Lieutenant Colonel), USAF, Maxwell AFB, Alabama.**

## SENTENCE SERMONS

CHRIST'S DEATH provides eternal redemption for all who believe.

**—Selected**

REDEMPTION WAS NOT an afterthought with God.

**—"Speaker's Sourcebook"**

JESUS LIVED that we might die and died that we might die.

**—"Speaker's Sourcebook"**

IT TOOK MORE than nails to hold Jesus to the cross. The bonds of love held Him there.

**—Rolla O. Swisher**

## EVANGELISTIC APPLICATION

CHRIST'S DEATH PROVIDES ETERNAL REDEMPTION FOR ALL WHO BELIEVE.

A great artist once sought to paint the scene of the Crucifixion. With marvelous skill he sketched the skull-shaped hill crowned by three crosses, and with true delineation pictured the two thieves hanging in agony upon their emblems of shame; but when he came to depict the figure upon the central cross, he found his hand had lost its cunning and that he was impotent to portray the figure of the world's great Redeemer.

Finally, in despair, he simply enveloped the central cross in a sunburst of glory, and left it thus. But what conception could have been more appropriate, for as the sun burns itself up in giving light, heat, and life to the planets of the solar system which it shepherds, so the Sun of Righteousness was consumed that man might have eternal life, and through His sacrificial death might learn that "without shedding of blood is no"—anything. The supreme fact of the age remains—"Christ died for our sins" (Walter B. Knight in *Knight's Master Book of New Illustrations*).

## ILLUMINATING THE LESSON

I heard of an infidel who said that if he believed as Christians say they believe, that a man's life in the world to come depends upon his life here in the world, then he would give men no rest, he would be at them day and night, urging them and entreating them to lead godly lives and to become men of faith that they might inherit eternal life. If this means much to us, then we must testify to the world, and both by our lives and by our words persuade men to live godly lives, that they not only may get the most out of this life but also may inherit life eternal (Clarence Edward Macartney in *Macartney's Illustrations*).

## DAILY DEVOTIONAL GUIDE

M. Song of Victory. Exodus 15:1-18
T. Song of Faith. Numbers 21:16-18
W. Song of Praise. Psalm 150:1-6
T. Song of Rejoicing. Romans 15:9-13
F. Song of Revelation. Revelation 5:6-10
S. Song of the Lamb. Revelation 15:3, 4

# Steadfast in the Faith

**Study Text:** Hebrews 10:19-39

**Supplemental References:** Exodus 34:1-7; Deuteronomy 17:2-6; Colossians 1:12-23; James 1:1-8; Jude 20-25

**Time:** Probably A.D. 65-70

**Place:** Written from Rome.

**Golden Text:** "Let us hold fast the profession of our faith without wavering" (Hebrews 10:23).

**Central Truth:** Because of Christ's sacrifice, access to God is now the privilege of every believer.

**Evangelistic Emphasis:** God always accepts those who come to Him in repentance and faith.

## Printed Text

**Hebrews 10:19.** Having therefore, brethren, boldness to enter into the holiest by the blood of Jesus,

**20. By a new and living way, which he hath consecrated for us, through the veil, that is to say, his flesh;**

21. And having an high priest over the house of God;

**22. Let us draw near with a true heart in full assurance of faith, having our hearts sprinkled from an evil conscience, and our bodies washed with pure water.**

23. Let us hold fast the profession of our faith without wavering; (for he is faithful that promised;)

**24. And let us consider one another to provoke unto love and to good works:**

25. Not forsaking the assembling of ourselves together, as the manner of some is; but exhorting one another: and so much the more, as ye see the day approaching.

**26. For if we sin wilfully after that we have received the knowledge of the truth, there remaineth no more sacrifice for sins,**

27. But a certain fearful looking for of judgment and fiery indignation, which shall devour the adversaries.

**28. He that despised Moses' law died without mercy under two or three witnesses:**

29. Of how much sorer punishment, suppose ye, shall he be thought worthy, who hath trodden under foot the Son of God, and hath counted the blood of the covenant, wherewith he was sanctified, an unholy thing, and hath done despite unto the Spirit of grace?

**30. For we know him that hath said, Vengeance belongeth unto me, I will recompense, saith the Lord. And again, The Lord shall judge his people.**

31. It is a fearful thing to fall into the hands of the living God.

## LESSON OUTLINE

I. A PURIFIED HEART
  A. The Most Holy Place
  B. A Great Priest
  C. The Hope
  D. The Meeting Place
II. THE DANGER OF APOSTASY
  A. The Knowledge of the Truth
  B. The Spirit of Grace
  C. A Dreadful Thing
III. FAITH IS THE VICTORY
  A. The Lasting Possessions
  B. The Lord's Coming
  C. The Saving Faith

## LESSON EXPOSITION

### INTRODUCTION

In the preceding verses of Chapter 10, the writer argues that the Jewish sacrifices availed for nothing more than external or ceremonial purifications. On the other hand, the one offering of Christ is internal and practiced; it purifies the soul from the uncleanness of sin and renders it capable of offering acceptable service to God.

In today's study, the author makes practical application of the truths he has already taught in this Epistle. Briefly he restates his position, showing that he still has in mind the solemn ceremonies of the great Jewish Day of Atonement.

Thus far he has discussed the restrictions imposed upon mankind in regard to entering the Holy of Holies. A veil hid this place where God's presence was manifested in sacred symbols. No one but the high priest dared pass beyond the veil—and he only in the prescribed manner. For a sinner to pass through was unthinkable. Yet, the veil is now done away with. Man now has free access to God. This extraordinary privilege has been made possible through the shed blood of God's Son.

The knowledge that Christ offered Himself for us should incite us to commit our lives more fully to Him. We should seek to draw closer and closer to Him. Maintaining the privileges we have found in Him requires an earnest, devoted, obedient life of love and service.

Also, Christ's example in fulfilling the will of God in His life should prompt us to find and fulfill that most holy will for our own live. It should bring us to the place of relying fully upon Him as our sacrifice and substitute, resulting in our salvation from sin.

### I. A PURIFIED HEART (Hebrews 10:19-25)

#### A. The Most Holy Place (vv. 19, 20)

**19. Having therefore, brethren, boldness to enter into the holiest by the blood of Jesus,**
**20. By a new and living way, which he hath consecrated for us, through the veil, that is to say, his flesh.**

By using the word **therefore** the writer shows he is making a transition in his thoughts from the preceding verses, and thereby is declaring them to be the ground for his present discussion.

The body of believers is referred to as brothers. This word denotes the spiritual relationship that exists between believers. After all, we are members of one family, the family of God.

Confidence to enter the Most Holy Place was a freedom not allowed under the Law. In pre-Christian times no one could enter the holy place but the high priest, and he could enter only once a year. The mass of people were utterly excluded from any entrance into the special presence of God.

But what a different situation we have under the gospel! Not only do we have the right, privilege, and liberty of access to God, but we also have the confidence to approach God. We are at liberty to enter into the immediate, gracious presence of God himself in Christ Jesus. And we make this approach unto God without no dread, fear, or terror.

But what has made possible this privilege that we enjoy? There is but one answer: "the blood of Jesus," which removed all barriers between God and believers. The blood made atonement for men's sins; it answered the Law; it removed the curse; it broke down the wall of partition; and it made boldness before God possible.

Entrance into the Holy of Holies by believers is called a "new" way. It was newly made, prepared, and consecrated under a new covenant. It is also said to be a "living" way. It leads to life, brings us to experience life, and is the only means of obtaining everlasting life. It is a "consecrated" way. He has set this way apart for believers. The only way of entrance into God's presence is by the blood of Jesus. One man expressed it: "We enter only through the death wounds of the Lamb."

B. A Great Priest (vv. 21, 22)

**21. And having an high priest over the house of God;**

**22. Let us draw near with a true heart in full assurance of faith, having our hearts sprinkled from an evil conscience, and our bodies washed with pure water.**

Jesus is our high priest; He exercises that office on our behalf. He rules over God's household. He takes the oversight of the church and orders all things unto the glory of God and the salvation of His own. The house of God includes the whole family of God in heaven and earth. But special attention is here given to the family on earth; they "have a high priest."

And how graciously does the Lord preside over the affairs of believers! They worship by His appointment. They are assisted in worship by His Spirit. He makes their worship acceptable unto God. He makes all their approaches to God effective by His intercession and glorious by the administration of His Spirit.

We are encouraged to draw near unto God. All the means available through Christ should be used to accomplish this goal. Our approach to Him must be in all sincerity of heart, for God requires "truth in the inward parts" (Psalm 51:6). Jesus said, "God is a Spirit: and they that worship him must worship him in spirit and in truth" (John 4:24).

We are to approach God with unfaltering faith fully trusting Him to receive us. Faith is essential because "without faith it is impossible to please [God]" (Hebrews 11:6). This unqualified assurance of faith refers to a firm and immovable persuasion concerning the priesthood of Christ, a confidence in His finished work that nothing can shatter. It is the expression of the full satisfaction of our souls that the work of Christ will give us acceptance before God. What joy such faith in Christ brings! What boldness such faith imports! What hope such faith inspires!

The application—sprinkling—of the blood of atonement removes an evil conscience from our hearts. The pure water might refer to the Word (Ephesians 5:25, 26), to the Holy Spirit (John 7:37-39), or to the Holy Spirit's using the Word in cleansing our lives from daily defilement. We need a continuous application of the Word to our heart by the Spirit.

C. The Hope (vv. 23, 24)

**23. Let us hold fast the profession of our faith without wavering; (for he is faithful that promised;)**

**24. And let us consider one another to provoke unto love and to good works.**

The profession of our faith involves the faith by which we believe and the faith which we believe. The first is the surrendering of ourselves unto Christ— we become subject to the demands of the gospel. The second is the avowal of our faith on all occasions, including willingness to cheerfully undergo afflictions, troubles, and persecutions because of our profession.

The admonition to maintain our grip firmly on the hope we profess suggests that there are difficulties to be faced. It implies putting forth our utmost strength and endeavors in maintaining our profession. And this must be done "without wavering." There can be no "halting between two opinions" (see 1 Kings 18: 21). Our resolve must be so strong that no matter what opposition we face our faith will be fixed and immovable.

When we are tempted to give up unseen blessings of Christianity for the visible things of this world, let us remind ourselves that He who has given us His promise will not fail us. If we trust in Him, we will never be disappointed.

The writer assumed that those to whom he was writing had a deep concern for others. In their church gatherings, the Christians discussed matters that were edifying. And this they did to incite one another to love and to good deeds.

The ultimate objective of our Christian fellowship is the consideration of one another's strengths and weaknesses. We should take every opportunity we have to encourage one another. Mutual edification is a part of the gospel prescription for victorious Christian living. Brotherly love and noble actions are attitudes worth promoting.

## D. The Meeting Place (v. 25)

**25. Not forsaking the assembling of ourselves together, as the manner of some is; but exhorting one another: and so much the more, as ye see the day approaching.**

By speaking of gathering ourselves together, the writer was referring to times of worship where prayer, preaching, singing, and the administration of sacraments were an integral part. Public worship served to admonish, exhort, and provoke unto love and good works, as well as to comfort, establish, and encourage those who were afflicted or persecuted. Thus, he admonished the readers not to forsake these meetings.

Forsaking God's house may be either total or partial. This neglect may stem from a fear of suffering. When lands, possessions, houses, relations, liberty, or even life itself becomes more important than Christ, the soul is in danger. This neglect may stem from spiritual slothfulness. When men fail to stir themselves up and to shake off the weight that lies upon them, they are likely to forsake this most important duty.

The writer of Hebrews inferred that some had already fallen—"as the manner of some is." During those early days some had begun to decline from their profession, often failing in worship attendance.

' Verse 24 encourages believers to carefully watch over one another. Verse 25 instructs believers to encourage and admonish and exhort one another. We should seize every opportunity to persuade and encourage one another to faithfulness in Christian service. And this we should do more earnestly as we see the day of His coming back again is drawing near. Knowing that the day of Christ's return is near should lead us to steadfastness. To see His coming as imminent, and not to be diligent in the duties of divine worship reveals a backsliding attitude.

## II. THE DANGER OF APOSTASY (Hebrews 10:26-31)

### A. The Knowledge of the Truth (vv. 26, 27)

**26. For if we sin wilfully after that we have received the knowledge of the truth, there remaineth no more sacrifice for sins,**

**27. But a certain fearful looking for of judgment and fiery indignation, which shall devour the adversaries.**

The words "if we" show that there is no respect of persons in this matter and that those who have equally sinned shall be equally punished. The apostasy of some believers should serve as a warning to each of us lest we become careless in our Christian experience.

The nature of the sin, against which this heavy doom was announced, was clear. The sin mentioned was the renouncing of the profession of faith which the writer urged the readers to retain, with all the acts and duties pertaining to it. It was to deliberately keep on sinning after they had received a knowledge of the truth.

It was a renunciation of the gospel; a deed done "wilfully"; that is, willingly. It was a definite decision to depart from God and to renounce openly the blood of the covenant.

Those who forsook the local assembly not only turned their backs on Christianity, but they reverted to Judaism. Thus, they showed a preference for another way of religion over and above the gospel. When such a choice is made, there is no means left whereby the soul may be saved. When the once-for-all sacrifice of Christ is decisively and conclusively rejected, God has no other way of salvation to offer.

For those who have forsaken the way of the Lord, there remains no sacrifice for sin, but there does remain a fearful expectation of judgment. Yet when men have hardened themselves in sin, no fear of punishment will either rouse or stir them up to seek for relief. Future wrath and judgment, without hope of relief, is the dreadful expectation of all Christ-rejecters. Their fate is a fury of fire, described as "fiery indignation."

B. The Spirit of Grace (vv. 28, 29)

**28. He that despised Moses' law died without mercy under two or three witnesses:**

**29. Of how much sorer punishment, suppose ye, shall he be thought worthy, who hath trodden under foot the Son of God, and hath counted the blood of the covenant, wherewith he was sanctified, an unholy thing, and hath done despite unto the Spirit of grace?**

The doom of the lawbreaker in the Old Testament forms a backdrop against which the writer contrasted the greater doom of the Christ-rejecter. A man who broke Moses' law, by becoming an idolater, died without mercy when his guilt was proven by the testimony of two or three witnesses (Deuteronomy 17:2-7).

The Christ-rejecter is counted worthy of much sorer judgment because his privilege is much greater. He sins not against Moses' law, but against the Son of God by showing utter disregard for His goodness, authority, and love. To tread something underfoot is the highest expression of scorn, contempt, and malice.

The Christ-rejecter also sins by being in opposition to the priestly office of Christ. He counts the precious blood of Christ as a worthless thing. He no longer esteems it as that wherewith the new covenant is sealed, confirmed, and established. To him the blood of bulls and goats brings greater glory to God than does the blood of Christ. This is

the height of contempt to esteem the precious blood of Christ whereby we are sanctified and dedicated unto God an "unholy thing!"

Then, also, the Christ-rejecter opposes the Spirit of grace in that he does Him despite. By the Spirit multitudes are converted unto God; the Scriptures are opened to their understanding; and mighty works, wonders, signs, and miracles are wrought.

Willful repudiation of God's beloved Son is a sin of immense magnitude. God will judge all who reject His Son. The abiding lesson for all of us is this: Let us not be numbered among those who must appear before God for judgment, for it is a dreadful thing to fall into the hands of the living God.

C. A Dreadful Thing (vv. 30, 31)

**30. For we know him that hath said, Vengeance belongeth unto me, I will recompense, saith the Lord. And again, The Lord shall judge his people.**

**31. It is a fearful thing to fall into the hands of the living God.**

The writer turns to the Old Testament to prove that God is to be the judge and not man. Vengeance is the sole prerogative of God. Sometimes we are inclined to take matters into our own hands. But the Lord encourages us to put matters into His hands. In His time and in His way, God will resolve the situation. God's time and God's way are always the best way.

John Phillips wrote: "We are dealing with serious issues when dealing with God's Son, God's salvation, and God's Spirit. They are not to be trifled with, ignored, or despised. And they are certainly not to be rejected with impunity." So it is understandable that God says He will judge and determine and solve and settle the cause and the cases of His people.

Then the writer asserts that it is an awful, terrifying thing to fall into the hands of the living God. Jesus warned His disciples to fear God rather than man: "Fear them not therefore: for there is nothing covered, that shall not be revealed; and hid, that shall not be known. What I tell you in darkness, that speak ye in light: and what ye hear in the ear, that preach ye upon the housetops. And fear not them which kill the body, but are not able to kill the soul: but rather fear him which is able to destroy both soul and body in hell" (Matthew 10:26-28). Ananais and Sapphira learned how dreaded the judgment of God could be. They came to a premature death at the hands of the living God. The early church was moved by this action. "And great fear came upon all the church, and upon as many as heard these things" (Acts 5:11).

III. FAITH IS THE VICTORY (Hebrews 10:32-39)

A. The Lasting Possessions (vv. 32-34)

(Hebrews 10:32-34 is not included in the printed text.)

The writer calls upon his readers to recall their earliest experiences when they first came to know Christ as Savior. This is a valuable exercise for every believer. It is important to look back occasionally and remember where we came from and where the Lord has brought us. When Satan tempts us to doubt our salvation, we can take him back to the time and the place where Christ first became real in our live.

Remembering their first encounters with the Lord, these believers stood their ground even in the face of great suffering. To publicly acknowledge Christ in those days led to public insult and persecution. They were less fortunate than most Christians today. Most believers today do not live in dread of bodily injury or prison or death because of their faith. I wonder how our consecration and commitment compare with the first-century believers.

These early Christians were able to sympathize with those who were persecuted and imprisoned. They stood side by side with them. They understood what they were facing and were able to encourage them and help them to live victoriously in the midst of their trying circumstances.

Also, these believers kept their eye on the ultimate goal. When their property was confiscated they joyfully accepted that. They did so because they knew that they had better and lasting possessions. They had caught the spirit of Paul who wrote: "I press toward the mark for the prize of the high calling of God in Christ Jesus" (Philippians 4:14). Do you face life's reverses with a similar attitude? Are you keeping your eye on that heavenly prize that awaits every faithful believer? Nothing this world offers can compare with what is in store for the child of God.

B. The Lord's Coming (vv. 35-38)

(Hebrews 10:35-38 is not included in the printed text.)

As long as our confidence in the future is based on God's Word, it will be richly rewarded. Paul wrote to the Galatians, "And let us not be weary in well doing: for in due season we shall reap, if we faint not" (Galatians 6:9). There may be times when it appears that all our efforts are futile, that nothing is going to come of our labors. But the history of believers shows that God honors the faithfulness of His people.

Our generation is not known for its persevering nature. For the most part, what is called the "now generation" and the "me generation" wants everything to happen immediately. It is also more interested in the present than the future. There is a fatalism about our time that seems to feel that if it doesn't get everything now, it won't get it at all. But the writer of Hebrews says that those who persevere in doing the will of God are the ones who will receive the promise. Serving God is a day-by-day adventure which calls for determination and stickability.

The ultimate goal every believer seeks to reach is the second coming of Christ. Many people scoff at the idea that Jesus is coming back, but the Bible clearly teaches this. When the time for His return arrives, He will come without delay.

It behooves us to be watching and longing for that day. We keep busy in His service as He has instructed us until He comes, but we also say with John, "Even so, come quickly, Lord Jesus."

C. The Saving Faith (v. 39)

(Hebrews 10:39 is not included in the printed text.)

The writer did not believe that his readers were inclined to look back. He admonished them not to be of that number who start out in the race but take their eye off the goal and fall by the wayside. The backward look only leads to destruction. So the believer is encouraged to keep his eyes on the future and to move steadily ahead.

To do this, perseverance is required. Almost anyone can get off to a good start and many people can excel in spurts and spasms. Great moments come in one way or another for almost everyone. William Barclay observed: "To everyone it is sometimes given to mount up with wings as eagles; in the moment of the great effort everyone can run and not be weary; but the greatest gift of all is to walk and not to faint."

When the writer speaks of being of those who believe and are saved, he is thinking of the time when we will be totally conformed to Christ at His coming. All that salvation entails will be realized at that time. It is a goal well worth persuading with perseverance. Following Jesus now will bring us to His immediate presence and to ultimate glory.

## REVIEW QUESTIONS

1. What makes possible our access into the presence of God?

2. What thoughts emerge in your mind as you reflect on the word "brethren," as used in verse 19?

3. Give your idea of what it means to be "steadfast in the faith."

4. What is meant by "apostasy?" Is there evidence of apostasy in our day?

5. What can the church do to make people more conscious of the return of Christ?

## GOLDEN TEXT HOMILY

"LET US HOLD FAST THE PROFESSION OF OUR FAITH WITHOUT WAVERING" (Hebrews 10:23).

The Jewish members of the Jerusalem Christian Church believed their salvation came through Jesus Christ whom they accepted as the Messiah. However, many still adhered to some of the Jewish rituals including animal sacrifices. Those Jews who remained in the Jewish faith strongly rejected the Christian doctrine, and resented those who embraced it. The breach between these two groups was great.

Paul had become convinced that his hope for a national Jewish repentance and acceptance of Jesus Christ as Savior would not come—at least not in his lifetime. Paul regretfully turned his efforts away from the Jews as a whole and toward the Gentiles (Acts 13:46; 28:28).

Remember that Judaism was both a religious and political system. The political system fell when Jerusalem was destroyed in A.D. 70. Following this destruction, the Jews were without a land, without a temple, and without a government. This placed a great strain on the faith of those Jewish Christians. How would they accept the destruction of their beloved city? Jesus said in His Olivet discourse that not one stone would be left upon another (Matthew 24:2; Luke 19:41-44). If they believed His teaching, they could only accept the overthrow as the inevitable judgment of God for the rejectors of Jesus as the Messiah. If, however, they turned totally from law to grace, and away from Jerusalem as the center of worship to their church, they would be regarded as traitors by their countrymen who were loyal to the law and temple.

The writer of Hebrews seemed to be using this letter to prepare the Jewish Christians for this crisis. The essence of the letter is to encourage the Christians to prevail in this time of testing. They must hold fast to the profession of their faith without wavering.—**Wayne S. Proctor, Pastor, Lexington, Kentucky**

## SENTENCE SERMONS

BECAUSE OF CHRIST'S sacrifice ac-

cess to God is now the privilege of every believer.
**—Selected**

THE CHRISTIAN WHO sells out to Christ is always unsatisfied, but not dissatisfied.
**—Eugenia Price**

ONLY ENTIRELY DEVOTED Christians are happy Christians.
**—Selected**

FAITH DOESN'T ALWAYS exempt us from ridicule and sacrifice, but it does gain the favor of God.
**—"Notes and Quotes"**

## EVANGELISTIC APPLICATION

GOD ALWAYS ACCEPTS THOSE WHO COME TO HIM IN REPENTANCE AND FAITH.

When an individual truly repents of his sin and places his faith in Jesus Christ, God forgives him of his sin and gives to him eternal life. The Bible clearly presents Jesus as the hope of mankind. He is the Bible's fullness, the Bible's center, the Bible's fascination. It is all about Jesus. The Old Testament conceals, infolds, promises, pictures, prophesies, localizes, symbolizes Christ. The New Testament reveals, unfolds, presents, produces, proclaims, universalizes, and sacrifices Christ.

The name of Jesus, the Supreme Personality, the center of a world's desire, is on every page in expression, or symbol, or prophecy, or psalm, or proverb. Through this book the name of Jesus, the revealed, the redeeming, the risen, the reigning, the returning Lord, runs like a line of glimmering light (adapted from Robert G. Lee in *Sourcebook of 500 Illustrations*).

## ILLUMINATING THE LESSON

Geologists knew that there were great reservoirs of oil deep down under the ground of West Texas. The ranchers lived in their modest homes and had large flocks of sheep that grazed the vast reaches of the semi-desert plain on the surface. The oil was underneath, but there was no access to it. Then great wells were sunk, and the oil gushed forth and out flowed the black gold. The wealth transformed the lives of those who had entered into its possession. The oil had been there all the time, but access to it determined possession more than a title deed; it made it a present reality.

The believer who is justified through the atoning work of the Savior has direct access to the grace of God. The Lord Jesus Christ has opened up a way—a new and living way—by which we come boldly to the very presence of God, who is the source of all grace. In Romans 8:32 we find that with Christ He has given us all things (Donald Grey Barnhouse in *Let Me Illustrate*).

## DAILY DEVOTIONAL GUIDE

M. Steadfastness Through Trust. Psalm 37:1-9

T. Steadfastness Through Repentance. Psalm 51:1-13

W. Steadfastness Through Prayer. Psalm 84:1-12

T. Steadfastness Through Obedience. John 15:1-11

F. Steadfastness Through Christ. 1 Corinthians 15:57, 58

S. Steadfastness Through Faith. James 1:1-8

# Living by Faith

**Study Text:** Hebrews 11:1-40

**Supplemental References:** Genesis 22:1-19; Psalm 27:1-14; Habakkuk 2:1-4; Matthew 8:5-10; Acts 14:21-28; Romans 4:9-25

**Time:** Probably A.D. 65-70

**Place:** Generally thought to have been written from Rome.

**Golden Text:** "Faith is the substance of things hoped for, the evidence of things not seen" (Hebrews 11:1).

**Central Truth:** The promises of God are appropriated by faith.

**Evangelistic Emphasis:** Salvation comes to all who believe in the sacrifice of Christ on Calvary.

## Printed Text

**Hebrews 11:1.** Now faith is the substance of things hoped for, the evidence of things not seen.

**2. For by it the elders obtained a good report.**

3. Through faith we understand that the worlds were framed by the word of God, so that things which are seen were not made of things which do appear.

**4. By faith Abel offered unto God a more excellent sacrifice than Cain, by which he obtained witness that he was righteous, God testifying of his gifts: and by it he being dead yet speaketh.**

5. By faith Enoch was translated that he should not see death; and was not found, because God had translated him: for before his translation he had this testimony, that he pleased God.

**6. But without faith it is impossible to please him: for he that cometh to** God must believe that he is, and that he is a rewarder of them that diligently seek him.

7. By faith Noah, being warned of God of things not seen as yet, moved with fear, prepared an ark to the saving of his house; by the which he condemned the world, and became heir of the righteousness which is by faith.

**8. By faith Abraham, when he was called to go out into a place which he should after receive for an inheritance, obeyed; and he went out, not knowing whither he went.**

9. By faith he sojourned in the land of promise, as in a strange country, dwelling in tabernacles with Isaac and Jacob, the heirs with him of the same promise:

**10. For he looked for a city which hath foundations, whose builder and maker is God.**

## LESSON OUTLINE

I. FAITH DEFINED

  A. Substance and Evidence

  B. The Elders

  C. Creation

II. FAITH ILLUSTRATED

  A. Abel and Enoch

B. Noah and Abraham
C. Strangers and Pilgrims
D. Isaac, Jacob, and Joseph

III. FAITH REWARDED

A. Moses
B. Those Delivered From Their Foes
C. Those Delivered to Their Foes
D. Something Better for Us

## LESSON EXPOSITION

### INTRODUCTION

Today's study deals with faith's perfect vision and its quality of endurance. It introduces us to men and women of the Old Testament who had 20-20 spiritual vision and who did not renounce their faith, despite tremendous shame and suffering.

The eleventh chapter of Hebrews is one of the greatest and best known chapters of the Bible. The writer furnishes a history of faith that reaches from the creation of the world to Christ and the church. Like a scarlet ribbon the history of faith winds its way through the history of mankind. Wherever God revealed Himself, even before Christ, faith existed.

As we review the list of the heroes of faith, may we be challenged to appropriate to ourselves the promises of God. The rewards of our spiritual fathers' faith should encourage us to exercise our own.

The chapter we are studying is a chapter of personal testimonies. We are given insight into how the followers of God responded to the various circumstances they faced. Every believer ought to be able to share with others the things that God has done for him.

### I. FAITH DEFINED (Hebrews 11:1-3)

A. Substance and Evidence (v. 1)

**11:1. Now faith is the substance of things hoped for, the evidence of things not seen.**

The faith with which this chapter deals is that persevering faith of Habakkuk 2:3, 4 and Hebrews 10:38, "Now the just shall live by faith." Such faith is not of ourselves, but of God. It is divine, supernatural, saving faith. Such faith

makes things hoped for as real as if we already had them, and provides unshakable evidence that the unseen, spiritual blessings of Christianity are absolutely certain and real. It gives the soul a taste of the goodness of the things promised and hoped for. It makes the things it represents so real that the believer beholds them as if they were present.

Abraham by faith saw the day of Christ and rejoiced. Other saints in the Old Testament also saw the King in His beauty. Faith, in being the proof of the reality of the things we cannot see, has always been the great means of preservation for the saints. It is faith alone that takes believers out of this world, even though they are in it; that exalts them above the world while they are still under its rage; that enables them to live upon the hope of things future and invisible; and that prevents them from fainting under opposition, temptation, and persecution.

Gromack said that in this verse faith "is that confident assurance that future hopes will come to pass. It is not wishful thinking or emotional fantasy; rather, it has present confidence because it is placed in God who has promised and who will not lie." Hewitt stated, "Faith does not bestow reality on things which have no substance or reality in themselves."

B. The Elders (v. 2)

**2. For by it the elders obtained a good report.**

Because they walked by faith and not by sight, the Old Testament worthies received divine approval. Most of Hebrews 11 is an illustration of how God bore witness through Old Testament saints. All true believers of that dispensation are here characterized as "elders" or saints of old. It is expressly declared that they won God's approval and were therefore accepted by Him. And it was through faith they obtained this report of pleasing God.

Clarence Edward Macartney wrote that after Sir Walter Raleigh was beheaded in the tower, they found in his Bible these true and striking lines, written the night before his death:

Even such is time, that takes in trust
Our youth, our joys, our all we have,
And pays us but with age and dust;
Who in the dark and silent grave,
When we have wandered all our
ways,
Shuts up the story on our days.
But from this earth, this grave, this
dust,
My God shall raise me up, I trust!

All the things of this world he had lost, but he had kept the faith; faith spoke to him of a hope and life beyond the grave.

When we live and make decisions that are based on faith and others observe how God honors that trust, they find faith attractive. What is more important though is that God takes note of our faith. He knows when it is genuine and He responds accordingly.

C. Creation (v. 3)

**3. Through faith we understand that the worlds were framed by the word of God, so that things which are seen were not made of things which do appear.**

By faith we accept the only factual account of creation: the divine revelation. God is the only One who was there; He tells us how it happened. If by faith we are assured that God created the world out of nothing, though this seems impossible, it will help us to believe that other things that seem impossible will take place at His command.

By faith, and faith only, do we understand that the universe was created at the bidding of God. He is responsible for "the ordering, disposing, fitting, perfecting, and adorning of the world." The beautiful order of the universe is a demonstration of the eternal power of God. This framing of the worlds was brought about by "the Word of God." "He spake, and it was done; he commanded, and it stood fast" (Psalm 33: 9).

The things that are visible (the created world) were made by those which are invisible (the eternal power and wisdom of God). All things we now behold in their order, glory, and beauty were made by the power of God; but we can comprehend this only through faith.

The world says, "Seeing is believing." God says, "Believing is seeing." Jesus said to Martha, "Did I not tell you that if you would believe you would see . . .?" (John 11:40, **New International Version**). The Apostle John wrote: "I write these things to you who believe . . . that you may know" (1 John 5:13, **New International Version**). In spiritual matters, faith precedes sight.

II. FAITH ILLUSTRATED (Hebrews 11: 4-22)

A. Abel and Enoch (vv. 4-6)

**4. By faith Abel offered unto God a more excellent sacrifice than Cain, by which he obtained witness that he was righteous, God testifying of his gifts: and by it he being dead yet speaketh.**

**5. By faith Enoch was translated that he should not see death; and was not found, because God had translated him: for before his translation he had this testimony, that he pleased God.**

**6. But without faith it is impossible to please him: for he that cometh to God must believe that he is, and that he is a rewarder of them that diligently seek him.**

Abel offered "the firstlings of his flock and of the fat thereof" (Genesis 4:4). His offering was of living creatures (that is, creatures that had lived) and therefore was made by shedding of blood. It was of the best of his flock, the "firstlings." And it was of the "fat thereof," which God also claimed as His own. He offered this sacrifice "unto God." And he offered it "by faith."

Somewhere, perhaps from his parents, Abel had learned that sinful man can approach God only on the ground of shed blood. The offering of his sacrifice of blood in approaching God was an expression of faith. It was not Abel's personal excellence that God looked upon in counting him righteous, but the excellence of the sacrifice that he brought and the demonstration of his faith. And so it is with us: we are not justified because of our character or good works, but solely because of the excellence of the sacrifice of Christ and our acceptance of Him.

Enoch was the first man, of which there is record, to leave this life without dying. There was no record of anyone ever having been translated. And then it happened! Enoch walked with God for three hundred years (Genesis 5:21-24) and then he walked into eternity. Before his translation he had this testimony—that he pleased God. The life of faith always pleases God; He loves to be trusted.

There are three factors in God's being pleased with us. (1) He is pleased with us personally. (2) He is pleased with our labors which we offer to Him. (3) He is pleased that our testimony is that of a righteous life.

Without faith it is impossible to please God. Faith is the only thing that gives God His proper place and puts man in his place. Faith glorifies God exceedingly because it proves that we have more confidence in His eyesight than in our own.

Faith not only believes that God exists, but it also trusts Him to reward those who seek Him. This diligent seeking of Him will be exhibited in prayer, patience and worship. All faith that does not set men on a diligent inquiry after God is vain.

B. Noah and Abraham (vv. 7-10)

**7. By faith Noah, being warned of God of things not seen as yet, moved with fear, prepared an ark to the saving of his house; by the which he condemned the world, and became heir of the righteousness which is by faith.**

**8. By faith Abraham, when he was called to go out into a place which he should after receive for an inheritance, obeyed; and he went out, not knowing whither he went.**

**9. By faith he sojourned in the land of promise, as in a strange country, dwelling in tabernacles with Isaac and Jacob, the heirs with him of the same promise:**

**10. For he looked for a city which hath foundations, whose builder and maker is God.**

Noah "found grace in the eyes of the Lord" (Genesis 6:8). In an act entirely motivated by faith, Noah prepared for the Flood and the saving of himself and his household in an ark. He had no physical evidence that an ark was needed (see Genesis 2:5, 6); all he had was a divine revelation. To human reason Noah's building of the ark was in every way incredible. But Noah's faith was rewarded: his household was saved, the world was condemned by his life and testimony, and he became an heir of righteousness on the basis of his faith.

Abraham was called of God. This call consisted of a command and a promise. The command was, "Get thee out of thy country" (Genesis 12:1). The promise was that all nations would be blessed in him. The promise was temporal in that Abraham, though without children at the time, was to father a great nation. The promise was spiritual in that it confined the promised seed unto him and his family in whom all the families of the earth were to be blessed. Abraham obeyed the command. He went out as he was called to do. What an illustration of faith! On the first call of God he responded with absolute obedience, without regard for what it might cost him or even of what the reward consisted. And the same is required of us. Our attitude must be one of complete trust.

Abraham built no house; he purchased no inheritance—only a burying ground. Why did he show such little interest in real estate in Canaan? Because he looked for the city that had the foundations, whose Architect and Builder was God. He did not have his heart set on present, material things, but on the eternal. This was the ultimte object of Abraham's faith, the sum and substance of what he expected from God. God being the architect, this city would be the model city—no slums, no polluted air, no polluted water. It would be built as the habitation of God and all those who enjoy His presence. Abraham expectantly and confidently "looked for" this city. He believed in an eternal rest with God in heaven. The troubles and inconveniences of his pilgrimage would be as nothing compared with the glory of that land. Such a city would be the blessed fruit of faith, trust, and hope.

C. Strangers and Pilgrims (vv. 11-16)

(Hebrews 11:11-16 is not included in the printed text.)

Sarah was ninety years old (Genesis 17:17) when the Lord announced that she and Abraham would become parents (Genesis 18:11). By faith, however, she was enabled to conceive, to carry the child to full term, and to bear the promised Isaac. Her faith was in the faithfulness of God who had promised her a son. Although Abraham was sexually sterile, he became the father of descendants as numerous as the stars in the sky and as countless as the sand on the seashore.

The writer says that all these people —the patriarchs—were still living by faith when they died. They did not see the tangible fulfillment of the promises, but they were given a glimpse of them from a distance and rejoiced in them. They recognized that they were foreigners and strangers here on earth. By acknowledging that, they make it clear that they are seeking a country of their own—a homeland. They could have gone back to the country they left. Instead, they were yearning for a better, a heavenly land. For this reason, the writer said, God is not ashamed of them, to be called their God. Indeed, He has already prepared a city for them, namely the Holy City which will be the eternal habitation of all saints (Revelation 21:2).

D. Isaac, Jacob, and Joseph (vv. 17-22)

(Hebrews 11:17-22 is not included in the printed text.)

Abraham's most severest test came when God instructed him to offer his son, Isaac, as a sacrifice. Isaac was the son of promise. Through him, the Lord had said that Abraham's posterity would be traced. Knowing this, Abraham obeyed God and prepared to offer his son. The patriarch's whole approach was guided by faith. He believed that God could raise his son up, even if he were dead. When he approached the place of the sacrifice, he informed his servants: "I and the lad will go yonder and worship, and will come again to you" (Genesis 22:5). The only way that both of them could return would be for Abraham to believe that God would restore his son to life.

It was faith that enabled Isaac to bless Jacob and Esau with regard to the future.

In an act of faith, Jacob, when he was on his deathbed, put his blessings on each of Joseph's sons. Leaning on the top of his staff, he bowed himself in worship before God.

Also, Joseph, in the hour of his death, acted by faith and confidently spoke of God bringing the people of Israel out of Egypt. Then he gave directions of what to do with his body and concerning his burial. The body was carried during the forty years of wilderness wanderings and later buried in Shechem.

III. FAITH REWARDED (Hebrews 11:23-40)

A. Moses (vv. 23-28)

(Hebrews 11:23-28 is not included in the printed text.)

Moses was born at the very height of the persecution and fury of Pharaoh; but in the wise disposal of providence Moses, who was to be the deliverer of the people, was preserved. By the faith of his parents, Moses was kept secretly for three months. The outward act of hiding the child was an indication of the inward work of their faith. They saw that Moses was a child of destiny, one whom God had designated for a special work. Their faith that God's purposes would be worked out gave them courage to defy the king's edict.

Attention shifts in verse 24 from the faith of his parents to the faith of Moses himself. By faith he was able to make several noble renunciations. Though reared in the luxury of Egypt's palace and assured of all the things that men strive for, he learned that it is usually not the possession of things but the forsaking of them that brings rest.

He came to this realization when he was fully grown and had reached the understanding of a man. It was then he refused to be known as the son of Pharaoh's daughter. He had been born of better blood than those of Pharaoh's family. He was a member of God's chosen earthly people.

The children of God are, in all their distresses, ten thousand times more honorable than any other society of men in the world. Moses chose to endure illtreatment with these people: he chose to identify with them and to trust his life to the guidance of God. He considered the worst of the people of God (their affliction) and the best of the world (the temporary pleasure of sin) and preferred the former. This he did "by faith."

Moses was dealing with Pharaoh, a bloody tyrant. Pharaoh, armed with all the power of Egypt, threatened Moses with immediate death if he persisted in the work that God had committed unto him. But instead of being terrified, Moses professed his determination to proceed and predicted destruction to the tyrant himself. Moses' concept of God's omnipresence, power, and faithfulness gave him a fixed trust that God would protect him and be faithful to him in the discharge of His promise.

And what did this faith get for him? Instead of occupying a line on some obscure cuneiform tablet, his name was memorialized in God's eternal Book. Instead of being installed in a museum like an Egyptian mummy, he became famous as a man of God.

B. Those Delivered From Their Foes (vv. 29-34)

(Hebrews 11:29-34 is not included in the printed text.)

By faith the children of Israel passed through the Red Sea as though they were passing over dry land. When the Egyptians tried to do the same thing, they were overcome by the water and drowned.

Faith caused the walls of Jericho to collapse after they had been encircled for seven successive days. Walking in circles didn't make a lot of sense from a human vantage point, but the people trusted God and obeyed Him and God honored their faith.

Then, we have a catalog of accomplishments faith has wrought. In fact, the writer said that there was not enough time to relate all the stories of the heroes of faith. Mention is made of Gideon, Barak, Samson, David, Samuel, all the prophets and others. Through faith they conquered kingdoms, ruled righteously, procured promised blessings, muzzled ravening lions, put out furious fires, escaped the devouring of swords, out of weakness found great strength, proved valiant in warfare, and put to flight foreign armies.

C. Those Delivered to Their Foes (vv. 35-38)

(Hebrews 11:35-38 is not included in the printed text.)

By faith, women had their dead restored to them by resurrection. Others were put to death by torture, refusing the deliverance offered to them. They were looking forward to a better life through the resurrection. Others were exposed to public taunts and floggings, even to being left bound in prison. Some were stoned to death, cut in pieces, and put to death with the sword. Many became refugees with nothing but sheepskins or goatskins to cover them. They lost everything and were destitute, oppressed, and ill treated. Yet they are characterized by the writer as men of whom the world was not worthy; men who were too good for this world. They roamed in lonely places and lived a hunted life in deserts and on mountainsides and in caves and the holes of the earth.

John Phillips observed: "Example after example is given to assure the Hebrews that, no matter what they might be called upon to face for their profession of faith in Christ, God is well able to deliver if He so wills. . . . If, the writer of Hebrews argues, men and women could bear such things for the faith in the old days when they lived in the shadowlands of faith, how much more should Christian believers, dwelling in the full blaze of light brought to men by Christ, be willing to dare all for Him!"

D. Something Better for Us (vv. 39, 40)

(Hebrews 11:39, 40 is not included in the printed text.)

God bore witness to the faith of Old Testament heroes, yet they died before receiving the fulfillment of the promise. They did not live to see the advent of the long-awaited Messiah or to enjoy the blessings of His ministry. God promised them that the Messiah would come, and they saw the fulfillment of the promise, but only afar off. Yet, they never lived to see its actual accomplishment in the coming of Christ.

God reserved something better for us. He arranged that Old Testament saints, though examples of faithfulness, should not be made perfect. They were not as privileged as we are. Yet, think of their thrilling triumphs and their tremendous trials! Think of their exploits and their endurance! They lived on the other side of the Cross; we live in the full glory of the Cross. Yet, how do our lives compare with theirs?

The difference between conditions of Old Testament days and those of our day is Jesus Christ. The coming of the promised Seed made possible something better for us. All consummation, all perfection, is in Christ alone: "For in him dwelleth all the fulness of the Godhead bodily. And [we] are complete in him, which is the head of all principality and power" (Colossians 2:9, 10). If we have Christ, we have all that we need.

## REVIEW QUESTIONS

1. What is a definition of faith?

2. Why did God accept Abel's sacrifice rather than Cain's?

3. What according to verse 6, is the most essential thing in pleasing God?

4. What was Abraham looking for in his journeyings?

5. Is there any such thing as "blind faith?" Explain your answer.

## GOLDEN TEXT HOMILY

"FAITH IS THE SUBSTANCE OF THINGS HOPED FOR, THE EVIDENCE OF THINGS NOT SEEN" (Hebrews 11:1).

The Bible teaches the just shall live by faith (Hebrews 10:38). Our faith will enable us to see Christ, even though He is invisible. To the world such a statement may be ridiculed, but our faith is not without substance. The foundation of our faith is in the person of Jesus Christ and His infallible Word.

No other person or religion has come close to the substance and assurance that Christ gave to us. Our text assures us that our faith is not the figment of man's imagination. The Christian's faith is grounded in the incarnation of God, coming to earth as a man. No historian can discredit the fact that Jesus Christ was a true historical figure. He came teaching about love, grace, and redemption. He opened the door by which man could be forgiven of his sins and be reconciled to God. Therefore the things we hope for become clearer and the things of which we have heard will become a reality.

Jesus also came teaching about a future kingdom, a blessed hope, that awaits all believers. We read and teach of the resurrection of the dead which has not yet taken place. However, these events are just as real to the Christian as if they had already happened. The authority of Christ is so absolute that it is not difficult for a believer to live in such expectation. Faith in the reality of God's Word and His life is our proof of things not seen.

As we serve Christ and study His Word our faith will increase. We will become keenly aware of the spiritual life and our soul will be lifted to a higher place. Those things which we have not seen will become as clear and glorious as those things which we now see.

Our faith in Christ is our assurance that we will experience those things of which He spoke.—**Jerry Puckett, Plant Superintendent, Church of God Publishing House, Cleveland, Tennessee.**

## SENTENCE SERMONS

FAITH ENDS WHERE worry begins and worry ends where faith begins.
—"**Speaker's Sourcebook**"

NEVER TRY TO arouse faith from within. You cannot stir up faith from the depths of your heart. Leave your heart, and look into the face of Christ.
—**Andrew Murray**

I SAID TO the man at the gate of the year, "Give me a light that I may tread safely into the unknown." He replied, "Go out into the darkness and put your hand into the hand of God. That shall be to you better than light and safer than a known way."
—**M. L. Haskins**

I CAN'T UNDERSTAND a religious truth until I first believe it.
—**Anselm**

## EVANGELISTIC APPLICATION

SALVATION COMES TO ALL WHO BELIEVE IN THE SACRIFICE OF CHRIST ON CALVARY.

Our sins were the palms that slapped Jesus, the fists that beat Him, the scourge that cut Him, the thorns that crowned Him, the nails that transfixed Him. This, in a sermon, I have said several times. The truth of it, John Trowbridge has expressed in these words:

A crown of thorns
And a purple robe—
Somebody fashioned them both.
Somebody platted the bloody crown,
Somebody fitted the gaudy gown,
Somebody fashioned them both.
A crown of thorns
And a purple robe—
And it was so long ago
They made the vesture our Savior wore,
And wove that crown that He meekly bore
And was it so long ago?

A crown of thorns
And a purple robe—
I read the words with a sigh:
But when I remembered my own misdeeds,
My soul awakes, and my conscience pleads,
And I say to myself, "Is it I?"
—**Robert G. Lee** in *Sourcebook of 500 Illustrations*

## ILLUMINATING THE LESSON

Walking through the mountains with his little daughter, a man crossed a stream on a fallen log. He urged his daughter to hold on tight. "If I take hold of your hand, I might let go," the little girl replied. "But if you take hold of mine, you will never let go of me."

That kind of faith is exhilarating! It is breathtaking. It is the kind of faith that claims and clings to the promises of God, knowing that He will never let us down and never let us go!

John Bunyan said, "Faith cannot sit still; faith is forcible. Faith is the principle of life by which a Christian lives, a principle of motion by which the soul walks forward toward heaven in the way of holiness."

It is said that faith is dead to doubt, dumb to discouragement, and blind to impossibilities. How we need to learn that faith fights our fears!

## DAILY DEVOTIONAL GUIDE

M. Faith Tried. Genesis 22:1-14

T. Faith Delivers. Joshua 6:15-17, 22-25

W. Faith Provides. 2 Kings 4:1-7

T. Faith Lost. Mark 4:35-41

F. Faith Heals. James 5:13-16

S. Faith Overcomes. 1 John 5:1-4

# Looking Unto Jesus

**Study Text:** Hebrews 12:1-17

**Supplemental References:** Genesis 25:24-34; 1 Corinthians 9:24-27; 1 Timothy 6: 11-16; 2 Timothy 4:6-8; 1 Peter 4:12-19

**Time:** Probably 65-70 A.D.

**Place:** Generally thought to have been written from Rome.

**Golden Text:** "Follow peace with all men, and holiness, without which no man shall see the Lord" (Hebrews 12:14).

**Central Truth:** All who faithfully run the Christian race will receive eternal reward.

**Evangelistic Emphasis:** All who look to Jesus in faith will be saved.

## Printed Text

**Hebrews 12:1.** Wherefore seeing we also are compassed about with so great a cloud of witnesses, let us lay aside every weight, and the sin which doth so easily beset us, and let us run with patience the race that is set before us,

**2. Looking unto Jesus the author and finisher of our faith; who for the joy that was set before him endured the cross, despising the shame, and is set down at the right hand of the throne of God.**

3. For consider him that endured such contradiction of sinners against himself, lest ye be wearied and faint in your minds.

**4. Ye have not yet resisted unto blood, striving against sin.**

5. And ye have forgotten the exhortation which speaketh unto you as unto children, My son, despise not thou the chastening of the Lord, nor faint when thou art rebuked of him:

**6. For whom the Lord loveth he chasteneth, and scourgeth every son whom he receiveth.**

7. If ye endure chastening, God dealeth with you as with sons; for what son is he whom the father chasteneth not?

**8. But if ye be without chastisement, whereof all are partakers, then are ye bastards, and not sons.**

11. Now no chastening for the present seemeth to be joyous, but grievous: nevertheless afterward it yieldeth the peaceable fruit of righteousness unto them which are exercised thereby.

**12. Wherefore lift up the hands which hang down, and the feeble knees;**

13. And make straight paths for your feet, lest that which is lame be turned out of the way; but let it rather be healed.

**14. Follow peace with all men, and holiness, without which no man shall see the Lord:**

15. Looking diligently lest any man fail of the grace of God; lest any root of bitterness springing up trouble you, and thereby many be defiled.

## LESSON OUTLINE

## LESSON EXPOSITION

INTRODUCTION

Living victoriously in Christ may at first appear to be a simple matter of allowing right to prevail over wrong or of following a prescribed code of do's and don'ts. However, victorious living involves much more than this. The race of life requires discipline. We don't always know what we should do. Sometimes we are in the dark as to where the Lord is leading us or what He desires for our life in a given situation. So, it is necessary for the Lord to teach us, to shape us, to fashion us into His likeness. Only through His constant presence and encouragement can we successfully run life's race. He is both the author and finisher of our faith; therefore, from beginning to end, we must have His coaching and His instruction.

Spiritual development comes as we progressively allow Christ more room to operate in our life. As we experience His love and His keeping power through the storms of life, He becomes more to us than mere example. He becomes the only star by which we may navigate the sea of life and safely secure the shores of eternity.

The clear call of the writer in this chapter is to a life of faith and patient endurance. He is interested in a positive response from his readers and seeks to guide them toward spiritual advancement.

## I. RUNNING THE CHRISTIAN RACE (Hebrews 12:1, 2)

A. Running With Patience (v. 1)

**1. Wherefore seeing we also are compassed about with so great a cloud of witnesses, let us lay aside every weight, and the sin which doth so easily beset us, and let us run with patience the race that is set before us.**

The writer assures us that a great cloud of witnesses surrounds us like a vast crowd of spectators in the grandstands. These witnesses are the Old Testament saints of chapter 11, who have gone on before us. The record of their earthly race has been placed in the Scripture for a purpose: to testify that faith will carry the believer safely through all he may be called to do or to suffer in the profession of the gospel.

---

Is it possible that our loved ones who have gone on to glory join these witnesses in observing our conduct? Is this not a powerful incentive to faithful service?

---

With the example of the heroes of the faith before us, we are admonished to rid ourselves of everything that would hinder us in our race. This laying aside includes a cheerful willingness, readiness, and resolution to part with anything and everything that might weight us down and cause us to stumble or faint before the race has ended. Just as an athlete must trim down and shape up before a race, we must watch that our hearts do not become "overcharged with surfeiting . . . and cares of this life" (Luke 21:34). We must trust God completely, being confident that the life of faith is sure to win.

No matter what assails us, we are admonished to keep on running in this race which God has marked out for us. To complete the race, we must run with determination, resolution, and courage. The Lord would have us proceed steadily down the course He has mapped out for us. As we pursue our journey with patience the Lord will be with us.

B. Looking Unto Jesus (v. 2)

**2. Looking unto Jesus the author and finisher of our faith; who for the joy that was set before him endured the cross, despising the shame, and is set down at the right hand of the throne of God.**

The writer leads us from our forerunners in faith to Jesus upon whom our faith depends from start to finish. When we set our eyes upon Him, we lose sight of those things that tend to discourage us, for He works faith into us by His Spirit and sustains it to fulfillment.

The "joy" that was set before Christ was His exaltation at the Father's right hand. Paul wrote: "Wherefore God also hath highly exalted him [Christ], and given him a name which is above every name: That at the name of Jesus every knee should bow, of things in heaven, and things in earth, and things under the earth; And that every tongue should confess that Jesus Christ is Lord, to the glory of God the Father" (Philippians 2:9-11). The Son's sufferings and obedience were the means of salvation and, thus, of His eternal glory, since salvation was the center and soul of all God's glory and the purpose for which the Father sent His Son to earth.

Jesus patiently endured the sufferings and shame of the cross on this account. The glorious effect of His sufferings blotted out the shame of His death in His own mind. Having suffered, He sat down at His Father's right hand in equal authority, glory, and power. Of Christ's exalted position, John Philips wrote: "There He is, crowned! There He is, smiling down from the utmost height upon those who, for His name's sake, would enter the race and follow His lead."

II. ACCEPTING THE FATHER'S CHASTENING (Hebrews 12:3-11)

A. Resisting Unto Blood (vv. 3, 4)

**3. For consider him that endured such contradiction of sinners against himself, lest ye be wearied and faint in your minds.**

**4. Ye have not yet resisted unto blood, striving against sin.**

If Christ, being so great, so excellent, so infinitely exalted above us, steadily endured the great opposition aimed at Him by sinful men, ought not we so to do? Think about that! The object of this caution is to keep our hearts from fainting and failing. Spiritual vigor and strength are required if we are to persevere; therefore, we are commended to arm ourselves with the same mind that was in Christ (1 Peter 4:1); to put on the whole armor of God, that we may be able to stand (Ephesians 6:11); and to watch, to stand fast in the faith, to quit ourselves like men, and to be strong (1 Corinthians 16:13).

Faith stirs up spiritual courage, resolution, patience, perseverance, prayer—all the things that are necessary to a successful race.

When we have a tendency to grow weary or fainthearted, we should think of what Christ suffered. No one ever endured such hostility from sinners as He. Our trials will seem trifling by comparison.

The writer suggests that the end of our sufferings may not come as soon as expected. We who suffer might yet expect to resist unto blood—the utmost persecution. But there is one consolation: although men may kill the body, when they have done so, they can do no more.

The author also reminds us that we are engaged in a ceaseless striving against sin. We ourselves may not have paid the extreme sacrifice of shedding our own blood, but many of the Old and New Testament saints did. Christ did.

B. Enduring Chastening (vv. 5-8)

**5. And ye have forgotten the exhortation which speaketh unto you as unto children, My son, despise not thou the chastening of the Lord, nor faint when thou art rebuked of him:**

**6. For whom the Lord loveth he chasteneth, and scourgeth every son whom he receiveth.**

**7. If ye endure chastening, God**

**dealeth with you as with sons; for what son is he whom the father chasteneth not?**

**8. But if ye be without chastisement, whereof all are partakers, then are ye bastards, and not sons.**

Why do testings, trials, and trouble come into the life of the believer? Are they an indication of God's anger or displeasure? Do they happen by chance? How should we react to them? These verses teach that nothing happens by chance to the Christian. Tragedies are blessings in disguise, and disappointments are His appointments. God harnesses the adverse circumstances of life to conform us to the image of Christ.

The word **chastening** in our language means "to subject to pain, suffering, deprivation, or misfortune in order to correct, strengthen, or perfect in character, in mental or spiritual qualities, or in conduct; to discipline; to purify; to cause to be more humble, modest, restrained, or cautious; to subdue." In the original language of the Bible, this word generally refers to "training, education, the cultivation of the soul, instruction that aims at the increase of virtue."

Chastening is God's child training. It involves much more than corporal punishment or chastening; basically it centers around the teaching-learning process.

This means that God assumes the role of a teacher to school us in spiritual development, to train us, to purify us, to purge from us all that mars the likeness of Christ, to lead us into all knowledge of the truth. Many lessons in God's school can be learned only through experience, so He leads us into a situation whereby we can glean knowledge firsthand. God is all-wise in His methods of teaching us.

C. Submitting to the Father (vv. 9, 10)

(Hebrews 12:9, 10 is not included in the printed text.)

The writer calls attention to the chastening parents use toward their children. Such chastening leads to respect for the authority of the parents. And yet that chastening may be imperfect. The parents may "underdiscipline, overdiscipline, fail to discipline at all, or discipline from wrong motives and in the wrong way and at the wrong time" (Phillips). On the other hand, God always disciplines correctly. He always has our best interest in mind.

In *Exploring Hebrews,* John Phillips wrote: "D. L. Moody told of a wealthy couple whose only child died as a baby. They were brokenhearted and inconsolable, and, trying to fill up the void left in their lives, they took a trip to the Holy Land. There they saw a shepherd trying to coax some sheep across a stream, but the fast-running water frightened the sheep and they held back. The shepherd stooped down and took a lamb and carried it across the river. The bleating ewe sheep watched her young lamb being taken away, and suddenly she lost all her fright of the stream. Looking where her treasure had gone, she followed, too, and soon the whole flock was on the other side.

"The incident spoke to the bereaved parents. Suddenly they realized what God was doing in their lives. He was making heaven more real, more significant to them. They had never entertained thoughts of heaven before and had been heedless of God's gentler dealings with them. Seeing in a flash the stern lesson their chastening had been intended to accomplish, they returned home to spend their lives focused on heaven rather than on earth."

D. Producing Righteousness (v. 11)

**11. Now no chastening for the present seemeth to be joyous, but grievous: nevertheless afterward it yieldeth the peaceable fruit of righteousness unto them which are exercised thereby.**

Suffering is a great teacher, so it may well be that God will chose to perfect our character through adversity and sorrow, just as He did many saints of old. Many of God's choice lessons are learned in the school of suffering. God can just as well lead us into the school of success or the school of affluence, if a curriculum calls for that particular discipline. Many of God's jewels are crystallized tears.

The patient endurance of chastening is of great value in the sight of God. He doesn't deal with us as an enemy, or as a judge, or as a stranger, but as a Father toward His child. The writer illustrates the Father-child relationship by declaring that every wise, careful, and tender earthly father will chasten, teach, and train his son. In any normal father-son relationship, the father trains his son because he loves him and wants the best for him.

Charles H. Spurgeon wrote: "I am afraid that all the grace I have got out of my comfortable and easy times and happy hours might almost lie on a penny. But the good I have received from my sorrows and pains and griefs is altogether incalculable. What do I not owe to the hammer and the anvil, the fire and the file. Affliction is the best bit of furniture in my house."

How an individual responds to spiritual discipline will determine its effect upon him. It can either make him better or it can make him bitter depending on how he reacts to it.

III. LIVING THE GODLY LIFE (Hebrews 12:12-17)

A. Being Strengthened (v. 12)

**12. Wherefore lift up the hands which hang down, and the feeble knees.**

Listless hands and shaky knees describe one who is heartless and fainting in the running of the race. His despondency is so great that he is ready to despair of all hope of success and to give up. This direction to "lift up" or strengthen encourages him not to "cast . . . away" his "confidence, which hath great recompence of reward," for he needs, "patience, that, after" he has "done the will of God," he "might receive the promise" (Hebrews 10:35, 36).

To such a one comes the consolation:
Never a heartache and never a groan,
Never a teardrop and never a moan,

Never a danger but there on the throne
Moment by moment He thinks of His own.

God still cares. Therefore, for a man to give up the race or to abandon himself to the luxury of fainting would be cowardly and dangerous. It would deprive him of courage or of the wish to get back in the race. Hence the admonition: "Get a grip on yourself! Stand up straight!" (writer's paraphrase).

Paul addressed this matter of fainting when He wrote: "And let us not be weary in well doing: for in due season we shall reap, if we faint not. As we have therefore opportunity, let us do good unto all men, especially unto them who are of the household of faith" (Galatians 6:9, 10).

Paul's cry is for the believer not to be frozen by fear and anxiety, but rather to persist in the power and authority of the Lord. Such faithfulness will ultimately be rewarded.

B. Being Upright (v. 13)

**13. And make straight paths for your feet, lest that which is lame be turned out of the way; but let it rather be healed.**

Quoting from Proverbs 4:26 and alluding to Matthew 3:3 and 7:13, 14, the writer stresses the importance of living a stable, nonfaltering life. The Hebrew Christians were halting between two opinions: Judaism and Christianity. He admonishes them, "Let your Christian walk be so firm and straight that a plain trial of "wheeltracks" might be established for those who follow behind you."

Those "lame" or "weak in the faith" (Romans 14:1) were leaning toward Judaism; and eventually, if they continued this way, they would lose the race. However, if they exercised their faith in Christ and pursued the habit of walking straight and consistently with Him, their feet would be strengthened in the right way and they would be restored to spiritual health.

The writer calls for a maturity in Christ that sustains one against the anxieties of life. Paul set such maturity as a worthy goal of the Christian life. He wrote of our spiritual development "Till we all come in the unity of the faith, and of the knowledge of the Son of God, unto a perfect man, unto the measure of the stature of the fulness of Christ: That we henceforth be no more children, tossed to and fro, and carried about with every wind of doctrine, by the sleight of men, and cunning craftiness, whereby they lie in wait to deceive; But speaking the truth in love, may grow up into him in all things, which is the head, even Christ" (Ephesians 4:13-15).

C. Being Peaceful (v. 14)

**14. Follow peace with all men, and holiness, without which no man shall see the Lord.**

Chastening is a very solitary thing. As with Job, it brings a sense of intense loneliness. To us who are so afflicted, God is all in all. Even in pain we experience a great calm, a great peace, "the peace of God" (Philippians 4:7). What a comfort! And, yet, something even more infinitely precious is our reward: "the God of . . . peace" (2 Corinthians 13:11)—Immanuel himself!

To "follow" connotes an earnest and diligent pursuit. If we are following peace with all men, we are doing nothing contrary to the Word of God. We are obeying the injunction to love our neighbor as ourselves to the extent that consideration for others has become for us a way of life.

Likewise, we are pursuing the way of holiness, knowing that without it no one will see the Lord. To live and die in an unholy condition is paramount to eternal exclusion from God, for God is holy.

This is not to say, however, that we earn the right to see God by living a holy life, for only the blood of Christ entitles us to heaven. Yet, that blood is able to wash us clean from all our sin and to keep us from falling and to present us "faultless before the presence of his glory with exceeding joy" (Jude 1:24).

Peace and holiness are two objectives the believer should actively seek to cultivate. The practical living out of a life of peace toward man and holiness toward God will attract others to the way of Christ.

D. Being Watchful (v. 15)

**15. Looking diligently lest any man fail of the grace of God; lest any root of bitterness springing up trouble you, and thereby many be defiled.;**

As believers we all have a responsibility to exercise watch care over others so that spiritual good may be promoted and so that spiritual and moral evil may be prevented. There is a danger, the writer says, of coming short of the grace of God—the grace that consists of all spiritual mercies and privileges. Coming short of attaining this grace could lead to the springing up of a "root of bitterness," a "departing from the living God" through "an evil heart of unbelief" (Hebrews 3:12). If we turn sour against the Lord and repudiate the Christian faith, our defection will be contagious. Others will be defiled by our complaints, our doubts, and our denials.

God uses various means to keep us on the right track. One of those things is chastening. J. H. Jowett wrote: "The purpose of God's chastening is not punitive but creative. He chastens "that we may share His holiness." The phrase "that we may share" has direction in it, and the direction points toward a purified and beautified life. The fire which is kindled is not a bonfire, blazing heedlessly and unguardedly, and consuming precious things; it is a refiner's fire, and the Refiner sits by it, and He is firmly and patiently and gently bringing holiness out of carelessness and stability out of weakness. God is always creating even when He is using the darker means of grace. He is producing the fruits and flowers of the Spirit. His love is always in quest of lovely things."

E. Being Cautious (vv. 16, 17)

(Hebrews 12:16, 17 is not included in the printed text.)

The word **fornicator** is used to refer

to one who has no real regard for spiritual values. Such a person was Esau. Esau had no appreciation for his birthright, but willingly bartered it for the momentary gratification of his appetite. Later, after also losing the paternal blessing, Esau felt remorse, but it was too late. Neither his birthright nor his blessing could be regained.

Esau treated spiritual matters casually. Escape from physical hunger was more important to him than his spiritual well-being. He placed no value on spiritual blessings and responsibilities.

What a warning Esau's fate should bring! What danger is involved in departing from the living God! Even Esau's remorse could not bring him back to where he once was. This should behoove us to tread softly when walking on sacred ground.

Gromack: warns us that we "can make a decision to disobey God for materialistic reasons and find it impossible to reverse the future consequences of that willful act." The author of Hebrews has already cautioned us: "For it is impossible for those who were once enlightened, and have tasted of the heavenly gift, and were made partakers of the Holy Ghost, And have tasted the good word of God, and the powers of the world to come, If they shall fall away, to renew them again unto repentance; seeing they crucify to themselves the Son of God afresh, and put him to an open shame" (Hebrews 6:4-6).

## REVIEW QUESTIONS

1. What are some of the "weights" believers encounter as they run the Christian race?

2. List some of the best ways one can use to resist temptation to sin.

3. Discuss the necessity of God's discipline. List some of the ways He disciplines His children.

4. Is it possible to "fall from God's grace?" Explain your answer.

5. What does the admonition to "follow peace with all men" suggest to you? Is personal peace possible in this life? Explain.

## GOLDEN TEXT HOMILY

"FOLLOW PEACE WITH ALL MEN, AND HOLINESS, WITHOUT WHICH NO MAN SHALL SEE THE LORD" (Hebrews 12:14).

The great exemplary lessons of the heroes of faith, and the strong admonition to endure the spiritual race precede the Golden Text. The obstacles and hindrances in the Christian life can be discouraging and sap our spiritual energy.

We also can become despondent in failing to see purpose in difficulties resulting from the chastening love of the Father (Hebrews 12:5-11). It's been said, the struggle of life can make us either bitter or better. The message is clear and urgent—don't be incapacitated by the blows of life, but pick yourself up and get moving down the road to restoration. "Lift up the hands which hang down . . . the feeble knees; And make straight paths for your feet . . . [so] that which is lame . . . [may] be healed" (Hebrews 12:12, 13).

Often our failures and difficulties not only turn us against God, but against people. Unless we are restored, we can ultimately be infected by a cancerous "root of bitterness" (Hebrews 12:15). Disliking ourselves, rationalizing our sin, and standing up for our rights causes us to be continually at variance with others. Cutting ourselves off from God's spiritual blessing and favor, we can begin to lose those characteristics that set us apart (holiness) as a believer.

In this spiritually perilous condition, the biblical writer gives the strong exhortation, which is both encouragement and warning. Instead of striking out and reacting to people, we should strive to live in peace with everyone, including those who are the source of our hurts. A supernatural love for others and a determined trust, inspite of circumstances, are distinguishing traits of those who see dimly through a dark glass now, but will one day see **Him face to face.** —**John J. Secret, Chaplain (Capt.), United States Air Force, APO, New York, New York**

## SENTENCE SERMONS

THOSE WHO FAITHFULLY run the

Christian race will receive eternal reward.

**—Selected**

GOD IS MORE interested in making us what He wants us to be than giving us what we ought to have.

**—Walter L. Wilson**

IF CHRIST IS the center of our lives, the circumference will take care of itself.

**—"Notes and Quotes"**

CHRISTIANITY IS EITHER relevant all the time or useless any time. It is not just a phase of life—it is life itself.

**—Richard C. Halverson**

## EVANGELISTIC APPLICATION

ALL WHO LOOK TO JESUS IN FAITH WILL BE SAVED.

There is no pang that rends the heart, I might almost say, not one, which disturbs the body, but what Jesus Christ has been with us in it all.

Feel you the sorrows of poverty? He "hath not where to lay His head."

Do you endure the grief of bereavement? Jesus wept at the tomb of Lazarus.

Have you been slandered for righteousness" sake, and has it vexed your spirit? He said, "Reproach hath broken my heart."

On what stormy seas have you been tossed which have not roared about His boat? Never glen of adversity so dark, so deep, apparently so pathless, but what in stooping down you may discover the footprints of the Crucified One (Charles H. Spurgeon in **Knight's Three Thousand Illustrations**).

## ILLUMINATING THE LESSON

Out of adversity and trial come the virtues of a Christian life, such as patience, courage, kindness, sympathy. Power and influence are won out of the struggle of life. In his **Heredity and Environment** Professor Conklin wrote: "What is needed in education more than anything else is some means or system which will train the powers of self-discovery and self-control. Easy lives and so-called "good environment" will not arouse the dormant powers. It usually takes the stress and strain of hard necessity to make us acquainted with our hidden selves, to rouse the sleeping giant within us. How often it is said that the worthless sons of worhty parents are mysteries; with the best of heredity and environment they amount to nothing, whereas the sons of poor and ignorant farmers, blacksmiths, tanners, and backwoodsmen, with few opportunities and with many hardships and disadvantages, become world figures. Probably the inheritance in these last named cases was no better than in the former, but the environment was better (Clarence Edward Macartney in **Macartney's Illustrations**).

## DAILY DEVOTIONAL GUIDE

M. The Blessing Lost. Genesis 25:24-34

T. Encouragement Given. 1 Chronicles 28:9-20

W. Request for Blessing. 1 Chronicles 29:10-19

T. Marks of Wisdom. James 3:13-18

F. Spiritual Appetite. 1 Peter 2:1-7

S. Precious Promises. 2 Peter 1:1-4

# February 16, 1986

# God's Everlasting Kingdom

**Study Text:** Hebrews 12:18-29

**Supplemental References:** Exodus 19:10-25; Daniel 2:36-45; Matthew 6:10-13; Revelation 11:15-19

**Time:** Probably A.D. 65-70

**Place:** Generally thought to have been written from Rome.

**Golden Text:** "Wherefore we receiving a kingdom which cannot be moved, let us have grace, whereby we may serve God acceptably with reverence and godly fear" (Hebrews 12:28).

**Central Truth:** Believers are to live in total assurance that God's kingdom will never be shaken.

**Evangelistic Emphasis:** The delay of God's judgment is an expression of His goodness and long-suffering toward the sinner.

## Printed Text

**Hebrews 12:18.** For ye are not come unto the mount that might be touched, and that burned with fire, nor unto blackness, and darkness, and tempest,

**19. And the sound of a trumpet, and the voice of words; which voice they that heard entreated that the word should not be spoken to them any more:**

20. (For they could not endure that which was commanded, And if so much as a beast touch the mountain, it shall be stoned, or thrust through with a dart:

**21. And so terrible was the sight, that Moses said, I exceedingly fear and quake:)**

22. But ye are come unto mount Zion, and unto the city of the living God, the heavenly Jerusalem, and to an innumerable company of angels,

**23. To the general assembly and church of the firstborn, which are writ-** ten in heaven, and to God the Judge of all, and to the spirits of just men made perfect,

24. And to Jesus the mediator of the new covenant, and to the blood of sprinkling, that speaketh better things than that of Abel.

**25. See that ye refuse not him that speaketh: for if they escaped not who refused him that spake on earth, much more shall not we escape, if we turn away from him that speaketh from heaven:**

26. Whose voice then shook the earth: but now he hath promised, saying, Yet once more I shake not the earth only, but also heaven.

**27. And this word, Yet once more, signifieth the removing of those things that are shaken, as of things that are made, that those things which cannot be shaken may remain.**

## LESSON OUTLINE

I. THE COVENANT OF GRACE
   A. Coming to Mount Sinai
   B. Coming to Mount Zion
   C. Coming to Jesus
II. OBEYING GOD'S VOICE
   A. Turning Not Away
   B. Shaking the Earth
   C. Lasting Relationships
III. AN UNSHAKABLE KINGDOM
   A. Receiving a Kingdom
   B. Consuming Fire

## LESSON EXPOSITION

INTRODUCTION

At the beginning of this lesson, the words of Charles Swindoll in his Bible study guide **Hebrews Volume II** should be considered. His comments are about Hebrews 12:18-29: "In any good piece of literature, there are always portions that require deep thought, sustained concentration. Because of our hurry-up, give-it-to-me-quick-and-easy mentality, we tend to pass by such profound sections in our reading; and in doing so, we miss some of the richest and most rewarding times in our lives. Now we have come to such a text in Hebrews. The meaning of this passage is not easy to grasp, nor does it appear (at least on the surface) to be very exciting. But within and between these lines are treasures that the hurried, casual approach will never mine. As we dig and probe, let's think. Let's ask our God to reveal Himself to us and show us otherwise hidden dimensions of His truth. Pause and pray for illumination before going any further with this study."

That is good advice at the start of any study. This lesson will mean more to us if we do what has been suggested.

For the most part, this lesson is a study in contrasts. The principle contrast is between Mount Sinai and Mount Zion. Sinai represents the place where the law was given; Sion speaks of the place where the righteous dwell.

This lesson also offers to the believer an undergirding optimism. It implants in his mind the thought that all will be

well. It assures him that God is in control and that Jesus is on the throne. With assurance like that we can face whatever circumstances life may bring and triumph over them.

George Moore used to write about Irish peasants. In his novels he told of the Irish peasants being employed to build roads that led to little jumping-off places, that served no purpose for them or for anyone else. He made this observation: "A road that leads to nowhere is difficult to make. Man to do a job, has to have the end clearly in sight."

The believer knows what lies at the end of the road. He knows at that point the battle will be won, the victory will be total, and God will manifest Himself in marvellous, matchless wonder.

I. THE COVENANT OF GRACE (Hebrews 12:18-24)

A. Coming to Mount Sinai (vv. 18-21)

**18. For ye are not come unto the mount that might be touched, and that burned with fire, nor unto blackness, and darkness, and tempest,**

**19. And the sound of a trumpet, and the voice of words; which voice they that heard entreated that the word should not be spoken to them any more:**

**20. (For they could not endure that which was commanded, And if so much as a beast touch the mountain, it shall be stoned, or thrust through with a dart:**

**21. And so terrible was the sight, that Moses said, I exceedingly fear and quake:)**

At Mount Sinai, there were fearful manifestations of God's power. The people were reminded of His awesome holiness, a God not to be trifled with. When you think of Sinai, you think of something tangible, and you see a mountain that is ablaze with fire, and you envision darkness and gloom and a raging storm. It is vividly described in Deuteronomy 4:11, "And ye came near and stood under the mountain; and the mountain burned with fire unto the midst of heaven, with darkness, clouds, and thick darkness."

Not only were there these terrifying sights, there were also fearful sounds. There was the blast and blare of a trumpet. The Bible says: "And it came to pass on the third day in the morning, that there [was] . . . the voice of the trumpet exceeding loud; so that all the people that was in the camp trembled. . . . And when the voice of the trumpet sounded long, and waxed louder and louder, Moses spake, and God answered him by a voice" (Exodus 19:16, 19).

In addition to the sound of the trumpet, they heard an audible voice. The sound of that voice struck terror to their soul. The people entreated Moses to go to God and to speak for God lest they be consumed by God's presence. "Now therefore why should we die? for this great fire will consume us: if we hear the voice of the Lord our God any more, then we shall die. . . . Go thou near, and hear all that the Lord our God shall say: and speak thou unto us all that the Lord our God shall speak unto thee; and we will hear it, and do it" (Deuteronomy 5:25, 27).

The people could not bear what they were seeing and hearing. So sacred was the place because of God's presence that even if a wild beast touched the mountain, it was to be stoned. This divine display of power and holiness frightened the people. They were reminded of their own unrighteousness and staggered beneath the burden of guilt and fear.

Even Moses, who had met God at the burning bush, was terrified and did tremble so appalling was the sight. This is Moses' confession: "For I was afraid of the anger and hot displeasure, wherewith the Lord was wroth against you to destroy you. But the Lord hearkened unto me at that time also" (Deuteronomy 9:19).

William Barclay observed: "In the giving of the law at Mount Sinai three things are stressed. (1) There is stressed **the sheer majesty of God.** The whole story stresses the shattering might of God, and in it there is no love at all.

(2) There is stressed **the absolute un-approachability of God.** So far from the way being opened to God, it is barred; and he who tried to approach God met death. (3) There is stressed **the sheer terror of God.** Here there is nothing but the awe-stricken fear which is afraid to look and even afraid to listen."

B. Coming to Mount Zion (vv. 22, 23)

**22. But ye are come unto mount Zion, and unto the city of the living God, the heavenly Jerusalem, and to an innumerable company of angels,**

**23. To the general assembly and church of the firstborn, which are written in heaven, and to God the Judge of all, and to the spirits of just men made perfect,**

What a contrast there is between the previous passage and these verses. What a difference there is between Mount Sinai and Mount Zion. What a difference the new covenant makes.

The believer has come to Mount Zion. In biblical terms Mount Sion represents the security and defense of God's people. It was the stronghold of the city of Jerusalem. Likewise, in the spiritual Zion, we have someone to fight our battles for us and to keep us in safety.

The believer has also come to the city of the living God. John Phillips noted that God first placed man in a garden; now He places him in a city. He observed that there are three things associated with a city—position, population, and progress. Then he added, "The city of the living God is like no city on earth. As to its **position,** it is settled in heaven; as to its **people,** it is the eternal home of the redeemed; and as to its **purpose,** it exists to make life rich and glorious for the saints throughout the endless ages of eternity. It is a place where God's order is fully observed."

Then, the believers have come to the heavenly Jerusalem. This is also the place John so vividly described in the Book of Revelation (see Revelation 21:10—22:5).

Also, the place to which the believers

have come is described as a place where there are myriads of angels, a countless hosts of angels. These same angels rejoice when just one sinner repents of his sin (see Luke 15:10). These angels are involved in divine service in which they minister to those who are to inherit salvation (see Hebrews 1:1-4).

Notice that the believers are joined to that festal assembly of heaven and to the congregation of the firstborn. Or, as someone has expressed it, "the solemn gathering of all God's elder sons." As such, they are united with all believers of all ages—Jew and Gentile—who are enrolled as citizens in heaven.

Observe that as God was present at Mount Sinai, He is also present in Mount Zion. He is here described as the Judge of all men.

Then believers have come into the company of just men who are now made perfect, of upright men who are now at last enjoying the fulfillment of their hopes. At one point these people encompassed the believer in an unseen cloud; now he is one of them.

C. Coming to Jesus (v. 24)

**24. And to Jesus the mediator of the new covenant, and to the blood of sprinkling, that speaketh better things than that of Abel.**

The crowning glory of heaven will be that we are brought into the presence of Jesus. The writer says that when we come to Mount Zion that we come to Jesus. It is Jesus who makes our relationship to God possible. He sustains us and enables us to become what we need to be to please God. The greatest thing about the future life will be to fall at His feet and pay homage to Him. At that point, we can acknowledge that we owe everything to Him. The credit for whatever accomplishments we have had go to Him, because it was in His power that they were done.

Also, believers have come to the sprinkling of Christ's blood. Jesus is the perfect priest and He has made the perfect sacrifice. He has made it possible for men who could not otherwise approach

God to do so. Nothing but the blood of Jesus was adequate to appease the wrath of God and bring men into fellowship with the Almighty One. When we consider that sin has broken the heart of God, and that that sin has been removed by the blood, we understand how much Christ has done for us. He died that we might live. He never did anything that deserved death, but we have—yet He died for us.

The writer compares the blood of Jesus with the blood of Abel. John Phillips wrote: "The blood of Abel cried out to God from the ground for vengeance. The blood of Jesus spoke of vengeance already past. It is the blood that slaked the fire of God's wrath. The fire on Israel's altar always cried for more, more, and more. But this blood has quenched the flame, and it speaks to God and man alike of justice satisfied fully and forever." The blood of Jesus opened the door that men could be friends with God. His death is the way to reconciliation.

II. OBEYING GOD'S VOICE (Hebrews 12:25-27)

A. Turning Not Away (v. 25)

**25. See that ye refuse not him that speaketh: for if they escaped not who refused him that spake on earth, much more shall not we escape, if we turn away from him that speaketh from heaven:**

To a great extent, the position or authority of the person speaking determines the weight of what he says. A person in a position of power has the clout to demand attention. The person who is an expert in any field commands respect when he speaks in the area of his discipline. For example, if the President of the United States announces a position on a given matter we listen because he speaks from a seat of power and what he does will affect all of us. If a person who has studied the operation of computers explains how they function we take note of what he says.

The ultimate authority in all things is God. To refuse to hear Him when He speaks is sheer folly. He possesses all wisdom and all power so that He knows what He is speaking about and He has the power to accomplish what He says or predicts to bring about.

In the Old Testament God spake to the prophet Habakkuk. The prophet felt that God was not responding quickly enough to the sin of the people. When God told him that He was going to use a more wicked nation than Judah to punish His people, Habakkuk was astonished. Then the Lord informed him that He was also going to punish this wicked nation whom He used to punish Judah. They too would have to give an accounting for their iniquity. Having explained all of that to the prophet, God declared: "But the Lord is in his holy temple: let all the earth keep silence before him" (Habakkuk 2:20). By which He is saying that God is in control and that God knows what He is doing and that His timing is always perfect.

In the Old Testament times there was no escape for those who would not listen when God spoke. In the New Testament there is no escape for those who refuse to hear Him who came from heaven to teach us.

B. Shaking the Earth (v. 26)

**26. Whose voice then shook the earth: but now he hath promised, saying, Yet once more I shake not the earth only, but also heaven.**

The power of God is awesome. When He spoke at Mount Sinai, the earth shook. Several passages of Scripture speak of this trembling. "And mount Sinai was altogether on a smoke, because the Lord descended upon it in fire: and the smoke thereof ascended as the smoke of a furnace, and the whole mount quaked greatly" (Exodus 19:18). "The earth shook, the heavens also dropped at the presence of God: even Sinai itself was moved at the presence of God" (Psalm 68:8). "The voice of thy thunder was in heaven: the lightnings lightened the world: the earth trembled and shook" (Psalm 77:18). "Tremble, thou earth, at

the presence of the Lord, at the presence of the God of Jacob" (Psalm 114: 7).

The God who spoke at Sinai has spoken again. His speech is in the form of a promise. This is not the promise of a mere man who may or may not be able to carry out his word. It is rather the Word of Him who never fails to do what He says He will do.

In the earliest stages of man's history, God promised that He would send a Redeemer. To the serpent in the garden, He said: "And I will put enmity between thee and the woman, and between thy seed and her seed; it shall bruise thy head, and thou shalt bruise his heel" (Genesis 3:15). Years passed and there was no sign that the promise would be fulfilled.

Prophets came and went, and they repeated the promise but nothing happened. Then as the apostle Paul expressed it: "But when the fulness of the time was come, God sent forth His Son, made of a woman, made under the law, to redeem them that were under the law, that we might receive the adoption of sons" (Galatians 4:4, 5). Thus, in God's time the promise was fulfilled exactly as the Lord had foretold.

The promise God made in this passage is that He will shake the earth again. Only this time, He will not limit the trembling to the earth. The starry heavens also will shake before His great power.

It is a matter of sad observation to me that inanimate objects tremble in the presence of God while many men defy Him.

C. Lasting Relationships (v. 27)

**27. And this word, Yet once more, signifieth the removing of those things that are shaken, as of things that are made, that those things which cannot be shaken may remain.**

The Holy Spirit gave the apostle Peter unusual insight into the day when God will shake the heavens and the earth. "But, beloved, be not ignorant of this one thing, that one day is with the Lord as a thousand years, and a thousand years as one day. The Lord is not slack concerning his promise, as some men count slackness; but is long-suffering to us-ward, not willing that any should perish, but that all should come to repentance. But the day of the Lord will come as a thief in the night; in the which the heavens shall pass away with a great noise, and the elements shall melt with fervent heat, the earth also and the works that are therein shall be burned up. Seeing then that all these things shall be dissolved, what manner of persons ought ye to be in all holy conversation and godliness, Looking for and hasting unto the coming of the day of God, wherein the heavens being on fire shall be dissolved, and the elements shall melt with fervent heat? Nevertheless we, according to his promise, look for new heavens and a new earth, wherein dwelleth righteousness" (2 Peter 3: 8-13).

John Phillips observed: "In a coming day, all that has been created is to be demolished. Man's defiance under grace makes this inevitable. The day is coming when this world will see such a demonstration of God's power as will leave nothing standing at all, except what is founded on His grace."

If men defied God in Old Testament times and died when they touched the mount He told them not to touch, what will become of those who defy His great grace which He has exhibited in Christ Jesus? What hope is there for any man who turns his back upon the only means of redemption available to mankind? Or, as Simon Peter terms it: "And if the righteous scarcely be saved, where shall the ungodly and the sinner appear?" (1 Peter 4:18).

The one hope that men have is to hear and heed the voice of the Lord.

III. AN UNSHAKABLE KINGDOM (Hebrews 12:28, 29)

A. Receiving a Kingdom (v. 28)

(Hebrews 12:28 is not included in the printed text.)

Believers have entered into a relationship with God that can never be destroyed. We have a place in His ulti-

mate kingdom, and that cannot be taken away. Everything around us may crumble, but our place is in Christ and that is a safe place. While the heavens depart and the elements melt, we are hidden in Him. Men of this world may not have much to look forward to, but believers have started a journey that will last forever. The best days and the best times are yet to be. We have only been given a glimpse of the magnificent glory that is yet to be revealed.

Knowing that the future is bright, we should work at constantly maintaining an attitude of grace and thanksgiving. When Paul was faced with what he called a thorn in the flesh which the Lord did not choose to remove from him, his attitude was what carried him through. "And he said unto me, My grace is sufficient for thee: for my strength is made perfect in weakness. Most gladly therefore will I rather glory in my infirmities, that the power of Christ may rest upon me" (2 Corinthians 12:9). He could have become depressed or even bitter over this experience, but he chose rather to surrender everyting into the hands of Christ.

Believers are admonished to render service that is well pleasing to God. We are to approach Him with holy reverence and awe. Godly fear is always in order when we come before a holy God.

B. Consuming Fire (v. 29)

(Hebrews 12:29 is not included in the printed text.)

Our God is a devouring, all-burning, consuming fire. Moses wrote: "For the Lord thy God is a consuming fire, even a jealous God" (Deuteronomy 4:24). When David was given a glimpse of God this is what he saw: "At the brightness that was before him his thick clouds passed, hail stones and coals of fire" (Psalm 18:12). And when John got a look at Jesus in His resurrected and soon-coming splendor, he wrote: "His head and his hairs were white like wool, as white as snow; and his eyes were as a flame of fire" (Revelation 1:14).

When Jesus comes back to earth

again, He will be accompanied by holy fire. "And to you who are troubled rest with us, when the Lord Jesus shall be revealed from heaven with his mighty angels, in flaming fire taking vengeance on them that know not God, and that obey not the gospel of our Lord Jesus Christ" (2 Thessalonians 1:7, 8).

Fire symbolizes the holiness of God. Since His holiness cannot abide the presence of sin, sin and those it infests will be consumed by His fiery indignation. Earlier, the writer of Hebrews had said that those who reject redemption in Christ have nothing to look forward to "but a certain fearful looking for of judgment and fiery indignation, which shall devour the adversaries" (Hebrews 10:27). The fires of doom await those who defy the offers of a merciful God.

## REVIEW QUESTIONS

1. What is the author's purpose in writing the verses we study today?

2. What is meant by the Covenant of Grace?

3. What 3 things, according to this lesson, are stressed in the giving of the law at Mt. Sinai?

4. What does Mt. Sion (Zion) represent to God's people?

5. What thoughts are conjured up in your mind with the expression "An unshakable kingdom?" Do we determine the brightness of our future by attitudes? Explain.

## GOLDEN TEXT HOMILY

"WHEREFORE WE RECEIVING A KINGDOM WHICH CANNOT BE MOVED, LET US HAVE GRACE, WHEREBY WE MAY SERVE GOD ACCEPTABLY WITH REVERENCE AND GODLY FEAR" (Hebrews 12:28).

Everything we know in this physical life is subject to change. Not one of us can say for certain that we will have specific things, be at a designated place, or accomplish what we intend to. Sickness, accidents, storms, financial reverses or changing circumstances, things we do not have any control over, can dramatically affect the direction of our life.

But God's kingdom is far different. God is not subject to physical circumstances or change. He is in total control and His kingdom will never be shaken or moved. The Lord has also made provision whereby each person can be part of His unchanging kingdom. How great God is!

Through salvation God provides specific things for each individual who accepts His provision. Cleansing from sin and a sure hope for the future are guaranteed to everyone who comes to God in true repentance (which means confessing and forsaking sin) and faithfully follows the Lord. Jesus said in John 14 that He was going to prepare a place in that unshakable kingdom for each of His children.

The greatest tragedy that could happen in our life would be to miss God's kingdom. The passage in Hebrews 2:3 asks the question, "How shall we escape, if we neglect so great salvation?"

Thank God for His unshakable kingdom and that all His children are part of it!

Even though we are—SURROUNDED BY GLOOM
If we have experienced—SAVING GRACE
There will be—SUDDEN GLORY
—**Philip Siggelkow, President, International Bible College, Moose Jaw, Saskatchewan, Canada.**

## SENTENCE SERMONS

BELIEVERS ARE TO LIVE in total assurance that God's kingdom will never be shaken.
—**Selected**

THE HIGHER a man is in grace, the lower he will be in his own esteem.
—**Charles Spurgeon**

GRACE WILL NOT COVER what cannot be helped until the blood covers what can be helped.
—**Keith Huttenlocker**

OBEDIENCE IS the beginning of all other Christian graces.
—**"Notes and Quotes"**

OBEDIENCE IS NOT idle holiness.
—**"Notes and Quotes"**

## EVANGELISTIC APPLICATION

THE DELAY OF GOD'S JUDGMENT IS AN EXPRESSION OF HIS GOODNESS AND LONGSUFFERING TOWARD THE SINNER.

Exhibited in one of the cases in the library of the Vatican is an ancient palimpsest. Centuries ago, men had written line after line on sheets of papyrus until their work filled an entire volume. Many years later, when paper was difficult to secure, someone found the old volume and wrote a new work across the original manuscript, in lines perpendicular to the first. Today the blacker ink of the second writing is more legible, but the text underneath is still clear enough to read with ease; scholars frequently take more delight in reading the older than they do the more recent writing.

Such is the heart and conscience of man. Across the fresh page in the youth of the race, God wrote the eternal truths of His being, His holiness, His justice, and the certainty of His wrath against sin. Men turned the page sidewise and wrote with blacker ink the history of their doings until, in some places, the earlier writing is almost effaced. But the day will come when the acid of God's judgment will eat away the writings of man, and the strong X ray of the light of God will bring to the surface the original writing by which man will be judged. (Donald Grey Barnhouse in *Let Me Illustrate*).

## ILLUMINATING THE LESSON

Christians do not face a fiery Sinai but rather the welcome of Zion. Someone has said, "We have already arrived in principle where in full reality we shall be forever. The future is already the present. In today we possess tomorrow. On earth we own heaven." These incomparable privileges and glories of the Christian faith are not to be treated lightly. Those who reject God's voice as it now speaks from heaven in the gospel are more responsible than those who broke the Law. Their ultimate doom is expressed in these words: "Then shall he say also unto them on the left hand, Depart from me, ye cursed, into everlasting fire, prepared for the devil and his angels" (Matthew 25:41).

## DAILY DEVOTIONAL GUIDE

M. The Kingdom Promised. 2 Samuel 7:12-17

T. The Kingdom Is Eternal. Daniel 2:44, 45

W. The Kingdom Is Universal. Daniel 7: 21-27

T. The Gospel of the Kingdom. Matthew 4:23-25

F. The Children of the Kingdom. Matthew 13:37-43

S. The King of Kings. Revelation 19: 11-16

# A Life That Pleases God

**Study Text:** Hebrews 13:1-25
**Supplemental References:** Psalm 118:1-29; Matthew 6:24-34; Ephesians 4:12-16; 1 Timothy 6:1-7; 1 Peter 2:1-5
**Time:** Probably A.D. 65-70
**Place:** Generally thought to have been written from Rome.
**Golden Text:** "Let us offer the sacrifice of praise to God continually, that is, the fruit of our lips giving thanks to his name" (Hebrews 13:15).
**Central Truth:** God is glorified when we live according to Christ's example.
**Evangelistic Emphasis:** God has an eternal purpose for every life.

## Printed Text

**Hebrews 13:1.** Let brotherly love continue.

**2. Be not forgetful to entertain strangers: for thereby some have entertained angels unawares.**

3. Remember them that are in bonds, as bound with them; and them which suffer adversity, as being yourselves also in the body.

**4. Marriage is honourable in all, and the bed undefiled: but whoremongers and adulterers God will judge.**

5. Let your conversation be without covetousness; and be content with such things as ye have: for he hath said, I will never leave thee, nor forsake thee.

**6. So that we may boldly say, The Lord is my helper, and I will not fear what man shall do unto me.**

7. Remember them which have the rule over you, who have spoken unto you the word of God: whose faith follow, considering the end of their conversation.

**8. Jesus Christ the same yesterday, and to day, and for ever.**

9. Be not carried about with divers and strange doctrines. For it is a good thing that the heart be established with grace; not with meats, which have not profited them that have been occupied therein.

**10. We have an altar, whereof they have no right to eat which serve the tabernacle.**

11. For the bodies of those beasts, whose blood is brought into the sanctuary by the high priest for sin, are burned without the camp.

**12. Wherefore Jesus also, that he might sanctify the people with his own blood, suffered without the gate.**

13. Let us go forth therefore unto him without the camp, bearing his reproach.

**14. For here have we no continuing city, but we seek one to come.**

15. By him therefore let us offer the sacrifice of praise to God continually, that is, the fruit of our lips giving thanks to his name.

**16. But to do good and to communicate forget not: for with such sacrifices God is well pleased.**

17. Obey them that have the rule over you, and submit yourselves: for they

watch for your souls, as they that must give account, that they may do it with joy, and not with grief: for that is unprofitable for you.

## LESSON OUTLINE

I. GODLINESS AND CONTENTMENT
   A. Love
   B. Concern
   C. Contentment
II. STRENGTHEN BY GRACE
   A. Immutability
   B. Truth
   C. Blessings
III. GIVING THANKS TO GOD
   A. Praise
   B. Goodness
   C. Obedience

## LESSON EXPOSITION

INTRODUCTION

The power of the blood of Christ and the supremacy of His priesthood is the theme of chapters 1-10 of Hebrews. Chapter 11 is, of course, the great faith chapter of the Bible. The Christian life is likened to the running of a race in chapter 12.

Today's lesson is taken from chapter 13, which underscores many of the privileges and duties of the Christian. Love, hospitality, care, sympathy, purity, and contentment are some of the graces we are called upon to develop. Christ's power is available to our lives that we may grow in Him. In chapter 13 we are encouraged to take an inward look (at ourselves), an outward look (at our neighbors), and an upward look (at our Lord). Indeed, it is a chapter that challenges us to manifest love and service to Christ and others.

Vance Havner, twentieth-century preacher, said, "Much of our orthodoxy is correct and sound, but it is like words without a tune and statutes without songs. It does not glow and burn, it does not stir the wells of the heart. . . . It is too much like a catechism and not enough like a camp meeting. . . . One man with a glowing experience of God is worth a library full of arguments."

And that was the secret of the Great Awakening—someone had a glowing experience with God. When a person catches a glimpse of the things that are eternal, all other interests are swept away. Motivated by a God-given love for others and a passion for souls, a person with a visionary, purposeful, and Spirit-implanted zeal goes forth to stir slumbering souls and to shake his world for God!

"Romanism trembled when Martin Luther saw God. The 'great awakening' sprang into being when Jonathan Edwards saw God. The world became the parish of one man when John Wesley saw God. Multitudes were saved when Whitefield saw God. Thousands of orphans were fed when George Mueller saw God" *(The Kneeling Christian)*. And the same thing can happen today, for "Jesus Christ [is] the same yesterday, and today, and for ever" (Hebrews 13:8).

I. GODLINESS AND CONTENTMENT (Hebrews 13:1-6)

A. Love (vv. 1, 2)
   **1. Let brotherly love continue.**
   **2. Be not forgetful to entertain strangers: for thereby some have entertained angels unawares.**

All believers have one Father, one Elder Brother, and one Spirit. We are members of the family of God, and thus we have a responsibility to love one another.

Next to faith in Jesus Christ, the life and beauty of the Christian religion consists in the mutual love of them who are partakers of the same heavenly calling. Jesus said, "By this shall all men know that ye are my disciples, if ye have love one to another" (John 13:35). Paul wrote: "Let love be without dissimulation. . . . Be kindly affectioned one to another with brotherly love; in honour preferring one another" (Romans 12:9, 10). And again, "But as touching brotherly love ye need

selves are taught of God to love one another" (2 Thessalonians 4:9). Peter wrote:
"Seeing ye have purified your souls in
obeying the truth through the Spirit unto unfeigned love of the brethren, see
that ye love one another with a pure
heart fervently" (1 Peter 1:22). He added:
"Finally, be ye all of one mind, having
compassion one of another, love as brethren, be pitiful, be courteous" (1 Peter
3:8). And again, "And to godliness brotherly kindness; and to brotherly kindness
charity" (2 Peter 1:7).

The writer of Hebrews called upon
Christians of his day to entertain strangers. This calling was sounded at a time
of severe persecutions, when believers
were driven from their own homes. Christian hospitality would provide for dis-
placed persons a refuge and hiding place.
It would also give those living at peace
an opportunity to exercise faith, love,
and kindness. In doing this, he went on
to say that some have entertained angels
without knowing it. Through being hospitable, some have had angels as their guests
and were not aware of it.

B. Concern (vv. 3, 4)

**3. Remember them that are in bonds,
as bound with them; and them which
suffer adversity, as being yourselves
also in the body.**

**4. Marriage is honourable in all, and
the bed undefiled: but whoremongers
and adulterers God will judge.**

Those in bonds were persons who
suffered for the gospel; many of them
were "prisoners of Christ"—an honorable
title. It was far better, safer, and more
honorable to be in bonds with and for
Christ than to be at liberty with this
Christ-rejecting world.

We today should "remember" our fellow Christians that are bound for the
gospel's sake and identify with them.
Those in bonds need food, warm clothing, reading matter, encouragement. We
are tempted to shield ourselves from
association with prisoners and, thus, from
the danger of guilt by association; but
we should remember that in visiting the

prisoner, we are doing the bidding of
Christ.

We should also show compassion for
the ill-treated and the persecuted. We
should remember that we too are in the
same body of believers and, therefore,
subject to similar afflictions.

Paul encouraged hospitality. "Distribut-
ing to the necessity of saints; given to
hospitality" (Romans 12:13). He recognized hospitality as a quality a pastor
should possess. "A bishop then must be
blameless, the husband of one wife,
vigilant, sober, of good behaviour, given
to hospitality, apt to teach" (1 Timothy
3:2).

Then, the writer of Hebrews turns his
attention to the sacredness of marriage.
Since marriage is ordained of God and
honorable in His sight, it is the duty of
those who enter into this relationship to
esteem it highly. God will penalize those
who violate its sacredness. Acts of
premarital sexual immorality and extra-
marital sexual affairs are outside the
realm of proper sexual behavior and are
therefore subject to the judgment of God.

C. Contentment (vv. 5, 6)

**5. Let your conversation be without
covetousness; and be content with such
things as ye have: for he hath said, I
will never leave thee, nor forsake
thee.**

**6. So that we may boldly say, The
Lord is my helper, and I will not fear
what man shall do unto me.**

Covetousness is an inordinate desire
for more riches than we have. Those
exhibiting such an attitude overrate the
value of material things, because they
have developed a love for them. In
contrast to this, we are admonished to
be satisfied with what we have. Such
contentment is based on our faith that
God will in no wise fail us, neither will
He in any wise forsake us. If our trust is
in God, and He is our helper, all will be
well.

John Phillips observed: "God is the ultimate Provider. He feeds the birds and
the beasts, sending springtime and harvest and soft, refreshing rain. Our ability

to work and our temporal employment are of His providing. God knows our needs, our circumstances, and all about us, and He has pledged Himself to take care of us."

God is in the business of meeting the needs of His people. Paul discovered this. He wrote: "But I rejoiced in the Lord greatly, that now at the last your care of me hath flourished again; wherein ye were also careful, but ye lacked opportunity. Not that I speak in respect of want: for I have learned, in whatsoever state I am, therewith to be content. I know both how to be abased, and I know how to abound: every where and in all things I am instructed both to be full and to be hungry, both to abound and to suffer need. I can do all things through Christ which strengtheneth me" (Philippians 4:10-13).

The apostle raised this question to the Romans, "If God be for us, who can be against us?"(Romans 8:31). He also shared with them his philosophy: "And we know that all things work together for good to them that love God, to them who are the called according to his purpose" (Romans 8:28).

II. STRENGTHENED BY GRACE (Hebrews 13:7-14)

A. Immutability (vv. 7, 8)

**7. Remember them which have the rule over you, who have spoken unto you the word of God: whose faith follow, considering the end of their conversation.**

**8. Jesus Christ the same yesterday, and to day, and for ever.**

The writer calls attention to those who preach the Word of God. He admonishes us to remember them because of what they do and teach. Those charged with the responsibility of the church are leaving us an example of faith and holiness to follow.

Quintilian, the Roman master of oratory said: "It is a good thing to know, and always to keep turning over in the mind, the things which were illustriously done of old." Epicurus advised his followers continuously to remember those of old time who lived with virtue.

The word conversation carries the thought of one's manner of life. It includes both the frame of our minds and the manner of our acting. The order of our conversation is of great importance in our Christian profession. We must exercise behavior worthy of imitation.

The unchangeableness of Christ is mentioned in verse 8. Christ is "the same yesterday, and to day, and for ever." This attribute of immutability is borne out by verb tenses in Scriptures: He "**was** in the beginning"; He "**was** with God"; He "**was** God" (John 1:1, 2). His "goings forth **have been** from old, from everlasting" (Micah 5:2). He said of Himself, "I **am** Alpha and Omega . . . which **is,** and which **was,** and which **is to come"** (Revelation 1:8). He is, He was, He ever will be all in all unto His church (Colossians 1:16-19; 2:9, 10). He is "the same": the author, the object, the finisher of our faith and the preserver and rewarder of all persons in all generations that believe!

Of Christ, Clarence Edward Macartney wrote: "All that He is today, He was yesterday. All that He was yesterday, He is today. All that He will be tomorrow, He is today. All that He is today, He will be forever."

B. Truth (vv. 9, 10)

**9. Be not carried about with divers and strange doctrines. For it is a good thing that the heart be established with grace; not with meats which have not profited them that have been occupied therein.**

**10. We have an altar, whereof they have no right to eat which serve the tabernacle.**

There are all sorts of outlandish teachings and they are to be avoided. When they are entertained, men become double-minded and unstable and turn from the truth. The neglect of this caution has been the hurt of the church in various places and ages. There is safety for all believers in keeping to the fundamental doctrines of God's Word. Such care leads to the establishing of the heart. Only God's grace can inspire and empower blessings to live holy lives.

Love for the Savior who died for us motivates us to "live soberly, righteously,
and godly, in this present world" (Titus
2:12).

The inadequacy of the whole system of
Mosaic institutions is contained in the
words "not with meats." "The kingdom
of God is not meat and drink; but righteousness, and peace, and joy in the
Holy Ghost" (Romans 14:17). Grace is
needed to enjoy the fruits of the kingdom.

The altar mentioned probably has reference to an altar for the slaying and
burning of victims: such as the altar of
the burnt offering, also, the altar of incense, or any other altar, such as the
cross on which Christ suffered and died.

No place was more important to the
Jew than the altar, of sacrifice. Thus,
the Hebrew sometimes mocked the Christian for having no altar. But the reply
of the believer was, "Christ is our altar. All the blessings that are found in
Him are our portion."

Those who have never accepted Jesus
know nothing of the better things of
Christianity. One must repent of his sins
and believe in Jesus Christ as his only
Lord and Savior to receive these benefits.

C. Blessings (vv. 11-14)

**11. For the bodies of those beasts,
whose blood is brought into the sanctuary by the high priest for sin, are
burned without the camp.**

**12. Wherefore Jesus also, that he
might sanctify the people with his
own blood, suffered without the gate.**

**13. Let us go forth therefore unto
him without the camp, bearing his reproach.**

**14. For here have we no continuing
city, but we seek one to come.**

Under the Levitical order, certain beasts
were slain and their blood was brought
into the holy of holies by the high priest
and offered as a sacrifice for sin. The
bodies were then carried to an area
away from the Tabernacle and burned.
The expression "without the camp" means
outside the outer fence that enclosed
the porch of the Tabernacle.

These animals that were taken outside
the camp and burned were a type of
the Lord Jesus Christ. He was taken
outside the walls of Jerusalem and crucified. Outside the walls He sanctified the
people through the shedding of His own
blood. Faith in that shed blood is our
only basis of hope.

Just as the former adherents of Judaism
could no longer rely upon the rituals of
the Law, even so we can trust nothing
to save us but the blood of Jesus. Church
membership alone will not do it! Tithing
alone will not do it! Good works alone
will not do it! Nothing but the blood of
Jesus will suffice for our sins! There may
be reproach connected to our faith in the
power of the blood, but we must bear it,
and gladly.

The Jews under the Mosaic dispensation had a city—Jerusalem—which was
the seat of divine worship. But believers
have no such city; they "seek one to
come." That city is to be their eternal
habitation.

Jesus spoke of preparing that city:
"In my Father's house are many man-
sions: if it were not so, I would have
told you. I go to prepare a place for
you. And if I go to prepare a place
for you, I will come again, and receive
you unto myself; that where I am, there
ye may be also" (John 14:2, 3).

The apostle John saw that city: "And I
John saw the holy city, new Jerusalem,
coming down from God out of heaven,
prepared as a bride adorned for her
husband" (Revelation 21:2). In verses
10-27 of that same chapter, John paints
a breathtaking portrait of the Holy City.

The heart of the believer is set on the
heavenly city, the new Jerusalem, where
the Lamb of God is all the glory. Entrance into that city is promised to the
believer. The way to it is made plain
by Jesus Christ.

III. GIVING THANKS TO GOD (Hebrews
13:15-17)

A. Praise (v. 15)

**15. By him therefore let us offer
the sacrifice of praise to God con-**

**tinually, that is, the fruit of our lips giving thanks to his name.**

All saints are priests in this dispensation of grace. We enter the sanctuary of God with the right to worship Him (1 Peter 2:5). We depart from the sanctuary into the world to witness for Him (1 Peter 2:9).

As priests unto God there are cetain sacrifices we offer unto Him. There is the sacrifice of our person (Romans 12:1). Then, there is the "sacrifice of praise" unto God. It is "by Him" alone that the offering of our sacrifices is made acceptable. All our praise and prayer must first pass through the priestly office of the Lord Jesus Christ before it reaches God the Father. It is Christ who removes all impurities and imperfections.

Our sacrifice is to be offered "continually." We are freed from appointed times, and seasons, and places; but this gives us both the right and the responsibility to maintain a constant attitude toward prayer and praise.

John Phillips asked some provocative questions: "Can we praise God without cost to ourselves? . . . How long does it take to perfect praise, to soberly think through the immense realities of the grace and the goodness and the glory and the government of God? Is praise the glib singing of a chorus, or is it hours spent in God's presence with heart uplifted in awe and worship at the wonders of His person and His works? Is praise the thoughtless line or two of a hymn song with others at a worship service, or is it the voice of testimony raised among men in glory to God at home, at work, at play?"

B. Goodness (v. 16)

**16. But to do good and to communicate forget not: for with such sacrifices God is well pleased.**

To "do good" concerns the whole course of our life. Patient continuance in "well doing" is the life of the believer, and this we are warned not to be weary of, nor faint in. Paul wrote: "And let us not be weary in well doing: for in due season we shall reap, if we faint not" (Galatians

6:9). This "well doing" consists in a gracious readiness to do good unto all. In all ways and things, spiritual and temporal, we are to be useful and helpful to mankind, embracing all opportunities for the exercise of pity, compassion, and loving-kindness.

To "communicate" is to distribute to others the good things we enjoy. "With such sacrifices God is well pleased."

The believer is not only encouraged to give gifts unto God, but also to offer his total self in the service of the Master. Paul wrote: "I beseech you therefore, brethren, by the mercies of God, that ye present your bodies a living sacrifice, holy, acceptable unto God, which is your reasonable service" (Romans 12:1). And again, "And this they did, not as we hoped, but first gave their own selves to the Lord, and unto us by the will of God" (2 Corinthians 8:5). Jesus commended men for attention given to those many would ignore: "And the King shall answer and say unto them, Verily I say unto you, Inasmuch as ye have done it unto one of the least of these my brethren, ye have done it unto me" (Matthew 25:40).

C. Obedience (v. 17)

**17. Obey them that have the rule over you, and submit yourselves: for they watch for your souls, as they that must give account, that they may do it with joy, and not with grief: for that is unprofitable for you.**

The writer calls attention to **past** leaders in verses 7 and 8; and now in verses 16 and 17 he instructs us of our duty to **present** leaders. He refers primarily to elders in the local church who act as representatives of God. God has given authority to them, and it is our duty as believers to submit to this authority. As undershepherds, they watch for our souls and will have to give account to God in a coming day. They will do it either with joy or with sadness, depending on the spiritual progress of those under their care. If their report brings sadness, the saints concerned will lose their reward.

Therefore, it is to everone's benefit to respect the lines of authority that God has laid down.

When Mr. Baldwin, as he then was, became Prime Minister of Great Britian, his friends thronged round him to congratulate him. His answer to their congratulations was: "It is not your congratulations I need; it is your prayers."

Every minister who takes his calling seriously will echo that reply. He would tell you that the prayers of the smallest saints are useful to him. He desires their prayers both with respect to his person and to the discharge of his office. He wants to live honorably, both for his own sake and for the sake of others who watch his life. He knows prayer is an essential element in his success.

## REVIEW QUESTIONS

1. How is the unchangeableness of Christ expressed in this lesson?

2. How can one "offer the sacrifice of praise continually?"

3. What should leaders do, or how should they lead, so that those under them will submit and obey with all good will and cooperation?

4. What are the outstanding qualities of the Shepherd-sheep relationship between God and man?

5. How is the "priesthood of all believers" alluded to in this lesson?

## GOLDEN TEXT HOMILY

"LET US OFFER THE SACRIFICE OF PRAISE TO GOD CONTINUALLY, THAT IS, THE FRUIT OF OUR LIPS GIVING THANKS TO HIS NAME" (Hebrews 13:15).

The **New International Version** of the Bible renders this verse: "Let us continually offer to God a sacrifice of praise —the fruit of lips that confess his name."

To confess the lovely name of Jesus is to live a life that pleases God. We are called upon to confess His name in both word and deed, in the good times and in the bad times. A sacrifice (of-fering) of praise is what God calls upon each born-again believer to give.

Our faith must be fixed upon Christ who is "the same yesterday, and today, and forever" (v. 8). With our faith fixed in Him, we shall not be carried about by every strange doctrine which comes along. Instead, we will live a committed life which will bring praise, honor, and glory to God the Father who sent His Son into the world that we might have eternal life.

We are not to be ashamed of the death of Christ or His redemption by blood. Instead, we are to share the reproach which sinful men place upon Him and in so doing confess He is Lord. We are not to let Him bear His cross of shame alone while we go free. Rather let us offer our sacrifice of praise with our lips and our life as we continue to confess He is indeed the Son of God.

Cast out! Despised and rejected of men! Bearing His reproach! All these descriptive phrases of Christ have a familiar ring to the faithful follower of the Lord Jesus. Even in this age of tolerance there are still times when you may be shut out—not in the camp—barred from the general fellowship. Yes, there is a social ostracism that Christians must endure, even in our day. This is often the posture of the believer who refuses to compromise His faith in Christ.

To be shut out from the circle of evil men is to be drawn near to God. A life set apart from sinful practices is one which lifts up the name of Jesus. Let us pursue the good life; the life which exalts the one who gave His life for us.

Let our prayer each day be: "May the words of my mouth and the meditation of my heart be pleasing in your sight, O Lord, my Rock and my Redeemer" (Psalm 19:14, **New International Version**).—**Henry J. Smith, D. Min., President, East Coast Bible College, Charlotte, North Carolina**

## SENTENCE SERMONS

GOD IS GLORIFIED when we live according to Christ's example.
**—Selected**

CONTENT MAKES poor men rich; discontent makes rich men poor.
—**Benjamin Franklin**

CONTENTMENT OFTEN SERVES as a brake on the wheels of progress. God has the correct formula: "Godliness with contentment is great gain."
—**"Speaker's Sourcebook"**

GIVING THANKS is a course from which we never graduate.
—**"Speaker's Sourcebook"**

GRATITUDE IS the memory of the heart.
—**"Speaker's Sourcebook"**

## EVANGELISTIC APPLICATION

GOD HAS AN ETERNAL PURPOSE FOR EVERY LIFE.

Jesus Christ who gives purpose to our life, is the great shepherd; He is the only shepherd; and He is the shepherd only of the sheep. He is great in His person, being the eternal Son of God; He is great in power to preserve His flock; He is great in the discharge of His office; and He is great in His glory and exaltation. He is incomparably great and glorious. He is the "shepherd of the sheep"; He laid down His life for the flock. It is the "God of peace" that brought Him again from the dead, giving evidence that peace was now made perfect through Christ.

If one is to find God's promise in life, he must begin with Jesus Christ. The danger of missing the mark looms darkly over the heads of all who refuse to seek His guidance. On the other hand, life's greatest fulfillment awaits those who turn to Christ for direction.

## ILLUMINATING THE LESSON

Freedom in Christ reminds one of the story Dr. William Barclay told in one of his books. Abraham Lincoln once bought a slave girl for the sole purpose of giving her her freedom. To the girl this was merely another transaction. She thought she was simply a pawn; she was someone else's property. Even when Lincoln handed her papers of freedom, she did not understand.

"You are free," Lincoln said to her gently.

"Free? Can I go wherever I want to go now?"

"Indeed, you can," Lincoln said.

"If I am free to go anywhere," came the stunning reply, "I will stay with you and serve you till I die."

She was bound by love and gratitude even though she was legally free. Jesus Christ has set us free; yet, we are His bondslaves because of our love and gratitude for Him.

## DAILY DEVOTIONAL GUIDE

M. A Walk That Pleases God. Genesis 5:21-24

T. Faith That Pleases God. Genesis 15:1-6

W. Prayer That Pleases God. 1 Kings 3:3-14

T. Holiness Pleases God. 1 Thessalonians 4:1-7

F. Works That Please God. Titus 2:7-15

S. A Sacrifice That Pleases God. 1 Peter 2:1-5

# INTRODUCTION
# TO SPRING
# QUARTER

The month of March begins the spring quarter of studies which are presented under the theme, "The Patriarchs." This study in the Book of Genesis which was begun in September, now continues after a break in the sequence as attention was focused on the Book of Hebrews.

The lessons in this series cover incidents in the lives of Isaac and Rebekah, Esau aríd Jacob, and Joseph and his brothers. Two lessons—Easter and Pentecost—are included in this quarter of studies and bring a departure from the regular studies as attention is placed on the resurrection of our lovely Lord, and on the outpouring of the Holy Spirit on the Day of Pentecost.

The studies of this quarter are certain to give new insights to the great patriarchs, as well as renew our appreciation for the sacrifice of Christ, and the coming of the Holy Spirit.

# Led by God

**(Isaac and Rebekah)**

**Study Text:** Genesis 24:1-67

**Supplemental References:** Numbers 9:15-23; Psalm 73:23-28; Acts 13:1-3

**Time:** Opinions vary, but many scholars set the date around 2026 B.C.

**Place:** Canaan and Mesopotamia

**Golden Text:** "The Lord, before whom I walk, will send his angel with thee, and prosper thy way" (Genesis 24:40).

**Central Truth:** The Lord is faithful to guide all who sincerely seek His will.

**Evangelistic Emphasis:** Spiritual blessings come to those who sincerely accept Christ as Savior.

## Printed Text

**Genesis 24:4.** But thou shalt go unto my country, and to my kindred, and take a wife unto my son Isaac.

**5. And the servant said unto him, Peradventure the woman will not be willing to follow me unto this land: must I needs bring thy son again unto the land from whence thou camest?**

6. And Abraham said unto him, Beware thou that thou bring not my son thither again.

**7. The Lord God of heaven, which took me from my father's house, and from the land of my kindred, and which spake unto me, and that sware unto me, saying, Unto thy seed will I give this land; he shall send his angel before thee, and thou shalt take a wife unto my son from thence.**

12. And he said, O Lord God of my master Abraham, I pray thee, send me good speed this day, and shew kindness unto my master Abraham.

**13. Behold, I stand here by the well of water; and the daughters of the men of the city come out to draw water:**

14. And let it come to pass, that the damsel to whom I shall say, Let down thy pitcher, I pray thee, that I may drink; and she shall say, Drink, and I will give thy camels drink also: let the same be she that thou hast appointed for thy servant Isaac; and thereby shall I know that thou hast shewed kindness unto my master.

**15. And it came to pass, before he had done speaking, that, behold, Rebekah came out, who was born to Bethuel, son of Milcah, the wife of Nahor, Abraham's brother, with her pitcher upon her shoulder.**

57. And they said, We will call the damsel, and inquire at her mouth.

**58. And they called Rebekah, and said unto her, Wilt thou go with this man? And she said, I will go.**

59. And they sent away Rebekah their sister, and her nurse, and Abraham's servant, and his men.

**60. And they blessed Rebekah, and said unto her, Thou art our sister, be thou the mother of thousands of millions, and let thy seed possess the gate of those which hate them.**

61. And Rebekah arose, and her damsels, and they rode upon the camels, and followed the man: and the servant took Rebekah, and went his way.

## LESSON OUTLINE

I. TRUSTING GOD'S DIRECTION
II. FOLLOWING GOD'S WAY
III. ACCEPTING GOD'S WILL

## LESSON EXPOSITION

INTRODUCTION

In this quarter's lessons we study the Hebrew patriarchs, those early fathers of the Hebrew people who laid the foundation for their faith and national character. Generally speaking, the patriarch of a clan is the eldest living male of that clan and therefore its spiritual and titular head. The Hebrews put great stock in old age and its accompanying virtues of wisdom and strength of character. Any man who was the eldest male member of his family was in that sense a patriarch.

When we speak of "the patriarchs" we generally mean something more specific than that bold definition. The patriarchs generally refer to only three men: Abraham, Isaac and Jacob. This is because these three were not only patriarchs to their family but to the nation that was to come. The Jewish people always looked back to these three as the fountainhead of their nation and faith.

In an earlier quarter we have already looked at the life of Abraham, greatest of the patriarchs, and have seen the most active part of his life and influence. We catch only a brief glimpse of him in this lesson and then our attention moves on to the second of the patriarchs, Isaac. For reasons we shall see, Isaac was the least renowned of the three patriarchs. He has been likened to a valley that appears naturally between towering peaks. Both Abraham and Jacob were men of strength and ability and resolve; each in his own right is a strong peak of strength. Isaac, on the other hand, never rises to the height of either his father or his son. He is nevertheless important, for his life was a great example to the Hebrews—and to Christians today.

So now we begin to examine the life of this valley, this low ground between the towering peaks.

## I. TRUSTING GOD'S DIRECTION (Genesis 24:1-9)

When Abraham was old and still bereaved over the death of Sarah, he seems to have sensed that his own death was near. God had prospered him in all things, both spiritual and material, so that he was one of the richest men of his time. His tent was quiet and sad, however, for his beloved Sarah was dead and their son Isaac had not yet married.

The aged patriarch gave a solemn commission to a trusted servant. In all likelihood this man was Eliezer, who is mentioned in Genesis 15:2. Eliezer was a native of Damascus who served as steward over all Abraham's household and other affairs. He was something like a manager of all that Abraham had. The physical gesture of putting one's hand under another's thigh was the Jewish equivalent to our shaking of hands or signing a contract or placing our hand upon the Bible as assurance of our good faith. The tone of what Abraham has to say indicates that he intended them to be carried out even if he should die. This was an absolute and binding oath that should be not put aside even if Abraham did not live long enough to see the fulfillment of Eliezer's mission.

**Genesis 24:4. But thou shalt go unto my country, and to my kindred, and take a wife unto my son Isaac.**

Abraham had lived among the Canaanites long enough to know that he did not want his son to marry one of their women. In verse 3 he said, "And I will make thee swear by the Lord, the God of heaven, and the God of the earth, that thou shall not take a wife unto my son of the daughters of the Canaanites, among whom I dwell." Abraham had seen enough of their pagan practices and perverted religion to know that a mixed marriage could bring nothing good to the cause of God. One of the most abominable practices of the Canaanites was that of human sacrifice. God had demonstrated in the grammatic offering of Isaac that He could not be worshiped by human sacrifice (22:2-13).

Discuss the potential problems that can accompany the marriage between a believer and nonbeliever.

---

Abraham directed Eliezer to go into the Chaldean area and there find a bride for Isaac from among Abraham's own people. In this oath Eliezer swears to Abraham: First, that he will not accept a Canaanite woman as a bride for Isaac; and second, that he will travel to Abraham's own country and there find a bride for Isaac. The spiritual purpose of this oath was to insure the purity of the Abrahamic faith. The term "my kindred" alludes to the family bonds that were observed through many generations by the Hebrew people.

**5. And the servant said unto him, Peradventure the woman will not be willing to follow me unto this land: must I needs bring thy son again unto the land from whence thou camest?**

Here Eliezer raises a question that is interesting for a couple of reasons. First, it should be observed that Isaac was at this time about 40 years old—yet the father and his steward are making all arrangements for Isaac's search for a bride. Second, it suggests the possibility that Isaac might leave Canaan to return to his father's homeland. The bride Eliezer might choose could be unwilling to make the long journey into Canaan, for it was a wild and forbidding area in comparison to the more developed north country. This does not mean that Eliezer expected the chosen bride to be reluctant to come, but he was simply covering all situations that might arise.

**6. Abraham said unto him, Beware thou that thou bring not my son thither again.**

**7. The Lord God of heaven, which took me from my father's house, and from the land of my kindred, and which spake unto me, and that sware unto me, saying, Unto thy seed will I give this land; he shall send his angel before thee, and thou shalt take a wife unto my son from thence.**

The very thought that Isaac might leave Canaan because of a bride's unwillingness to go there seems to have horrified Abraham. His response to that suggestion is strong and emphatic, that Isaac was in no wise to leave Canaan and move into Haran—for Canaan had been promised to Abraham and his descendants. It was in Canaan that Isaac must live, as would his descendants until the seed of Abraham should become a mighty people. Canaan was their heritage from the Lord, their promised land, the center of their lives for all times.

Abraham recalled how God had taken him from his birthplace in Ur of the Chaldees and from the region of Haran, where his kinsman then resided, and led him southward into Canaan. It was God's promise that his land of Canaan would be an inheritance to Abraham's descendants forever.

Abraham seemed to realize that God would intervene directly in the choice of Isaac's wife by saying, "He will send his angel before you and you shall take a wife for my son from there." In verse 8 Abraham explains that any refusal of the bride to come to Canaan will relieve Eliezer from his oath but it must not cause Isaac to go out of Canaan. In this way the aged patriarch worked to secure the succession of his family in the land the Lord had promised.

*The Broadman Commentary* says: "Abraham's last wishes therefore are his final act of obedience to the inaugural vision of his vocation. The beginning and the end of Abraham's life cohere in the promises of the Lord, the God of heaven and earth. God is thus pictured as living and ruling everywhere, and the idea suits the story."

II. FOLLOWING GOD'S WAY (Genesis 24:10-19)

Abraham's servant went into Mesopotamia to the city where Nahor lived, which was probably Haran. He took with him a caravan of ten camels loaded with gifts of choice and valuable sorts. The fact that there were ten camels within the caravans gives some indication of Abraham's immense wealth. It was the custom for the groom's father to pay for his son's bride. This was a form of dowry that would benefit both the bride and her family. During his long journey to the north country the servant, aware of the magnitude of his responsibility, devised a plan for ascertaining God's will concerning the woman to be chosen. Certainly it was responsibility too grave for him to undertake without divine assistance. At a well outside the city the servant made ready to discover the will of God. He caused his caravan of camels to kneel beside the well that provided the city's water.

**12. And he said, O Lord God of my master Abraham, I pray thee, send me good speed this day, and shew kindness unto my master Abraham.**

It is fitting that the servant should seek the will of the Lord in a matter that would involve the lives of two persons and all of those who would follow after them. God is truly interested in the most ordinary and personal parts of our lives. Eliezer's prayer is in direct accord with Proverbs 3:5, and 6: "Trust in the Lord with all thine heart; and lean not unto thine own understanding. In all thy ways acknowledge him, and he shall direct thy paths." It is noteworthy that the servant's prayer was not based upon his own righteousness, but upon that of his master Abraham.

**13. Behold, I stand here by the well of water; and the daughters of the men of the city come out to draw water.**

It was late in the day, time for the women of the city to come to the well for their household water, when Eliezer sat beside the well. The women of the city were always those who went to the water source to get their household supply; in the event a grown daughter lived in her father's household it became her responsibility to get the water. In verse 13 we read the word **daughters** and in verse 11 we read the word **women.** This indicates that married women and unmarried alike would make their way to the well. The word **daughter** is mentioned in verse 13 because Eliezer would be interested only in those unmarried persons he might encounter.

**14. And let it come to pass, that the damsel to whom I shall say, Let down thy pitcher, I pray thee, that I may drink; and she shall say, Drink, and I will give thy camels drink also: let the same be she that thou hast appointed for thy servant Isaac; and thereby shall I know that thou hast shewed kindness unto my master.**

Here the word **damsel** is used, which becomes even more specific regarding the person Eliezer might chose for Isaac's bride. The word **damsel** connotes a person young in years and virgin in purity.

The servant's plan was to request a drink of water from various damsels who would come to the well. All of them would be obligated to give a stranger a drink of water, and any refusal to do so would bring shame upon her father's household and even the village in which she lived. Custom required the citizens of any place to give water to the stranger who happened by. It was therefore no test for the servant to ask the damsels for a drink of water; the test was that one of them would offer to draw water for his camels also. This was such an extraordinary gesture, but Eliezer would know by it that God had chosen such a person to be the bride of Isaac.

---

Discuss the practice of setting out "fleeces" before the Lord to gain guidance.

---

**15. And it came to pass, before he had done speaking, that, behold, Rebekah came out, who was born of Bethuel, son of Milcah, the wife of Nahor, Abraham's brother, with her pitcher upon her shoulder.**

God was busy answering the servant's prayer even while he was still praying. Among those damsels who came to the well was one named Rebekah, whose beauty and virginity are referred to in verse 16. Like most, or all, of the people of the region, Rebekah was a relative of Abraham; her father was Abraham's nephew, son of Abraham's brother. In the patriarchal days it was not uncommon for relatives to marry one another, but it was rather to be expected. In fact, Abraham, Isaac, and Jacob all married persons related to them.

The servant permitted Rebekah to water his camels, probably as a thorough test that she was indeed the choice of God to be the bride of Isaac. It would be difficult for us to imagine the magnitude of work required to water the caravan of ten camels; likewise it would have been impossible for her to imagine what reward she would soon receive for her labor. She was to receive great material treasure plus the joy of becoming a bride and the exalted honor of being in the Messianic ancestry.

When her task of watering the camels was finished, the steward immediately adorned her with a ring and two bracelets of gold. With much rejoicing that God had prospered his journey by manifesting that bride for Isaac, the steward yielded to Rebekah's invitation and her brother Laban's to stay in their house. It would not have been a small or ordinary house, for it was sufficient to accommodate both the steward and all his camels. Eliezer related the entire story to Rebekah's family and said, "And now if ye will deal kindly and truly with my master, tell me: and if not, tell me; that I may turn to the right hand, or to the left" (v. 49). With this polite speech, the steward encouraged Rebekah's father and brother to send her to Canaan with him so she might become the wife of Isaac.

III. ACCEPTING GOD'S WILL (Genesis 24:50-67)

Laban and Bethuel recognized that it was no near coincidence that had brought the steward to their home or prompted his solicitation that Rebekah become Isaac's bride. The event was too wonderful to be happenstance; therefore, it must be the work of the Lord. They readily gave approval for her to proceed to Canaan and become the bride of Isaac. The servant showered Rebekah with treasures from his store; and he also gave great treasure to her mother and brother.

When the servant wanted to leave immediately for Canaan, the family urged him to let Rebekah to remain with them for a few days. Feeling that his mission was accomplished, and probably recognizing that Abraham did not have long to live, the steward appealed to them to let Rebekah and him go into Canaan without delay.

**57. And they said, We will call the damsel, and inquire at her mouth.**

It is significant to note that Laban and Bethuel had not asked Rebekah's desires concerning the marriage (vv. 50, 51). The fact that Bethuel included Laban in that decision indicates that the father must by then have been old and already referring to his son in certain matters of importance. Even though Rebekah's desire was not sought regarding the marriage, they do defer to her at this time as to her readiness to accompany the steward.

**58. And they called Rebekah, and said unto her, Wilt thou go with this man? And she said, I will go.**

When the question was put to Rebekah of whether or not she was ready to accompany Eliezer to Canaan, her answer was unwavering. Having witnessed the marvelous way that God had revealed her to the steward, she was in no frame of mind now to delay in fulfilling that which the Lord had accomplished. Her readiness to leave home and family for marriage and a new life stemmed from something deeper than a maiden's desire to be married. She believed in what had been accomplished and was ready to follow wherever the hand of the Lord might lead her. This faith and her readiness to act upon it reflect her worthiness to become a participant in the Abrahamic covenant. Just as her response at the well showed her to be God's choice for Isaac, her readiness to go now show her to be worthy of her place in the great Hebrew lineage.

Do you feel that the Lord had given Rebekah some indication that it was the right course of action? Explain.

**59. And they sent away Rebekah**

**their sister, and her nurse, and Abraham's servant, and his men.**

After so long a journey from Canaan to Haran, Eliezer spent only one night with Rebekah's family (v. 54). It is on the following day that the family sent Rebekah their sister with Abraham's servant into Canaan. Only Rebekah's nurse and serving maid accompanied her into her new life. Her departure meant that she was leaving her home forever: She would never see her parents again, and would never again return to her homeland. The quickness with which the decision and departure were made indicate faith rather than rashness, for both Rebekah and her family were convinced that it was the hand of God that had chosen her for this high purpose.

**60. And they blessed Rebekah, and said unto her, Thou art our sister, be thou the mother of thousands of millions, and let thy seed possess the gate of those which hate them.**

Rebekah's family pronounced a blessing upon her, wishing her that she might be the mother of thousands of ten thousands. They did not know it then, but that is precisely what would happen as Rebekah and Isaac formed one link in the long chain that would give birth to the Jewish people. Countless millions of souls have issued from Rebekah; her descendants still constitute a major portion of the world's population. All that God had done for her and would yet do for her came about because she was willing to serve a traveler who asked her for a drink of water.

**61. And Rebekah arose, and her damsels, and they rode upon the camels, and followed the man: and the servant took Rebekah, and went his way.**

The camels that had brought great treasure from Canaan to Haran now took great treasure back from Haran into Canaan. Rebekah and her attendants rode like precious cargo on the camels that plodded their way through the bleak deserts of Canaan.

The story of Rebekah's arrival at the tents of Abraham and the meeting of her groom Isaac is one of the beautiful stories of biblical literature. Isaac's evening meditation became an experience of joy and excitement when he lifted up his eyes and saw the caravan making its way toward him. The ceremony of taking Rebekah into his tent was the only ceremony of marriage observed at that time. The groom simply took his bride into his tent, which was a public admission that he accepted this woman as his wife. With this simple act Isaac and Rebekah began a life together that would found a new nation and would bless the world forever. Isaac's joy in his bride made him forget the deep sorrow he had felt since the death of his mother, Sarah.

**REVIEW QUESTIONS**

1. What was the Hebrew concept of a "patriarch?"

2. What request did Abraham make regarding the selection of a wife for his son Isaac?

3. What was Abraham's response to his servants question "Peradventure the woman will not be willing to follow me . . . must I bring thy son again to the land from whence thou came?"

4. What request did Abraham's servant make of the Lord that enabled him to know which was the right woman?

5. List some practical applications you draw from this lesson.

**GOLDEN TEXT HOMILY**

"THE LORD, BEFORE WHOM I WALK, WILL SEND HIS ANGEL WITH THEE, AND PROSPER THY WAY" (Genesis 24: 40).

Too often Christians talk about demons. In a sense they are bringing glory to them when they do this. Why not talk more about the ministering spirits of God? For example, if your class has ten students and if each one has a guardian angel, and I believe each does, this means in your classroom there are, counting you as a teacher, 11 ministering spirits of God. The atmosphere of your classroom is filled with the ministering spirits of God.

The same applies wherever we may go. We should pray every day for the angels of the Lord that encamp about us to protect us from sin, harm and danger. I believe most of us pray this prayer; however, have we been neglectful in recognizing the promise of our golden text, "The Lord . . . will send his angel with thee, and prosper thy way"? The *New International Version* says, "The Lord, before whom I have walked, will send his angel with you and make your journey a success."

This is a promise of God which I believe is conditional. "The Lord, before whom I walk" would seem to be the prerequisite to this promise. Please consider the following statements:

God wants us to be prosperous and successful. (The prosperity of the Christian is God's blessing.)

God is not stingy toward His children in outward things—when they are for our good.

Prosperity should be a part of our life when we are "led by God." This is especially true when it brings praise to God and it will benefit us.

Everything we receive from God is by faith. The songwriter wrote: "Every promise in the Book is mine," but the promises must be believed. Why not take time now to make the promise of Genesis 24:40 personal? Read it: The Lord, before whom I walk, will send His angel with me, and will prosper my way.—**Fred Swank, Pastor, Monroe, Michigan.**

## SENTENCE SERMONS

THE LORD IS FAITHFUL to guide all who sincerely seek His will.

—**Selected**

TRUST GOD FOR GREAT THINGS; with your five loaves and two fishes. He will show you a way to feed thousands.

—**Horace Bushnell**

TRUST GOD where you cannot trace Him. Do not try to penetrate the cloud He brings over you; rather look to the bow that is on it. The mystery is God's; the promise is yours.

—**John Macduff**

I HAVE NEVER committed the least matter to God, that I have not had reason for infinite praise.

## EVANGELISTIC APPLICATION

WALKING WITH GOD IS MORE THAN A BEAUTIFUL FIGURE OF SPEECH; WHILE IT IS INDEED A FIGURE, IT IS ALSO A VERY REAL POSSIBILITY.

One of the great realities of life is that God and man can be in step, in cadence, in harmony and in fellowship. Though we do not see Him or hear His steps, we can know that we are at His side on the issues of life.

Exactly what does this marvelous expression "walking with God" mean? For one thing, walking implies motion. Lethargy, laziness, sloth are impossible for one who is up and about his Father's business. The expression also implies direction. We are to walk, not wander. Our walk leads to a destination, a purpose in this life and a goal in eternity. For example, Enoch's walk led to translation; Noah's, to preservation; and Abraham's to generation.

The point we must not miss is this: God is the one who leads the way. He sets the pace and He points out the direction. The steward learned that no man walks with God who walks in his own way.

He hath shewed thee, O man, what is good; and what doth the Lord require of thee, but to do justly, and to love mercy, and to walk humbly with thy God? (Micah 6:8).

## DAILY DEVOTIONAL GUIDE

M. Called by God. Genesis 12:1-4

T. Led by God. Exodus 13:17-22

W. Committed to God. Psalm 37:1-9

T. Following God's Direction. Matthew 2:1-12

F. Obeying God's Call. Acts 16:6-10

S. Knowing God's Will. Ephesians 1:15-23

**March 9, 1986**

# The Danger of Self-Indulgence

**(Esau)**

**Study Text:** Genesis 25:19-34

**Supplemental References:** 1 Samuel 1:12-20; Hosea 12:23; Romans 9:6-13; Hebrews 12:15-17

**Time:** Around 1950-1850 B.C.

**Place:** Near Hebron in Canaan

**Golden Text:** "I have set before you life and death, blessing and cursing: therefore choose life" (Deuteronomy 30:19).

**Central Truth:** Only those who reject worldly values can avoid ultimate loss.

**Evangelistic Emphasis:** The gospel of Christ presents every person with the opportunity to choose life or death.

## Printed Text

**Genesis 25:22.** And the children struggled together within her; and she said, If it be so, why am I thus? And she went to enquire of the LORD.

**23. And the LORD said unto her, Two nations are in thy womb, and two manner of people shall be separated from thy bowels; and the one people shall be stronger than the other people; and the elder shall serve the younger.**

24. And when her days to be delivered were fulfilled, behold, there were twins in her womb.

**25. And the first came out red, all over like an hairy garment; and they called his name Esau.**

26. And after that came his brother out, and his hand took hold on Esau's heel; and his name was called Jacob: and Isaac was threescore years old when she bare them.

**27. And the boys grew: and Esau was a cunning hunter, a man of the field; and Jacob was a plain man, dwelling in tents.**

28. And Isaac loved Esau, because he did eat of his venison: but Rebekah loved Jacob.

**29. And Jacob sod pottage: and Esau came from the field, and he was faint.**

30. And Esau said unto Jacob, Feed me, I pray thee, with that same red pottage; for I am faint: therefore was his name called Edom.

**31. And Jacob said, Sell me this day thy birthright.**

32. And Esau said, Behold, I am at the point to die: and what profit shall this birthright do to me?

**33. And Jacob said, Swear to me this day; and he sware unto him: and he sold his birthright unto Jacob.**

34. Then Jacob gave Esau bread and pottage of lentiles; and he did eat and drink, and rose up, and went his way: thus Esau despised his birthright.

## LESSON OUTLINE

I. A PROPER REQUEST

II. CONTRASTING LIFE-STYLES

III. A TRAGIC CHOICE

## LESSON EXPOSITION

INTRODUCTION

Following Isaac's marriage to Rebekah, his father, Abraham, died and was buried in the area of Hebron. Isaac and Ishmael buried their father, according to Genesis 25:9. Ishmael was a son born before Isaac, but he was the son of Hagar, an Egyptian servant, and was therefore not the legitimate heir of Abraham. Isaac, being the son of Sarah, was Abraham's heir. It is interesting to note that both sons honored their father in burial. In days to come the descendants of Isaac and Ishmael would become bitter enemies.

In this lesson we see how Isaac also became the father of two sons who would likewise become bitter enemies. With this lesson we see the development of rivalry between brothers, a rivalry that will grow in intensity until even today there is violent hostility between the descendants of the two. With the lives of Jacob and Esau we also see the marked contrast between two lifestyles, one self-indulgence and the other contemplative and spiritual. These distinctions would become increasingly manifest in the lives of the two sons and the descendants that should follow them.

I. A PROPER REQUEST (Genesis 25:19-22)

(Verses 19-21, not in printed text.)

Frequently in Scripture the generations, or genealogies, of Hebrew families are recorded. Genesis 25 contains a record of Abraham's descendants through Ishmael and Isaac. Ishmael's descendants settled in the desert lands beyond Canaan and became a nomadic people. Ishmael was of mixed Hebrew and Egyptian blood and his descendants would show constant hostility toward the descendants of Isaac.

Isaac was of pure blood, being the son of Abraham and Sarah. Furthermore, he married Rebekah, who was also of Abraham's family, so his descendants were the true heirs of the Abrahamic covenant. Unfortunately there would be bitter conflict between his two sons, a conflict that has not been resolved unto this day.

**21. And Isaac intreated; the Lord for his wife, because she was barren: and the Lord was intreated of him, and Rebekah his wife conceived.**

Rebekah was barren when she married Isaac and for a time it seemed that they would be childless. Isaac prayed earnestly that God would give him children so that his line would continue upon the earth. It was of utmost importance to the Jewish people that children be born in order to propitiate their family through succeeding generations. It was considered a tragedy when any woman was childless; and childless women regarded their situation with shame. In the patriarchal system, the husband was regarded as the priest of his household, so it became his responsibility to entreat the Lord for all matters concerning his family. For that reason Isaac prevailed upon the Lord to heal the barrenness of Rebekah and give him sons. In answer to Isaac's entreaty, God answered the prayer and Rebekah conceived twins.

In verse 22 we see the twins struggling against each other even before birth. It perplexed Rebekah that the children struggled in her womb, so she sought the Lord for the reason why. Since unborn children always move in their mother's womb, there must have been something special about the activity Rebekah felt in order for her to recognize the struggle that was underway. Isaac and Rebekah had been married for 20 years when this pregnancy occurred, which would only intensify her anxiety about the strange movements she felt within her body.

II. CONTRASTING LIFE-STYLES (Genesis 25:23-28)

**23. And the Lord said unto her, Two nations are in thy womb, and two**

**manner of people shall be separated from thy bowels; and the one people shall be stronger than the other people; and the elder shall serve the younger.**

God's answer to Rebekah was direct and significant, both for the immediate time and for all time to come. It is possible that Rebekah did not know until this answer from the Lord that she would give birth to twins. It is all together possible that she thought of her condition as a single pregnancy which gave her all the more concern about the strange activities she felt within her body. God speaks of two nations and two manner of people, emphasizing the discord and disunity that would exist between them. The words "separated from thy bowels" refers to a condition that will exist after their birth rather than to the fact of their being born. The children born to her would be separate from one another and the division between them would widen with the passing of time.

---

Discuss the divine prophecy regarding the two nations that would emerge from the sons. How are the two nations impacting the world today?

---

This divine prophecy would be fulfilled in every detail. From one child, Jacob, would come the nation of Israel; from the other child, Esau, would come the nation of Edom. From Jacob would come the vast Hebrew people that have existed to the present day; from Esau would come the multitudes of Arab peoples. Every passing year would see them grow farther and farther apart.

Even stranger than the division that would exist between the two sons was the disruption of the patriarchal order, which called for the eldest son to be primary in all affairs of the family. The divine prophecy stated that the order would be set aside and the elder son would be servant to the younger.

The entire prophecy suggests a spiritual conflict between the two children and the divine purpose in the reordering of their rank. Sibling rivalries bring great distress to parents. Rebekah must have felt a particular concern when she knew even before their birth what extraordinary rivalry would exist between her children.

**24. And when her days to be delivered were fulfilled, behold, there were twins in her womb.**

**25. And the first came out red, all over like an hairy garment; and they called his name Esau.**

When the two sons were born, the prophecy was fulfilled in every detail. The first child born was exceedingly red and hairy, so much so that he looked like a woolen garment. He was named **Esau** or **Edom** (36:1, 8, 19), which was the Hebrew word for "red." Another name for Esau was **Seir** (36:8), which in the Hebrew language means "hairy."

This description of Esau does not suggest in any way that he was born a monster, but that his physical appearance was highly contrasted to that of Jacob. This physical appearance, however, did suggest the kind of rugged and physical person he would be.

**26. And after that came his brother out, and his hand took hold on Esau's heel; and his name was called Jacob: and Isaac was threescore years old when she bare them.**

When the second child was born he did a strange thing: even on the birth bed he laid hold on Esau's heel. He was named **Jacob,** which means "God will protect"; it all refers to the fact that he would supplant Esau. The Prophet Hosea (12:3) states that Jacob took Esau by the heel even while they were in the womb, which may account for the struggle that Rebekah felt before they were born. In any event, this seizing by the heel was a gesture that neither infant could understand, but later events would manifest it to be of spiritual significance. There were characteristics in Esau that would disqualify him for the rights of the firstborn and there were qualities in Jacob that could be refined admirably for that purpose.

It is by the statement that Isaac was 60 years old when the boys were born and the fact that he was 40 years old when he married Rebekah (25:20) that we know that they had been married 20 years before Esau and Jacob were born. During those 20 years they had no doubt longed very much for sons. Yet they could scarcely comprehend even now what a great purpose they had served in the plan of God. Esau and Jacob were no ordinary sons, for in totally opposite ways each would leave an indelibale mark upon the history of mankind.

**27. And the boys grew: and Esau was a cunning hunter, a man of the field; and Jacob was a plain man, dwelling in tents.**

The differences between Esau and Jacob became apparent almost immediately. One modern translation says, "When the boys grew up, Esau was a skillful hunter, a man of the field, while Jacob was a quiet man, dwelling in tents" (v. 27). The statement "dwelling in tents" indicates that Jacob was a shepherd, leading a pastoral life, gathering food and wool from his flocks. Esau, on the other hand, was a skillful hunter, pursuing game through the field with bow and arrow or spear.

The two lifestyles centered in differences in the two young men: Esau was physical and visceral, while Jacob was contemplative and thoughtful by nature. Esau was accustomed to the rugged life of the hunter, pursuing his prey across rugged terrain, sleeping in the open field and finding food when he was hungry. Jacob followed the more peaceful flocks of sheep, slept regularly in his tent, and was more systematic and regular about raising and tending his food supply.

**28. And Isaac loved Esau, because he did eat of his venison: but Rebekah loved Jacob.**

The differences in the two boys brought about differences in the home, for Isaac favored Esau and Rebekah was partial to Jacob. This is understandable, for Esau was what we call a man's man, rugged and muscular in his actions, direct and vigorous in his pursuit of sustenance, while Jacob was gentler and quieter, more methodical in his habits, more reasoned in his communications, more given

to habits and behavior that could be understood by his mother. In chapter 27 the scriptures give us a full discussion of how the differences between Esau and Jacob brought about difference between Isaac and Rebekah.

III. A TRAGIC CHOICE (Genesis 25:29-34)

**29. And Jacob sod pottage: and Esau came from the field, and he was faint:**

**30. And Esau said to Jacob, Feed me, I pray thee, with that same red pottage; for I am faint: therefore was his name called Edom.**

There came an occasion when Esau returned home from the hunt famished and weary. Jacob, at home with his flocks, was boiling pottage, a soup made of lentils. Later Esau would complain that Jacob tricked him at this point (27:36). It is believed by some scholars that Jacob made the soup to look red, containing meat and life-giving potency. Esau, seeing such food in the pot, was overwhelmed with the desire for it. Esau was obviously a robust man and a hearty eater. His craving for the red stew in the pot for a second time associated his name with the color red—Edom.

**31. And Jacob said, Sell me this day thy birthright.**

Seeing the famished state of Esau, Jacob set about to bargain with Esau. He would feed his brother from the pottage if Esau would give to him the family birthright. In this action we see the most pronounced difference between the two men: the cunning of Jacob and the carelessness of Esau, the long-range plans of Jacob and Esau's desires for immediate gratification. Jacob was given to the long view of life and Esau was shortsighted. Jacob was greedy and self-seeking, while Esau was vulnerable and unthinking. There was really no match between the two: a person of Jacob's characteristics will almost always have an advantage over men like Esau.

**32. And Esau said, Behold, I am at the point to die: and what profit shall this birthright do to me?**

Whether or not he was at the point

of dying from hunger we do not know, for the word **faint,** or **famished,** certainly indicates that he was at a point of great weakness. At least Esau was so faint from hunger that he was willing to strike any deal in order to get food. The tragic, blind, unthinking, permanent tragedy is that he was willing to trade away a spiritual right for the immediate gratification of the flesh. It is tragedy when anyone is willing to surrender spiritual principles for carnal desires.

A birthright was of utmost importance in the patriarchal system. The birthright gave to the firstborn son special strength within the family—the right to leadership of the clan and a double portion of the family estate. These were time-honored rights that fell upon the firstborn son; he was expected to live in a way that recognized and honored his position within the family. It is unthinkable that Esau should trade away so much for so little. His excuse that he was about to die and the birthright would therefore be useless to him cannot justify his careless disregard for the birthright.

**33. And Jacob said, Swear unto me this day; and he sware unto him: and he sold his birthright unto Jacob.**

Jacob, being as cunning as he was, was aware that Esau would think better of the creed once his painful hunger was satisfied. He therefore shrewdly required Esau to make the deal binding and permanent before he ate the food. While we may condemn the ethics of Jacob at this point, we must acknowledge his shrewdness and understanding of human nature. He was not responsible for Esau's carelessness and inability to look ahead, and he took full advantage of a temperament that was already in his twin brother.

For the immediate gratification of his flesh, Esau therefore sold the most precious right in the patriarchal structure. The nearness of the food blinded him to the blessings of the birthright in the distance.

---

Did the prophecy concerning the birthright sway Esau's attitude? Could he have thought more positively about the birthright? Explain.

**34. Then Jacob gave Esau bread and pottage of lentiles; and he did eat and drink, and rose up, and went his way: thus Esau despised his birthright.**

Esau quickly filled himself with pottage but went away from the scene far emptier than he had been when he arrived. He had been outwitted by his younger brother. It cannot truly be said that Jacob deceived Esau, for Esau fully understood what the birthright meant. He would have realized fully, as much as Jacob, what he was giving up for an immediate mess of pottage.

The whole story concludes with the words "thus Esau despised his birthright." This means that he held it in low regard, a matter of such little consequence to him because it was in the future that he was willing to trade it away for a meal of soup in the present. Thus the scripture places the greater blame for this pivotal incident in Jewish history upon Esau, who was quite willing to give very much for very little. Now, although he was born first, Esau will no longer be regarded as the firstborn of Isaac. Hereafter the promised line will be through Jacob and not through him. In the grand design of God's prophecy we see the first step that will give Israel (Jacob) supremacy over his kinsmen (v. 23). We now see the long line toward the Messiah shift to Isaac's secondborn, Jacob. For many centuries the world has witnessed the consequences of the incident that happened at the door of Jacob's tent on that fateful day.

**REVIEW QUESTIONS**

1. How long had Isaac and Rebekah been married when she conceived Esau and Jacob? Did this length of time have anything to do with Isaac's prayer for heirs?

2. What answer did the Lord give Rebekah regarding the struggle of the two unborn sons?

3. What were the occupations of the twin boys?

4. How was the patriarchal order reversed in the case of Esau and Jacob?

5. List the sequence of events that led up to Esau's giving away his birthright.

## EVANGELISTIC APPLICATION

THE GOSPEL OF CHRIST PRESENTS EVERY PERSON WITH THE OPPORTUNITY TO CHOOSE LIFE OR DEATH.

The physical body is important in our spiritual welfare, much more than a fleshly housing for the soul. While we live on earth we must be concerned with and motivated by our physical selves, for separation of the flesh and the spirit on earth can never be successful. The spirit and the body are bound together, they influence one another, catch one another's diseases and share in the same determinations of life. Yet they struggle against one another in an unending spiritual conflict. The Christian concern is that the spirit be dominant over the flesh so that our lives will extend beyond physical life. We can succeed in spiritual dominion only by being filled with the Spirit, which is why temperance, or control of self, is a matter of the Spirit.

The body is never ignored in the Word of God but its purity is linked with that of the soul. Paul said, "And the very God of peace sanctify you wholly; and I pray God your whole spirit and soul and body be preserved blameless unto the coming of our Lord Jesus Christ" (1 Thessalonians 5:23). And in another place he called upon Christians to " . . . present your bodies a living sacrifice, holy, acceptable unto God, which is your reasonable service" (Romans 12:1).

## ILLUMINATING THE LESSON

Samson was a man born to glory and accustomed to power. Little by little, however, his inclinations toward the world, the flesh and sin dulled his spiritual keenness and confused his spiritual vision. Stupefied by his own lustful desires and familiarity with the world, he betrayed his calling, violated his holiness and slept in the arms of Delilah. Even when he was to the danger of his situation he remained cocksure because of past triumphs,

. . . awoke out of his sleep, and said, I will go out as at other times before, and shake myself. And he wist not that the Lord was departed from him (Judges 16:20).

Notice the expression "he wist not." The change in Samson had been so gradual that he was unaware that it had taken place. Through the years he had been so accustomed to spiritual power and was so familiar with God's glory that he had come to take them for granted. It probably never occurred to him that he could lose his position in the Lord. But he did.

Sin does not flagrantly storm a man's soul with some great show of force; it creeps in quietly, little by little until its work is done. A lax attitude here, an unrepaired breach in our holiness there, a compromise with evil now and a wink at sin is all we need to lose our power with God. Sin comes as a creeping sneak thief, first to rob us of our souls.

## GOLDEN TEXT HOMILY

"I HAVE SET BEFORE YOU LIFE AND DEATH, BLESSING AND CURSING: THEREFORE CHOOSE LIFE" (Deuteronomy 30:19).

The story of one's life may be told in terms of the choices made. Many times the choices we make not only affect our own history but that of many others as well. The choice seems to us to be personal but in the long run turns out to be personal and social.

A few examples of this from the Bible will illustrate the sobering truth. Adam made a choice. It was a personal decision yet it has affected the entire human family. Moses chose to suffer affliction with the people of God rather than enjoy the pleasures of sin for a season. Abraham, Isaac, Jacob, Nehemiah, Esther and on and on the list could grow. We know about these people on the basis of how they chose. Their choices continue to influence the unfolding pages of history.

It is the freedom to choose that makes man a morally responsible creature. The freedom to choose means that we are responsible for the choices we make and for the most part responsible for the consequences of those choices. When the options facing us are somewhat balanced we would prefer some one else decide for us. But the truth of the matter is that no one can decide for us—we must do that ourselves.

A Chinese proverb states, "Take what you want and pay for it." This makes life similar to a supermarket or smorgasboard. We are free to claim whatever we want but must be prepared to pay the price. Sometimes we get a bargain and at other times we lose.

Looking at the text one wonders if it really is a choice. Life or death? Blessing or cursing? What fool would not choose life and blessing? To add to the weight of this choice the text admonishes readers and hearers to choose life. If such a choice is logical why the need to be urged to make the right decision? I am not sure I know the answers to that puzzle. But we do know that this choice confronts mankind every day. And we also know that despite the logic of choosing life and blessing many have chosen death and cursing. Life and blessing are available to us all but they are not thrust or forced upon us. Neither are we doomed to death and cursing. Whichever it is for you it is a matter of choice. Choose wisely for our choice will not only affect your history

it will determine your eternal destiny! —**R. B. Thomas, D. Litt., Director of Academic Advising, Lee College, Cleveland, Tennessee.**

## SENTENCE SERMONS

ONLY THOSE WHO REJECT worldly values can avoid ultimate loss.
**—Selected**

CHARACTER IS NOT MADE in a crisis —it is only exhibited.
**—Robert Freeman**

NO MAN'S ACTIONS stop with himself.
**—Selected**

HOWEVER MUCH we may deceive others and ourselves, we never deceive God.
**—"Speaker's Sourcebook"**

## DAILY DEVOTIONAL GUIDE

M. A Poor Choice. Genesis 13:8-13
T. A Godly Choice. Joshua 24:14-28
W. A Selfish Choice. 1 Samuel 15:1-23
T. A Wordly Choice. Luke 14:16-24
F. A Wise Choice. John 6:60-69
S. A Present Choice. Revelation 3:14-22

# March 16, 1986

# Living in Peace

**(Isaac)**
**Study Text:** Genesis 26:1-33
**Supplemental References:** Genesis 21:22-34; Psalm 133:1-3; Acts 15:1-21
**Time:** Date is uncertain, but generally considered to have been around 1930 B.C.
**Place:** In Philistine's section of Canaan
**Golden Text:** "Follow peace with all men, and holiness, without which no man shall see the Lord" (Hebrews 12:14).
**Central Truth:** God honors those who seek to live in harmony with others.
**Evangelistic Emphasis:** The demonstration of God's peace is an effective witness to the power of the gospel.

## Printed Text

**Genesis 26:17.** And Isaac departed thence, and pitched his tent in the valley of Gerar, and dwelt there.

**18. And Isaac digged again the wells of water, which they had digged in the days of Abraham his father; for the Philistines had stopped them after the death of Abraham: and he called their names after the names by which his father had called them.**

19. And Isaac's servants digged in the valley, and found there a well of springing water.

**20. And the herdmen of Gerar did strive with Isaac's herdmen, saying, The water is our's: and he called the name of the well Esek; because they strove with him.**

21. And they digged another well, and strove for that also: and he called the name of it Sitnah.

**22. And he removed from thence, and digged another well; and for that they strove not: and he called the name of it Rehoboth; and he said, For now the Lord hath made room for us, and we shall be fruitful in the land.**

23. And he went up from thence to Beer-sheba.

**24. And the Lord appeared unto him the same night, and said, I am the God of Abraham thy father: fear not, for I am with thee, and will bless thee, and multiply thy seed for my servant Abraham's sake.**

25. And he builded an altar there, and called upon the name of the Lord, and pitched his tent there: and there Isaac's servants digged a well.

**26. Then Abimelech went to him from Gerar, and Ahuzzath one of his friends, and Phichol the chief captain of his army.**

27. And Isaac said unto them, Wherefore come ye to me, seeing ye hate me, and have sent me away from you?

**28. And they said, We saw certainly that the Lord was with thee: and we said, Let there be now an oath betwixt us, even betwixt us and thee, and let us make a covenant with thee;**

251

March 16, 1986

29. That thou wilt do us no hurt, as we have not touched thee, and as we have done unto thee nothing but good, and have sent thee away in peace: thou art now the blessed of the Lord.

**30. And he made them a feast, and they did eat and drink.**
31. And they rose up betimes in the morning, and sware one to another: and Isaac sent them away, and they departed from him in peace.

## DICTIONARY

**Gerar (GE-rar)—Genesis 26:17**—An ancient city south of Gaza (GAY-za).

**Philistines (fil-LISS-teens)—Genesis 26:18**—One of the dominant powers in Canaan at this time. They were called "the peoples of the sea" because they had come to Canaan from the Island of Crete in the Mediterranean Sea.

**Esek (EE-sek)—Genesis 26:20**—A Hebrew word meaning "quarrel" or "fight."

**Sitnah (SIT-nah)—Genesis 26:21**—A Hebrew word meaning "accusation."

## LESSON OUTLINE

I. BLESSED BY GOD

II. PERSECUTED BY MEN

III. REACTING PEACEABLY

## LESSON EXPOSITION

INTRODUCTION

Very few incidents in the life of Isaac are related in the Scriptures. Compared with Abraham and Jacob, of whom much is recorded, Isaac passes with little attention. In those incidents that are recorded, we see Isaac as a man of peace, a man who endeavored to get along with those whom he encountered.

There was a great famine in the land of Canaan during the days of Isaac, similar to a famine that had occurred in the time of Abraham (compare 12:10 with 26:1). As Abraham did, Isaac seems to have started to the land of Egypt for relief from the famine. He and his household stopped in the land of Philistia and were received cordially by Abimelech, king of the Philistines. While he sojourned in Philistia, the Lord appeared unto Isaac and instructed him not to go into Egypt but to remain where he was. God then confirmed to Isaac the great covenant He had established with Abraham (Genesis 26:2-5).

In Gerar, chief city of the Philistines, Isaac was overcome with fear that someone would kill him in order to marry the beautiful Rebekah. As Abraham his father had done in the very same place (Genesis 20:1-8), Isaac skirted the truth and declared that Rebekah was his sister. Abimelech discovered the truth, however, and the matter ended peaceably. Isaac and his household remained in Philistia under the protection of Abimelech, and there the Hebrew patriarch lived in peace and prospered.

I. BLESSED BY GOD (Genesis 26:12-18)

(Verses 12-16 are not in the printed text.)

Isaac prospered beyond his wildest imagination while he dwelled in the land of the Philistines. In verse 12 it is said that Isaac sowed crops while he was in Philistia. This is the first record of Hebrew planting and harvesting in the promised land. Until this time the Hebrews had not been farmers, but only shepherds. Isaac did both and became immensely rich. In fact, his wealth increased a hundredfold, so that the Philistines became envious of his wealth and might. Abimelech recognized that Isaac was becoming the most powerful man in Philistia and instructed him to leave Gerar: "Go away from us; for you are much mightier than we."

**17. And Isaac departed thence, and pitched his tent in the valley of Gerar, and dwelt there.**

Compelled to leave Gerar by Abimelech the king, Isaac and his household departed the city and camped in a place known as "the valley of Gerar." The significance of this is that Isaac followed a source of water and camped where there would be water supply. There he would be able to feed his great flocks and herds and also continue the farming he had begun in Gerar. Here in the valley he would require much water in order to till the soil and graze his herds and flocks.

**18. And Isaac digged again the wells of water, which they had digged in the days of Abraham his father; for the Philistines had stopped them after the death of Abraham: and he called their names after the names by which his father had called them.**

During the lifetime of Abraham he had dug wells in strategic places of the region. These wells provided water for his flocks and herds while he lived, but they were filled in by the Philistines after his death. Isaac unplugged these old wells of Abraham and caused them to give water again. Because water was life in the desert, significant names were given to all wells that were dug in the land. Isaac called the wells that he redug by the names they had been given by Abraham. In so doing, he asserted ownership of those wells and reminded the Philistines of his rights to them. One of Abraham's wells was named **Beer-lahai-roi** (Genesis 16:14), which means "the well of him that lives and sees me." Another well was named **Beer-sheba** (Genesis 21:30, 31), which means "the well of the covenant." Both of these had special meaning in the life of Abraham and special meaning to Isaac, son of Abraham.

II. PERSECUTED BY MEN (Genesis 26: 19-22)

**19. And Isaac's servants digged in the valley, and found there a well of springing water.**

After uncovering the wells of Abraham, Isaac proceeded to dig other wells on his own. The first of these was dug in the Gerar Valley. The diggers struck a generous water supply and soon the well was springing forth for the needs of the sojourner. The wells in Palestine were not generally deep wells such as we have in our land; they were only deep enough to tap the water table that lay below the surface of the earth. Possible well sites were in valleys where surface water flowed during rainy seasons.

**20. And the herdmen of Gerar did strive with Isaac's herdmen, saying, The water is our's: and he called the name of the well Esek; because they strove with him.**

The herdmen of Gerar laid claim on the new well dug by Isaac. It is important to note that they made no objection when Isaac redug the wells of Abraham. They fully understood that those wells belonged by right to Abraham and his descendants; Abraham and Abimelech had made a covenant to that effect regarding the well at Beer-sheba (Genesis 21:29-32). The contention of the Philistian herdmen was that any additional wells belonged to them. The construction of this verse indicates that the well already existed, or at least had been sufficiently dug so that water was springing up in it when Isaac's servants found it. The position of Isaac's men may have been that their digging brought the water source to the surface of the ground. Whatever the contention may have been, it was hotly contested by both sides and Isaac abandoned his claim to the well, naming it **Esek,** which means "contention" or "a quarrel."

It is noteworthy that the Philistines did not contest the claim of Isaac on the wells that Abraham had dug; it is equally noteworthy that he yielded to their claims that the well of Esek belonged to them. Although the contention had been sharp, it had not led to violence or hurt.

If peace is to prevail it must be pursued by all parties involved. This is why it is said in Romans 12:18, "If it be possible, as much as lieth in you, live peaceably with all men."

---

Can you think of incidents when contention arose over very insignificant matters? How can it best be resolved?

**21. And they digged another well, and strove for that also: and he called the name of it Sitnah.**

A second well was dug in the Gerar Valley with the same results as the first. Following the contention that ensued, this well was named **Sitnah,** meaning "accusation." The obvious position of the men of Gerar was that any well dug in Gerar Valley belonged to them. That would be a natural position for them to take, especially in light of the great wealth Isaac had accumulated in their land. In their view, they were not depriving a stranger of sustenance or necessary provision, but they were unwilling for him to accumulate further wealth without restraint.

**22. And he removed from thence, and digged another well; and for that they strove not: and he called the name of it Rehoboth; and he said, For now the Lord hath made room for us, and we shall be fruitful in the land.**

At this point Isaac's mild nature manifested itself in a commendable and positive manner. He did not argue or contend with the Philistines any further; he simply moved to another place and dug a new well there. He named this third well **Rehoboth,** which refers to space. This implies that he moved a great distance away from the Gerar Valley. The Philistines did not raise an objection to this well, for it was moved a sufficient space from where they lived and secured their water.

Students of human behavior have long insisted that the possession of water rights is older and more important than the possession of land rights. When water is scarce, the possession of land means very little, and some of the fiercest contention among men concerns the accessibility of water.

Isaac's peaceable nature led to a satisfactory solution to what might have been an outbreak of conflict. The mild man also proved himself to be worthy of his position as son of the illustrious Abraham and father of the aggressive Jacob. He had uncovered his father's wells and called them by names his father had given them, which honored his father's memory. He then went further and dug wells of his own. He earned his place among the great patriarchs of the Jewish people.

In naming his well Rehoboth, Isaac said that God had made room for them and that the land would be bountiful to them.

III. REACTING PEACEABLY (Genesis 26: 23-33)

**23. And he went up from thence to Beer-sheba.**

**24. And the Lord appeared unto him the same night, and said, I am the God of Abraham thy father: fear not, for I am with thee, and will bless thee, and multiply thy seed for my servant Abraham's sake.**

From Rehoboth Isaac made his way to Beer-sheba, a site long associated with his father Abraham. Significantly, the Lord appeared unto Isaac and confirmed still again the Abrahamic covenant that through Isaac a mighty people would be born upon the earth. This covenant concerning the seed of Abraham formed the bedrock of God's promises to His people. It kept them and directed them and strengthened them in all time to come. The fact that God appeared to Isaac on the very night that he went up to Beer-sheba is like a divine confirmation that Isaac had done properly when he left in peace from Gerar.

**25. And he builded an altar there, and called upon the name of the Lord, and pitched his tent there: and there Isaac's servants digged a well.**

Isaac responded to the divine visitation by building an altar and worshiping the Lord on the site where God had spoken to him. The fact that he pitched his tent there reveals that he remained in the place for a considerable period of time. Moreover, his servants dug another well. Isaac had been drawn to Beer-sheba because of his familiarity with the place and the association with Abraham; he now sought to settle roots there because God has visited with him. Like Abraham, Isaac was nomadic, moving from place to place with his herds and flocks. His venture in farming in Gerar was a new occupation that would bring a new dimension into the Jewish life but now in Beer-sheba he follows the practices of a shepherd.

**26. Then Abimelech went to him from Gerar, and Ahuzzath one of his friends, and Phichol the chief captain of his army.**

Interestingly, Abimelech, king of Gerar, and two others visited Isaac in Beer-sheba. Even though he had been virtually expelled from Gerar, these important persons of Gerar now sought him out. His pursuit of peace had not proved him to be weak and had not earned him the scorn of the Philistines; it opened the door for them to approach him in peace.

**27. And Isaac said unto them, Wherefore come ye to me, seeing ye hate me, and have sent me away from you?**

Isaac reminded Abimelech and his companions of the manner in which they had sent him out of the city of Gerar and then had pushed him beyond the valley of Gerar. In the light of recent events, he naturally wondered why they were seeking him out. With Abimelech the king were Ahuzzath, the king's chief advisor, and Phichol, the military leader of Gerar. There must be a reason that such important company should seek out the nomad shepherd Isaac.

**28. And they said, We saw certainly that the Lord was with thee: and we said, Let there be now an oath betwixt us, even betwixt us and thee, and let us make a covenant with thee;**

The men of Gerar had observed, and been impressed by, the way Isaac had prospered and behaved himself while in their land. They correctly attributed his good fortune to the blessings of God and wished to form a treaty with him. A covenant of peace was both desirable and advisable, for the two would live together as neighbors in Canaan and there was generally free traffic among them. Furthermore, the widespread wells

in the region, and the tensions that these wells had already engendered, made a peace treaty advantageous both to Gerar and to Isaac. It should be noted that the emissaries from Gerar did not approach Isaac with an attitude of superiority but they immediately asserted that it was he who was in the superior position. They had seen that God was with him and that a divine blessing attended his life.

Discuss the practice of associating prosperity with a godly life. Are there forms of prosperity other than material benefits? Explain.

**29. That thou wilt do us no hurt, as we have not touched thee, and as we have done unto thee nothing but good, and have sent thee away in peace: thou art now the blessed of the Lord.**

They sought Isaac's assurance that he would do them no harm and reminded him that they had done him no harm when he was in Gerar. That was an accurate reminder, for Abimelech had treated Isaac with hospitality, so that the only difficulties he encountered were restriction of operation and contested rights. The manner in which he had behaved himself during the tension proved that he was a man of peace. Now they wanted the same assurance that he would be peaceable toward them.

The men of Gerar returned to their observation that Isaac was blessed of the Lord. By basing their approach upon this fact, they gave recognition to the God of heaven and that Isaac was a true servant to Him. Thus the mild-mannered Isaac had impressed the people as a man of peace so that they wanted to have peace with him.

**30. And he made them a feast, and they did eat and drink.**

Discuss the value of a godly life as a testimony to the ungodly.

Isaac responded to their entreaties by preparing a feast as a token of their peace and friendship together. This was a customary manner of celebrating a treaty and of underscoring the goodwill that existed between the parties.

**31. And they rose up betimes in the morning, and sware one to another: and Isaac sent them away, and they departed from him in peace.**

The men of Gerar had very likely pitched their tents near to those of Isaac. When morning came they arose and pledged peace to one another. The mission of the Philistines had brought success and would advance their security and Isaac's prosperity. When the treaty of peace was completed Isaac sent the men of Gerar on their way in peace. It is noteworthy that the word peace is mentioned both in this verse and in verse 29. It is said that Isaac went away from them in peace and now they departed from him in peace.

Once again there was a divine affirmation that Isaac was in the good pleasure of the Lord. On the same day that the men of Gerar departed, the servants of Isaac came to him with the good news that the well which they were digging had yielded water. Isaac responded by naming the new well Shebah, which referred to the treaty that had been formed that very morning. The name Shebah was also a repetition of Beer-sheba which was already the name of the place. The meekness of Isaac had paid great dividends, and many years later the Messiah was to say that the meek shall inherit the earth.

## REVIEW QUESTIONS

1. What was the reason for Isaac's journey to Philistia?

2. Why had Isaac told the men of Philistia that Rebecca was his sister? Is there ever justification for telling an untruth? Explain.

3. What was the point of contention between Isaac's servants and the herdmen of Gerar?

4. How was the contention over the wells resolved?

5. What significance did Isaac place on the name "Rehoboth," that he gave one of the wells?

6. What impact did Isaac's peaceableness have on Abimelech?

## EVANGELISTIC APPLICATION

### "The Christian's Peace"

THE DEMONSTRATION OF GOD'S PEACE IS AN EFFECTIVE WITNESS TO THE POWER OF THE GOSPEL.

The Christian has a deep, silent, hidden peace, which the world sees not—like some well in a retired and shady place, difficult of access. He is the greater part of his time by himself, and when he is in solitude, that is his real state. What he is when left to himself and to his God, that is his true life. He can bear himself; he can (as it were) joy in himself, for it is the grace of God within him, it is the presence of the Eternal Comforter, in which he joys. He can bear, he finds it pleasant, to be with himself at all times— "never less alone than when alone." He can lay his head on his pillow at night, and own in God's sight, with overflowing heart, that he wants nothing,—that he "is full and abounds,"—that God has been all things to him, and that nothing is not his which God could give him. Many hard things may be said of the Christian, and may be done against him, but he has a secret preservative or charm, and minds them not.—John Henry Newman.

## ILLUMINATING THE LESSON

In his little book on **New Testament Christianity,** J. B. Phillips, New Testament translator and scholar, says:

But as we study New Testament Christianity, we are aware that there is an inner core of tranquillity and stability. In fact, not the least of the impressive qualities which the Church could demonstrate to the pagan world was this ballast of inward peace. It was, I think, something new that was appearing in the lives of human beings. It was not mere absence of sensitivity nor a complacent self-satisfaction, which can often produce an apparent tranquillity of spirit. It was a positive peace, a solid foundation which held fast amid all the turmoil of human experience. It was, in short, the experience of Christ's bequest when He said:

"Peace I give unto you: not as the world giveth, give I unto you" (John 14:27).

## GOLDEN TEXT HOMILY

"FOLLOW PEACE WITH ALL MEN, AND HOLINESS, WITHOUT WHICH NO MAN SHALL SEE GOD" (Hebrews 12:14).

In the areas of Christian living and dedication there are numbers of attributes which are not complete without another. Peace and holiness are the examples here set forth. There can be no satisfying peace with God or man without possessing His holiness. There can be no true holiness unless man is at peace with God and man.

In the first of this chapter, admonition is given that we be concerned about the weights and sins that "so easily beset us" (v. 1). A lack of peace and holiness could be two of those weights.

It appears that this scripture concerning "peace with all men" is related to peacefulness among those of the "household of faith" rather than all people. However, how great is that person who would set as a goal in life to be at peace with all persons without compromise of his own life of dedication.

Knowing all men as He does, God has said that if possible, live peaceably with all men (Romans 12:18). Sadly enough, there are those even in the church who are not content to let peace reign. God calls them busybodies (1 Timothy 5:13). We are to avoid disputings, quarrelings, and offensive actions as much as possible.

Anyone can create chaos, but "blessed are the peacemakers" (Matthew 5:9). When one is seen to be creating animosity among individuals or in groups he is carnal, no matter his claims otherwise. The passage is Romans 14:19 admonishes us to seek "the things which make for peace" and edify one another. There are those who actually relish an offense to themselves, even though none is intended. This feeds their own self-righteousness.

Our attitude toward others will affect the life of the church to which we belong. When one is at peace with God, he will desire only the best for another's good—not his destruction. So if we are to see peace with God, in homes, and with others, some definite steps must be taken on our part to bring it about. All mischief needs to be stopped. Peace will come when we become obedient to God.

Peace is not something that just happens—we must work and strive for it. "Seek peace, and pursue it" is the advice given in Psalm 34:14.

Our God is a God of peace. Paul wrote, "The very God of peace sanctify you" (1 Thessalonians 5:23). Holiness makes for peace.

Yes, the second attribute we must possess to see God is holiness, or sanctification of life. This saying is so simple yet so pointed and powerful!

This wonderful state of being or way of life is a growing conformity to the likeness of Christ. He not only saves from the guilt of sin but from its power, too. Holiness thrives in an atmosphere of peace.

How sad that in many circles the mention of holiness only brings negative responses. Holiness means a willing obedience to God. How wonderful to know at the end of a day that you have pleased Him.

Holiness not only means being sanctified but also sanctifying those around us. It not only denotes whiteness, but a continued whitening.

One's daily life reveals his philosophy about an afterlife. Word of mouth is ineffective here. God says that if we have hope in a life hereafter we will purify ourselves (1 John 3:3).

Concerning a life of consecration, sanctification, or holiness, certain specifics are made known. Yet there are areas in which the Word of God does not deal in detail. It is here that each individual must "work out [their] own salvation with fear and trembling" (Philippians 2:12).

God has not called us to dictate to others which way they are to take in these unspecified concerns. However, it is so hard for some to sit by and let others reach their own maturity in Christ. The temptation is great to tell them that if they don't conform to our idea of holiness they are all wrong.

Charles W. Conn, in his book **Why Men Go Back**, has a chapter entitled, "Hardness Is Not Holiness." How true.

Christ never had problems in dealing with publicans and sinners. They knew their need. It was the ultraconservative, self-righteous religionists of His day who caused Him heartache. He referred to them as "whited sepulchres," "full of dead men's bones," "generation of vipers."

How many hungry souls have been driven from the Father's table because someone let it be known that they should not eat with unwashed hands? God forgive the church for its loss of souls due to overbearingness in areas where it need not trod. God forbid that we have blood of others on our hands when we stand before Him because we opened wounds rather than pouring in healing oil. Animosity on the part of some, divisiveness from others, and wrong attitudes have driven many from the fold or hindered many who longed to enter. What an indictment: "If that person is a Christian I want no part of it."

Why cannot the lesson be learned anew today, "He that is without sin among you, let him cast a stone" (John 8:7)? How easy to see splinters of weakness in others but not our own greater weaknesses! Maybe one is not guilty of the same sin as the woman kneeling before Christ, ready to be stoned by her accusers; yet possibly guilty of greed, envy, hatred, malice, false accusations, bitterness, backbiting and strife. If a person is guilty of one, he is guilty of all. All are in need of the sanctifying anew of His grace and forgiveness.

So much is needed to bring about a life of holiness (or sanctification) for us. Christ suffered without the gate for our sanctification. We, too, are sanctified by the Word, by the Holy Spirit, and by the blood of Christ. Yet we too must do our part.

If we are truly, completely set apart unto Him, our greatest aim will one day be realized when we enter into His presence forever. Righteousness and peace have kissed. All is at rest. Home at last!—**Fred E. Whisman, Cost Analyst, Church of God Publishing House, Cleveland, Tennessee.**

## SENTENCE SERMONS

GOD HONORS those who seek to live in harmony with others.

**—Selected**

IT IS ONLY one step from toleration to forgiveness.

**—Sir Arthur Pinero**

THAT BEST PORTION of a good man's life—his little, nameless, unremembered acts of kindness and love.

**—Wordsworth**

PEACE—GOOD WILL effectively asserted against greed.

**—Anonymous**

## DAILY DEVOTIONAL GUIDE

M. Covenant of Peace. Genesis 21:22-34

T. Dwelling in Peace. Psalm 133:1-3

W. Quietness and Rest. Isaiah 32:15-18

T. Formula for Peace. Matthew 5:1-12

F. Peaceful Solution. Acts 15:1-21

S. The Gift of Peace. John 20:19-23

# Trouble in the Home

**(Jacob)**

**Study Text:** Genesis 27:1-40

**Supplemental References:** 2 Samuel 14:21-33; Luke 15:11-24; Galatians 4:22-31; Ephesians 6:1-4

**Time:** Date is uncertain but generally considered to have been between 1930-1900 B.C.

**Place:** Southern Canaan near Beer-sheba

**Golden Text:** "Be kindly affectioned one to another with brotherly love" (Romans 12:10).

**Central Truth:** The family that gives priority to God's will can avoid broken relationships.

**Evangelistic Emphasis:** God's grace can restore broken relationships.

## Printed Text

**Genesis 27:21.** And Isaac said unto Jacob, Come near, I pray thee, that I may feel thee, my son, whether thou be my very son Esau or not.

**22. And Jacob went near unto Isaac his father; and he felt him, and said, The voice is Jacob's voice, but the hands are the hands of Esau.**

23. And he discerned him not, because his hands were hairy, as his brother Esau's hands: so he blessed him.

**24. And he said, Art thou my very son Esau? And he said, I am.**

25. And he said, Bring it near to me, and I will eat of my son's venison, that my soul may bless thee. And he brought it near to him, and he did eat: and he brought him wine, and he drank.

**26. And his father Isaac said unto him, Come near now, and kiss me, my son.**

27. And he came near, and kissed him: and he smelled the smell of his raiment, and blessed him, and said, See, the smell of my son is as the smell of a field which the Lord hath blessed:

**28. Therefore God give thee of the dew of heaven, and the fatness of the earth, and plenty of corn and wine:**

29. Let people serve thee, and nations bow down to thee: be lord over thy brethren, and let thy mother's sons bow down to thee: cursed be every one that curseth thee, and blessed be he that blesseth thee.

**30. And it came to pass, as soon as Isaac had made an end of blessing Jacob, and Jacob was yet scarce gone out from the presence of Isaac his father, that Esau his brother came in from his hunting.**

31. And he also had made savoury meat, and brought it unto his father, and said unto his father, Let my father arise, and eat of his son's venison, that thy soul may bless me.

**32. And Isaac his father said unto him, Who art thou? And he said, I am thy son, thy firstborn Esau.**

33. And Isaac trembled very exceedingly, and said, Who? where is he that

hath taken venison, and brought it me, and I have eaten of all before thou

camest, and have blessed him? yea, and he shall be blessed.

---

## LESSON OUTLINE

I. DISAGREEMENT
II. DECEPTION
III. DESPAIR

## LESSON EXPOSITION

### INTRODUCTION

In Genesis 27 we see the fragmentation of the family in clear detail. The rivalry that began between Jacob and Esau at their birth comes to full fruit in this chapter. There is no more dramatic account of sibling rivalry than that which tore these two brothers apart. Tragically, roots of the hostility fed within the family so that even the mother and father were divided on the issues that divided the brothers.

Rivalry between brothers is not uncommon, but it is uncommon for that rivalry to reach the intensity which we observe here. The elements within the family are tragic: a deceived father, a scheming mother, a cheated older brother, and a pampered younger son. A real flaw existed within the family in order for all of these cracks to develop. The mild-mannered Isaac was no match for the scheming of Rebekah and the trickery of Jacob. The self-indulgent, undisciplined Esau made him a perfect target for Jacob's cunning.

As tragic as the family breakup was, it nevertheless resulted in the grand design that was foreseen at the time Jacob and Esau were born. It is an occasion when God brought ultimate good out of human weakness and error. The fact that God often overrides our human tragedies does not make them less tragic. Here is a home in disarray and two brothers so divided that they will never enjoy the pleasures of brotherhood or be to each other what they could have been. In the end, God will take these ugly human threads and weave them into a design for His own glory.

### I. DISAGREEMENT (Genesis 27:5-17)

(Verses 5-17 are not in the printed text.)

Isaac was about 100 years old when this event took place. He was 60 years old when Esau and Jacob were born (Genesis 25:26) and we know that Esau and Jacob were now 40 years of age (Genesis 26:34). At that age, Isaac certainly would be justified in feeling that death was not far away. His eyes were dim and he felt the weariness of his years. In reality, however, he would live for another 80 years after the events of this chapter took place (see Genesis 35:28).

Feeling that the time of death was near, Isaac wanted to give his eternal blessing to Esau. He proposed to Esau that the son would hunt for fresh game in the field and prepare his favorite dish for him. He would then give the patriarchal blessing to Esau.

Isaac and Esau were close enough that they understood each other's desires and Isaac's request was very simple. Rebekah, however, overheard them discussing this plan and related it to Jacob. She made no secret of the fact that Jacob was special to her. In Genesis 27:6 it speaks of "Jacob her son," whereas verse 5 spoke of "Esau his son." These terms are not used consistently in the account, but they do show that each parent was partial to a particular son.

---

Why is it so easy for a parent (or parents) to become partial to a particular child? What are the consequences of such practice?

---

Rebekah, who was equally cunning as her son Jacob but far more deceptive, devised a plan to trick her husband and secure Isaac's blessing for her darling son. She of all people would understand the physical limitations of Isaac, and was willing to take advantage of his disabilities in order to thwart his intention to bless Esau. Rebekah shows evil genius in her plan and becomes the real villain in the episode.

While the unwitting Esau was hunting

game in the field, Rebekah, with the assistance of Jacob, slaughtered two young goats from the flock and prepared from them the tasty food that Isaac so greatly desired. She compounded the deception by using the hairy stubble of the goats to disguise the smooth skin of Jacob and give him the rough, hairy feel of Esau. Jacob doubted that the ruse would work and feared that his father, discovering the trickery, would place a curse rather than a blessing upon him. It was at this point that the depth of Rebekah's deceiving nature was seen. She said, "On me be your curse, my son; only obey my word, and go, fetch them to me" (v. 13, **Amplified**).

The carefully designed plan worked. Rebekah clothed Jacob in Esau's garments, which would have had the smell of the field upon them, and disguised Jacob's skin as Esau's skin, and used her cooking skills to prepare the savory dish for Isaac.

The division of the family was deep and permanent, with Rebekah and Jacob on one side and Isaac and Esau on the other; yet it was Jacob who would be heir to his father and would be listed for all time as one of the patriarchs: Abraham, Isaac and Jacob. It is difficult now to imagine what disagreements must have occurred in the family for the gulf to become so deep between them. Isaac was old and dottery; Rebekah was scheming and deceiving; Esau was self-indulgent and unwitting; Jacob was shrewd and cunning.

II. DECEPTION (Genesis 27:18-29)

(Verses 18-20 are not in the printed text.)

At this point Jacob's ability to deceive came forth also. When he took the food to Isaac and Isaac asked his identity, Jacob lied that he was "Esau your firstborn." Isaac then showed the first sign of doubt and misgiving about the situation; he asked how the hunt, the kill, the preparation of the food had been done so quickly. Jacob's reply to that was a mixture of lie and cynicism: "Because the Lord your God granted me success." This matched Rebekah's cynical use of the Lord's name in verse 7.

The invocation of the Lord's name to accomplish deception must be one of the lowest and most cynical forms of deceitfulness. Every advantage was taken of Isaac: physically, his bad eyesight; as a parent, his fondness for Esau; and spiritually, his devotion to God.

**21. And Isaac said unto Jacob, Come near, I pray thee, that I may feel thee, my son, whether thou be my very son Esau or not.**

Isaac's misgiving about his son's identity continued. He somehow sensed that something was wrong and called Jacob to him so he could feel of him and thereby determine if he spoke the truth.

**22. And Jacob went near unto Isaac his father; and he felt him, and said, The voice is Jacob's voice, but the hands are the hands of Esau.**

When Jacob complied with Isaac's request, the father said, "The voice is Jacob's voice, but the hands are the hands of Esau." The old man knew that something was wrong, but he was not able to clear up his suspicions or verify what was truth. Under any normal circumstance, a husband, incapacitated by loss of sight, should be able to call in his wife for assistance. Unhappily, this was not the case with Isaac, for Rebekah was the chief perpetrator of the fraud.

**23. And he discerned him not, because his hands were hairy, as his brother Esau's hands: so he blessed him.**

**24. And he said, Art thou my very son Esau? And he said, I am.**

Isaac's suspicions continued, for he knew in his heart something was wrong. One of the most pathetic questions in Scripture is when Isaac asked Jacob, "Are you really my very own son Esau?" Jacob's bold assurance that he was constitutes one of the great deliberate lies of his career.

Despite the fact that God's grace worked eventual benefit from the tawdry scene does not in any way lessen the wrong that Rebekah and Jacob carried out. At this time in their lives Esau seemed to be morally superior to Jacob. At least the Scripture never records any similar deliberate evil from the part of Esau. The one thing that will eventually tip the balances in favor of Jacob is the fact that he did indeed love God and would eventually trust himself to the sovereignty of God. Esau may have been a better man but Jacob was a better believer. One of the glories of the Word of God is the fact that it reveals the unworthy and undesirable side of some who became heroes of the faith.

**25. And he said, Bring it near to me, and I will eat of my son's venison, that my soul may bless thee. And he brought it near to him, and he did eat: and he brought him wine, and he drank.**

Unable to prove his doubts, and unwilling to continue his hesitation, Isaac called for the meal that had been prepared for him. He ate the food and drank the wine prepared for him, finding that the food at least had the taste of his son Esau's provision. The smell and taste of the food must have replaced the other inputs of his senses so that they were laid aside for the moment.

**26. And his father Isaac said unto him, Come near now, and kiss me, my son.**

When the meal was complete and Isaac's hunger had been satisfied, he seemed to have reverted to his earlier suspicions and doubts. He called upon Jacob to approach him and kiss him. It is strange how many deceptions are worked through the means of a kiss. In fact, this token of affection has been universally used through the centuries in the cause of deceit and dishonor.

**27. And he came near, and kissed him: and he smelled the smell of his raiment, and blessed him, and said, See, the smell of my son is as the smell of a field which the Lord hath blessed.**

Jacob complied with Isaac's request for a kiss, but Isaac had a purpose in making the request. It gave him an opportunity to smell of the clothing worn by the son. This seems to be the final point of Isaac's doubt, for Jacob, wearing Esau's clothing, did indeed smell like Esau. His clothing did not have the smells of a sheepfold, as Jacob's would have had, but of the field, the wild, where Esau was accustomed to being in his chase of game. Now three of Isaac's senses confirmed to him that the son in his presence was indeed Esau: the sense of touch confirmed it; the sense of taste confirmed it; now the sense of smell confirmed it. Only the sense of hearing denied it; and the sense of sight was unavailable to him. So, despite his inner misgivings, Isaac proceeded with the paternal blessing.

**28. Therefore God give thee of the dew of heaven, and the fatness of the earth, and plenty of corn and wine:**

**29. Let people serve thee, and nations bow down to thee: be lord over thy brethren, and let thy mother's sons bow down to thee: cursed be every one that curseth thee, and blessed be he that blesseth thee.**

Isaac's blessing upon Jacob was of three parts: (1) for his prosperity, (2) for his dominion, (3) and a curse upon his enemies. Esau was a skillful hunter, and yet Isaac's blessing was for him to be rich in agriculture. The dew of heaven, the fatness of the earth, and plenty of grain and wine are all related to the growing of crops and the fertile soil. This is possibly an occasion where even the words spoken were beyond the understanding of the one who spoke.

The blessing of dominion called for nations and family to bow down to the blessed. Use of the words **brethren** and **sons** when Jacob had only one brother can be understood to mean only that the blessing was to extend beyond the immediate family to all the kindred both then and in later generations. A curse was pronounced upon anyone who should ever curse Jacob and a blessing upon everyone who would bless him.

How remarkably we have seen the conditions of this blessing carried out through the generations that have followed this strange incident. Obviously God guided the words that were spoken so that they would apply to all generations to come, for God saw beyond the deceitful scene in which they were spoken to all the ages that would follow.

## III. DESPAIR (Genesis 27:30-40)

**30. And it came to pass, as soon as Isaac had made an end of blessing Jacob, and Jacob was yet scarce gone out from the presence of Isaac his father, that Esau his brother came in from his hunting.**

**31. And he also had made savoury meat, and brought it unto his father, and said unto his father, Let my father arise, and eat of his son's venison, that thy soul may bless me.**

Almost at the time the blessing was ended, Esau returned from the field with his game and prepared the food for his father. So narrowly did the deception achieve its ends before it would have been revealed. Jacob got the blessing that Isaac intended to give to Esau, but he was almost caught before it was completed. One can only imagine the joy with which Esau brought food to his father expecting to receive the paternal blessing in exchange. How narrowly he missed the blessing that now belonged to Jacob. It is upon these narrow slices of time and barely achieved events that the world turns and mankind has come to this hour. If Esau had come in a few moments earlier, the history of Esau and Jacob might have been different.

**32. And Isaac his father said unto him, Who art thou? And he said, I am thy son, thy firstborn Esau.**

**33. And Isaac trembled very exceedingly, and said, Who? where is he that hath taken venison, and brought it me, and I have eaten of all before thou camest, and have blessed him? yea, and he shall be blessed.**

---

Discuss the overall attitude Esau had toward spiritual matters. Did he have anything to do with shaping his mother's attitude?

---

Isaac trembled when he learned that Esau's blessing had gone to Jacob. Esau cried out in anguish and bitterness. Both of them knew that the blessing was irreversible, forever lost to the one for whom it had been intended. The resulting scene of sorrow and bewilderment is one of the most piteous scenes in the history of man. Esau's cry was heartrending, one that has echoed through human history, an exceedingly great and bitter cry: "Bless me, even me also, O my father."

Isaac would try to pronounce a blessing upon Esau, but nothing he could do would reverse his blessing of abundance and dominion and victory on Jacob. Esau accused Jacob of having stolen from him twice: first his birthright and now his paternal blessing. It could not yet have dawned on him how completely he had been supplanted by Jacob, for this would only become manifest through the years to come. But in a distant kind of way, he was aware that he had now lost all the benefits that came to the firstborn. It was not only a personal loss to him, but the descendants of the two boys would see and feel it as they became nations and cultures and peoples.

In this wretched and tearful scene Esau repeatedly asked if there were not a blessing for him. In verse 34 he said, "Bless me, even me also, O my father" and in verse 38 he asked, "Hast thou but one blessing, my father? bless me, even me also, O my father." Then the tearful, frustrated and defrauded firstborn son lifted up his voice and wept.

In Hebrews 12:16, 17, this incident is spoken of in a way that shows the spiritual implications of the episode: "Lest there be any fornicator, or profane person, as Esau, who for one morsel of meat sold his birthright. For ye know how that afterward, when he would have inherited the blessing, he was rejected: for he found no place of repentance, though he sought it carefully with tears."

Even though Esau seems to have been more ethical than Jacob at the time, he was also more profane, less inclined to a recognition of God. He had married pagan wives (Genesis 26:34), which had greatly grieved Isaac and Rebekah. Although he was the defrauded one he seemed to be far inferior to Jacob in spiritual sensitivity and devotion to the Abrahamic covenant.

When Isaac pronounced the blessing upon Esau, it was but a pale effort in light of the great blessing he had given to Jacob. "And Isaac his father answered and said unto him, Behold, thy dwelling shall be the fatness of the earth, and of the dew of heaven from above; And by thy sword shalt thou live, and shalt serve thy brother; and it shall come to pass when thou shalt have the dominion, that thou shalt break his yoke from off thy neck" (vv. 38, 39).

## REVIEW QUESTIONS

1. How old was Isaac when the events of today's lesson took place?

2. What evidences are there in this lesson of parental partiality toward a particular son?

3. Who was the person most responsible for the trickery in this household disruption? Explain.

4. How did Jacob contribute to the deception?

5. What reactions do you have about this lesson?

## GOLDEN TEXT HOMILY

"BE KINDLY AFFECTIONED ONE TO ANOTHER WITH BROTHERLY LOVE; IN HONOUR PREFERRING ONE ANOTHER" (Romans 12:10).

Paul presents one of the best keys for effective and purposeful relationships in his exhortation of love. The word used for affection, **philostorgos**, means "brotherly love, tenderness, and affection; putting another first." This meaning of **affection**, its motivation of doing the good received from God, is contrary to the worldly definition with its overtones of affection displayed today in perverse and selfish manners.

The revolutionary concept of Christian affection is that it is kind, feeling an obligation to others. This kindness of affection is brotherly love, affection that not only cares but also cares about what happens to other people, willing to do something to make love a reality. Affection of this nature can only grow out of our relationship with Christ as we demonstrate the love that He first has given us.

When Jesus told His followers to "love one another as I have loved you," this saying was not fully understood. The disciples could not appreciate the ultimate gift of Christ's love. For Jesus, this greatest love was expressed by giving up His life upon the Cross. How could the disciples comprehend this event until it happened? For the rest of their lives, the disciples would be witnesses of a greater love than the world had ever known.

How can we experience sacrificial love toward our brothers and sisters? How can we love as Christ loved? First, the covenant of marriage offers individuals the opportunity of placing another first, learning tenderness with commitment.

Second, the blossoming family of kinship provides many learning experiences to overcome self and to appreciate another in love, growing as friends.

Third, the church is to be that unique creation of God whereby brotherly love is expressed beyond kinship, where love's very foundation is established to be the gift of Christ himself in relationship.

And finally, our goal is Jesus' command to love even our enemies, those who may yet remain at enmity with God because of sin. Letting brotherly love continue means expressing our fullness of love outwardly to those in need—in marriage, in family, in church and in the world.—**Mrs. Florie Brown Wigelsworth, Chaplaincy Staff, Mississippi Department of Corrections, Parchman, Mississippi**

## SENTENCE SERMONS

THE FAMILY THAT GIVES priority to God's will can avoid broken relationships.
**—Selected**

THE CHRISTIAN HOME is the Master's workshop where the processes of character molding are silently, lovingly, faithfully, and successfully carried out.
**—Richard M. Milnes**

A HAPPY FAMILY is but an earlier heaven.
**—Sir John Bowring**

HOME INTERPRETS HEAVEN; Home is heaven for beginners.
**—Charles Henry Parkhurst**

THE HOME IS A LIGHTHOUSE which has the lamp of God on the table and the light of Christ in the window, to give guidance to those who wander in darkness.

**—Henry Rische:**
**"The Windows of Home"**

## EVANGELISTIC APPLICATION

### "The Love of Christ for the Church"

GOD'S GRACE CAN RESTORE BROKEN RELATIONSHIPS

What is love? Love is one of the dethroned words in human speech; it goes about without its crown. And we have got to restore something of its lost majesty and authority before we have even a passable canon for interpreting the love of our Lord. We cannot make any headway in Scriptural exposition until we have redeemed our minds from all little and belittling conceptions of love, and until we have reenthroned the word in its essential and appointed sovereignty.

Let us, then, begin here. The primal and central element in all true love is holiness. When sin is in the heart love is frightfully stricken. Sin half-slays love and makes her blind. Holiness is the innermost secret of Fatherhood, and in love's temple the holy of holies is holiness itself.

And the second element in all true love is benevolence, the genius of sacrifice, the spirit of self-impartation. Love can never be self-contained. The very life of love is found in movement away from self. Love leaves home to be at home. Stop its exodus, you kill its genesis. "God so loved . . . that he gave!" "Greater love hath no man than this, that a man lay down his life for his friends."

And the third great element in all true love is sympathy, a fine sensitiveness of discernment, an exquisite fellow-feeling, a sort of mystical divining-rod which discovers the waters moving in another man's life, a vicarious strength which apprehends another's spiritual estate, and thrills to hidden joys and sorrows.

## ILLUMINATING THE LESSON

On no subject has human thought more centered than upon the family. There is nothing more important in our entire social life. For a nation will not be better than its homes. Christianity did not invent the family or marriage, but it has been probably the greatest agency in giving ideals to the home. This is all the more remarkable when one recalls that Jesus was not married, and that so much of the New Testament literature was written by Paul who, like his Master, had no home. But how incomplete would the gospel be without the figures drawn from fatherhood, sonship, marriage, and childhood! The more one reads the New Testament the more does one feel how sacred the family is, because it so often serves as a symbol of the relations of the Church with Christ. When the New Testament writers wish to express the very closest and holiest union of believers with their Lord it is to the family that they turn for symbols.

## DAILY DEVOTIONAL GUIDE

M. An Unfaithful Son. 2 Samuel 15:1-12

T. A Father's Prayer. Job 1:1-5

W. A Mother's Concern. Mark 7:24-30

T. The Waiting Father. Luke 15:11-32

F. A Holy Influence. 1 Corinthians 7:12-16

S. Family Instructions. Ephesians 5:33 through 6:4

# Victory Over Death

## (Easter)

**Study Text:** 1 Corinthians 15:1-58
**Supplemental References:** Matthew 28:1-10; Mark 16:9-20; Luke 24:1-10; John 20:1-18
**Time:** 1 Corinthians was written around A.D. 55.
**Place:** 1 Corinthians was written in and sent from Ephesus.
**Golden Text:** "But thanks be to God, which giveth us the victory through our Lord Jesus Christ" (1 Corinthians 15:57).
**Central Truth:** Christ's resurrection is the guarantee of the believer's victory over death.
**Evangelistic Emphasis:** The death and resurrection of Jesus Christ provides eternal life for all who believe.

### Printed Text

**1 Corinthians 15:3.** For I delivered unto you first of all that which I also received, how that Christ died for our sins according to the scriptures;

**4. And that he was buried, and that he rose again the third day according to the scriptures:**

5. And that he was seen of Cephas, then of the twelve:

**12. Now if Christ be preached that he rose from the dead, how say some among you that there is no resurrection of the dead?**

13. But if there be no resurrection of the dead, then is Christ not risen:

**14. And if Christ be not risen, then is our preaching vain, and your faith is also vain.**

20. But now is Christ risen from the dead, and become the firstfruits of them that slept.

**21. For since by man came death, by man came also the resurrection of the dead.**

22. For as in Adam all die, even so in Christ shall all be made alive.

**23. But every man in his own order: Christ the firstfruits; afterward they that are Christ's at his coming.**

24. Then cometh the end, when he shall have delivered up the kingdom to God, even the Father; when he shall have put down all rule and all authority and power.

**25. For he must reign, till he hath put all enemies under his feet.**

54. So when this corruptible shall have put on incorruption, and this mortal shall have put on immortality, then shall be brought to pass the saying that is written, Death is swallowed up in victory.

**55. O death, where is thy sting? O grave, where is thy victory?**

57. But thanks be to God, which giveth us the victory through our Lord Jesus Christ.

## LESSON OUTLINE

I. PROOF OF CHRIST'S RESURREC-TION

II. IMPORTANCE OF CHRIST'S RESUR-RECTION

III. PROMISE OF THE BELIEVER'S RES-URRECTION

IV. GLORY OF THE RESURRECTION

## LESSON EXPOSITION

INTRODUCTION

We interrupt our study of the patriarchs for the special Easter lesson. This is a highlight of the Christian year and great emphasis should at all times be given to the subject of our Lord's resurrection. Everything written in the Old Testament, including the events of the patriarchs that we have been studying, looks forward to the Resurrection; everything in the New Testament looks back to that central event of history. The resurrection of Christ is the proof perfect of all things contained in the Word of God.

The resurrection of Christ is the basis of our own belief in life after death. The resurrection from the dead became a crucial point in early Christian teaching. Understanding of the Resurrection was imperfect, however, and the apostles endeavored constantly to clarify the Christian assurance of resurrection. The believers in Corinth were particularly in need of correction and instruction because of numerous erroneous notions that had crept in.

The entire fifteenth chapter of First Corinthians is devoted to a discussion of the Resurrection. Because of the Corinthians' need of understanding, the Christian world has been blessed with Paul's extensive statement on the question. His clarifications to them constitute a statement on the Resurrection to all Christians.

I. PROOF OF CHRIST'S RESURRECTION (1 Corinthians 15:1-11)

(Verses 1, 2, 6-11 are not in the printed text.)

Belief in the Resurrection makes steadfast Christians. As Paul said, It is a "gospel which I preached unto you, which also ye have received, and wherein ye stand." According to Acts 17:2, 3, Paul based his ministry upon the death and resurrection of Christ. Nothing makes a person more careful about this life than belief in life after death.

**3. For I delivered unto you first of all that which I also received, how that Christ died for our sins according to the scriptures.**

Paul begins his discussion by showing proof of Christ's resurrection. His ministry in Corinth had been that Christ died for the sins of the world and thereby made provisions for man's salvation. This theme is recurrent in all Paul's writings and preaching. We find references to it in numerous scriptures. (See Galatians 2:20; 6:14; Acts 17:3, 31; 1 Corinthians 1:18; 2:2.)

**4. And that he was buried, and that he rose again the third day according to the scriptures.**

The preaching of the Crucifixion is incomplete unless it contains a preaching of the Resurrection. The story of Christ's suffering consists of two essential parts, each as important as the other. First of all, He died for our sins; second, He was raised from the dead. It is the second that gives validity to the first and it is the first that made possible the second. Paul based his teaching of the Crucifixion and Resurrection upon the Scriptures. Observe that in both instances he uses the expression "according to the scriptures."

---

Discuss the need to give strong emphasis to both the death and resurrection of Christ in our witness for Him.

---

**5. And that he was seen of Cephas, then of the twelve.**

The greatest proof that Christ arose from the dead is the fact that He was seen by so many following the resurrection. Paul begins the list of those who saw the Lord in verse 5 and continues it through verse 8. He first of all appeared to Cephas (Peter), and then to all of the apostles. He was seen by more than 500 of His followers all at once, most of whom were still alive at the time Paul wrote this letter to the Corinthians. It is interesting that his particular appearance is not recorded in any other place in the Scriptures. This is also the only record that Jesus appeared to James following His resurrection, but there are other records of His appearance to His apostles and the later appearance to Paul himself. (Paul always considered that his Damacus Road experience was a true and actual appearance of Jesus Christ to him). All of these appearances (called **christophanies**) constituted irrefutable proof that Christ had risen from the dead. This had been the ministry of Paul as well as the other apostles and it was the basis of all Christian belief.

II. IMPORTANCE OF CHRIST'S RESURRECTION (1 Corinthians 15:12-19).

(Verses 15-19 are not in the printed text.)

**12. Now if Christ be preached that he rose from the dead, how say some among you that there is no resurrection of the dead?**

Paul's argument was that it was pointless to preach that Christ arose from the dead and not to believe that there is a resurrection of the dead. It would be inconsistent to preach that Christ was raised from the dead but that we will not be raised. The two go hand in hand. The resurrection presupposes the resurrection of His followers and the resurrection of man must be built upon the foundation of Christ's resurrection.

**13. But if there be no resurrection of the dead, then is Christ not risen:**

**14. And if Christ be not risen, then is our preaching vain, and your faith is also vain.**

In his well-developed argument, Paul makes the point that if there is no resurrection of the dead then Christ was not risen from the dead. The purpose of His resurrection was to secure to us our resurrection, so to believe in one without the other would be futility and

error. This would also mean that Christian preaching is vain and Christian faith is baseless. Paul's point is that Christian belief in the Resurrection must be the bedrock of all our faith and commitment. Take away the glorious fact of the Resurrection and Christianity would become little more than admiration of the teachings of another man.

---

Discuss the utter powerlessness of a gospel that is not based on the death and resurrection of Christ.

---

Paul continues by saying that Christians would be "false witnesses of God, because we have testified of God that He raised up Christ." It was the teaching of the Resurrection, though laughed at by many (Acts 17:32), that made Christianity a powerful force in the pagan world. Men saw in Christ's resurrection cause for hope and a faith that answered the deepest longings of the soul. The fact of His resurrection was like a strong light in time of darkness, for it revealed God's intention that we should survive this present existence for a better life to come. For that reason, the Corinthians should be reminded that without a resurrection, those among them who had died are perished, for "if in this life only we have hope in Christ, we are of all men most miserable" (v. 19).

Christians in Paul's day were imprisoned, persecuted, killed and made the **offscouring** of the world (1 Corinthians 4:13), so there was little cause for hope in this life. If a man took unto himself such abuse and pain in this life without there being a reward in the life to come, then he would be foolish to accept the gospel of Christ at all.

III. PROMISE OF THE BELIEVER'S RESURRECTION (1 Corinthians 15:20-34)

**20. But now is Christ risen from the dead, and become the firstfruits of them that slept.**

His arguments now completed, Paul turns to positive assurances regarding the resurrection and what it means to Christians. The fact of the matter is that

Christ did arise from the dead and that in so doing He became the first of many who shall be resurrected. The resurrection of Christ is not a single event, standing alone in the history of God upon the earth. His resurrection from the dead was but the first step of all Christians' resurrection unto eternal life.

**21. For since by man came death, by man came also the resurrection of the dead.**

**22. For as in Adam all die, even so in Christ shall all be made alive.**

Sin and death entered the world through the fall of Adam and these twin curses must be removed by the life of Jesus. Paul's reasoning is that since death had come through a man, the correction of death must also come through a man. It was therefore necessary that Christ come to the earth in the form of a man in order that He might die and conquer death by resurrection. Until death should be conquered by Christ, who died as a man, all other men would die without hope beyond the grave. Because of Adam's sin all men upon the earth would die without hope; however, because of Christ's victory over both sin and death, all men who believe in Him can expect resurrection unto eternal life.

**23. But every man in his own order: Christ the firstfruits; afterward they that are Christ's at his coming.**

Paul repeats his position of verse 20 that Christ was the firstfruit, that is, the forerunner of all that will follow Him. Christ's resurrection from the dead is to be followed by the resurrection of His followers when He returns to earth again. Because of the example He set for us we can know what to look forward to. His resurrection moved the expectation of eternal life out of an abstract idea into concrete assurance. It is no longer something that men might long for, as many of the Old Testament's servants of God did, but it is something that we can believe in because we have the evidence before us. Our faith is affirmed because ". . . He shewed himself alive after his passion by many infallible proofs,

being seen of them forty days, and speaking of the things pertaining to the kingdom of God" (Acts 1:3).

**24. Then cometh the end when he shall have delivered up the kingdom unto God, even the Father; when he shall have put down all rule and all authority and power.**

**25. For he must reign, till he hath put all enemies under his feet.**

In our resurrection the Lord will deliver the kingdom, meaning those who have followed Him, unto the Father. With our resurrection the Lord will put down all rule and all authority and power. The resurrection of the dead will spell the end of sin and death and all the human horrors that came to earth with Adam.

The second Adam, Jesus Christ, will gain total authority upon the earth and will put all enemies under His feet. He gained the victory first for Himself and then for His followers. The last enemy to be conquered by Christ is death itself (v. 26). But His victory will be complete and eternal.

IV. GLORY OF THE RESURRECTION (1 Corinthians 15:35-58)

From verse 35 to 50 Paul draws a powerful analogy of the human resurrection to the sowing of the seed and the planting of the human body in death. Just as the seed will spring forth in new life, so will the human body burst forth from the grave into eternal life. In the resurrection we will not have a natural body but a spiritual body that will never again know disease or pain or death. Ours will be a spiritual body because we must inherit the kingdom of God and sinful flesh cannot enter there. Our bodies in resurrection will be real and true bodies, but they will be of spirit rather than of the earth.

From verses 51 to 55 Paul gives a statement of Christian faith that is nothing short of majestic in its beauty and content. Not all Christians will die before the Lord comes, he says, but some of us will be alive and will be changed into our immortal bodies while living. This will happen so quickly that we will probably not be aware that it has happened, except that we are suddenly changed into our immortality. As the living are caught up in what we refer to as the Rapture, the dead will come forth from their graves. Both the living and the dead in this instance will be changed from corruptible bodies capable of dying into incorruptible bodies that shall live forever (vv. 52, 53).

**54. So when this corruptible shall have put on incorruption, and this mortal shall have put on immortality, then shall be brought to pass the saying that is written, Death is swallowed up in victory.**

Why is it so easy to lose sight of the resurrection while one is still young?

The corruptible body is subject to pain, disease and human limitations. Mortal bodies are those that are subject to death. In the resurrection both the capability of corruption and death will be put away and the resurrected believers will no longer be subject to disease, infirmity, pain or death.

Paul is so caught up in the glory of what he is writing that his heart sings out quotations from the prophets. It was Isaiah who said, "He will swallow up death in victory; and the Lord God will wipe away tears from off all faces; and the rebuke of his people shall he take away from off all the earth: for the Lord hath spoken it" (Isaiah 25:8). It was Hosea who said, "I will ransom them from the power of the grave; I will redeem them from death: O death, I will be thy plagues; O grave, I will be thy destruction" (Hosea 13:14).

One of the active consequences of faith in the resurrection is a steadfast life. No man can be slack in his living who truly believes that the Lord is coming and that the dead will rise in resurrection (v. 58).

**REVIEW QUESTIONS**

1. What erroneous view did Paul attempt to correct by his correspondence about the resurrection?

2. As a matter of review, list some of the biblical proofs of Christ's resurrection.

3. What attitude did Paul suggest he would have to take toward faith and preaching if Christ had not been raised from the dead?

4. What contrast did Paul give in this lesson concerning Adam and Christ?

5. How important to you is the resurrection of Christ?

**GOLDEN TEXT HOMILY**

"BUT THANKS BE TO GOD, WHICH GIVETH US THE VICTORY THROUGH OUR LORD JESUS CHRIST" (1 Corinthians 15:57).

In our daily Christian walk we often face trials, battles, temptations and even death.

Physicians through medical science work hard to find answers and cures for the disease of mankind. It seems that it is an endless job. When an antidote for a old disease is found a new disease develops and death comes again.

Automobile manufacturers place new safety devices in our automobiles in an effort to lower the death rate. Safer freeways are designed and lower speed limits set to try to lower the death rate on our highways. However, each year thousands are killed in automobile accidents.

Death to the sinner is a time of dread and anxiety for he does not know the peace of God's presence. Death to the child of God is an entrance to eternal life with God. Physical death will come to the children of God, but not a spiritual death.

Recently I sat in the hospital room of a dear Christian friend, Fredia Coffey Underwood, was dying with cancer. Her husband (Reverend A. E. Underwood), my wife, and other members of her family were there. Sister Underwood had been in a coma for some time, but about 9:30 p.m. she began to praise the Lord and continued this praise until 6:30 a.m. She then slipped back into a coma and in a few hours went to be with her Lord.

I have never before witnessed the glory of the Lord as it was manifested in that hospital room that night. Although Sister Underwood lost the battle with cancer and physical death, she did not lose the battle with spiritual death.

"Death is swallowed up in victory. O death, where is thy sting? O grave, where is thy victory? The sting of death is sin; and the strength of sin is the law. But thanks be to God, which giveth us the victory through our Lord Jesus Christ" (1 Corinthians 15:54-57).

## SENTENCE SERMONS

CHRIST'S RESURRECTION is the guarantee of the believer's victory over death.
**—Selected**

EVERYTHING SHOULD BE VIEWED in the light of the resurrection day.
**—"Notes and Quotes"**

OUR LORD HAS WRITTEN the promise of the resurrection not in books alone, but in every leaf in springtime.
**—Martin Luther**

THE EMPTY TOMB proves Christianity, but an empty church denies it.
**—Selected**

## EVANGELISTIC APPLICATION

THE DEATH AND RESURRECTION OF JESUS CHRIST PROVIDES ETERNAL LIFE FOR ALL WHO BELIEVE.

*Jesus Christ is the only one who ever proved His authority to promise eternal life!*

As He stood at the graveside of His friend Lazarus, Jesus gave the promise, "I am the resurrection, and the life: he that believeth in me, though he were dead, yet shall he live" (John 11:25).

Jesus was not the first to ever promise His followers eternal life; nor was He the last. Then why do we believe Him and not the others? Jesus Christ stands alone as the one man who ever demonstrated His authority to make such a claim. Not only did He raise Lazarus, but He Himself also personally, literally, undeniably rose from the grave.

This is the one characteristic that distinguishes Christianity from all of the religions of the world. The disciples of all of the world's religions can take you to the tomb of their prophet and say, "Here is the remains of the one who promised us eternal life."

Not so with the Christian. We know where they buried Him, but He is not there. He is risen; He lives forevermore.

## ILLUMINATING THE LESSON

The story is told of a missionary service in Scotland which was attended by a young Scotch lad of singular earnestness and sincerity. When the plates were passed for the offering, the lad was grieved because he had nothing to give for missions. As the usher passed him, he asked the man to place the plate on the floor. Taken aback at something so unusual, the usher did as the lad requested; then the boy stepped into the offering plate with his bare feet and said with heart-warming sincerity, "I'll give myself; I have nothing else to give."

His gift stuck. The lad actually did give himself to God and the ministry of foreign missions, for that boy was Robert Moffatt, who would one day do so much to bring Africa to God.

While we may not give ourselves to God in such a dramatic and spectacular manner, we still have the opportunity of giving ourselves to Him. Robert Moffatt was not looking for something from God, but was crushed because he had nothing to give to God. His hurt was not that God had given him so little, but that he had so little to give God. Robert Moffatt was not looking for something for himself, but was looking for something in himself to give to God.

## DAILY DEVOTIONAL GUIDE

M. The Promised Resurrection. Psalm 16:9-11

T. Everlasting Life. Daniel 12:1-3

W. The Living Christ. Luke 24:13-35

T. The Resurrection and the Life. John 11:27-44

F. Alive in Christ. Ephesians 2:1-10

S. The Lord of Glory. Revelation 1:11-18

# Meeting God

**(Jacob)**

**Study Text:** Genesis 27:41 through 28:22

**Supplemental References:** Genesis 35:1-15; John 1:43-51; 4:7-29

**Time:** Around 1920-1910 B.C.

**Place:** Beersheba, Bethel

**Golden Text:** "I am with thee, and will keep thee in all places whither thou goest, and will bring thee again into this land; for I will not leave thee, until I have done that which I have spoken to thee of" (Genesis 28:15).

**Central Truth:** God often reveals His grace in the midst of life's troubles.

**Evangelistic Emphasis:** God seeks to save sinful people even while they are running from Him.

## Printed Text

**Genesis 28:12.** And he dreamed, and behold a ladder set up on the earth, and the top of it reached to heaven: and behold the angels of God ascending and descending on it.

**13. And, behold, the Lord stood above it, and said, I am the Lord God of Abraham thy father, and the God of Isaac: the land whereon thou liest, to thee will I give it, and to thy seed;**

14. And thy seed shall be as the dust of the earth, and thou shalt spread abroad to the west, and to the east, and to the north, and to the south: and in thee and in thy seed shall all the families of the earth be blessed.

**15. And, behold, I am with thee, and will keep thee in all places whither thou goest, and will bring thee again into this land; for I will not leave thee, until I have done that which I have spoken to thee of.**

16. And Jacob awaked out of his sleep, and he said, Surely the Lord is in this place; and I knew it not.

**17. And he was afraid, and said, How dreadful is this place! this is none other but the house of God, and this is the gate of heaven.**

18. And Jacob rose up early in the morning, and took the stone that he had put for his pillows, and set it up for a pillar, and poured oil upon the top of it.

**19. And he called the name of that place Beth-el: but the name of that city was called Luz at the first.**

20. And Jacob vowed a vow, saying, If God will be with me, and will keep me in this way that I go, and will give me bread to eat, and raiment to put on,

**21. So that I come again to my father's house in peace; then shall the Lord be my God:**

22. And this stone, which I have set for a pillar, shall be God's house: and of all that thou shalt give me I will surely give the tenth unto thee.

## LESSON OUTLINE

I. RUNNING FROM TROUBLE

II. ENCOUNTER WITH GOD

III. RESPONDING TO GOD

## LESSON EXPOSITION

### INTRODUCTION

When we last looked at the rivalry between Jacob and Esau, we saw the two brothers fatally and finally divided from each other. The cunning Jacob had cheated Esau out of his paternal blessing and the hapless firstborn son was left in anguish and grief. He said that he had been twice cheated by his younger brother, first of his birthright and then of his paternal blessing.

Now we see the two brothers as the rift between them deepens as two roads that meet at a junction then grow farther and farther apart. Jacob has secured all the rights of the firstborn and he will for all time be the successor of Isaac. It will be through him and his line that the Messiah of the Jews will come.

There is no denying the fact that the youthful Jacob was of doubtful character, willing to cheat his brother in the two most important issues of the patriarchal system. Yet in this lesson we see him grow older and more compassionate and responsible. He comes to have a greater consciousness of God and of his fellowmen. He begins in the scripture portion of this lesson to reach upward to the heights of his grandfather Abraham and his father Isaac. The battering of life will mellow him so that he becomes the suitable progenitor of Israel. In short, he meets God and responds well to that meeting.

### I. RUNNING FROM TROUBLE (Genesis 27:41 through 28:10)

(These verses are not in the printed text.)

Esau's sorrow over his lost blessing deepened into a genuine hatred of Jacob. He determined to kill his brother, a resolution that he shared with his Hittite wives or with some confederate.

He had to share his decision with someone, for Rebekah heard about it. Always doting and protective toward Jacob, she now became understandably concerned lest one brother kill another. She told Jacob about Esau's intention and counseled him to flee to Haran, her home city in Mesopotamia. There he could find refuge with her brother Laban until Esau's fury could be moderated. She would send to Haran for Jacob when she felt it was safe for him to return to Canaan.

In order to persuade Isaac that Jacob should go to Haran, Rebekah told her husband that she was distressed because of Esau's two Hittite wives (see 26:34, 35 and 27:46). She expressed a fear that Jacob might marry a Hittite wife if he stayed in Canaan. This was a legitimate concern despite the circumstances that gave rise to it, for even Abraham had sent his servant to Padanaram to find a wife, Rebekah, for Isaac. Certainly Isaac would agree with her that Jacob should go to the same place to find his wife. This would preserve the purity of the Abrahamic line.

In chapter 28:1, Isaac called Jacob to him and commanded him not to marry a Canaanite woman. Jacob and Esau were more than 40 years old at this time, and yet in the patriarchal society they were obligated to seek and follow the directions of their father. (Isaac himself was past 40 when Abraham sent his servant into Padanaram to select a bride for him.) Esau had violated this patriarchal principle by marrying Hittite women without seeking the counsel of Isaac. This had brought distress to Isaac and Rebekah and had contaminated the pure Hebrew line. Lest that happen to Jacob, he should go to his mother's country and select a bride from among her kinsmen. The marrying of cousins was not only practiced but was expected.

Isaac blessed Jacob and sent him away to find his wife. When Esau observed these things he became aware of how deeply his marriage to the Hittite women had displeased Isaac. He also saw that his father was becoming reconciled to the fact that the familial line would extend through Jacob. Despite their character differences, the fitness of Jacob over Esau to be Isaac's heir becomes more apparent. Esau observes that Jacob is obedient to his father and that he does not intend to take a Canaanite wife. Possibly out of frustration, and possibly because Ishmael was also Abraham's son, Esau therefore married a third wife, the daughter of Ishmael. Whatever his reason for doing this, he further deepened the separation from the patriarchal line, for Ishmael was not the legitimate heir of Abraham. Now Ishmael and Esau's bloodlines would merge and their descendants would be united as a people against the descendants of Jacob. The stage was becoming set for the millenia-old conflict between Israel and the other people of Palestine. Jacob was fleeing from immediate trouble with his brother Esau, but the conditions were fixed that would extend their conflict unto the present time.

II. ENCOUNTER WITH GOD (Genesis 28: 11-15)

(Verse 11 is not in the printed text.)

Jacob began his journey from Beersheba to Haran all alone. There is rugged, rocky terrian north of Beersheba and Jacob must have found the journey difficult. Evening caught Jacob at some undisclosed place in the wilderness. He arranged the stones, which were plentiful thereabout, into a place for sleeping (probably spreading his garments and pack upon the stones) and there lay down to sleep. That barren spot was about to become one of the great spiritual centers for Jacob and the Jewish people after him.

---

In addition to dreams, what are some of the methods God uses to get our attention?

---

**12. And he dreamed, and behold a ladder set up on the earth, and the top of it reached to heaven: and behold the angels of God ascending and descending on it.**

During the night Jacob dreamed an obviously spiritual dream, one that God used to communicate with Jacob. The Scriptures are filled with accounts of God speaking to men through dreams. The ladder that touched earth and heaven, with angels of God ascending and descending on it, clearly represented a relationship between earth and heaven, with a flow of communication between the two. In this particular instance the symbolism seems to refer to the establishment of the nation Israel, which God is about to accomplish.

**13. And, behold, the Lord stood above it, and said, I am the Lord God of Abraham thy father, and the God of Isaac: the land whereon thou liest, to thee will I give it, and to thy seed.**

At the top of the ladder stood the Lord, who confirmed the covenant He had made with Abraham in Genesis 17: 4-10, and to Isaac in Genesis 26:2-5.

**14. And thy seed shall be as the dust of the earth, and thou shalt spread abroad to the west, and to the east, and to the north, and to the south: and in thee and in thy seed shall all the families of the earth be blessed.**

God said to Abraham that his descendants would be like the stars of the heavens and the sands of the sea; He said to Isaac that his descendants would be like the stars of heaven; and here He tells Jacob that his descendants shall be like the dust of the earth. There is apparent significance in the manner of the promise only in the comparison of the number of stars in heaven to the dust of the earth. At a time when man's naked eye could see only about three thousand stars in the heaven, God compared the number of stars to the dust of the earth. Now astronomers can penetrate the sky with their powerful telescopes and see indeed that there are as many stars in the heaven as there are grains of sand upon the seashores.

In all accounts of the covenant, the Lord promises that the seed of Abraham will bless all the families of the earth. It is interesting that so much of the world has for so long hated the people whom God intended to be a blessing to the earth. Nonetheless, the promises of God have been true: those nations that have befriended Israel as a nation, or the seed of Abraham as a people, have been blessed and benefited throughout the generations of time. The fact that the Jewish people have existed through all the persecution that has been brought against them and are still a vital and numerous people is clear proof of the everlasting truth of God's holy Word.

What are some of the criteria by which one evaluates the credibility and relevance of dreams? Are all dreams from God? Explain.

**15. And, behold, I am with thee, and will keep thee in all places whither thou goest, and will bring thee again into this land; for I will not leave thee, until I have done that which I have spoken to thee of.**

The Lord added two particular promises to Jacob. First, he would be with him and keep him while he was out of the land of Canaan and would bring him back home in safety. Second, he would be with Jacob to prosper him and cause him to see the beginning of the fulfillment of the covenant. Although Abraham had been promised a great multitude of descendants, he lived long enough to see only Isaac and Ishmael. The same promise was extended to Isaac, but he lived only long enough to see Esau and Jacob. Now the promise to Jacob is that he will see the beginning of the covenant blessing in his prosperity and in his descendants.

III. RESPONDING TO GOD (Genesis 28:16-22)

**16. And Jacob awaked out of his sleep, and he said, Surely the Lord is in this place; and I knew it not.**

Jacob awoke from his sleep shakened and moved by the experience of his dream. As carnal as he had been in the past, he recognized that he had now entered into the divine presence. His use of the word **surely** is significant

and unusual, for the word is used only here and in Exodus 2:14. It indicates surprise or astonishment, something that was in no wise expected. Jacob had fled from Beersheba with no thought beyond escaping the wrath of Esau, but here he encounters the divine presence of the Lord God of Israel. The appearance of God to the patriarchs and others in the Book of Genesis never seemed startling or unusual. Somehow it was accepted as normal and something to be expected. Only in this instance is there the suggestion of astonishment and fear. Jacob associated the appearance of God with the place where he had slept.

**17. And he was afraid, and said, How dreadful is this place! this is none other but the house of God, and this is the gate of heaven.**

Alone and startled awake in a strange place, Jacob thought long about what he had seen. He was afraid, filled with that fear that is more like awe and that brings a soul into a state of worship and respect of God. Modern translations of the Bible use the word **awesome** instead of **dreadful,** for that is a clearer meaning of the word. It was an awesome place there among the stones where he lay, there under the stars of heaven, there where he had just seen steps ascending into heaven. He called it the "house of God" and the "gate of heaven," and for him it was both of these things. The unworthy supplanter had been brought at last into an awesome awareness of God.

It was an experience that shook him thoroughly, knowing as he did that this was no ordinary dream. God had only used the means of the dream to communicate with one who would be so important to the divine plan. He had gone to sleep filled with fear of Esau, but he awoke with a more wonderful kind of fear—awe—for the Lord. He had heard many times about the God of Abraham and Isaac but now He was something much more personal and intimate to Jacob.

**18. And Jacob rose up early in the morning, and took the stone that he**

**had put for his pillows, and set it up for a pillar, and poured oil upon the top of it.**

When the morning came Jacob arose from where he had lain and built an altar with the stone on which he had slept. He poured oil on the pillar he erected as an act of worship and reverence. This was reminiscent of the building of altars by Noah following the flood (Genesis 8:20), by Abraham after the Lord appeared to him near this very place (Genesis 12:8), and by Isaac when the Lord appeared in Beersheba unto him (Genesis 26:25).

**19. And he called the name of that place Beth-el: but the name of that city was called Luz at the first.**

Jacob called the place **Bethel,** which means "the house of God." The locality had previously been called Luz, but now it would become an important religious shrine.

**20. And Jacob vowed a vow, saying, If God will be with me, and will keep me in this way that I go, and will give me bread to eat, and raiment to put on.**

Now Jacob is moved to do something he has not done before: He makes a solemn vow to the Lord, which was the first genuine spiritual direction he had taken in his life. It appears in this verse that he tried to bargain with God and made his vow conditional on certain blessings from the Lord. That was not necessarily his intention: he was more likely stating what he would do as soon as he was in a position to do so. He was now leaving Canaan and would probably be in Padanaram for a number of years. But as soon as he returned to the land, he would make remembrance of his great encounter with God.

**21. So that I come again to my father's house in peace; then shall the Lord be my God.**

It was Jacob's destiny to live in the land of Canaan and be the forebearer of the Israelites. His compact with God was to the effect that when he returned to the land he would set about the

accomplishing of those things to which God had directed him.

**22. And this stone, which I have set for a pillar, shall be God's house: and of all that thou shalt give me I will surely give the tenth unto thee.**

The two specific points of Jacob's vow was that he would make Bethel into a place of worship, a place of remembrance of God. Moreover, he would give a tithe of all his wealth into the service of the Lord. At the time he made this vow to consecrate a tenth of his wealth to God's cause, the practice of tithing had not been instituted. Jacob was so overwhelmed by his spiritual experience that he wanted to respond with a gesture both selfless and generous. As Abraham had done in Genesis 14:20, Jacob's inner pulse was that of giving a tithe of his possessions.

It is much the same with us in modern times. When God blesses us and we are warmly aware of His benefits to us, we want to express our enlarged awareness of Him with offerings to Him. We therefore make offerings of ourselves, our time, our families, our means, our energies and even our thoughts. The truly spiritual person seeks to express thanksgiving for what he has received by giving something himself.

### REVIEW QUESTIONS

1. What two incidents had given rise to the rift between Esau and Jacob?

2. What excuse did Rebekah give for Jacob's need to flee Haran to escape the wrath of Esau?

3. What was the nature and meaning of the dream Jacob had as he journied toward Haran?

4. How did Jacob respond to the divine message?

5. What were the two specific points of the vow Jacob made to the Lord?

### GOLDEN TEXT HOMILY

"I AM WITH THEE, AND WILL KEEP THEE IN ALL PLACES WHITHER THOU GOEST, AND WILL BRING THEE AGAIN INTO THIS LAND; FOR I WILL LEAVE THEE, UNTIL I HAVE DONE THAT WHICH I HAVE SPOKEN TO THEE OF" (Genesis 28:15).

Jacob awakened with a start. The afterglow of the angelic vision and the re-verberation of the divine voice which had spoken lingered in his consciousness with remarkable clarity. An inexplicable sense of peace and tranquility charged the very atmosphere of this hallowed spot. The impact of this dream-vision would not soon be forgotten, especially in view of the long and difficult sojourn he was to experience in an unfamiliar distant land.

God reminded Jacob of this Bethel experience at the outset of his perilous flight from Laban and the land of Pada-naram, en route to his beloved Canaan once again (Genesis 31:13). Jacob later reminded God of this same promise as he awaited his inevitable encounter with his brother Esau, whose vengeful wrath he had fled many years before (Genesis 32:12). Rather than a bloodbath, how-ever, the encounter became the scene of restoration as brother embraced broth-er.

Finally in Genesis 35:1, God instructed Jacob to return to Bethel once again. In welcome obedience, Jacob returned to the sacred spot where God had ex-tended the original promise of His abid-ing presence to him. In spite of every pitfall, danger, and threat, the God of Bethel had faithfully brought him back to the point of promise just as He declared He would do.

What a fountainhead of comfort this encouraging narrative should be to the weary pilgrim today. Time has not altered the promises of God. Through His be-loved Son He has promised to be with us even until the end of the world (Mat-thew 28:20). He who brought Jacob back to Bethel will never leave us to be trod-den under the feet of a careless world which marches to the fiendish orders of the archenemy of man's soul. He has re-served far better things for us!—**Jimmy D. Wood, Martinsville, Virginia**

## SENTENCE SERMONS

GOD OFTEN REVEALS HIS grace in the midst of life's troubles.

**—Selected**

MANY MEN OWE the grandeur of their lives to their tremendous difficulties.

**—Charles W. Spurgeon**

OUT OF DIFFICULTIES grow miracles.

**—Jean De La Bruyere**

LIFE-CHANGING ENCOUNTERS with God prepare us to face with success the difficult crisis of life.

**—Selected**

## ILLUMINATING THE LESSON

Forth into the darkness passing
Nothing can I hear or see,
Save the Hand outstretched to guide me
And the Voice that calls to me.

"I will bring the blind by pathways
That they know not, nor have known;
'Tis a way untried, untrodden
But they shall not walk alone."

Lead the way then, where Thou pleasest,
Only keep me close to Thee,
Craving not to see the distance,
Well content that Thou dost see.

Have I not my all committed
To Thy keeping long ago?
Knowing Him Whom I have trusted,
More I do not need to know!

## DAILY DEVOTIONAL GUIDE

M. Fleeing God. Exodus 2:11-22

T. Overcoming the Enemy. 1 Samuel 17:48-58

W. Preserved by God. 1 Samuel 21:10 through 22:5

T. Obeying God. Matthew 4:18-22

F. Encountering God. John 14:1-11

S. Seeing God in Christ. 2 Corinthians 5:19-21

# A Transformed Life

**(Jacob)**

**Study Text:** Genesis 32:1-32

**Supplemental References:** Joshua 5:13-15; Psalm 34:4-8; Luke 11:5-13

**Time:** Middle 1800's B.C.

**Place:** Mahanaim, east of the Jordan River.

**Golden Text:** "I will not let thee go, except thou bless me" (Genesis 32:26).

**Central Truth:** Those willing to die to sin and self realize fulness of life in Christ Jesus.

**Evangelistic Emphasis:** Crisis in the life of a believer deepen faith and makes his witness more effective.

## Printed Text

**Genesis 32:9.** And Jacob said, O God of my father Abraham, and God of my father Isaac, the Lord which saidst unto me, Return unto thy country, and to thy kindred, and I will deal well with thee:

**10. I am not worthy of the least of all the mercies, and of all the truth, which thou hast shewed unto thy servant; for with my staff I passed over this Jordan; and now I am become two bands.**

11. Deliver me, I pray thee, from the hand of my brother, from the hand of Esau: for I fear him, lest he will come and smite me, and the mother with the children.

**12. And thou saidst, I will surely do thee good, and make thy seed as the sand of the sea, which cannot be numbered for multitude.**

24. And Jacob was left alone; and there wrestled a man with him until the breaking of the day.

**25. And when he saw that he pre-** vailed not against him, he touched the hollow of his thigh; and the hollow of Jacob's thigh was out of joint, as he wrestled with him.

26. And he said, Let me go, for the day breaketh. And he said, I will not let thee go, except thou bless me.

**27. And he said unto him, What is thy name? And he said, Jacob.**

28. And he said, Thy name shall be called no more Jacob, but Israel: for as a prince hast thou power with God and with men, and hast prevailed.

**29. And Jacob asked him, and said, Tell me, I pray thee, thy name. And he said, Wherefore is it that thou dost ask after my name? And he blessed him there.**

30. And Jacob called the name of the place Peniel: for I have seen God face to face, and my life preserved.

**31. And as he passed over Penuel the sun rose upon him, and he halted upon his thigh.**

## DICTIONARY

hollow . . . thigh—Genesis 32:25—where the thigh joins the abdomen.
Peniel (pe-NIGH-el)—Genesis 32:30—The word means "face of God."

---

### LESSON OUTLINE

I. FACING THE PAST
II. PERSISTENCE IN PRAYER
III. POWER WITH GOD

### LESSON EXPOSITION

INTRODUCTION

The incident recorded in Genesis 32 occurred more than 20 years after Jacob's experience at Bethel. During those 20 years he lived in Padanaram with Laban, his mother's brother, and became a very wealthy man. Jacob married Laban's two daughters, Leah and Rachel, and became the father of 11 sons (a twelfth son will be born on his way back to Canaan). Jacob served Laban 14 years to pay for his wives Leah and Rachel, and then served him another six years to pay for herds and flocks and other possessions that made him rich. The passage in Genesis 30:43 says *(King James Version),* "Thus the man grew exceedingly rich, and had large flocks, maidservants and menservants, and camels and asses" *(King James Version).*

Because of Jacob's skills he made Laban a rich man while he also increased his own possessions. Laban was one of the most devious and unadmirable men in the Book of Genesis, and Jacob had difficulty in getting away from him. Jacob managed to do so, however, and left Padanaram with his great family and enormous holdings of livestock, servants, tents, and household effects. He left in response to an angel of God that appeared to him with this message: "I am the God of Beth-el, where thou anointedst the pillar, and where thou vowed a vow unto me: now arise, get thee out from this land, and return unto the land of thy kindred" (Genesis 31:13).

The call back to Bethel was strong and urgent in Jacob's heart. He must return to Canaan, for there is where he must fulfill the conditions of the covenant. It would be his offspring that would truly launch the nation of Israel. Moreover, it was in Canaan that he had first encountered God and it was in Canaan that his spiritual development would continue until he became "a prince with God."

In this chapter we see Jacob back in Canaan with his wives, his children and his vast possessions. It is now that he will begin to manifest himself as one of the patriarchs, as a worthy father of the Hebrew people.

I. FACING THE PAST (Genesis 32:1-20)

(Verses 1-8, 13-20 are not in the printed text.)

In Canaan, somewhere north of Jabbok, not far from the Jordan River, Jacob encountered the angels of God. He named the place **Mahanaim,** which means "two camps," because he interpreted the appearance of the angels as signifying that two hosts were present: the visible host of persons and beasts that accompanied him and the invisible host of angels that were about them. The incident sharped Jacob's spiritual sensitivity and resumed his spiritual development begun at Bethel 20 years earlier.

No doubt remembering the division between himself and Esau, Jacob sent messengers to Esau in the land of Seir, or Edom, with tidings of his sojourn in Padanaram and his present circumstance. It was admittedly an appeal for peace and reconciliation. He said, "that I may find grace in thy sight" (v. 5). The messengers returned to Jacob with the information that Esau was on his way to meet Jacob and that 400 men were with him. Jacob's interpretation of this, whether it was true or not, was that Esau's movement was hostile and the 400 men must be men of war. Verse 7 says that he was greatly afraid and distressed. He remembered the reason for his going into Padanaram was to escape the murderous wrath of Esau, and now he had no way of knowing whether or not that wrath had subsided.

Jacob's response to the grime tidings was to divide all the host with him into two companies. In that way, if Esau should attack one company the other could escape intact. It was a clever maneuver, especially since those accompanying Jacob were not men of war or even equipped to withstand attack. If Esau should attack them, those he struck would easily be destroyed. Hopefully, the other would remain intact and unhurt.

**9. And Jacob said, O God of my father Abraham, and God of my father Isaac, the Lord which saidst unto me, Return unto thy country, and to thy kindred, and I will deal well with thee.**

Most important of all was the fact that Jacob began to pray. He reminded the Lord that he was returning to Canaan at the specific instruction of the Lord and that the Lord had promised to deal well with him. Jacob must have assumed that part, for God did not specifically promise Jacob that he would deal well with him (31:11-13). Such a promise may be inferred but it is not specifically stated. The fact that Jacob mentioned this indicates that he was at a point of desperation when he called on the Lord.

---

Do you feel that God uses adverse circumstances to draw people closer to Him? Was that the case with Jacob?

---

**10. I am not worthy of the least of all the mercies, and of all the truth, which thou hast shewed unto thy servant; for with my staff I passed over this Jordan; and now I am become two bands.**

Real humility and thanksgiving come through clearly in Jacob's prayer. He acknowledges his unworthiness for the least of the Lord's mercies and he compares his status now with what it was when he went north into Padanaram. As he went northward across Jordan he had

only the staff he carried with him; but now on his return to Canaan his possessions are so great that they are divided into two bands. He attributes this great increase of wealth to the blessings of the Lord.

**11. Deliver me, I pray thee, from the hand of my brother, from the hand of Esau: for I fear him, lest he will come and smite me, and the mother with the children.**

This is obviously a prayer of crisis, when Jacob felt that he and his company might be slaughtered by Esau and his 400 men of war. Even though it was a prayer of crisis it was earnestly made and the sincerity of it broke up the deep wells of humility within Jacob. Sometimes in life we all pray most earnestly in times of emergency, but that is good for such prayers awaken in us finer qualities than have come to the surface before. For instance, Jacob's concern for protection must of necessity extend far beyond himself to include us all, "the mothers with the children."

**12. And thou saidst, I will surely do thee good, and make thy seed as the sand of the sea, which cannot be numbered for multitude.**

Once again Jacob reminds the Lord of His promises to him, although the Lord's promise was not precisely like Jacob quotes it. In Genesis 28:13, 14 God had said, "The land on which you lie I will give to you and to your descendants; and your descendants shall be like the dust of the earth." The Lord had further said in 28:15, "I will bring you back to this land; for I will not leave you until I have done that of which I have spoken to you." This prayer was preparatory for a great spiritual struggle and victory.

From this vast possessions he then selected a present for his brother Esau: "Two hundred she goats, and twenty he goats, two hundred ewes, and twenty rams, Thirty milch camels with their colts, forty kine, and ten bulls, twenty she asses, and ten foals" (32:14, 15). Jacob's servants were instructed carefully on how to take these offerings to Esau.

Jacob admittedly feared the encounter with Esau and hoped that his gift to him would appease any anger that remained from their earlier days when Jacob had cheated him.

II. PERSISTENCE IN PRAYER (Genesis 32:21-26)

(Verses 21-23 are not in the printed text.)

Jacob arranged his gift of 580 animals into three droves. Each of the three droves was to be accompanied by servants who would drive or lead them. The three were kept at some distance from each other so they would not arrive at Esau's camp at the same time.

Jacob watched this vast gift pass before him on its way to Esau and then he encamped for the night.

Before the night ended Jacob and his company broke camp and crossed the brook Jabbok to continue their southward journey. In his immediate company were Leah and Rachel, his wives, and Zilpah and Bilhah, the two handmaids, and his 11 sons. It should also be observed that Jacob had one daughter, Dinah, but in the custom of that day she is not listed in the enumeration of his wives and sons. We find Dinah mentioned in Genesis 30:21, 34:1 and other portions of that chapter. Although Dinah was not listed among the descendants of Jacob she still is mentioned more than most daughters of Scripture.

Jacob sent his family on ahead of him while he tarried at the side of the brook presumably to pray. The dramatic incident that followed gives indication that he tarried behind for spiritual meditation.

**24. And Jacob was left alone; and there wrestled a man with him until the breaking of the day.**

All alone by the brook Jabbok, Jacob encountered an unidentified person who engaged him in a struggle. Although this person is called "a man," it is understood that he was an angel. The word **angel** means simply "messenger," and this was clearly a messenger from God to Jacob.

If Jacob and the angel struggled together until the breaking of the day, that means that he broke camp while it was still fully dark and almost immediately encountered the angel.

**25. And when he saw that he prevailed not against him, he touched the hollow of his thigh; and the hollow of Jacob's thigh was out of joint, as he wrestled with him.**

The struggle was not one of survival, but Jacob clung to the heavenly messenger for spiritual reasons. It is clear that the angel was testing the resolve of Jacob by endeavoring to pull out of his grasp. The struggle was intense, for Jacob's will of worship was tested to the fullest. If he was to take his place among the patriarchs of Israel then he must be determined upon his service to the Lord. From this and the verses that follow the nature of the struggle is seen as Jacob's taking hold of the angel and contending for a divine blessing. The angel's struggle to be free was the way of testing Jacob's sincerity and determination. The servant of God must put forth great effort to claim the blessings and accompaniments that come from a life of service to God. These would certainly come to Jacob, if he proved himself to be determined to attain and hold them.

The angel touched Jacob's thigh so that it was thrown out of joint, which would greatly incapacitate him in his struggle. Still Jacob struggled on and refused to release the angel. He was intent upon the purpose of finding his appropriate position with the almighty God. There had been kindled in him an overwhelming spiritual awareness and he was not about to let this opportunity pass him, even though it meant that he struggled with pain from a disjointed thigh. All those who obtain the great blessings and benefits of God must manifest an equal determination and refuse to be stopped by pain or other circumstances.

**26. And he said, Let me go, for the day breaketh. And he said, I will not let thee go, except thou bless me.**

The man of God implored Jacob to

release him because the dawn was breaking. At this point the record shows the reason for the struggle: Jacob was intent upon finding favor with the Lord. The blessing Jacob sought was clearly not for more possessions, for he had great abundance in that regard. It would not have been merely in the matter of protection, or Jacob in no way makes references to such need. The patriarch had come at last to a point where he recognized his responsibility and need before the Lord. With this incident he at last takes his place alongside Abraham and Isaac as a champion of God. This was a crisis of responsibility and obligation in life. Jacob knew very well that he by this time was the heir to Isaac and it would be through him that the line of Abraham would continue through the generations. He is therefore intent on the kind of relationship with the God of Abraham and Isaac that will make him fit for his appointed place.

---

Discuss the encounter Jacob had with the angel of God. Was it only a dream? How do you interpret the total incident?

---

III. POWER WITH GOD (Genesis 32:27-32)

**27. And he said unto him, What is thy name? And he said, Jacob.**

**28. And he said, Thy name shall be called no more Jacob, but Israel: for as a prince hast thou power with God and with men, and hast prevailed.**

The angel of the Lord asked Jacob his name not because God did not know it but in order to make a point of what he was about to do. For 60 years he had been **Jacob,** a "supplanter," but now he would be **Israel,** a "prince with God." It is from this name that both the people and the land will be named. Even to this day the land is Israel and the people are Israelis. That name carries back to Jacob, third of the great patriarchs.

**29. And Jacob asked him, and said, Tell me, I pray thee, thy name. And he said, Wherefore is it that thou dost ask after my name? And he blessed him there.**

Jacob, in turn, asked the angel his name. Without answering the question, the man of God there blessed Jacob.

**30. And Jacob called the name of the place Peniel: for I have seen God face to face, and my life is preserved.**

Jacob realized that he had struggled with God in the form of an angel or of man, and his soul was overawed by that realization. He had been in touch with divinity. He named the place where the struggle had occurred **Peniel,** which means "face of God," and said, "it is because I saw God face to face, and yet my life was spared." Jacob had prevailed in prayer and determination with the God of heaven in the form of a man; his life would be forever changed and exalted because of it.

All who come face to face with God, even though it is in time of peril or crisis, and prevail in that prayer will be forever touched and lifted up because of it. He who had been Jacob is now Israel, and that name will be known around the world for centuries upon centuries. Through this man who had held firmly to the Lord, the nations of all the world would be blessed, just as the Lord had said.

**31. And as he passed over Penuel the sun rose upon him, and he halted upon his thigh.**

Record of the incident closes by telling that Jacob's walk was effected with a limp following the enounter. As the sun rose over Peniel, Jacob limped away, the limp being visible proof that he had wrestled with God. Each step he should take hereafter would remind him of the encounter; each time a person saw him limp as he walked would recall what he heard about the encounter. Through the years the Jews have heard about it and have set it in their lore by refusing to eat the tendon attached to the socket of the hip of any animal used for food.

Jacob in a striking way had an experience similar to Paul's on the Damascus road; Paul had said, "I am crucified with Christ: nevertheless I live; yet not I, but Christ liveth in me: and the life which I now live in the flesh I live by the faith of the Son of God, who loved me, and gave himself for me" (Galatians 2:20).

## REVIEW QUESTIONS

1. How long after the act of deceiving his father did the event of today's lesson happen?

2. Discuss the conditions Laban had imposed on Jacob before he was able to leave with his wives and livestock.

3. What message had Jacob received from the angel of God that caused him to leave Padanaram?

4. What efforts had Jacob made in an attempt to restore peace and achieve a reconciliation with his brother Esau?

5. How did Jacob respond to the message that Esau was enroute to meet him? How had Esau planned for the meeting?

## GOLDEN TEXT HOMILY

"I WILL NOT LET THEE GO, EXCEPT THOU BLESS ME" (Genesis 32:26).

Many biblical historians have had difficulty interpreting this story. Possibly the story was told over and over for many years before it was finally crystallized and put down in the form we have today.

Did Jacob actually wrestle with a man or an angel? Or was this simply a spiritual battle for Jacob? Angels have appeared as men before, for we know that an angel appeared as a man and ate with Abraham.

Jacob was a shrewd man who tried to bargain with God. Even the name of Jacob means "wrestler." As Jacob sought God that night, his request for a blessing was not granted at first. God needed to make some changes in Jacob's life. There is a time in every person's life that he must face himself, God, and reality. Jacob came to the place in his life where God could mold him. Therefore, God changed his name from Jacob to Israel and then changed his nature. Isn't this what God really does to a sinner who desires to know Him? He changes his name from sinner to saint. The changed person leaves off the old

nature and takes on the new nature provided by the righteousness of God.

Jacob was persistant in seeking God. Therefore, he did not turn the angel loose; he held on even in the midst of the struggle. So should we, like Jacob, strive not to turn loose until our battles are won through prayer.

After wrestling, Jacob was given a sign to remember the struggle, a crippled thigh. He also had a new walk, a distinguishable difference in his life, even his friends saw and knew of the change in Jacob. Paul said, "If any man be in Christ, he is a new creature: old things are passed away; behold, all things are become new" (2 Corinthians 5:17).—**James R. Burroughs, Chaplain (Major), U. S. Army, Fort Jackson, South Carolina**

## SENTENCE SERMONS

THOSE WHO ARE WILLING to die to sin and self realize fulness of life in Christ Jesus.

**—Selected**

IF PROBLEMS SWEEP you off your feet, it is time to get on your knees.

**—Fred Beck**

A REFORMED SINNER is one who changed the circles under his eyes for one over his head.

**—Selected**

WHEN YOU PRAY, rather let your heart be without words, than your words without heart.

**—John Bunyan**

## EVANGELISTIC APPLICATION

CRISIS IN THE LIFE OF A BELIEVER DEEPENS FAITH AND MAKES HIS WITNESS MORE EFFECTIVE.

Pearl Buck has told the story of a monkey who wanted to get away from God, but though he had struggled, he had never succeeded. He was a fine jumper, and one day he decided that he would give a great leap that would certainly take him out of God's hand. He jumped as far as he could and landed on the top of a great mountain in a strange country. "Ah," he cried, "I have escaped him this time." Then he heard

God's voice very near him: "Dear little monkey, you have jumped only to the base of my thumb. You are still in God's hand."

## ILLUMINATING THE LESSON

Tolstoy has described a man sitting in a boat which has been pushed off from an unknown shore; he has been shown the opposite shore, and given a pair of oars, and left alone. Straight out into the stream he rows; but then the current gets hold of him and deflects him. Other boats are there; some have thrown their oars away, a few are struggling against the stream, most are gliding with it quite content. "Is this the way?" he asks some of them; and a chorus of voices replies: "Of course it is. What did you think? There can be no other way." And so he drifts on; but suddenly he grows conscious of a sound, menacing, terrible—the roar of rapids. The man comes to himself, remembers what he had forgotten—the oars, the course, the opposite shore—and madly he begins to row upstream against the current, crying: "Fool that I was to drift!" He rows on until safety is reached. "Now," says Tolstoy, "that current is the tradition of the world, the oars are free will, the opposite shore is God."

## DAILY DEVOTIONAL GUIDE

M. Vision of God. Joshua 5:13-15

T. Victory Over Sin. 1 Kings 18:30-40

W. Protected by God. Psalm 34:4-8

T. Continuing in Prayer. Luke 11:5-13

F. Manifest Power. Acts 13:4-12

S. Pressing Forward. Philippians 3:8-14

# April 20, 1986

# Jealousy in the Family

**(Joseph's Brothers)**
**Study Text:** Genesis 37:1-36
**Supplemental References:** Numbers 5:11-15; 1 Samuel 18:6-16; Mark 10:35-41; 1 Corinthians 3:1-4; James 3:13-18
**Time:** Around 1820-1800 B.C.
**Place:** Grazing lands near Shechem
**Golden Text:** "Charity suffereth long, and is kind; charity envieth not; charity vaunteth not itself, is not puffed up" (1 Corinthians 13:4).
**Central Truth:** Satan seeks to destroy the purposes of God by creating a spirit of jealousy.
**Evangelistic Emphasis:** God's grace can deliver from the bondage of jealousy.

## Printed Text

**Genesis 37:3.** Now Israel loved Joseph more than all his children, because he was the son of his old age: and he made him a coat of many colours.

**4. And when his brethren saw that their father loved him more than all his brethren, they hated him, and could not speak peaceably unto him.**

18. And when they saw him afar off, even before he came near unto them, they conspired against him to slay him.

**19. And they said one to another, Behold, this dreamer cometh.**

20. Come now therefore, and let us slay him, and cast him into some pit, and we will say, Some evil beast hath devoured him: and we shall see what will become of his dreams.

**21. And Reuben heard it, and he delivered him out of their hands; and said, Let us not kill him.**

22. And Reuben said unto them, Shed no blood, but cast him into this pit that is in the wilderness, and lay no hand upon him; that he might rid him out of their hands, to deliver him to his father again.

**23. And it came to pass, when Joseph was come unto his brethren, that they stript Joseph out of his coat, his coat of many colours that was on him;**

24. And they took him, and cast him into a pit: and the pit was empty, there was no water in it.

**31. And they took Joseph's coat, and killed a kid of the goats, and dipped the coat in the blood;**

32. And they sent the coat of many colours, and they brought it to their father; and said, This have we found: know now whether it be thy son's coat or no.

**33. And he knew it, and said, It is my son's coat; an evil beast hath devoured him; Joseph is without doubt rent in pieces.**

34. And Jacob rent his clothes, and put sackcloth upon his loins, and mourned for his son many days.

## DICTIONARY

**coat of many colors—Genesis 37:3**—Jacob had planned for Joseph to be his successor and the coat (a pricely one) was evidence of it.

**rent—Genesis 37:33, 34**—Torn, ripped

**sackcloth—Genesis 37:34**—A coarse, thick, haircloth worn next to the skin in times of extreme distress.

---

**LESSON OUTLINE**

I. SEEDS OF JEALOUSY

II. VICTIM OF JEALOUSY

III. RESULTS OF JEALOUSY

**LESSON EXPOSITION**

INTRODUCTION

After the events of last week's lesson, Jacob and Esau were reconciled to each other without violence or bitterness. There was no way that two 60-year-old men could effect the closeness and intimacy of brothers, but they did establish a courteous relationship. Jacob returned to Bethel, site of his first encounter with God (Genesis 35:1-15). From Bethel Jacob and his great company traveled southward toward Hebron and Beersheba. Near Bethlehem his beloved wife Rachel bore him her second and his twelfth son. Rachel died as a result of the childbearing, but before she died she named her son **Benoni,** which means "son of my sorrow." After Rachel's death, Jacob named his twelfth son **Benjamin,** "son of the right hand."

Jacob's sons were 12 in number, and these would be the heads of the 12 tribes of Israel. His wife Leah bore him six sons: Reuben, Simeon, Levi, Judah, Zebulun and Issachar. His wife Rachel bore him two sons, Joseph and Benjamin. Rachel's maid Bilhah bore him two sons, Dan and Naphtali. Leah's maid Zilpah bore him two sons, Gad and Asher. The birth order of the 12, as listed in Genesis 49, was Reuben, Simeon, Levi, Judah, Zebulun, Issachar, Dan, Gad, Asher, Naphtali, Joseph and Benjamin.

Jacob's wild, youthful years came back to haunt him in the persons of his children. The same sibling rivalry that had destroyed his relationship with Esau would divide his own 12 sons. They formed confederates among themselves, mainly along the lines of who their mothers were. They would unify to form a mighty nation, but as individuals there was always rivalry among them. Genesis 37 tells the most familiar story of the ill will that existed among Jacob's sons. The aftermath of this act of spite will continue for many years.

I. SEEDS OF JEALOUSY (Genesis 37: 1-11)

(Verses 1, 2, 5-11 are not in the printed text.)

Jacob's father, Isaac, died after Jacob returned to Canaan (Genesis 35:27-29), which made Jacob the true patriarch of the Abrahamic line. This record opens with a statement that Jacob lived in the land of his father's sojournings, the land of Canaan. All of the following history concerns Jacob and his 12 sons as they composed the beginning of a people and a nation.

Joseph was 17 years old when the incidents of this chapter occurred. He worked as a shepherd along with the sons of Bilhah and Zilpah. These were Dan, Naphtali, Gad and Asher. Joseph and his four half brothers apparently did not get along well, for Joseph gave his father a bad report concerning them.

**3. Now Israel loved Joseph more than all his children, because he was the son of his old age: and he made him a coat of many colours.**

Israel, or Jacob, had a particular attachment to Joseph; the firstborn son of Rachel. During Jacob's years in Haran it was very clear that Rachel was the one wife he truly loved: He was willing to neglect Leah and the two handmaids in favor of Rachel. For many years she did not bear Jacob sons, but then Joseph was born. This made Joseph a particular favorite with his father. The old man therefore made Joseph a special garment of many colors. The *New International Version* calls it "a richly ornamented robe," which probably explains the *King James Version* description of it as "a coat of many colors."

**4. And when his brethren saw that their father loved him more than all his brethren, they hated him, and could not speak peaceably unto him.**

Jacob's conspicuous preference for Joseph understandably engendered envy in Jacob's other sons. This led to a resentment of Joseph, which deepened to outright hatred. This is a normal dynamic of family tension, when an aging father shows preference for a younger son because that son supplies some psychological need in the man who feels that his youth has slipped away. The older children do not recognize that the father is clinging to a lost youth, and so they become envious and resentful.

---

Discuss the unwise practice of obvious favoritism of parents toward a son or daughter. How does other children react?

---

The tension between Joseph and his brethren deepened when he related to them a dream that placed him in a position superior to them. The first dream was of an agricultural nature, with the brothers" sheaves of grain bowing down before Joseph's sheaf. Then Joseph had a second dream of similar nature in which the sun and moon and 11 stars bowed down to him. It was impetuous of Joseph, who was an immature 17 years of age, to tell these things to his brothers. These dreams represented God's message to him.

The second dream brought Joseph a rebuke from his father and both dreams deepened the hatred of his brothers. Joseph was therefore placed in a lonely position, with dreams that he could not understand and that infuriated his breth-

ren. His relating the dreams was like casting pearls before swine, which we are warned not to do (Matthew 7:6); it placed him in danger at the hands of his brothers. An explosive jealousy seethed within them as he, wearing his grand coat, told of dreams that gave him preeminence over them. Jacob the father did not understand these matters either. He rebuked Joseph for telling them, but he nevertheless kept them in mind as the days went by.

II. VICTIM OF JEALOUSY (Genesis 37: 12-28)

(Verses 12-17, 25-28 are not in the printed text.)

Jacob's brothers took their flocks northward to Shechem for grazing. This was a dangerous thing to do, for the last time Jacob's family was in Shechem they had experienced trouble and danger at the hands of the inhabitants (chapter 34). Jacob was probably worried about his sons, so he called upon Joseph to go there and see about their welfare. This was not uncommon, for Joseph customarily accompanied his shepherding brothers.

Joseph was probably pleased to make the trip; at least he showed no hesitation about making it. It was approximately 50 miles from Hebron to Shechem and the paths between the two follow some very pleasant areas. For the most part, Joseph would have followed the well-marked trails, but shepherds do not stay on the trails in the course of pasturing their flocks. Therefore, he occasionally left the trails to locate pasture lands off the beaten path. When a passerby saw Joseph searching for someone he told him that his brothers had gone to Dothan, about 15 miles north of Shechem, with their flocks. It was at Dothan that Joseph finally found them.

**18. And when they saw him afar off, even before he came near unto them, they conspired against him to slay him.**

Joseph had made the 65-mile trip across the desert without danger, but as he neared his brothers danger arose against him like a dark cloud. Instead of their hearts being glad when they saw him coming, they began a conspiracy to put him to death. Their hate had escalated beyond sullen resentment and ugly words to an actual contemplation of murder. Joseph should have been safer with his brothers than in the desert with strangers, but what should have been sanctuary became instead a center of danger.

**19. And they said one to another, Behold, this dreamer cometh.**

**20. Come now therefore, and let us slay him, and cast him into some pit, and we will say, Some evil beast hath devoured him: and we shall see what will become of his dreams.**

Ancient Dothan stood at the edge of a broad, fertile plain, so a person could be seen while he was still far away. As Joseph in his coat approached the brothers, their conversation about him was strong and contemptuous. He was bitterly denounced as a dreamer. The Hebrew language actually says "this master of dreams," which is considerably stronger than the translation here.

For some of the brothers to suggest that they kill Joseph indicates that the feeling against him was held by all the brothers. If there had been even one favorable to Joseph, there is danger that he would tell Jacob of such talk. The brothers felt quite safe in killing him and lying that a wild beast had devoured him. What then, they reasoned, would become of his arrogant dreams? When Joseph, like the imprudent youth he was, told his brothers of his dreams he did not realize that he was planting the seeds of his own destruction. The dreams were probably regarded to be signs of his attitude of superiority. If they would kill him they would be rid of both him and his arrogant dreaming.

---

How can the feeling of superiority affect relationships? Any idea how to deal with persons who manifest a superior attitude?

**21. And Reuben heard it, and he delivered him out of their hands; and said, Let us not kill him.**

**22. And Reuben said unto them, Shed no blood, but cast him into this pit that is in the wilderness, and lay no hand upon him; that he might rid him out of their hands, to deliver him to his father again.**

It was Reuben, Jacob's eldest son, who showed a spark of responsibility and mercy. That is understandable, for in the firstborn there is often a sense of responsibility and concern for the younger siblings not found in those of later birth. Being the firstborn often conditions a person to be exemplary and protective to a degree that is surpassed only by the parents themselves.

Reuben's intention was to rescue Joseph from his murderous brothers and get him back home to Jacob. Near at hand was a pit, probably a dry cistern, where Reuben suggested they put Joseph for the time being. He would then devise a way of helping Joseph escape back to his father.

**23. And it came to pass, when Joseph was come unto his brethren, that they stript Joseph out of his coat, his coat of many colours that was on him.**

As soon as Joseph arrived at the place where his brothers were gathered, they seized him and stripped from him the ornamented coat that had become the object of their jealousy and hatred. The cloak had come to represent those things about Joseph that they regarded with violent hate.

**24. And they took him, and cast him into a pit: and the pit was empty, there was no water in it.**

Joseph was then thrown into the pit, from which he could not escape. The water pits, or cisterns, were dug out of the ground much like a bottle, large at the bottom but with only a small opening at the top. This left anyone in the pit with no way of climbing up; he would have to be pulled up if he were ever to be released. It is probably because of the security of the pit that the brothers were willing to set aside killing him for the time being.

The pit was apparently out of earshot and probably out of sight of the brothers as they sat down to eat. As they ate they saw a caravan making its way across the desert in a southward direction. These were Ishamelites on their way from Gilead with spices, balm and myrrh, all products of Gilead, on their way to Egypt. Gilead was east of the Jordan River, a mountainous country where shrubs and plants that bore these substances grew in abundance. Dothan would have been on the caravan route that led from Gilead to Egypt. This proved to be significant in this situation of Joseph, for Judah proposed that he be sold to the Ishamelites for profit. Apparently Judah had no more wished to kill Joseph than did Reuben. If they would sell Joseph to the Ishmaelites as a slave then they would realize a profit and would not be guilty of the death of their brother. The plan appealed to the men and they concluded to sell him.

Meanwhile a group of Midianite merchants who were also passing by heard the cries of Joseph in the pit. They lifted him out without the brothers being aware of what had happened. The Midianites then sold Joseph to the Ishmaelites for 20 pieces of silver. The Ishmaelites would be able to sell the young Hebrew as a slave for a handsome profit once they arrived in Egypt.

III. RESULTS OF JEALOUSY (Genesis 37:29-36)

(Verses 29, 30, 35, 36 are not in the printed text.)

It was Reuben who returned to the pit to draw Joseph out so they could sell him to the Ishmaelites. In the way of Eastern mourning, Reuben tore his clothing in distress. The fact that he felt a personal responsibility for the safety of Joseph is seen in his words, "The child is not; and I, whither shall I go?" (v. 30). This is further indication that as the firstborn of Jacob, he would be held accountable for Joseph's safety.

**31. And they took Joseph's coat and killed a kid of the goats, and dipped the coat in the blood.**

Joseph's ten older brothers killed a goat and dipped his robe in its blood so they could pretend that he had been killed by some beast. Such a ruse would not be successful in modern times, with blood analysis and other scientific examinations, but this would be compelling proof in that day that Joseph had been killed by a beast.

**32. And they sent the coat of many colours, and they brought it to their father; and said, This have we found: know now whether it be thy son's coat or no.**

The sons followed through with their plans and carried the bloodstained garment to their father. The culprits asked him to examine the robe and determine whether or not it was his son's. Note that they did not call him their brother, but rather, Jacob's son.

**33. And he knew it, and said, It is my son's coat; an evil beast hath devoured him; Joseph is without doubt rent in pieces.**

Jacob reached the conclusion that they wished him to, that a wild beast had killed and devoured Joseph. He visualized Joseph as being torn to pieces by the beast. This was a terrible thing to inflict upon a loving father in order to cover their own vile tracks.

Do you feel that the incidents leading up to Joseph's being sold and taken to Egypt were so predetermined by God they had to happen? Explain.

**34. And Jacob rent his clothes, and put sackcloth upon his loins, and mourned for his son many days.**

Jacob went through the Eastern custom of mourning by tearing his garments and putting sackcloth upon himself. As he mourned for many days his sons and daughters endeavored to comfort him but their efforts failed and Jacob spoke some of the saddest words in the human experience: "For I will go down into the grave unto my son mourning" (v. 35).

Joseph's brothers were frustrated in all of their desires. They did not succeed in their intention to kill him; they did not reap a reward from selling him; they did not have the satisfaction of knowing that he was dead. Now they had to watch while a grief-stricken father poured out lamentation for his son. There has never been a more complete frustration of anyone's intention to do evil.

As for Joseph, his life had a definite change of direction. In Egypt, the Midianites sold him to Potiphar, the Pharaoh's captain of the guard. As a slave in Potiphar's house, Joseph would be in a position to be used of the Lord in great and extraordinary ways. Future events would only add to the irony of the brothers' hatred and their desire to see him out of the way. His life would be living proof that "all things work together for good to them that love God, to them who are the called according to his purpose" (Romans 8:28).

## REVIEW QUESTIONS

1. How old was Joseph when the incidents of this lesson happened?

2. What were the conditions that gave rise to jealousy toward Joseph?

3. How had the stage been set for the brothers of Joseph to take revenge on him?

4. Discuss the extent of the trip Joseph made to check on his brothers. What was their reaction to the visit?

5. List the practical lessons for today that can be drawn from today's study.

## GOLDEN TEXT HOMILY

"LOVE IS PATIENT AND KIND; LOVE IS NOT JEALOUS OR BOASTFUL" (1 Corinthians 13:4, *King James Version*).

The Apostle Paul supplies for us the fundamental excellencies of love: its patience toward evil and kindly activity in good (13:4). The word **patient** in the New Testament always describes patience with people and not patience with circumstances. It is used in reference to God and His relationship to me. In our dealings with others, the love of God is best exemplified with the same pa-

tience that God exercises with us. This is the more excellent way to which the apostle refers to earlier.

It is the simple truth that such patience is not the sign of weakness as some might suppose to believe. Rather, it is a clear indication of the workings of divine grace in the heart of the individual.

The fruit of such kindness is seen as a product of Christian duty, which is doing good to others. There are many ways in which we are to do good as we have opportunity. We may do good to others by promoting their esteem and acceptance among others, by sinners in mind of their misery and danger and by being the instruments of awakening them to conversion and bringing them to Christ. Thus we may be of the number of those whom we read about in Daniel 12:3: "They that turn many to righteousness [shall shine] as the stars for ever and ever."

We are obliged to do by the example of our heavenly Father, for He "is kind unto the unthankful and to the evil" (Luke 6:35). The command is that we "be merciful, as [our] Father also is merciful" (v. 36).—**Larry D. Cripps, LT, Chaplain Corps, U. S. Navy. Presently assigned to 4th Marines, 3d Marine Division, FMF, Camp Schwab, Okinawa, Japan, as Assistant Regimental Chaplain.**

## SENTENCE SERMONS

SATAN SEEKS TO DESTROY the purposes of God by creating a spirit of jealousy.
**—Selected**

SUSPICION AND JEALOUSY never did help any man in any situation.
**—Abraham Lincoln**

THOSE WHO ARE GREEN with envy often become red with anger.
**—"Notes and Quotes"**

ONE MUST BE emptied of jealousy to be filled with love.
**—"Notes and Quotes"**

MORE HEARTS pine away in secret anguish for unkindness from those who should be their comforters than for any other calamity in life.
**—Edward Young**

## EVANGELISTIC APPLICATION

GOD'S GRACE CAN DELIVER FROM
THE BONDAGE OF JEALOUSY.

Serving the Lord is not to be taken as
immunity from oppression, assault,
affronter, hardship, or even momentary
failure at times! In the language of a
recent hit tune. "He never promised you
a rose garden." Even Jesus, our example
in all things, was tempted—He suffered;
He died; His way was the way of blood.
Any notion that the Christ-way is for the
sissy, the chicken, or the timid should be
dispelled immediately!

The Bible speaks of "enduring to the
end" to be saved. It talks of being
vigilant, sober, watching, moving straight
forward all the time!

In John Bunyan's *Pilgrim's Progress*,
two fellows, Timorous and Mistrust spent
their time in flight, trying to run away
from evil! Theirs was a hopeless effort as
they ran into even greater evils because
of lions in their way. On the other hand,
Christian—you and I, if you please—
continued his forward course with per-
serverance, and things were not as bad
as they seemed! Indeed, Bunyan wrote:

This hill, though high I covet to
    ascend;
The difficulty will not me offend
For I perceive the way of life lies
    here:
Come, pluck up heart, let's neither
    faint nor fear:
Better though difficult, the right way
    to go,
Than wrong, though easy, where the
    end is woe.

Songwriter Andrae Crouch says it best,
he being a modern-day psalmist; "I've
had many tears and sorrows—questions
for tomorrow—so many times I didn't
know right from wrong. But in every

situation—God gave blessed consolation
—my trials only come to make me strong.
And through it all . . . I've learned
to depend upon the Lord."

Through what? The "snare of the fowl-
er" or man-made danger! Yes, through
that! And through noisome pestilence
or perhaps epidemics! Through the arrow that flieth by day, or deeds or words
of evil doers. THROUGH IT ALL!

Do not be beaten down with the perilous nature of living today! Like Job,
you'll get a "fair trial from God." "But
he knoweth the way that I take: When
he hath tried me, I shall come forth as
gold."—**A. M. Long**

## ILLUMINATING THE LESSON

"Remorse ruins serenity; our infideli-
ties, which we so eagerly anticipate and
which pass from expectation through enjoyment into memory, haunt us evermore," Harry Emerson Fosdick has written. "Ill will spoils serenity, as does the
cherished grudge, the mean vindictive-
ness. Jealousy wrecks serenity, as in
the old story where, from the day he began enviously eyeing David, Saul never
had a peaceful moment more. Engross-
ing ambition, where a man's ego becomes the clamorous center of the universe—that exiles serenity."—**The Power
to See It Through**

## DAILY DEVOTIONAL GUIDE

M. Foolishness of Jealousy. 1 Samuel
    18:5-9
T. The Strength of Love. Song of Sol-
    omon 8:6, 7
W. False Ambition. Mark 10:35-41
T. Disruptive Jealousy. 1 Corinthians 3:
    1-4
F. Jealousy. Philippians 2:1-11
S. Wisdom From Above. James 3:13-18

# Resisting Temptations

**(Joseph)**

**Study Text:** Genesis 39:1-23

**Supplemental References:** 2 Samuel 11:1-5; Proverbs 5:1-14; 6:20-32; 7:6-27; Matthew 4:1-11; James 1:2-15; 4:7-10

**Time:** Probably between 1800 and 1780 B.C.

**Place:** Egypt

**Golden Text:** "Blessed is the man that endureth temptation: for when he is tried, he shall receive the crown of life, which the Lord hath promised to them that love him" (James 1:12).

**Central Truth:** The believer can resist temptation by the power of God.

**Evangelistic Emphasis:** For those who have yielded to temptation, forgiveness is available through Christ.

## Printed Text

**Genesis 39:11.** And it came to pass about this time, that Joseph went into the house to do his business; and there was none of the men of the house there within.

**12. And she caught him by his garment, saying, Lie with me: and he left his garment in her hand, and fled, and got him out.**

13. And it came to pass, when she saw that he had left his garment in her hand, and was fled forth,

**14. That she called unto the men of her house, and spake unto them, saying, See, he hath brought in an Hebrew unto us to mock us; he came in unto me to lie with me, and I cried with a loud voice:**

15. And it came to pass, when he heard that I lifted up my voice and cried, that he left his garment with me, and fled, and. got him out.

**16. And she laid up his garment by her, until his lord came home.**

17. And she spake unto him according to these words, saying, The Hebrew servant, which thou hast brought unto us, came in unto me to mock me:

**18. And it came to pass, as I lifted up my voice and cried, that he left his garment with me, and fled out.**

19. And it came to pass, when his master heard the words of his wife, which she spake unto him, saying, After this manner did thy servant to me; that his wrath was kindled.

**20. And Joseph's master took him, and put him into the prison, a place where the king's prisoners were bound: and he was there. in the prison.**

21. But the Lord was with Joseph, and shewed him mercy, and gave him favour in the sight of the keeper of the prison.

**22. And the keeper of the prison committed to Joseph's hand all the prisoners that were in the prison; and whatsoever they did there, he was the doer of it.**

23. The keeper of the prison looked not to any thing that was under his hand; because the Lord was with him, and that which he did, the Lord made it to prosper.

## LESSON OUTLINE

I. PROSPERITY

II. TEMPTATION

III. VICTORY

## LESSON EXPOSITION

INTRODUCTION

Jacob continued to see his own wild ways repeated in his children for many years. This should not be interpreted as divine retribution, but a natural outcome of early parental example. The children of Jacob did many things that were worse than Jacob did, which is also a natural consequence, for children frequently out do their parents in whatever they do.

Genesis 38 tells the unfortunate story of Judah's marriage to a Canaanite woman and their unworthy offspring.

There had been earlier occasions of sorrow that regarded daughter Dinah, who was abused in Genesis 34 by a man named Shechem, and of the violence that the sons of Jacob brought upon the city of Shechem. The most tragic circumstance in Jacob's household, however, was the hatred that existed between his sons. The patriarch had failed to bind them together in brotherly love and affection. They regarded themselves more as rivals than as companions and finally stooped to the base treatment of Joseph that was described in Genesis 37.

Now we see Joseph in servitude in Egypt while his brothers live and practice a lie in Canaan. Jacob is destined to spend years in grief over a son he believes to be dead.

It is a sorry situation that offers no relief, and the story will grow darker still before it begins to turn upward. In the end, however, it will be seen that God took all the dark threads of family misfortune to weave a pattern for His glory. In the same way God will take the dark threads of our lives and form them into beauty if we commit them to Him.

I. PROSPERITY (Genesis 39:1-6)

(Verses 1-6 are not in the printed text.)

Although he was a slave, Joseph was so successful in his affairs for Potiphar that he soon rose in station. Potiphar, a ranking officer of the Pharaoh's guard, was a wealthy man who obviously had a large estate. Every time he placed Joseph over any part of his business, that business prospered and grew. God gave Joseph special gifts that made him successful in his affairs.

It is interesting that the word **prosperous** is used twice. The word **prosper** means "success," so that anything that was successful was said to prosper. In Numbers 14:41 Moses says that transgression shall not prosper; in Deuteronomy 28:29 he says if the Hebrews turned from the commandments of the Lord they should not prosper in their ways. In Proverbs 28:13 Solomon says, "He that covereth his sins shall not prosper"; and Isaiah 54:17 says, "No weapon that is formed against thee shall prosper." It is important that we observe that the word in no wise refers to wealth in these references, but only to ultimate success. In the same sense, those who succeed in life are said to prosper. Isaiah, speaking of Christ, says "the pleasure of the Lord shall prosper in his hand" (53:10). Isaiah uses the word **prosper** most emphatically: "So shall my word be that goeth forth out of my mouth: it shall not return unto me void, but it shall accomplish that which I please, and it shall prosper in the thing whereto I sent it" (55:11).

Throughout the Word of God, the word **prosper** means the accomplishment of good and the success of an endeavor. It may or may not involve material possessions. When Joseph was called "a prosperous man" he was a slave in the household of Potiphar and certainly not a wealthy man. His accomplishments turned out well and he rose in station until he became the overseer of Potiphar's vast estate. Joseph was so skilled in the management of the Egyptian's affairs that "the blessing of the Lord was upon all that he had in the house, and in the field" (v. 5).

How do you account for the special skills and wisdom Joseph manifested? Did he have special training?

It pleased this Egyptian official to trust the management of all his business to Joseph, for he had seen in him scrupulous honesty and astuteness in his decisions. Joseph came to know more about Potiphar's affairs, and the tally of his holdings, than Potiphar himself did. This is stewardship at its highest level.

II. TEMPTATION (Genesis 39:7-18)

(Verses 7-10 are not in the printed text.)

Verse 6 says that "Joseph was a goodly person, and well favored." This has reference to his physical appearance: he was a strikingly attractive man. When a man is mentally astute and physically attractive he attracts admiration and attention among those who see him. Generally that attention is good and amounts only to popularity, but it also has the result of making that man the object of desire to unworthy and wanton women. In this case, the unfortunate thing occurred with dangerous results: for it was Potiphar's wife who lusted after Joseph and urged him to make carnal love to her.

If she had been anyone else Joseph could have rebuffed her and that would have ended the matter. With his master's wife, however, Joseph would have defiled himself by yielding and incurred her hatred by resisting. He therefore reasoned with her with what amounted to an appeal not to ask him to do that which was wrong. Potiphar, being an active captain of the Pharaoh's guard, was frequently away from home, no doubt for extended periods of time. To yield to her approaches would be to sin against his master. More than that, to follow her invitation would be to sin against God.

**11. And it came to pass about this time, that Joseph went into the house to do his business; and there was none of the men of the house there within.**

' After days of avoiding the carnal

suggestions of Potiphar's wife, probably by staying away from her as much as possible, he found it necessary to go personally into the house for some business that needed attention. Joseph would not have lived in Potiphar's house but in quarters provided for the Egyptian's servants. Only those servants who did the household work would have routinely gone into the living quarters. On this particular day none of the servants were present. It is all together possible, even likely, that the scheming woman arranged for them to be away.

**12. And she caught him by his garment, saying, Lie with me: and he left his garment in her hand, and fled, and got him out.**

Now Potiphar's wife turned from seductive words to physical force: she took Joseph by his clothing and endeavored to pull him to her. It was in that moment that the preconditioning of his mind took over. He did not tarry and debate whether or not he should yield to her temptations, for that decision had already been made. He tore away from her with such vigor that his garment was left in her hand. This suggests how forceably she had taken hold of him and with what equal force he tore away from her.

Those who wait until the moment of temptation to decide whether or not to resist are the ones who most frequently yield to temptation. The only safe course is for the Christian to settle it in his mind beforehand that his answer is no, he will not yield to the temptation of sin. Daniel and his three Hebrew friends experienced the benefits of setting their minds against sin beforehand. In Daniel 3:18 they said to Nebuchadnezzar, "We will not serve thy gods, nor worship the golden image which thou hast set up." Daniel, in defiance of the king's decree that no man should pray except to him, went into his house and knelt upon his knees three times a day and prayed and gave thanks unto God. These men did not vacillate when the time of temptation came, because they had already established in their hearts what they would do (Daniel 1:8).

What is the secret to being fully prepared to resist any temptation?

**13. And it came to pass, when she saw that he had left his garment in her hand, and was fled forth,**

Potiphar's wife was outraged that Joseph would resist her in such a fashion. One can only imagine her astonishment and frustration as she held Joseph's garment without him being in it. He had fled with such determination that he was gone from the room and the house and temptation.

**14. That she called unto the men of her house, and spake unto them, saying, See, he hath brought in an Hebrew unto us to mock us; he came in unto me to lie with me, and I cried with a loud voice:**

In her frustration and wrath, Potiphar's wife called for her household servants and fabricated a lie about Joseph. Her words also had a touch of ridicule toward her husband, for it was he who had placed Joseph in command of the house as well as the field (v. 5). It was also possible that such a statement might gain her the sympathy or support of the household men, for they may well have been jealous of the fact that Joseph had been brought in as supervisor over them.

**15. And it came to pass, when he heard that I lifted up my voice and cried, that he left his garment with me, and fled, and got him out.**

The woman's lie that she had cried out with a loud voice probably did not ring true even with the servants. They were not so far away that she could not have called to them, so certainly they would have heard her if she had screamed with the terror of a woman about to be assaulted. Her lie was so patent that no further mention of the men of the house is made nor is it likely that her attempt to seduce Joseph was her first act of carnal evil. Everything she did had the marks of a promiscuous woman who lived without morals or faithfulness to her husband. A woman who has always

been faithful in marriage is not likely to make so determined an effort at infidelity as she did nor would she likely be so enraged that she was willing to hurt her husband and sacrifice the life of an innocent young man. Hers was certainly not a single evil act or even an evil of the moment. It was an evil of habit that came from a lifestyle of deceit.

**16. And she laid up his garment by her, until his lord came home.**

Further indication of the woman's habitual evil is the fact that she could so deliberately keep the garment and nurse her lie until Potiphar came home from his official service to Pharaoh. The wording in this verse indicates that he had been gone for a period of time. He did not come in from a day's absence but "[he] came home," which implies a longer absence.

**17. And she spake unto him according to these words, saying, The Hebrew servant, which thou hast brought unto us, came in unto me to mock me:**

By the time Potiphar came home, his wife had no doubt practiced the lines of her story and was able to give them easily and freely. She repeated the story she had told to the men of the house, even the mildly accusative line that it was he who had brought the Hebrew servant into their life. She wanted him to feel the full responsibility, and possibly the guilt, of having brought over his business the man who had endeavored to rob him of his greatest treasure, his wife. Here she uses the words "to mock me" but in speaking to the menservants she had said "to mock us." In the first instance she had been trying to gain their loyalty. In the latter instance she only wants to show herself as the victim of Joseph's treachery.

**18. And it came to pass, as I lifted up my voice and cried, that he left his garment with me, and fled out.**

Her lie regarding Joseph's fleeing out of the house and leaving his garment with her remained the same as she had told to the men of the house. Now her trap was cleverly laid and Joseph's trial is complete. In saving his honor, he had incurred the wrath of a woman and risked the loss of position and life.

III. VICTORY (Genesis 39:19-23)

**19. And it came to pass, when his master heard the words of his wife, which she spake unto him, saying, After this manner did thy servant to me; that his wrath was kindled.**

Potiphar reacted to the report of his wife much as she expected him to. His wrath was kindled, no doubt mingled with hurt and confusion. He had trusted Joseph completely and had felt complete faith in him.

The scheming wife worked at creating in Potiphar a sense of responsibility for Joseph's behavior. She called Joseph "the Hebrew servant, which **thou** hast brought unto us" (v. 17). In verse 19 she said, "After this manner did **thy** servant." There is reproach against her husband in such words. She was implying that if Potiphar had not brought the Hebrew servant into the household this terrible thing would never have happened.

**20. And Joseph's master took him, and put him into the prison, a place where the king's prisoners were bound: and he was there in the prison.**

Potiphar had Joseph put in prison. Harsh as being falsely imprisoned is, it was an act of clemency, for those guilty of such crimes were usually put to death. For a slave to attempt the violation of his master's wife would certainly have resulted in his death. The fact that Potiphar did not execute Joseph indicates that he did not fully believe his wife's story. Something in what she told him did not apparently ring true.

**21. But the Lord was with Joseph, and shewed him mercy, and gave him favour in the sight of the keeper of the prison.**

Even in this new misfortune the hand of the Lord is clearly seen. To begin with, Joseph was placed among the king's prisoners, members of the king's staff who had fallen into disfavor. The Lord showed Joseph further mercy by giving

him the goodwill of his jailer. This would assure Joseph of better treatment than he might otherwise expect and would also set the stage for further benefits.

**22. And the keeper of the prison committed to Joseph's hand all the prisoners that were in the prison; and whatsoever they did there, he was the doer of it.**

Joseph became a trusted prisoner, what is called a trustee in modern times, which included some supervision over the other prisoners. This kept him out of a common cell and out of solitary confinement; it gave him the opportunity for communication with the prisoners on a continuing basis. It also made him responsible for the prison activities. Step by step along the course, God would take the many bad things that happened to Joseph and make them into ultimate good.

**23. The keeper of the prison looked not to any thing that was under his hand; because the Lord was with him, and that which he did, the Lord made it to prosper.**

Once again we encounter the word **prosper,** which means that Joseph's activities in prison turned out well. He was so successful in the discharge of his prison assignments that the keeper never had to bother himself with them. He knew that if Joseph was in charge of a matter it would be done well; he knew that Joseph's reports would be accurate, fair and dependable. The key to this success was the fact that the Lord was with him. The Lord gave these blessings and grace to Joseph for his own sake in one way, for certainly he deserved it, but He was also working for the protection and preservation of all the family of Jacob. Israel was becoming a people and God's hand was upon them.

**REVIEW QUESTIONS**

1. Review briefly the events that led up to Joseph's being in Egypt and his favored position in Potiphar's household.

2. Was Joseph too careless in frequenting the household of Potiphar when "none of the men of the house" were present?

3. Why was Potiphar's wife so anxious to bring false accusation against Joseph?

4. Discuss the word "prosperous" as it relates to Joseph's period of servitude in Egypt.

5. Should Joseph have been given a time to give his side of the story? Why would Potiphar not allow for such a defense?

## GOLDEN TEXT HOMILY

"BLESSED IS THE MAN THAT ENDURETH TEMPTATION: FOR WHEN HE IS TRIED, HE SHALL RECEIVE THE CROWN OF LIFE, WHICH THE LORD HATH PROMISED TO THEM THAT LOVE HIM" (James 1:12).

There is a difference between resisting temptation (James 1:13) and enduring trial or testing (vv. 2, 12). Resisting temptation has to do with our saying no to a tendency in us which by varying degrees of frequency and intensity is awakened, and then seeks to lure us toward making a choice contrary to what we believe is pleasing to the Lord. There is no sin in being tempted, for temptation is something we each face as one of the realities of being human. James reminds us in verse 13 that under no circumstances are we ever tempted by God. God does, however, always provide ways for us to be victorious in the face of temptation (1 Corinthians 10:12, 13).

Are there times when God himself may put us through "testing"? Yes! Never with the hope that we'll fail, but that we'll grow in faith. Those are the times we must trust, pray, and in spite of everything, continue to march.

"Endureth temptation" in verse 12 is correctly translated as "perseveres under trial" *(New International Version)*, or "endures the temptations and trials" *(Phillips Translation)*. God puts us through a lifelong process of strengthening and refinement that takes the mix of life and uses it with the goal of making us better fit for real-world living and ministry.

At those junctures in our pilgrimage where we do fail a test, it is only because of our choosing and not because God in some way withholds the means

by which we could pass. Taking the lifelong view, we need to also remember that failing a test doesn't mean we fail the course, for salvation is not by works but by grace.

Reality for most of us is not straight **A's.** James says that the person who passes a test is blessed!—**Robert J. Jenkins, D. Min., Chaplain (Major) United States Army**

## SENTENCE SERMONS

THE BELIEVER can resist temptation by the power of God.
**—Selected**

KITES RISE HIGHEST against the wind —not with it.
**—Sir Winston Churchill**

ONE OF THE HIGH TESTS of our personal living, is not how we travel on the highway, but how we take the forced detours.
**—"Megiddo Message"**

TEMPTATIONS ARE like tramps. Treat them kindly and they return bringing others with them.
**—"The Link"**

BETTER TO SHUN the bait than struggle in the snare.
**—John Dryden**

## EVANGELISTIC APPLICATION

FOR THOSE WHO HAVE YIELDED TO TEMPTATION, FORGIVENESS IS AVAILABLE THROUGH CHRIST.

The seal is significant of property and also suggestive of treasure. We do not seal the unimportant letter. The affixing of a seal distinguishes the valuable. When the Holy Spirit seals the soul it testifies that we are of infinite value to God. Everybody counts! We are precious in the sight of the Lord.

A country minister told me of an untutored countryman who dwells in the Yorkshire dales; I mean untutored by the schools, but grandly trained and finished of the Spirit. He is a man of deeply spiritual nature, and enjoys most intimate communion with His Lord. His prayers are quaint and unconventional, and he speaks with delightful and yet reverent familiarity to his God. A little while ago, in one of his public prayers, he communed in this wise: "Lord, I must be worth something! There must be some hidden treasure within me! Burglars never visit empty houses, and the devil is always visiting me!" The reasoning was perfectly sound, and based upon New Testament teaching. Much sought implies much treasure. When the burglar is about there is something to be gained. When the Evil One sees the Lord's seal, he beholds a treasure he longs to loot.

## ILLUMINATING THE LESSON

In 1840 Bishop Selwyn, who was a missionary among the cannibal Maoris of New Zealand, wrote: "I am in the midst of sinful people, who have been accustomed to sin uncontrolled from their youth. If I speak to a native on murder, infanticide, cannibalism, and adultery, they laugh in my face and tell me I may think these acts are bad, but

they are good for a native, and they cannot conceive any harm in them. But on the contrary when I tell them that these and other sins brought the Son of God, the great Creator of the universe, from his eternal glory to this world to be incarnate and to be made a curse and to die—then they open their eyes and ears and mouths, and wish to hear more, and presently they acknowledge themselves sinners, and say they will leave off their sins."

## DAILY DEVOTIONAL GUIDE

M. Falling Into Temptation. 2 Samuel 11: 1-5
T. Tragedy of Immorality. Proverbs 5:1-14
W. The Snare of Sin. Proverbs 7:6-27
T. Victory Over Temptation. Matthew 4: 1-11
F. Power in the Lord. Ephesians 6:11-13
S. Resisting the Devil. James 4:7-10

# God's Providential Care

**(Joseph)**
**Study Text:** Genesis 40:1 through 41:57
**Supplemental References:** Psalm 105:16-22; Daniel 2:46-49; 5:29; 6:25-28; Acts 23:12-30; 27:27-44; 2 Corinthians 1:3-11; Philippians 2:5-11
**Time:** Opinions vary, but generally thought to be around 1775 B.C.
**Place:** Egypt, probably Memphis
**Golden Text:** "We know that all things work together for good to them that love God, to them who are called according to his purpose" (Romans 8:28).
**Central Truth:** In all things God is working to accomplish His purpose in the life of the believer.
**Evangelistic Emphasis:** God often places His faithful servants in a position of usefulness as a witness to the lost.

## Printed Text

**Genesis 41:33.** Now therefore let Pharaoh look out a man discreet and wise, and set him over the land of Egypt.

**34. Let Pharaoh do this, and let him appoint officers over the land, and take up the fifth part of the land of Egypt in the seven plenteous years.**

35. And let them gather all the food of those good years that come, and lay up corn under the hand of Pharaoh, and let them keep food in the cities.

**36. And that food shall be for store to the land against the seven years of famine, which shall be in the land of Egypt; that the land perish not through the famine.**

37. And the thing was good in the eyes of Pharaoh, and in the eyes of all his servants.

**38. And Pharaoh said unto his servants, Can we find such a one as this** **is, a man in whom the Spirit of God is?**

39. And Pharaoh said unto Joseph, Forasmuch as God hath shewed thee all this, there is none so discreet and wise as thou art:

**40. Thou shalt be over my house, and according unto thy word shall all my people be ruled: only in the throne will I be greater than thou.**

41. And Pharaoh said unto Joseph, See, I have set thee over all the land of Egypt.

**42. And Pharaoh took off his ring from his hand, and put it upon Joseph's hand, and arrayed him in vestures of fine linen, and put a gold chain about his neck;**

43. And he made him to ride in the second chariot which he had; and they cried before him, Bow the knee: and he made him ruler over all the land of Egypt.

---

**LESSON OUTLINE**
I. REVELATION FROM GOD

II. FAVOR WITH MEN
III. DIVINE PROVISION

299

## LESSON EXPOSITION

INTRODUCTION

Joseph reached the bottom of his misfortunes during the time he was in prison in Egypt. Genesis 40 tells the well-known story of the dreams of the Pharaoh's butler and baker, who were also in prison with Joseph. Each of these men related his dream to Joseph, and Joseph was able to tell the meaning of the dream. When Joseph interpreted the butler's dream to mean that he would be released from prison within three days, Joseph asked the butler to remember him to the Pharaoh. If the Pharaoh could hear how he had been stolen out of Canaan and that he had done nothing in Egypt worthy of imprisonment, perhaps the Pharaoh   would show him clemency.

The baker's dream did not end up so well for him. Three days following his dream the baker was executed.

With the butler, it is said that he was restored to his full position "and he gave the cup into Pharaoh's hand" (Genesis 40:21). Joseph hoped that he might gain clemency when the butler related this case to the Pharaoh, but that was not to be the case. Verse 23 says, that the chief butler did not remember Joseph, but forgot him. This brought Joseph to the low point of the series of misfortunes which had befallen him.

This story is one of the greatest examples in Scripture of how God can take a series of misfortunes and work them to eventual good. There were five definite stages in Joseph's misfortune, not one of which was good: (1) he was hated by his brethren, and there is nothing good in hate; (2) he was sold as a slave into Egypt, and there is nothing good about slavery; (3) he was lied about by Potiphar's wife, and there is nothing good about being lied about; (4) he was falsely imprisoned, and there is nothing good about unjust imprisonment; (5) he was forgotten by the butler, and there is nothing good about being isolated and forgotten. With such a series of misfortunes, it does not seem likely that any good could come to Joseph.

But such reasoning does not take God into consideration. God in His providence did make good of a bad situation. Two years after the butler was released, the Pharaoh himself dreamed a disturbing dream and the butler told him about his experience with Joseph (Genesis 41:1-13). The Pharaoh sent for Joseph and related his dream to him. It was at this point that the affairs of Joseph turned upward at last and it was seen "that all things work together for good to them that love God, to them who are the called according to his purpose" (Romans 8:28).

I. REVELATION FROM GOD (Genesis 41:25-36)

(Verses 25-32 are not in the printed text.)

The Pharaoh's dream had been of seven fat cows grazing on the banks of the Nile River. Then seven lean cows (poor and very gaunt, such as he had never seen in all the land of Egypt) ate up the seven well-fed cows. A second dream was of seven full and good ears of corn that were swallowed up by seven thin and withered ears of corn. Joseph said to the Pharaoh that the dream was not two, but only one. He also tells Pharaoh that the dreams are from God and for a purpose.

---

Discuss the nature of Pharaoh's dreams. How would Joseph have known that the dreams were one and from God?

---

The interpretation of the dream was that Egypt would enjoy seven years of unusual and continuous abundance. These seven years were represented by the seven fat cows and the seven full ears. Following the plenteous years there would be seven years of extreme famine, represented by the cows and the ears that were lean and famished. The fact that the lean cows and ears had devoured the fat ones signified that the famine would be so great that it would wipe out all benefits of the seven good years.

**30. And there shall arise after them**

seven years of famine; and all the plenty shall be forgotten in the land of Egypt; and the famine shall consume the land;

**31. And the plenty shall not be known in the land by reason of that famine following; for it shall be very grievous.**

Joseph told Pharaoh that the dream had come to him twice in order to emphasize that it was a thing "established by God, and God will shortly bring it to pass" (v. 32). The meaning was that the fulfillment of the dream was both inescapable and off or even delayed. There was a reason, however, that the Lord had shown this to Pharaoh, and that was so he could prepare for it.

**32. Now therefore let Pharaoh look out a man discreet and wise, and set him over the land of Egypt.**

Joseph then turned from interpreter to advisor. Pharaoh would certainly be pleased to hear the counsel of a man capable of interpreting the dream to him.

How do people generally react to dreams today? Are there reasons to be skeptical about dreams? Explain.

The fact that God had given him the dream was proof that God wished him to prepare for it. The event would be unavoidable but the result of it could be changed if Pharaoh would be prudent with the knowledge he had. He should therefore appoint a person of skill and wisdom to direct the land of Egypt during the seven good and seven evil years.

**34. Let Pharaoh do this, and let him appoint officers over the land, and take up the fifth part of the land of Egypt in the seven plenteous years.**

Serving under the general director of the conservation program would be officers who, it would appear, would serve in the various parts of the land. This management structure would see that in all parts of Egypt steps were taken to avert total catastrophe when the bad years came. The management team would requisition 20 percent of all crops produced in the land during the seven good years. Although this was a stiff amount of their produce to give to the government, it was probably offset in considerable measure by the abundance that would be produced during the good years. The fact that one-fifth saved during the seven good years would suffice to supply the land for the seven bad years gives some indication of just how bounteous those good years would be.

**35. And let them gather all the food of those good years that come, and lay up corn under the hand of Pharaoh, and let them keep food in the cities.**

The Egyptian farmers were not to be trusted to do this conservation and preservation work on a voluntary basis. The officers would have to collect the grain and store it in the various cities under the supervision of the Pharaoh's officers. The grain reserve would be kept in government granaries so that the people could not abuse the wealth of the good years.

**36. And that food shall be for store to the land against the seven years of famine, which shall be in the land of Egypt; that the land perish not through the famine.**

Although the program would be under the supervision of the government, specifically the general director of it, the grain would be for the use of the people and not merely the government. It would be for their preservation during the lean years, and it would assure the survival of the land in time of famine. Joseph was suggesting that the force of the government be employed to see that every farmer followed a rigid program of saving for the future.

It was a sound program that would achieve its purpose and then would be made into a law of the land of Egypt (47:26).

II. FAVOR WITH MEN (Genesis 41:37-45)

**37. And the thing was good in the eyes of Pharaoh, and in the eyes of all his servants.**

Joseph's proposal seemed sound and

practical to Pharaoh. It had become clear to the king that Joseph was a man of God, whose counsel should be followed. If he could interpret the dreams of the ruler, then certainly God would equally direct him in providing a solution to the problem that was forthcoming. The Egyptian aids to the king were also impressed with the proposal.

**38. And Pharaoh said unto his servants, Can we find such a one as this is, a man in whom the Spirit of God is?**

Pharaoh discussed the matter with his men and wondered where a man who possessed the Spirit of God could be found. His concern that a man with the Spirit of God be found is interesting, since he was certainly not a man of spiritual understanding. Certainly he was no servant of Jehovah God, yet Joseph had mentioned God freely in his interpretation of the dream and in his solution to the catastrophe. These are the things he said: "God shall give Pharaoh an answer of peace" (v. 16); "God hath shewed Pharaoh what he is about to do" (v. 25); "What God is about to do he sheweth unto Pharaoh" (v. 28); "The thing is established by God, and God will shortly bring it to pass" (v. 32). With such an emphasis upon God's hand in this matter it was impressed upon Pharaoh that he needed a godly man to administer the program.

**39. And Pharaoh said unto Joseph, Forasmuch as God hath shewed thee all this, there is none so discreet and wise as thou art:**

Pharaoh and his men probably tried to think of an Egyptian who would fill this need of having the Spirit of God. Naturally there was no such man, for the priests of Egypt were more along the order of magicians. It probably did not take very long for them to reach the conclusion that Joseph was the most suitable person to head up the nationwide preservation program. It was he who had been able to interpret the dream and it was he who had emphasized that God had given the dream to Pharaoh for a purpose. Joseph had spoken with such clarity and conviction and had followed

with such sensible predictions and proposals that the king was obviously impressed with him as a person who could succeed in the work that needed to be done. He saw Joseph as a divinely endowed person; that is, one in whom the Spirit of God dwelt.

It is not likely that Joseph had expected or desired that he be the person to direct the program. His wish was much more immediate, and that was to be released from prison and allowed to return to Canaan to his family. There is no reason to imagine that he hoped to become an important person within the Egyptian nation. The Pharaoh no doubt saw this sincerity and lack of self-seeking in Joseph's demeanor. This made the Hebrew all the more desirable.

**40. Thou shalt be over my house, and according unto thy word shall all my people be ruled: only in the throne will I be greater than thou.**

**41. And Pharaoh said unto Joseph, See, I have set thee over all the land of Egypt.**

The king elevated Joseph to a position of importance second only to his own. He was to be more than an advisor, but a ruler with full authority from the king. Whatever Joseph would do would have the full force of the king behind it. In monarchies such men are known as prime ministers or viceroys.

**42. And Pharaoh took off his ring from his hand, and put it upon Joseph's hand, and arrayed him in vestures of fine linen, and put a gold chain about his neck;**

Joseph was arrayed in the appropriate clothing to signify his high office. It would have been similar to the purpose of a uniform in our way of understanding. Being viceroy to the king made it necessary that his vestments be rich and impressive. The king's signet ring was actually a royal seal which was used to impress official documents and orders and decrees. Anything that bore the king's seal had his royal power behind it.

The gold chain that was put about Joseph's neck was possibly an emblem that denoted his office, but it is more likely that this was a personal reward to

Joseph for the service he had already rendered. The clothing he wore was probably the only designation of his absolute powers. The king would certainly do something to reward him personally, and the gold chain is not known to have any other use than that.

**43. And he made him to ride in the second chariot which he had; and they cried before him, Bow the knee: and he made him ruler over all the land of Egypt.**

In all processions the Pharaoh rode in the first chariot because he was the king. Second only to his chariot would be that designated for Joseph. This must be a continuing visible evidence that Pharaoh had made him second in the kingdom, second in power, second in status and second in importance. This is what we generally call protocol, those visible matters that indicate rank and importance.

The final aspect of Joseph's elevation was the order that all the Egyptians bow to him. Bowing was done to royalty and government officials of the highest order. The Egyptian people would not only see Joseph as second in importance to the king, but they must make a constant gesture in recognition of that fact.

**44. And Pharaoh said unto Joseph, I am Pharaoh, and without thee shall no man lift up his hand or foot in all the land of Egypt.**

Following the details of Joseph's installation as viceroy of Egypt, Pharaoh declares him to have authority over life and behavior in Egypt. He will be more than an administrator of a preservation program but will also have authority in the day-to-day affairs of the people. The Egyptians can do nothing whatsoever that is contrary to the Hebrew director-general. Joseph also received a new name in Egyptian, Zaphnath-paaneah (v. 45), which means "God speaks and lives." Joseph was still more fully integrated into the Egyptian nation when he married Asenath, daughter of the priest of On. He who had been betrayed, enslaved, lied about, imprisoned and forgotten has risen to extraordinary heights

in ways he could never have dreamed of.

III. DIVINE PROVISION (Genesis 41:46-57)

(Verses 46-57 are not in the printed text.)

The seven plenteous years brought abundance to Egypt just as Joseph had predicted they would. In verse 47 it is said that the earth brought forth by handfuls; and in verse 49 it is said that the corn was as the sand of the sea, very much, until he left numbering; for it was without number. The plan worked as Joseph had proposed it should. The grain was gathered into granaries and stored in great abundance, so that when the seven years of famine came Egypt was able to have sufficient and even to share with other countries that came to buy corn. Verses 56 and 57 state: "And the famine was over all the face of the earth: And Joseph opened all the storehouses, and sold unto the Egyptians; and the famine waxed sore in the land of Egypt. And all countries came into Egypt to Joseph for to buy corn; because that the famine was so sore in all lands."

In his personal life Joseph prospered as well. He was 30 years old when he interpreted the Pharaoh's dream (v. 46), which would have made him 37 when the famine began. During those seven years Asenath, his wife, had borne two sons. The first was **Manasseh** (v. 51), which means "God hath made me forget." The good fortune that had befallen Joseph in Egypt had erased from his mind the toil and abuse he had suffered previously. His second son was named **Ephraim** (v. 52), which means "bountiful or fruitful."

Joseph's predictions occurred even in his own life as fully as in the land of Egypt. His forgetting the pain of the past does not mean that he could no longer recall it, but that it had been more than atoned for by the good that had befallen him. His two sons would bring him great joy and through them he would receive a double allotment of the land of Canaan. Each of his brothers would have one tribe named after them for all time to come, but Joseph would have two: Ephraim and Manasseh.

Discuss the significance of the names "Manasseh," and "Ephraim."

As important as any other part, Joseph was now in a position to aid his own family and provide for its preservation in the same way that the land of Egypt was preserved. He who was hated by his brethren would become the means of their salvation from starvation and ruin. Thus the dreamer was the means of preserving two peoples and seeing his own life blessed in the meantime. He is proof that all things do work together for good to them who love God, who are the called according to His purpose.

## REVIEW QUESTIONS

1. Review Joseph's experience with the butler in the Egyptian prison.

2. What were the characteristics evident in Joseph that caused Pharaoh to promote him?

3. What authority did Pharaoh place in the charge of Joseph?

4. How did Joseph prepare for the famine that was to come upon the land?

5. List any unusual evidence of God's providential care of Joseph as seen in today's lesson.

## GOLDEN TEXT HOMILY

"WE KNOW THAT ALL THINGS WORK TOGETHER FOR GOOD TO THEM THAT LOVE GOD, TO THEM WHO ARE THE CALLED ACCORDING TO HIS PURPOSE" (Romans 8:28).

This is a remarkable statement for the Apostle Paul to make, especially when we consider how much he suffered because of his love for God and His truth. He had been imprisoned, stoned, beaten with stripes, and yet after all of this he could say, "All things work together for good to them that love God." It is important and imperative that Christians have faith in the character of God and not in the circumstances we see or understand.

God is a loving Heavenly Father who only does what is best for His children. **We, His children, must believe this fact.**

There is a purpose in all things.

God allows things to happen in our life to lift us from indifference.

We must strive to learn to avoid murmuring by remembering that even unfavorable circumstances are intended by God to work out His highest goal in our life.

We must believe and accept the fact that we, as Christians, will profit sooner or later from God's providential dealings.

We can look forward to the day when we can look back on the path which God has led us and realize in a beautiful way **that God did all things well.**

There are many Christians everywhere who, with feelings of deep humility and gratitude, are ready to acknowledge that they never had any serious thoughts of eternity and that they never really knew the greatness of the love of Christ **until** the day adversity came into their life.

Let us thank God for the discipline of trial, because our trials have often proved to be our greatest blessings.—**O. W. Polen, D.D., Editor in Chief, Church of God Publications, Cleveland, Tennessee**

## SENTENCE SERMONS

GOD GOVERNS in the affairs of man, and if a sparrow cannot fall to the ground without His notice, is it probable that an empire can rise without His aid?
—**Benjamin Franklin**

IT IS NOT the circumstances of our lives that give them character, but our relationship to God under any circumstance.
—**"Speaker's Sourcebook"**

IN ALL THINGS God is working to accomplish His purpose in the life of the believer.
—**Selected**

OUT OF SUFFERING have emerged the strongest souls, the most tempered

characters are seared with scars.
—**E. H. Chaplain**

## EVANGELISTIC APPLICATION

GOD OFTEN PLACES HIS FAITHFUL SERVANTS IN A POSITION OF USEFULNESS AS A WITNESS TO THE LOST.

The chief thing that St. Paul had in his mind when he spoke about forgetting the things that are behind was not his past sins but rather his past attainments. He had already made some progress in the life of faith. Most of us would say he had made a great deal, and would feel almost envious of him, thinking, Would God we were only half as far on as he was! What patience, what courage; what zeal, what self-denying love, what readiness to bear the cross, what untiring faith he had manifested in weariness and watching, in hunger and thirst, in cold and nakedness! Now, that was just what St. Paul especially wished to forget. Past attainments in grace were not, in his view, things to dwell on; they were only stages to be left behind.

In that old foot-race on the isthmus of Corinth the men who competed for the prize did not stop every now and then to look back with complacency upon that portion of the course which they had already traversed. Nor, when they had run a certain distance, did they sit down and say, "It is enough." The coveted crown would never have been theirs, had they done so. Moreover they would have been disgraced in the estimation of all the onlookers. They forgot the things which were behind, and reached forth unto those which were before. Even so in his life-course did St. Paul.—**A. C. Price**

## ILLUMINATING THE LESSON

It seems hard to imagine that a son of a slave would be offered a job at one hundred thousand dollars a year. And it seems incredible that the same man would turn the offer down. But that is what happened to George Washington Carver. The offer was made by the famous inventor, Thomas Edison. And Henry Ford tried to persuade Carver to become a scientist for the Ford Motor Company. But Carver, unimpressed with the offers of money and prestige, chose to live in the South, living in relative property, wearing the same suit for forty years. He had already given up a promising position at Iowa State University to work with Booker T. Washington and his struggling Tuskegee Institute. When friends chided him for turning down the big salaries, Carver always had an answer for them. They argued that he could help his people if he had all that money. Carver invariably replied, "If I had all that money I might forget about my people."

And on his tombstone were carved fitting words: "He could have added fortune to fame, but caring for neither, he found happiness and honor in being helpful to the world."—**Selected**

## DAILY DEVOTIONAL GUIDE

M. Divine Provision. 1 Kings 19:1-8
T. Remembering God's Blessings. Psalm 105:16-22
W. God's Favor Revealed. Daniel 6:25-28
T. Divine Deliverance. Acts 27:27-44
F. The Comfort of God. 2 Corinthians 1:3-11
S. Secure in God. Romans 8:31-39

# Forgiveness and Reconciliation

**(Joseph)**

**Study Text:** Genesis 42:1 through 45:28

**Supplemental References:** Matthew 6:14, 15; 18:21-35; 2 Corinthians 5:17-20; Psalm 32:1-11; Hosea 14:1-9

**Time:** Probably between 1800-1775 B.C.

**Piace:** Egypt

**Golden Text:** "If ye forgive men their trespasses, your heavenly Father will also forgive you" (Matthew 6:14).

**Central Truth:** A forgiving attitude is necessary for human reconciliation.

**Evangelistic Emphasis:** Those whom God forgives should seek to share the message of reconciliation.

## Printed Text

**Genesis 45:1.** Then Joseph could not refrain himself before all them that stood by him; and he cried, Cause every man to go out from me. And there stood no man with him, while Joseph made himself known unto his brethren.

**2. And he wept aloud: and the Egyptians and the house of Pharaoh heard.**

3. And Joseph said unto his brethren, I am Joseph; doth my father yet live? And his brethren could not answer him; for they were troubled at his presence.

**4. And Joseph said unto his brethren, Come near to me, I pray you. And they came near. And he said, I am Joseph your brother, whom ye sold into Egypt.**

5. Now therefore be not grieved, nor angry with yourselves, that ye sold me hither: for God did send me before you to preserve life.

**6. For these two years hath the famine been in the land: and yet there are five years, in the which there shall neither be earing nor harvest.**

7. And God sent me before you to preserve you a posterity in the earth, and to save your lives by a great deliverance.

**8. So now it was not you that sent me hither, but God: and he hath made me a father to Pharaoh, and lord of all his house, and a ruler throughout all the land of Egypt.**

9. Haste ye, and go up to my father, and say unto him, Thus saith thy son Joseph, God hath made me lord of all Egypt: come down unto me, tarry not:

**10. And thou shalt dwell in the land of Goshen, and thou shalt be near unto me, thou, and thy children, and thy children's children, and thy flocks, and thy herds, and all that thou hast.**

11. And there will I nourish thee; for yet there are five years of famine; lest thou, and thy household, and all that thou hast, come to poverty.

**12. And, behold, your eyes see, and the eyes of my brother Benjamin, that it is my mouth that speaketh unto you.**

13. And ye shall tell my father of

all my glory in Egypt, and of all that ye have seen; and ye shall haste and bring down my father hither.

**14. And he fell upon his brother**

**Benjamin's neck, and wept; and Benjamin wept upon his neck.**

15. Moreover he kissed all his brethren, and wept upon them: and after that his brethren talked with him.

---

**LESSON OUTLINE**

I. CONFRONTING PAST SINS

II. FORGIVENESS SHOWN

III. RECONCILIATION

**LESSON EXPOSITION**

INTRODUCTION

Just as Joseph's experience in Egypt was a dramatic upturn from misfortune to good fortune, so his ability to forgive his brothers is one of the great lessons of forgiveness in the Word of God.

When Joseph proposed and administered the program of conservation that saved Egypt in time of famine, he was not aware that he would also be preserving his own family and the Hebrew race. Four chapters of the Book of Genesis—42 through 45—tell the story of how Jacob and his sons were preserved because of Joseph's presence and status in Egypt. In these chapters Joseph's brothers make two journeys to Egypt and then Jacob and all the family make the journey into Egypt.

On the first occasion, ten of Jacob's sons—all but Benjamin—visited Egypt to buy grain. Joseph recognized his brothers but they did not recognize him. He at first imprisoned his brothers as spies but released them after three days. Then Joseph sent nine of the brothers back into Canaan with orders to bring Benjamin with them on their next trip. He kept Simeon in Egypt as surety that the brothers would return. In all of this Joseph did not reveal himself to the brothers.

As the famine tightened its grip in Canaan, Jacob sent his sons back to buy more food in Egypt. The sons would not return without Benjamin, for they feared the Egyptian governor (Joseph) who had ordered them to bring him. To gain the favor of this Egyptian ruler, Jacob instructed his sons to take gifts to him, along with double the money they would need, and their youngest brother, Benjamin. All of this brought grief to the old man: He believed Joseph to be dead, Simeon was a hostage in Egypt, and now Benjamin would be taken from him into Egypt. All of this, added to his distress over the famine, caused him great distress. Both Reuben and Judah acted in an admirable way when they tried to assume responsibility for the welfare of Benjamin.

The brothers then went into Egypt and encountered the great man (Joseph) once again. On the first visit Joseph tested his brothers' honesty by having their money replaced in their sacks. They told him about finding the money (Genesis 43:20-22) and returned it to him. On this second trip Joseph also tested them by placing his silver cup in Benjamin's sack of grain (44:2), then he had his servants to overtake his brothers and accuse them of having stolen the cup. When it was found in Benjamin's sack, his brothers tore their clothes in grief and all of them sadly returned into Egypt.

It might seem that Joseph was playing a cruel and cynical game with his brothers, but actually he was testing them to see if they were the same as when they treated him so vilely in Dothan. When the drama is over everything will be clear and he and his brothers will have a restored relationship.

---

Discuss the somewhat cruel testings that Joseph carried out against his brothers and father. Was he justified in doing this to his father and brothers? Explain.

---

I. CONFRONTING PAST SINS (Genesis 44:18-34)

(Verses 18-34 are not in the printed text.)

Judah and his brothers came to Joseph's house and fell down before him in obeisance. Judah did not endeavor to make any excuses, but said, "God hath found out the iniquity of thy servants: behold, we are my lord's servants, both we, and he also with whom the cup is found" (v. 16). Joseph refused to accept a guilty plea from anyone other than the person who had been found with the silver cup. That was Benjamin. Joseph said that he would keep Benjamin as a slave, but the other brothers could return to their father in Canaan.

Judah and his brothers were not about to return to Canaan. They believed that God had caught up with them and the crime they had committed on the plains of Dothan. They did not realize that the supposed Egyptian to whom they were speaking would know what that crime had been. In truth, however, no one could have known better of the guilt that bore upon their consciences.

Fully aware of their difficult situation, Judah approached the official and began a most piteous appeal for understanding with the statement that the Egyptian's authority approached that of the Pharaoh. Judah carefully rehearsed the events that had led them to this sorry hour, explaining that the brothers had been reluctant to bring Benjamin into Egypt because he was the child of their father's old age. There is a tremendous sadness in Judah's words: "My lord asked his servants, 'Do you have a father or a brother?' " And we answered, 'We have an aged father, and there is a young son born to him in his old age. His brother is dead, and he is the only one of his mother's sons left, and his father loves him' " (vv. 19, 20, *New International Version*).

Judah reminded the governor that he had insisted that the youngest brother accompany them on their return trip to Egypt or he would not be willing to receive them. The Egyptian's requirement had placed the ten brothers in a difficult position when they were in Canaan with their father. He had not wanted Benjamin to go into Egypt, for he feared for his safety, and he was still bereaved over the loss of his son Joseph whom he

believed to be dead. The brothers had insisted that Benjamin must accompany them or they would not be able to obtain food.

Only with great heaviness of heart had Jacob finally agreed for Benjamin to accompany his brothers. "And thy servant my father said unto us, Ye know that my wife bare me two sons: And the one went out from me, and I said, Surely he is torn in pieces; and I saw him not since: And if ye take this also from me, and mischief befall him, ye shall bring down my gray hairs with sorrow to the grave" (vv. 27-29).

These are some of the saddest words in the entire Old Testament. Jacob still regarded Rachel as his one truly beloved wife; her firstborn son had surely been torn to pieces and now the brothers had proposed to take Jacob and Rachel's youngest son as well. The degree of the brothers' compassion is that none of them was a son of Rachel and yet they could speak of their father and Rachel and their two sons without apparent reluctance.

Judah himself had become surety for Benjamin's safety. In a gesture of true nobleness he said, "Now then, please let your servant remain here as my lord's slave in place of the boy, and let the boy return with his brothers. How can I go back to my father if the boy is not with me. No! Do not let me see the misery that will come upon my father" (vv. 33, 34, *New International Version*).

At long last Judah and all his brethren had come face to face with their crime against Joseph; they were sadder but better men because they had faced themselves. One can only imagine the turmoil of grief and care that must have twisted and wrenched inside them. They had truly come to have human feelings and the flowers of love had taken root in their heart.

II. FORGIVENESS SHOWN (Genesis 45: 1-15)

**1. Then Joseph could not refrain himself before all them that stood by him; and he cried, Cause every man to**

go out from me. And there stood no man with him, while Joseph made himself known unto his brethren.

**2. And he wept aloud: and the Egyptians and the house of Pharaoh heard.**

Now came the glorious time of revelation and reconciliation. Joseph's heart was broken as he heard Judah's piteous plea that issued from the remorse and contrition of the brothers. Unwilling for the Egyptians present to see such a personal and sacred scene, he ordered them to leave the room and revealed to the brothers who he was. All the pent-up emotions burst forth in tears and great weeping, so much so that the Egyptians heard the weeping and the emotional disclosure of who he was. The Egyptians heard his identity, but the brothers seemed unable to comprehend what he was saying.

**3. And Joseph said unto his brethren, I am Joseph; doth my father yet live? And his brethren could not answer him; for they were troubled at his presence.**

As if to assure them, Joseph repeated the statement of who he was and added the question, "Is my father still living?" For more than 20 years the brothers had believed that Joseph was dead, which made it almost impossible for them to comprehend that he was alive; added to their lack of comprehension is their fear of this all-powerful Egyptian with whom they have been dealing. They are overwhelmed by such a barrage of unexpected developments.

**4. And Joseph said unto his brethren, Come near to me, I pray you. And they came near. And he said, I am Joseph your brother, whom ye sold into Egypt.**

---

Why do you suppose Joseph mentioned being sold into Egypt?

---

With an almost paternal tenderness Joseph called the brothers to come near him and repeated once again that he was "Joseph your brother, the one you sold into Egypt!" We know from the following verse that Joseph did not make this

statement in order to be cruel to his brothers, but only to make it clear to them that he was indeed Joseph their brother. Bear in mind that he was wearing Egyptian clothing in an Egyptian court surrounded by Egyptian servants and administering Egyptian affairs of state. There is no way they could have immediately correlated this powerful man with the 17-year-old lad whom they had abused in Dothan more than 20 years earlier.

**5. Now therefore be not grieved, nor angry with yourselves, that ye sold me hither: for God did send me before you to preserve life.**

The brothers should not be angry with themselves because they had sold him, or intended to, for his being in Egypt was clearly within the providence of God. Nothing that happened to get Joseph into Egypt was good, and yet he now says "God did send me before you to preserve life." Although everything had seemed bad at the time, Joseph could now see that even the bad had worked together to bring about the will of God. So it is with all persons who will commit the affairs of their lives—bad and good alike—unto God.

**6. For these two years hath the famine been in the land: and yet there are five years, in the which there shall neither be earing nor harvest.**

The famine had existed for two years when these events happened; there were five years yet to come. From this dating we know that Joseph was 39 years old (see 41:46).

**7. And God sent me before you to preserve you a posterity in the earth, and to save your lives by a great deliverance.**

**8. So now it was not you that sent me hither, but God: and he hath made me a father to Pharaoh, and lord of all his house, and a ruler throughout all the land of Egypt.**

It was a theme that Joseph could not repeat often enough: it was God who had sent him into Egypt, and the events that got him there were only God's way of bringing about His will. He viewed his going into Egypt as only a matter of going before his father and brethren in order to preserve them. He sees it clearly that they will be moving into Egypt also and will there be preserved as a people of God. He was only their forerunner and bore them no malice that it was their unkindness that had driven him there.

Discuss the evidences of God's care for His people Israel in today's lesson.

Not only would the house of Jacob be preserved, but so would the land of Egypt. It was by divine decree that Joseph was like a father to Pharaoh, a lord of all his house and a ruler throughout the land of Egypt.

**9. Haste ye, and go up to my father, and say unto him, Thus saith thy son Joseph, God hath made me lord of all Egypt: come down unto me, tarry not.**

For the fourth time Joseph emphasized that it was God who had sent him into Egypt and made him lord of the land. The brothers should hasten back to Canaan and notify Jacob that his son Joseph was alive. Then he and all his household should move into the land without delay. It was not enough that he could send food into Canaan for his father and family, but they must come to him in Egypt and there be nourished and strengthened with life and provision. At no time did Joseph suggest any ill will toward his brothers; the events were too clearly the handwork of God for him to waste any time in bringing greater grief to them than they had already suffered.

**10. And thou shalt dwell in the land of Goshen, and thou shalt be near unto me, thou, and thy children, and thy children's children, and thy flocks, and thy herds, and all that thou hast.**

The land of Goshen was a broad valley in the northern part of Egypt running east and west on the western side of the Nile. It was the most ideal pastoral land in Egypt, perfect for the grazing of flocks and herds. (See Genesis 47:6.)

Why do you think Joseph gave his brothers the choice Goshen valley for their homeland?

This was also a strategic place, lying between the cities of Egypt and the Sinai Desert and Canaan. It was well removed from the populated areas so the people of Jacob could live and grow and prosper to themselves.

**11. And there will I nourish thee; for yet there are five years of famine; lest thou, and thy household, and all that thou hast, come to poverty.**

Without the bounty of Egypt the Hebrews would be reduced to poverty. With provisions from the granaries and the pasture land of Goshen, the Hebrews should fare well in the time of famine. Although they had already felt the tragedy of the famine, it had not yet run one third of its course. Two years had reduced the entire countryside to poverty and depression, but there were five more years yet to come.

**12. And, behold, your eyes see, and the eyes of my brother Benjamin, that it is my mouth that speaketh unto you.**

There is great and tender affection between Joseph and Benjamin, his only full brother. Once again Joseph emphasizes that it is he, Joseph their brother, who is the governor of Egypt and is extending invitation and provision to them. He wished Benjamin and the other ten to know of a certainty who he was and how significant it was to them that he had survived and prospered in the land of Egypt.

**13. And ye shall tell my father of all my glory in Egypt, and of all that ye have seen; and ye shall haste and bring down my father hither.**

Joseph's concern for his father, Jacob, is touching. He instructs his brothers to assure Jacob that he is well and to tell him "of all my glory in Egypt." His careful instructions in this regard are understandable, for the brothers, who had seen Joseph and his circumstance in

Egypt, had found it difficult to comprehend. Certainly Jacob, who had not heard or seen, would find it almost beyond belief that the great man in Egypt of whom his sons had spoken was in reality his lost son.

If Judah was solicitous for his father's welfare (44:34), then Joseph was far more so. Yielding to the human wish to see his father as soon as possible, Joseph urged haste upon his brothers. With reunion so close at hand and with his expectations so high, Joseph was overwhelmed with a desire to see his father as soon as possible.

**14. And he fell upon his brother Benjamin's neck, and wept; and Benjamin wept upon his neck.**

**15. Moreover he kissed all his brethren, and wept upon them: and after that his brethren talked with him.**

At last the brothers were completely convinced of Joseph's identity and they all indulged in a time of reunion and brotherhood. It is clear that Joseph's strongest relationship was to his one full brother, Benjamin. So he embraced him and kissed him and wept upon his neck first of all. When he embraced his ten older brothers and expressed the same affection for them that he had for Benjamin, it was very possibly the first emotional expressions of love and fraternity that they had exchanged. Until now the principle bond between Joseph and his older brethren was the fact that they loved the same father. With their reconciliation complete, an independent bond of brotherhood was made between them.

III. RECONCILIATION (Genesis 45:16-28)

Joseph's Egyptian servants had heard his first weeping and revelation of his identity to his brothers. The news now spread widely through the Pharaoh's court that the men who had come from Canaan were Joseph's brothers. This pleased the Pharaoh very much.

In secular history we know that at this period Egypt was controlled by a people called **Hyksos,** or "shepherd kings," who

had defeated and now occupied the land. These people, being shepherds themselves, had great feeling for the Hebrews and their desire to have pasture lands.

The interlude of the Hyksos rule over Egypt helps explain the hospitality the Hebrews received at this time and the hostile attitudes that existed in the time of Moses. At the time of the Exodus the control of the land had been wrested away from the Hyksos and the original Egyptians were not kindly disposed toward the Hebrews.

Now the Pharaoh joined his invitation to that of Joseph's and strongly urged the Hebrews to come into the land. He promised to give them the good of the land of Egypt and to cause them to eat the fat of the land. Moreover, Joseph sent wagons to his family to assist them with the move. He also gave them money, clothing and provisions for the journey.

When the 11 sons returned to their father in Canaan and told him that Joseph was alive and the governor over all the land of Egypt, the old man's heart fainted with unbelief. This is an expression that means the tidings were too wonderful for him to believe. It does not mean that he disbelieved, but, as we of our day say, it was too good to be true. When the old man saw the provisions and wagons that Joseph had sent he comprehended that his sons were telling the truth. Such glad news requires time to be fully absorbed, but at last Jacob was able to say: "It is enough; Joseph my son is yet alive: I will go and see him before I die" (v. 28).

**REVIEW QUESTIONS**

1. Under what conditions did Joseph choose to reveal himself to his brethren?

2. What was Joseph's first question after revealing his identity?

3. How did Joseph identify himself in verse 4?

4. What was Joseph's interpretation of his past experiences at the hands of his brothers?

5. What message does Joseph send to his father?

## GOLDEN TEXT HOMILY

"IF YE FORGIVE MEN THEIR TRES-PASSES, YOUR HEAVENLY FATHER WILL ALSO FORGIVE YOU" (Matthew 6:14).

**Forgiveness.** It is somehow interwoven into the fabric of the heart/an attitude that makes us forgiving, being reconciled to other men and women, even as we are reconciled to God. He who is forgiven must be forgiving toward others. There may be times when we are wronged so much that to have a forgiving heart seems impossible; in such times, it is a Christian discipline to intentionally **begin** to forgive.

Furthermore, it is not the offense against us that creates those feelings of anger, hurt and frustration. The Bible says, "As he thinketh in his heart, so is he" (Proverbs 23:7). The feelings, then, are actually a result of what we "think in our heart," or **say** to ourselves, about the circumstances! We may base a theology of forgiveness on this truth. Although a deep hurt received at the hand of another might come into our thoughts "seventy times seven" times in a day (Matthew 18:21-35), the heart that is disciplined in God's loving, intentional forgiveness will be able to cope with remembering and still have forgiving thoughts.

Jesus cautions us in His explanation of the Lord's Prayer that we must institute a self-talk of forgiveness lest we, through an ungodly attitude, block God's forgiveness for us. It is the nature of God to love enough to be first in granting us forgiveness. As we walk with Him, let us extend to others the olive branch of peace, having a heart so bathed in God's love and so disciplined by that love that we easily forgive. If you forgive men when they sin against you, your heavenly Father will also forgive you.
**—Chaplain John Renfro, USNR, Naval Air Station, Memphis, Tennessee**

## SENTENCE SERMONS

FORGIVENESS IS THE FRAGRANCE the violet sheds on the heel that has crushed it.
**—Mark Twain**

DOING AN INJURY puts one below your enemy; revenging one makes you even with him; forgiving it sets you above him.
**—Selected**

THOSE WHO BRING sunshine into the lives of others cannot keep it from themselves.
**—J. M. Barrie**

A FORGIVING ATTITUDE is necessary for human reconciliation.
**—Selected**

## EVANGELISTIC APPLICATION

THOSE WHOM GOD FORGIVES SHOULD SEEK TO SHARE THE MESSAGE OF RECONCILIATION.

Love is needed for the perfecting of religion. If no relationship of earth is perfect till love has entered with its benediction, how can a man's relationship to God be perfect, if love is wanting? For true religion is not a thing of doctrine, nor of eager and intellectual speculation; it is the tie that binds the life on earth to the infinite and eternal life beyond the veil. Only when a man can lift his eyes, and say with a cry of victory, 'God loves me'; only when he believes, though all be dark, that the God who reigneth is a God of love; only then does his religion become real, a very present help in time of trouble.

It is just that which makes ours the perfect religion. For the perfecting of religion love is needed, and that love is needed, and that love has been revealed in Christ. God commendeth His own love to us, in that while we were yet sinners Christ died for us. God so loved the world that He gave His only begotten Son, that whosoever believeth in Him should not perish. When we have looked upon the face of Christ, there are a thousand things we still may doubt; but there is one thing we can never doubt again, and that is the love of God.—
**J. M. Jones, "The Cup of Cold Water."**

## ILLUMINATING THE LESSON

Convincing Beauty of the Christ-Life. —The grandest sight on this earth is not the march of the all-conquering storm whose cloudy battalions go rushing through the sounding heavens; the most beautiful thing on earth is not the garden which opens and sends forth from its censers fragrance; it is not the stateliness of the tree which you sit under through the long summer's day; those are not the most beautiful things on earth that art carves out of stone. The beauty of the soul, that lies in its secret chambers; the rich, deep, just and loving natures—these are the beautiful things of this world. There is nothing so beautiful as Christ in men; and when one begins to reflect the nature of Christ in his life, religion needs no apology; there is no call for argument.—**Henry Ward Beecher**

## DAILY DEVOTIONAL GUIDE

M. Trusting in the Lord. Ruth 1:1-5, 15-18

T. A Family in Conflict. 1 Samuel 14:36-45

W. A Sinner Forgiven. Luke 7:36-50

T. Judgment Against the Family. Acts 5:1-11

F. Care in God's Family. Acts 6:1-6

S. Called to Reconciliation. 2 Corinthians 5:17-20

# Spiritual Understanding

## (Pentecost Sunday)

**Study Text:** 1 Corinthians 2:1-12

**Supplemental References:** Ezekiel 3:12-15; Joel 2:28, 29; Zechariah 4:6-9; Acts 2:1-4; Romans 8:1-11, 26, 27; 1 Corinthians 12:4-11; 14:1-40

**Time:** Probably written in the spring of 57 A.D.

**Place:** Written at Ephesus

**Golden Text:** "The Holy Ghost, whom the Father will send in my name, he shall teach you all things" (John 14:26).

**Central Truth:** We are completely dependent upon the Holy Spirit for understanding spiritual matters.

**Evangelistic Emphasis:** The Holy Spirit convicts the sinner and brings him to a saving knowledge of Christ.

### Printed Text

**1 Corinthians 2:1.** And I, brethren, when I came to you, came not with excellency of speech or of wisdom, declaring unto you the testimony of God.

**2. For I determined not to know any thing among you, save Jesus Christ, and him crucified.**

3. And I was with you in weakness, and in fear, and in much trembling.

**4. And my speech and my preaching was not with enticing words of man's wisdom, but in demonstration of the Spirit and of power:**

5. That your faith should not stand in the wisdom of men, but in the power of God.

**6. Howbeit we speak wisdom among them that are perfect: yet not the wisdom of this world, nor of the princes of this world, that come to nought:**

7. But we speak the wisdom of God in a mystery, even the hidden wisdom, which God ordained before the world unto our glory:

**8. Which none of the princes of this world knew: for had they known it, they would not have crucified the Lord of glory.**

9. But as it is written, Eye hath not seen, nor ear heard, neither have entered into the heart of man, the things which God hath prepared for them that love him.

**10. But God hath revealed them unto us by his Spirit: for the Spirit searcheth all things, yea, the deep things of God.**

11. For what man knoweth the things of a man, save the spirit of man which is in him? even so the things of God knoweth no man, but the Spirit of God.

**12. Now we have received, not the spirit of the world, but the spirit which is of God; that we might know things that are freely given to us of God.**

314

## LESSON OUTLINE

I. DEMONSTRATION OF THE SPIRIT

II. REVELATION THROUGH THE SPIRIT

III. INSTRUCTION BY THE SPIRIT

## LESSON EXPOSITION

INTRODUCTION

The church in Corinth had many misunderstandings regarding the gospel of Christ; much of Paul's communication with the Corinthians has to do with clarifying difficult points with them. The apostle had an ongoing paternal relationship with the Corinthians and dealt with them with great patience and simplicity of language.

The Corinthian people were not highly regarded by the rest of the world in their day, for they were given to superficiality, childishness and carnal pretentions. Many of these characteristics were to be found in the church there as well as in the populace as a whole. Yet they were a people in whom the Spirit of God dwelt and manifested Himself. The potential of the Corinthians was enormous, for they always had the great teaching of Paul available to them and they seemed eager to know the truth.

In this lesson Paul explains to them the manner of his preaching to them. He wishes them to recall the simplicity of the gospel and reminds them that "the preaching of the cross is to them that perish foolishness; but unto us which are saved it is the power of God" (1:18), and "if our gospel be hid, it is hid to them that are lost" (2 Corinthians 4:3).

I. DEMONSTRATION OF THE SPIRIT (1 Corinthians 2:1-5)

**1. And I, brethren, when I came to you, came not with excellency of speech or of wisdom, declaring unto you the testimony of God.**

In chapter one Paul discussed wisdom, which was one of the pretentions of the Corinthians. They admired wisdom greatly and supposed themselves to be wise. In 1:20 he said, "Where is the wise man? Where is the scribe?

Where is the debator of this age? Has not God made foolish the wisdom of the world?"(*King James Version*).

In chapter two he continues the discussion of wisdom, in particular the differences between carnal wisdom and divine wisdom. We find the word itself six times in the first seven verses.

Paul reminds the Corinthians that he did not come to them with learned discourses and clever reasoning but with simplicity in the presentation of the gospel. He did not captivate their minds with the use of carnal or secular widsom but gave only the straightforward account of the gospel. With his great learning, Paul could have resorted to secular reasoning, he could have even dazzled their minds with a display of his understanding and depth of knowledge. Although he could have done so, he did not, for their acceptance of the truth was more important to him than their acceptance of him as a learned man.

**2. For I determined not to know any thing among you, save Jesus Christ, and him crucified.**

What happens to persons who place too much emphasis on their own capabilities, rather than proclaiming the message of Christ?

Paul correctly understood that Christ and His cross were the foundation of all gospel truth. He therefore determined that this, and this alone, would be his gospel. In Galatians 2:20 he says, "I am crucified with Christ: nevertheless I live; yet not I, but Christ liveth in me: and the life which I now live in the flesh I live by the faith of the Son of God, who loved me, and gave himself for me." He furthermore says in Galatians 6:14, "But God forbid that I should glory, save in the cross of our Lord Jesus Christ, by whom the world is crucified unto me, and I unto the world."

Paul reckoned that he had shared in the crucifixion of Christ and understood that all men must share in it if they are to be His true disciples. The preaching of crucifixion was certainly not an attractive gospel to carnal men. The preaching of the cross is directly opposed to human reasoning—and yet it is the one truth that avails in the redemption of man.

**3. And I was with you in weakness, and in fear, and in much trembling.**

Paul mentions three words here—**weakness, fear** and **trembling.** These should be understood in the light of 1 Corinthians 1:25, which says, "The foolishness of God is wiser than men; and the weakness of God is stronger than men." The apostle's meaning is that his presence and ministry in Corinth would have appeared inferior to those who regarded worldy wisdom and earthly power. He had neither pompous speech nor impressive appearance, for he was only an earthen vessel for the glorious treasure of the gospel. (See 2 Corinthians 4:3-7.)

**4. And my speech and my preaching was not with enticing words of man's wisdom, but in demonstration of the Spirit and of power:**

Who are you more likely to respond to: the man with enticing and capable speech delivery who is dependent on himself, or the one who is limited in his speech delivery, but is an obvious dedicated servant?

Paul did not come into Corinth preaching the gospel with sophisticated oratory or clever reasoning; he came simply preaching the cross with spiritual conviction and scriptural proof. As he had done in another place, Paul "reasoned with them out of the scriptures, Opening and alleging that Christ must needs have suffered, and risen again from the dead; and that this Jesus, whom I preached unto you, is Christ" (Acts 17:2, 3). This was Paul's constant message, supported by the evidence of scripture, and delivered with the persuasive power of the Holy Ghost.

It is still the world's most powerful message—that "God so loved the world, that He gave His only begotten Son, that whosoever believeth in him should not perish, but have everlasting life."

**5. That your faith should not stand in the wisdom of men, but in the power of God.**

The purpose of Paul's single-minded preaching was that the Corinthians should be won to a faith in Christ and not beguiled by the clever presentation of wisdom. What passes for carnal wisdom in one time may be disproved and discarded in another, but the gospel of the Lord Jesus Christ never changes. Paul wanted Christians to have a steadfast faith in "Jesus Christ the same yesterday, and today, and forever" (Hebrews 13:8).

II. REVELATION THROUGH THE SPIRIT (1 Corinthians 2:6-10)

**6. Howbeit we speak wisdom among them that are perfect: yet not the wisdom of this world, nor of the princes of this world, that come to nought:**

In the preceeding five verses Paul used the word "I" but here uses "we." What he has to say at this point is the position of the worldwide Christian community. It is, in other words, a truth held by the entire church as that truth had been revealed by Jesus Christ.

The *New International Version* translates this verse as follows: "We do, however, speak a message of wisdom among the mature, but not the wisdom of this age or of the rulers of this age, who are coming to nothing." The wisdom taught by the church is not the wisdom that is based upon man's own efforts and conjectures. Nor is the wisdom of Christ arrived at by the reasoning powers of rulers or learned men. That wisdom is doomed to pass away. The *Broadman Commentary* says: "The wisdom of this age is the interpretation of life based on man's own strivings. It will die because it has no future beyond **this** age, this present evil world." Corinth was a Greek city, and Paul had recently been to such Greek cities as Philippi, Thessalonica, Berea and Athens, where Greek philosophy and wisdom were viewed with respect and veneration. In chapter 1:22 the apostle said, "For the Jews require a sign, and the Greeks seek after wisdom: But we preach Christ crucified, unto the Jews a stumblingblock, and unto the Greeks foolishness."

**7. But we speak the wisdom of God in a mystery, even the hidden wisdom, which God ordained before the world unto our glory:**

The wisdom of the gospel was something the world could never comprehend. Paul calls it a **mystery,** which means a truth that can be understood only by the revelation of God. The *Scofield Reference Bible* says, "A **mystery** in scripture is a previously hidden truth, now divinely revealed, but in which a supernatural element still remains despite the revelation."

Why is the wisdom of God necessarily connected with mystery so far as we are concerned?

Men do not arrive at the truth of the gospel, or the truth of Christ through carnal reasoning and wisdom: it comes as a revelation by the power of the Holy Spirit to men of faith. The wisdom of Christ comes as revealed truth, not wisdom that can be obtained by study or self-effort. It is because of this wide difference between carnal knowledge and spiritual knowledge that Paul wrote to Timothy that in the last days men will be "ever learning, and never able to come to the knowledge of the truth" (2 Timothy 3:7).

Christ is the glory of the Christian, and we receive Christ through faith. The Christian life is more than an intellectual exercise, more than the accumulation of knowledge and wisdom, but it is an adventure of the spirit for those who will receive it.

**8. Which none of the princes of this world knew: for had they known it, they would not have crucified the Lord of glory.**

The princes of this world did not receive the wisdom of God during the days of the apostles, and very rarely does this occur in our own time, because of their many kinds of blindness. They could not understand the gospel of Christ because they were absorbed in

carnal things. They were so aware of their own power they did not recognize that they had need. They were such pretenders of wisdom that they could not admit to wisdom that comes by revelation. Such princes as Agrippa and Herod were made aware of the gospel but their minds were closed to it. (See Acts 26:1-28, where Paul spoke to Agrippa, and Luke 23:6-11, where Herod saw Jesus face-to-face before He was crucified.)

It was the princes of this world who crucified Jesus. They attempted to put out the light of the world because their heart was dark. They tried to abolish the truth of the gospel because their own heart could not comprehend it. They tried to eliminate the power of God because they were so proud of their own earthly power.

**9. But as it is written, Eye hath not seen, nor ear heard, neither have entered into the heart of man, the things which God hath prepared for them that love him.**

The meaning of this often-quoted verse is that spiritual truth cannot be discovered by human wisdom. There is no gate of human understanding, not by eye or ear or intuition, that will reveal the glories of God to a carnal man. There is a truth so high that it cannot be reached by earthly endeavors of learning, but that is fully known and understood by mature men of faith.

This verse is often quoted to show the glories of heaven, and it may include that, but it also means far more. It speaks of the glory of life in Christ, even here on this earth, which is beyond the understanding of carnal conjecture. The joy of having one's sins forgiven, of being alive in Christ, of having His peace within one's heart, of being a part of the Christian brotherhood, and of having an integrated and purposeful life is something at which carnal men can only guess. But even their guesses do not come about because of their learning, but because they see in the example of Christians the wonderful "things which God hath prepared for them that love Him."

**10. But God hath revealed them unto**

**us by his Spirit: for the Spirit searcheth all things, yea, the deep things of God.**

God gives the Holy Spirit to men and the Spirit, in turn, gives wisdom and understanding to men. Unspiritual persons do not have the Holy Spirit and therefore cannot know the divine reality of the spiritual life. Encased in his carnality, the natural man is isolated from spiritual wisdom.

Those who receive the Holy Spirit, however, have spiritual realities revealed to them in a never-ending flow of inspiration and teaching. This spiritual sensitivity comes through faith in Christ and the enablement of the Holy Spirit. Persons in Christ are able to see things they could never see before. An instance of this, mentioned in 1 Corinthians 1:18, is that carnal wisdom views the cross as foolishness while spiritual wisdom sees it as the power of God unto salvation. The Spirit of the Lord in man will reveal to him the deep and treasured wisdom of all spiritual reality. This refers as much to the richness of the revelation as to its profoundity.

III. INSTRUCTION BY THE SPIRIT (1 Corinthians 2:11, 12)

**11. For what man knoweth the things of a man, save the spirit of man which is in him? even so the things of God knoweth no man, but the Spirit of God.**

One of the great instructions of Greek wisdom is "Know thyself." From this one of the great exercises of human reasoning is an effort for one to understand oneself. Paul draws a parallel between knowledge of oneself to knowledge of the Spirit of God. Just as no one can know what is really in a man except the man himself, so no one can comprehend the wisdom of God except the Spirit of God. Paul speaks of "two kinds of spirits: the Spirit of God or the Holy Spirit and the spirit of the world, which is man centered. The spirit of the world, human wisdom, and the unspiritual man are different ways of describing persons who do not know divine reality which the Holy Spirit reveals to those who are open to it" *(Broadman Commentary)*. One of the most fruitless endeavors in life is for a man without the Spirit of God to undertake to understand the things of God.

**12. Now we have received, not the spirit of the world, but the spirit which is of God; that we might know the things that are freely given to us of God.**

It is necessary to bear in mind at all times that we must receive before we can understand. We receive the Lord through faith and following our union with Him we are able to comprehend the Word of God, with all its beauty and power, and the ways of God, with their purposes and effects. These things are given to us with the Spirit of God so that we can enjoy them without measure.

Paul states in verse 13 that the Christian message should be presented in the wisdom of the Holy Ghost rather than in the wisdom of man. He draws the parallel between natural wisdom and spiritual wisdom suggesting that Christians may become mature in understanding and faith. "Which things also we speak, not in the words which man's wisdom teacheth, but which the Holy Ghost teacheth; comparing spiritual things with spiritual. But the natural man receiveth not the things of the Spirit of God: for they are foolishness unto him: neither can he know them, because they are spiritually discerned."

**REVIEW QUESTIONS**

1. What, according to verse 5, is lacking in the wisdom of men so far as a basis for faith is concerned?

2. Differentiate the two kinds of wisdom of verses 6 through 8.

3. What limitations keep man from seeing the riches of God's provision for those who love Him?

4. Why is it unwise to try to give full explanation of spiritual things to unbelievers?

5. What are some of the most important messages you have received from this lesson?

## GOLDEN TEXT HOMILY

"THE HOLY GHOST, WHOM THE FATHER WILL SEND IN MY NAME, HE SHALL TEACH YOU ALL THINGS" (John 14:26).

In this passage, Christ reveals for the disciples a transition that will take place in their relationship to God. They had been with Christ face to face. They had lived with Him and had enjoyed His constant care and instruction. Christ had taught them what the kingdom of God is all about. He had revealed more of the nature and the person of God.

Now He is about to depart and He tells His disciples that the Holy Spirit will continue the ministry of training and guiding them as they endeavor to live in Christian life. He will continue to reveal the plan and purpose of God and will continue to enlighten and illuminate the Word of God to their hearts. As this happens, the Word of God will come alive and bring them to a clearer understanding of their role in the kingdom of God.

As this scripture is applied to us today, we must recognize our responsibility in this relationship we have with the Holy Spirit. The Holy Spirit is a teacher, but teaching is a two-way process. For teaching to take place, there must be a learner who studies the text, listens carefully, and then, in some measure, applies what he has learned to his life situation. The Holy Spirit will teach us, but we are not passive recipients of spiritual truths. To gain the full impact and benefit of the Holy Spirit's role as teacher in our life, we must study God's Word, listen carefully to the Spirit of God, and then apply the Word of God. By doing this, we are actively receiving the work of the Holy Spirit and we can be assured of a wealth of spiritual understanding to be made available to us.—**David W. Smartt, Chaplain (Captain), United States Army, Fort Stewart, Georgia**

## SENTENCE SERMONS

IF THE CHURCH is to rise to its fullest stature in God, if it is to meet all foes in the spirit of triumph, it must rely, not upon its number or skills, but upon the power of the Holy Spirit.
**—Arthur J. Moore**

THE BASIC DIFFERENCE between physical and spiritual power is that men use physical power, but spiritual power uses men.
**—Justin Wroe Dixon**

NOT BY MIGHT, nor by power, but my spirit, saith the Lord of Hosts.
**—Zechariah 4:6**

## EVANGELISTIC APPLICATION

THE HOLY SPIRIT CONVICTS THE SINNER AND BRINGS HIM TO A SAVING KNOWLEDGE OF CHRIST.

When Christ committed His mission and ministry to His followers He promised to send them the Holy Spirit to serve as their guide, to instruct and empower them (John 14:12-18; 16:13). Through the Holy Spirit we have all the spiritual equipment and provision we require to be what we should and to do what we must. It is in the Holy Ghost, and by the Holy Ghost in us, that Christ Himself is still in the world today (John 14:18). It is in the Holy Ghost that we are empowered and equipped to function as the body of Christ and bear fruit as the branch of the Vine.

While Jesus was on earth He was limited to being in one place at one time, and His life was bound by the measure of His years. But the Holy Ghost is not restricted by space or time— the Spirit is in all the earth forever. He manifests His power and performs His purpose wherever there is a yielded and believing heart.—**Charles W. Conn, A BALANCED CHURCH**

## DAILY DEVOTIONAL GUIDE

M. Spiritual Insight. Ezekiel 3:12-17

T. Promise of Power. Joel 2:28, 29

W. Work of the Spirit. Zechariah 4:6-8

T. The Promise Fulfilled. Acts 2:1-4

F. Life in the Spirit. Romans 8:1-11

S. Worship in the Spirit. 1 Corinthians 14:1-40

# God's Plan Fulfilled

**(Jacob and Joseph)**

**Study Text:** Genesis 48:1 through 50:26

**Supplemental References:** Genesis 12:1-3; Deuteronomy 30:15-20; Romans 8:29-39; 2 Timothy 4:6-8; Philippians 1:20-26; Revelation 19:1-8

**Time:** Probably around 1800 to 1760 B.C.

**Place:** Egypt

**Golden Text:** "Blessed be the Lord . . . there hath not failed one word of all his good promises" (1 Kings 8:56).

**Central Truth:** God's people can rejoice in the certain triumph of His plan.

**Evangelistic Emphasis:** The church can witness in confidence, knowing that no promise of God shall fail.

## Printed Text

**Genesis 49:28.** All these are the twelve tribes of Israel: and this is it that their father spake unto them, and blessed them; every one according to his blessing he blessed them.

**29. And he charged them, and said unto them, I am to be gathered unto my people: bury me with my fathers in the cave that is in the field of Ephron the Hittite,**

30. In the cave that is in the field of Machpelah, which is before Mamre, in the land of Canaan, which Abraham bought with the field of Ephron the Hittite for a possession of a burying-place.

**31. There they buried Abraham and Sarah his wife; there they buried Isaac and Rebekah his wife; and there I buried Leah.**

32. The purchase of the field and of the cave that is therein was from the children of Heth.

**33. And when Jacob had made an end of commanding his sons, he gathered up his feet into the bed, and yielded up the ghost, and was gathered unto his people.**

**50:15.** And when Joseph's brethren saw that their father was dead, they said, Joseph will peradventure hate us, and will certainly requite us all the evil which we did unto him.

**16. And they sent a messenger unto Joseph, saying, Thy father did command before he died saying,**

17. So shall ye say unto Joseph, Forgive, I pray thee now, the trespass of thy brethren, and their sin; for they did unto thee evil: and now, we pray thee, forgive the trespass of the servants of the God of thy father. And Joseph wept when they spake unto him.

**18. And his brethren also went and fell down before his face; and they said, Behold, we be thy servants.**

19. And Joseph said unto them, Fear not: for am I in the place of God?

**20. But as for you, ye thought evil against me; but God meant it unto good, to bring to pass, as it is this day, to save much people alive.**

21. Now therefore fear ye not: I will nourish you, and your little ones. And he comforted them, and spake kindly unto them.

## DICTIONARY

**Ephron (EE-frohn)—Genesis 49:29**—A Hittite from whom Abraham purchased a field which contained a cave he wanted for the burial place of Sarah.

**Hittite (HIT-tight)—Genesis 49:29**—A group of people originating in Asia Minor and penetrating all parts of the ancient world except Egypt. They were third only to the Mesopotamians and the Egyptians in political importance in ancient times.

**Machpelah (mac-PEE-lah)—Genesis 49:30**—A field near Hebron which Abraham purchased from Ephron the Hittite for 400 shekels of silver in order to use a cave in it for a burial place for Sarah.

**Mamre (MAHM-ree)—Genesis 49:30**—A place a few miles north of Hebron. Possibly named for a person by the name of Mamre who was an Amorite and who was confederate with Abram.

## LESSON OUTLINE

I. RECEIVING BLESSINGS
II. FACING DEATH WITH FAITH
III. RECOGNIZING GOD'S PROVIDENCE

## LESSON EXPOSITION

INTRODUCTION

Jacob lived in Egypt for 17 years, during which he saw his family grow into a great multitude. His descendants also became very wealthy, thriving in the land of Goshen (Genesis 47:27, 28).

When the time came that Jacob knew he would die, he asked Joseph not to leave his body in Egypt after he died. Jacob knew that his descendants would depart from Egypt one day to return to Canaan; at such a time he wished his remains to be removed from this foreign land and returned to Canaan, the land of promise. Joseph, upon knowing of his father's illness, took his two sons, Manasseh and Ephraim, to Jacob for his paternal blessing.

For Jacob, the time had come for him to bless his sons and arrange for their succession following his death. His name had been changed to Israel, and these sons were the children of Israel. His sons would become the 12 tribes of Israel, of whom the entire nation of Israel would consist. His bequests to and pronouncement upon these sons would be important for the land of Israel in all the years to come.

Why is it important to deceased persons to be buried where their graves will be attended?

First among the acts of Jacob was the designation of two tribes for Joseph, one for each of his sons, Manasseh and Ephraim, rather than a single tribe in Joseph's name. In 48:5, Jacob said, "and now thy two sons, Ephraim and Manasseh, which were born unto thee in the land of Egypt before I came unto thee into Egypt, are mine; as Reuben and Simeon, they shall be mine." The tribe of Levi would be omitted from the tribal allotments, so the two sons of Joseph restored the list of tribes to 12. The descendants of Levi would serve the entire nation as priests and spiritual leaders and would therefore not be reckoned as a regular tribe.

In seeing Ephraim and Manasseh, the sons of Joseph, Jacob recalled his beloved wife, Rachel, the grandmother of these two sons of Joseph. It is a touching fact of Scripture that Jacob loved Rachel from the time he first saw her until the time of his death. This love for her gave him a special feeling of tenderness toward those children that issued from her.

I. RECEIVING BLESSINGS (Genesis 48: 8-12)

(Verses 8-12 are not in the printed text.)

Although we are told in 47:28 that Jacob lived in the land of Egypt for 17 years, the events described here appear to have happened shortly after his arrival in Egypt. Manasseh and Ephraim had been born to Joseph before Jacob came to Egypt, and verse 12 indicates that the two stood between the knees of Jacob. This indicates that they were still small at the time of this paternal blessing upon them.

Verse 8 also indicates that Jacob sees the two boys for the first time. His eyes are dim, however, because of his advanced age, and he must ask the identity of Manasseh and Ephraim. Jacob embraced and kissed his grandsons while stating his intention to bestow a paternal blessing upon them. During the years that Joseph was believed to be dead, Jacob had not felt that he would ever see his son again—but he now sees him and his two sons as well. This was an emotional experience for Jacob, who bowed himself in gratitude to the Lord.

Jacob recounted blessings of the Lord upon him by stating that he had little hope ever to see Joseph again, but God had brought it to pass that he should do so. God had not only blessed him by giving him his son again but also by giving him grandsons whom he now received as his own.

According to the Oriental custom of that time, he in effect adopted the two sons as his own: "They shall be mine" (v. 5). By this act of adoption Jacob gave Manasseh and Ephraim status equal to Reuben, Simeon and his other sons.

The passage in Genesis 48:12-22 relates Jacob's blessing to Manasseh and Ephraim in which he made them full partners of the children of Israel. Jacob pointed out to Joseph that this in effect gave him a portion above that of his brethren (v. 22).

II. FACING DEATH WITH FAITH (Genesis 49:28 through 50:14)

(Verses 50:1-14 are not in the printed text.)

In chapter 48:21 Jacob said to Joseph, "Behold, I die: but God shall be with you, and bring you again unto the land of your fathers." In 49:1, Jacob calls his sons together and gives them his final blessing, which was really a prophecy of the kinds of tribes they would be. The sections are as follows:

| | |
|---|---|
| Reuben (vv. 3, 4) | Gad (v. 19) |
| Simeon (vv. 5-7) | Asher (v. 20) |
| Judah (vv. 8-12) | Naphtali (v. 21) |
| Zebulun (v. 13) | Joseph (vv. 22-26) |
| Issachar (vv. 14, 15) | Benjamin (v. 27) |
| Dan (vv. 16-18) | |

Joseph summarized the characteristics of his sons with amazing insight and candor. He saw their strong points and weak points with equal clarity and prophesied the course that each son would follow. It is clear from Jacob's prophecy that it is through Judah that the nation's kings will come and ultimately the Messiah (v. 10). In the providence of God, it would not be the firstborn Reuben or even the favorite son Joseph who would produce the royal line, but this fourth-born son. Thus God, at His will, chose whom He would, and chooses whom He will, for the work of His kingdom.

**28. All these are the twelve tribes of Israel: and this is it that their father spake unto them, and blessed them; every one according to his blessing he blessed them.**

The repeated references to 12 tribes of Israel is according to divine plan. The number 12 in Scripture is a number of perfection, one that we find in numerous usages. The 12 tribes of Israel were to establish the nation of God's people; the 12 apostles were those who laid the foundation of the church; and in the Book of Revelation we read of 12 gates, 12 angels, 12 foundations and 12 manner of fruits (Revelation 21:12-14; 22:2).

Jacob's name had been changed to Israel, so the 12 tribes of Israel means the 12 tribes (or sons) of Jacob. It is typical of God that He should so refine a coarse vessel such as Jacob into one for whom an entire nation would be named. He has both the ability and good pleasure to change inferior things into vessels of great treasure.

**29. And he charged them, and said unto them, I am to be gathered unto my people: bury me with my fathers in the cave that is in the field of Ephron the Hittite,**

**30. In the cave that is in the field of Machpelah, which is before Mamre, in the land of Canaan, which Abraham bought with the field of Ephron the Hittite for a possession of a burying-place.**

Jacob carefully instructed Joseph in the manner of his burial. Realizing that his death was near, the aged patriarch wanted this son to understand the importance of burying him with his fathers. One of the most time-honored traditions of the Hebrew people was the burying of each generation along with those of past generations. Throughout the history of the Jews we read of such things as "and Jotham slept with his fathers, and was buried with his fathers in the city of David his father" (2 Kings 15:38).

In the Oriental manner, Jacob repeated to Joseph the manner in which Abraham had secured a burying place for his family. There were no written records in those days, so the oral record had to be carefully handed down from generation to generation and person to person. Jacob rehearsed to Joseph the fact that Abraham had bought a field near Mamre with a cave called Machpelah to be a sacred tribal burying place.

There was no such thing as cemeteries as we know them and each head of family had the responsibility of providing a place for the burying of his dead. These burial plots were regarded as sacred and were never to be disturbed. They contained the remains of many generations of a particular family, which were frequently visited by the present generation. Jacob wanted to be buried in Abraham's burying place so he could "sleep" with his fathers and remain linked with them. This was of utmost importance to the Jews, so much so that Jacob, aware that he would die in Egypt, still wanted his remains carried back before they were permanently interred.

**31. There they buried Abraham and**

Sarah his wife; there they buried Isaac and Rebekah his wife; and there I buried Leah.

Jacob reminded Joseph that three generations were buried at Machpelah. Abraham, Isaac and Jacob had all buried their wives there. (Jacob's wife Rachel had been buried near Bethlehem.) Abraham and Isaac were buried at Machpelah, and there Jacob wished to be buried also. A Hebrew's strong desire to be buried in the family burying place can be seen from the fact that he did not choose to be buried near Rachel, his favorite and beloved wife, but at Machpelah where the less favorite and less loved Leah was buried. This means that a sense of tribal tradition was stronger than sentiment and affection.

**32. The purchase of the field and of the cave that is therein was from the children of Heth.**

Still in the tradition of ancient historical records, Jacob makes an oral recounting of how Abraham came to have the family burying place. He had purchased it from the children of Heth. The account of Abraham's purchase of the field and the cave is found in chapter 23:4-20.

So sacred was the burying place that it still exists in Hebron today. Its sanctity and importance have been preserved through the centuries, which adds importance to the plan of Abraham and the determination of Jacob. A Hebrew burying place was no simple matter for it represented the greatest possession of the Jewish family.

**33. And when Jacob had made an end of commanding his sons, he gathered up his feet into the bed, and yielded up the ghost, and was gathered unto his people.**

In a dramatic fashion, Jacob died at the close of his prophecy to his sons and his instructions concerning his own intimate burial. Jacob was 147 years old, as compared to Abraham's 175 years and Isaac's 180 years. It is said in chapter 48:1 that Jacob was sick and in 48:10 that his eyes were dim for age.

Jacob's life had been tumultuous, filled with adventure and peril, marked by the most ignoble deeds and those of highest character. In his lifetime he had gone all the way from total self-will and self-seeking to a life of grieving and serving, but most of all Jacob's life was marked by his ability to believe God and to put his trust in him. That was the characteristic that gave him rise from his ignoble beginnings to his triumphant end.

III. RECOGNIZING GOD'S PROVIDENCE (Genesis 50:15-21)

When Jacob died Joseph had the Egyptian physicians to embalm him and then mourn for him 40 days. The Egyptians were masters at embalming, so skilled that the mummies of their kings remain unto this time. Since Joseph was the leader in Egypt, it is not at all unlikely that he was embalmed in similar fashion.

The Pharaoh permitted Joseph and his brethren to take the body of Jacob into Canaan and bury him in the cave of Machpelah so that he was gathered unto his people.

**15. And when Joseph's brethren saw that their father was dead, they said, Joseph will peradventure hate us, and will certainly requite us all the evil which we did unto him.**

Joseph's brethren feared that his anger toward them had been held in check by the presence of Jacob their father. They felt such guilt over the wrong they had done to Joseph that they could not truly comprehend the thoroughness of his forgiveness. They believed that somehow he would still avenge himself on them. It was far easier for Joseph to forgive his brethren than it was for the brethren to forgive themselves. The depth of their guilt remained with them all of their days, with probably a mixture of fear of him and remorse for what they had done. Wicked men flee when no one pursues them (Proverbs 28:1), and in a similar way those who are riddled with guilt rarely escape from the knowledge of their crimes.

**16. And they sent a messenger unto Joseph, saying, Thy father did command before he died saying,**

**17. So shall ye say unto Joseph, For-**

**give, I pray thee now, the trespass of thy brethren, and their sin; for they did unto thee evil: and now, we pray thee, forgive the trespass of the servants of the God of thy father. And Joseph wept when they spake unto him.**

The depth of the brothers' sense of guilt and fear is seen in their contrivance of this message. They acknowledge their sin in the most telling terms, and appeal to Joseph anew for forgiveness, but yet they do it in their father's name rather than their own. It seemed to be beyond them to accept the fact that Joseph had truly forgiven them and put the matter out of his heart. Notice that the words **trespass, sin** and **evil** are all used in their appeal for forgiveness. Notice also that they use the term **thy** father rather than the word **our** father. They were reluctant even to presume upon the brotherhood of Joseph. Instead, they appealed to his love for his father.

**18. And his brethren also went and fell down before his face; and they said, Behold, we be thy servants.**

**19. And Joseph said unto them, Fear not: for am I in the place of God?**

Joseph wept when his brethren sent the message unto him. He wept because his brethren were unable to accept his forgiveness; he wept because of the depth of remorse they felt; and he wept because of the memory of his father. The brethren followed their message by going to Joseph in person and falling down before him and declaring themselves to be his servants. These men had lived with him for more than 17 years in Egypt and had every right to know the degree to which Joseph accepted them and loved them. Yet, they had maintained through those years a nagging fear that Joseph showed forgiveness only for Jacob's sake.

---

What steps should be taken to be reconciled to one who has been done wrong? Who should make the initial contact?

---

When they called themselves his servants and fell down before him, they were fulfilling precisely his dream in which they had bowed down to make obeisance to him (37:9). How often that dream must have haunted them, especially the way they had ridiculed him because of it. It is not likely that they thought of the dream now, for their hearts were too filled with fear of what he might do to them. Joseph had no thought of vengeance, however, and let them know that he would not take the place of God by exacting it of them. Vengeance should come from God and not from man.

**20. But as for you, ye thought evil against me; but God meant it unto good, to bring to pass, as it is this day, to save much people alive.**

Once again Joseph reminded his brothers that what they had intended to be evil God had turned into good. Many years earlier he had assured them of this (45:5-7), but they had not been able to comprehend even yet that this verse was so. Joseph's life is one of the greatest proofs in human experience that "all things do work together for good to them that love God, to them who are the called according to his purpose" (Romans 8:28). The good that resulted from his experiences could have come about in other ways, but God used his misfortunes for that purpose.

**21. Now therefore fear ye not: I will nourish you, and your little ones. And he comforted them, and spake kindly unto them.**

Joseph gave a final assurance to his brothers that he would keep them and nourish them, both them and their families. He comforted and provided for them for the remainder of their days.

Joseph lived to be 100 years old and lived to see his great grandchildren grow up in the land of Egypt. Before his death, he, like Jacob, made the children of Israel vow that they would not leave his remains in Egypt. That promise was kept when the children of Israel left Egypt about 400 years later. It is recorded thusly: "Moses took the bones of Joseph with him: for he had straitly sworn the children of Israel, saying, God will surely visit you; and ye shall carry up my bones away hence with you" (Exodus 13:19).

## REVIEW QUESTIONS

1. What request had Jacob made of Joseph concerning his burial site?

2. What is meant by the statement in verse 33 "He gathered up his feet into the bed, and yielded up the ghost"?

3. What acts of repentance toward Joseph had his brothers made?

4. What was Joseph's reaction to his brother's apologies?

5. Discuss the providential care God manifested for Jacob's family in Egypt. How do you relate Joseph's earlier hardships to the plan of God?

## GOLDEN TEXT HOMILY

"BLESSED BE THE LORD . . . THERE HATH NOT FAILED ONE WORD OF ALL HIS GOOD PROMISES" (1 Kings 8:56).

In our rapidly changing society, there seem to be very few absolutes, very few things that are unchangeable. The result is there is very little here in which we can have lasting confidence. Yet, down through history, we can see that God's Word, His promises to us, cannot fail. When we meet God's conditions, His promises are ours. Over and over throughout both testaments we are assured that God **is** faithful!

It is because He is faithful that His promises have not, cannot and will not fail. The Hebrew term in the Golden Text is "have not fallen" or "remain unfulfilled." But, what about the times when we look at our circumstances and apparently His promise has "fallen" or "remains unfulfilled"? Then, we need to be aware of our perspective as compared with God's. Paul tells us that even if we doubt His faithfulness, that does not change God. He remains faithful (1 Timothy 2:13). During these moments we must remember that we are in God's hands and therefore we **can** rest on His promise that "all things work together for good to them that love God" (Romans 8:28).

Just as God was with Joseph in the pit, in the prison and in the palace, so He is with us, no matter how bleak our circumstances. The lessons we learn about the ways of God in those difficult times are what make it possible for us to reign in life through Christ Jesus.

Joshua, referring to God's promises, said they "all came to pass" (21:45). It may have taken time, but in God's time, they were fulfilled. Let us continue to trust in God's timing.—**Paul C. Stewart, Chaplain, (CAP.), United States Air Force, Spokane, Washington.**

## SENTENCE SERMONS

GOD'S PEOPLE CAN REJOICE in the certain triumph of His plan.
**—Selected**

WE WIN BY TENDERNESS; we conquer by forgiveness.
**—Frederick W. Robertson**

DEATH IS THE OPENING of a more subtle life. In the flower, it sets free the perfume; in the Chrysales, the butterfly; in man, the soul.
**—Paul Vasile**

ANY ONE THING in the creation is sufficient to demonstrate a Providence to a humble and grateful mind.
**—Epictetus**

SOMETIMES PROVIDENCES, like Hebrew letters, must be read backwards.
**—John Flavel**

## EVANGELISTIC APPLICATION

THE CHURCH CAN WITNESS IN CONFIDENCE, KNOWING THAT NO PROMISE OF GOD SHALL FAIL.

By God working in us "to will and to do," we are to understand that He makes us willing, and gives us power, who were formerly unwilling and unable, to surrender ourselves to the work of our own salvation. Nor is there involved in this any violation of the true liberty of the human will. The will is incapable of coercion. There can be no forcing of volition. The very freest act of the human soul is that by which it gives itself under God's grace to Himself. When God works in the soul "to will" there is no violence done to the rational nature. On the contrary, there is the fullest unison with the freedom and responsibility of the moral being. And so it is also when God works in us "to do." Our doing is not compulsory action. It is not a course of conduct to which we are forcibly driven, but one to which we are freely drawn. We are not like slaves, compelled by the lash to do what we have a repugnance to do. We are like freemen, influenced by grace to do what we have the inclination and resolve to do. Thus the carrying out of our salvation is willing action. But the will and action, though **by us as** agents, are not **from us** in their motive cause. The will is wrought **in us** by God, and the action is wrought **by us,** as the instruments of the inworking agency of God.—**Selected**

## DAILY DEVOTIONAL GUIDE

M. A Promised Blessing. Deuteronomy 30:15-20

T. God's Faithfulness. 2 Samuel 22:47-51

W. Victory Through Christ. Romans 8:29-39

T. Faith in God's Promises. Hebrews 11:17-22

F. A Faithful Witness. 2 Timothy 4:6-8

S. Our God Reigns. Revelation 19:1-8

# INTRODUCTION
# TO SUMMER
# QUARTER

The lessons for the summer quarter (June, July, August) are presented under the theme, "Critical Issues." As this theme suggests, the studies focus on issues which the human family faces in a very real way. These issues range from that of personal integrity to that of the cooperate effort of the church to carry out its mission in harmony with the plan of Christ Jesus the Lord.

Few, if any, families or individuals are so isolated as to be void of the pressures of a jet-age society. On the contrary, most people, even Christian persons, are bombarded by the reality of suffering, the appeals of materialism, the indirect results of a growing drug population, the evils of the occult, and the death of loved ones who have not surrendered their lives to Christ.

In a day when many persons are overwhelmed by such critical issues, it is comforting to the Christian that he can offer help. It is certain that this series of lessons will give the conscientious student of the Word a solid foundation for facing contemporary issues and for helping others.

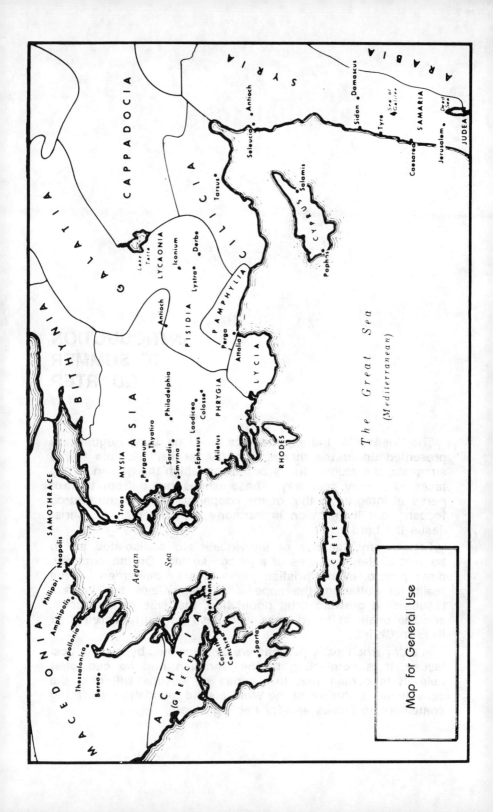

Map for General Use

# June 1, 1986

# Personal Integrity

**Study Text:** Deuteronomy 25:13-15; Psalm 24:3-6; Proverbs 11:3-5; Micah 6:8; Romans 13:8-12; 14:10-12; Philippians 4:8, 9; 1 John 1:6, 7

**Supplemental References:** Job 27:4-6; Psalm 26:1-3; Proverbs 2:3-9; 16:11; Isaiah 33:14-17; 56:1; Ezekiel 18:5-9; Luke 3:13, 14; Acts 24:16; 2 Corinthians 4:1, 2; 8:21; Colossians 3:22, 23; 1 Peter 2:11, 12; 3:10-16

**Golden Text:** "He hath shewed thee, O man, what is good; and what doth the Lord require of thee, but to do justly, and to love mercy, and to walk humbly with thy God?" (Micah 6:8).

**Central Truth:** The Christian's integrity in his relationship with God and man is a testimony of Christ's saving and keeping power.

**Evangelistic Emphasis:** Heaven is prepared for those who accept Christ as Savior and live by God's standards in this present world.

## Printed Text

**Deuteronomy 25:13.** Thou shalt not have in thy bag divers weights, a great and a small.

**14. Thou shalt not have in thine house divers measures, a great and a small.**

15. But thou shalt have a perfect and just weight, a perfect and just measure shalt thou have: that thy days may be lengthened in the land which the Lord thy God giveth thee.

**Psalm 24:3. Who shall ascend into the hill of the Lord? or who shall stand in his holy place?**

4. He that hath clean hands, and a pure heart; who hath not lifted up his soul unto vanity, nor sworn deceitfully.

**5. He shall receive the blessing from the Lord, and righteousness from the God of his salvation.**

6. This is the generation of them that seek him, that seek thy face, O Jacob. Selah.

**Proverbs 11:3. The integrity of the upright shall guide them: but the per-** verseness of transgressors shall destroy them.

4. Riches profit not in the day of wrath: but righteousness delivereth from death.

**5. The righteousness of the perfect shall direct his way: but the wicked shall fall by his own wickedness.**

**Romans 13:8.** Owe no man any thing, but to love one another: for he that loveth another hath fulfilled the law.

**9. For this, Thou shalt not commit adultery, Thou shalt not kill, Thou shalt not steal, Thou shalt not bear false witness, Thou shalt not covet; and if there be any other commandment, it is briefly comprehended in this saying, namely, Thou shalt love thy neighbour as thyself.**

10. Love worketh no ill to his neighbour: therefore love is the fulfilling of the law.

**11. And that, knowing the time, that now it is high time to awake out of**

329

**sleep: for now is our salvation nearer than when we believed.**

12. The night is far spent, the day is at hand: let us therefore cast off the works of darkness, and let us put on the armour of light.

**Philippians 4:8. Finally, brethren,** **whatsoever things are true, whatsoever things are honest, whatsoever things are just, whatsoever things are pure, whatsoever things are lovely, whatsoever things are of good report; if there be any virtue, and if there be any praise, think on these things.**

---

## LESSON OUTLINE

I. INTEGRITY IS A DIVINE COMMAND
II. INTEGRITY BRINGS FELLOWSHIP WITH GOD
III. INTEGRITY MARKS THE CHRISTIAN'S LIFE

## LESSON EXPOSITION

INTRODUCTION

Integrity means "conformity to sound moral principles." Thus, integrity reflects an honesty and an uprightness of character.

Is not this what Jesus called for in Matthew 5:33-37? He said we should have such an impeccable character that we would not have to persuade people to believe our words and actions by making exaggerated oaths.

Jesus knew that personal integrity was important in our personal relations. When we possess integrity, it enhances our relationships with others. Integrity is at the heart of the moral life. If we possess integrity, it means that we keep our promises, that we can be trusted, that we are loyal, and that we are dependable. Integrity is a moral force that affects our human destiny, that brings freedom in personal relationships and that makes human community possible.

Everything in our life depends on personal integrity. On that single thread-integrity hangs everything from nuclear disarmament to a family reunion. When we have integrity, we are most of all like God, who is faithful to His nature and actions.

I. INTEGRITY IS A DIVINE COMMAND (Deuteronomy 25:13-15; Romans 13:8-12; 14:10-12)

**Deuteronomy 25:13. Thou shalt not** **have in thy bag divers weights, a great and a small.**

**14. Thou shalt not have in thine house divers measures, a great and a small.**

**15. But thou shalt have a perfect and just weight, a perfect and just measure shalt thou have: that thy days may be lengthened in the land which the Lord thy God giveth thee.**

When a merchant purchased a product, it was possible for him to obtain more than he actually paid for by using a large weight or measure, and when he sold the product, he could make a larger profit by exchanging the weight or measure for a smaller size. This practice was prohibited in the Mosaic law. The merchant was required to use only the legally approved size of weight or measure when buying and selling commodities.

Verse 15 ties the commercial practice with religion, which was characteristic of Hebrew religion. Other near Eastern religions separated religion and morality, but in Hebrew religion they were inseparable. This is evident in the Holiness Code given in Leviticus 19:9-18. The passage contains regulations for Hebrew society, but they are all founded on the basis of God being Lord. The people were to obey the stipulations from God, because they had formed a covenant with Him. Hence, integrity in business dealings indicated integrity before God.

Furthermore, the verse ties the duration of Israel's stay in the promised land with honest commercial practices. If the people were honest in their business dealings, then they would remain in the promised land. If they were dishonest, God would remove them from the land.

**Romans 13:8. Owe no man any thing,**

**but to love one another: for he that loveth another hath fulfilled the law.**

**9. For this, Thou shalt not commit adultery, Thou shalt not kill, Thou shalt not steal, Thou shalt not bear false witness, Thou shalt not covet; and if there be any other commandment, it is briefly comprehended in this saying, namely, Thou shalt love thy neighbour as thyself.**

**10. Love worketh no ill to his neighbour: therefore love is the fulfilling of the law.**

Love is the capstone of the moral structure leading to integrity. We should not be indebted to anyone, except for our obligation to love our neighbor. Since he is loved by God, we will always be in debt to serve him with love.

In verse 9, Paul listed the last five commandments of the Ten Commandments. These commandments pertain to the relationship between persons. They deal with personal relations, marriage and family relations, and economical relations. However, instead of giving us an exhaustive list of commandments, Paul summarized our responsibility to our neighbor by quoting Leviticus 19:18: "Thou shalt love thy neighbour as thyself." We need no other commandment because love will seek to do what is right and will not serve its own end.

**11. And that, knowing the time, that now it is high time to awake out of sleep: for now is our salvation nearer than when we believed.**

**12. The night is far spent, the day is at hand: let us therefore cast off the works of darkness, and let us put on the armour of light.**

In his writings Paul used three themes to encourage holy living. The athletic theme (1 Corinthians 9:24-27) admonishes us to prepare ourselves for the Christian life like an athlete who trains himself for his sporting event. Personal sacredness (1 Corinthians 6:12-20) is a theme that exhorts us to live godly because we are God's possessions and we are indwelt by Him. The second coming of Christ (Romans 13:11, 12) is a motive that encourages us to live holy

because of the immediacy of the return of Christ. We should awake from our spiritual sleep and be up, doing Christian works and living a Christian life in dynamic love.

The soon return of Christ motivates us to moral living. Verse 12 declares that we should have moral discernment between light (that which is moral) and darkness (that which is immoral). Verse 13 exclaims that we should conduct ourselves as Christians. Verse 14 admonishes us to live out what we have experienced inwardly.

---

How may the expectation of the return of Christ affect our integrity?

---

In the context of Romans 14:10-12, Paul is writing to Christians at Rome about two groups of Christians who had difficulty getting along with each other because of their views about matters that were really matters of personal convictions. One of the groups could be called liberated Christians because their conscience allowed them to eat meat that had been offered to idols, and their conscience had released them from having to observe certain holidays and festivals. The second group could be called overcautious Christians because their conscience did not allow them to eat meat that had been offered to idols, and because they had to observe certain holidays and festivals. If they did not follow the dictates of their conscience, they felt like they were under the condemnation of sin. However, as Paul says in the chapter, it was not God who impressed upon them the sense of condemnation, but their own conscience.

These two groups would argue with each other. The liberated Christians would insult the overcautious Christians because of the convictions of the overcautious. The overcautious Christians would condemn the liberated Christians because the latter did not live according to the convictions of the former.

Hence, in verses 10-12, Paul asked why they judged each other. It was not appropriate for one Christian to judge another Christian. In fact, we do not need to be concerned with judging each other. Everyone will bow before Christ, everyone will confess Christ to God, and everyone will give an account of himself to God.

In those matters of personal convictions, we should not judge the spirituality of our fellow Christians, but we should all be very concerned with the integrity of our own life. We should not judge a brother for a speck of sawdust in his eye when there may be a plank in our own eye (Matthew 7:1-5). We should be concerned with our own personal, spiritual life because each one of us will give an account to God for his life.

These passages show integrity to be the demand of God. We must have personal integrity because of the relationship between religion and morality, because of our love debt to others, because of the immediacy of the return of Christ, and because of our giving an account to God for our life.

---

Discuss the value of conscience in the Christian life. Can one's conscience steer in error? Explain.

---

II. INTEGRITY BRINGS FELLOWSHIP WITH GOD (Psalm 24:3-6; 1 John 1:6, 7)

**Psalm 24:3. Who shall ascend into the hill of the Lord? or who shall stand in his holy place?**

**4. He that hath clean hands, and a pure heart; who hath not lifted up his soul unto vanity, nor sworn deceitfully.**

**5. He shall receive the blessing from the Lord, and the righteousness from the God of his salvation.**

**6. This is the generation of them that seek him, that seek thy face, O Jacob. Selah.**

Psalm 24 is one of the psalms (compare Psalm 15) which shows that integrity of character brings fellowship with God. Verse 3 asks, "Who shall ascend into the hill of the Lord? or who shall stand in his holy place?"

' Verse 4 answers the questions in verse

3: Those who have clean hands, a pure heart, and have not sworn deceitfully can have fellowship with God. "Clean hands" refers to following the rituals in worship and giving proper treatment to one's neighbors. "A pure heart" refers to proper thoughts, will, motives, and intentions. A lack of deceitfulness refers to not being deceptive, fraudulent or underhanded with others. Verse 4 gives a comprehensive view of integrity that includes a loyalty and faithfulness to God and man, and it is this kind of person who will have a relationship with God.

Verse 5 gives the results of having personal integrity. As shown by the parallelism in the verse, the man of integrity has the smile of God upon him. He is accepted by God; he is helped by God to live an upright life; and his affairs in this life proceed under God's blessings. The man of integrity is successful because God pronounces a verdict in favor of integrity.

In the context of 1 John 1:6, 7, John dealt with three erroneous claims (1:6, 8, 10) presented by false teachers. The errors concern the fact of sin in our conduct, its origin in our nature, and its consequence in our relationship to God. They are the misconceptions of men who want fellowship with God on easy terms. They want to separate religion from morality.

The false claim in verse 6 is the assertion that we have fellowship with God, while at the same time we habitually practice immorality ("walk in darkness"). However, since God is light, from a moral perspective that is, holy, religion without morality is an illusion.

If we talk about being righteous without doing righteousness, we do two things. First, we lie. Second, we do not do the truth. The truth of the gospel is that those who have fellowship with God will not be immoral.

Verse 7 describes what will happen "if we walk in the light, as he is in the light." God is in the light because He is always true to His nature. As imitators of God, we will be faithful to our nature and our activity will be consistent with our nature. We should be the person God created us to be. Nothing more; nothing less.

If we do imitate God, two things will happen. First, we will have fellowship with God. Second, we will have fellowship with each other. When we have integrity of character, such as, pure motives and intentions, loyalty, and reliability, there is a freedom and a willingness to have association with each other. These fibers of the fabric of integrity enhance the relationship between each other.

These two passages show that we must have integrity of character if we are to have fellowship with God. No one can have fellowship with God and practice immorality. If he says he can, he is deceived.

What is the relationship between integrity of character and fellowship with God?

III. INTEGRITY MARKS THE CHRISTIAN'S LIFE (Proverbs 11:3-5; Micah 6:8; Philippians 4:8, 9)

**Proverbs 11:3. The integrity of the upright shall guide them: but the perverseness of transgressors shall destroy them.**

**4. Riches profit not in the day of wrath: but righteousness delivereth from death.**

**5. The righteousness of the perfect shall direct his way: but the wicked shall fall by his own wickedness.**

Guidance is the subject of verse 3. It deals with the contrast between the righteous and the wicked. Integrity is contrasted with perversion, and "straight men" with "crooked men." Integrity guarantees safe guidance, but perversion leads to destruction.

The contrast between wealth and righteousness in verse 4 is similar to Proverbs 10:2. The "day of wrath" probably refers to God's judgment upon the ungodly. Hence, wealth without righteousness does not give protection against God's judgment. The only safeguard of life and guard against death is righteousness.

In verse 5 the perfect man is the sincere man, whose piety is without defect or hypocrisy. The righteousness of a sincere man guarantees him unfailing guidance on the way of life. On the other hand, the wicked man, who is denied a passage along a safe and clear road and is like a person stumbling in the dark, fails because of his wickedness.

The Prophet Micah gives a clear picture of integrity in chapter 6 of his book. God invites the people to plead their case before the mountains, where He pleads His case against them (vv. 1, 2). The mountains and the earth present a cosmic setting for conducting the case. In this setting God appears like a Hebrew entering the gate of a city calling for the elders to hear his complaint against his neighbor.

In review of His case against Israel, God gives the history of His relationship to Israel (vv. 3-5). He had repeatedly and powerfully redeemed His people, bringing them from Egypt and preserving them in the face of the hostility of the Moabites. In return the people had repeatedly and perversely turned to other gods and indulged in forbidden practices. They used wicked balances, deceitful weights, violence, and lies to amass their wealth (vv. 9-12). God's judgment for their sin against their neighbor would be the following: they would eat and not be satisfied; they would try to save money but would not be able to because of monetary inflation; their agricultural pursuits would not increase; and they themselves would be scorned and held in contempt (vv. 13-16).

In the midst of his sermon, Micah, speaking on behalf of the people, asked what would meet God's approval (vv. 6-8). Was God seeking quality in worship (offering a one-year-old calf)? Or was it quantity of worship (thousands of rams or ten thousands of rivers of oil)? Or was it the sacrifice of the first child in a family?

It seems the people would have been

willing to have done any of these, if these were what God wanted. Isaiah, who lived at the same time of Micah, indicated the people were not slack in their offering of proper sacrifices and in quantity of sacrifices. Later, in the time of Jeremiah, some Israelites did sacrifice their own children. But the answer to each of these questions was no! What God required was justice, mercy, and humility.

*Justice* which is the theme of Micah 2, 3, and 6:10, 11, means "fulfilling a right and equitable standard of dealing between people." Justice may be based on merit. It is right to pay an architect who designed a skyscraper more than a laborer who cleaned up the work site. Justice may be based on need. It is fair to give a person who has a physical handicap special consideration which may not be given to others, in order that the handicap person may have the same opportunity as others.

Mercy is a consistent practice of love. It characterizes our actions which fulfill obligations inherent in a relationship, even when no laws cover that relationship. A husband owes certain duties to his wife, not because they are defined in the marriage contract, but because they are inherent in the common understanding and practice of the relationship. Obligations may be inherent in relationships without being defined in legal codes; mercy will fulfill those obligations.

We must approach God in humility and continue to walk in humility. There is no sacrificial offering that can open the way to God. Only God opens the way, and it is by God's kindness that man may have a relationship with God (Ephesians 2:8-10). Thus, we see the necessity of walking humbly before God.

**Philippians 4:8. Finally, brethren, whatsoever things are true, whatsoever things are honest, whatsoever things are just, whatsoever things are pure, whatsoever things are lovely, whatsoever things are of good report; if there be any virtue, and if there be any praise, think on these things.**

"Finally" means "besides." Before his conclusion Paul had one more exhortation (4:8, 9). He had already given several instructions: (1) persevere in the faith (v. 1); (2) settle differences (v. 2); (3) help others (v. 3); (4) rejoice in the Lord (v. 4); (5) be known for moderation (v. 5); and (6) pray rather than worry (vv. 6, 7). Now he spoke to them about integrity of thought and deed (vv. 8, 9).

Paul gave a list of virtues that we should think and act upon and exhorted that under the guidance of the Holy Spirit, these virtues be a part of our Christian life.

Think upon what is true. True refers to what is real and not false. We should think upon reality. Television includes programs about reality and fantasies. Watching too much fantasy on television may blur our perception of reality so that we are unable to determine the difference between the two. It also may numb our moral sensitivity so that we become indifferent to the events of real life. It may lead us to retreat from real life, causing us to "drop out" of the world as God made it. It is necessary that we discipline our thoughts to deal with reality.

Thinking upon what is true includes a spiritual dimension. Barnabas thought on that which was real—the things of God—ministering to the needs of others. It led him to true life. Ananias had thoughts of grandeur and personal glory. They led him to phoniness rather than integrity. The true, genuine life will be lived in a right relationship with God and neighbor.

Think upon what is honest. In the verse "honest" means "a thought that is ennobling and reverential to the individual." The idea may be explained by the contrast between serious and frivolous. We should be serious in thought and deed. We are not opposing humor and laughter. We all know what good medicine laughter is for us (Proverbs 17:22). We are referring to a fixation on the trivia of life. We become what we think. If we are preoccupied with petty matters, our character will be affected by them; but, if we reflect on lofty ideas, our character will be ennobled.

Think upon what is just. Think upon

what is right according to God's will rather than what is convenient to our desires. The good Samaritan exemplified justice because he ministered to his neighbor, while the priest exemplified convenience because he neglected his neighbor for selfish reasons.

Think upon what is pure. Our thoughts should be unadulterated. The word is quite often associated with sexual thoughts, meaning these should be holy and chaste. We should not look upon the opposite sex as an object to be exploited or manipulated, but we should respect the individual as a person.

There is a broader use of the word "pure." The motives and intentions of our plans should serve the well-being of all concerned. When David sent for Uriah, his scheme had impure motives and intentions that led to tragedy (2 Samuel 11:1-25). Our thoughts should be unmixed; we should meditate only on those things that will minister to our neighbors and ourselves.

Think upon what is lovely, which means what is friendly and pleasing. Think upon those amiable ideas that will promote and maintain harmony between our neighbor and ourselves. Instead of destructively criticizing our neighbor, let us imagine ways in which we can improve our relationship with him.

Think upon what is a good report. A good report is well-sounding and appealing. It is a thought that would not disturb devotion or give rise to a scandal. It is not chronically negative. It is unlike Tobiah and Sanballat who found fault with everything that Nehemiah and Ezra did. Instead, it looks for the good in life.

It is essential that we feed our body; it is also essential that we feed our mind. We need to feed our mind plenty of food served through teaching, preaching, and example. Paul said the Philippians had learned, received, heard, and seen. They had been given information and they had received it. They had seen an example of integrity of thought and action in Paul. They were now to practice what they had heard and seen.

Verse 8 exhorts us to proper meditation. The integrity of our thought will affect the development of character in us. Proper thought is developed through proper feeding, such as the above virtues, and is given birth through action.

Verse 9 exhorts us to proper action. Our meditation is not just abstract thought, but it is thinking with a purpose. True believers meditate until they understand. Then they act upon their meditation, putting it into constant practice.

The result of integrity of thought and action will be the presence of God, who will bring peace to our life. We can have fellowship with God, and we dwell in His presence because our thoughts and actions do not condemn us when the light of His nature falls upon us. We know that we have conformed to His standard of righteousness when we have integrity of thought and action. Consequently, our conscience is free of guilt and shame. We have peace with God and ourselves.

**REVIEW QUESTIONS**

1. What does integrity mean?
2. Why is integrity a divine command?
3. Why does integrity allow us to have fellowship with God?
4. What was Micah's answer to the question of what God expects of us?
5. How do our thoughts affect our actions?

**GOLDEN TEXT HOMILY**

"HE HATH SHEWED THEE, O MAN, WHAT IS GOOD; AND WHAT DOTH THE LORD REQUIRE OF THEE, BUT TO DO JUSTLY, AND TO LOVE MERCY, AND TO WALK HUMBLY WITH THY GOD?" (Micah 6:8).

God had delivered His people, Israel, from Egyptian bondage, but they had failed to respond to His mighty saving acts. They had turned aside from God and had trusted in external forms of worship to no avail. The popular view was that God demanded an unceasing supply of offerings to atone for sins. So people asked the Prophet Micah, "Will the LORD be pleased with thousands of rams, or with ten thousands of rivers of oil?" (Micah 6:7).

As always, God did not want more and more offerings but heartfelt devotion to Him. Our response to the living God is to be grounded in His great mercy. What God has done prompts us to live the life of faith. That requires us to do justly, to love kindness, and to walk humbly with God. "To do justly" requires righteous living. The Scripture teaches us to "trust in the LORD, and do good" (Psalm 37:3). Genuine concern and love for others are to spring from personal faith in God. "To love kindness" requires a right heart. Only the person with a pure and sanctified heart abides with God (Psalm 15:1, 2). Regardless of how noble our deeds may be, without pure motives we cannot please God. "To walk humbly" requires the forsaking of pride and self-will and developing a whole-hearted devotion to walk carefully with God. As the Prophet Isaiah says, "The meek . . . shall increase their joy in the LORD, and the poor among men shall rejoice in the Holy One of Israel" (29:19).

Faith without works is dead. Good deeds are important, but basic is the devotion of the heart to God. Our hearts should be set on fire with love in response to God's grace and mercy in Christ. The fruit of this is the doing of justice, the pursuit of kindness, and the exercise of a humble walk with the Lord.
—**French L. Arrington, Ph. D., Professor of New Testament Greek and Exegesis at the Church of God School of Theology, Cleveland, Tennessee.**

## SENTENCE SERMONS

IT IS OFTEN surprising to find what heights may be obtained merely by remaining on the level.

—**"Speaker's Sourcebook"**

THE CHRISTIAN'S INTEGRITY in his relationship with God and man is a testimony of Christ's saving and keeping power.

—**Selected**

WHEN A MAN gets in the straight way, he finds there is no room for crooked dealings.

—**"The Presbyterian"**

## EVANGELISTIC APPLICATION

HEAVEN IS PREPARED FOR THOSE WHO ACCEPT CHRIST AS SAVIOR AND LIVE BY GOD'S STANDARDS IN THIS PRESENT WORLD.

If you were tried by a court of law for being a Christian, would there be enough evidence to convict you? Many of us have heard this question before. It is a question that makes us evaluate our life. Have we really been living what we say? Do we have integrity?

More specifically, do our employees know that what we say is the truth or do we have to "stand on a stack of Bibles to convince them we are truthful? Do our spouses know that we love them when we tell them so, or do we have to constantly convince them because we mistreat them? Do our neighbors know that we have wholesome thoughts by the jokes we tell?

If we can answer these questions affirmatively, let us maintain our integrity. If we cannot, let us recall 1 John 1:7 which says, "The blood of Jesus Christ . . . cleanseth us from all sin." We can have integrity of character because God will forgive us of our sins, cleanse us from them, declare us to be righteous before Him and our neighbor, and help us maintain our new integrity. Then, we will have peace in our life because we are living as we were meant to be—in a right relationship with God and neighbor.

## DAILY DEVOTIONAL GUIDE

M. Holding Fast to Integrity. Job 27:3-6
T. Understanding God's Ways. Proverbs 2:3-9
W. God's Estimate of a Just Person. Ezekiel 18:5-9
T. Maintaining a Good Conscience. Acts 24:10-16
F. Honesty Before God and Men. 2 Corinthians 8:16-21
S. God's Special People. 1 Peter 2:1-12

# Responsible Citizenship

**Study Text:** Daniel 1:1-8; Matthew 5:13-16; 22:17-21; Acts 4:18-20; 5:27-39; Romans 13:1-7; 14:7, 8; Philippians 2:14-16; 1 Peter 2:13-17

**Supplemental References:** Ezra 6:8-10; Jeremiah 29:7; Matthew 17:24-27; 1 Thessalonians 1:7, 8; 1 Timothy 2:1, 2; 6:1-5; Titus 3:1-9

**Golden Text:** "Let your light so shine before men, that they may see your good works, and glorify your Father which is in heaven" (Matthew 5:16).

**Central Truth:** God does not intend for Christians to live in isolation but to exert their influence in this world.

**Evangelistic Emphasis:** Citizenship in God's kingdom comes only through a born-again experience.

## Printed Text

**Matthew 5:13.** Ye are the salt of the earth: but if the salt have lost his savour, wherewith shall it be salted? it is thenceforth good for nothing, but to be cast out, and to be trodden under foot of men.

**14. Ye are the light of the world. A city that is set on an hill cannot be hid.**

15. Neither do men light a candle, and put it under a bushel, but on a candlestick; and it giveth light unto all that are in the house.

**16. Let your light so shine before men, that they may see your good works, and glorify your Father which is in heaven.**

**Romans 13:1.** Let every soul be subject unto the higher powers. For there is no power but of God: the powers that be are ordained of God.

**2. Whosoever therefore resisteth the power, resisteth the ordinance of God: and they that resist shall receive to themselves damnation.**

3. For rulers are not a terror to good works, but to the evil. Wilt thou then not be afraid of the power? do that which is good, and thou shalt have praise of the same:

**4. For he is the minister of God to thee for good. But if thou do that which is evil, be afraid; for he beareth not the sword in vain: for he is the minister of God, a revenger to execute wrath upon him that doeth evil.**

5. Wherefore ye must needs be subject, not only for wrath, but also for conscience sake.

**6. For for this cause pay ye tribute also: for they are God's ministers, attending continually upon this very thing.**

7. Render therefore to all their dues: tribute to whom tribute is due; custom to whom custom; fear to whom fear; honour to whom honour.

**14:7. For none of us liveth to himself, and no man dieth to himself.**

8. For whether we live, we live unto the Lord; and whether we die, we die unto the Lord: whether we live therefore, or die, we are the Lord's.

**1 Peter 2:13. Submit yourselves to every ordinance of man for the Lord's sake: whether it be to the king, as supreme;**

14. Or unto governors, as unto them that are sent by him for the punishment

of evildoers, and for the praise of them that do well.

**15. For so is the will of God, that with well doing ye may put to silence the ignorance of foolish men:**

**16.** As free, and not using your liberty for a cloke of maliciousness, but as the servants of God.

**17. Honour all men. Love the brotherhood. Fear God. Honour the king.**

---

## LESSON OUTLINE

I. THE CHRISTIAN AND GOVERNMENT

II. CONFLICTING OBLIGATIONS

III. THE CHRISTIAN'S INFLUENCE

## LESSON EXPOSITION

INTRODUCTION

It is of God's ordering that there should be human government and human laws. Without them there could be no order, security, or progress among mankind. Imperfect as they may often be, and in some instances oppressive and unjust, still they in general exist for a purpose of good and form part of the Divine order for the government of the world. In this sense all are from God and are ordained of God; and in submitting to them we are submitting to God.

The duty of Christians as citizens is in our day not sufficiently recognized. Many Christians keep aloof from public life because of political corruption and party strife. Others enter into public duties but seem to leave their religious convictions behind. The result is a sad want of Christian statesmanship and of Christian influence on legislature.

Our lesson today focuses on the Christian's responsibility as citizens in this world while retaining citizenship in the heavenly kingdom. We cannot take an isolationist position, but are called on to exert our influence in this world.

I. THE CHRISTIAN AND GOVERNMENT (Matthew 22:17-21; Romans 13:1-7; 1 Peter 2:13-17)

**Romans 13:1. Let every soul be subject unto the higher powers. For there is no power but of God: the powers that be are ordained of God.**

At the time of his writing the letter to the church at Rome, Paul had seen the benefits of the Roman government to society. It had provided justice, a network of highways for commerce, and stability in government. Paul himself had experienced the benefits of Roman citizenship. It had given him certain rights and privileges, as well as protection.

The positive experience with the Roman government may have influenced Paul in his instruction to the Christians at Rome. He encouraged them to be obedient to the government, which was opposite of the attitude that many Jews had. The Jews had been expelled from Rome, perhaps because of unfriendliness to the Roman rule or because of their rebellion. Since Christianity was associated with Judaism in the minds of the Roman officials, Paul insisted that the Christians be obedient to the government rather than have the attitude of the Jews.

Furthermore, it was highly desirable to Christians that the world continue until the return of Christ. The Roman government acted as a restraining power, which gave Christians a peaceful existence and the opportunity of preaching the gospel. Accordingly, it was their duty to maintain the machinery of the state, and to recognize in it God's own appointed means of preserving the stability and moral order of the world, and of putting God's wrath into operation before the "day of wrath."

In verse 1, Paul recognized that God is the Lord over all things, even nations and history. His view is consistent with the Old Testament view. God raised up the Assyrian Empire for His purpose, and then destroyed it. God placed Cyrus on the Persian throne so that the Hebrews could return home. Paul acknowledged that God is behind all authority.

God provides man with civil authority, just as He provides him with sun and rain, in order to protect man from the consequences of unbridled aggression and anarchy. Thus, civil authority has its appointed place in the providential order which God has established for man.

**2. Whosoever therefore resisteth the power, resisteth the ordinance of God: and they that resist shall receive to themselves damnation.**

Some Christians in the early church considered themselves above the law, because they were citizens of the kingdom of God. They believed it was all right if they disobeyed the civil authority, but Paul said such a belief was wrong because God ordained the civil authority. God is the source of the power of the civil authority, and a violation of the laws of the civil authorities is a wrong committed against God as well.

If someone does disobey the government, he will be judged. When resistance is offered to the state, divine judgment comes into operation at once by means of the government's judicial procedures.

**3. For rulers are not a terror to good works, but to the evil. Wilt thou then not be afraid of the power? do that which is good, and thou shalt have praise of the same:**

**4. For he is the minister of God to thee for good. But if thou do that which is evil, be afraid; for he beareth not the sword in vain: for he is the minister of God, a revenger to execute wrath upon him that doeth evil.**

"Rulers are not a terror to good works, but to the evil" refers to the punishment of evildoing. Paul recognized the authority of the state to punish those who violated the law. The "terror" which rulers are to evil works is the fear punishment evokes in the hearts of men when they recognize the authority of the government to punish evildoers. This fear can be of two kinds: the fear that inhibits wrongdoing and the fear that results when wrong has been committed.

"Thou shalt have praise of the same" does not refer to a tangible reward. Evildoers receive their punitive rewards, but those who do well do not receive any meritorious reward. The term "praise" could be expressed by saying that good behavior secures good standing in the state, which is a status Paul encouraged us to attain.

Verse 4 gives the primary purpose of civil authority. The term "minister of God," which is related to verses 1 and 2 where authority is said to be of God, refers to a specific task of civil authority. The ruler is to serve for the good in the sense that he provides order and protection in society by restraining evil. The title shows that the ruler deserves respect because he is God's servant within the government.

The next clause, "but if thou do that which is evil, be afraid," points to the fear referred to in verse 3.

The third clause, "for he beareth not the sword in vain," gives the reason why this fear is to be considered. The sword which the ruler carries is the sign of his authority and of his right to inflict punishment when it is required.

The last clause of verse 4, "for he is the minister of God, a revenger to execute wrath upon him that doeth evil," is parallel to the first clause in verse 4. In the first clause the authority is a minister that brings good, and in the last clause he judges evil. The ruler executes judgment upon the criminal, because he is the agent executing God's wrath.

---

Should we consider the punishment administered by present governments to be God's punishment on the evildoer as well?

---

**5. Wherefore ye must needs be subject, not only for wrath, but also for conscience sake.**

Verse 5 gives two reasons why Christians should obey the civil authorities. If we fail to do so, God's wrath will fall upon us through the powers of the government. Also, there is the obligation to fulfill God's will. As Christians, we are bound to recognize the divine authority of the government as God's servant, so that our conscience itself will impel us to give obedience.

**6. For for this cause pay ye tribute also: for they are God's ministers, attending continually upon this very thing.**

**7. Render therefore to all their dues: tribute to whom tribute is due; custom to whom custom; fear to whom fear; honour to whom honour.**

In verse 6, the term "ministers" is different from the one used in verse 4. This term refers specifically to the service of the Lord and sometimes to the highest forms of ministry in the worship of God (Acts 13:2; Philippians 2:17; and Hebrews 1:7). The designation enhances the dignity of the ministry of the rulers and the respect we should give them.

The term "very thing" refers to the collection of taxes. If the ruler is to perform his ministry, he must have material means with which he can do it. Hence the payment of taxes is necessary on the part of citizens.

Verse 7 indicates that honor is due to earthly rulers because they have been appointed by God. It follows, then, that to treat them with less than their due of honor is dishonor to God.

**1 Peter 2:13. Submit yourselves to every ordinance of man for the Lord's sake: whether it be to the king, as supreme;**

**14. Or unto governors, as unto them that are sent by him for the punishment of evildoers, and for the praise of them that do well.**

Peter was writing to churches that, like other churches, had not yet been persecuted by the state. One of the positive aspects of the Roman government was its toleration of different religions. When the Romans conquered an area, they allowed the people to continue practicing their religious beliefs. Until the time of Peter's writing the letter, Christianity was considered a part of Judaism, which was an officially accepted religion by the state. Consequently, Christianity had the approval and protection of the government.

When Christians were persecuted, and they were, it was by a religious or social group and limited to a particular area. The persecution of the church in Jerusalem is an example (Acts 3-5). Until the end of the reign of Nero, the church did not experience official persecution from the Roman government.

In the phrase "ordinance of man" Peter is referring to the particular laws of society and not to a Christian theology of the state. His interest is that Christians would submit themselves to the civil laws, that is, they would voluntarily accept the laws of the land.

"For the Lord's sake" may mean one of several things. First, it may mean that Christians will obey civil laws, because they recognize the state is an institution from God. This interpretation is equivalent to what Paul wrote in Romans 13:1-7. Second, it may mean we should follow the example of the Lord. This interpretation is a recurring theme in the letter, and it is based on the acceptance of Pilate's judgment by Jesus rather than revolting against civil authority. Third, it may mean that through the obedience of Christians to the civil laws, Christ would be commended to nonbelievers and reproach would not be brought on Christ, which is suggested in verse 15.

**15. For so is the will of God, that with well doing, ye may put to silence the ignorance of foolish men.**

Verse 15 recognizes that submission to civil authorities is the will of God so that the testimony of Christianity will not be harmed. One of the purposes for Luke writing the Acts of the Apostles was to refute the idea that Christianity was attempting to overthrow the Roman government. Peter attempts the same thing in this letter. By the Christian obeying the civil laws, no one could indict them for rebellion and subversion nor could they slander the character of Christians. At times nonbelievers had accused Christians of incest, murder, and even cannibalism. A good way of ending doubt and avoiding bad testimony is to do what is expected of you. Peter counseled the Christians to do that by their submission to the government. When they did obey the civil laws, the non-believers who looked for an excuse to persecute and slander Christianity would not have one.

**16. As free, and not using your liberty for a cloke of maliciousness, but as the servants of God.**

**17. Honour all men. Love the brotherhood. Fear God. Honour the king.**

Peter wrote in verse 16 that Christians have freedom in Jesus Christ; however, the freedom did not mean lawlessness. Christian freedom is the liberty to do what God wants us to do, and it is not license to practice rebellion. God's will is that we obey the laws of the land so that we do not harm the testimony of the gospel. Christian freedom, in this case, means that we will submit to the civil authorities.

Peter concludes the appeal to submission to civil authorities with four practical expressions. We should honor all men because Christ did. We should love all Christians. We should approach God with worship. And we should respect civil rulers.

---

Should we obey all laws, including the speed limit?

---

As these verses gave practical instruction to the Christians during biblical times, they give us practical guidance for our lives. First, we should obey our government for several reasons. If we do not obey the government, God will punish us through the means of the government, our conscience will condemn us, and we will harm the testimony of the gospel. Second, we should keep in mind that Paul and Peter instructed the Christians to obey a government that was on the whole, good. They did not indicate in these verses what Christians should do if a government went beyond its divinely given authority.

II. CONFLICTING OBLIGATIONS (Daniel 1:1-8; Acts 4:18-20; 5:27-29)

Both the Old Testament and the New Testament recognize there may be times

when the religious sphere and the political sphere conflict. It was noted in the discussion of Romans 13:1-7 and 1 Peter 2:13-17 that both Paul and Peter had a positive attitude toward civil authority, and they had reasons, both theological and practical, for their attitude. However, not all of the biblical writers had the same positive attitude about particular governments. The Book of Revelation certainly does not reflect the same attitude as the writings of Paul and Peter. When Revelation was written, the church was being persecuted by the Roman government, and the church found hope in God. This is not to say there is a contradiction in Scripture, but a recognition that Paul and Peter were addressing one situation and John another.

Some biblical passages that deal with conflicting obligations for God's people in the religious sphere and the political sphere are: Daniel 1:1-8, Matthew 22:15-21, Acts 4:18-20, and Acts 5:27-29.

Daniel writes that he, along with other Hebrews, had been deported from Israel to Babylon by Nebuchadnezzar the king of Babylon. Nebuchadnezzar chose the elite of the Hebrew captives to work in his empire. Daniel, Shadrach, Meshach, and Abednego were some of those who were chosen. As part of their training for their position in the empire, the captives were required to eat the diet provided by the king's officers. Daniel and the three Hebrew young men refused to eat the diet, because they believed to so eat would have compromised their faith. (The food may have been part of Babylonian religious practices. To have eaten would have implied an acceptance of that religion.) They believed it was more important to observe their Hebrew faith rather than the king's demands.

In Matthew 22:15-21, Jesus is asked a question by the Pharisees and Herodians. It is ironic that these two factions should ask Jesus a question because of their differences. The Pharisees despised the Roman rulership in Palestine. The Herodians supported the Romans, because it meant their patron, Herod, would remain in power and they would benefit.

They asked Jesus if a Jew should pay

taxes to Caesar. On the one hand, the question implied God's people were not subject to pagan Gentiles and on the other hand, one was giving divine honors to Caesar through the payment of taxes. This was a provocative question for two reasons. If Jesus said a Jew should not pay taxes, He would be guilty of treason. If He said yes, He would be supporting the foreign power, which would have jeopardized His relationship with the Jews.

Jesus said to give to Caesar what belonged to him and to give to God what belonged to Him. The coin, which bore Caesar's image, belonged to him and was to be returned. We, being made in God's image, belong to Him and should be given back to Him. Jesus did not divide life into two parts, one religious and one political. That would have ranked Caesar with God. We have an obligation to Caesar, but we have a higher obligation to God. In this situation it meant the Jews had an obligation to pay taxes to Caesar, whom God permitted to rule. They also had an obligation to give their total selves to God, who owned them.

Prior to Acts 4:18-20, Peter and John were used by the Lord to heal a man at the temple gate called Beautiful. The miracle drew a large crowd, and Peter took the opportunity to preach the gospel to the crowd. The priests, the captain of the temple guard, and the Sadducees were among the listeners.

These religious leaders apprehended Peter and John and questioned them about their preaching. Although the religious leaders could not charge them for any crime, they prohibited them from preaching the gospel. Peter and John refused to comply with the prohibition. They charged that whenever a duty conflicted with an obligation to God, they must fulfill the obligation to God.

The passage in Acts 5:27-29 is similar to Acts 4:18-20. The apostles had been preaching throughout Jerusalem, and the religious leaders summoned the apostles to appear before them. The leaders questioned the disobedience of the apostles to the leaders' prohibition. Peter replied, even more forcefully than before, that the apostles must obey God rather than man.

III. THE CHRISTIAN'S INFLUENCE (Matthew 5:13-16; Romans 14:7, 8; Philippians 2:14-16)

**Matthew 5:13. Ye are the salt of the earth: but if the salt have lost his savour, wherewith shall it be salted? it is thenceforth good for nothing, but to be cast out, and to be trodden under foot of men.**

**14. Ye are the light of the world. A city that is set on a hill cannot be hid.**

**15. Neither do men light a candle, and put it under a bushel, but on a candlestick; and it giveth light unto all that are in the house.**

**16. Let your light so shine before men, that they may see your good works, and glorify your Father which is in heaven.**

Christ described the influence of Christians by two metaphors, salt and light. Salt seasons food so that it is more pleasant to the taste, and it prevents food from spoiling. These are the characteristics of the Christian that Christ had in mind. Christians are to penetrate society so that they can prevent it from decaying. Paul wrote about a degenerate society in Romans 1:18-32. Christians are placed in the world by God to prevent the world from completely decaying. "Christian" salt cannot remain in a box; it must be rubbed into secular society, like salt is rubbed into meat, to stop it from going bad.

Light penetrates darkness so that we may see. The idea of the metaphor that Jesus is presenting is our responsibility to lead the world to truth, righteousness and justice.

As salt and light to the world, our Christian responsibility is twofold. As salt, we are to hinder social decay. As light, we are to dispel spiritual darkness. This calls us to social action (James 1:27) and evangelism (Acts 1:8).

Although God has instituted civil authority and the family as social structures for stabilizing society and restraining evil, Christians have a responsibility to see that these structures are not only preserved but also operated with justice.

We need to help those who suffer from a sick society, but we also need to change the structures which cause them to suffer. Just as doctors are concerned with treating a patient and with preventive medicine, we must be concerned with the disadvantaged in society and the causes for injustices. Hence, we need to feed and clothe the disadvantaged, but we also must plead for their civil rights.

However, the world needs an addition to a social ministry. It needs the gospel that proclaims a new life. While we need good works of love, such as caring for the homeless, we also need works of faith, such as witnessing. The gospel has the power to transform an individual and give him a new life wherever he is.

We should never put our two vocations, our social and evangelistic responsibilities, over against each other as if we had to choose between them. The world needs both. It is decaying and needs salt; it is dark and needs light.

If we do not do both, what is our value? When salt has lost its power, it is useless. In biblical days, when salt lost its effectiveness, it was thrown away. Should that happen to a Christian, if he loses his effectiveness? No one would light a candle and then hide it. No Christian should do such with his life.

Should Christians be involved in politics?

**Romans 14:7. For none of us liveth to himself, and no man dieth to himself.**

**8. For whether we live, we live unto the Lord; and whether we die, we die unto the Lord: whether we live therefore, or die, we are the Lord's.**

Paul is giving advice about resolving difficulties between the two groups. Verses 7 and 8 show that the believer lives "unto the Lord." This is a principle that controls the believer's obedience and devotion to the Lord (Romans 12:1, 2). Paul inferred that out of our devotion and obedience to Christ will come an attitude of caring for our fellow Christian.

Paul also speaks of our Christian influence with others in Philippians 2:14-16. An application of these verses to our social relationships is appropriate, as indicated by the words "murmurings" and "disputings." The Philippians had some quarrels among themselves. Paul calls them to holiness so that God's purpose for them as a witnessing community may be fulfilled. For believers a blameless life must couple itself with inward sincerity, purity, and simplicity. Here we catch a glimpse of God's intentions for His people. There should be no feature in their character or conduct that would undermine the testimony of the church.

The Christians at Philippi were to have lives of integrity, because they were to be witnesses to a hostile world. The influence of the church as a witnessing community is described in the language of the influence of light in a dark place. They could influence the world because they possessed the word of salvation, which is life and which gives life, and because they hold its light out in front of them toward others.

The lesson offers several guidelines for responsible citizenship in our country. First, we should obey our government for the sake of our conscience. We recognize the need of obeying important laws, like respecting the civil rights of others, but we may think it is harmless to disobey what we may consider insignificant laws, like paying taxes on all earned income. While we may think disobedience to these types of laws is harmless, the disobedience may have adverse effects on our testimony as a Christian. Furthermore, while our so-called "harmless" actions may not seem to be significant when considered individually, they, as a whole, may dull our conscience so that we may not be able to discriminate clearly between right and wrong.

Second, we should recognize that our foremost allegiance is to the kingdom of God. While civil authorities are established by God to provide order and protection in society, they are not to take over the authority of God. Whenever they do, we must obey God. This is clearly evident in obeying the command from God to preach the gospel. It is also true when civil authorities oppress the rights of their citizens and deprive them of their rights and threaten the peace of the world. However, since it is very difficult to determine when civil authorities have overstepped their divinely sanctioned roles, we must be very prayerful about what we should do. As a general rule, it is our duty to obey the government.

Third, we should influence our society. We should be a stabilizing and preserving force in our society. While society may be disintegrating because its overemphasis of sex, materialism, and violence, we should offer an alternative through the testimony of our personal lives, our families, and our church community. We should be guiding society into higher morality. It is a sad commentary on the power of the church when society leads the way in advocating civil rights for its citizens. As God and His prophets defended the disadvantaged in the Old Testament, the church must lead society in its protection of the lives of all men.

## REVIEW QUESTIONS

1. Who established civil authority?
2. What are some reasons for obeying civil authorities?
3. What should we do when there is a conflict of duty between our obligation to God and to civil authorities?
4. What do the metaphors salt and light mean for the Christian?
5. What is the role of a Christian in society?

## GOLDEN TEXT HOMILY

"LET YOUR LIGHT SO SHINE BEFORE MEN, THAT THEY MAY SEE YOUR GOOD WORKS, AND GLORIFY YOUR FATHER WHICH IS IN HEAVEN (Matthew 5:16).

Our golden text is one of many scriptures that teach us that our responsibility to man is directly related to our relationship with God. Other texts show this direct relationship between our responsibility to man and our relationship with God. In Romans 10:9, the Apostle Paul states: "If thou shalt confess with thy mouth [to

man] the Lord Jesus, and shalt believe in thine heart that God hath raised him from the dead, thou shalt be saved." This relation is further shown in Acts 1:8 declares: "But ye shall receive power after that the Holy Ghost is come upon you: and ye shall be witnesses unto me [to man] . . ." A person who has a relationship with God is obligated to man by that very relationship. This relationship to God and responsibility to man are inseparable. In other words, a relationship to God where there is no responsibility to man does not exist. Consider the Great Commission in Mark 16:15: "And he [Jesus] said unto them, [His disciples who have a relationship with Him], Go ye into all the world, and preach the gospel to every creature [every man]." As responsible, born-again Christian citizens we have an obligation to exert our influence in this world.—**Terry A. Beaver, Pastor, Bradley, Illinois**

## SENTENCE SERMONS

LET NO MAN imagine that he has no influence. Whatever he may be and wherever he may be placed, the man who thinks becomes a light and a power.

**—Henry George**

GOD DOES NOT intend for Christians to live in isolation but to exert their influence in this world.

**—Selected**

"YOU ARE LIGHT for all the world. A town that stands on a hill cannot be hidden."

**—Jesus (Matthew 5:14 NEB)**

IN THE FOOTPRINTS on the sands of time some people leave only the marks of a heel.

**—"Speaker's Sourcebook"**

## EVANGELISTIC APPLICATION

CITIZENSHIP IN GOD'S KINGDOM COMES ONLY THROUGH A BORN-AGAIN EXPERIENCE.

Citizenship in a republican, democratic, or totalitarian nation may come by birth, but citizenship in the kingdom of God comes by a born-again experience. The experience is not a second entrance into the world through a woman's womb; it is the work of the Holy Spirit, as He transforms the motives and intentions of an individual.

Jesus described the entrance into the kingdom of God by the first four Beatitudes (Matthew 5:3-6). One who comes into God's kingdom will recognize his spiritual poverty. He will be deeply sorry for his sin. He will have an obedient will. He will have a desire for a righteous relationship with God and his neighbor. When these attitudes and motivations are present in a person, the Holy Spirit is creating a new life in the individual.

This citizenship far surpasses any worldly citizenship we may have. It indicates our eternal fellowship with God and His people.

## ILLUMINATING THE LESSON

It is said that England was spared the similar fate of the French Revolution in the 18th century because of the Wesleyan revival. John Wesley and his followers preached a gospel that changed the lives of people and social conditions. The gospel took hold in individuals and changed their lifestyles; it also made the Christians conscious of depressed social conditions and motivated them to change the conditions. This is the power of the gospel.

## DAILY DEVOTIONAL GUIDE

M. Act Wisely. Psalm 101:1-4

T. Avoid Offense. Matthew 17:24-27

W. Follow the Lord. 1 Thessalonians 1:5-10

T. Pray for All Men. 1 Timothy 2:1-6

F. Speak No Evil. Titus 3:1-7

S. Be Sober and Prayerful. 1 Peter 4:1-7

# The Biblical View of Marriage

**Study Text:** Genesis 2:18-25; Matthew 19:3-9; 1 Corinthians 7:10-16; Ephesians 5:21-33

**Supplemental References:** Deuteronomy 24:1-4; Matthew 1:18-25; Mark 10:2-12; Romans 7:2, 3

**Golden Text:** "Therefore shall a man leave his father and his mother, and shall cleave unto his wife: and they shall be one flesh" (Genesis 2:24).

**Central Truth:** God designed marriage to unite man and woman in a complete and lifelong commitment to each other.

**Evangelistic Emphasis:** Christian marriage should provide the model for a strong witness of the gospel.

### Printed Text

**Genesis 2:18.** And the Lord God said, It is not good that the man should be alone; I will make him an help meet for him.

**21. And the Lord God caused a deep sleep to fall upon Adam, and he slept: and he took one of his ribs, and closed up the flesh instead thereof;**

22. And the rib, which the Lord God had taken from man, made he a woman, and brought her unto the man.

**23. And Adam said, This is now bone of my bones, and flesh of my flesh: she shall be called Woman, because she was taken out of Man.**

24. Therefore shall a man leave his father and his mother, and shall cleave unto his wife: and they shall be one flesh.

**25. And they were both naked, the man and his wife, and were not ashamed.**

**Ephesians 5:21.** Submitting yourselves one to another in the fear of God.

**22. Wives, submit yourselves unto your own husbands, as unto the Lord.**

23. For the husband is the head of the wife, even as Christ is the head of the church: and he is the saviour of the body.

**24. Therefore as the church is subject unto Christ, so let the wives be to their own husbands in every thing.**

25. Husbands, love your wives, even as Christ also loved the church, and gave himself for it;

**26. That he might sanctify and cleanse it with the washing of water by the word,**

27. That he might present it to himself a glorious church, not having spot, or wrinkle, or any such thing; but that it should be holy and without blemish.

**28. So ought men to love their wives as their own bodies. He that loveth his wife loveth himself.**

29. For no man ever yet hated his own flesh; but nourisheth and cherisheth it, even as the Lord the church:

**30. For we are members of his body, of his flesh, and of his bones.**

31. For this cause shall a man leave his father and mother, and shall be joined

unto his wife, and they two shall be one flesh.

**32. This is a great mystery: but I speak concerning Christ and the church.**

33. Nevertheless let every one of you in particular so love his wife even as himself; and the wife see that she reverence her husband.

---

## LESSON OUTLINE

I. ORIGIN OF MARRIAGE

II. DIVORCE AND REMARRIAGE

III. MUTUAL CONSIDERATION

## LESSON EXPOSITION

INTRODUCTION

The deepest claim of life upon the individual is that he should give and receive mature love. Love at a mature level might exist between any two persons, but the love and understanding which concerns us in this lesson is that which exists between husband and wife.

The institution of marriage is as old as the family of man. It was first instituted in the Garden of Eden. It was guarded in tones of thunder upon Mount Sinai, and in the gentle accents of the Sermon on the Mount. Jesus Christ honored a marriage in Cana of Galilee, where He wrought His first miracle, and the Apostle Paul declares it to be honorable in all.

Few persons question the biblical view of marriage, and most would agree that they want their marriage to reflect standards set forth by God's Word. It is, however, when persons act with personal self interests to the exclusion of consideration of the marriage companion, that difficulties emerge.

Our lesson today is certain to make one more keenly aware of standards given by God. When His standards are followed, harmony in marriage is a certain reward.

I. ORIGIN OF MARRIAGE (Genesis 2:18-25)

**Genesis 2:18. And the Lord God said, It is not good that the man should be alone; I will make him an help meet for him.**

The sentence, "it is not good that man should be alone," recognizes the fundamental characteristic of man's nature. Man is an individual-in-relationship. This is the essential meaning of man being created in the image of God. God does not exist in isolation. In the creation story and throughout the Bible, God is with and for men. He is a community-creating God. Since God is not alone, it is understandable that God would say, "It is not good that man should be alone; I will make him an help meet for him." So, "God created man in his own image . . . male and female created he them" (Genesis 1:27).

The point in connecting man's maleness or femaleness with the image of God is to say that no human being can find the fulfillment of his humanity in himself. As man is made for woman and woman is made for man, human beings can be human only in relation with another person.

By being a person man desires a relationship with another person. This desire is uniquely fulfilled through a marital relationship. It is in a marriage that the personal character of male and female is revealed to each other. In a marriage there is disclosed more fully than is possible in any other relationship between two people what it means to be a man and a woman. There is a recognition of the complementary character of the sexes, the dependence of one person upon another person and, the freedom to give to another person.

The meaning of the phrase, "help meet," is noteworthy. The root word of the phrase appears twenty-one times in the Old Testament. On sixteen occasions it refers to a superior person helping an inferior person. (Psalm 121:1, 2 is an example.) The phrase is a relational term and designates a partnership. It literally means a helper according to what is equal and adequate to man. Hence, woman is essentially like man. She is the person that confronts him and completes him. Man's need for fellowship is fulfilled in woman with whom he can communicate and share life.

Woman is created to be the partner and companion of man. She complements him in every way and completes him. She is a mirror of him in which he recognizes himself. She was created in every way the equal of man, one to whom he could relate at every level.

**19. And out of the ground the Lord God formed every beast of the field, and every fowl of the air; and brought them unto Adam to see what he would call them: and whatsoever Adam called every living creature, that was the name thereof.**

**20. And Adam gave names to all cattle, and to the fowl of the air, and to every beast of the field; but for Adam there was not found an help meet for him.**

The giving of a name was a way of declaring man's power and authority over the rest of creation. The idea in the verses is parallel to Genesis 1:28.

The statement that Adam was unable to find a mate for himself among the other creatures was not an indication that he was looking for one among them. Rather, it serves to underline man's sense of loneliness. He had named the creatures, but there were none with whom he could have fellowship.

**21. And the Lord God caused a deep sleep to fall upon Adam, and he slept: and he took one of his ribs, and closed up the flesh instead thereof;**

**22. And the rib, which the Lord God had taken from man, made he a woman, and brought her unto the man.**

**23. And Adam said, This is now bone of my bones, and flesh of my flesh: she shall be called Woman, because she was taken out of Man.**

While a deep sleep came upon Adam (compare Genesis 15:12, Job 4:13), God took a rib from Adam and made a partner for him. When Adam awoke, he recognized that his companion had come from himself and not from anything brought to him. He gave her a name that placed her above other creatures.

These verses indicate that the woman is not of inferior substance to the man, for she is of man. It also indicates the unity of the human race. The origin of all humans is man and woman. Nowhere does the Scripture say there should be segregation among mankind because of different origins. In fact, these verses advocate a oneness among men.

**24. Therefore shall a man leave his father and his mother, and shall cleave unto his wife: and they shall be one flesh.**

**25. And they were both naked, the man and his wife, and were not ashamed.**

The formation of the one-flesh relationship constitutes a vital aspect of the marriage relationship. As indicated in verse 18, marriage helps us to appreciate human life. In marriage we share our need to know another person and to be known by that person. It includes a sharing of our past experiences, our present circumstances, and our future expectations. It is a sharing of our total selves. This is the idea of one flesh.

Verse 24 denotes in strong terms the importance of leaving and cleaving. The verb "leave" means "abandon" or "forsake." The verb "cleave" suggests strong personal attachment, such as being "glued" or "welded" or "united with another person." Hence, the one-flesh relationship represents the most intimate union possible to man.

The one-flesh relationship involves not just the physical but the whole being and impacts one's personality at its deepest level. In the one-flesh union personality becomes completely identified with another. As the couple come together physically, emotionally, and intellectually, there is a wholeness that did not exist before. They are fused into one.

Another characteristic of one flesh is fidelity. Fidelity suggests faithfulness, loyalty, trust, and commitment of both marriage partners to the marriage. This characteristic is essential to the marriage relationship. Its importance is evident by contrasting fidelity with infatuation. The latter is based on feeling and self-gratification. It is characteristic of a number of relationships today. It is evident in a marriage partner saying he will give the marriage a couple of years in order to see if the marriage is suitable with him. Unfortunately, this attitude is not able to bear the strain of difficult times that will inevitably come to a marriage. Furthermore, it prevents a real oneness from occurring between the couple, because they are afraid of giving themselves completely to the marriage, since there is the possibility of being rejected by the other person. On the other hand, fidelity enhances the marriage. Since the couple know they are committed to each other, they are able to endure difficult times in their marriage, and they are able to realize a true oneness in the relationship. When fidelity is present, there is an attitude of cooperation in the marriage instead of a fear of rejection.

A third aspect of one flesh is permanency. This characteristic is the result of the oneness that occurs in the union of the will and the feelings of the couple. When they leave others and cleave to each other, they are implying by the union of their personalities that this will be a permanent relationship. No one else will ever be a part of this intimate relationship. An intrusion of another person into the relationship contradicts the very nature of the oneness between the couple, because one individual can only be committed to another individual in this union. He cannot serve two.

There is practical insight in this survey of Genesis 2:18-25. First is the recognition of the equality and partnership of woman and man in marriage. Woman exists as an equal to the man by being created in God's image. Woman is not seen as subordinate in marriage but is man's equal and companion. Do our marriages reflect this biblical perspective?

Second, we recognize three important characteristics of marriage. One is the union of the couple, which is an incorporation of their total lives into the marriage. Another is fidelity, which is a commitment of their will to the marriage

regardless of what may happen to them. The last is permanency, which is recognition of the responsibility to maintain the marriage indefinitely.

---

Why is marriage monogamous?

---

II. DIVORCE AND REMARRIAGE (Matthew 19:3-9; 1 Corinthians 7:10-16)

The passage in Matthew 19:3-9 deals with the answer Jesus gave to the question the Pharisees asked Him about divorce. There was a controversy in the days of Jesus surrounding divorce, and the Pharisees asked Jesus for His teaching on the subject. The controversy centered around two ways of interpreting Deuteronomy 24:1-4. One interpretation, given by Rabbi Shammai, taught that the only reason for divorce was a serious marital offense. The other interpretation, given by Rabbi Hillel, said a man could divorce his wife for any reason. If she was unable to cook and she burned the biscuits, her husband could divorce her.

Instead of answering the Pharisees' question, Jesus referred them to the creation of mankind as male and female (Genesis 1) and to the institution of marriage (Genesis 2). This biblical definition implies that marriage is monogamous ("a man . . . his wife") and permanent ("cleave"). Jesus emphasized these two aspects in Matthew 19:6.

The Pharisees responded by asking why Moses granted divorce (Deuteronomy 24:1-4). The Pharisees actually emphasized the giving of a divorce certificate (as if it were the most important part of the Mosaic provision) rather than the reason for divorce.

Jesus did not deny that the regulation given by Moses was from God, but He recognized that it was given because of the hardness of the hearts of the people. Divorce was not a divine instruction, but a divine concession to human weakness.

It seems that Jesus, in His second reply to the Pharisees, was dealing with a husband's irresponsible behavior (compare Matthew 5:31, 32). Instead of divorcing the spouse for a trivial reason, cultivate the relationship with the spouse. In other words, if she burns the biscuits, give her cooking lessons (or cook the biscuits yourself) instead of divorcing her.

In 1 Corinthians 7:10-16, Paul wrote to Christians who were married to believers and to Christians who were married to nonbelievers.

A Christian woman should not separate from her Christian husband. If separation seems to be the only answer, the woman should remain single or be reconciled to her husband. It is implied that a Christian husband who is married to a Christian woman has the same responsibility. He should not divorce his wife. If he does, he should remain unmarried or return to his wife. Paul is prohibiting separation or divorce from being a stepping-stone to another marriage.

After addressing Christian couples, Paul spoke to Christians who were married to nonbelievers. This situation had come into being through the conversion of one of the partners rather than a Christian marrying a nonbeliever.

The Christian is not to initiate a divorce in a marriage with a nonbeliever. If the nonbeliever is content to live with the Christian, the marriage should continue. On the other hand, if a nonbeliever does not want to continue the marriage, the Christian is not obligated to continue the marriage.

Does a marriage exist, as God intended, where one spouse abuses the other spouse?

III. MUTUAL CONSIDERATION (Ephesians 5:21-33)

**Ephesians 5:21. Submitting yourselves one to another in the fear of God.**

The relationship between fellow Christians and, particularly, Christian husbands and wives is considered in these verses (5:21-33). Verse 21 is a summary of the responsibility of Christians to each other.

"Submitting" means to surrender one's own rights or will. It points to voluntary subordination. The basis for the demand is the submission of the Christian community to Christ. It requires renouncement of self-will and preference given to others in order that community may exist.

This submission is addressed to a Christian audience. Although Christians are free in Christ, their freedom is surrendered voluntarily and they become slaves to all for the sake of Christ. An example for Christians is seen in the submission of Jesus and His humility. As applied to marriage, submission shows a wife and husband are to serve each other voluntarily.

**22. Wives, submit yourselves unto your own husbands, as unto the Lord.**

**23. For the husband is the head of the wife, even as Christ is the head of the church: and he is the saviour of the body.**

**24. Therefore as the church is subject unto Christ, so let the wives be to their own husbands in every thing.**

Paul wrote that a wife was to be submissive to her husband. The submission of a wife in marriage is to be done voluntarily. One reason lies in the fact that there is no verb in Ephesians 5:22, and it must be inferred from verse 21. The wife's submission portrays her submission to Christ. A second reason the submission is voluntary rests in the difference in the meaning of "submission" of Christians in Ephesians 5:21 and "obedience" of children in Ephesians 6:1. Obedience is demanded, while submission is voluntary. A wife is not forced to submit to her husband. She submits in a voluntary way as an expression of love.

Why did Paul ask women to submit to their husbands? Although women were required by law to be subject to their husbands Paul introduced a new element in the way submission was to be viewed. Wives were to submit "as unto the Lord."

In Ephesians 5:21-33 Paul discussed other responsibilities of a wife in marriage. They are summarized in the following list:

1. A wife is to submit to her husband as a service to the Lord (vv. 21, 22, 24).

2. A wife is responsible to the Lord for her part in the marriage relationship (v. 22).

3. A wife is responsible to her husband in her marital role (v. 24).

4. A wife is a partner in the one-flesh relationship (v. 31).

5. A wife is to respect her husband (v. 33).

Each of these responsibilities can only be carried out through the expression of Christian love.

**25. Husbands, love your wives, even as Christ also loved the church, and gave himself for it;**

**26. That he might sanctify and cleanse it with the washing of water by the word,**

**27. That he might present it to himself a glorious church, not having spot, or wrinkle, or any such thing; but that it should be holy and without blemish.**

**28. So ought men to love their wives as their own bodies. He that loveth his wife loveth himself.**

**29. For no man ever yet hated his own flesh; but nourisheth and cherisheth it, even as the Lord the church:**

**30. For we are members of his body, of his flesh, and of his bones.**

**31. For this cause shall a man leave his father and mother, and shall be joined unto his wife, and they two shall be one flesh.**

**32. This is a great mystery: but I speak concerning Christ and the church.**

**33. Nevertheless let every one of you in particular so love his wife even as himself; and the wife see that she reverence her husband.**

Christian men in marriage have a serious challenge given to them in Ephesians 5:25-33. Husbands are challenged to serve their wives as Christ served the Church. The commandment for husbands to love their wives as Christ loved the Church calls for faithfulness, commitment and caring. Paul told the men who lived in a patriarchal society that they were to have greater respect and love for their wives, and to live in the way of Christ rather than the way their culture demanded.

Paul's emphasis was on the husband serving the wife as Christ served the Church. Christ sacrificed Himself for the Church. This should be the attitude of the husband. He sacrifices his goals and ambitions so that the wife may be treated properly. This is not an attitude of self-seeking or of demanding, but it is an attitude of seeking the benefit of the wife.

The husband's responsibilities in marriage are many. Those found in Ephesians 5:21-33 are summarized in the following list:

1. A husband is to submit to his wife as a service to the Lord (v. 21).

2. A husband is given the responsibility by the Lord to be head of his wife (v. 23).

3. A husband is commanded to love his wife with a sacrificial love as Christ loved the Church (v. 25).

4. A husband is responsible to help his wife grow in the Lord (v. 26).

5. A husband is to love his wife as the part of himself which she is (vv. 28, 33).

6. A husband is to give his wife loving and tender care (v. 29).

7. A husband is a partner in the one-flesh relationship (v. 31).

8. A husband is to forsake all others for his wife (v. 31).

These responsibilities of a husband in marriage can only be carried out under the Lordship of Christ.

Did Paul teach that men are superior to women?

Submission to others requires a husband and wife to be servants. The idea of service to others is also found in the teachings of Jesus. He told His disciples: "Whoever wants to become great among you must be your servant, and whoever wants to be first must be your slave" (Matthew 20:26, 27; New International Version).

Submission in Ephesians 5:21-33 refers to a voluntary yielding in love. It means a husband and a wife must submit to each other. Both husband and wife have models to follow. The wife is to submit to her husband as a service to the Lord. The husband is to follow the example of Christ's love for the Church in his love for his wife.

The idea of submission to each other or mutual submission is often misunderstood. It is inaccurate to understand the leadership role of the husband only in terms of his wife's submission. The danger lies in creating a hierarchy of command which sets up the husband as the absolute authority in all family matters. The wife and children may be seen as servants to carry out every command and wish of the head male in a family.

The primary responsibility of a husband as head of his wife is to be a servant to his wife. Husbands are challenged to love their wives with a self-sacrificing love just as Christ loved the Church.

The lesson gives guidance to husbands and wives about their relationship in marriage. A review of these teachings follows.

The Creation account portrays man and woman in marriage as equals and companions. Since man's creation in the image of God includes being created male and female, woman is created as man's equal. An understanding of the meaning of "help meet" shows woman is man's equal companion in marriage. Man and woman in marriage are also portrayed as equal partners in the forming of the one-flesh relationship.

Jesus referred to the Creation narratives in His discussion of the roles of man and woman in marriage. Perhaps He wanted to emphasize the original intention of God for marriage. Husband and wife are to treat their marriage as a permanent relationship. They should seek to cultivate and enhance their marriage.

The writings of Paul introduced a new element in his discussion of the submission of the wife to her husband. The wife is to submit or yield voluntarily in love to her husband as a way to serve Christ. Likewise, the command for husbands to love their wives as Christ loved the Church proves to be a new concept. It contrasts with the ways men of their society treated women as objects or slaves.

Marriage can be a growing and enriching experience through its cultivation. The love of Christ should be shown in the way a husband and wife treat each other. Each must be willing to put the interests and concerns of the other above their own. Such a model requires self-sacrifice and love. Can servants of Christ act otherwise?

## REVIEW QUESTIONS

1. Why should a woman be equal with a man?

2. What is meant by a one-flesh relationship?

3. What does submission mean?

4. What are responsibilities of a wife to her husband?

5. What are responsibilities of a husband to his wife?

## GOLDEN TEXT HOMILY

"THEREFORE, SHALL A MAN LEAVE HIS FATHER AND HIS MOTHER, AND SHALL CLEAVE UNTO HIS WIFE; AND THEY SHALL BE ONE FLESH" (Genesis 2:24).

The first six days' record of creation repeats the words, "and God said, Let there be . . . and there was . . . and it was good." Now in Genesis 2:18, for the first time, God surveys what He has done and says IT IS NOT GOOD—that is, that man should be ALONE. God determines to make a help or helper, who would be meet or suitable for him. The actual meaning is literally, "a helper corresponding to him."

The account of this given in the *Amplified Bible*, Genesis 2:21 and 22 reads, "And the Lord God caused a deep sleep to fall upon Adam, and while he slept He took one of his ribs—apart of his side—and closed up the (place with) flesh instead of it; And the rib or part of his side which the Lord God had taken from the man He built up and made into a woman and brought her to the man." Here we see that man's mate did not originate as did the animal species, but her very body was dependent upon him for its existence. At the same time she was so designed as to provide for Adam that which he was lacking. Adam was able to recognize her as woman (Hebrew; ishshah) because she was taken out of man (Hebrew; ish).

D. S. Baily calls this one flesh relationship ‚a mysterious union which is the greatest basis for marriage. "For in this unique union, man and woman become one, yet each does not lose his individuality. In marriage, one finds oneself in another so that each becomes the alter ego of the other." (D. S. Baily, **The Mystery of Love and Marriage.** New York: Harper & Bros. 1952). This union of man and woman is so total that it should include mental, emotional, and physical oneness.

A beautiful parallel can be drawn here as we look at Calvary. Christ gave life to His bride, the church, when water and blood flowed from His riven side. Christ is truly one with His bride, and the bride's very existence is dependent upon His sacrificial act. The New Testament likens the oneness relationship between Christ and His church to marriage (Ephesians 5:25-32).

Christ, Himself, in Matthew 19:5 enhances the authority of the marriage commitment when He makes it clear that the relationship of husband and wife is the strongest, and most indissoluble of all human relationships—stronger even than that of parent and child. By leaving of father and mother, which applies to the woman as well as to the man, the union is shown to be a spiritual oneness, a vital communion of heart as well as body, in which it finds its consummation. A marriage is therefore, a holy appointment of God.—**Edward E. Call, Head Librarian, West Coast Christian College, Fresno, California.**

## SENTENCE SERMONS

A GOOD MARRIAGE is the peaceful coexistence of two nervous systems.
**—Emil Krotky**

MARRIAGES MAY BE MADE in heaven, but man is responsible for the maintenance work.
**—"Changing Times"**

GOD DESIGNED MARRIAGE to unite man and woman in a complete and lifelong commitment to each other.
**—Selected**

TAKE GOD INTO your plans. Then after marriage you won't be bothered with alibis and alimony.
**—"Notes and Quotes"**

## EVANGELISTIC APPLICATION

CHRISTIAN MARRIAGE SHOULD PROVIDE THE MODEL FOR A STRONG WITNESS OF THE GOSPEL.

Emil Brunner recognized marriage as a means of God transforming our lives. Our spouse sees us for who we are and we see him for who he is. In some ways this is uplifting because we enjoy intimate fellowship with each other. In other ways it is threatening because there are the risks of disappointments and rejection. We may be hurt or we may do the hurting. Either can try the love and the loyalty of the marriage. If the couple imitate God by forgiving and reconciling, their lives will be transformed by the energy that flows from their imitation of God.

This fact that the couple could reconcile differences is a testimony of the power of the gospel.

## DAILY DEVOTIONAL GUIDE

M. Find a Spiritual Wife. Genesis 24:1-8

T. Seek a Godly Husband. Ruth 3:1-11

W. A God-Directed Union. Matthew 1:18-25

T. Jesus Blesses a Marriage. John 2:1-11

F. Jesus' Teaching on Divorce. Mark 10:2-12

S. A Hospitable Couple. Acts 18:1-3, 24-26

# June 22, 1986

# Marriage Relationships

**Study Text:** Genesis 2:18; 1 Corinthians 7:1-5; Ephesians 6:1-4; Colossians 3:18, 19; 1 Peter 3:1-7

**Supplemental References:** Deuteronomy 6:4-9; Psalm 127:3-5; Proverbs 1:8, 9; 22:6; 31:10-31; 1 Corinthians 13:4-7; Colossians 3:20, 21; Hebrews 13:4

**Golden Text:** "Let every one of you in particular so love his wife even as himself; and the wife see that she reverence her husband" (Ephesians 5:33).

**Central Truth:** Wholesome relationships are fostered in a marriage that honors God and seeks the best for every family member.

**Evangelistic Emphasis:** A Christian's conduct is an effective witness to unsaved members of the family.

## Printed Text

**Colossians 3:18.** Wives, submit yourselves unto your own husbands, as it is fit in the Lord.

**19. Husbands, love your wives, and be not bitter against them.**

**1 Peter 3:1.** Likewise, ye wives, be in subjection to your own husbands; that, if any obey not the word, they also may without the word be won by the conversation of the wives;

**2. While they behold your chaste conversation coupled with fear.**

3. Whose adorning let it not be that outward adorning of plaiting the hair, and of wearing of gold, or of putting on of apparel;

**4. But let it be the hidden man of the heart, in that which is not corruptible, even the ornament of a meek and quiet spirit, which is in the sight of God of great price.**

5. For after this manner in the old time the holy women also, who trusted in God, adorned themselves, being in subjection unto their own husbands:

**6. Even as Sara obeyed Abraham, calling him lord: whose daughters ye are, as long as ye do well, and are not afraid with any amazement.**

7. Likewise, ye husbands, dwell with them according to knowledge, giving honour unto the wife, as unto the weaker vessel, and as being heirs together of the grace of life; that your prayers be not hindered.

**1 Corinthians 7:3. Let the husband render unto the wife due benevolence: and likewise also the wife unto the husband.**

4. The wife hath not power of her own body, but the husband: and likewise also the husband hath not power of his own body, but the wife.

**5. Defraud ye not one the other, except it be with consent for a time, that ye may give yourselves to fasting and prayer; and come together again, that Satan tempt you not for your incontinency.**

**Ephesians 6:1.** Children, obey your parents in the Lord: for this is right.

**2. Honour thy father and mother; which is the first commandment with promise;**

354

3. That it may be well with thee, and thou mayest live long on the earth.
**4. And, ye fathers, provoke not your** **children to wrath: but bring them up in the nurture and admonition of the Lord.**

## LESSON OUTLINE

I. THE HUSBAND'S ROLE
II. THE WIFE'S ROLE
III. MARITAL RESPONSIBILITIES
IV. FAMILY RESPONSIBILITIES

## LESSON EXPOSITION

INTRODUCTION

In Colossians 3:18—4:1 there is a list of household duties. It was common in the first century throughout the popular culture to find these tables of instruction. Although New Testament writers may have borrowed from the lists there were differences. While popular culture gave the ethical exhortations as guidelines, the New Testament told how the admonitions could be fulfilled by the power of God. The instructions were given to bring glory to God. Furthermore, they became a pattern for glorifying God in our conduct.

I. THE HUSBAND'S ROLE (Colossians 3:19; 1 Peter 3:7)

**Colossians 3:19. Husbands, love your wives, and be not bitter against them.**

This verse is in the midst of practical exhortation given by Paul after he contrasted the life of a Christian with the life prior to his conversion. Paul instructed the Christians at Colossae not to live as they did when they were nonbelievers. They must renounce that life and follow the new life in Christ. Paul proceeded, then, to give specific commands that indicated the Christian was living as he should. One of the commands is in verse 19.

In verse 19, Paul did not use a word that expressed the opposite of submission. Submission is contrasted, instead, with love. Love for the wife is emotion, devotion, action, and sacrifice for her.

It is noteworthy that Paul told the husbands to love their wives, because in New Testament times husbands considered their wives to be objects or slaves. Paul recognized that the wife deserved attention and treatment as a person. Thus, the husband was to love the wife.

The warning "be not bitter against them" is a reminder that Christian love is to be exercised in everyday living. Husbands should not be embittered toward their wives by nursing resentment and harsh feelings. They should not be so embittered that it spills over into a nasty display of temper or a harsh look thrown at the wives. Rather, their face and temperament should radiate the love they have for their wives. Even though they may not have feelings of "love," they should act in Christian love toward their wives.

**1 Peter 3:7. Likewise, ye husbands, dwell with them according to knowledge, giving honour unto the wife, as unto the weaker vessel, and as being heirs together of the grace of life; that your prayers be not hindered.**

Peter dealt with the responsibilities of Christian wives in 3:1-6. Then in verse 7 he turned to the responsibilities of Christian husbands.

By the phrase "dwell with them according to knowledge" Peter meant husbands should live with their wives according to the dictates of the nature of marriage. This may have specific reference to a Christian view of marriage as opposed to a pagan view regarding the relationship of husband and wife.

The word "honor" means "precious." The husband is to consider his wife as a precious helper sent from God and should show reverence for her as a person would respect a priceless jewel.

This honor is to be given in natural and spiritual relations. The husband should recognize the natural limitations of his wife and give her corresponding consideration. Spiritually, he should recognize the full equality as fellow sharers in the grace of God and in His gift to them of eternal life. The husband should recognize that in the spiritual sphere the wife is not weaker or inferior but a joint heir.

On the other hand, if a husband does not honor his wife, his spiritual life will be hurt. The thought includes all manner of hindering. A husband who treats his wife in the wrong way will himself be unfit to pray. There will be no family altar, and he himself may not pray at all. His worship in the sanctuary will be affected as well.

---

Why should a husband honor his wife?

---

Peter gave several guidelines for a Christian husband to follow in his relationship with his wife. A marriage should be based on Christian principles, such as equality, cooperation, self-giving, and serving. A husband should respect his wife as a person. He should recognize the spiritual equality between his wife and himself. Lastly, if these guidelines are not followed, the husband will have spiritual problems.

II. THE WIFE'S ROLE (Genesis 2:18; Colossians 3:18; 1 Peter 3:1-6)

In order to understand and appreciate the role of a wife in marriage it is helpful to review Genesis 2:18. In the verse, the phrase "an help meet for him" is based on two Hebrew words. The first word, "meet," refers to relationships, and describes woman as a partner equal to man. The second word, "help," describes assistance given to someone. The word describes beneficial relationships such as God being the helper of Israel. Hence, it must be recognized that God intended for the wife to be an equal partner in the marriage and for the wife to complement her husband.

**Colossians 3:18. Wives, submit yourselves unto your own husbands, as it is fit in the Lord.**

"Submit" does not imply that the woman is inferior to man naturally or spiritually, neither does it mean a requirement imposed on a wife by the rule of her husband. The phrase "in the Lord"

points to the lifestyle of one who is a Christian. Thus, the wife in marriage is addressed as a responsible person and she is called upon to voluntarily accept a role in the family. She should have the attitude of submission to her husband as she has to Christ. Submission to Christ comes not out of fear but out of respect for Him and an eagerness to serve Him.

The phrase "in the Lord" reminds Christians that our marital relationship should be seen in light of our relationship with Christ and in the divine plan for marriage (compare Genesis 2:18-25). In that context submission by the wife will not seem harsh, because it will be reciprocated by the husband's love. There must be no selfseeking by the husband, because Christian love, as shown by Christ, seeks the good of the other.

**1 Peter 3:1. Likewise, ye wives, be in subjection to your own husbands; that, if any obey not the word, they also may without the word be won by the conversation of the wives;**

**2. While they behold your chaste conversation coupled with fear.**

According to Peter's greeting in Chapter 1 he addressed exiles of the Dispersion. These were persecuted Jewish Christians outside of Palestine who lived under Roman rule. Christianity presented a threat to the pagan society because of its treatment of each other as equals, including husbands and wives, as well as masters and slaves. Although they were free in Christ they were to act as bondservants; to be an example as followers of Christ in their conduct toward others.

Christian women were advised by Peter how to react in a particular situation. There existed a danger of a Christian woman pressing her freedom in Christ in a way that would bring injury to herself and the faith. Peter recommended a specific strategy for Christian women with nonbelieving husbands. Peter told them to follow the Old Testament pattern of modesty. Such an evangelistic strategy would be the most persuasive for these men, since they were accustomed to patriarchal arrangements in the home. Peter devoted attention to this case because of the difficult position into which the women were placed after conversion. This was especially true since women in that time were expected to follow the religion of their husbands.

Wives are told to submit to their husbands. Subordination in this instance refers to an acceptance of the woman's role in the home as wife.

The situation indicates that a Christian wife was married to a nonbeliever. The family was probably totally nonbelievers until the wife became a Christian. There is a possibility that some nonbelieving husbands were even actively hostile to the gospel. Peter suggests that the husbands may be won to the Lord by the wife's Christian conduct.

**3. Whose adorning let in not be that outward adorning of plaiting the hair, and of wearing of gold, or of putting on of apparel;**

**4. But let it be the hidden man of the heart, in that which is not corruptible, even the ornament of a meek and quiet spirit, which is in the sight of God of great price.**

In verses 1 and 2, Peter exhorted the Christian wives to win their husbands to the Lord by their conduct. In verses 3-6, Peter explained what he meant by conduct.

In verse 3, Peter told the women not to depend upon gaudy dress in their effort to win their husbands to the Lord. The women were making the mistake of thinking that if they dressed conspicuously and immodestly (overdressing, using too many accessories), they would win their husbands to the Lord.

In verse 4, Peter described the beauty of Christian women. She depends upon an adornment that proceeds from her character and is representative of her spiritual life. The phrase "the hidden man of the heart" refers to the personality of the woman as she is made beautiful by the ministry of the Holy Spirit in her life, by glorifying Jesus Christ, and by manifesting Christ in her life.

Peter further described the beauty of her character by the graces of meekness and quiet spirit. Meekness describes the gentle way in which a wife submits to her husband. Quiet spirit describes her docile attitude toward her husband and the world. These virtues do not suggest weakness of will but strength of character.

It is this spiritual adornment that will persuade the nonbelieving husband to follow the Lord.

Although the Christian woman is forbidden to use her apparel to win her husband to the Lord it does not mean she is not to dress with neatness and good taste or that she be so drab and plain that she is conspicuous. That only harms the woman and does not bring glory to Christ. The woman should be guided by the principle that first of all she desires to be clothed in spiritual virtues, and second, that the apparel she wears will be in keeping with the purity of Jesus Christ.

**5. For after this manner in the old time the holy women also, who trusted in God, adorned themselves, being in subjection unto their own husbands:**

**6. Even as Sara obeyed Abraham, calling him lord: whose daughters ye are, as long as ye do well, and are not afraid with any amazement.**

In verses 5 and 6, Peter appealed to women in the Old Testament as examples for the wives to follow. The wives in the Old Testament were called holy because they trusted in God. Their devotion was not to corruptible, earthly vanities, but to God. This devotion to God made them beautiful as persons.

A specific feature of their holiness was their submission to their husbands. Sarah is an example. The fact that she obeyed Abraham and called him lord indicated her quality of character. "Daughters ye are" suggests that these wives, by adorning themselves with the same attitude of character, would become her children and would imitate her as a child imitates his mother.

As well as being submissive, these women were to continue doing good ("as long as ye do well") and were not to panic ("not afraid with any amazement"). The Christian wives were not to let anything frighten them from their course. Other women might insult the Christian wives because of their noble attitude. Even their husbands might resent them. However, it was these virtues of the inner person the wives were to cultivate.

Peter gave several guidelines for Christian women who were married to non-Christians to follow. They should concentrate on winning their husbands by Christian graces rather than improper dress. They should be submissive to their husbands by being gentle and docile. They should serve their husbands. They should have a strong character that would not panic in crisis.

What are some virtues of Christian character found in a Christian woman?

III. MARITAL RESPONSIBILITIES (1 Corinthians 7:1-5)

In 1 Corinthians 7, Paul gave the Corinthian believers some practical advice to questions about marriage. In verse 1, Paul referred to a slogan ("It is good for a man not to touch a woman") that the Corinthians used to ask Paul questions in a letter ("Now concerning the things whereof ye wrote unto me"). Hence, this was not Paul's attitude toward marriage and sex, but he reminded the Corinthians of their questions and then gave them his answers in the following verses.

It should be noted that the slogan in verse 1 represents a problem the Corinthians had in understanding the Christian meaning of marriage. There were those in the Corinthian Church who believed Christians should not engage in marriage and sex. They believed anything that had to do with the body was evil and was to be suppressed.

In 1 Corinthians 7, Paul is addressing the first view. This view believed the most intimate act of the marriage relationship was sinful, because the body is evil and any expression of the natural desires was evil. Paul categorically denounced this view. Paul recognized the natural desires to be God-given to serve noble purposes in marriage. Sex is the basis of the most intimate relationship in life between husband and wife.

If the sentence "it is good for a man not to touch a woman" is Paul's view, the statement only recognizes the legitimacy of being single—but it does not say it is better to remain single.

In 1 Corinthians 7:2, Paul recognized that men and women have sexual desires. These desires are a part of our being human. They find proper fulfillment, as Paul contended, in marriage.

In the verse, Paul did not advocate marriage only to be a means of avoiding sexual immorality. He knew that some Corinthians were suppressing their natural desires because they thought they should abstain from marriage and sex in order to be spiritual. However, it was creating problems for them because they were constantly facing temptation in Corinth.

Paul advised the Corinthians to marry. They were not to attempt to live an unnatural lifestyle. They had a desire to marry, which was given by God, and it was acceptable to fulfill that desire. One would not be less spiritual if he did marry. In marriage he would find the proper fulfillment of his desires.

**1 Corinthians 7:3. Let the husband render unto the wife due benevolence: and likewise also the wife unto the husband.**

**4. The wife hath not power of her own body, but the husband: and likewise also the husband hath not power of his own body, but the wife.**

**5. Defraud ye not one the other, except it be with consent for a time, that ye may give yourselves to fasting and prayer; and come together again, that Satan tempt you not for your incontinency.**

"Due benevolence" means that each spouse, husband and wife, must fulfill his role in the marriage. The man should fulfill his duty as a husband, and the woman should fulfill her duty as a wife.

In verse 4, Paul said the woman does not have sole authority over her body, and neither does the husband have sole authority over his body. When they enter into marriage, they imply that they have given up exclusive rights to their bodies and that they have accepted mutual ownership of each other. Therefore, there should be mutual consideration for the spiritual and physical needs of both husband and wife.

Paul recognized that marriage is spiritual and physical. For one spouse to make the marriage only spiritual means the other spouse is being robbed ("defraud ye not one the other"). In the Corinthian Church there were those who spiritualized their marriage and neglected the physical aspect of the marriage, namely, sexual relations. This practice robbed the other spouse of a significant dimension of marriage and created marital and sexual problems.

In 1 Corinthians 7:1-5, Paul answered a question the Corinthians had about marriage, particularly about sex in marriage. Paul replied that marriage is the proper place for sexual relations and that sexual relations are good (compare Hebrews 13:4). Also, both spouses, husband and wife, have a responsibility to meet the natural desires of the other. Although they may abstain for a limited time because of spiritual reasons they must return to normal marital relations. The responsibility to fulfill the spiritual and physical needs of each spouse calls for mutual consideration.

IV. FAMILY RESPONSIBILITIES (Ephesians 6:1-4)

From antiquity there were codes of household duties that suggested proper attitudes and responsibilities for each of the groups that made up the households. The table of household duties gave the ways different people in the household should relate to the other members of it. Early Christians borrowed from these tables of instruction although they adapted them to Christianity. The New Testament includes some of these codes: Ephesians 5:21-33, Colossians 3:18—4:1, and 1 Peter 2:18--3:7.

In Ephesians 5:21—6:9, Paul addressed each group of individuals in the household: wives and husbands (5:21-33), children (6:1, 2), parents (6:4), slaves (6:5-

8), and masters (6:9). The material in the household code instructs Christians as to how they should relate to one another in the household. Their daily lives together are to reflect their new life in Christ. One does not live one way in the church and another way at home. In many ways the home is a unit of God's larger purposes.

**Ephesians 6:1. Children, obey your parents in the Lord: for this is right.**

"Obey" means for the child to accept and to follow the commands of his parents. The child should not display an attitude of stubborn resistance or talking back to his parents, but by his compliance with their commands manifest an attitude of respect and reverence for his parents.

"In the Lord" indicates that Paul had in mind a Christian home. Paul thinks a child should obey his parents, but he assumes that in a Christian home the parents will not request the child to do something contrary to God's will.

"For this is right" is the reason for the child to obey his parents. Obedience is God's intention for the child. God has entrusted the parents with the responsibility of rearing the child; they are God's representatives to the child. If they are to be successful in their responsibility, the child must obey them. Also, obedience to the parents is, in a way, obedience to God, since they are His representatives.

Should a child obey every request of his parents?

**2. Honour thy father and mother; which is the first commandment with promise;**

**3. That it may be well with thee, and thou mayest live long on the earth.**

The command to obey is followed by the command to honor. "Honour" means "to esteem with respect." A child should think of his parents with the highest reverence. He should be grateful for parents who will share their experience and wisdom with the child so that he may develop and mature. He should reverence his parents, as they are God's representatives to the child.

In verse 3, Paul may have had in mind personal blessings that the child would receive for obeying and honoring his parents. A child who has obeyed and honored his parents will have an appreciation for life that will make his life enjoyable and rich, because through his attitude toward his parents he has developed the same attitude about life in general. On the other hand, Paul may have been suggesting that through the training of the child in habits of obedience and respect, there would be stability in a community and a nation.

**4. And, ye fathers, provoke not your children to wrath: but bring them up in the nurture and admonition of the Lord.**

While a child has obligations to his parents, parents have obligations to the child. First, parents must not deal harshly with the child by making unreasonable demands on the child and unnecessary rules for him. If the commands of the parents are unbearable, the child will resent the parents and will eventually rebel against parental authority ("provoke not your children to wrath"). Parents should discipline the child in such a way that when firmness is necessary, it will be with a loving desire for the welfare of the child.

There is a positive command for parents. They should rear their child in "the nurture and admonition of the Lord." "Nurture" means "discipline," and "admonition" means "instruction." The idea in the command is the responsibility parents have to rear their child so that he will be a responsible person before God. An example of fulfilling the responsibility is Lois and Eunice (2 Timothy 1:5; 3:14, 15).

The principles Paul gives in Ephesians 6:1-4 in regard to family relations are these: (1) a child should obey his parents; (2) a child should respect his parents; (3) parents should not make their child angry by imposing on him ridiculous rules; and (4) parents are to help the child mature into a responsible person.

These Scripture passages give advice on responsibilities in the family. The husband should put his wife before himself and should respect her as an equal before God. He should not mistake the comparison Paul made between the husband and the Lordship of Christ (Ephesians 5:21-33) to mean the husband is a dictator, but he should understand it to mean that the husband is to sacrifice himself for his wife, as Christ did for the Church. The wife should have an attitude of cooperating with her husband. She should not mistake her freedom in Christ to mean that she can do as she pleases, but she should understand her freedom in Christ to mean that she is willing to do what is best for the family. The parents should nurture their child so that he will develop into a responsible person before God and in society. This means that the parents will be examples of God before their child and will give sensible instruction to him. The child should obey and respect his parents, remembering that they are God's representatives to him.

**REVIEW QUESTIONS**

1. What are the responsibilities of a husband in marriage?

2. What will happen to a husband if he does not respect his wife?

3. What are the responsibilities of a wife in marriage?

4. What are the duties of a child to his parents?

5. What are the duties of parents to their child?

**GOLDEN TEXT HOMILY**

"LET EVERY ONE OF YOU IN PARTICULAR SO LOVE HIS WIFE EVEN AS HIMSELF; AND THE WIFE SEE THAT SHE REVERENCE HER HUSBAND" (Ephesians 5:33).

Upon completion of his analogy comparing the marital relationship to Christ and the church, the Apostle Paul points out that this has a practical application as well.

Husbands are instructed to love their

wives. To insure that there are no exceptions, it is addressed to every one of you in particular; that is, every one of you individually is to love his wife. The original word that is used here is not the word that means love of attraction or desire, but rather the word that is used means true Christian love. It is the same word that is used in referring to God's love for us.

The husband is not only to love his wife, but he is to love her as himself. Many of the problems people have are caused by a low self-image or poor self-esteem, which may go under the guise of humility. However, this is not a Christian concept. Jesus taught that we are to love ourselves and base our relationships upon this: "Thou shalt love thy neighbour as thyself" (Matthew 22: 39). Here the apostle used the same terminology in referring to a husband's love for his wife.

The wife's duty to her husband is reverence. The word used in the original is the one from which we get our word **phobia** and may be translated fear, as it is in the **American Standard Version.** However, this conjures up the thought of frightful emotion which is foreign to the concept intended here. Most recent translations use the word **respect,** which seems to be the best way of conveying this thought in our current language.

Many marriages are in constant tension or break up because the husband and wife act as though they are in competition rather than in partnership. A wife should respect her husband and not compete with him for status or prestige from friends, children, or other family members.

This admonition does not imply that the husband has the right to make a servant of his wife. They are dependent upon one another and each has a different role in the relationship and in the family.—**Richard Y. Bershon, Chief, Chaplain Service, VA Medical Center, Tomah, Wisconsin.**

## SENTENCE SERMONS

SUCCESS IN MARRIAGE consists not only in finding the right mate, but also in being the right mate.
—**"Speaker's Sourcebook"**

WHOLESOME RELATIONSHIPS are fostered in a marriage that honors God and seeks the best for every family member.
—**Selected**

## EVANGELISTIC APPLICATION

A CHRISTIAN'S CONDUCT IS AN EFFECTIVE WITNESS TO UNSAVED MEMBERS OF THE FAMILY.

A minister told a story in a sermon about the influence he had on a girl without knowing it at the time. A tragedy had occurred in the minister's life, and the girl, who was an agnostic but had attended the minister's church, waited for the pastor's faith in God to crumble. Instead, she saw him continue on and even grow in his faith. She wrote the pastor a letter and said that when she saw him playing on a ball field and enjoying life, she knew that the pastor had a relationship with a real God. Since then, she, too, had found that relationship with God.

Christians in a family where there are unsaved members can likewise have an influence on them. When the unsaved in the family see the joy and victory that the Christian has, it will be a sermon to them that the Holy Spirit will use to convict them of their unbelief. This is an idea Paul presents in 1 Corinthians 7:12-16. Thus, the Christian should persevere in the faith, because he will be a light penetrating the spiritual darkness of unsaved family members. Perhaps they will be rescued by the light.

## DAILY DEVOTIONAL GUIDE

M. Teaching God's Words. Deuteronomy 6:4-9
T. Children Are God's Gift. Psalm 127: 3-5
W. Wise Counsel. Proverbs 1:7-19
T. The Exceptional Wife. Proverbs 31: 10-31
F. The Qualities of Love. 1 Corinthians 13:4-7
S. Benefits of Discipline. Hebrews 12:5-11

# Dangers of Materialism

**Study Text:** Deuteronomy 8:10-18; Psalm 62:10; Proverbs 23:4, 5; Isaiah 5:8; Matthew 6:19-21, 24; 13:22; Mark 8:34-37; 10:17-31; Luke 6:24; 12:13-32; 19:8; 1 Timothy 6:6-11, 17, 18; James 2:1-9; 4:1-3; 5:1-6; 1 John 2:15-17; 3:17

**Supplemental References:** Psalm 37:16; Matthew 4:8-10; Mark 12:41-44; Acts 8:20; 20:35; Hebrews 13:5, 6; James 1:9-11

**Golden Text:** "Take heed, and beware of covetousness: for a man's life consisteth not in the abundance of the things which he possesseth" (Luke 12:15).

**Central Truth:** Preoccupation with material things interferes with a person's relationship with God and others.

**Evangelistic Emphasis:** We should be concerned first with receiving eternal life through Jesus Christ.

## Printed Text

**Matthew 6:19.** Lay not up for yourselves treasures upon earth, where moth and rust doth corrupt, and where thieves break through and steal:

**20. But lay up for yourselves treasures in heaven, where neither moth nor rust doth corrupt, and where thieves do not break through nor steal:**

21. For where your treasure is, there will your heart be also.

**24. No man can serve two masters: for either he will hate the one, and love the other; or else he will hold to the one, and despise the other. Ye cannot serve God and mammon.**

**Matthew 13:22.** He also that received seed among the thorns is he that heareth the word; and the care of this world, and the deceitfulness of riches, choke the word, and he becometh unfruitful.

**Mark 8:34. And when he had called the people unto him with his disciples also, he said unto them, Whosoever will**

come after me, let him deny himself, and take up his cross, and follow me.

35. For whosoever will save his life shall lose it; but whosoever shall lose his life for my sake and the gospel's, the same shall save it.

**36. For what shall it profit a man, if he shall gain the whole world, and lose his own soul?**

37. Or what shall a man give in exchange for his soul?

**1 Timothy 6:9.** But they that will be rich fall into temptation and a snare, and into many foolish and hurtful lusts, which drown men in destruction and perdition.

**10. For the love of money is the root of all evil: which while some coveted after, they have erred from the faith, and pierced themselves through with many sorrows.**

11. But thou, O man of God, flee these things; and follow after righteousness, godliness, faith, love, patience, meekness.

## LESSON OUTLINE

I. WARNINGS AGAINST MATERIALISM

II. EFFECTS OF MATERIALISM
- A. Forgetfulness of God
- B. Selfishness
- C. False Evaluation of Others
- D. Eternal Loss

III. CHOOSING BIBLICAL VALUES

## LESSON EXPOSITION

INTRODUCTION

God is the creator of all, and all that He has created is good. He created the material world in which man lives, and He created man with material needs. The purpose of material goods, then, is to serve man's needs. They are not to be an end in themselves.

Materialism has changed the function of material objects. It believes life's highest value is an accumulation of material goods. This is a distortion of reality, and, even worse, it is idolatry.

Materialism enslaves men with consumption, fashions, and gadgets. Here we see men threatened with the loss of their own humanity in the worship of mammon. Instead of community there are extremes of poverty and wealth. Instead of justice there is injustice. Instead of mutual service there is exploitation.

Obsession with material objects affects man like salt water affects a sailor's thirst. Salt water never quenches his thirst; it makes him want more.

I. WARNINGS AGAINST MATERIALISM (Psalm 62:10; Luke 6:24, 25, 12:13-32; 1 Timothy 6:17, 18)

In Psalm 62, the psalmist addressed the right and wrong object of faith. He said we may do away with one idol, like too much respect for mortal celebrities, only to idolize another object, such as riches.

In verse 10, the psalmist was not forbidding riches, but indicating the danger of letting just and unjust acquisitions take the place of God in our lives. He recognized that wealth is as jeopardous to our lives as extortion ("oppression" and "robbery").

God can be trusted. This was the strong conviction of the psalmist. Notice how often this theme is stated in the first nine verses of the psalm. The language came from a person persecuted by his enemies who had found refuge in the temple where a scripture had reassured him. His firm confidence was based on his experiencing protection by the Lord and comfort by the scripture. He knew what was the right object of his faith. It was God—his rock, salvation, and stronghold.

In Luke 6:24 and 25, part of Luke's account of the Sermon on the Mount, are three woes. These woes do not mean a curse but an acknowledgment of a fact that all men can see. The woes introduce three groups—the rich, the well-fed, and the boastful—that are criticized by Jesus.

The rich are to be pitied because they already have their reward and consolation. Their blessing has come in the form of what money can buy them. The idea underlying the judgment is the consumption of goods by the rich without helping the needy (compare Luke 16:19-31). They had purchased items for their own comfort, while neglecting the needs of the disadvantaged. They were satisfied with their wealth and had no need to store treasures in heaven by giving to the needy.

The criticism against the well-fed was that they were satiated with food and were unconcerned about those without food. They had plenty to eat and were satisfied with what they had, while neglecting their responsibility for the not-so-fortunate people. There will be a day when they, too, will know hunger (compare Isaiah 65:13, James 4:9).

The boastful are smug in the presence of their enemies, not because God is their protector, but because they feel self-sufficient. Because of their smugness, they were indifferent to the needs of those around them. They felt no responsibility to help the powerless. If they could defend themselves and their property, everyone else should defend himself and his own. However, life will change for them one day, and their arrogance will turn to weeping and mourning.

These verses are addressed to those who revel in earthly possessions those who seek life and happiness in material things. They are so self-exalted and rich in their own eyes that they do not go to Christ, therefore they remain in spiritual poverty. Prosperity without God does not endow real life. Unfortunately, those who place their aspirations on earthly possessions will not have any in the future, and perhaps even more tragically, they do not really possess life in this world.

The verses suggest that the rich, in order to receive life, should sell what they have and give the proceeds away. Is that what the verses mean? No. Luke did not present poverty as an ideal in itself nor wealth as intrinsically evil. Recall the parable of the Publican and Tax Collector (Luke 18:10-14). The Pharisee belonged to a group Luke described as full of self-justification (Luke 16:14, 15), and the tax collector was a man of material means. In the parable the man acceptable and justifiable before God was the tax collector because of his utter dependence upon God's mercy. The point is that what is right before God is not our riches or poverty, but our attitude toward God.

According to 1 Timothy 6:17-19 wealth is not a sin. There were some wealthy people who were Christians. They were not condemned for their wealth, and they were not told to give it away. Rather, we are told that God gave them the wealth to enjoy.

The passage does recognize two perils that threaten the wealthy. First, they may be tempted to think too highly of themselves or to think that they are better than others. Second, they may depend on their wealth rather than God. This would be foolish because wealth is easily lost. It may be here today and gone tomorrow.

The verses instruct the wealthy in the use of their riches. Since these wealthy people belonged to Christ, they were to share their wealth with others. They were not to think of themselves as living in isolation, but they were to remember that they were a part of a fellowship and had a responsibility to share with the fellowship. A wise use of their wealth would lay a good foundation for their future life.

Wealth is not a sin. Wealth brings great responsibility. If wealth is used for selfish purposes, it will ruin the person, but if it is shared, it will bring comfort and enjoyment in this life and the life to come. (Of course, it must be acknowledged that one's future life is determined by his acceptance of God.)

What are some ways we may share our wealth?

II. EFFECTS OF MATERIALISM (Deuteronomy 8:10-18; Matthew 13:22; Isaiah 5:8; James 2:1-9; 4:1-3; 5:1-6; 1 John 3:17; Mark 10:17-31; 1 Timothy 6:6-11)

A. Forgetfulness of God (Deuteronomy 8:10-18; Matthew 13:22)

Materialism has several effects on a person's life. One effect is forgetfulness of God. Sometimes, when a person is blessed with abundant earnings, he forgets the source of his wealth. He thinks he himself has amassed his wealth, or now that he is self-sufficient he does not need the crutches of faith he leaned upon to pull himself into financial security.

The Hebrews were warned against this attitude in Deuteronomy 8:10-20. They were instructed to remember the Lord when they prospered in the promised land. They should remember His mighty acts of deliverance and provisions for them, because it was by Him that they were able to prosper. If they did forget the source of their material blessings, they were warned that God would punish them.

**Matthew 13:22. He also that received seed among the thorns is he that heareth the word; and the care of this world, and the deceitfulness of riches, choke the word, and he becometh unfruitful.**

This verse is part of a parable Jesus gave about people's response to the gospel. There was a man who sowed a field with seed. The seed represented the different responses given to the gospel. The man's life became so cluttered with material wants and wishes that he served money more than he served God.

B. Selfishness (Isaiah 5:8; James 4:1-3; 5:1-6; 1 John 3:17)

When a person is materialistic, he has an everconsuming appetite for more things. Although he may have a sufficiency for his necessities he constantly sees something else he wants. He can never accumulate enough, even when he has more than his neighbor. The desires scream to be fed. He consumes more and more, but thinks he has less and less. His unsatiated desires prevent him from seeing his neighbor's needs.

C. False Evaluation of Others (James 2: 1-9)

The passage in James 2:1-9 suggests that materialism gives a false evaluation of others. It is an irony that the ones who exploit men and blaspheme God are the ones who are shown favoritism. The partiality is not based on who the persons are but on what they are. Materialism makes people worship and show deference to the rich regardless of their morality or their spiritual values.

D. Eternal Loss (Mark 10:17-31; 1 Timothy 6:6-11)

In the context of 1 Timothy 6, Paul refuted false teachers and gave Timothy some instruction. The false teachers taught that godliness was a means to financial profit. Their motive for godliness was not pure but was carnal. They advocated godliness for material benefits.

Paul refuted their teaching by explaining that contentment was the result of godliness. Contentment signifies an inner attitude of satisfaction with ourselves and our lives in the world. Paul was not praising poverty and denouncing wealth. He said real contentment, which is independent of poverty or wealth, is found in a right relationship with God. Contentment comes when we escape the servitude to things, when we find our wealth in the fellowship of our neighbor, and when we realize that our most precious possession is our relationship with God.

Verses 7 and 8 reinforce verse 6. When we were born, we did not come with any material possessions, and when we die, we will not carry any material possessions with us. Hence, the gaining of any material acquisitions is only of temporary significance. The few things we need in life should not disturb us. If we have food, clothing, and shelter, the result should be contentment.

**1 Timothy 6:9. But they that will be rich fall into temptation and a snare, and into many foolish and hurtful lusts, which drown men in destruction and perdition.**

The people to whom Paul referred were not necessarily wealthy, but they desired to be wealthy. Paul said they had placed themselves in a dangerous position. Their inordinate desire for wealth was a lure ("fall into temptation and a snare") that led to lust ("into many foolish and hurtful lusts"), and ultimately to total moral ruin ("drown men in destruction and perdition").

To "fall into temptation and a snare" means more than to be tempted. It means a constant enticement that results in yielding to the lure. For the person whose chief purpose is to acquire wealth, there will always be opportunities of questionable nature whereby he can take advantage and acquire even more wealth.

"Many foolish and hurtful lusts" indicate that greed produces desires and actions that are evil. They harm one's character and spiritual life, and they take away interest in Christian activity.

"Drown men in destruction and perdition" describes the inevitable, downward course which results from avarice. "Drown" illustrates greed as a monster that plunges its victim into an ocean of complete destruction. It represents the eternal result of all who are possessed by an inordinate desire for wealth.

**10. For the love of money is the root of all evil: which while some coveted after, they have erred from the faith, and pierced themselves through with many sorrows.**

"Root" suggests that Paul was thinking that greed is a source of evil rather than the fruit of evil. "All" indicates different kinds of evil. "Coveted after" indicates the lustful attitude some have toward money. Riches can be the source of good, but the lustful desire for wealth, which characterized the people Paul mentioned, is evil. Thus, greed leads men away from the faith ("erred from the faith") and into "many sorrows." These sorrows may be different types, such as guilty conscience, disillusionment, and spiritual unrest.

**11. But thou, O man of God, flee these things; and follow after righteousness, godliness, faith, love, patience, meekness.**

Paul told Timothy to flee greed and to cultivate righteousness, godliness, faith, love, patience, and meekness. By pursuing these good virtues he would escape evil.

"Righteousness," in this context, does not refer to imputed righteousness, which every believer has on the merits of Christ's death, but practical righteousness. As we present ourselves to the control of the Spirit, we will be transformed in nature so that we will be in right relationship with God and neighbor.

"Godliness" refers to living a daily life of consecration to God that is evident in motives, intentions, and actions, especially toward our neighbors.

"Faith" is the trust we have in God to sustain us. "Love" refers to treating our neighbor as ourselves. "Patience" refers to remaining steadfast in our discipleship under God. "Meekness" means a true evaluation of ourselves. We do not think too highly or too lowly of ourselves.

Paul did not condemn wealth and praise poverty. He denounced avarice and advocated contentment. Greed leads to our destruction, but contentment leads to stability of life. Instead of accumulating things, we should cultivate virtues.

How may we prevent the effects of materialism in our lives?

III. CHOOSING BIBLICAL VALUES (Proverbs 23:4, 5; Matthew 6:19-21, 24; Mark 8:34-37; Luke 19:8; 1 John 2:15-17)

**Matthew 6:19. Lay not up for yourselves treasures upon earth, where moth and rust doth corrupt, and where thieves break through and steal:**

**20. But lay up for yourselves treasures in heaven, where neither moth nor rust doth corrupt, and where thieves do not break through nor steal:**

**21. For where your treasure is, there will your heart be also.**

Jesus directs our attention to the durability of the two treasures. The earthly treasures are perishable and insecure. In ancient days no earthly treasure was permanent. Moths would eat the people's clothes, rats would eat their stored grain, and thieves would steal from the houses. But neither is earthly treasure permanent today. Although we have made improvements with insecticides and burglar alarms we have to contend with inflation, recession, and depression.

On the other hand, "treasures in heaven" are endurable and secure. These treasures are enjoying the glory of God, fellowshiping with God and neighbor, and having a Christlike character. No element of nature, no pest, nor thief can take these valuables from us. They are secure in God's presence (compare Romans 8:31-39 and 1 Peter 1:3-5).

In these verses Jesus forbids selfish accumulation of goods. He does not prohibit private property, savings, or the enjoyment of God's gifts of material blessings to us. The prohibition to "lay not up for yourselves treasures upon earth" does not mean neglecting sensible provision for the future or living a beggar's existence. It means being covetous like misers who hoard and materialists who always want more. Jesus recognizes covetousness makes us hardhearted to the needs of the world's underprivileged, distorts our perception of true values, and binds our affection and will to perishable objects. The admonition Jesus gives, "lay up for yourselves treasures in heaven," focuses our affection and will upon lasting values.

**24. No man can serve two masters: for either he will hate the one, and love the other; or else he will hold**

**to the one, and despise the other. Ye cannot serve God and mammon.**

Jesus explains the choice between two masters. It is a choice between God and mammon, that is, between the Creator and any object of our own creation. We cannot serve both.

In the verse Jesus presents a picture of a slave and a slave owner. A person can work for two employers without conflict, but a person cannot be the slave of two owners. He must be owned by one or the other. It is the same with us. We are either owned by God or our own creation.

**Mark 8:34. And when he had called the people unto him with his disciples also, he said unto them, Whosoever will come after me, let him deny himself, and take up his cross, and follow me.**

The self-sacrifice which Jesus practiced is the standard for His followers. Self-renunciation is more than the denial of something that is dear to us. The cross was an instrument of death to Jesus. Unfortunately, to some people the cross is merely a charm or an article for adornment, but to those who follow the example of Jesus it is a symbol of death to the old life and a testimony of our fellowship with Jesus.

**35. For whosoever will save his life shall lose it; but whosoever shall lose his life for my sake and the gospel's, the same shall save it.**

In verse 35, Jesus uttered one of His great paradoxes: to gain life was to lose life. This calls for a radical adjustment in the thinking of his self-seeking disciples, past and present. Men of the world try to find life in materialism, but men of the cross assume the responsibility of making the world morally fit and look to the future for their reward.

**36. For what shall it profit a man, if he shall gain the whole world, and lose his own soul?**

**37. Or what shall a man give in exchange for his soul?**

Verses 36 and 37 contrast the worldly life with the life of the cross. Suppose a person did gain the world. It would not

mean he had genuine life. He may be like the rich man and build larger barns (Luke 12:16-21), indicating that materialism does not satisfy man's desire. Even worse, he will not be able to take it with him when he dies. A Spanish proverb says: "A shroud does not have pockets."

To take up the cross denotes the beginning of holiness in life. The objects of importance to the world become trivial to the life of the cross. The focus of the life of the cross is on Christ and not on accumulation or consumption of things.

---

Why is it impossible to serve God and mammon?

---

This lesson recognizes that God has provided material things to serve real human needs and that He intends for us to enjoy those gifts from God. Those of us who are blessed with material prosperity have a responsibility to share the blessing with others. Our stewardship becomes a ministry to God's people (Acts 4:34-37).

The lesson does not make renunciation of all material possessions a universal condition for entry into the Kingdom. The rich fool was condemned for the folly of thinking that wealth was the aim of life and not for his riches. In the parable about Lazarus, the rich man was condemned because of his callous indifference toward the beggar at his gate and not for his wealth.

On the other hand, the lesson recognizes the perils of an inordinate desire for riches. First, it distorts life's true aim. Life is more than food, raiment, or investments. If we trust in riches, we are vulnerable to the thieves of time and death. Second, covetousness can poison the rich with greed and the poor with envy. The Bible is not interested in the transfer of property from one covetous man to another.

Wealth is disvalued by the Bible. It is an incident to life, not an essential. The true pearl of great price is life under God's rule. All other treasures are handled with a detachment that neither seeks wealth nor despises it. Such spiritual detachment, the ability to be rich without avarice or pride, or to be poor without covetousness or anxiety, is indeed a blessing. Those who have this attitude live in the Kingdom.

## REVIEW QUESTIONS

1. What are some characteristics of the three groups described in Luke 6:24 and 25?

2. Does 1 Timothy 6:17-19 describe wealth as sin?

3. What are some effects of materialism?

4. What are some differences between "treasures on earth" and "treasures in heaven"?

5. What is the attitude reflected in Mark 8:34-37?

## GOLDEN TEXT HOMILY

"TAKE HEED, AND BEWARE OF COVETOUSNESS: FOR A MAN'S LIFE CONSISTETH NOT IN THE ABUNDANCE OF THE THINGS WHICH HE POSSESSETH" (Luke 12:15).

The Greek word rendered "covetousness" (**plenoexia**) describes a moral charateristic which is extremely ugly. Perhaps the word **greediness** most nearly expresses it. It is used ten times in the New Testament in a variety of ways. Christ's warning seems to have these various expressions in view, for the Greek text, followed by modern versions, reads, "Be on your guard against greed of every kind" (**New English Bible**).

However, it is clear that, in context, Jesus was thinking specifically of greed for money and material things. He was replying to a man in His audience who interrupted the sermon with a request that Jesus would intervene in his quarrel with his brother over the family inheritance. Jesus discerned that this man was so eaten up with greed for more that he could not wait until the conclusion of the service to seek His assistance.

Instead of opening his heart and mind to the pearls of wisdom which were falling from Christ's lips this man was probably thinking: How can I use this great man for my own material prosperity?

What are we really thinking about when we settle down in a church service to listen to the preacher? How often and easily our dominant desires and interests will surface during these moments. If we have enthroned the modern gods of pleasure and money in our hearts we may actually be quietly and secretly worshiping them even in the stillness of the church service.

Jesus warns us that when we enthrone the god of money we miss out on our true life. In the words of Jeremiah, we "have forsaken . . . the fountain of living waters, and hewed out cisterns, broken cisterns, that can hold no water" (Jeremiah 2:13).—**Noel Brooks, D.D., (Retired), Writer, ADULT SUNDAY SCHOOL TEACHER quarterly, International Pentecostal Holiness Church, Bristol, England.**

## SENTENCE SERMONS

LET US SOAR above our worldly possessions. The bee does not less need its wings when it has gathered an abundant store; for if it sinks in the honey it dies.

**—St. Augustine**

PREOCCUPATION WITH material things interferes with a person's relationship with God and others.

**—Selected**

THE MOST TERRIBLE thing about materialism, even more terrible than its proneness to violence, is its boredom, from which sex, alcohol, drugs, all devices for putting out the accusing light of reason and suppressing the unrealizable aspirations of love, offer a prospect of deliverance.

**—Malcolm Muggeridge**

ON MONEY AND POSSESSIONS: It all depends on whether you have things, or they have you.

**—Robert A. Cook**

## EVANGELISTIC APPLICATION

WE SHOULD BE CONCERNED FIRST WITH RECEIVING ETERNAL LIFE THROUGH JESUS CHRIST.

In the conclusion of His teaching on the Christian attitude toward material needs, Jesus declared that the primary ambition of the Christian must be entrance into the kingdom of God (Matthew 6:33, 34). Later in the Sermon on the Mount Jesus underscored the importance of being committed to God first of all. Jesus said there will be some who have prophesied, exorcised devils, and done wonderful works in His name, but they will not enter heaven. When they ask why they cannot, Jesus will say because they did not do the will of God (Matthew 7:21-23).

From these scriptures we see that what we do or what we have are not as important as obeying God's will. After Jesus refused to become the kind of Messiah the people wanted Him to be (John 6), which was one who would meet their material desires, they left Him. Jesus, then, asked His apostles if they would leave. Peter remarked there was no place for them to go, because Christ had the words of eternal life. The words to eternal life that Jesus gave were, "Seek ye first the kingdom of God, and his righteousness" (Matthew 6:33).

## ILLUMINATING THE LESSON

In his book, *The Morals Game*, Edward Stevens gives a method for determining our values. He suggests we write on a sheet of paper what we have done with our money and time over the last week or month. To whatever we devote most of money and time indicates our values and priorities. Follow Stevens' suggestion. Does your use of money and time reflect your Christian beliefs?

The futility of riches is stated very plainly in two places: the Bible and the income tax form. (Gilcrafter)

## DAILY DEVOTIONAL GUIDE

M. Living by God's Word. Deuteronomy 8:1-6
T. Righteousness Better Than Wealth. Psalm 37:16-24
W. Showing Unselfishness. Proverbs 28:20-27
T. God Rewards Liberality. Acts 10:1-4
F. A Cheerful·Giver. 2 Corinthians 9:6-11
S. Riches—False and True. Revelation 3:17-21

# The Sacredness of Human Life

**Study Text:** Genesis 1:26-28; 2:7; 9:5, 6; Exodus 20:13; 21:22; 1 Samuel 31:2-5; Job 33:4; Psalms 8:4, 5; 90:10; 139:13-16; Isaiah 44:2; Jeremiah 17:10; Luke 12:42-48; Acts 1:15-20; 16:25-28; 1 Peter 1:17; 4:15; 1 John 3:15

**Supplemental References:** Genesis 4:8-11; 6:8; Leviticus 24:17; Deuteronomy 8:3; Ecclesiastes 12:12, 13; Isaiah 45:11, 12; Acts 17:24-29

**Golden Text:** "God created man in his own image, in the image of God created he him; male and female created he them" (Genesis 1:27).

**Central Truth:** Life is a gift from God and must be respected and treated as sacred.

**Evangelistic Emphasis:** The Giver of physical life provides spiritual life to all who trust in Christ.

## Printed Text

**Genesis 1:26.** And God said, Let us make man in our image, after our likeness: and let them have dominion over the fish of the sea, and over the fowl of the air, and over the cattle, and over all the earth, and over every creeping thing that creepeth upon the earth.

**27. So God created man in his own image, in the image of God created he him; male and female created he them.**

28. And God blessed them, and God said unto them, Be fruitful, and multiply, and replenish the earth, and subdue it: and have dominion over the fish of the sea, and over the fowl of the air, and over every living thing that moveth upon the earth.

**9:5. And surely your blood of your lives will I require; at the hand of every beast will I require it, and at the hand of man; at the hand of every man's brother will I require the life of man.**

6. Whoso sheddeth man's blood, by man shall his blood be shed: for in the image of God made he man.

**Psalm 139:13. For thou hast pos-** sessed my reins: thou hast covered me in my mother's womb.

14. I will praise thee; for I am fearfully and wonderfully made: marvellous are thy works; and that my soul knoweth right well.

**15. My substance was not hid from thee, when I was made in secret, and curiously wrought in the lowest parts of the earth.**

16. Thine eyes did see my substance, yet being unperfect; and in thy book all my members were written, which in continuance were fashioned, when as yet there was none of them.

**Luke 12:42. And the Lord said, Who then is that faithful and wise steward, whom his lord shall make ruler over his household, to give them their portion of meat in due season?**

43. Blessed is that servant, whom his lord when he cometh shall find so doing.

**1 Peter 1:17. And if ye call on the Father, who without respect of persons judgeth according to every man's work, pass the time of your sojourning here in fear.**

## LESSON OUTLINE

I. LIFE, GIVEN BY GOD
II. LIFE, ABUSED BY MAN
   A. Abortion
   B. Murder
   C. Suicide
III. LIFE, A STEWARDSHIP

## LESSON EXPOSITION

INTRODUCTION

Creation has value because of its relationship to God. He created all, cares for all, and declared all of creation to be good. Thus, we are not free to exploit and neglect creation, but we are called upon to reverence it. While creation does have value, there is something unique about the sacredness of man, which is the focus of the lesson.

I. LIFE, GIVEN BY GOD (Genesis 1:26-28; 2:7; Job 33:4; Psalm 8:4, 5)

**Genesis 1:26. And God said, Let us make man in our image, after our likeness: and let them have dominion over the fish of the sea, and over the fowl of the air, and over the cattle, and over all the earth, and over every creeping thing that creepeth upon the earth.**

**27. So God created man in his own image, in the image of God created he him; male and female created he them.**

**28. And God blessed them, and God said unto them, Be fruitful, and multiply, and replenish the earth, and subdue it: and have dominion over the fish of the sea, and over the fowl of the air, and over every living thing that moveth upon the earth.**

This passage indicates the sacredness of man. First, it shows man's sacredness because God created man. Although God created man with special powers that make him foremost among the creation and God gave man over them, man is a created being like all other creatures. There is a gulf between the Creator and the creature man. Since man is dependent upon God, he has no ground for boasting in himself; however, the sacredness of man is evident in God, the Creator and Sustainer of creation, determining to create man, sustaining man, and relating to man.

The sacredness of man is supported by Genesis 2:4-7. The passage stresses the fact that man has life as a divine gift, bestowed directly by God through the breath of life. While the life of all other created beings is ascribed to the divine breath of God, man was distinguished from the other creatures by the direct impartation of the divine breath. While it seems the animals receive the divine breath by group, man receives it by a special act of God. According to the language Moses uses, it seems he is presenting an intimate picture of God carefully shaping the body of man, lovingly leaning over man, and gently breathing into man the divine breath of life. This intimate creation of man by God shows the sacredness of man.

In Genesis 1:26-28 a second affirmation is made about the sacredness of man. Man differs from all other creatures in that he alone is made "in the image of God." Man is created in the image of God; he does not fashion himself into it. He is a creature, but God has bestowed on him a dignity and a worth that is far greater than that of any other living thing.

Man being created in the image of God means man exists in a special relationship to God which sets him apart from other living things. The image of God in man points to the personal relationship which exists between God and man. What makes him **man** is that he stands in a personal relationship with God.

We should respect man because he originated from God. Our dignity is a result of God's dealings with us. Since God affirms us and gives us dignity, we should act with a holy awe toward anyone who bears the image of God. How we treat, nourish, and relate to each other should be done with the greatest respect, because we are dealing with one on whom God has placed His image. This respect will manifest itself in our social, economical, and international relations, as we seek to preserve and develop human life.

II. LIFE, ABUSED BY MAN (Exodus 20:13; 21:22; Psalm 139:13-16; Isaiah 44:2; Genesis 9:5, 6; 1 Peter 4:15; 1 John 3:15; 1 Samuel 31:2-5; Acts 1:15-20; 16:25-28)

A. Abortion (Exodus 21:22; Psalm 139:13-16; Isaiah 44:2)

When discussing the issue of abortion, some people refer to Exodus 21:22-25 although it does not discuss an induced abortion. The passage presents an incident in which two men were fighting and a pregnant woman was hit. The result of the woman's injury is the important matter of the verses, because some people believe the compensation or punishment that occurs due to injury has implications about the value of nascent life.

The passage says if a pregnant woman has a miscarriage due to being hit by two men who are fighting, but she does not die, the two men only pay a fine. If the woman dies, the two men are to be executed. Since the men are only fined if a miscarriage occurs but are executed if the woman dies, the passage implies maternal life has more value than nascent life. Although there seems to be a difference of value between the mother and the child, the Hebrews did not consider abortion for convenience as morally acceptable, because they had a very positive attitude about the sacredness of man, family, and children. They considered a child to be a blessing from God and would not think of destroying nascent life. Rather than seeking for a reason to destroy an unborn child for the sake of convenience, they affirmed and supported the person because of their recognition of the sacredness of man, since God had made man in His image. Consequently, the passage should not be used to support an argument for abortion-on-demand.

In Psalm 139, the king sought an encounter with God from which he would gain strength to persevere against his enemies. He invited God to search him, because he was confident that God would find him to be loyal to Him. Finally, he petitioned God to destroy his enemies.

**Psalm 139:13. For thou hast possessed my reins: thou hast covered me in my mother's womb.**

After recognizing the impossibility of escaping from God, although it was an attempt only in thought, the psalmist turned to God in a personal way through the idea of creation. He applied this idea of creation to himself, which became a means of expressing a positive relationship with an omniscient and omnipresent God. It was a recognition that God knows everything about our life and is constantly present with us. This recognition consoled the writer during his crisis.

The Old Testament idea of creation makes clear that man's existence belongs to God and has no meaning without Him. It recognizes that God is actively involved from the beginning, not only knowing about it but effecting creation. By seeing himself included in God's creation, he has an attitude of awe and trust toward God and even his own life.

**14. I will praise thee; for I am fearfully and wonderfully made: marvellous are thy works; and that my soul knoweth right well.**

The change in the psalmist's attitude takes a form of a testimony that expresses an attitude of awe and trust. Because he is a creature of God, the writer senses the infinite difference between himself and God. He knows that he does not possess an independent being that he could place over against God; he will always be dependent on God. He recognizes that God holds his life in His hands and with whom he has known himself to be secure since his childhood.

**15. My substance was not hid from thee, when I was made in secret, and curiously wrought in the lowest parts of the earth.**

**16. Thine eyes did see my substance, yet being unperfect; and in thy book all my members were written, which in continuance were fashioned, when as yet there was none of them.**

A note of trust prevails over the fear

suggested in the beginning of the psalm. He is unable to explain the divine mystery of God's providential rule, but it gives him a sense of security. He submits to the mystery of God in awe and trust. He recognizes that the power to which he owes his existence and which alone decides about his life is God. This does not frighten him because he knows that his Creator will sustain him.

Although these verses do not give us a biological lesson on the beginning of human life, they do suggest what should be our attitude toward man. The psalm recognizes that God knows us because He has created us and He relates to us. He knows us more intimately than any other person. He knows our deeds and our thoughts, even those thoughts hidden deep within us. He knows us in this intimate and personal way, because He has chosen to do so. It was a free and gracious act on His part. God, who created and sustains men intimately and personally, gave man dignity by choosing to relate to man. Since God deals with man in this manner, we should stand in respect and reverence of man, which calls on us to affirm and support man.

These verses do not tell us what to do in all situations regarding maternal life and nascent life. We should recognize that conflicts may occur between maternal life and nascent life. In exceptional situations very serious consideration must be given to the decision.

On the other hand, the verses do indicate the sacredness of man because of God's dealings with man. In His own way God is at work in our lives. Thus, we should recognize that nascent life, too, is sacred.

---

Is there a time when abortion is morally acceptable?

---

B. Murder (Genesis 9:5, 6; Exodus 20: 13; 1 Peter 4:15; 1 John 3:15)

**Genesis 9:5. And surely your blood of your lives will I require; at the hand of every beast will I require it, and at the hand of man; at the hand**
of every man's brother will I require the life of man.

**6. Whoso sheddeth man's blood, by man shall his blood be shed: for in the image of God made he man.**

According to these verses, man is under God's protection. The verses do not specify how man will be protected; a pattern for law and order is not given.

There are two views on how the verses should be interpreted. First, it is believed that God will protect and punish man through His providential ruling. If an animal or a man kills someone, God will take the life of the animal or man in His own way. The death may occur through natural processes or through direct divine intervention. Second, it is suggested that the phrase, "by man shall his blood be shed," implies that God gave society the authority and responsibility to avenge the death of man.

While these verses do not clearly indicate how justice will occur in the case of murder, they do indicate the reason why murder is wrong: "for in the image of God made he man." This phrase stresses the heinousness of the crime. An assault upon man's life, who is made in God's image, is a virtual assault upon God.

When the Hebrew read the sixth commandment, "Thou shalt not kill" (Exodus 20:13), he understood it to mean murder. If a person accidentally killed another person, he could find refuge in a City of Refuge, but if a person deliberately killed someone, he himself was to be executed.

People who were marked for killing were, however, exceptions to the rule. They forfeited their life only by some specific and grievous offense. They could not be killed because of who they were. The capital offenses given in Israel's civil laws were exceptions to the rule that everyone who bore God's image had a right to live.

In 1 John 3:15 the principle given by Jesus in the Sermon on the Mount (Matthew 5:21-26) is repeated. If murder is a horrible crime, malicious anger and insult are horrible too. These are horrible crimes because we are not reverencing another person as we should. The ultimate penalty for such an attitude is spiritual death.

Is capital punishment the same as murder?

C. Suicide (1 Samuel 31:2-5; Acts 1: 15-20; 16:25-28)

Generally speaking, there are three attitudes toward suicide. The first condemns suicide as a moral wrong. It believes suicide is a sin against one's own nature. It is the nature of every living thing to want life; to destroy our own life is to act in an unnatural way. In addition, it is argued that suicide is a sin against one's community. To cause our death deprives our family of our relationship with them. Also, suicide is believed to be a sin against God. He alone has the right to take our life, since He gave it.

A second attitude toward suicide justifies the act. It contends that any responsible person has the right to end his life whenever death seems a reasonable alternative to the cruel circumstances of one's life.

The third attitude excuses suicide as a tragedy. Advocating compassion and understanding, it excuses a person who commits suicide as a victim of forces beyond his control rather than a person who consciously and deliberately chooses death over life. It recognizes that people may be victims of tragic situations. For another person to give a moral judgment against their suicide would be inhumane and naive.

There are different reasons why people commit suicide. Some do so because of their pride. They think by taking their lives they are playing the role of God. They believe they have determined their destiny by their suicide rather than allowing God to determine their destiny.

Others commit suicide as a benevolent act. A soldier who hurls his body across a "live" grenade to save his friends, knowing that it will cause his death, is an example of a benevolent suicide. Perhaps the word "suicide" is not really the proper word in this situation; the word "sacrifice" may be a better term. The person does not choose to die in order to die; he chooses to do so as a means to help another person live.

Still others commit suicide as a means of escape from despair. Their bodies may be in unremitting, excruciating physical pain and they believe suicide is their cure. Others may be in such mental anguish that they have lost hope and have been stripped of joy and see death as their comfort. It may be shame from a sense of failure or worthlessness that drives some people to suicide.

Do the conditions of life ever make the choice of death a reasonable choice?

III. LIFE, A STEWARDSHIP (Psalm 90:10; Jeremiah 17:10; Luke 12:42-48; 1 Peter 1:17)

**Luke 12:42. And the Lord said, Who then is that faithful and wise steward, whom his lord shall make ruler over his household, to give them their portion of meat in due season?**

In the previous verse Peter asked a question of privilege and responsibility of the apostles in their ministry. Jesus did not answer Peter's question directly, but He focused on the responsibility of all servants. He stressed that a greater privilege means a greater responsibility. His words are closely linked with the previous warning not to be worldly minded but to be heavenly minded (Luke 12:22-34). The disciples must be loyal to Christ, expect His advent, and be faithful in their daily tasks.

**43. Blessed is that servant, whom his lord when he cometh shall find so doing.**

A steward was a slave who managed an estate. If he was "faithful and wise," he would properly manage the estate. He would be promoted on the unexpected return of his master, if he had been productive and fulfilled his responsibility.

If a steward does not expect his master to return, he may think he will not give an account to his master for his leadership, becoming a harsh taskmaster and careless manager. The unexpected return of his master will bring fatal punishment upon him.

Jesus declared the certainty of punishment for irresponsible stewardship. Those who have enjoyed particular privileges and know the will of God will have to bear the full responsibility of their misconduct, because they have knowingly sinned against God and their neighbor. Those who enjoyed fewer privileges will receive some punishment, because they disregarded their conscience.

Those who are looking for the second coming of Christ and who have fulfilled their responsibility will have joy and reward for their faithfulness.

**1 Peter 1:17. And if ye call on the Father, who without respect of persons judgeth according to every man's work, pass the time of your sojourning here in fear.**

The verse suggests that if we call ourselves the children of God, who is a just Judge, we should have reverent behavior and attitude during our earthly life. This extends to our action and attitude toward our neighbor. Being obedient to the will of God is quite often thought only in terms of evangelism and discipleship; however, being a "faithful and wise steward" includes a reverence for the sacredness of man. If anyone should respect human life, it should be those of the redeemed community. God has created a community in which its members would be mutually responsible for one another and for those not of the church.

Jesus was the foundation stone and at the same time builder of the new community. Jesus showed the attitude of God toward each individual. He refused to accept the hierarchical categorizing of men. One of the charges frequently laid upon Him was that He fellowshiped with those of whom other members of society looked down on. Jesus saw in each of these outcasts the image of God, and related to them.

Those who followed Jesus discovered the ministry God had for each man as he came into the church. Man had raised sexual, racial, economical, and social walls of separation that kept him from seeing the humanity of his neighbor. Jesus came breaking down these dividing walls of hostility, reconciling all men, who will, to God in body (Ephesians 2:11-22).

On this common ground before the church there is "no difference between the Jew and the Greek: for the same Lord over all is rich into all that call upon him" (Romans 10:12). Thus, there should be no prejudice or discrimination toward another person regardless of sex, race, economic level, or social status, because everyone who bears the image of God (and all men do) must be treated and ministered to as God has to all who are part of His redeemed community.

In this lesson we have presented reasons for the sacredness of man. When we speak of man's sacredness, we are not referring to the force of life within him. While God breathes life into all living things, it is persons, not the vital drive within the individual, whom He loves as His children.

We must see each individual as someone who lives each moment in relationship with God. We need to see the religious connection if we want to recognize the essence of human sacredness. The concrete person, beautiful or ugly, productive or idle, smart or stupid, is the one God made, whom God loves, whose life is in God's hands, and for whom His Son died on the Cross. This is the person who walks humbly on the earth in the image and likeness of the Creator who made him. He is, with all gifts and in spite of all his sins, the sacred person among all other valuable living creatures (Lewis Smedes, *Mere Morality*).

We who by faith know that God is the Creator of all and that He wills only the good for man should respond to Him with praise and gratitude for life, and for the good gifts which He has given to us. This means that we will accept ourselves with our talents and potential and that we will accept our neighbor with his endowments as good, regardless of his social standing, intelligence or nationality.

Thus sacredness of man means we will reverence human life by accepting the uniqueness of each individual, providing for the development of each person's potential, and protecting the life of each person.

## REVIEW QUESTIONS

1. What two reasons are given for the sacredness of man?

2. How does Psalm 139 describe God's relationship to man?

3. What are two interpretations to the phrase "by man shall his blood be shed" (Genesis 9:6)?

4. What are three attitudes toward suicide?

5. In what ways can we be a steward of life?

## GOLDEN TEXT HOMILY

"GOD CREATED MAN IN HIS OWN IMAGE, IN THE IMAGE OF GOD CREATED HE HIM; MALE AND FEMALE CREATED HE THEM" (Genesis 1:27).

The Book of Genesis sets forth all great principles of truth—truths dealt with and developed throughout the following books of the Bible. High among these principles is the truth of God's creation of man. Man was preceded by divine consultation—"Let us make man"—and created as the culmination of all God's creative works, His masterpiece. The word **created** repeated three times in Genesis 1:27, should be regarded as significant negation of modern evolutionist theories as to the descent of man and as emphatic declaration of man's divine origin. Man . . . woman . . . are **God-created;** mankind did not **evolve.**

Thus is set forth the value of human life. Individuals and nations who grasp and accept this fact cherish and protect human beings—from animals is debasing, allowing him to blame every low impulse within himself as his "animal nature coming out." Contrariwise, conceiving himself to be the creation of God, in God's image, is ennobling, calling forth his best in life.

The divine Trinity's consultation included "make man in our image" . . . "after our likeness" . . . created He them. This is a moral likeness—"righteousness and true holiness" (Ephesians 4:24)—and an intellectual likeness—"renewed in knowledge after the image" (Colossians 3:10). This "image and likeness" was lost in Adam's fall and is to be renewed in the new birth (1 Corinthians 15:49). Finally, "we shall be like him" (1 John 3:2). Man was created like God with purity, innocence. God is holy, just, wise, good, perfect; so must be the soul He placed in man. In it could be nothing impure, unjust, ignorant, evil, base, mean, or vile. In the first man Adam, what glory was lost! Man became a fallen, morally imperfect being. In the second Adam—Christ—perfection of God's creation is restored, purchased and redeemed by His own blood.

God made Adam and Eve like Himself, giving them an understanding mind that they may know the things of God, a feeling heart that they might love the things of God, and a will that they might make decisions to delight in the things of God.

Emerging from Genesis 1:27 are the facts of man's relationship with God—"in His own image"—and the distinction of humanity's sexuality—both male and female under the divine creation and blessing of God, but each distinctive physically and in their roles as male and female.—**Karl W. Bunkley (Retired), Former General Sunday School President, International Pentecostal Holiness Church, Oklahoma City, Oklahoma.**

## SENTENCE SERMONS

STEWARDSHIP IS NOT SO MUCH what you are doing but what God is doing through you.

—**"Notes and Quotes"**

LIFE IS A GIFT from God and must be respected and treated as sacred.

—**Selected**

IT IS REQUIRED in stewards, that a man be found faithful.

—**Apostle Paul (1 Corinthians 4:2)**

STEWARDSHIP IS the acceptance from

God of personal responsibility for one's life and life's affairs.

**—Roswell C. Long**

### EVANGELISTIC APPLICATION

THE GIVER OF PHYSICAL LIFE PROVIDES SPIRITUAL LIFE TO ALL WHO TRUST IN CHRIST.

You may have seen a beggar holding out his skinny hand for a morsel of bread, but have you ever seen a rich man following the poor, offering him a handful of gold? God does this very thing in offering His Son to us. He knows how wretched our life is, and He wants to give us a new life through Christ Jesus (2 Corinthians 5:17).

### ILLUMINATING THE LESSON

The most basic form of human encounter is looking another in the eye. There are many ways we deny our own humanity and other's humanity by not seeing. Sometimes we do not even bother to look (as when we cannot remember which waitress in a restaurant is ours). Sometimes we do not see concrete people but only abstract categories—Negroes, Catholics, conservatives, or liberals (Shirley Guthrie, *Christian Doctrine*).

If we see our neighbor and ourselves as God sees us, we will see someone who is finite and limited but who is deserving of our love and attention, because he is God's image.

### DAILY DEVOTIONAL GUIDE

M. Caring for the Oppressed. Psalm 70: 1-5

T. God Our Creator. Isaiah 45:5-12

W. God's Care for Human Life. Jonah 4: 1-11

T. God Values Human Life. Matthew 10: 28-31

F. Serving God Faithfully. Luke 16:10-13

S. Accountable to God. Acts 17:24-31

# Understanding Suffering

**Study Text:** Job 2:1-10; Romans 8:16-25; 2 Corinthians 1:3-11; 2 Timothy 3:12; Hebrews 11:24, 25, 36, 37; 1 Peter 2:19, 20; 3:13-17; 4:15

**Supplemental References:** Job 13:13-16; 23:1-12; 2 Corinthians 1:1-7; Philippians 3:1-11; 1 Peter 2:21-25; 4:12-19

**Golden Text:** "The sufferings of this present time are not worthy to be compared with the glory which shall be revealed in us" (Romans 8:18).

**Central Truth:** The believer is not exempt from suffering but God gives grace and sufficient strength to sustain him.

**Evangelistic Emphasis:** We can have eternal salvation through faith in Jesus Christ who suffered and died for our sins.

## Printed Text

**Job 2:1.** Again there was a day when the sons of God came to present themselves before the Lord, and Satan came also among them to present himself before the Lord.

**2. And the Lord said unto Satan, From whence comest thou? And Satan answered the Lord, and said, From going to and fro in the earth, and from walking up and down in it.**

3. And the Lord said unto Satan, Hast thou considered my servant Job, that there is none like him in the earth, a perfect and an upright man, one that feareth God, and escheweth evil? and still he holdeth fast his integrity, although thou movedst me against him, to destroy him without cause.

**4. And Satan answered the Lord, and said, Skin for skin, yea, all that a man hath will he give for his life.**

5. But put forth thine hand now, and touch his bone and his flesh, and he will curse thee to thy face.

**6. And the Lord said unto Satan, Behold, he is in thine hand; but save his life.**

7. So went Satan forth from the presence of the Lord, and smote Job with sore boils from the sole of his foot unto his crown.

**8. And he took him a potsherd to scrape himself withal; and he sat down among the ashes.**

9. Then said his wife unto him, Dost thou still retain thine integrity? curse God, and die.

**10. But he said unto her, Thou speakest as one of the foolish women speaketh. What? shall we receive good at the hand of God, and shall we not receive evil? In all this did not Job sin with his lips.**

**2 Timothy 3:12.** Yea, and all that will live godly in Christ Jesus shall suffer persecution.

---

**LESSON OUTLINE**

I. CAUSES OF SUFFERING

II. COPING WITH SUFFERING

III. DELIVERANCE FROM SUFFERING

## LESSON EXPOSITION

### INTRODUCTION

The world is full of pain and suffering. In glaring instances, the faithful ones suffer acutely and the guilty or evil ones are spared. Disasters appear to strike the evil and the good indiscriminately, whether in the case of a bridge that plunges twelve cars of people into the waters, or the downing of KAL flight 007.

From a practical point of view, men are weighed down by the poignant burden of suffering whether from natural disasters like earthquakes, hurricanes, or floods; from the manifold pains of sickness and incurable disease; or problems generated by careless living.

In the field of theology this is called the problem of evil. It grows out of the fact of suffering, but it is set by our belief in God. Our lesson today will not answer every question about suffering. It is hoped that it will aid in a better understanding of suffering.

Job, a righteous and prosperous man (Job 1:1-3), and his large family lived in the land of Uz. When the Lord in heaven boasts of Job's piety, Satan cynically insists that Job has served God only because he has been well rewarded. Because of the challenge, the Lord permits Satan to subject Job to a series of trials that result in the loss of his family and wealth; however, this catastrophe is unable to destroy Job's faith. Job utters no words of complaint against his Maker, but silently accepts these blows as the will of God. Satan is disconcerted by his apparent failure and appears before God a second time.

I. CAUSES OF SUFFERING (Job 2:1-10; 2 Timothy 3:12; Hebrews 11:24, 25, 36, 37; 1 Peter 4:15)

**Job 2:3. And the LORD said unto Satan, From whence comest thou? And Satan answered the LORD, and said, From going to and fro in the earth, and from walking up and down in it.**

Satan will not admit that he has been mistaken about Job's integrity, but the Lord claims that Job held to his integrity.

**Job 2:4. And Satan answered the LORD, and said, Skin for skin, yea, all that a man hath will he give for his life.**

**5. But put forth thine hand now, and touch his bone and his flesh, and he will curse thee to thy face.**

Satan complains that the trial has not been severe enough. He accuses Job of callousness and indifference to the suffering of others. Satan insists that if Job be struck in his own person, his piety will crumble. So far the calamity has affected only the lives of others. His own skin has been untouched. Let his own person be involved and he will not hold fast to his integrity.

**Job 2:6. And the LORD said unto Satan, Behold, he is in thine hand; but save his life.**

**7. So went Satan forth from the presence of the LORD, and smote Job with sore boils from the sole of his foot unto his crown.**

**8. And he took him a potsherd to scrape himself withal; and he sat down among the ashes.**

The Lord extends the offer to Satan to attack Job himself. The sufferer is stricken with a loathsome skin disease. He takes his place among the lepers on the ash heap outside of the city. There, in this place of discarded things, sat the man who once had been, "the greatest of all the men of the east" (1:3).

**Job 2:9. Then said his wife unto him, Dost thou still retain thine integrity? curse God, and die.**

The loss of family, wealth, and now her husband's health leaves the faith of Job's wife in ruins. She thinks God has treated Job badly and deserves a curse. Thus, she recommends that Job curse God, even if death is the result of his blasphemy.

**Job 2:10. But he said unto her, Thou speakest as one of the foolish women speaketh. What? shall we receive good at the hand of God, and shall we not receive evil? In all this did not Job sin with his lips.**

Job sees a support for his faith taken from him. He can no longer count on her spiritual support in this spiritual battle. He never curses God, but his human relationships are broken.

His attitude is the same as before (Job 1:21). It is right for God to give good gifts and to retrieve them (Job 1:20-22); it is also right for God to send good and evil (Job 2:10). Job bows before the sovereign hand of God whether it bestows or takes away, whether it caresses or strikes. In all of the calamity, Job continued to remain silent in his affliction.

The Book of Job is a universal book because it speaks to a universal experience: suffering. Four friends of Job, Eliphaz, Bildad, Zophar and Elihu, represent all that orthodox theology could say about the calamities that had devastated Job's life. With the possible exception of Elihu, their interpretation of suffering was in terms of personal sinfulness. This is a striking reminder of the inadequacy of human understanding of the problem of suffering. All the human persons in the drama address the problem of suffering in total ignorance of Satan's allegations against Job's piety and of the divine permission to prove his point, if he can. Job and the others were trying to fit together the pieces of a puzzle without having all the pieces within their grasp. Consequently, the Book of Job is a commentary on the inadequacy of man to reduce the complexity of the problem of suffering to some consistent pattern.

While the author does not recognize a simple answer to the problem of suffering, he does advocate hope. He believes in a God who has the answer to human need. The word of man is unable to penetrate the darkness of Job's mind; the Word of God brings abiding light. God does not answer the questions about suffering, but He answers the need of Job's heart. He does not explain the battle of strategy to Job, but He makes Job a conqueror in it.

**2 Timothy 3:12. Yea, and all that will live godly in Christ Jesus shall suffer persecution.**

In the context of this passage (2 Timothy 3:10-17), Paul gives Timothy an exhortation to be steadfast during persecution. Paul reminds Timothy of his doctrine and life. **Manner of life** (v. 10) denotes general behavior which a man's closest friends will know. **Purpose** (v. 10) means chief aim. Paul had as his aim the preaching the gospel and winning the approval of God. His **faith** (v. 10) enabled Paul to triumph in every circumstance. His **longsuffering** (v. 10) caused him to endure until the fruit of his labor appeared. His **love** (v. 10) enabled him to win many to Christ. **Patience** (v. 10) caused Paul to remain firm under the most discouraging circumstances.

The appeal to the events in Antioch, Iconium, and Lystra may have been because Timothy could remember them from childhood in Lystra. Paul's suffering from persecution may have made a deep impression on his mind. While he reminisced about the persecution, Paul also mentions God's deliverance for him.

Those who determine to live a life of Christian devotion should not be surprised by persecution. They should expect persecution even more so as the contrast between good and evil increases and evil men get worse in their departure from the truth and in their power to mislead others.

Against the background of this militant error, the Christian leader must stand firm on what he knows as the truth, like a rock resisting the increasing fury of waves. He is to continue in the things which he has learned. Timothy can be satisfied with what he has already received. The basis of this confidence is twofold. It is assured by Timothy's knowledge of his teachers and the Scriptures. The character of the teachers reflects the character of what is taught. Since Timothy knew the integrity of Paul, his mother, and his grandmother and he knew the message they had taught him, he should be steadfast in the Christian life. Likewise, we should abide in the strength of the gospel when we are persecuted.

The Apostle Paul in writing to the Hebrews alludes to the suffering of Moses as a choice based on values (Hebrews 11:24, 25). The cruel oppression and hardship suffered by the Hebrews, Moses knew well. But he weighed their sufferings over against the pleasures of sin, because he perceived that the sufferers were the people of God and that they would come out best in the end. He therefore reasoned that the advantages of the Egyptian court were both superficial and temporary. His choice was prompted by his standard of value "Esteeming the reproach of Christ greater riches than the treasures in Egypt" (v. 26).

The passage in Hebrews 11:36 and 37 picks up the history of those who suffered through many eras as cruel men brought suffering and shame to God's people who were busy in kingdom work.

The spirit of worldly men is unchanging. Let a Christian persevere in kingdom service and he will suffer. He may not be stoned, but he will be pelted with the sneers of thoughtless and evil men. Compare also, 1 Peter 4:15.

Is it important to determine the cause of suffering?

II. COPING WITH SUFFERING (1 Peter 2:19, 20; 3:13-17; 2 Corinthians 1:3-11)

In 1 Peter 2:18-25, Peter accepts slavery as a prevailing human social arrangement in which the Christian, whose role is a servant, should find and fill his place by active submission. It is the Christian's awareness of God, his knowledge of what is pleasing to Him, and his sense of calling in Christ that should inspire him and enable him to be submissive. He should be submissive even when it is difficult and painful because of harsh matters and unjust treatment.

Peter commands uncomplaining service and loyalty from the Christian although it may involve the painful endurance of unjust treatment. He says submission to punishment when one has done wrong is not what he is commanding. He says it is the patient, uncomplaining submission to suffering even when one has done what he should that is pleasing to God.

Peter indicates that submission to suffering corresponds to the example in Christ. He endured the suffering which He did not deserve. He accepted the suffering patiently and submissively. His action was pleasing in God's sight.

The divine purpose for the Christian is to become a member of God's family. This purpose is to find its immediate outworking in circumstances and experiences like those of the slave. If a slave becomes a Christian, it is normally God's immediate purpose that he should not cease to be a slave because he has become a Christian. He should glorify God by beginning to behave in relation to his master as only a Christian slave would.

Although slavery is a thing of the past, the principle Peter set forth for slaves is applicable to us in our world. There are relationships in business, employment, and government in which others are set over us. It is our Christian duty to be submissive, cooperative and uncomplaining, even if we have been hurt by unfair treatment. The injustice is not the end of our condition. Christ was submissive to those who abused Him even to the point of death, but the Father raised Him from the dead. We may suffer even though we have done what we should do, but our heavenly Father will ultimately vindicate us by receiving us into eternal fellowship with Him.

In 1 Peter 3:13-17, Peter writes that those who do good have God on their side; therefore, there is no one who can really hurt them (compare Romans 8:31). In this world there is always a possibility that Christians may have to suffer for the sake of righteousness; this may be God's will for them. When it is, they should regard such suffering as a privilege. It is not an occasion for alarm, distress, or backsliding. In suffering they should maintain a reverence for Christ and be ready to confess their hope in Him. They should be careful not to deserve their suffering by doing evil; instead, they should be conscientious in their conduct by which they could silence their persecutors.

When Christians do suffer, they should

382                                                    July 13, 1986

recognize that God will bring forth some good from it. It may glorify God, it may be for the benefit of others, or it may be for the personal good of the one suffering.

Peter illustrated this point by Jesus Christ. He suffered at the hands of men doing good: healing people, feeding people, and forgiving people of their sins. Yet He suffered according to the will of God and for the benefit of men.

Paul wrote to the Corinthians (2 Corinthians 1:3-11) about his suffering. There were three distinct ideas about suffering that Paul presented to the Corinthians. First, Paul had learned to praise God, because God had comforted him during his suffering. During the trial caused by suffering, Paul was conscious of God's gracious love and His sustaining strength. He cited a particular experience in Asia as an example of God's unfailing support. It was a kind of danger where Paul reminded them that he had been exposed to death on several occasions. The result was despair, but he learned confidence in God. He learned that he could depend on God who knows the future even when he did not know what was before him.

Paul wrote that Christians participate in the sufferings of Christ. These sufferings are not in the sense of atonement but in the sense of suffering while doing God's will to preach the gospel. While we share in the sufferings of Jesus, we also are comforted through Christ. He is the water of life and the bread of life that sustains us in life, even in the crisis of suffering.

Finally, Paul wrote that Christians' participation in sufferings is not futile. We endure sufferings for the spiritual benefit of fellow Christians. What Paul had in mind could be illustrated by the care a parent has for his child (1 Thessalonians 2:7). The parent may sacrifice, endure hardships, or suffer deprivations so that the child can be taken care of well.

How can we cope with suffering?

III. DELIVERANCE FROM SUFFERING
(Romans 8:16-25)

While one recognizes that Christians may suffer, he has no doubt that the future for the Christian will far outbalance his present sufferings (Romans 8:18-27). This assurance of future blessing is not vain. Paul supports his conviction with three facts.

First, he points to the unity of creation. Man and nature are so closely related that by man's sin nature suffered. Man fell of his own free will, but nature was corrupted with him by decree of God. Creation was subjected to frustration, but it has hope of deliverance. Man's redemption means that creation itself will be redeemed.

Second, we have assurance of full redemption from suffering and a promise of future glory through our hope. By emphasizing hope, Paul does not minimize the role of faith. Hope emerges through a faith attitude. Paul makes the point that faith in God produces hope for the consummation of salvation. Since hope is produced, there is assurance that we will receive the fulness of salvation.

Finally, there is the work of the Holy Spirit in the life of the Christian. The indwelling of the Spirit is a testimony that God has begun a work in our life. In all of the trials we presently endure, the Holy Spirit aids us. He is there testifying of our adoption into a new family, which brings us strength from the fellowship. He is there calling God our Father, indicating the tender relationship between God and man. He is there interceding on our behalf by presenting our needs to God.

Through the indwelling Spirit we are given victory over our sufferings and a guarantee of the coming glory. The indwelling Spirit is a firstfruit of the harvest. It is like the farmer who checked on his crop and found some of the fruit ripe; he knew then that he would harvest the crop. By the indwelling of the Spirit, we know that we will see the harvest. We have the assurance that we will see God fully redeem us even though we are presently in trials of sufferings.

In summary, several observations can be made about suffering from a Christian view. First, a Christian view does not attempt to simplify suffering by limiting the cause of suffering to one source. It recognizes that suffering may be due to natural calamities, sinful attitudes, or to a testing of faith—to name a few causes. Suffering is a complex issue as indicated in the story of Job. His friends gave him orthodox reasons for his suffering. They were the standard explanations given for suffering, but they were not the right answers in Job's case.

Second, while a Christian view of suffering is not preoccupied with answering the question of why we do suffer, it does emphasize the God who is there within the suffering, who sustains during the suffering, and who will lead us out of the suffering. A Christian view of suffering does not focus on the situation, but it focuses upon the One who is the Lord of the situation. A Christian view of suffering is not paralyzed by the current painful circumstance, but it anticipates the future glory-heaven where there will be no sorrow.

Third, a Christian view of suffering recognizes that suffering can be used for our own good:

(1) It can refine our faith (1 Peter 1:5-7).

(2) It can make us mature (James 1:2-4).

(3) It can be an opportunity to manifest the works of God (John 9:1-3).

(4) It can conform us to the image of Christ (Romans 8:28, 29).

(5) It can produce in us perseverance and character (Romans 5:3-5).

---

To what extent can we be delivered from our temporal sufferings?

## REVIEW QUESTIONS

1. Were the answers Job's friends gave him adequate for his questions?

2. What was the cause for Paul's sufferings that he mentioned in 2 Timothy 3:12?

3. Will Christians always suffer?

4. If a person is not suffering, can he be a Christian?

5. What is some good that can be gained when we suffer?

## GOLDEN TEXT HOMILY

"THE SUFFERINGS OF THIS PRESENT TIME ARE NOT WORTHY TO BE COMPARED WITH THE GLORY WHICH SHALL BE REVEALED IN US" (Romans 8:18).

Human life is so constituted that the choicest things are the costliest; the most valuable, the most expensive; the most pleasurable, the most painful.

Liberty follows slavery; freedom follows bondage; pleasure follows pain; joy follows sorrow; and happiness follows duty.

The wonder and brightness of the stars are revealed by the dark night. Tempered steel comes from hot furnaces. Pure gold is the result of fire. The fragrance of expensive perfume comes from crushed flowers.

In every life there are many areas of suffering. Clouds gather. Thunders roar. Lightnings flash. There are many times of darkness, distress, sorrow, bereavements, remorse, and guilt. But there is also glory for every suffering.

For the suffering of sin, there is the glory of salvation.

For the suffering of inner pollution, there is the glory of cleansing.

For the suffering of need, there is the glory of the unlimited supply of God's grace.

For the suffering of weakness, there is the glory of His strength.

For the suffering of loneliness, there is the glory of good cheer.

For the suffering of perplexities, there is the glory of God's guidance.

For the suffering of misunderstanding, there is the glory of His understanding.

For the suffering of human want, there is the glory of divine plenty.

For the suffering of temptation, there is the glory of deliverance.

For the suffering of death, there is the glory of immortality.

Suffering? Yes. But also glory.

The glory comes only to those who endure the suffering.

No cross—no crown.

No suffering—no glory.

That is God's order. He always leaves us in the sunlight.—**Eugene Christenbury, Ed.D., Associate Professor of Education, Lee College, Cleveland, Tennessee**

## SENTENCE SERMONS

THE BELIEVER IS NOT EXEMPT from suffering but God gives grace and sufficient strength to sustain him.

**—Selected**

THE SCHOOL of suffering graduates rare scholars.

**—"Speaker's Sourcebook"**

TO HAVE SUFFERED much is like knowing many languages: It gives the sufferer access to many more people.

**—"Speaker's Sourcebook"**

SUFFERING IS A MISFORTUNE, as viewed from the one side, and a discipline as viewed from the other.

**—Samuel Smiles**

## EVANGELISTIC APPLICATION

WE CAN HAVE ETERNAL SALVATION THROUGH FAITH IN JESUS CHRIST WHO SUFFERED AND DIED FOR OUR SINS.

God has made Jesus Christ to be sin for us so that we may receive the righteousness of God. It is in Jesus Christ, specifically through His suffering, that we have eternal life. There is no other person who can suffer vicariously for us and commend us to God.

For some this seems harsh. They understand the death of Christ to be an attempt on Christ's part to turn the wrath of God away from man. They picture Christ as a hero who appeases a tyrant. But nothing could be further from the truth. We do not see a hero appeasing a tyrant; we see God himself taking upon Himself our sins so that He may fulfill the justice He requires for sin. What great love expression this is. The one without sin dying for the sinner; the one offended dying for the offender.

## ILLUMINATING THE LESSON

A survivor of the Holocaust recounted this experience she had in a concentration camp. Life was unbearable in her bunkhouse. A reason was the infestation of fleas in her living quarters. When she complained about the fleas, another prisoner pointed out that it was because of the fleas that they were able to keep their Bible. It was a camp policy to search the dorms on a regular basis; however, the guards overlooked this particular dorm because of the fleas. Consequently, the guards never found the Bible. While the prisoners did suffer from the fleas, it was because of the fleas that they had the Bible to encourage them.

## DAILY DEVOTIONAL GUIDE

M. Partakers of Suffering. 1 Peter 4:12-19
T. Consolation in Suffering. 2 Corinthians 1:1-7
W. Fellowship of Suffering. Philippians 3:1-11
T. Christ's Sufferings. 1 Peter 2:21-25
F. Tried Through Suffering. Job 23:1-12
S. Faithful Through Suffering. Job 13:13-16

# Caring for Others

**Study Text:** Deuteronomy 5:16; 15:7-11; 2 Samuel 9:1-13; Psalm 68:6; Matthew 11:28-30; 25:34-40; 1 Timothy 5:1-4, 16; James 5:13-16; 1 John 3:17, 18

**Supplemental References:** Psalms 27:9, 10; 41:1; 71:6-9, 17, 18; Proverbs 28: 27; 19:7; Acts 2:44, 45; James 2:1-8, 14-18

**Golden Text:** "Let us not love in word, neither in tongue; but in deed and in truth" (1 John 3:18).

**Central Truth:** Christian love demands that we cheer the lonely, help the poor and handicapped, and honor our elders.

**Evangelistic Emphasis:** When we perform deeds of Christian love we may find fertile soil for the gospel message.

## Printed Text

**Deuteronomy 5:16.** Honour thy father and thy mother, as the Lord thy God hath commanded thee; that thy days may be prolonged, and that it may go well with thee, in the land which the Lord thy God giveth thee.

**1 Timothy 5:1. Rebuke not an elder, but intreat him as a father; and the younger men as brethren;**

2. The elder women as mothers; the younger as sisters, with all purity.

**3. Honour widows that are widows indeed.**

4. But if any widow have children or nephews, let them learn first to shew piety at home, and to requite their parents: for that is good and acceptable before God.

**Deuteronomy 15:7. If there be among you a poor man of one of thy brethren within any of thy gates in thy land which the Lord thy God giveth thee, thou shalt not harden thine heart, nor shut thine hand from thy poor brother:**

8. But thou shalt open thine hand wide unto him, and shalt surely lend

him sufficient for his need, in that which he wanteth.

**11. For the poor shall never cease out of the land: therefore I command thee, saying, Thou shalt open thine hand wide unto thy brother, to thy poor, and to thy needy, in thy land.**

**1 John 3:17.** But whoso hath this world's good, and seeth his brother have need, and shutteth up his bowels of compassion from him, how dwelleth the love of God in him?

**18. My little children, let us not love in word, neither in tongue; but in deed and in truth.**

**James 5:13.** Is any among you afflicted? let him pray. Is any merry? let him sing psalms.

**14. Is any sick among you? let him call for the elders of the church; and let them pray over him, anointing him with oil in the name of the Lord:**

15. And the prayer of faith shall save the sick, and the Lord shall raise him up; and if he have committed sins, they shall be forgiven him.

**16. Confess your faults one to an-**

other, and pray one for another, that ye may be healed. The effectual fervent prayer of a righteous man availeth much.

---

## LESSON OUTLINE

I. HONORING OLDER ADULTS
II. CHEERING THE LONELY
III. PROVIDING FOR THE DESTITUTE
IV. HELPING THE HANDICAPPED

## LESSON EXPOSITION

### INTRODUCTION

Volumes could be and have been written about the compassion of Christ within the church. This is to be expected for the Christian church ceases to be the expression of Christ in the world when compassion does not flow from it.

But a new and wonderful thing is happening: The compassion so warmly expressed by Christ has moved beyond the confines of the church to that of the masses throughout the world. Many who do not even attend church are showing great concern for the elderly, the lonely, the destitute, and the handicapped.

Even to minister to those within the church family is now requiring full-time staff persons in many cases. Certainly all Christians must follow the example of the Lord to share in the vital ministry of caring for others. From those within our own households to those distant points around the world, our challenge is to follow Christ in showing compassion.

### I. HONORING OLDER ADULTS (Deuteronomy 5:16; 1 Timothy 5:1-4, 16)

**Deuteronomy 5:16. Honour thy father and thy mother, as the LORD thy God hath commanded thee; that thy days may be prolonged, and that it may go well with thee, in the land which the LORD thy God giveth thee.**

This commandment does not suggest that children have warm, affectionate feelings toward their parents. It does not tell children to feel happy about their parents. It commands children to honor their parents.

Why does the commandment tell us to honor our parents? First, let us eliminate some of the wrong reasons for a child to honor his parents. The duty to honor is not a result of the sinfulness of the child. Children are no more sinful than their parents. It would be no more risky to give children freedom than it would be to give parents authority. Both are sinful. Even in a perfect world, children would need to honor their parents. In addition, children do not owe their parents honor out of gratitude for what they have done for them. While some children may abound with pleasant memories of the parental care that surrounded them in their childhood, others are engulfed with resentment because of abusive parental care.

Children have a duty to honor their parents, because parents have authority from God. It is God's intention, through this commandment, that parents nurture and guide children.

The authority of parents is expressed through family life. A family is a group of people bound together in a covenant of care for one another. Though blood is a family's natural bond, it does not create a family. What binds people together as a family is the covenant of loyalty to one another from birth to death.

When two people bring a child into the world, they are called to be the child's caretakers. This calling is the first ingredient of a family. The child gradually learns to trust his parents to be his caretakers. This is the second ingredient to a family. The trust between the child and the parents grows until the parents tell the child what they believe to be true and right about life and its meaning.

The Bible sees this circle of covenanted care in the family as the right setting for the nurture of children into commitment to what is right and true about life. Parents are parents in order to take care of the child's initiation into faith and morals.

Honor, on the part of the child, then

is a willingness to listen to the voice of one's father and mother because they are God's representatives to the child. They serve as teachers and guides into faith and morals on the behalf of God. It is from his parents that the child learns who he is and what God expects of him.

Honor is not a sentimental thing. A Hebrew child showed respect for his father by listening to his stories about faith in God with a mind toward believing and obeying. A Hebrew child continued to honor his parents long after their roles were reversed. When the parents moved into the twilight years and the children moved into maturity, the child remained a child called to honor his parents. The power of the parents might diminish, but they always stood for God before the child (Proverbs 19: 26).

---

Do all parents deserve honor?

---

**1 Timothy 5:1. Rebuke not an elder, but intreat him as a father; and the younger men as brethren;**

**2. The elder women as mothers; the younger as sisters, with all purity.**

1 Timothy is one of the three Pastoral Epistles (2 Timothy and Titus are the other books). The letter is written to Timothy who is pastoring the church in Ephesus. The letter gives counsel and directions to Timothy concerning faith, doctrine, and practical matters, as they relate to the church and to Timothy.

In 1 Timothy 5:1, 2, Paul instructs Timothy about pastoral care of old and young members. He mentions four groups: elderly men, elderly women, young men, and young women. Since Timothy was a relatively young man, these designations were significant for the instruction given. The pastoral care should be practiced with love and care. Admonition is necessary for all people from time to time, including older people; however, a disrespectful assault upon an older man by a younger minister merely makes the accuser open to rebuke. There may be occasions when correction is needed, but the matter should

be handled by the minister in a way that comforts and encourages.

Pastoral care should be performed in a way that is typical of the care in a family. The minister should treat the members as gently as he treats his family. He should be as respectful of the older members as he is of his parents; he should be as considerate of the younger members as he is of his brothers and sisters.

All pastoral care should be done in purity. This is not so much a warning against immorality as it is a warning against impropriety. Thoughtlessness or indiscretion will ruin the ministry of any pastor. When his pastoral duties require him to deal with young women, he should behave as he would want other men to act toward his own sister. (Titus 2:3-5 entrusts the teaching of younger women to older Christian women.)

**1 Timothy 5:3. Honour widows that are widows indeed.**

**4. But if any widow have children or nephews, let them learn first to shew piety at home, and to require their parents: for that is good and acceptable before God.**

When determining the widows who need care and assistance from the church, it should be determined not only who needs help, but also who is deserving. Whenever possible, widows should be provided for by their own children or families, which is an obvious Christian duty. Nonetheless, Paul does recognize that the church has a responsibility to provide for widows who need help and who are deserving. Paul says a widow who is serving in the ministry (or the work of the church), who is over 60 years old, who has been married only once, who does not intend to remarry, who is well spoken of, and who has no one to care for her is qualified. In this situation the church has a responsibility to care for the widow.

---

Should twentieth century churches have a program to assist the widows?

---

On the otherhand, younger women are

not qualified. They may be tempted to remarry or fall into making house-to-house visitation a time of idle talk and gossip. It is better for younger women to remarry and help in the responsibilities of a home. In this way, they may be able to help some of the widows that the church would be unable to help.

Paul also admonishes Timothy to show care and love for older adults (2 Timothy 5:1-4). Although Paul is addressing Timothy's pastoral duties, the principle is applicable to all of us. We have a responsibility to care for the needs of our older citizens. We have a responsibility to show them respect in the way we talk with them and act toward them. We should not be harsh, because we open ourselves up to rebuke and we may cause ill feelings. We should be respectful because it will uplift the body of Christ.

In addition, Paul gave some practical advice to Timothy on the church's responsibility to care for the widows. Paul recognized that the church had a duty to care for those widows who were in need and had no one to care for them. Benevolence was a natural result of Christian love. If we see our sister in need, we are obligated to minister to that need. There are no if's, and's, or but's; we have an obligation to take care of her needs.

Some people would question if we are to follow those regulations listed in 1 Timothy 5:3-16 precisely or if we should adopt regulations that would be more fitting to our time. This may be a significant question to consider; however, the more fundamental question, especially with more people living longer, is: Are we doing anything to fulfill our responsibility to the deserving widow?

II. CHEERING THE LONELY (Psalm 68:6; Matthew 11:28-30)

In Psalm 68:6 we find part of the introduction (vv. 1-6) to Psalm 68. This psalm may have been composed for David's procession with the ark into Jerusalem. The two main parts of the psalm celebrate God's victorious march from Egypt to Jerusalem and the power and

majesty of God evident in the rise of God's people and the number of worshipers of God.

Protection of the helpless and judgment on the lawless are marks of the true kinship; the ark brings its reminder of the Exodus to bear on this as well. The Exodus was a classic example of provision of the homeless, liberation for the prisoners and punishment for the rebels.

In these events, as well as in the Gospel accounts, God's pattern of action stands out. He is on the side of the lonely. He seeks them out in order to bring them into fellowship with Him and with His chosen people. It is in this community, which God has made possible by His mighty acts of redemption, that we can know the joy of fellowship.

In Matthew 11:28-30, Jesus stands as the Great Teacher who alone can give knowledge of God, and, consequently, comfort for the lonely. Although Jesus was reviled, slandered, and rejected by many (Matthew 11:16-24), He still stands in the fullness of His wisdom and the gentleness of His love and invites all to come to Him. He will place His yoke of instruction upon them and they will find rest for their souls. The yoke probably should not be pictured as the ordinary yoke that a laborer lays across his shoulder (containers on both ends) hoping that he will find rest at the end of the day when it is taken off of him. Jesus says it is not toil and labor that lead to rest, but following after Him. Because Jesus himself is among those who are tired and burdened, He can inspire the disciple to follow His life of total openness to God and thus attain true peace (compare Jeremiah 6:16).

III. PROVIDING FOR THE DESTITUTE (Deuteronomy 15:7-11; Matthew 25:34-40; 1 John 3:17, 18)

**Deuteronomy 15:7. If there be among you a poor man of one of thy brethren within any of thy gates in thy land which the LORD thy God giveth thee, thou shalt not harden thine heart, nor shut thine hand from thy poor brother:**

**8. But thou shalt open thine hand unto him, and shalt surely lend him sufficient for his need, in that which he wanteth.**

In Deuteronomy 15:11, the Hebrews are instructed of their responsibilities to the poor at the end of every seven years. They were to forgive the debts of the poor. In addition they should have an attitude of generosity toward them. They should lend to the poor so that his need would be met. On the other hand, their motive should be pure. They should provide for the poor because the poor, who likewise bear the image of God, deserve to be treated as God's children.

The Hebrews were not to be reluctant to lend to the poor in the sixth year, because they know they would have to forgive the debt the next year. This kind of attitude is repulsive to God. Regardless of the cost of giving to the poor, the Hebrews had a responsibility of ministering to the poor's need. If they did not act because it would be costly, it would be sin. Later, Israel did neglect the poor, and God judged her for her neglect among other reasons. (See Isaiah 1:10-17; Ezekiel 16:48-52; Amos 5:9ff, and Micah 6:10-15.)

The Christian's responsibility toward the needy is emphasized in Matthew 25: 34-40. The lesson in the passage is that God will judge us in accordance with our reaction to human need. God does not judge us according to the knowledge we have amassed or the fortune that we have accumulated. He judges us on the help that we have given.

The help we give is in simple things: giving a hungry man a meal, offering a thirsty woman a drink, greeting a stranger, or visiting a prisoner. It is not giving away thousands of dollars, but it is giving ordinary help to meet basic human needs.

This simple, human help to our neighbor in need is given to Jesus Christ himself. If we wish to delight a parent's heart, then we should do something for his child. Is there any greater way to please God?

---

How should the church provide for the destitute?

---

**1 John 3:17. But whoso hath this world's good, and seeth his brother have need, and shutteth up his bowels of compassion from him, how dwelleth the love of God in him?**

**18. My little children, let us not love in word, neither in tongue; but in deed and in truth.**

Love is practical. We can know love in the Christian sense because of what we see on Calvary. True love is not only revealed on the cross it is expressed in our lives. None of us can offer the supreme redemptive sacrifice, but we constantly have the opportunity to share our possessions with those in need (compare James 2:15-16). The transition from the plural **brethren** in verse 16 to the singular **brother** in verse 17 is significant. It is easier to talk about helping mankind than it is to love individual men and women—especially those unlike us.

Loving everybody in general may be an excuse for loving nobody in particular. John gave two reasons why we cannot escape our responsibility. If we see our brother's need and if we have the means to help meet his need, then we have an obligation to our brother. We may say that we do not have the means to help the brother. If that is true, then we are not obligated, but we must be very cautious that we do not use that as an excuse to be selfish. If we do, we stand under the condemnation and judgment of God. Since we have seen the love of God demonstrated in Jesus Christ and have experienced His love through adoption, we must help our brother in need.

John concludes this section (1 John 3:14-18) with an exhortation that statements about love are not enough. Love is essentially not talk but action. If our love is to be genuine (**in truth**), it will be active (**in deed**).

This passage is about hatred and love. Hatred characterizes the world. Cain is its example. Hatred murders and brings spiritual death. Love characterizes the church. Christ is the example. Love originates in God, leads to self-sacrifice, and is indicated by eternal life.

IV. HELPING THE HANDICAPPED (2 Samuel 9:1-13; James 5:13-16)

**James 5:13. Is any among you afflicted? let him pray. Is any merry? let him sing psalms.**

**14. Is any sick among you? let him call for the elders of the church; and let them pray over him, anointing him with oil in the name of the Lord:**

**15. And the prayer of faith shall save the sick, and the Lord shall raise him up; and if he have committed sins, they shall be forgiven him.**

Instead of being angry at God for their trials through afflictions, James exhorts Christians to turn constantly to prayer. Prayer is a characteristic that distinguishes a Christian from a non-Christian. He knows that the heavenly Father invites him with extended arms to draw close to Him through prayerful communion. The believer can turn immediately for inspiration, peace, and power to Him who holds the universe in the palm of His hand and orders all things in accordance with His will. The natural man is unaware of this opportunity. He is elated in times of peace and depressed in times of difficulty. The Christian can always turn to his heavenly Father who knows his need even before he prays. He knows the power of prayer will change discouragement into encouragement, restlessness into tranquility, disappointment into a divine appointment.

There is power through prayer that we can offer the handicapped, there is personal assistance as well. In 2 Samuel 9:1-13 there is recorded the story of David fulfilling his covenant with Jonathan. Sometime after the death of Jonathan, David discovered that Jonathan had a son who was alive. Because of his great love for Jonathan, David invited Jonathan's son, Mephibosheth, to come to the palace. While some considered it dangerous for Mephibosheth to go to the palace because he was the grandson of David's enemy, Saul, David had no intention of harming

Mephibosheth. When the young man came to see David, he was told that David would take care of him and that he would be part of David's household.

In addition to the love that David showed for a son of a friend, the act of kindness was significant because Mephibosheth was lame. David was not prejudiced against Mephibosheth because of his handicap; he did not let the handicap come between Mephibosheth and himself. David showed love and compassion toward him by taking care of him.

We should act the same way towards those with physical handicaps or with intellectual limitations.

**REVIEW QUESTIONS**

1. What does "honor thy father and mother" mean?

2. What are some qualifications for determining if a widow should be assisted by the church?

3. To what extent do Christians have a responsibility for assisting the poor?

4. What are some ways that we can help the handicapped?

5. How should we deal with those who have handicaps, but refuse to be assisted?

**GOLDEN TEXT HOMILY**

"LET US NOT LOVE IN WORD, NEITHER IN TONGUE; BUT IN DEED AND IN TRUTH" (1 John 3:18).

As I study 1 John 3:18, several words stand out as though they were highlighted by the Holy Spirit. The first word is "love" (**agapao**) which is used in this New Testament context to convey God's will for His children concerning their attitude toward one another (compare John 13:34) and toward all men (compare 1 Thessalonians 3:12; 1 Corinthians 16:14; and 2 Peter 1:7). This word "love" expresses the essential nature of God (1 John 4:8). This love can only be known from the actions it prompts. It is practical love given by God that causes people to be drawn to Him.

John proclaims that this type of love cannot be shared properly with others through our "words" (**logo**) which are the expressions of our thoughts or our good intentions. Neither can it be conveyed by our "tongue" (glossa—the very word from which we transliterate glossolalia or speaking in tongues). John exhorts us that the love he is proclaiming can only be shared in "work" (**ergon**) and in "truth" (**alethes**). This is a practical Christianity which encompasses every activity undertaken for Christ's sake (2 Thessalonians 1:11); it is the practical effect that faith in Christ has upon us (James 1:25). This "work" expresses the "truth" that Christ is indeed Lord of our life by revealing Him in concrete ways. Love knows no enemies, least of all any person in need!

This command to Christian love is demonstrated in the model that the Christian has been given to imitate—nothing less than the selfless love of Christ himself (John 13:34). This duty of love cannot be fulfilled merely by profession or good intentions. It must be proven by our deeds. This is the "love" that has God for its source and model.—**Chaplain, Ralph S. Douglas, (LT), U.S. Naval Station, Guam.**

## SENTENCE SERMONS

IT IS NOT ENOUGH to help the feeble up, but to support him after.
**—William Shakespeare**

HE WHO HAS CONFERRED a kindness should be silent, he who has received one should speak of it.
**—Seneca**

CHRISTIAN LOVE DEMANDS that we cheer the lonely, help the poor and handicapped, and honor our elders.
**—Selected**

THE LONELY NON-CHURCH goer cannot be reached by the non-going church.
**—Selected**

## EVANGELISTIC APPLICATION

WHEN WE PERFORM DEEDS OF CHRISTIAN LOVE WE MAY FIND FERTILE SOIL FOR THE GOSPEL MESSAGE.

Have you ever been so hungry that you were unable to do anything? Because you were hungry, you could not concentrate, you could not think on anything but food.

There are people who are literally starving today because of a lack of food. Can we blame them if they are more interested in a morsel of bread than they are in the Bread of Life? But if we gave them a morsel of bread, they may see in that act of compassion Christ who gives all the sustenance of life. If we give them a cup of water in the name of Christ, they may recognize that Christ gives all blessings.

## ILLUMINATING THE LESSON

We have property so that we can be caretakers of God's earth and God's people. The principle of love requires that we use the property God has given to us. Love requires us and enables us to move toward our neighbors in ways that they will receive what they deserve as human beings.

---

The quality of mercy is not strained,
It droppeth as the gentle rain from
   heaven
Upon the place beneath. It is twice
   blessed,
It blesseth him that gives, and him that
   takes,
'Tis mightiest in the mightiest, it becomes
The throned monarch better than his
   crown . . .
It is enthroned in the hearts of kings,
It is an attribute of God himself.
**—William Shakespeare**

## DAILY DEVOTIONAL GUIDE

M. The Lord's Care. Psalm 27:7-14

T. Honoring Parents. Proverbs 23:22-25

W. Promise of Strength. Isaiah 40:28-31

T. Caring for Parents. Mark 7:10-13

F. Sharing in the Church. Acts 2:43-47

S. The Royal Law of Love. James 2:1-8

# The Biblical View of Death

**Study Text:** Luke 16:19-31; Romans 6:9, 10; 1 Corinthians 15:51-57; 2 Corinthians 5:1-8; Hebrews 2:11-16; Revelation 14:13; 21:4-7

**Supplemental References:** Psalms 23:1-6; 116:12-19; 2 Corinthians 1:8-11; 1 Thessalonians 4:13-17; Revelation 2:8-11; 20:1-6

**Golden Text:** "When this corruptible shall have put on incorruption, and this mortal shall have put on immortality, then shall be brought to pass the saying that is written, Death is swallowed up in victory" (1 Corinthians 15:54).

**Central Truth:** Death is a fearful reality for the unsaved, but to the saved it is the beginning of a glorious eternity free from pain, sadness, and tears.

**Evangelistic Emphasis:** Accepting Jesus Christ as Saviour and Lord removes the cause for fearing death.

## Printed Text

**Luke 16:19.** There was a certain rich man, which was clothed in purple and fine linen, and fared sumptuously every day:

**20.** And there was a certain beggar named Lazarus, which was laid at his gate, full of sores,

**21.** And desiring to be fed with the crumbs which fell from the rich man's table: moreover the dogs came and licked his sores.

**22. And it came to pass, that the beggar died, and was carried by the angels into Abraham's bosom: the rich man also died, and was buried;**

**23.** And in hell he lift up his eyes, being in torments, and seeth Abraham afar off, and Lazarus in his bosom.

**24. And he cried and said, Father Abraham, have mercy on me, and send Lazarus, that he may dip the tip of his finger in water, and cool my tongue; for I am tormented in this flame.**

**25.** But Abraham said, Son, remember that thou in thy lifetime receivedst thy good things, and likewise Lazarus evil things: but now he is comforted, and thou art tormented.

**26. And beside all this, between us and you there is a great gulf fixed: so that they which would pass from hence to you cannot; neither can they pass to us, that would come from thence.**

**27.** Then he said, I pray thee therefore, father, that thou wouldest send him to my father's house:

**28. For I have five brethren; that he may testify unto them, lest they also come into this place of torment.**

**29.** Abraham saith unto him, They have Moses and the prophets; let them hear them.

**30. And he said, Nay, father Abraham: but if one went unto them from the dead, they will repent.**

**31.** And he said unto him, If they hear not Moses and the prophets, neither will they be persuaded, though one rose from the dead.

**Romans 6:9. Knowing that Christ being raised from the dead dieth no more; death hath no more dominion over him.**

10. For in that he died, he died unto sin once: but in that he liveth, he liveth unto God.

**Revelation 14:13.** And I heard a voice **from heaven saying unto me, Write, Blessed are the dead which die in the Lord from henceforth: Yea, saith the Spirit, that they may rest from their labours; and their works do follow them.**

## LESSON OUTLINE

I. TERROR FOR THE LOST
II. DEATH CONQUERED BY CHRIST
III. VICTORY FOR THE SAVED

## LESSON EXPOSITION

### INTRODUCTION

The life of man never ceases to be, and the grave is only the tunnel through which he passes in order to reach the life beyond. The nature of his future existence is determined by personal character and this in turn by the attitude of the soul toward the atoning work of the Lord Jesus Christ.

Although death is a period of dread for the unregenerate person, for the Christian death is a crowning day for his entry to eternal life with the Lord. Through the resurrection of Christ, the believer's future state was assured. "But if the Spirit of him that raised up Jesus from the dead dwell in you, he that raised up Christ from the dead shall also quicken your mortal bodies by his Spirit that dwelleth in you" (Romans 8:11).

The biblical perspective of death is often overlooked in this materialistic world. Hopefully our study today will sharpen our thoughts about this inevitable encounter.

I. TERROR FOR THE LOST (Luke 16:19-31)

**Luke 16:19.** There was a certain rich man, which was clothed with purple and fine linen, and fared sumptuously every day:

**20.** And there was a certain beggar named Lazarus, which was laid at his gate, full of sores,

**21.** And desiring to be fed with the crumbs which fell from the rich man's table: moreover the dogs came and licked his sores.

Jesus pictures a rich man. This man had all he wanted in life and lived a life of enjoyable ease. But Jesus condemned him. His condemnation was not in a grave sinful deed but in his selfishness. He lived only for himself.

In contrast is the poor man Lazarus. He lay at the gate of the rich man's extravagant house. He was in misery; his body was covered with sores that were licked by dogs; he had nothing to eat, but what may come from the rich man's table. The one man had all he wanted; the other had nothing.

**22.** And it came to pass, that the beggar died, and was carried by the angels into Abraham's bosom: the rich man also died, and was buried;

**23.** And in hell he lift up his eyes, being in torments, and seeth Abraham afar off, and Lazarus in his bosom.

Although nothing is explicitly said about the religious state of the rich man or of Lazarus, it can be assumed that Lazarus was a servant of God because he was taken to Abraham's bosom. This expression indicates a state of joy. Some people think it compares to the relationship between a child and a parent (compare John 1:18). The joy of the saved is pictured as a great feast.

There is not corresponding joy for the rich man after his, death. He is in a place of punishment where he is in torment. He is able to see Lazarus and the joy of Lazarus.

**24.** And he cried and said, Father Abraham, have mercy on me, and send Lazarus, that he may dip the tip of his finger in water, and cool my tongue; for I am tormented in this flame.

**25.** But Abraham said, Son, remember that thou in thy lifetime receivedst thy good things, and likewise Lazarus evil things: but now he is comforted, and thou art tormented.

**26. And beside all this, between us and you there is a great gulf fixed: so that they which would pass from hence to you cannot; neither can they pass to us, that would come from thence.**

The rich man addresses Abraham as "Father Abraham," which shows the respect he has, but there is an arrogance in his attitude to Lazarus. He assumes he can have the poor man sent across to do him a service. He has not realized that worldly values no longer apply.

Although Abraham used the tender word, "Son," he does not give the rich man hope. Abraham points to the reversal. In life the rich man had had his good things. He had had what he chose. He could have chosen the things of God, but he had chosen fine clothes, feasting, and merriment. He could have given alms; Lazarus was close enough. Instead Lazarus had received evil things.

According to Abraham, a different set of values operate now. The balance is redressed; justice is done. Another factor is presented: the great chasm between the rich man and Lazarus is fixed. This means that in the afterlife there is no passing from one side to the other side. The rich man can know how Lazarus is doing, but he can never cross the gulf that is between them.

Living without God, both here and in the future, is not an eternal life at all; it is a kind of eternal living death. It is living in hostility toward God and toward other people; therefore, denying one's own true self, forever. It is living forever without loving. It is never coming to a rest, but living forever in the frantic, self-destroying attempt to be what one is not and never can be (Matthew 8:12; 13:42; Luke 13:28).

Verses 27-31 further intensify the fixed position after death. But the appeal is made that his brothers be warned by one returning from the dead in the hope that they could avoid the place of torment.

What are your thoughts about hell?

II. DEATH CONQUERED BY CHRIST (Romans 6:9, 10; Hebrews 2:11-16; Revelation 21:4-7)

**Romans 6:9. Knowing that Christ being raised from the dead dieth no more; death hath no more dominion over him.**

**10. For in that he died, he died unto sin once: but in that he liveth, he liveth unto God.**

Death did at one time rule over Christ, because He was identified with the wages of sin which is death. However, His resurrection from the dead is a guarantee that He defeated the power of death and this victory over death is final. Death can never again be lord over Him. The finality of the resurrection of Christ, emphasized in strong terms, indicates the decisiveness of the break with the power of sin and death.

According to Hebrews 2:11-16, the primary purpose of the incarnation of Jesus was to be the Savior of mankind, but this could be accomplished only through His death. In this way, man's sin and guilt could be removed.

In this passage, salvation is presented as deliverance. The word **destroy** means to make something so powerless that it does not appear to exist. Christ by the offering of Himself has made a perfect atonement for sin and consequently has destroyed the power of sin, death, and the devil. Natural death remains, but it has lost its sting for believers. They need not fear death because they participate in the resurrection of Jesus.

In Revelation 21:4-7, the ultimate victory fellowship that Christians have because Christ defeated death is described. The essential blessing is fellowship with God, but other blessings flow from this central reality. God will wipe away every tear from their eyes. In this context, tears represent all human sorrow, tragedy, and evil. There will be a mode of living in which the sorrows and evils in the old order are left far behind. The most fearful cause of tears is the awful reality of dying; but in the presence of God, death will not exist. The end of death has already been described when death and Hades were thrown into the lake of fire (Revelation 20:14). The triumph over death is not, however, an end in itself; it is a blessing which flows from fellowship with God. Not only is death destroyed; there shall be neither mourning nor crying nor pain, because these things will have passed. In the new order, all the evils that have burdened and cursed human existence will flee from the presence of God.

---

What should be a Christian's attitude toward death?

---

III. VICTORY FOR THE SAVED (1 Corinthians 15:51-57; 2 Corinthians 5:1-8; Revelation 14:13)

Paul expresses certainty of the Christian's victory over death in 1 Corinthians 15:51-57. Because of the death and resurrection of Christ, death no longer has power over God's people. Paul mocked death:

O death, where is thy sting?
O grave where is thy victory?
The sting of death is sin;
and the strength of sin is
the law. But thanks be to
God, which giveth us the
victory through our Lord
Jesus Christ.

The Christian is no longer under the fear of death, "For the law of the Spirit of life in Christ Jesus made me free from the law of sin and death" (Romans 8:2).

Paul also speaks of the Christian hope in 2 Corinthians 5:1-8. Paul recognizes that his earthly body suffers during his time on earth and that it cannot ultimately withstand the forces of time; however, Paul is not without hope. He is convinced that the shelter that awaits him after death is superior to that provided by the present body. It is a shelter made with God's hands and is made to last for eternity.

The apostle's intense desire to be clothed with the new shelter is not because of a fanatical desire to be rid of his body. There is nothing intrinsically evil about the body nor is the body itself in opposition to God. Paul does not want to be unclothed at all, but he desires to be better clothed when he moves into the existence after death.

Paul insists that nothing he has said is the result of wishful thinking. God has called men to be His people in order that He may bring them to His glory. God has made the elect aware of His purposes and has given them the assurance that a blessed life awaits them after death by the presence within them of the Holy Spirit. The testimony of the Holy Spirit within us guarantees to us our glorification by God over death.

The presence of the Holy Spirit, Paul asserts, is the source of courage for the future and the present. This courage comes to the aid of the Christian when he contemplates his death. The natural sense of loss one has at leaving his earthly body is overcome by the certainty that the best is yet to come.

**Revelation 14:13. And I heard a voice from heaven saying unto me, Write, Blessed are the dead which die in the Lord from henceforth: Yea, saith the Spirit, that they may rest from their labors; and their works do follow them.**

The saints who remain faithful to Jesus are not only summoned to endurance; they are assured of blessedness upon their death. This blessing is pronounced primarily upon those who are about to suffer martyrdom, not upon the saints in general. However, it need not be understood as a blessing that is not shared by all believers. This is the same rest promised to the martyrs in Revelation 6:11. The word **henceforth** does not mean that other saints are not blessed, but that those who shortly will fall before the beast are God's children, contrary to all outward appearances. To die **in the Lord** is the state of all believers, who both live and die in Christ (1 Corinthians 15:18; 1 Thessalonians 4:16). It does not designate a special group of Christians. Those who are blessed enter into their rest. In other words, all Christians enter into the rest of God. The word **labor** means work to the point of weariness. Their afflictions by the beast have worn the saints down to a point of exhaustion. Nevertheless, they have died **in the Lord** and their deeds follow them beyond the grave. Deeds here include their endurance, obedience to the commandments of God, and faith in Jesus mentioned in the previous verse.

A biblical view of death does not pretend that death is not bad. For the biblical writers, death is real, total, and terrible. Jesus himself did not face death with calmness. He faced it "with strong crying and tears" (Hebrews 5:7) and bloodsweating dread (Luke 22:44; Mark 14:32-42). There is not pious denial of the horror of death in genuine Christian teaching.

Second, the Christian hope is not in the indestructibility of man, but in the creative power of God who by the power of His word can call life into being out of nothing and make dead men live. God alone has immortality (1 Timothy 6:16). If there is life beyond death for men, it is not because they possess in themselves some immortal quality death cannot destroy, but because God gives them eternal life. It is not because they are strong enough to conquer death, but because Christ is, and because He has triumphed over death for them.

Finally the Bible teaches that we were created body, as well as soul, and that physical as well as spiritual life is willed and blessed by God himself. The biblical hope is not for the soul's escape from the body into some spiritual realm. Our hope is for the renewal of our total human existence. We have this hope in Jesus Christ. The Apostle John wrote in the revelation of Jesus Christ (Revelation 1:18):

> I am he that liveth, and was dead; and, behold, I am alive for evermore, Amen; and have the keys of hell and of death.

Should Christians be afraid of dying?

## REVIEW QUESTIONS

1. What is the future like for the lost?

2. Who conquered death?

3. What will the future be like for Christians?

4. What was Paul's attitude toward death?

5. Summarize a biblical view of death given in this lesson.

## GOLDEN TEXT HOMILY

"WHEN THIS CORRUPTIBLE SHALL HAVE PUT ON INCORRUPTION, AND THIS MORTAL SHALL HAVE PUT ON IMMORTALITY, THEN SHALL BE BROUGHT TO PASS THE SAYING THAT IS WRITTEN, DEATH IS SWALLOWED UP IN VICTORY" (1 Corinthians 15:54).

"I want to live forever." That statement was made by a young man in answer to the judge's question, "What would you want if you could have one desire fulfilled?" According to 2 Timothy, Christ has destroyed death and has brought us life and immortality. "Hey, Rev, I know about heaven: everyone goes there, I want life on earth forever!" I warned him not to be deceived by human leaders or philosophical ideas. Without Christ there is no eternal life; if you've never believed on Him, you're bound for hell. In the Garden of Eden, Satan's purpose was not to make Eve ungodly, but to convince her that she was "godlike" and could live forever.

Man has always sought immortality. To the unregenerated, death and hell are indeed fearful subjects. But because of God's love, Christians can claim eternal life—not by our merit, nor by intellect, but through Jesus' sacrificial death. He has proclaimed victory over the second death—the death we should fear most. "Blessed and holy are those who have part in the first resurrection. The second death has no power over them" (Revelation 20:6, **New International Version).**

We must get our priorities in order: the salvation of our soul is the number one task. Jesus' greatest mission was man's salvation, as shown when the paralytic was brought to Him. Jesus said, "Your sins are forgiven." Life's most critical issue is: where will I spend eternity. Because Christ has risen from the dead, death has no more dominion over us. If our sins have been forgiven, we can face death with peace in our hearts, knowing we have life eternal.—**Chaplain James L. Durel, Director of Prison Ministries, Chicago, Illinois.**

## SENTENCE SERMONS

WHEN ROBERT INGERSOLL (infidel) died, the printed notice of his funeral said, "There will be no singing."

**—"Speaker's Sourcebook"**

DEATH TAKES no bribes.

**—Benjamin Franklin**

WE WHO WOULD teach men to die, would at the same time teach them to live.

**—Michel De Montaigne**

DEATH IS A FEARFUL reality for the unsaved, but to the saved it is the beginning of a glorious eternity free from pain, sadness, and tears.

**—Selected**

## EVANGELISTIC APPLICATION

ACCEPTING JESUS CHRIST AS SAVIOUR AND LORD REMOVES THE CAUSE FOR FEARING DEATH.

Death: It is an event that every human being shall experience. But we who accept Jesus Christ as Savior and Lord do not need to fear death. We do not need to fear death because Jesus died and was raised from the dead. He now has the keys to death. We who sleep in Christ need not fear because we shall rise when the trumpet of the Lord shall sound. Death does not have a hold on us nor can it grasp a hold on us, because we have eternal life through Jesus Christ (John 20:31; 1 John 5:11-13).

## ILLUMINATING THE LESSON

The futility of life is an idea presented in Albert Camus's book *The Stranger.* The main character in the book recognizes that no matter what one does with his life, each person has the same ending, death. A person may be famous or infamous, a celebrity or unknown, ruler or a follower, but each person will die.

According to Camus, death is the ultimate experience in life. But according to the Bible, life in Jesus Christ is the ultimate relationship in life. In Jesus Christ we conquer death. We have eternal life. We receive eternal life when we accept Him who has the keys to death, hell, and the grave. We need not fear the sting of death nor the victory of the grave because we live in Him who reigns forever and forever.

## DAILY DEVOTIONAL GUIDE

M. No Fear of Death. Psalm 23:1-6

T. The Saint's Death Is Precious. Psalm 116:12-19

W. Jesus Abolished Death. 2 Timothy 1:8-14

T. Delivered From Death. 2 Corinthians 1:8-11

F. Faithful Unto Death. Revelation 2:8-11

S. No Terror of Second Death. Revelation 20:1-6

# Biblical Morality

**Study Text:** Genesis 3:7, 21; 19:4, 5; Leviticus 18:6-19; Isaiah 5:20; Matthew 5:27, 28; Romans 1:24-27; 13:13, 14; 1 Corinthians 6:15-20; Ephesians 5:3-5; 1 Thessalonians 4:3; 5:22; 1 Timothy 2:9, 10; Titus 1:15

**Supplemental References:** Genesis 9:20-27; Proverbs 6:20-25; Matthew 7:21-23; 1 Corinthians 6:9, 10; Galatians 5:19-25; 1 John 2:15-17

**Golden Text:** "Ye are bought with a price: therefore glorify God in your body, and in your spirit, which are God's" (1 Corinthians 6:20).

**Central Truth:** God expects His children to think and act according to the biblical standards of morality.

**Evangelistic Emphasis:** A pure life radiates a powerful witness to the unsaved.

## Printed Text

**Isaiah 5:20.** Woe unto them that call evil good, and good evil; that put darkness for light, and light for darkness; that put bitter for sweet, and sweet for bitter!

**1 Timothy 2:9. In like manner also, that women adorn themselves in modest apparel, with shamefacedness and sobriety; not with broided hair, or gold, or pearls, or costly array;**

10. But (which becometh women professing godliness) with good works.

**Romans 13:13. Let us walk honestly, as in the day; not in rioting and drunkenness, not in chambering and wantonness, not in strife and envying;**

14. But put ye on the Lord Jesus Christ, and make not provision for the flesh, to fulfil the lusts thereof.

**1 Corinthians 6:15. Know ye not that your bodies are the members of Christ? shall I then take the members of Christ, and make them the members of an harlot? God forbid.**

16. What? know ye not that he which is joined to an harlot is one body? for two, saith he, shall be one flesh.

**17. But he that is joined unto the Lord is one spirit.**

18. Flee fornication. Every sin that a man doeth is without the body; but he that committeth fornication sinneth against his own body.

**19. What? know ye not that your body is the temple of the Holy Ghost which is in you, which ye have of God, and ye are not your own?**

20. For ye are bought with a price: therefore glorify God in your body, and in your spirit, which are God's.

**Ephesians 5:3. But fornication, and all uncleanness, or covetousness, let it not be once named among you, as becometh saints;**

4. Neither filthiness, nor foolish talking, nor jesting, which are not convenient: but rather giving of thanks.

**5. For this ye know, that no whoremonger, nor unclean person, nor covetous man, who is an idolater, hath any inheritance in the kingdom of Christ and of God.**

**1 Thessalonians 5:22.** Abstain from all appearance of evil.

## LESSON OUTLINE

I. MODESTY
II. PURITY
III. VIRTUE
IV. SANCTITY

## LESSON EXPOSITION

INTRODUCTION

God made man a free creature for a high destiny. God administers the natural and moral orders within which alone man can grow into intelligence and moral character. He blesses man's efforts of righteousness with approval and joy and judges errors with pain and frustration. But even in man's waywardness, God's pursuing love has taken availing steps toward his restoration.

There is a real moral struggle going on in the world moving toward ultimate destiny. History is seen in the Bible as a dramatic conflict between the forces of good and the forces of evil. "We are not contending against flesh and blood, against the principalities, against the powers, against the world rulers of this present darkness, against the spiritual hosts of wickedness in the heavenly places" (Ephesians).

Such evil forces militate against humanity's efforts to live by biblical standards of morality. A look at the subjects of modesty, purity, virtue, and sanctity from God's perspective will suffice to remind us again of our need to lean on His plan for our lives.

I. MODESTY (Genesis 3:7, 21; Leviticus 18:6-19; 1 Timothy 2:9, 10)

In Genesis 3:7 and 21, the account of the Fall and subsequent consequences are given. Faced with the choice between his own desires and the will of God, man rejected God's purpose for him and went his selfish way. Both the Hebrew and Greek words for sin mean "to miss the mark" or to fail. Sin is not only the practice of immorality but also the denial of the will of God in life.

How mistaken are those who think that in Christianity God's principal purpose is to provide eternal life. The thrust of Scrip-

ture is that God will not permit man to live forever until he has enabled him to become a good steward of his existence. This stewardship includes his spiritual wellbeing.

In Leviticus 18:6-19 a list of the family connections within which sexual relationships were forbidden was given. These family relationships were frequently termed "blood relationships" as many of them undoubtedly were. It appears that the social setting which centered in the larger family—parents, grandparents, and even other kinfolk living in one household—might have generated the tendency to marry since polygamy was common in that day. Certainly, modesty in apparel was a necessity in such a household.

**1 Timothy 2:9. In like manner also, that women adorn themselves in modest apparel, with shamefacedness and sobriety; not with broided hair, or gold, or pearls, or costly array;**

**10. But (which becometh women professing godliness) with good works.**

In the context of these verses, Paul gives general advice for the conduct of prayer and worship in the church; then he makes general observations about Christian women. Paul instructs the women to cultivate godliness in their lives.

Paul advises Christian women to adorn themselves with modest apparel, modesty (shamefacedness), and self-control (sobriety). Apparel probably refers to a woman's disposition and attire reflect a right attitude of the mind. Modesty and self-control indicate dignity and a seriousness of purpose as opposed to levity, foolishness, and frivolity.

Paul says Christian women should avoid anything designed merely to promote a display of themselves for the purpose of attracting attention, admiration, or envy. He illustrates his point by cautioning the women in his day from plaiting their hair, using expensive jewelry, and wearing costly clothing. Paul knew of the spiritual danger that accompanied a display of oneself. It would breed pride which would ultimately lead to one's spiritual fall.

# 400 August 3, 1986

Paul adds that women are not denied all adornment, but the greatest asset she possesses is a devout and godly life. A woman's adornment does not lie in what she herself puts on, but in the loving service she gives. Actually, this is Paul's emphasis in his instructions to Christian women. He is not so much giving them a prohibition as he is admonishing them to bear Christian works in their lives.

Paul is exhorting the women to be free from conceit, vanity, and coarseness. What they wear will reflect their disposition and the attitude of their mind. They should be careful not to allow their dress to feed carnality. Instead, they should be concerned with performing good works. They should practice moderation and self-control. When women reflect the fruit of the Spirit in their lives, they will not need to be concerned with their dress. It will be as God desires.

Does Paul's advice to women apply to men?

II. PURITY (Matthew 5:27, 28; Romans 13:13, 14; 1 Corinthians 6:15-18; 1 Thessalonians 4:3; Titus 1:15)

**Romans 13:13. Let us walk honestly, as in the day; not in rioting and drunkenness, not in chambering and wantonness, not in strife and envying.**

**14. But put ye on the Lord Jesus Christ, and make not provision for the flesh, to fulfil the lusts thereof.**

**As in the day** refers to the consummation of our redemption, God's judgment upon the world, and the restoration of the world as God desires. This day of Christ, though not yet come, is nevertheless throwing its light backward upon the present. We are to live as Christ would have us to live in heaven. His light is dispelling the darkness we live in. We were called out of spiritual and moral darkness to walk in the light of the day of Jesus Christ.

Paul is pressing home the moral incompatibility of this world, characterized by darkness, and heaven, characterized by light. In that light, believers must now live. **Let us walk honestly** means that we are to walk as if we already lived in the day of the Lord; therefore, we are not to practice rioting, drunkenness, strife, or envy. These are moral practices of the world. They have no place in the life of a Christian who is no longer of this world. They are the result of the moral darkness of the world. We are to radiate the moral light of the kingdom of God.

The positive exhortation in verse 14 points to the contrast which the lordship of Christ creates and demands. The figure is that of putting on Christ. To put on Christ is to be identified with Him not only in His death but also in His resurrection. It is to be united to Him in the likeness of His resurrection. Complete negation of immorality and the perfection of purity and virtue seen in Christ is required of the believers. When we think of Christ, we see the contrast between the voices described in verses 13 and the example for moral behavior given in verse 14.

Neither are we to make provision for the fulfillment of the flesh. The flesh is not the body. It is the sinful inclinations that we have. We are not to yield to them, but we are to put on Jesus Christ.

In this passage, we have seen two themes that give us guidance in being pure. First is the day of the Lord. We are to live now like we will live in heaven. We are to live like we live in heaven, because we already know in a measure what heaven will be like. It will be living in a right relationship with God, our fellowman, and ourselves. We are called upon, then, to leave the moral darkness of this fallen world and to walk in the light of what God has revealed to us in the Bible about our future life with Him in heaven.

Second is Jesus Christ. We are to put on the virtues of Jesus Christ. We have seen and experienced the love, mercy, generosity, grace, kindness, patience and faithfulness of Jesus Christ. As we put on Jesus Christ, we will put on these virtues; therefore, we are to practice these same virtues toward our neighbor.

---

How do we "put on Jesus Christ"?

---

**1 Corinthians 6:15. Know ye not that your bodies are the members of Christ? shall I then take the members of Christ, and make them the members of an harlot? God forbid.**

**16. What? know ye not that he which is joined to an harlot is one body? for two, saith he shall be one flesh.**

**17. But he that is joined unto the Lord is one spirit.**

**18. Flee fornication. Every sin that a man doeth without the body; but he that committeth fornication sinneth against his own body.**

For Paul, believers are united to Christ. They are members of His body. It is this which makes sexual sin wrong. They are taken away from Christ and made members of a harlot. The sexual union is such an intimate union that it makes one body out of the two. Thus, there is profanation of the body of Christ.

Paul commands the Corinthians to flee sexual immorality. Paul does not say sexual sin is the worst of all sins, but he recognizes that sexual sins have a unique effect upon the individual. Other sins of the body, such as gluttony, involve the use of that which is outside the body, but a sexual sin involves the total person. It takes its toll on the whole person, because it involves the total person.

Paul forbids sexual immorality, because it endangers one's relationship to Christ. A believer cannot give himself totally to Christ when he is in a false union with another person. That person will have an allegiance with the believer that belongs to Christ.

Purity means a state of being free from what harms, weakens, or leads to error. We are called to purity. We are called to flee those activities that threaten our spiritual life and moral quality. As we await the day of the Lord, we should live in the purity of the light of that day. As we put on Jesus Christ, we

should live in the purity of His life. As we are part of the body of Christ, we should live in the purity of His body. All three of these moral images give us insight as to how we should be pure and the moral strength we need to be pure. We need to appropriate from God the strength that He has provided for us in these images.

II. VIRTUE (Genesis 19:4, 5; Romans 1: 24-27; Isaiah 5:20; 1 Thessalonians 5:22)

In Romans 1:24 through 27, following his remarks about the low estate into which mankind drifts, Paul describes the punishment: From idolatry sprang sensuality. Originally man was chaste, but when he cast God off, his animal passions were unchained and God inflicted punishment for the sin of idolatry.

When God "gave them up" the original corruption in the blood showed itself in foul moral ulcers, and human virtue proved to be less than that of the beasts of the field, among which the barriers of sex are not crossed.

**Isaiah 5:20. Woe unto them that call evil good, and good evil; that put darkness for light, and light for darkness; that put bitter for sweet, and sweet for bitter!**

Isaiah addresses those who no longer have moral values. Clear cut terms, such as good and evil, light and darkness, or bitter and sweet, are perverted to mean their opposites. As men sink deeper and deeper into sin, moral values become clouded until no distinction can be made between right and wrong. They turn to expediency and utilitarianism instead of moral convictions.

**1 Thessalonians 5:22. Abstain from all appearance of evil.**

A series of exhortations that deal with the Holy Spirit are given in 1 Thessalonians 5:19-22. Paul instructed the Thessalonians to accept what the Lord gives through prophetic revelations, but he also asks them to discern whether or not the revelations are from God. The instruction is both positive and negative. If the prophecy is true, then the Thessalonians are to accept it. If it is not from God, then the Thessalonians are to avoid the prophecy. Paul means more here than a false prophecy. He means **every** kind of evil. There is one source for a true prophecy—God, but there are many different sources for evil. Christians are to avoid all of these sources of evil.

In light of these passages, we should see that the Bible calls for virtue. Virtue may be defined as moral excellence, integrity of character, or uprightness of conduct. It is based on a knowledge of good that makes one act in accordance with what is good. It is a habit of involving the choice of moral excellence. It is an action that will produce conformity to a standard of righteousness.

Virtue will require a knowledge between good and evil, right and wrong. It will require a testing of the moral quality of an act, desire, or choice. It will require choosing moral excellence and will require doing what will support the integrity of one's character.

A person with virtue has a knowledge of right and wrong. He discriminates between good and bad. Because of his uprightness of conduct, he has integrity of character.

IV. SANCTITY (Ephesians 5:3-5; 1 Corinthians 6:19, 20)

**Ephesians 5:3. But fornication, and all uncleanness, or covetousness, let it not be once named among you, as becometh saints;**

**4. Neither filthiness, nor foolish talking, nor jesting, which are not convenient: but rather giving of thanks.**

**5. For this ye know, that no whoremonger, nor unclean person, nor covetous man, who is an idolater, hath any inheritance in the kingdom of Christ and of God.**

In Ephesians 4:17-24, Paul speaks in general terms of the transformed life of a Christian. In Ephesians 4:25ff, he gives some specific guidelines on what he believes characterizes a Christian life.

In Ephesians 5:3, Paul prohibited sexually immorality (fornication). Sexual immorality may be regarded as unclean-

ness or covetousness because of the effects it has on the individual. It is uncleanness because of not controlling one's impulses in accordance with God's intention. It is covetousness because it is exploitation of another person for one's own desire. Such a lifestyle contradicts what God intends for His children; therefore, Paul commands the Ephesians to control themselves.

In Ephesians 5:4, Paul uses three words to describe conversation that Christians should not indulge in. **Filthiness** refers to that which would make a morally sensitive man ashamed. **Foolish talking** is conversation that is senseless or that is not profitable. **Jesting** is the witty talk that is on the borderline of being improper. Paul says Christians should not participate in conversation that fits one of these three words. It is out of place for the Christian. Paul is not opposing wholesome humor, but he is rejecting coarse, vulgar, senseless talk.

On the other hand, Paul exhorts the Ephesians to give thanks. Thanksgiving is the best kind of speech. It helps us to acknowledge the beauty of God's gifts to us. It helps to maintain our purity. It helps to uplift us. It is the kind of conversation that is becoming to a Christian.

In Ephesians 5:5, Paul gives a solemn warning that no one who is guilty of the above sins will share in the kingdom of God. Only those who have put off the world and put on Christ will be in the kingdom. These traits do not testify that a person has put off the world and put on Christ. In fact, they testify that the person is still in the world.

**1 Corinthians 6:19. What? know ye not that your body is the temple of the Holy Ghost which is in you, which ye have of God, and ye are not your own?**

**20. For ye are bought with a price: therefore glorify God in your body, and in your spirit, which are God's.**

In the context of this passage, Paul is refuting sexual immorality that was practiced by the Corinthians. He says they should not be immoral, because they are the temple of God. If they are immoral, they defile the temple in which God dwells through the Holy Spirit.

The principle Paul is advocating is wider in its application. Every Christian is a temple in which God dwells. This gives a dignity to our lives. Wherever we go, we are the temple of God. Anything, whether it is what we say or do or wherever we go, that defiles the temple of God or is offensive to God is unacceptable. In all things we must glorify God.

Verse 20 indicates why. We have been purchased. by God and He indwells us with His Holy Spirit as His temple: We should live holy lives. What we say should give testimony that we are indwelt by God. What we do should bear witness that we are the temple of God. Where we go should be a place suitable for God to attend.

This lesson discusses biblical morality. There are three images presented in the lesson that urge us to live as God intends us to live. These images are not so much rules as they are motivators to modesty, purity, virtue, and sanctity.

The theme **day of the Lord** urges upon us to live godly lives as we expect the imminent return of Christ. The expectation of His return will help us to place our priorities in their rightful place. It will shed light on what kind of life we should live, because we understand better what God expects of us since we have a glimpse of the kingdom of God.

The theme **put on the Lord Jesus Christ** suggests that we will imitate Jesus Christ. We should clothe ourselves with the pure motives, intentions, and actions evident in the life of Jesus. Instead of following an eternal law, we respond to the image of Christ.

The theme **temple of God** bears upon us that we must live holy because God indwells us. We cannot lightly consider our conversation or action. We must recognize that we have a special dignity about us and we should live to indicate that dignity.

These images of biblical morality are positive. They instill within us a sense of hope, virtue, and dignity. They do not so much restrain us as they lead us to more fruitful and fulfilling lives.

## REVIEW QUESTIONS

1. Does Paul emphasize what a woman should not wear or does he emphasize that a woman should do good works in 1 Timothy 2:9, 10?

2. What does virtue mean?

3. What are three images of biblical morality?

4. What are some forms of idolatry in our day?

5. Are the three images of biblical morality positive or negative?

## GOLDEN TEXT HOMILY

"YE ARE BOUGHT WITH A PRICE: THEREFORE GLORIFY GOD IN YOUR BODY, AND IN YOUR SPIRIT, WHICH ARE GOD'S" (1 Corinthians 6:20).

We are living in "The Age Between." That is, we are between redemption and glorification. We who have confessed our sin and believed on Jesus are saved, but because we are not in a heavenly state we are still subject to temptation.

Keep in mind that to be tempted is not the same as sinning, for Christ himself was tempted, yet he lived without sin. The Christian continually confesses his need of God's help to live in a manner that brings glory to His holy name. He does all within his own power to live each day without participating in sin.

A holy life is the gift of God to all who believe. It is a gift of supreme expense, because it is the purchase of the blood of our Lord and Savior Jesus Christ. His blood was poured out to save us all completely; therefore, we are to glorify Him through a complete life, a life that has integrity in what we say and what we do, a life that reflects the wholeness and wellness that only God gives.

Some Christians emphasize the need to live according to a list of external requirements. Others emphasize only internal, personal attitudes. However, in reality the life that glorifies God combines our personal conduct with proper attitudes.

If we say we are Christ's and do not have love toward others, then we mock our Lord's sacrifice. But if we have love in our heart and do works of love, we bring glory to God and honor to the price that was paid for our salvation.—**Calvin Eastham, Registrar and Director of Public Relations, School of Theology, Cleveland, Tennessee.**

## SENTENCE SERMONS

GOD EXPECTS His children to think and act according to the biblical standards of morality.

**—Selected**

WRONGS DO NOT leave off where they begin, but still beget new mischief in their course.

**—Samuel Daniel**

NONE PREACHES BETTER than the ant, and she says nothing.

**—Benjamin Franklin**

THERE WAS NEVER YET any truly great man that was not at the same time truly virtuous.

**—"Speaker's Sourcebook"**

## EVANGELISTIC APPLICATION

A PURE LIFE RADIATES A POWERFUL WITNESS TO THE UNSAVED.

Friendship evangelism requires a pure life. Friendship evangelism is witnessing to those people we are around constantly. They may be our neighbors or our fellow employees. Because we are with them so much, they see the kind of person we are. They know if we live up to our Christian testimony. A pure life can radiate to them the love of God, and it will be a powerful witness to the unsaved.

## ILLUMINATING THE LESSON

A businessman was well known for his witnessing. He did personal witnessing, spoke in local churches on witnessing, and conducted seminars on witnessing. He was very successful in winning to the Lord people who did not personally know him, but he was not successful in winning to the Lord those who worked for him. To them he was a poor testimony of a Christian because of the way he mistreated his employees. His action toward them spoke louder than his words.

Speaking the truth in word and deed is important in giving a witness to Christ. Our modesty, purity, virtue, and sanctity in action can tell people of the transforming power of God's grace.

## DAILY DEVOTIONAL GUIDE

M. Concern for Modesty. Genesis 9:20-27
T. Counsel for a Son. Proverbs 6:20-25
W. Conduct Will Be Judged. Matthew 7:15-23
T. Show Love to All. Romans 13:8-10
F. Walk in the Spirit. Galatians 5:16-25
S. Keep God's Commandments. 1 John 2:3-6, 15-17

# Evils of the Occult

**Study Text:** Deuteronomy 18:10-14; 1 Chronicles 10:13, 14; Isaiah 8:18-20; Acts 8:9-24; 16:16-21; 19:18-20; Colossians 3:1-4

**Supplemental References:** Exodus 7:8-13; 2 Chronicles 33:1-13; Psalm 95:1-7; Galatians 5:16-26; 1 Peter 2:1-10; Revelation 4:6-11

**Golden Text:** "If ye continue in my word, then are ye my disciples indeed; and ye shall know the truth, and the truth shall make you free" (John 8:31, 32).

**Central Truth:** Those who obey God refuse to participate in any form of occult practice.

**Evangelistic Emphasis:** Forgiveness and deliverance are available to those who come to God through Jesus Christ.

## Printed Text

**Isaiah 8:18.** Behold, I and the children whom the Lord hath given me are for signs and for wonders in Israel from the Lord of hosts, which dwelleth in mount Zion.

**19. And when they shall say unto you, Seek unto them that have familiar spirits, and unto wizards that peep, and that mutter: should not a people seek unto their God? for the living to the dead?**

20. To the law and to the testimony: if they speak not according to this word, it is because there is no light in them.

**Acts 8:9. But there was a certain man, called Simon, which beforetime in the same city used sorcery, and bewitched the people of Samaria, giving** out that himself was some great one:

10. To whom they all gave heed, from the least to the greatest, saying, This man is the great power of God.

**11. And to him they had regard, because that of long time he had bewitched them with sorceries.**

12. But when they believed Philip preaching the things concerning the kingdom of God, and the name of Jesus Christ, they were baptized, both men and women.

**13. Then Simon himself believed also: and when he was baptized, he continued with Philip, and wondered, beholding the miracles and signs which were done.**

## LESSON OUTLINE

I. THE OCCULT CONDEMNED BY SCRIPTURE
II. THE OCCULT DECEIVES PEOPLE
III. DELIVERANCE FROM THE OCCULT

## LESSON EXPOSITION

INTRODUCTION

The term **occultism** is used to cover a wide range of systems of disclosing what is hidden, obscure, or unknown, whether of the past, present, or future. In a more restrictive sense, occultists themselves claim that the term refers to a science which is capable of revealing by nonobjective scientific procedures, the true nature of the world and of man.

Of course, Jehovah, the true God of

the universe, is the only One who has knowledge of the future and other phenomena so baffling to humanity. But the lack of revelation coupled with the obvious occurrences of phenomena that elude the present techniques of science to explain them, leaves an open field for the occultist. Our lesson today deals with the evils of the occult.

I. THE OCCULT CONDEMNED BY SCRIPTURE (Deuteronomy 18:10-14; 1 Chronicles 10:13, 14; Isaiah 8:18-20)

In Deuteronomy 18:10 through 14, the account is given of God's warning to the Israelites against adopting the sensuous practices of the Canaanites after they had taken possession of their inheritance. The occult, superstitions, sorcery, divination and so-called spiritual orgies of the heathen peoples were to be avoided.

The infectious nature of the occult practices in Canaan is indicated in the frequent warnings Jehovah gives His people. Verse 12 says "all that do these things are an abomination unto the LORD."

There was no compromise in the dedication which was required by God, "Thou shalt be perfect" (v. 13). His standards have never been lowered.

In 1 Chronicles 10:13 and 14, God's judgment on seeking counsel of wicked ones is given: "So Saul died for his transgression which he committed against the LORD, even against the word of the LORD, which he kept not, and also for asking counsel of one that had a familiar spirit, to enquire of it; And enquired not of the LORD: therefore he slew him, and turned the kingdom unto David the son of Jesse."

**Isaiah 8:18. Behold, I and the children whom the LORD hath given me are for signs and for wonders in Israel from the LORD of hosts, which dwelleth in mount Zion.**

**19. And when they shall say unto you, Seek unto them that have familiar spirits, and unto wizards that peep, and that mutter: should not a people seek unto their God? for the living to the dead?**

**20. To the law and to the testimony: if they speak not according to this word, it is because there is no light in them.**

The Prophet Isaiah announces that his children and he are signs and wonders to the people. As signs, they are pledges of something that was to be accomplished. Isaiah's name is said to signify that salvation is found only in God. Shearjashub, a son of Isaiah, signifies that the nation would not be completely destroyed, but that a remnant would be saved. Maher-shalal-hash-baz, another child of Isaiah, indicated the immediate coming of destruction on the nations. As wonders, they were special manifestations of the power of God of future events. They are manifestations of the power of God and the faithfulness of God to His promises.

God gives the people signs and wonders about the future through Isaiah. He instructs them about the future and tells them what to expect. But the people do not accept God's instructions. Unbelievers are suggesting they consult the spiritualistic media. Since they do not have a saving word from God, they will resort to the words of diviners and soothsayers. They turn from faith to superstition.

The unbelievers encourage seeking advice from fortune tellers, mediums, and the dead. The use of the descriptive terms, "peep and mutter," indicate that unclear and unwholesome words come from those consulted. Their advice is poor and ill-gotten. If God, who is omniscient, cannot be trusted for advice on the future, how can these be trusted?

Isaiah gives a response to the tempting suggestions of the unbelievers. God's people should not seek spirits for direction, but they should seek God. While unbelievers seek to know the future through ways that are futile, we should seek to know what is before us by turning to God.

God's people should turn to the Bible for advice about their lives. The Scripture is the revelation of God expressing His will for man's obedience. It is the standard by which all opinions are to be judged. If anyone does not speak in the light of the Scripture, then he abides in the darkness of sin and unbelief. But the children of God dwell in light, because they are illuminated by the light of the gospel.

Believers must not turn to the occult for instruction. The occult cannot give clear-cut information. It "peeps and mutters." But the Scripture can give guidance to our lives, because it is the Word of God. We can depend upon it, because God has proven Himself to be true, faithful, and unchanging in the past. God has proven Himself to speak so that His children may understand Him. And God has proven Himself to know all things. Thus, we can trust in the Word of God and condemn the occult.

---

Can the occult give a person advice?

---

II. THE OCCULT DECEIVES PEOPLE (Acts 8:9-24)

**Acts 8:9. But there was a certain man, called Simon, which beforetime in the same city used sorcery, and bewitched the people of Samaria giving out that himself was some great one:**

**10. To whom they all gave heed, from the least to the greatest, saying, This man is the great power of God.**

**11. And to him they had regard, because that of long time he had bewitched them with sorceries.**

**12. But when they believed Philip preaching the things concerning the kingdom of God, and the name of Jesus Christ, they were baptized, both men and women.**

**13. Then Simon himself believed also: and when he was baptized, he continued with Philip, and wondered, beholding the miracles and signs which were done.**

This passage describes Simon's first contact with the Christian message. (Early Christian literature records numerous accounts of a man named Simon, but it is uncertain if the Simon of these accounts is the same as the Simon of Acts 8.) Simon practiced "magic."

The Samaritans were susceptible to such influence because of their background. They were a mixed people religiously. The people were amazed at Simon's pretensions, because he announced himself as someone great and supported his claim by a display of magic. Simon appeared to the Samaritans as one deserving reverence for his supernatural demonstrations. He had been able to deceive them through his "power."

The preaching of Philip in Samaria introduced a greater power than Simon had. Philip's preaching centered on Jesus Christ. The people turn from Simon to the gospel. Simon himself professes to believe and is baptized. It is uncertain what kind of faith Simon had. It may have been a saving faith or it may have been a recognition on Simon's part of a greater power than his.

Later, Simon was an observer of what happened when the apostles prayed and laid their hands on believers. Simon was fascinated. Here was a power he wanted to possess. Perhaps he thought it would add credibility to his trade and increase his prestige.

Peter was shocked when Simon offered to pay for the gift. Peter gave Simon a stern rebuke and called for repentance.

---

How can a person be deceived by the occult?

---

III. DELIVERANCE FROM THE OCCULT (Acts 16:16-21; 19:18-20; Colossians 3:1-4)

The power of God over the occult is recorded in Acts 16:16-21. In this passage we are given hope for deliverance from any of the evils of the world.

The passage recounts an incident that a missionary party had with a demon-possessed girl. The missionaries were on their way to a place of prayer when they were stopped by a demon-possessed girl whose condition gave her the ability to tell the future. The girl was a source of profit to those who owned her.

In spite of not having contact with the missionaries, the girl was able to tell the public that they were in the service of God. She even told the public that the message they were proclaiming was the way of salvation.

This harassment of the missionaries went on for several days. Finally, Paul addressed the spirit in the girl and commanded it to come out of her. The spirit left the girl.

There are numerous accounts of Jesus exorcising demons in the gospels. These exorcisms show that God has power over the occult.

Another passage that shows the power of God over the occult is Acts 19:11-20. The ministry of Paul in Ephesus was accompanied by a ministry of miraculous works, including exorcisms.

Certain Jewish exorcists, noting the power that Paul had, determined to use the formula Paul used, "the name of the Lord Jesus," when they exorcised demons. These exorcists looked upon Paul as a competitor. They were in the practice to make money and they thought Paul's formula was a trick of the trade.

Their plans were ruined when an evil spirit refused to recognize them as having any control over him. Their use of the name Jesus was superficial. Consequently, they were given a severe beating.

The effect of this incident was drastic on the public. They were gripped with fear. No longer would they take the name of the Lord lightly.

The effect on the church at Ephesus was even greater. It caused the believers to confess the hold that the occult had on them. They gathered up their books of magic and burned them. The value of what was burned was "fifty thousand pieces of silver." While the exact amount cannot be calculated, it apparently was a very large figure.

The Christian attitude toward God is reflected in Colossians 3:1-4. We should not turn to the occult for advice or guidance about our lives. We should turn to

God. We should recognize our relationship with Him; we should affirm our commitment to Him.

In Colossians 3:1-4, it says believers were raised with Christ. We have died with Christ and we now live with Christ as we participate in His resurrection. On the basis of Christians sharing in the resurrection life of Christ, Paul exhorts us to seek the life of a Christian. We must continually guide our activities and energies in a new direction. Every Christian is to be concentrating his efforts upon developing these characteristics which have their source in the spiritual life from God.

The passage particularly emphasizes the importance of one's mind-set. It requires that the thoughts and attention of the Christian be continually directed toward the goal of the Christian life. A person's actions are the result of his thinking. That is why Paul regards it as extremely important that the Christian have the proper mental attitude.

---

How is a demon exorcised from a person?

---

This lesson deals with three major points. First, it recognizes that the Scripture condemns the occult. This is evident from the study of Isaiah 8:18-20. The occult is also condemned in Deuteronomy 18:10-14. An event of people destroying occult material is recorded in Acts 19:18-20. This shows the attitude of these Christians toward the occult.

At the heart of the Scripture's condemnation of the occult is the revelation of God's will that we have. We need not turn to the occult, because we have a revelation of what God has done, what He is doing, and what He will do. Based upon His integrity and immutability, we can have assurance that our present life and our future is secure.

The occult cannot give us advice as God has. It does not give clear-cut information. What it gives is jibberish. But God has given us a complete revelation in Jesus Christ.

Second, the occult can deceive people. Simon is an example. The people thought he was a great man of God because he was able to do mighty works. He baffled them with his powers. They reverenced him.

Third, there is deliverance from the occult. The Samaritans who received the message of Jesus Christ which Philip preached is an example. The girl who was demon-possessed is an example. And the burning of the witchcraft articles in Ephesus is an example.

The important thing for a Christian to do is to commit himself to the Lord. We need to focus our thought and attention upon God. When we concentrate upon God, He will keep us from occult powers. We will develop a sensitivity to the Lord's directing and become stronger as Christians.

## REVIEW QUESTIONS

1. Why is the occult condemned in Scripture?

2. What was Isaiah's response to those suggesting consultation with the occult?

3. What are some factors that make it possible for people to be deceived by the occult?

4. What was the influence of the gospel on Ephesus?

5. Are you better able to aid those who look to occultism for answers?

## GOLDEN TEXT HOMILY

"IF YE CONTINUE IN MY WORD, THEN ARE YE MY DISCIPLES INDEED; AND YE SHALL KNOW THE TRUTH, AND THE TRUTH SHALL MAKE YOU FREE" (John 8:31, 32).

For the past two days, Jesus had been teaching in the Temple. As a result of what He said, many believed on Him (John 8:28-31). To those Jews who believed on Him, Jesus said, "If ye continue in my word, **then** are ye my disciples indeed; And ye shall know the truth, and the truth shall make you free" (John 8:31, 32).

Jesus began this statement with a conditional clause, "If ye continue in

my word," followed with a promise of three results: (1) **"then** are ye my disciples indeed"; (2) "ye shall know the truth"; and (3) "the truth shall make you free." Let us look first at the condition and then at the results of fulfilling that condition.

The condition: "If ye continue in my word." The Jews have begun in His Word by believing on Him. But they must continue in His Word. The Greek word **meno,** translated "continue," is used approximately 112 times in the New Testament. The word is used by Christ in John 15:4, translated **"abide** in the vine," and by Paul in Acts 27:31, translated **"abide** in the ship." To continue in His Word means to live according to its truths and standards. When a person does that, then Jesus said these three things would result:

First, "Then are ye my disciples indeed." The Greek word translated "disciple" is **mathetes** which means a learner or pupil. The Greek word translated "indeed" is **alethos** and means surely, true or truth. The point that Jesus made is that a true disciple of His is one who not only has believed on Him as the Son of God, but who also continues in His Word.

Second, "And ye shall know the truth." Jesus was not talking about truth in general, but a specific truth which involves man's sinful, lost condition and God's plan of salvation through the death and resurrection of His Son, Jesus Christ. God's Word is God's truth about God's way of salvation and His plan of blessings for all who believe on Jesus Christ. Jesus said that we shall know the truth by continuing in the truth—the Word of God.

Third, "And the truth shall make you free." The Jews understood Jesus to be talking about physical and political freedom. "We be Abraham's seed, and were never in bondage to any man: how sayest thou, Ye shall be made free?" (John 8: 33). But Jesus was not talking about physical or political bondage and freedom, rather, a spiritual bondage and freedom. "Whosoever committeth sin is the servant of sin" (v. 34). Freedom from sin comes through a knowledge of Jesus

Christ and by continuing in His Word. "If the Son therefore shall make you free, ye shall be free indeed" (v. 36). True freedom is not only being free physically and politically, but spiritually and morally as well.—**Kenneth K. Foreman, D.D., Executive Director Christian Education, Pentecostal Church of God, Joplin, Missouri.**

## SENTENCE SERMONS

THOSE WHO OBEY GOD refuse to participate in any form of occult practice.

—**Selected**

SUPERSTITION IS the restless effort of a guilty but blind conscience to find rest and peace and good by unauthorized propitiations and ceremonies.

—**R. Watson**

THE HUMAN HEART needs something to cling to, something to which it may hold fast, a prop which its tendrils may firmly clasp; therefore when it leaves HIM, for whom it was made, when it sinks into unbelief, then it clings to superstitions and darkness.

—**Schlier**

## EVANGELISTIC APPLICATION

FORGIVENESS AND DELIVERANCE ARE AVAILABLE TO THOSE WHO COME TO GOD THROUGH JESUS CHRIST.

The sad story of a man who was demon-possessed is told in Mark 5:1-19. He lived in a cemetery; he could not be bound by any chain; he howled night and day; and he cut himself with stones. People had tried to calm him, but their effort was always in vain. There simply was not hope for him.

One day the man saw Jesus. The day marked the beginning of a new day for him, because Jesus exorcised the demons from the man.

He was free of his trouble. He was a new man. He clothed himself and went to his home because of the work Jesus did in his life.

The same power is available to anyone today. Jesus can set a person free, and he will be free indeed (John 8:30-32; 1 John 1:9—2:2).

## ILLUMINATING THE LESSON

Jehoshaphat, the king of Judah, and Ahab, the king of Israel, were making plans to attack Ramoth-gilead (2 Chronicles 18:4-34). Ahab wanted to consult the Lord about the battle; however, he wanted to only consult and listen to the prophets who would give him the answer that he wanted. He found many prophets who would agree with him, but Micaiah would not give the answer Ahab wanted. Instead, he gave the answer God told him.

When we look to others for counsel, we should be careful that we are not wanting them to give the answer we are wanting. We need to listen for God's answer. Otherwise, we may be deceived.

## DAILY DEVOTIONAL GUIDE

M. Superiority of God's Power. Exodus 7:8-13
T. Witchcraft Forbidden. 2 Chronicles 33:1-13
W. Kneeling Before God. Psalm 95:1-7
T. Walking in the Spirit. Galatians 5:16-26
F. God Our Deliverer. 1 Peter 2:1-10
S. Worship in Heaven. Revelation 4:6-11

# Challenges Facing the Church

**Study Text:** Matthew 28:19; Luke 9:23-26; John 4:35-42; Acts 8:4, 25; 10:13-16, 34, 35, 44-48; Romans 15:5, 6; Ephesians 4:11-16; Colossians 3:16, 17

**Supplemental References:** Psalm 86:9-13; Isaiah 55:1-5; Matthew 9:9-13; Acts 8:29-40; 9:26-31; 2 Timothy 2:1-7

**Golden Text:** "Go ye therefore, and teach all nations, baptizing them in the name of the Father, and of the Son, and of the Holy Ghost" (Matthew 28:19).

**Central Truth:** God gives abundant grace and wisdom for the many challenges facing the Church today.

**Evangelistic Emphasis:** Every Christian should make winning the lost a top priority in his life.

## Printed Text

**John 4:35.** Say not ye, There are yet four months, and then cometh harvest? behold, I say unto you, Lift up your eyes, and look on the fields; for they are white already to harvest.

**36. And he that reapeth receiveth wages, and gathereth fruit unto life eternal: that both he that soweth and he that reapeth may rejoice together.**

37. And herein is that saying true, One soweth, and another reapeth.

**38. I sent you to reap that whereon ye bestowed no labour: other men laboured, and ye are entered into their labours.**

39. And many of the Samaritans of that city believed on him for the saying of the woman, which testified, He told me all that ever I did.

**40. So when the Samaritans were come unto him, they besought him that he would tarry with them: and he abode there two days.**

41. And many more believed because of his own word;

**42. And said unto the woman, Now we believe, not because of thy saying: for we have heard him ourselves, and know that this is indeed the Christ, the Saviour of the world.**

**Ephesians 4:11.** And he gave some, apostles; and some, prophets; and some, evangelists; and some, pastors and teachers;

**12. For the perfecting of the saints, for the work of the ministry, for the edifying of the body of Christ:**

13. Till we all come in the unity of the faith, and of the knowledge of the Son of God, unto a perfect man, unto the measure of the stature of the fulness of Christ:

**14. That we henceforth be no more children, tossed to and fro, and carried about with every wind of doctrine, by the sleight of men, and cunning craftiness, whereby they lie in wait to deceive;**

15. But speaking the truth in love, may grow up into him in all things, which is the head, even Christ:

**16. From whom the whole body fitly joined together and compacted by that which every joint supplieth, according to the effectual working in the measure of every part, maketh increase of the body unto the edifying of itself in love.**

## LESSON OUTLINE

I. CHALLENGED TO EVANGELISM
II. CHALLENGED TO CHANGE
III. CHALLENGED TO DISCIPLESHIP

## LESSON EXPOSITION

INTRODUCTION

The church has one ministry. It is described in the New Testament as the ."ministry of reconciliation." The reality of that ministry is expressed by the Apostle Paul in 2 Corinthians 5:18: "And all things are of God, who hath reconciled us to himself by Jesus Christ, and hath given to us the ministry of reconciliation."

The ministry of the church, however, has many facets. It includes the telling of the gospel to mankind, the cultivation and practice of worship, deeds of mercy and works of love, efforts of Christians to live as citizens of this world while having citizenship in heaven, the education and edifying of the faithful, and the sharing with humanity the meaning of God's activity in the world.

No part of the ministry can be singled out and given priority over other facets of the ministry of the church. All parts are important and must move forward together for the glory of God, if that church is worthy of the name of Christ.

The task of the church is heavy, rightfully imposing on every member a share of the work. Statistics show, however, that the major work of the church is carried out by relatively few workers. When such is the case, it is apparent that the church is not effective in its responsibility to educate the people of their God-given opportunities.

Our lesson focuses on some of the challenges facing the church today. These challenges include evangelism, change, and discipleship.

I. CHALLENGED TO EVANGELISM (Matthew 28:19, 20; John 4:35-42; Acts 8:4, 25)

The final words of Jesus to the disciples as He stood on the mount just before His ascension are recorded in Matthew 28:19, 20: "Go ye therefore, and teach all nations, baptizing them in the name of the Father, and of the Son, and of the Holy Ghost: Teaching them to observe all things whatsoever I have commanded you: and, lo, I am with you alway, even unto the end of the world." Those penetrating words set into motion a wave of evangelistic efforts that are still in progress. William Barclay says, "It must have been a staggering thing for eleven humble Galileans to be sent forth to the conquest of the world. Even as they heard it, their hearts must have failed them. But no sooner was the command given than the promise followed. They were sent out—as we are—on the greatest task in history, but with them there was the greatest presence in the world" (**The Gospel of Matthew,** Vol. 2, William Barclay).

**John 4:35. Say not ye, There are yet four months, and then cometh harvest? behold, I say unto you, Lift up your eyes, and look on the fields; for they are white already to harvest.**

Jesus is the Great Sower. The seed sown in the heart of the Samaritan woman was springing up already. The harvest of the souls at Sychar immediately followed the sowing. This is contrary to the natural order. In the natural order a farmer plants the seed, then waits for the harvest. Natural law does not always prevail in the spiritual world. The spiritual in Sychar was ready to be harvested.

The disciples could see for themselves that the fields were ready to be harvested. When Jesus says the harvest is ready, He refers to the spiritual receptiveness of the Samaritan woman, the measure of faith which she has exhibited, and the eagerness with which her friends and neighbors were coming to inquire of Jesus for themselves. It may be likely that the disciples could see the multitude coming from the town, when Jesus spoke to them. Hence, they could see that the harvest was ripe and ready to be gathered.

**John 4:36. And he that reapeth receiveth wages, and gathereth fruit unto life eternal: that both he that soweth and he that reapeth may rejoice together.**

The Christian gathers the fruit of the spiritual fields and is rewarded. His reward is twofold. First, he has joy because he is working in the spiritual harvest. Second, he has joy because the fruit that he gathers is eternal. Finally, both the person who sows the seed (Jesus Christ) and the person who gathers the harvest rejoice together.

**John 4:37. And herein is that saying true, One soweth, and another reapeth.**

**38. I sent you to reap that whereon ye bestowed no labour: other men laboured, and ye are entered into their labours.**

Jesus is the sower, but He permitted His disciples to reap. This is a paradox. The sower usually harvests the crop. If someone does harvest where he has not sown, he is very thankful. In this case Jesus has sown the seed and has commissioned His disciples to harvest the crop. The disciples have not labored in Sychar; the seed was sown there by Jesus. The disciples should be thankful that Jesus has sown the seed and commissioned them to harvest the crop.

**John 4:39. And many of the Samaritans of that city believed on him for the saying of the woman, which testified, He told me all that ever I did.**

**40. So when the Samaritans were come unto him, they besought him that he would tarry with them: and he abode there two days.**

**41. And many more believed because of his own word;**

**42. And said unto the woman, Now we believe, not because of thy saying: for we have heard him ourselves, and know that this is indeed the Christ, the Saviour of the world.**

The first believers at Sychar were won by the testimony of the woman and not by visible miracles or signs. Others were drawn to Him because of His teachings (cf. v. 42). This illustrates the normal way in which men are drawn to Christ.

In this passage we are challenged to evangelize. We are told that the harvest is ready. God had been preparing the world to hear the gospel. He has sent the Holy Spirit to convince the world of its lack of righteousness, its sinfulness, and its certain judgment. He has poured out the Holy Spirit upon the world so that whosoever will can participate in the blessings of God. God has sown the seed and we are to reap the harvest.

While miracles and signs are important in the ministry of the church, we can witness to others regardless of our ability to perform a miracle or give a sign. The woman in the passage testified of what Jesus had said to her and she was able to bring her friends to Jesus. We can tell others of our relationship with Jesus.

When we testify of Jesus, we will have joy. We will have joy because we are working in the spiritual harvest. We are doing what God wants us to do. We are sharing our life with others. The fruit that we gather is eternal. And we are working with God.

Two passages in the Book of Acts (8:4 and 25) reveal the impact of persecution on the early Christians. Although they were exposed to severe hardships, their zeal for sharing the gospel message was not diminished.

List some ways that persons are discouraged to witness for the Lord in our day.

II. CHALLENGED TO CHANGE (Acts 10: 13-16, 34, 35, 44-48)

God challenges us to change. He challenges us to change our belief in customs that give us a sense of pride. Our confidence should not be in customs and neither should our spirituality be determined by customs. Spirituality is discovered in a personal relationship with God. When we are enslaved to our customs or we allow customs to dictate to whom we will witness, God challenges us to change. We are challenged to obey God and no custom.

An example is Peter (Acts 10). God appeared to Peter in a vision, while Peter was on the roof of a house in Joppa. In the vision, Peter was instructed to eat food that was unacceptable to a Jew.

He was instructed three times to eat the food and each time he refused.

While Peter reflected on the vision, the Holy Spirit told him that three men had come to the home looking for him, and he was to go with them. When Peter met the three men, they told Peter that Cornelius, a centurion, had sent them to find Peter and take him with them, because an angel had divinely directed Cornelius.

When Peter spoke to Cornelius, he commented on the radical change in his own thinking. He was now in a position to understand the character and purpose of God he had not previously perceived. The uniqueness of the covenant people had blinded him to the breadth of God's operations. Although the Abrahamic covenant had mentioned all the families of the earth would be blessed, the Jews were so impressed with their distinctiveness as the chosen people that they had relegated others to a subordinate position. So it was a radical change in Peter that had allowed him to remark that God is without partiality.

Why is it difficult to change? What are some prejudices that people practice today?

III. CHALLENGED TO DISCIPLESHIP (Luke 9:23-26; Romans 15:5, 6; Ephesians 4:11-16; Colossians 3:16, 17)

In Luke 9:23-26 the terms of being a disciple of Christ are listed. Generally the word "disciple" connotes an apprentice or learner giving himself to discipline under his teacher. But such a definition falls short of describing a disciple of Christ. The followers of Jesus had to face a simple but ultimate test: Will you die for Christ? "They were called on to stake their lives on the faith that the last word was not spoken by the Sanhedrin, by Pontius Pilate, nor by the soldiers who casually drove spikes into another condemned man's hands. They were called on to believe, as Jesus did, that beyond the hard cruel realities of this age, there stood the greater, ultimate reality of the Kingdom of God" (**The Broadman Bible Commentary,** Vol. 9).

To affirm allegiance to Christ requires one to **deny** himself. The disciple is to give up all claims on his own existence, surrendering his personal ambitions for prominence or power. Also, he must **take up his cross** (Luke adds **daily**). This takes the cross out of the past and makes it a part of the daily contemporary existence. To **follow Christ** requires sacrifice of one's own ambition unless the ambitions are to serve Christ.

In Romans 15:5, and 6, the apostle Paul prays that all parties in their use of the Scriptures may have granted to them by God both patience and comfort. These graces are the gift of God and are essential qualities that will make them "like minded" toward one another—a mind in harmony with Christ.

**Ephesians 4:11. And he gave some, apostles; and some, prophets; and some, evangelists; and some, pastors and teachers;**

**12. For the perfecting of the saints, for the work of the ministry, for the edifying of the body of Christ:**

**13. Till we all come in the unity of the faith, and of the knowledge of the Son of God, unto a perfect man, unto the measure of the stature of the fulness of Christ:**

**14. That we henceforth be no more children, tossed to and fro, and carried about with every wind of doctrine, by the sleight of men, and cunning craftiness, whereby they lie in wait to deceive;**

**15. But speaking the truth in love, may grow up into him in all things, which is the head, even Christ:**

**16. From whom the whole body fitly joined together and compacted by that which every joint supplieth, according to the effectual working in the measure of every part, maketh increase of the body unto the edifying of itself in love.**

In this passage Paul challenges the readers to discipleship. He says that Christ has given gifts to the church so that the church may mature and may defend itself against heresy.

According to Ephesians 4:7, 8, the church officers listed in Ephesians 4:11

are given by Christ as a gift of grace. This "gift" is different from an occasional token of God's good will that may be received, consumed, and forgotten. By this gift Christ establishes order within the church so that the church may mature.

Four things can be said of this gift of grace for the church. First, the gift of grace that is seen in the church officers provides for all the saints equally. No one member possesses anything that is not given to the whole body. Second, the gift of grace is unfolded in different ministries. Third, the gift consists of particular servants instead of impersonal services. Last, all the ministers listed are persons who fulfill their service by speaking. (This does not exclude other types of ministry in the church. It is simply emphasizing these ministries in the epistles.)

An apostle is the first minister that Paul mentioned. An apostle is someone who is sent by another person. In its biblical usage, the term suggests three meanings. An apostle may be anyone who is sent by Christ to preach the gospel. Second, an apostle is a minister in a new field. No one has preached the gospel in a particular area and the person is commissioned to take the gospel to that area. Third, an apostle is someone who has seen Christ and has worked in association with the twelve chosen disciples of Jesus. Earlier in the epistle (Ephesians 2:20; 3:5), Paul speaks of an apostle in the latter sense.

A prophet applies the gospel to specific contemporary circumstances, makes predictions of the immediate future, and speaks under the direct prompting of the Spirit of God (Acts 11:27ff; 13:1ff; 21:4, 9).

An evangelist is a missionary. Although his work is narrower than that of an apostle in preaching in a new region it does resemble the work of an apostle.

The two terms **pastors** and **teachers** mean the same person. The person could be defined as a teaching shepherd. The teaching shepherd fulfills pastoral tasks in a congregation.

Three phrases in verse 12 are used to describe the purpose of the spiritual gifts mentioned in verse 11. The ministry of the church is given "for the perfecting of the saints." The phrase suggests bringing disciples in the church to a place of maturity so that they can fulfill their roles in the body of Christ. Thus, discipleship is not an end in itself. It is for a purpose. It is so the disciples may be "fitted for the work of the ministry." Every Christian has a work of ministry in the body of Christ (compare Ephesians 4:7). What is done for and by the disciples, is for the edifying of the body of believers. The Church is built up as each member uses his particular gifts in spiritual service to his fellow-believers.

The three phrases in verse 12 describe growth as what is going on in the body of Christ. Verse 13 indicates maturity is the goal of that growth. The maturity is described in three ways. First, it is "the unity of the faith." Where the gospel is preached, people of different backgrounds will be in one mind and one accord. Second, the faith that is preached is more than a system of doctrines; it is "the knowledge of the Son of God." When the New Testament speaks of a knowledge of God, it means a personal relationship with Him. Third, fellowship with Jesus Christ means the full experience of life in Christ; therefore, it is a development "unto a perfect man, unto the measure of the stature of the fulness of Christ." The different words used in this phrase suggests maturity. **Perfect** suggests full development (compare 1 Corinthians 2:6). **Man** means adulthood (compare 1 Corinthians 13:11). **Stature** shows age or physical size (compare John 9:21, 23; and Luke 19:3).

There must no longer be the immaturity of children who are unstable in face of the pressures of different doctrines and standards of life. There must be stability in the lives of Christians, as one would expect from adults (v. 14).

Christian leaders are not to use the deceitful tools of false teachers. They are to be ambassadors of truth. They must act in love. What is supported and the manner in which it is supported is the opposite of the men spoken of in verse 14. The Christian is to present the truth in order to bring spiritual benefit to others, and he is to do it in love.

When the gospel is taught in love, the disciples will grow in stability and maturity. This growth is "in Christ." It is a development that recognized that all things find their bearing in relation to him.

From Christ, as Head, the body derives its whole capacity for growth. Each part of the body functions and grows as it is "energized" by God in the whole body. Each member does not seek its own growth but the growth of the whole body.

In Ephesians 4:11-16, Paul talks about discipleship in the body of Christ. He says four things. First, Christ has graciously given leaders to the church for the discipling of the church. The list of the types of the leaders is not exhaustive. It is an example list of those that Christ has placed in the church to lead. Second, the leaders are to disciple the believers so that the believers will be mature in Christ. Third, maturity comes from Christ. Fourth, individual members are not to seek spiritual growth in isolation from other members of the body. Edification in the body of Christ is a corporate effort.

Does Christ give leadership roles to the church in the twentieth century?

## REVIEW QUESTIONS

1. When did Jesus say the spiritual harvest was ready?
2. What is the twofold reward of the farmer?
3. Is it wrong to change tradition?
4. Who are the leaders Paul listed in Ephesians 4:11?
5. What is the purpose of discipleship?

## GOLDEN TEXT HOMILY

"GO YE THEREFORE, AND TEACH ALL NATIONS, BAPTIZING THEM IN THE NAME OF THE FATHER, AND OF THE SON, AND OF THE HOLY GHOST" (Matthew 28:19).

In death and resurrection, Christ began a new dispensation (Hebrews 10:7-9). Why, when Christ was dying on the cross, being taunted by malefactors on either side, and a surly centurion before Him, did He not make a show of His power and authority? This Galilean whose whole life was a pageant of inexplicable events who had the power to summon angels for protection, who had raised a girl and two men from the dead, had boldly said: "I have power to lay it down [His life] and I have the power to take it again" (John 10:17, 18). Why did He die? Because He chose to die! (Hebrews 10:5-9). Out of kind consideration for the people, He died that ignominious and frightful death of crucifixion. On that cross we see God in Christ reconciling the world unto Himself; that is the gospel message that He has committed unto us: a ministry of reconciliation, (2 Corinthians 5:18, 19). One may call to mind and use a dozen verbs to emphasize and reemphasize the power and force of the Lord's commandment, but none carried more weight than that little word, go. Go ye therefore, and teach all nations—"Go ye into all the world, and preach the gospel to every creature" (Mark 16:15). Go and teach, and go and preach, are unalterable terms. Nothing else is acceptable to the Lord.

Since we are Christ's by call and profession, we need to observe ourselves and break decisively with everything He cannot approve. Between God and man's soul, there can be no real love without that inward self-surrender. There can be no withholding of things held dear and precious. There is a law of exchange that brings about such a glorious relationship: Himself for me, and my all for Him! Do we, or do we not, accept the "I-am-crucified-with-Christ concept?" This is the crux of the whole Christian philosophy. What does He require? How much do I owe? God's salvation message is ours—not to alter, supplement, or annotate, but to speak with power and clarity (Acts 4:33).

This charge, given in Matthew 28:19, carries with it an obligation of sacrifice and service. Christ gave His back to the persecutor's rod, His face to those who smote Him and plucked out His beard, and His lovely brow to a thorny crown. He could have had heaven's finest robes and a crown of eternal worth, but He humbled Himself to become a servant to all men and to wash His disciples' feet.

The church is not living in divine will when it neglects this divine charge. Individuals are remiss when they refuse to participate in world evangelism! No new convert can keep his Light of life who does not let it shine, nor his testimony if he refuses to witness in Christ's name.

We're all adept at singing the old hymns: "Throw out the life line, someone is sinking today" and "Rescue the perishing, care for the dying." And to these phrases we must ask ourselves the question: Do our actions perjure our emotional testimony in songs?

The conversion prayer of H. B. Candles would be a model for all Christian witnesses:

Write Thy name, dear Jesus, upon my head that I may think after Thee, and, upon my lips that I may speak for Thee. Put Thy sandles upon my feet that I may walk before Thee and be perfect. Lift up my hands that I may work for Thee. Touch my ears that I may hear Thee well. Put Thy robe on my shoulders that I may bear Thy burdens. Touch my eyes so that I may see Thy glory, and Thy love in my heart, that I may be wholly Thine—always and everywhere!

Reaching the unconverted of our communities should be a task of paramount importance to the church. Without it, we fail and come short of the Lord's glorious will.—**Chancel E. French, Assistant Pastor, North Cleveland Church of God, Cleveland, Tennessee.**

## SENTENCE SERMONS

THE CHURCH MUST NOT conduct business as usual but as business extraordinary.
—**A. O. Jenkins**

THE CHURCH MUST have a compassion or else it will pass on.
—**"Notes and Quotes"**

IF THE CHURCH AIMS to hit sin, it should pull the trigger.
—**"Speaker's Sourcebook"**

MOST CHURCHES ARE full of well-fed saints who need spiritual exercise.
—**"Speaker's Sourcebook"**

THE MOST EXPENSIVE piece of furniture in the church is the empty pew.
—**St. John's Newsletter**

## EVANGELISTIC APPLICATION

EVERY CHRISTIAN SHOULD MAKE WINNING THE LOST A TOP PRIORITY IN HIS LIFE.

Every Christian should make winning the lost a top priority in his life. As Christians, we hold the Bread of Life and the Water of Life. We can point the lost to the Way. We can give the lost Light. We can share the Word of God with the lost. We can share the Comforter with the lost. Where else can the lost find Life unless we tell them?

## ILLUMINATING THE LESSON

How do we handle the challenges that confront us today? Ask the apostle Paul, who had a "thorn in the flesh." Paul would tell you God's grace is sufficient. Ask Corrie Ten Boom, who survived the Holocaust. She would tell you God's grace is sufficient. God's grace is sufficient for us in the twentieth century. Time does not exhaust God's grace. There is always an abundant supply of God's unfailing love.

---

Voltaire, the atheist, once said that he could and would destroy in a few years what it took Christ eighteen centuries to establish. His old printing press was later used to print Bibles. His log cabin was later owned by a Bible society and filled with Bibles.

## DAILY DEVOTIONAL GUIDE

M. Call to Glorify God. Psalm 86:9-13
T. Accept the Invitation. Isaiah 55:1-5
W. Invitation to Follow. Matthew 9:9-13
T. Share the Word. Acts 8:29-40
F. Change Attitudes. Acts 9:26-31
S. Be a Good Soldier. 2 Timothy 2:1-7

# Confronting Life's Problems

**Study Text:** Proverbs 23:29-35; Romans 6:11-14; 12:1, 2; 14:17-21; 1 Corinthians 3:16, 17; Ephesians 5:18; Philippians 4:4-7; 2 Timothy 1:7

**Supplemental References:** Genesis 26:23-25; Psalm 34:1-7; Romans 8:35-37; 1 Corinthians 6:12-20; Ephesians 5:1-13; Philippians 4:8, 9

**Golden Text:** "Likewise reckon ye also yourselves to be dead indeed unto sin, but alive unto God through Jesus Christ our Lord" (Romans 6:11).

**Central Truth:** God provides the believer with grace to resist the evil around him.

**Evangelistic Emphasis:** God wants the believer to share the message of deliverance with people enslaved by sin.

## Printed Text

**Romans 6:11.** Likewise reckon ye also yourselves to be dead indeed unto sin, but alive unto God through Jesus Christ our Lord.

**12. Let not sin therefore reign in your mortal body, that ye should obey it in the lusts thereof.**

13. Neither yield ye your members as instruments of unrighteousness unto sin: but yield yourselves unto God, as those that are alive from the dead, and your members as instruments of righteousness unto God.

**14. For sin shall not have dominion over you: for ye are not under the law, but under grace.**

**14:17.** For the kingdom of God is not meat and drink; but righteousness, and peace, and joy in the Holy Ghost.

**18. For he that in these things serveth Christ is acceptable to God, and approved of men.**

19. Let us therefore follow after the things which make for peace, and things wherewith one may edify another.

**20. For meat destroy not the work of God. All things indeed are pure; but it is evil for that man who eateth with offence.**

21. It is good neither to eat flesh, nor to drink wine, nor any thing whereby thy brother stumbleth, or is offended, or is made weak.

**Ephesians 5:18. And be not drunk with wine, wherein is excess; but be filled with the Spirit.**

## LESSON OUTLINE

I. ALCOHOLISM

II. DRUG ABUSE

III. FEAR AND DEPRESSION

IV. VICTORY THROUGH CHRIST

## LESSON EXPOSITION

INTRODUCTION

There are various ways to confront the problems of life. Some retreat to a magic mountain or a Shangri-La, while others take up every moment with "busyness." Far too many in our day, perhaps because of fear of the pressure-packed age in which we live, attempt to find escape through the anodyne of alcohol or drug abuse.

The best solution to the problems of life, however, is that which men of faith through the ages have found in their own lives to give the peace that passes all understanding. It is a faith in the goodness of God and of His mercy toward all men.

Although answers are never easy, our lesson today is certain to point up some of the problems that might be present in our own homes, or in the homes of our friends and loved ones. Certainly, our opportunity to find the biblical answer to such problems, will enable us to better serve our fellowman.

I. ALCOHOLISM (Proverbs 23:29-35; Romans 14:17-21; Ephesians 5:18)

Alcoholism is a problem that is not peculiar to any segment of society, any economic level, or any geographical region. All persons are potential victims of the direct or indirect effect of alcoholism. It is not a business problem that can be locked up in the office or left on the job, but one that is taken home to affect family and community life.

The consequences of drunkenness are graphically described in Proverbs 23:29-35. No translation or paraphrase can do justice to the concise, abrupt, and energetic manner of the original text of verses 29 and 30 which says in essence: "Oh that men should put an enemy in their mouths to steal away their brains! that we should with joy revel, pleasure, and applause, transform ourselves into beasts" **(Pulpit Commentary).** The sparkling wine in the cup (v. 31) has an end result that is like being bitten by a poisonous snake (v. 32). The adder mentioned here should probably be identified as the **dabovia xanthina,** a highly venomous viper and the largest snake of Palestine.

The general conditions described in verses 33 through 35 are all too common to a person who has seen the deplorable condition of one in a drunken condition: the speech is befuddled, when he tries to sleep he heaves and tosses

like a sailor trying to sleep on the deck of a ship in rough waters, and is insensitive to mistreatment and pain because of his intoxication (v. 35). But when he awakes, he is back to drinking. The terrible cycle goes on and on. Before one hangover is finished, the alcoholic is anticipating drinking again: "As soon as I can wake up, I shall want another drink," (v. 35).

**Romans 14:17. For the kingdom of God is not meat and drink; but righteousness, and peace, and joy in the Holy Ghost.**

**18. For he that in these things serveth Christ is acceptable to God, and approved of men.**

**19. Let us therefore follow after the things which make for peace, and things wherewith one may edify another.**

**20. For meat destroy not the work of God. All things indeed are pure; but it is evil for that man who eateth with offence.**

**21. It is good neither to eat flesh, nor to drink wine, or any thing whereby thy brother stumbleth, or is offended, or is made weak.**

The kingdom of God is not established on the distinction of what you eat and what you do not eat. The kingdom of God is based on righteousness, peace, and joy in the Holy Spirit. When men submit to God's reign, they receive the righteousness of God as God's free gift. In the kingdom of God there is peace because men's lives are whole and sound again; there is joy in the Holy Spirit, who is our foretaste and assurance of the bright new world of God.

The duty of the strong in this passage is clear. God expects them to be peacemakers. Christ, who builds His church, works through men who edify each other. Men who make peace and serve their overcautious brothers are doing "constructive" work. What arguments over food cannot do, love can do. The overcautious brothers, admitted into the church without argument, are edified. They grow strong in the love of their stronger brothers.

This calls for self-sacrifice on the part of the strong. Their love must be a self-denying love. If they refuse to make the sacrifice and assert their freedom —freedom to eat—they will destroy the work of God. The weak are God's own workmanship.

The strong may argue that it is "right" for them to evidence their strength and freedom of their faith by eating what they please, but Paul answers that nothing is so right as showing love for your brother. Paul contends that we must put aside some things in order that we protect and edify our fellow believer.

Is the church doing enough to combat the forces of evil brought about by alcoholism? What other things could be done?

**Ephesians 5:18. And be not drunk with wine, wherein is excess; but be filled with the Spirit.**

Man has tried to rise above his cares and gain happiness through alcoholic beverages. It was a danger to the church in the New Testament. The specific objection to being "drunk with wine" in Ephesians 5:18 is that it involves excess. The word **excess** denotes the uncontrolled action of the drunken man and his wastefulness. It is wasteful because one cannot make good use of the fleeting opportunities when he is drunk. The context of the passage exhorts the reader to use his time wisely because time is a precious commodity. Once it is lost, it can never be replaced. As Christians, we should be making every attempt to use constructively all the time God has given us for His kingdom. Both the wastefulness and the lack of self-control are things which should not be seen in the lives of Christians.

Instead of being drunk with wine, Christians should be filled with the Holy Spirit. Paul does not take joy out of a person's life when he forbids being drunk and exhorts him to be filled with the Spirit. He replaces wine with a alternative that is higher and better than wine. The fullness of the Holy Spirit in a believer's life will lift him above the depression of a monotonous life. When one is full of the Holy Spirit, there will be singing, praising, and worshiping of the Lord, and there will be unity among the believers as they submit to each other (Ephesians 5:19-21).

What a contrast Paul paints. Those who are drunk on wine are wasteful. They waste time, energy, effort, and money on wine that can never satisfy the thirst of man's soul. They lack self-control. It is wine that controls their lives. On the otherhand, those who are full of the Holy Spirit, worship God and have fellowship with each other. It is these two things—worship and fellowship—that can restore and refresh a soul as it desires.

II. DRUG ABUSE (Romans 12:1, 2; 1 Corinthians 3:16, 17)

Although the New Testament does not give an explicit prohibition of drug abuse, the tone of the New Testament definitely forbids the abuse of drugs. In Romans 12:1, 2 and 1 Corinthians 6:12-20 we find examples of New Testament passages that indicate drug abuse is wrong.

The first two verses of Romans 12 are a dedication passage. The basis of our dedication is God's revelation. Notice the emphasis throughout the previous eleven chapters in Romans: mercy! God has been merciful toward us. This word sums up all of God's activity on our behalf. Mercy is a revelation of God's love for us.

On the basis of this revelation of God's care for us, Paul exhorts us to make an act of consecration. We are to present our bodies to God. By **body** Paul means the whole human person, including its means of expressing itself in common, everyday life. God gets no service unless it is manifested through the body.

We are to present our bodies as "living sacrifices." Our sacrifices are not dead like the ones in the Old Testament. These sacrifices are alive. God died for our sins. He does not call on us to die for our sins, but He calls on us to live for Him. We present our bodies as living sacrifices by giving them to God with eagerness and joy.

This offering is holy, acceptable, and reasonable. It is holy because we have been made holy through Jesus Christ. It is acceptable because it is well pleasing to God. It is reasonable because it makes sense to the man who recognizes that God has bought him, and because it is the response of a moral creature.

Paul gives a positive exhortation: present yourselves to God. Then, he gives a negative exhortation: do not be conformed to the world, but be transformed by the renewing of your mind. The Christian should not be conformed to this age. He should not imitate the values of the world that oppose God and that do not reflect his inner nature. He should be transformed by the renewing of his mind. Who he is should be changing so that he will reflect on the outside, through his being and actions, who he is on the inside.

These two verses suggest that drug abuse is wrong. It is wrong because we cannot present a body as a living sacrifice to God when it is addicted to drugs. It is wrong because drug abuse contradicts the lifestyle of a Christian. The source of joy and peace for a Christian is God, not drugs. Drug abuse is temporal; fellowship with God is eternal.

In 1 Corinthians 3:16-18, Paul speaks to the perils and penalties of destroying God's temple. He had previously spoken about the **true** church of which Christ was the foundation, but now he moves to the inner sanctuary of that temple for, in reality, the real temple of God is not a building constructed by hands, but rather redeemed human personalities (Acts 7:48; 17:24).

The verb here translated "destroy" means to corrupt, to deprave, or to destroy. Paul warns that if anyone is instrumental in aggravating the factions that were existing in the Corinthian church, they were to know that God would destroy them.

Drawn down to the individual Christian, the warning still echoes, "If any man defile the temple of God, him shall God destroy; for the temple of God is holy, which temple ye are" (v. 17).

Paul says all things may be permitted for a Christian, but all things are not expedient. In this world we must use wisdom. Something in itself may be harmless to our faith, but an overindulgence in it may prove to be detrimental to our faith. Some things need to be avoided altogether so that we may concentrate on maturing our Christian faith. They will not nurture our development in Christ but will distract from our focus upon Christ (1 Corinthians 6:12).

In addition some things in life have a greater effect on us than we expect. We may think we master the activity because of its temporary duration, but the impact is much longer and hinders our role in the body of Christ (1 Corinthians 6:13-18).

Perhaps the most important reason Paul gives is God's ownership of our lives. We have been bought by God and are now indwelt by God; therefore, we are to glorify God with our body and with our spirit. Although this passage refers to sexual promiscuity, the advice Paul gives is applicable to the use of drugs. We need to abstain from the use of drugs because it will distract from our Christian growth.

III. FEAR AND DEPRESSION (Philippians 4:4-7; 2 Timothy 1:7)

Paul gives some advice on handling fear and depression in Philippians 4:4-7. First, we should always rejoice in the Lord. There are some situations in which people are not going to be happy, but people in the Lord have reserves of strength which allow them to be above their circumstances. Paul was not giving a theory. He experienced what he is telling the Philippians while he was imprisoned at Philippi. We are able to rejoice because we are in the Lord. The person who is in the Lord knows that he is secure; therefore, he can rejoice.

Second, we should be moderate to all men. Matthew Arnold defines moderation as "sweet reasonableness"; L. H. Marshall suggests it means "fairmindedness"; and R. P. Martin considers it to mean "graciousness." It seems Paul says we should have a gracious disposition toward others. We should have a real, positive attitude toward all who bear the image of God.

Third, "be careful for nothing," which means we should not be overly concerned with life. To care for people's well-being, including our own, is commendable, but to be in a state of chronic anxiety is not trusting God.

Fourth, we should pray. Our prayers should include worship, requests, and thanksgiving. And the peace of God will keep us. His peace will protect, defend and make an impregnable defense for us.

Paul gives Timothy advice (2 Timothy 1:7) that is applicable for us. Paul tells Timothy that God has not given us a disposition of fearfulness. Fearfulness is a condition that arises from our fallen condition and is not a fruit of the Holy Spirit in our lives.

The result of the Holy Spirit in our lives is power, love, and a sound mind. "Power" is the ability required to meet difficulties and to overcome adversity. "Love" is a demonstration of concern for another person. "Sound mind" is self-control. It is the power to resist self-indulgent laxity and the passionate impulses of the fallen heart.

Notice that God does not give us the disposition of fearfulness. It is a result of our fallen condition. It is destructive. It causes us to be timid, withdrawn, and frightful. With this kind of disposition, we cannot blossom as God desires for us.

God gives us a disposition characterized by power, love and a sound mind. These factors are constructive. They will help nurture us into healthy persons as God intends for us.

What are some of the major sources of fear in our day?

When we are troubled with fear and depression let us remember what Paul says in Philippians and in 2 Timothy 1:7. God does not want us to live skeletal lives. He wants us to enjoy this life He has created for us.

IV. VICTORY THROUGH CHRIST (Romans 6:11-14)

**Romans 6:11. Likewise reckon ye also yourselves to be dead indeed unto sin, but alive unto God through Jesus Christ our Lord.**

**12. Let not sin therefore reign in your mortal body, that ye should obey it in the lusts thereof.**

**13. Neither yield ye your members as instruments of unrighteousness unto sin: but yield yourselves unto God, as those that are alive from the dead, and your members as instruments of righteousness unto God.**

**14. For sin shall not have dominion over you: for ye are not under the law but under grace.**

Romans 6, Paul deals with victory over sin for the Christian. He asks if a Christian should continue in sin so that grace may abound. He promptly exclaims, "NO!" Next, he asks if those who are dead to sin should continue in sin. To which he declares, no. If Christians are to have victory over sin, how do they find the release from the power of sin? There are three key words to Paul's answer: **know** (Romans 6:3, 6, 9); **reckon** (Romans 6:11); and **yield** (Romans 6:13).

Paul says we are to know victory over sin in our lives by knowing that we died with Christ on the cross. When He died; we died. When He was buried; we were buried. Paul is talking about a spiritual reality. In Jesus Christ, we have died to the old life and we have been resurrected to a new life in Christ by the same power that resurrected Jesus Christ.

Since we know this truth, we are to reckon that it has happened in our lives. We are to continually, second by second, minute by minute, hour by hour, day by day, consider it to be done. We did die with Christ, we were buried with Him and we were raised with Him. God declares it so, now we must reckon it to be so.

Now we should yield ourselves to God. We should not give our instruments-our bodies to the enemy—we should give them to God. It should be a once-and-for-all yield. At one great crisis point in our lives, once and for all yield to God. When we do yield, we should not think we must sin once in a while in order for us to prove we are human. God forbid—and He does. To really be human as God intends for us means we will live for God and our neighbor which means not living in sin.

Paul concludes with a promise (Romans 6:14). When we **know, reckon,** and **yield,** sin will not have power over us. It will not have dominion over us because the grace of God breaks the power of sin.

## REVIEW QUESTIONS

1. List the analogies the writer of Proverbs uses in 23:29-35 to describe the actions of a drunken person.

2. List some of the difficulties that are brought upon a family household because of drunkenness.

3. Some drugs are useful in restoring people to health. Where must the line be drawn in the use of drugs?

4. Some nutritionists suggest that much of the depression (psychological depression) people experience is the result of poor eating habits. Do you agree or disagree? Explain.

5. What practical applications do you draw from the study of this lesson?

## GOLDEN TEXT HOMILY

"LIKEWISE RECKON YE ALSO YOURSELVES TO BE DEAD INDEED UNTO SIN, BUT ALIVE UNTO GOD THROUGH JESUS CHRIST OUR LORD" (Romans 6:11).

How do we look upon our true sense of identity and nature after we have been born again? I often wonder if most of us fail to realize the change within our nature and the new power of God within when JESUS became our Savior and Lord.

There are some very important truths that we must live by after we have been born again. They are **new** truths. Some of these truths relate to our past. It is vitally important to know what the Bible says about our past. It is equally important for us to confess them. What about the truths that have to do with the subjects of forgiveness, justification, reconciliation, and regeneration? We are to live by them.

Then there are truths that relate to the believers future. They also must be embarrassed. We know that there is life after death. There is heaven awaiting. Our bodies will be resurrected into glorified bodies. We will someday see Jesus face to face. On and on the list could go.

But what about biblical truths that relate to us today and are good for us today—not in the past, not in the future, but now! In this selected study verse, Paul is giving us a very important truth to know, to confess, and to live by every day.

Here is the truth. As born-again believers we are to be dead to the power of sin that once reigned in our bodies. We do not have to continue under the rule of Satan. The Bible tells us that the power of sin has been rendered dead. We are now free from that power that once was within us. In the name of Jesus that power is now dead.

But one of the major problems we have is that Satan tells us that we are not free from his power, and that we have no choice but to yield to his sway. May God help us to confess with our mouths and believe in our hearts that this claim of Satan is a lie.

If we truly believe that in Christ we are alive unto God then we are to "reckon" or "calculate" or come to a fixed and settled conclusion that sin is no longer in charge. Sin cannot be in charge if Christ is Lord.

Verse nine tells us that if we can firmly believe that death no longer has any power over our resurrected Christ then "likewise" we should know to believe that sin has no legal power over the believer.

It is true that the devil tempts us to sin but it is nothing more than a temptation.

That is all Satan can do to us. For in Christ we have the choice and power to say no. Why? Because we have reckoned ourselves to be dead to the power of sin and alive to God.

Because of the wonderful work of Christ in the earth we as believers are no longer alive unto sin, and we are no longer dead to God. It is now just the opposite. We are—and let us not forget it—dead to sin and alive to God. All because of Christ and faith.—**Ted Gray, Pastor, Henrietta, Texas**

## SENTENCE SERMONS

NO PERSON SETS OUT to become an alcoholic or drug addict. It is the mind-set that such provides relief from pressures weighing in upon a person, that extends the experimentation until there is no recourse.

**—Selected**

GOD PROVIDES THE BELIEVER with grace to resist the evil forces around him.

**—Selected**

"HE LIES THERE that never feared the face of man," so mused the Regent Morton over the open grave of John Knox. To fear God and to fear nothing else in God's universe—this indeed is to be a man.

**—John Roadmender**

SOMETIMES I'M ASKED by kids why I condemn marijuana when I haven't tried it. My answer: the greatest obstetricians in the world have never been pregnant.

**—Art Linkletter**

## EVANGELISTIC APPLICATION

GOD WANTS THE BELIEVER TO SHARE THE MESSAGE OF DELIVERANCE WITH PEOPLE ENSLAVED BY SIN.

Imagine hearing the last request of a dying father who had been hurt by his son. The father asks you to tell his son that he forgave him for the wrongful action. Would not we be eagerly willing to fulfill the request?

Has not God done the same to us? He died for man. When He died, He forgave man and He asked us to tell others of this forgiveness.

## ILLUMINATING THE LESSON

In some countries when a person does something that is wrong in his family, he is ostracized by the family. He is considered dead. Whenever anyone mentions him, the family does not acknowledge the comment, because to them the person is dead.

In a sense, this is what we are to do when we become a Christian. We are to consider the old person we were to be dead. We are not to acknowledge him. We are to live our new identity which is in Jesus Christ.

## DAILY DEVOTIONAL GUIDE

M. Fear Not. Genesis 26:23-25

T. Delivered From Fear. Psalm 34:1-7

W. Temples of God. 1 Corinthians 6:12-20

T. Walk in the Light. Ephesians 5:1-13

F. Keep the Mind Pure. Philippians 4:8, 9

S. More Than Conquerors. Romans 8:35-37

# Christian Priorities

**Study Text:** Joshua 24:15; Psalm 90:12; Proverbs 22:29; Matthew 6:33; Mark 6:31, 32; Luke 2:41-52; John 19:25-27; 1 Corinthians 10:31; 2 Corinthians 6:2; Ephesians 5:16; Colossians 4:5; 2 Thessalonians 3:10-12

**Supplemental References:** Ruth 1:15-17; 1 Kings 18:21; Psalm 39:4; Matthew 19:27-30; 1 Thessalonians 4:11; 1 Timothy 5:8

**Golden Text:** "Seek ye first the kingdom of God, and his righteousness; and all these things shall be added unto you" (Matthew 6:33).

**Central Truth:** Putting God first helps keep all life's priorities in proper order.

**Evangelistic Emphasis:** The first priority of every person should be to accept Christ as Savior.

## Printed Text

**Joshua 24:15.** And if it seem evil unto you to serve the Lord, choose you this day whom ye will serve; whether the gods which your fathers served that were on the other side of the flood, or the gods of the Amorites, in whose land ye dwell: but as for me and my house, we will serve the Lord.

**Psalm 90:12. So teach us to number our days, that we may apply our hearts unto wisdom.**

**Proverbs 22:29.** Seest thou a man diligent in his business? he shall stand before kings; he shall not stand before mean men.

**Matthew 6:33. But seek ye first the kingdom of God, and his righteousness; and all these things shall be added unto you.**

**Luke 2:49.** And he said unto them, How is it that ye sought me? wist ye not that I must be about my Father's business.

**50. And they understood not the saying which he spake unto them.**

51. And he went down with them, and came to Nazareth, and was subject unto them: but his mother kept all these sayings in her heart.

**52. And Jesus increased in wisdom and stature, and in favour with God and man.**

**1 Corinthians 10:31.** Whether therefore ye eat, or drink, or whatsoever ye do, do all to the glory of God.

**Ephesians 5:16. Redeeming the time, because the days are evil.**

**Colossians 4:5.** Walk in wisdom toward them that are without, redeeming the time.

**2 Thessalonians 3:10. For even when we were with you, this we commanded you, that if any would not work, neither should he eat.**

11. For we hear that there are some which walk among you disorderly, working not at all, but are busybodies.

**12. Now them that are such we command and exhort by our Lord Jesus Christ, that with quietness they work, and eat their own bread.**

## LESSON OUTLINE

I. SERVING GOD
II. FAMILY COMMITMENTS
III. IMPORTANCE OF WORK
IV. STEWARDSHIP OF TIME

## LESSON EXPOSITION

INTRODUCTION

Whether consciously or unconsciously all persons establish developmental priorities in each phase of life from the cradle to the grave. Such priorities are essential if one is to achieve the normal pattern of living—learning to walk, getting an education, being married, establishing a home, preparing for retirement, and so forth.

But beyond the physical, social, economic, and psychological tasks of development, there is an overarching need for spiritual priorities, which should aid in governing all other priorities we establish. Our lesson today focuses on four important matters all Christians must have in proper order if their lives are to be fruitful and fulfilling.

I. SERVING GOD (Joshua 24:15; Matthew 6:33; 1 Corinthians 10:31)

**Joshua 24:15. And if it seem evil unto you to serve the Lord, choose you this day whom ye will serve; whether the gods which your fathers served that were on the other side of the flood, or the gods of the Amorites, in whose land ye dwell: but as for me and my house, we will serve the Lord.**

Joshua does not suggest that serving God is a matter of indifference or that the listeners had the liberty to refuse to serve God if they saw fit. He uses rhetorical speech to impress upon the listeners a sense of duty to serve God and the absurdity of not serving God. Joshua's objective is to bring the people to a decision for God. He suggests that the service of idols compared with the service of God is so irrational that no person in his right mind would choose an idol over God.

As for Joshua, he is certain what he is going to do. He is going to serve

God. This decision suggests several things. First, the service of God is nothing below the most distinguished of men. Second, we are to be concerned for others, particularly our households, as well as ourselves. Third, those who are leaders should be first in the service of God. And fourth, we should resolve to serve God no matter what others may do.

**Matthew 6:33. But seek ye first the kingdom of God, and his righteousness; and all these things shall be added unto you.**

In Matthew 6:31, there is a prohibition given against being anxious about food, drink, and clothing; the next verse then adds that nonbelievers are concerned with these items. While nonbelievers are concerned with material things, Christians cannot be. Christians are to seek God first.

When one places God first, he will be concerned for the extension of the kingdom of God. The extension of the kingdom of God comes through evangelism and social responsibility. It is through evangelism that a person acknowledges the lordship of Jesus Christ and it is through social responsibility that the acknowledgement is manifested. If one is in the kingdom of God, he will be in a right relation with his neighbor. There will be a righteous business ethic, legal ethic, and social ethic.

When a relationship with God is our dominant ambition, then secondary ambitions will be healthy. Christians should be eager to develop their gifts, increase their opportunities, and extend their influence so that they may bring glory to God. If that truly is one's ambition, all other things will be given to them.

**1 Corinthians 10:31. Whether therefore ye eat, or drink, or whatsoever ye do, do all to the glory of God.**

In the context of this verse, Paul instructs the readers on how a Christian should act in the matter of eating meat offered to idols. He gives two principles for Christians to follow. First, we should glorify God in all we do. Second, we should be concerned with the well-being of our fellow Christian. These are basic principles that fit all of life.

It should be noted that Paul seeks to promote the glory of God in the ordinary things of life. God must reign in our religious activities. But for Him to be truly Lord in our lives, He must reign in our everyday affairs and receive glory from them.

---

Does seeking God first prohibit us from achievements in this world?

---

II. FAMILY COMMITMENTS (Luke 2:41-52; John 19:25-27)

**Luke 2:49. And he said unto them, "How is it that ye sought me? wist ye not that I must be about my Father's business?"**

**50. And they understood not the saying which he spake unto them.**

**51. And he went down with them, and came to Nazareth, and was subject unto them: but his mother kept all these sayings in her heart.**

**52. And Jesus increased in wisdom and stature, and in favour with God and man.**

In Luke 2:41-52, an account of the childhood of Jesus is given. In the passage there are several points given about family commitment. First, Joseph and Mary were concerned for the religious training of Jesus. They took Him to Jerusalem to observe the Feast of Passover and to celebrate the twelfth birthday of Jesus. It was a custom among the Jews to recognize the responsibilities and obligations to which the parents had committed the child on the twelfth birthday.

Second, Mary showed parental concern when she committed to memory the things Jesus had told her at the temple. This shows the love Mary had for Jesus.

Third, Jesus was obedient to His parents. He left the rabbinic teachers with whom He was having an enjoyable dialogue and returned home with His parents. In John 19:25-27 there is recorded some of the last words from the lips of the dying Savior. They tend to emphasize the tenderness of One, who yet racked with pain and suffering, would not forget His mother's love and well-being.

Mary was now advancing in life; her husband Joseph was apparently dead. As Jesus looked upon her from the Cross, He saw that the prediction was now fulfilled: "A sword shall pierce through thine own soul also" (Luke 2:35). He had loved her all of His life, and His love was never more grateful, more tender, more compassionate, than now. He was bearing the burden of the world's sin and sorrow; yet there was room in His heart for affectionate thoughts of His beloved mother.

There is a grace and beauty in the language in which Jesus commended His mother and friend John to each other: "When Jesus therefore saw his mother, and the disciple standing by, whom he loved, he saith unto his mother, Woman behold thy son! Then saith he to the disciple, Behold thy mother" (John 19:26, 27). He acknowledged His mother's fidelity to Himself; He foresaw the desolation which must come to her and He provided her not only a protector and a home, but that solace which would come with common memories and mutual sympathy. Thus it was secured that Mary should be removed from the distressing scene and should be assured of constant and affectionate tenderness.

---

Discuss the role children should play in regard to aging parents.

---

III. IMPORTANCE OF WORK (Proverbs 22:29; 2 Thessalonians 3:10-12)

Theodore Roosevelt once said, "No man needs sympathy because he has to work, because he has a burden to carry. Far and away the best prize that life offers is the chance to work hard at work worth doing." It is unfortunate when individual workmen feel they are doing work that does not contribute to some worthwhile end.

In Proverbs 22:29, the capable and diligent worker is praised. While the word **diligent** is used for a scribe in Psalm

45:1 and Ezra 7:6, the Hebrews honored the industrious person whatever the trade or profession might be. A **diligent** man was honored by kings.

The word **mean** used in the last phrase of this verse is translated **obscure** by some scholars. The thought is conveyed in the Septuagint that the diligent worker was not likely to have to work for the obscure or indifferent master, but that his diligence in habits of work fitted him for service to the king.

**2 Thessalonians 3:10. For even when we were with you, this we commanded you, that if any would not work, neither should he eat.**

**11. For we hear that there are some which walk among you disorderly, working not at all, but are busybodies.**

**12. Now them that are such we command and exhort by our Lord Jesus Christ, that with quietness they work, and eat their own bread.**

In the Thessalonian passage, Paul is dealing with some people who refuse to work. Paul admonishes them to work. He appeals to the example he set before them when he was with them. He worked diligently at that time. He also gave a maxim, "If anyone does not want to work, neither let him eat."

The people who were not working, were characterized as "disorderly." It indicates they were loafing and not doing any work for their living. Paul even called them busybodies. Moffat translates the phrase as "busybodies instead of busy." These people were not simply idle, they were meddling in the affairs of others.

Paul tactfully exhorted the offenders to change their ways. He seeks reconciliation. He wants to win them back into a committed place in the church. Paul urges them to work with quietness. It seems the thought of the second coming of Jesus had excited the offenders. In fact, they may have quit working because they thought the second coming was going to occur at any moment. So Paul directs them to that calmness of disposition which should characterize those who trust in the Lord.

Unfortunately the offenders may have gotten caught up in the excitement of the Redeemer coming that they forgot that He is the Creator who ordained work for man. Work should not be looked upon with disdain. God ordained man to work when man was in the Garden of Eden.

There are several good purposes of work. First, it is an expression of our love for our neighbor. We are able to produce something that may serve our neighbor's needs. Second, work is a means whereby we can gain identity. Through work we are able to express our abilities and talents. Third, we are able to glorify God through what we produce.

While we may be excited about the second coming of Christ, we must continue our ministry through work. We should look forward to seeing our Redeemer, but we should also recognize that our Redeemer is our Creator who has ordained that we work.

How may our work serve our neighbor?

IV. STEWARDSHIP OF TIME (Psalm 90:12; Mark 6:31, 32; 2 Corinthians 6:2; Ephesians 5:16; Colossians 4:5)

**Psalm 90:12. So teach us to number our days, that we may apply our hearts unto wisdom.**

The transitoriness of life is discussed in Psalm 90:7-12. The transitoriness of life is explained in terms of man's sin and God's wrath. Verse 12 is a short prayer asking that God may help us to take note of the brevity of human life and of the few days that are ours so that we may get a "wise heart." This suggests that wisdom consists in an awareness of what is wrong with man and a turn to God as the only dwelling where man can be safe.

A picture of the busy life of the disciples is given in Mark 6:31, 32. The disciples had been on a mission. When they returned, they reported to Jesus that the demanding crowds were so insistent that they had no time even to eat.

In response to their report, Jesus took them to a lonely place on the other side of the lake that they might have a time of peace and rest. "Here we see," says William Barclay, "what might be called the rhythm of the Christian life. The Christian life is a continuous going into the presence of God from the presence of men and coming out into the presence of men from the presence of God. It is like the rhythm of sleep and work. We cannot work unless we have our time of rest; and sleep will not come unless we have worked until we are tired" (**The Gospel of Mark,** Revised Edition).

**Ephesians 5:16. Redeeming the time, because the days are evil.**

Paul issues a very practical statement in Ephesians 5:16. Wisdom involves making the right use of time. It is not just using the 24 hours a day that God has given us. It means using every second of the day in a right and productive way.

Paul adds the reminder that "the days are evil." He recognizes that it is so easy to misuse time and opportunity. The Christian must not become reckless in his use of time. He should use everyday for the glory of God, especially every chance to turn someone from darkness to light.

**Colossians 4:5. Walk in wisdom toward them that are without, redeeming the time.**

Paul instructs us to use wisdom in our dealings with those outside the church. This means to live so that we do not misrepresent the gospel.

As in Ephesians 5:16, Paul instructs us to make the most of time. Every moment is a precious gift to be exploited and capitalized to the fullest. The English phrase "redeeming the time" means "buying up the opportunity," which suggests letting no fleeting chance to witness to the lost, but using every occasion wisely to lead to Christ unbelievers.

Does the way you use your time indicate your primary values?

**REVIEW QUESTIONS**

1. Did Joshua's position influence the people's decision to serve God?

2. What were two principles given in 1 Corinthians 10:31?

3. How were the people who were not working in Thessalonica characterized?

4. What may have been the reason for some of the Christians in Thessalonica not working?

5. Why is it important to use our time wisely?

**GOLDEN TEXT HOMILY**

"SEEK YE FIRST THE KINGDOM OF GOD, AND HIS RIGHTEOUSNESS AND ALL THESE THINGS SHALL BE ADDED UNTO YOU" (Matthew 6:33).

It is natural to have concern about food, drink, raiment (v. 25) and for the poverty stricken people to which Jesus spoke, concern often turned into worry. As in all matters relative to God's blessings and benevolence it would take faith; first, to avoid worry, and secondly to actually believe that God would supply these things. It takes a great deal of faith to accept verse 32, "For your heavenly Father knows that you have need of all these things," for only through faith can I actually conceive of God even caring about my temporal needs. Now the only way this faith can develop is to "seek first the kingdom of God." As I turn my attention to the things of God, faith soars and therefore I will not worry. The conjunction "but" supplies a contrast of the worldling, whose only thinking can be of the needs of this life, to those who are sustained by the knowledge that when one's priorities are spiritual there is absolutely no need to worry. It should be pointed out that the passage is in no way meant to encourage irresponsibility, but, beginning with verse 25, rather to provide the believer with what is said in other words, "my God shall supply all your needs according to His riches in glory" (Philippians 4:19). When a Christian understands this, his energies are free from worry of the cares of life to truly set his "affection on things above and not on things on the earth" (Colossians 3:2).—**Thomas Griffith, Jr., D. Min., is Administrative Dean, West Coast Christian College, Fresno, California.**

## SENTENCE SERMONS

GENERALLY THE LAST THING one knows is what to put first.

—**Blaise Pascal**

PUTTING GOD FIRST helps keep all life's priorities in proper order.

—**Selected**

SERVICE CAN NEVER become slavery to one who loves.

—**J. L. Massee**

ONLY A BURDENED HEART can lead to fruitful service.

—**Alan Redpath**

USE TIME for the things that outlast time.

—**"Speaker's Sourcebook"**

## EVANGELISTIC APPLICATION

THE FIRST PRIORITY OF EVERY PERSON SHOULD BE TO ACCEPT CHRIST AS SAVIOR.

Ask yourself which have more value: eternal relationships or temporal things? It is obvious that eternal relationships have more value. Therefore, we should seek God and trust Him to provide temporal things.

Is not this the lesson to be learned in the story of the rich man who decided to increase his material wealth rather than investing in eternal relationships (Luke 12:13-21)? The man had nothing when he died, but he could have had a relationship with God if he had given it priority.

## ILLUMINATING THE LESSON

Putting God first helps keep all of life's priorities in proper order. We recognize Him as Creator who owns all things, including our breath of life. We recognize Him as Judge who seeks reconciliation with all. We recognize Him as Redeemer who brings us into a new community. This recognition gives us a proper perspective on life, because we know that all things focus upon God. We are able to look beyond ourselves and see God as the center of life.

## DAILY DEVOTIONAL GUIDE

M. Choosing to Serve God. Ruth 1:11-18
T. Acknowledging God's Rule. 1 Kings 18:21-39
W. Taking Heed to Our Ways. Psalm 39:1-7
T. Rewards of Following Christ. Matthew 19:23-30
F. Putting Christ First. Philippians 3:7-14
S. Submitting to God's Will. James 4:13-17